GREAT
FORTUNE

RCA Building, 1933, by John C. Wenrich

GREAT FORTUNE

THE EPIC OF
ROCKEFELLER CENTER

DANIEL OKRENT

VIKING

VIKING
Published by the Penguin Group
Penguin Group (USA) Inc., 375 Hudson Street, New York, New York 10014, U.S.A.
Penguin Books Ltd, 80 Strand, London WC2R 0RL, England
Penguin Books Australia Ltd, 250 Camberwell Road, Camberwell, Victoria 3124, Australia
Penguin Books Canada Ltd, 10 Alcorn Avenue, Toronto, Ontario, Canada M4V 3B2
Penguin Books India (P) Ltd, 11 Community Centre, Panchsheel Park,
New Delhi – 110 017, India
Penguin Books (N.Z.) Ltd, Cnr Rosedale and Airborne Roads,
Albany, Auckland, New Zealand
Penguin Books (South Africa) (Pty) Ltd, 24 Sturdee Avenue, Rosebank,
Johannesburg 2196, South Africa

Penguin Books Ltd, Registered Offices: 80 Strand, London WC2R 0RL, England

First published in 2003 by Viking Penguin, a member of Penguin Group (USA) Inc.

1   3   5   7   9   10   8   6   4   2

Grateful acknowledgment is made for permission to reprint the following copyrighted works:
Excerpt from "At the Roxy Music Hall" by Lorenz Hart and Richard Rodgers. © 1938 (renewed)
EMI Robbins Catalog Inc. All rights reserved. Used by permission of Warner Bros. Publications
U.S. Inc., Miami, Florida. "I Paint What I See" by E. B. White. Reprinted by permission. ©
E. B. White. Originally published in *The New Yorker*. All rights reserved.

LIBRARY OF CONGRESS CATALOGING IN PUBLICATION DATA
Okrent, Daniel, date.
Great fortune : the epic of Rockefeller Center / Daniel Okrent.
p.   cm.
Includes bibliographical references and index.
ISBN 0-670-03169-0
1. Rockefeller Center—History.   2. New York (N.Y.)—History—1898–1951.   3. New York
(N.Y.)—Buildings, structures, etc.   4. Architecture—New York (State)—New York—
History—20th century.   5. Rockefeller family.   6. New York (N.Y.)—Biography.
7. Interviews—New York (State)—New York.   8. Oral history.   I. Title.
F128.8.R7O38 2003
974.7'1—dc21   2003050187

This book is printed on acid-free paper. ∞

Printed in the United States of America
Designed by Nancy Resnick
Maps by Anita Karl and Jim Kemp

TO LAWRENCE F. H. OKRENT,
who got me interested in
everything that's interesting

Jim said he would not mind standing all day in Radio City, where the French and British shops and the travel offices were, and the evergreens at Christmas and the tulips in the spring and where the fountains in summer sprayed ceaselessly around Mr. Manship's golden boy and where exhibition fancy skaters salved their egos in the winter. If he grew tired of the skaters, Jim said he would not mind standing and staring up and up, watching the mass of building cut into the sky. It made him know what people wanted and what they thought.

—John P. Marquand, *So Little Time*

They all laughed at Rockefeller Center
Now they're fighting to get in.

—Ira Gershwin

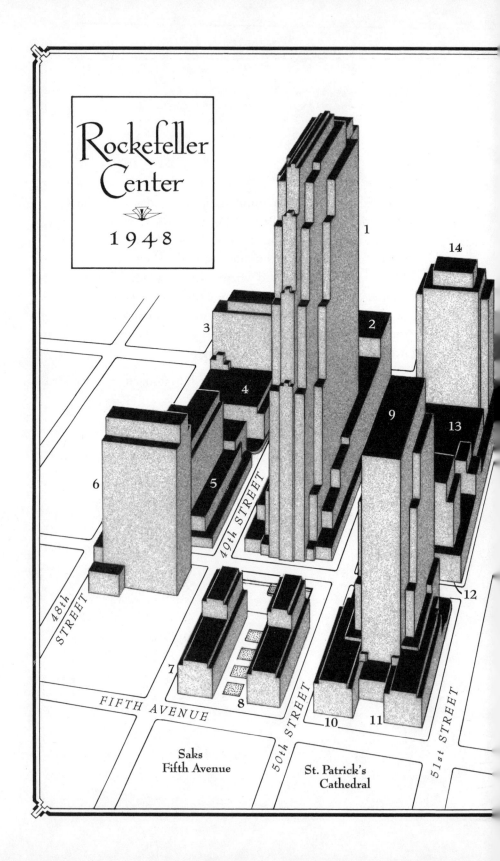

Rockefeller Center

1948

1

14

3

2

4

9

13

49th STREET

5

6

12

48th STREET

7

8

10

11

FIFTH AVENUE

50th STREET

51st STREET

Saks
Fifth Avenue

St. Patrick's
Cathedral

Names in bold are those generally used in the text;
each is followed by other names by which the buildings have been known.

1. RCA Building
General Electric Building
30 Rockefeller Plaza

2. RCA Building West
1250 Sixth Avenue

3. U.S. Rubber Building
Simon & Schuster Building
1230 Sixth Avenue

4. Center Theater
RKO Roxy
1236 Sixth Avenue

5. Eastern Airlines Building
Holland House
10 Rockefeller Plaza
20 Rockefeller Plaza
40 West 49th Street

6. Time & Life Building
General Dynamics Building
1 Rockefeller Plaza

7. La Maison Française
610 Fifth Avenue

8. British Empire Building
British Building
620 Fifth Avenue

9. International Building
630 Fifth Avenue
45 Rockefeller Plaza

10. Palazzo d'Italia
626 Fifth Avenue

11. International Building North
636 Fifth Avenue

12. Associated Press Building
50 Rockefeller Plaza

13. Radio City Music Hall
1260 Sixth Avenue

14. RKO Building
The Americas Building
American Metal Climax Building
1270 Sixth Avenue

15. Esso Building
Warner Communications Building
AOL Time Warner Building
75 Rockefeller Plaza
15 West 51st Street

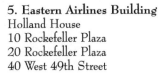

SIXTH AVENUE

15

52nd STREET

FIFTH AVENUE

CONTENTS

A NOTE TO THE READER

PLACES: I wish the names of buildings were as simple as, say, designing, erecting, and occupying a group of remarkable structures in the heart of America's largest city in the middle of the Great Depression. In most instances my proper nouns are the ones in use during the periods I'm writing about. Therefore, at different points in this book different names are used to describe one thing: Metropolitan Square, Radio City, Rockefeller City, Rockefeller Center; looking back from today, it's always Rockefeller Center. For individual buildings I've generally used the names they were known by when built—thus, the building now called 1270 Avenue of the Americas is referred to here as the RKO Building; the Time & Life Building I refer to is the original version, south of the skating rink, and not the current one on Sixth Avenue. (The illustration on pages viii–ix should clarify any nomenclatural murkiness.) By "Rockefeller Center" itself, I mean those buildings completed before World War II. The two later buildings in the original style (Sinclair and Esso) and all those across Sixth Avenue, from 46th Street to 51st Street, are formally part of Rockefeller Center, but not of the *concept* that became Rockefeller Center.

NUMBERS: Dates of buildings vary by source—some authorities use the date when construction begins, some the date when it ends. When in doubt, I've gone with the dates provided by Norval White and Elliot Willensky in their indispensable *AIA Guide to New York City*. The height of buildings, in feet as well as in stories, is often the concoction of developers and their publicists, who like to count rooftop air vents, water tanks, radio antennae, and anything else that can stretch the "official" number. I've generally allowed them their fun, except where it's material, as in the case of the sixty-six- (or maybe sixty-seven-, but not remotely seventy-) story RCA Building. Same with quantity of buildings: Rockefeller Center management has always counted the six-story eastern appendages of the International Building as separate structures, but the whole thing is clearly one building, and I count it as such.

PEOPLE: The only nomenclatural issue here has to do with the family at the book's heart, the Rockefellers. The three men bearing the name John Davison Rockefeller are here referred to in two instances by the names by which they are known to the family archivists—Senior and Junior. The third, depending on context, is either Johnny or John.

Some readers may think a more material issue concerning people has to do with gender: save for a very few lesser characters, this saga has an all-male cast. This is a reflection of the era, and not of any authorial bias.

Finally, a comment on memory: Interviews are great for color and for a sense of personality. But even those conducted much closer to the events described here—those compiled by the Columbia University Oral History Project, for instance, or by the excellent architectural historian Carol Herselle Krinsky—are flawed by that most unreliable of research tools, memory. Contemporary documents, however, are precise. When I've encountered a conflict of facts, either I point it out in context or go with the one that seems to me, after six years' immersion in this project, to be accurate. In a jump ball, the document almost always wins.

—D. O.
New York, March 2003

GREAT
FORTUNE

PROLOGUE

MAY 21, 1928

All the men entering the gleaming marble hall of the Metropolitan Club had arrived at Fifth Avenue and 60th Street on the wings of their wealth. The guest list was a roll call of New York's richest: corporate titans Marshall Field, Clarence Mackay, and Walter P. Chrysler; Wall Street operators Jules S. Bache, Bernard Baruch, and Thomas Lamont; various Lehmans and Whitneys, Guggenheims and Warburgs, men whose very surnames provided all the definition they needed. Financier Otto Kahn was there, for Otto Kahn was ubiquitous in New York if opera was on the agenda, as it was on this balmy night. But an interest in Verdi or Wagner was not the primary qualifier for inclusion on the invitation list. According to a young architect named Robert O'Connor, whose father-in-law was scheduled to be the featured speaker, the evening's host had simply invited everyone he knew who had more than ten million dollars.

Not all of them belonged to the Metropolitan Club, but there was no better venue for a convocation of the New York plutocracy. J. P. Morgan had founded the Metropolitan in 1891, after his friend John King, president of the Erie Railroad, was blackballed by the Union Club (Morgan said it was an act of spite; others insisted that certain members were offended by King's dreadful table manners). Morgan's stature had guaranteed a membership distinguished not solely by heredity or by financial success but by an unprecedented confluence of both. By 1928 the Metropolitan membership included two Vanderbilts, three Mellons, five Du Ponts, and six Roosevelts. It also included three men who were parties of interest to the evening's proceedings. One was the host, an aristocrat named R. Fulton Cutting, known to some as "the first citizen of New York." Another was Nicholas Murray Butler, president of Columbia University and a member of the Metropolitan's board of governors, who knew that the future of his institution was to a large degree dependent on the evening's outcome. The third was Ivy Ledbetter Lee, a preacher's son from Georgia representing the man who, even in his absence, was the lead player in the evening's drama.

No one expected John D. Rockefeller Jr. to attend the meeting at the Metropolitan Club that Monday night, and he didn't disappoint. He wasn't much of a clubman, generally preferring to spend his evenings at home in his nine-story mansion on West 54th Street; just the night before, he and his wife, Abby, had welcomed to a typical "family supper" another Ivy Lee client, Colonel Charles Lindbergh—"a simple, unostentatious, cleancut, charming fellow," Rockefeller wrote. Rockefeller usually sought to insulate himself from the endless entreaties for access to the family treasury, and the Metropolitan Club event was clearly in that category. He got a lot of invitations of this kind, and almost always chose to deputize one of his associates to serve as a sort of scout.

Oddly, in this instance the scout—Lee—was collaborating with the supplicants. Odder still was the shadow play that was the evening's presentation, offered ostensibly for the benefit of the assembled guests but mostly for the man who wasn't there. The speaker was Benjamin Wistar Morris, an architect of middling accomplishment but excellent breeding. On this particular evening Morris was working for the board of the Metropolitan Opera Real Estate Company (R. Fulton Cutting, president), a group of men whose money was substantial, very old, and dearly husbanded. The elaborate clay model of an opera house and other buildings on the table in front of Morris; his impressive stereopticon slides; his reasoned, detailed, and admirably practical speech—how could anyone not be convinced of the enormous civic virtue that would arise from the development of a small plot of land in the center of a slummy midtown block?

Morris's plan, Lee later reported to Rockefeller, would leave most of this land a plaza for the benefit of the public. "The Opera Company itself is able to finance the building of [a] new structure," he added. Wasn't it, Lee suggested, worth putting up the $2.5 million necessary to acquire this land from Columbia University, its improbable owner, so New York could finally have a new opera house?

SEPTEMBER 30, 1939

This time Rockefeller showed up. Seated in the front of a large gymnasium on the fourth floor of a new sixteen-story office building, he waited for his thirty-one-year-old son, Nelson, to finish the introductions. The audience this time consisted of some two thousand carpenters, charwomen, elevator operators, violinists, bookkeepers, rental agents, skating coaches, and widely assorted others on the Rockefeller payroll. One of those in attendance said that Nelson's natural charm, amplified by his boundless energy, "gave the meeting something of a feeling of a college rally of students and faculty a night or two before the big game."

His father would not sustain the pep rally; it wasn't his way. He was a constitutionally shy man, and on those occasions when he was compelled to speak in public he was far more likely to adopt the mien of the Bible-school teacher he had long been than to attempt to become a cheerleader. Facing the crowd that had been lifted so high by his buoyant son, Rockefeller chose to give a history lesson. Eleven years earlier, he said, "I was asked to join with others in acquiring [a] plot to be given to the city for a street and public square, in order to provide an adequate setting for the opera house." But, he continued, "the opera people withdrew entirely from the undertaking—an undertaking which they themselves had initiated and which I had become interested in solely at their instance." As a result, he went on to explain, things didn't turn out exactly as he had thought they would.

CHAPTER ONE

In an era when nearly every college president bore a triple-barreled name, none carried as potent a charge as Nicholas Murray Butler. To his intimates the president of Columbia University was "Murray"; to the associates who saw him found the school's Teachers College in 1887 at the age of twenty-five he was "Nicholas Miraculous." His employees simply called him President (when they didn't refer to him as "Czar Nicholas"), his acquaintances, Doctor. The editors of *Life* named him "one of the most erudite men of his time." None of this necessarily contradicted Senator Robert M. La Follette, who said Butler was a "bootlicker of men of fortune." Theodore Roosevelt was even blunter: he considered him "an aggressive and violent ass."

It was inevitable that a man so comfortable within the embrace of the American patriciate would provoke such epithets. He had built a career, a reputation, and an unblemished belief in his own virtue upon a nearly holy devotion to the marriage of money and power. Wherever Butler traveled, his focus italicized by the vivid smear of his luxuriant eyebrows, he looked benevolently upon the deeds, and the needs, of America's last ruling class. Rising from a middle-class New Jersey upbringing, he had become a pillar of the Republican Party (and a plausible candidate for its presidential nomination in 1920), a ubiquitous presence on the circuits of international power (he was Gladstone's houseguest as a young man, dined with Kaiser Wilhelm in his early forties, met with Mussolini when Italian fascism was still new), a joiner and a leader so prolific in his associations and so enamored of his own renown that, year after year, he made certain that his was

The Heart of This Great City Is Now Settled for All Time. It is the district from 34th to 59th Sts., 3rd to 10th Avenues.

—REAL ESTATE RECORD AND BUILDERS' GUIDE, 1920

the longest entry in *Who's Who*. This annual exercise in self-celebration cataloged honorary doctorates (writer Alva Johnston, who thought well of him, called Butler "a harvesting machine of university degrees"); club memberships (in New York alone, he belonged to the Century, the Union, the University, the Lotos, and the Metropolitan); publications (mostly repurposed speeches, few of them substantive, none of them memorable); and a sufficiency of other details that each year consumed more than a column and a half of tiny type, a mutable monument to his floodlit success.

Whatever it was he was seeking, the man worked at it. He produced all those speeches without the aid of ghostwriters, and his workday was frighteningly efficient. Letters poured from the President's House on Morningside Heights or from his office in Low Library in a volume that would overwhelm the hardiest archivist. He dictated each morning until noon, pacing back and forth, his coattails flying behind him, his secretaries desperately trying to keep up. Even the most trivial letters were answered within a day of their receipt at 60 Morningside Drive—or at his summer place in Southampton, on Long Island, or at the hotels in which he lived on his annual visits to Europe. In London he always stayed at the Berkeley, where he would receive wires from the States addressed in care of the hotel's comically inappropriate cable address: SYBARITE, LONDON.

Butler's European trips were largely the product of his long-held presidency of the Carnegie Endowment for International Peace, a platform from which he helped negotiate the Kellogg-Briand Pact of 1928. This was a document that renounced war, a deeply Butlerian notion insofar as the nobility of its sentiment balanced precisely with its specious futility. Still, it was an accomplishment that earned him the Nobel Peace Prize three years later, which was a nice thing but probably not nearly as gratifying to Butler as the honor that would endure for forty-three years of his long life. The presidency of Columbia University had brought Butler everything he had—the club memberships, the patronage of the Republican hierarchy, the offer of railroad presidencies extended by E. H. Harriman and J. P. Morgan. But it had also brought him a problem that by his own admission had vexed the university's board of trustees (and, therefore, Butler himself) since the day he had been installed as Columbia's president in 1902: what to do with the eleven acres of midtown Manhattan that Columbia owned—land that produced so very little, and that if properly exploited could be worth so very, very much.

Butler was not the first Columbia president to salivate over the potential revenue from the land, originally almost four full blocks stretching from

47th to 51st Street, from Fifth Avenue nearly all the way to Sixth. For decades the land had looked to Columbia's officers and trustees much like a lamb chop must look to a wolf. But long before the institutional drooling had begun, the property was more nuisance than asset, acquired almost as a sort of booby prize in a state distribution of public lands.

Originally part of the Dutch-controlled Common Lands assembled by Peter Minuit in 1624, the acreage that Butler would eventually turn into Columbia's dowry became, by the end of the seventeenth century, property of the City of New York. But the city, such as it was, still lay huddled around the southern tip of Manhattan, and this twenty-acre chunk of hilly slopes and rocky promontories might as well have been in Poughkeepsie.

To David Hosack, though, it was a convenient and comfortable ride up the carriage road that ran along the spine of Manhattan Island. Hosack was a man of parts, most of them glittering: physician, scholar, gentleman botanist, *salonnier*, friend to both Alexander Hamilton *and* Aaron Burr. Through a provident marriage and his own native talents, he had by 1800 become one of the foremost citizens of the growing city. His portrait was painted by Rembrandt Peale; Tocqueville wrote of the pleasures of Hosack's table. He was also a professor at the College of Physicians and Surgeons— precursor of Columbia's medical school—and longed for a piece of land that he could turn into a garden of materia medica, a sort of natural pharmacy.

Finding the ideal conditions for his garden about three and a half miles up the carriage road from the heart of inhabited New York, in 1801 he purchased the plot from the city for slightly less than five thousand dollars. Within three years the Elgin Botanical Garden, named after Hosack's father's birthplace in Scotland, bloomed with species from all over the world, some of them rare items contributed by Thomas Jefferson. A sixty-two-foot-long greenhouse anchored a row of structures running west from present-day Fifth Avenue. The entire plot was, Hosack noted with satisfaction, encircled by a "belt of forest trees and shrubs judiciously chequered and mingled," which were in turn enclosed by an imposing stone wall, two and a half feet thick and seven feet high.

Many years later a student of Hosack's recalled his mentor as "a man of profuse expenditure" who "had he the wealth of Astor" would still never have had enough. Over the nearly ten years he owned the Elgin plot, Hosack tried to prove his student's point, spilling nearly $100,000 into the garden until his wife's fortune could no longer bear the leakage. Unable to find a buyer for land he could no longer afford, he turned to the state legislature, where he had many friends, for relief.* After two years' effort, Hosack was able to persuade the lawmakers to give him $75,000 for a parcel of land that no one wanted.

Including the state of New York. Soon the spot to which the city's grandees had once proudly brought their European visitors became a near ruin. When the trustees of Columbia College came hat in hand to the state government seeking funds, just as their brethren at Union and Hamilton Colleges had done recently and successfully, the tapped-out legislature considered its empty pockets and instead gave Columbia land. The college trustees, whose existing buildings were confined to a plot of land on Park Place, some four miles away in downtown Manhattan, were more bemused than gratified. The trustees turned over responsibility for the plot to the son of a past Columbia president, but Clement Moore proved a better light poet ("'Twas the Night Before Christmas") than an agricultural manager, and the place sank into utter decrepitude. By 1823 the best Columbia could do with Hosack's Folly was rent it to a private individual for $125 a year and taxes.

The evanescent Eden that was the Elgin Garden would manifest itself in the life of the city several times over the next century. Many of the surviving plant specimens were shipped off to the Bloomingdale Asylum in distant Morningside Heights, where they were planted on what would decades later become the site of Low Library, the dominant building on Columbia's eventual campus. The Elgin itself became the model for the New York Botanical Garden in the Bronx; Hosack's large collection of horticultural texts was incorporated into its library. And both the carriage road that led to the garden and the pathway that fronted its south-facing expanse found their eventual forms in the city's decision, in 1807, to appoint a commission to plan New York's future. When they emerged from their deliberations four years later, the commissioners put forth a scheme to organize mile after mile of empty Manhattan terrain on a grid of 12 numbered avenues running north and south, and 155 similarly labeled streets crosshatching the island east and west. It was, wrote architect Rem Koolhaas in 1994, "the most courageous act of prediction in Western civilization: the

---

*It isn't surprising that Hosack would prove to be a better lobbyist than he was a plantsman. He was sufficiently politic to have attended the dying Hamilton after his fateful duel with Burr, and then to have subsidized Burr's flight to Europe following his treason trial in 1808.

land it divides, unoccupied; the population it describes, conjectural; the buildings it locates, phantoms; the activities it frames, non-existent."

But the grid gave names to the carriage road, which became Sixth Avenue, and to the pathway in front of the greenhouse, which became 50th Street. And what was soon known as Columbia's Upper Estate (to distinguish it from the Lower Estate, its property downtown near City Hall) was now fixed on the map, and in the city's history.

In 1838, when the first crosstown streets of the city's courageous imaginings were finally opened up in the area, Columbia's nearly valueless land suddenly had a future. But there was no agreement at Columbia regarding what that future might be. The original downtown campus, a relic of the school's beginnings as King's College in 1747, was at best inadequate, and the prospect of a move to the leafy precincts of the Upper Estate was enticing. But so was the new opportunity, presented by the area's incipient development, to do what colleges must do: make money. One faction believed the property was too valuable to use for education; the opposing view found its expression in the complaint of trustee Samuel B. Ruggles, who in 1854 wondered "at what point in the coming half century our speculating, land-loving, avaricious propensities are to cease, and our legitimate educational duties are to commence."

Land-loving avarice pinned educational duties to the mat. One chunk of the property, sixteen lots at the northwest corner of Fifth Avenue and 48th Street, had already been sold to the Dutch Reformed Church. A few years later the remaining frontage along Fifth Avenue between 48th and 49th Streets went to the Goelet family, landowners whose substantial Manhattan holdings—fifty-five acres in all—derived from the two Goelet brothers who had inherited the land from the man whose two daughters they had wisely married. Proceeds from the sales covered taxes, made a contribution to Columbia's operating costs, and built, at last, the new campus on a two-acre plot down the road, east of Madison Avenue at 49th Street. Continuing income was expected to come, someday, from long-term ground leases on all that land in the Upper Estate.

But in the late 1850s, ambitions flowering within the Roman Catholic archdiocese of New York—hardly a Columbia ally—suddenly spiked the land's value. Brownstone houses rose in what Edith Wharton called a "chocolate-coloured coating of the most hideous stone ever quarried," but which nonetheless produced perfectly lovely rents. Hosack's land became the virtual guarantor of Columbia's future solvency, not the last time it would play so noble a role.

The man who decreed a new St. Patrick's Cathedral on the plot facing the northernmost block of the Upper Estate was John J. "Dagger John" Hughes, the first archbishop of New York. Hughes was part cleric, part politician (antecedent of the Tammany bosses, he successfully ran slates of his own candidates for public office), and all Irishman. The city's established German Catholics had made way for the wave upon wave of Irish immigrants who had flowed into New York in the previous two decades, and the Vatican had provided them with one of their own as a leader. Hughes almost instantly made the church the center of Irish life in New York, both the symbol of his people's aspirations and the instrument by which they would achieve them.

The trustees and officers of Columbia may have been, every one of them, Protestant members of the city's commercial and genealogical elite, and may have included among their number, ex officio, the city's Episcopal bishop, but they could hardly have objected to the grand plans that Hughes revealed on August 15, 1858. The Irish place in the city virtually certified by Hughes's action, a crowd of 100,000 deliriously happy Catholics watched as the archbishop presided over the laying of the cornerstone for a building which, he said at the time, would cost more than $1.5 million. Never mind that the final cost, after more than two decades of construction, would exceed $4 million; never mind that, at the time of the cornerstone ceremony, Hughes had in hand pledges amounting to all of $73,000. Wrote one historian, "Hughes believed that if you took on a challenge, you would perforce rise to meet it."

Once met, Hughes's challenge transformed New York. By the Civil War, Fifth Avenue had already begun to evolve into the city's grandest thoroughfare, even if the grandeur largely resided below 23rd Street. But with the declarative punctuation of a lavish Gothic cathedral (even a Catholic one) inscribed at 50th Street, the northward rush accelerated. Almost as an ironic comment on the great gray cathedral, in a handsome residence one block north, with a staff of seven servants, lived Madame Restell, whose eminence as New York's leading abortionist had made her as wealthy as she was infamous. But just south of St. Patrick's rose a more congenial neighbor, the Buckingham Hotel. The Buckingham boasted in its advertising that "there is no noise, no confusion of porters or waiters, no loungers or patrons of the bar who are not guests of the house." This was exactly the sort of reassurance that a thirty-eight-year-old oilman from Cleveland might have sought before moving his young family into the hotel in 1877. Occupying a suite that looked out directly upon the filigreed towers of the cathedral, John Davison Rockefeller may have appreciated the general calm of the Buckingham and its neighborhood, but at least one member of his family did not: years later, John D. Rockefeller Jr. said, "I can still hear the noise of the steel tires [of the carriages] rumbling along the street. It was fearfully noisy."

Around the same time, starting with the "Vanderbilt Colony" in the lower 50s, hothouse blooms of mythic splendor began to burst into life on Fifth. The Millionaires' Mile grew into a lush garden of limestone turrets, marble finials, and formal porte cocheres. Behind Gothic windows outlined in lead and stone stretched grand ballrooms, mirrored galleries, rooms harboring Rembrandts, Flemish tapestries, furniture made for Marie Antoinette. Henry Clay Frick, whose own palace uptown on Fifth and 70th had not yet been built, estimated that the maintenance cost on just one of the Vanderbilt houses ran to $1,000 a day. Beside the Vanderbilt mansions—there were four in the space of two blocks, which was quite an accomplishment given the size of these beauties—stood houses for Astors, for Goelets, for the entire mercantile aristocracy of the Mauve Decades. Nathan Silver, in his *Lost New York,* called it "a visual summary of free enterprise and the history of architecture." And, he might have added, of the gaudy rivalries of the superrich, expressing themselves in a can-you-top-this orgy of rabid self-indulgence. Richard Morris Hunt, the favored architect to the wealthy, said, "If they want a house with a chimney on the bottom, I'll give them one."

The side streets throughout the 40s and 50s were substantially different, the better blocks lined with what Wharton considered "narrow houses . . . lacking in external dignity, so crammed with smug and suffocating upholstery," but also featuring some relatively noble exemplars of Victorian luxury. One, directly across from the shaded lawns of St. Luke's Hospital on 54th Street, just west of Fifth, was a present from railroad king Collis P. Huntington to his beloved mistress Arabella, the "unofficial Mrs. Huntington"—ergo, the recipient of gifts far grander than those bestowed on any old official wife. Four brownstone stories, dressed outside in demure threads of ivy and inside in the relatively understated style championed by the English aesthete Charles L. Eastlake, every cent of Huntington's investment nonetheless showed: the rosewood and mother-of-pearl inlays in the maple cabinets, the stenciled canvas ceilings, the ebonized cherry furniture as solid and as worthy as a government bond. But in 1884 Arabella the Unofficial tired of 4 West 54th Street and swapped it for nine pieces of uptown real estate that belonged to John D. Rockefeller Sr. The new owner probably enjoyed nothing about his 54th Steet mansion quite so much as the opportunity it gave him, each winter, to skate leisurely around the frozen surface of its capacious yard. The Columbia land harbored few houses as grand as Rockefeller's, but by 1879 every one of its 203 lots was developed and under long-term lease.

For all the wonders of Fifth Avenue, there lurked to the west a street that acquired disrepute at nearly the same rate that Fifth achieved glory. Once Dr. Rufus Henry Gilbert had opened the Sixth Avenue Elevated Railway on a series of piers and joists that ran from the Battery all the way up to 58th Street, Sixth turned into a hell of clattering noise, smoke, and sunless gloom. Gilbert, a physician who had spent years ministering to the tubercular victims of the Industrial Revolution, saw his railway as a means for the slum dwellers of downtown New York to escape to the bright meadows of Central Park, which had been completed the previous decade. His noble goal was about as hardy as one would expect in nineteenth-century New York. A gang of swindlers, stock manipulators, and profiteers soon seized control of the Gilbert Patent Railway from the hapless doctor, and by its third birthday the el was firmly in the control of a syndicate of robber barons, including Jay Gould and Russell Sage. The latter, who lived in a Fifth Avenue mansion at 52nd Street, would begin his day by having his carriage deliver him to the el station at 50th Street. At least John D. Rockefeller, emerging from 4 West 54th after the shave administered by his personal barber, walked to his daily encounter with the el.

Beneath the tracks, in the foul, murky shadows of the ungainly superstructure, there grew a netherworld of sin and sleaze—dance halls, brothels, crime-ridden bars. A Brooklyn clergyman called Sixth Avenue "a gaslit carnival of vice," and that was one of the nicer things anyone said about it. In a way, it was a perfect release valve for the palace-lined Fifth; without having to bear the clutter of public transportation, the smooth asphalt of Fifth Avenue evolved into a fine road for carriages and a handsome promenade route to Central Park.

But the presence of the el so near to hand, the promise of open vistas beside the park, and the inevitable northward march of the city's commercial enterprises led in time to the decline even of Fifth. As various Vanderbilts and assorted Astors relocated to mansions in the stretch of the avenue that faced Central Park, the blocks in the 40s and lower 50s attracted retail and other businesses. By the second decade of the twentieth century, the area had taken on the complexion of commerce. The stores that had replaced the mansions on Fifth may have been suitably exclusive, but they were still stores; however refined the crowds they attracted might have been, they were still crowds. In the space of six years land values on Fifth Avenue, bid up by the merchants flocking to midtown, more than tripled. As the Automobile Age accelerated, the city mandated a fifteen-foot widening of the roadway to accommodate the press of traffic. One Vanderbilt mansion gave up its garden to the project, another its handsome stone steps. St. Patrick's lost the grassy bank that buffered it from the street.

Nothing, however, changed the neighborhood so much as Columbia's decision to vacate its Madison Avenue buildings for the land it had purchased on upper Broadway in Morningside Heights. When the university abandoned its Collegiate Gothic structures east of Madison, Columbia's relationship to the Upper Estate changed radically. "The attention of the trustees," Butler wrote, "was divided between the important problems relating to the reorganization of the college and its development into a university and those growing out of the renewal of the leases on the Upper Estate." Translated out of Butlerese, this meant that expansion on the grand scale of McKim, Mead & White's Olympian campus on Morningside Heights had somehow to be financed, and the Upper Estate was the only cash cow in sight.

The milking commenced in 1904, shortly after Butler's presidency began. Over the protests of Columbia treasurer J. M. Nash, the southernmost block, between 47th and 48th Street, was sold for $3 million to pay for the land Columbia had acquired uptown. On a more sustained basis, the college attempted to renegotiate the remaining Upper Estate leases as they came up for renewal, but failed to wrest them entirely free of terms that had been set at the time of their original execution. Hurried along by some well-aimed lawsuits, and simultaneously seeking to maximize the value of the leases that did expire, Columbia stopped enforcing its 1859 restrictive covenants barring apartment houses and commercial or industrial use.

This last act proved to be a tactical error that would, over time, mutate into a brilliant strategic coup. For with the suspension of the covenants, the Upper Estate began a plummet that turned it into a tawdry collection of rooming houses, brothels, speakeasies, and shoe repair shops able to bring in by 1928, at the very peak of an unprecedented economic boom, a pathetic $300,000 a year in ground rents. But because of the accident of these eleven acres remaining under a single ownership for the entire 127 years since Hosack acquired them, it was possible for someone to think about taking over the whole thing and building something grand—at the very least a new opera house, ideally with a handsome plaza in front of it.

To Nicholas Murray Butler and Columbia treasurer Frederick A. Goetze, who was Butler's primary fiscal adviser, custodian of funds, and financial agent, correspondence was as natural, and as essential, as breathing. Every day Butler's letters to "Mr. Goetze," as he always called him, crossed in the mails on their way down to the Treasurer's Office on Wall Street with uptown-bound replies, queries, and comments respectfully addressed "Dear President." Letters posted by either man on a Tuesday were answered on Wednesday, and these in turn met their reply on Thursday, steady droplets in a pelting rain of paper. Read through their correspondence—Goetze worked with Butler for more than four decades, three of them as treasurer—and you may find reference to a telephone conversation one or the other had with a third party, but if the two men ever spoke on the phone to each other, it would have defied logic: in the wake of their oceanic correspondence, there would have been nothing left to say.

On January 20, 1928, a Friday, Butler's daily letter to Goetze included this bit of news: "I am told on good authority that a group of stockholders of the Metropolitan Opera House Company think that the best place for the Opera House would be on our property." Goetze's reply was speeding back to Morningside Heights by Saturday morning. He acknowledged that he had fielded an expression of interest from R. Fulton Cutting of the Metropolitan Opera less than two weeks earlier but wasn't very enthusiastic about it—the idea of an opera house on Columbia property, Goetze felt, was an especially bad one. "We have only to look at the neighborhood of Broadway and 40th Street to get an idea of how the [current] opera house has depressed that section for business purposes."

Not likely what Butler wished to hear. Though he himself wasn't connected to the Metropolitan, there was no institution in New York whose prime movers were closer to the center of the world Butler inhabited. On Monday evenings, the parterre boxes of the Opera House on Broadway accommodated a skein of New York notables whose names glittered as brightly as their jewels: the "Triple Entente" of Vanderbilts, Morgans, and Astors; the old New York clans like the the Goelets and the Cuttings; the industrialists-turned-aristocrats who bore such names as Harriman and Harkness. Together, the boxholders owned the Metropolitan Opera House, but that was not the same as controlling the Metropolitan Opera itself. That was the property of a man who couldn't have been in some ways more like them (aristocratic, fabulously wealthy, supremely confident) and in at least two others more different (he was Jewish, and he actually liked opera). And had Otto Kahn not been "slapped down [by the boxholders] in a manner distinguished for cold rudeness and disregard of fact," had they not "insulted, abused, flayed, and embarrassed" him, Rockefeller Center would never have been built.

Like so many Manhattan sagas, the story of opera in New York is a tale of real estate and money, specifically the convulsions that arise from not enough of the former and too much of the latter. In 1854 the old Knickerbocker families who comprised society in New York—Beekmans and Schuylers and Bayards—built the city's first opera house, the Academy of Music, at the corner of 14th Street and Irving Place. The Academy's sixteen prime boxes were enough for the founding families but could not accommodate the members of the rising merchant dynasties who may not have particularly cared for opera but definitely cared about any club they were not allowed to join.

In 1880 a well-connected lawyer named George H. Warren announced that he had mustered "the Astors, the three Vanderbilts, the Morgans, myself and others" to build a new opera house. Three years later, architect J. C. Cady's yellow-brick pile opened on Broadway between 39th and 40th Street. The Metropolitan Opera House was a design anthology of styles so inconsistent with one another, so extreme in their efforts to ape the tastes of the Europeans whom New York plutocrats admired (and misunderstood), that the *New York World,* at the house's opening, said that "a more amazing example of wealth working without taste or conviction or public spirit was never seen." The *World* also said the building looked like "an enormous malt-house"—the first instance of its being likened to a brewery, a characterization that would be used again and again over the eighty-plus years of its life.

Inside, nothing defined the Met so thoroughly as the dreadful sight lines and awkward seat positions that demanded a "sidesaddle, neck-craning posture" for operagoers who actually wished to see what was happening onstage. From nearly a thousand of the less expensive seats in the dress circle, the balcony, and the family circle—25 percent of the entire house—one could barely see the stage at all, blocked as it was by the justification for the house's very existence: the two tiers of boxes comprising the Diamond Horseshoe, "in which ladies expose their diamonds, chests and boredom, and old gentlemen sleep." Every Monday night during the opera season, each of the seventy founding families enjoyed what really mattered—what one writer called "exceptional sightlines from box to box."

To say merely that Otto Kahn differed from the Met's founding families because he was Jewish and because he loved opera may mislead. Given his upbringing, his place in the world of finance, the nature of his business associations, and his absolute lack of adherence to anything remotely resembling the practice of Judaism (Kahn and his equally aristocratic German-Jewish wife, the former Addie Wolff, had all their children christened in the Episcopal church), Kahn's religion was in most ways no more relevant to his stature in New York than was the shape of his silvery mustache. He was suspended so comfortably between the world into which he had been born and the world in which he lived that the social historian Dixon Wecter called him "the flyleaf between the Old and the New Testaments." To the founding families, much more offensive than either his ethnicity or the depth of Kahn's passion for opera was Kahn's wish to share that passion with a broad section of New York's citizenry.

Kahn was an unlikely populist. He was born in Mannheim, Germany, in 1867 to a wealthy family, and immigrated to New York in 1893, after several years as a banker in London. Working at the elbow of Jacob Schiff, the great financier who built the merchant banking firm of Kuhn, Loeb & Company to near preeminence in the last years of the nineteenth century, he became one of the towering figures in American financial history. It was largely through syndicates organized by Kahn's firm that the first John D. Rockefeller expanded his oil fortune by acquiring large pieces of the Southern Pacific and Pennsylvania Railroads, and got hold of his chunk of the meat-packing trust dominated by Armour and Swift. Kahn was only thirty when he attracted the attention of the rail baron E. H. Harriman and guided Harriman's successful effort to consolidate control of the Union Pacific, the Baltimore & Ohio, the Missouri Pacific, and several other lines.

Such activities will make a man very rich, a condition that Otto Kahn rather enjoyed. His most endearing indulgence was the purchase of two seats for every musical or theatrical performance he attended: one for himself, the second for his coat and hat. But Kahn spent his serious money on houses. His best-known residence was the three-million-dollar palazzo—

those are 1914 dollars—he built on Fifth Avenue, its walls soon lined with Botticellis and Titians. Although it was one of the largest private homes in New York, occupying the entire blockfront between 91st and 92nd Street (after his death it became the Convent of the Sacred Heart), it was a bungalow compared to the manor house at Kahn's 443-acre country estate in Huntington, on Long Island. There, atop the man-made hill constructed from fill brought in on Kahn's private railroad, and not far from Kahn's personal eighteen-hole golf course, sat the 107-room house that would become most familiar from one of the great opening sequences in American movies, the aerial shot in which it served as the stand-in for the palace of Orson Welles's Charles Foster Kane.

When Kahn took over control of the faltering Metropolitan Opera Company in 1908, he did it with the tacit support of the men who had founded the Met. That same year he brought in from Italy a young conductor named Arturo Toscanini as well as impresario Giulio Gatti-Casazza, who would build the company into one of the foremost presenters of opera in the world. Gatti was at first reluctant, complaining that the stage was inadequate, the seating abominable, the production equipment antiquated. Kahn persuaded him to leave his position with La Scala by promising him that "in two or three years a new Metropolitan Opera House will be built."

This was not merely a promise on which Kahn would fail to deliver; it was a promise he was never in a position to make. Though he would eventually own 83 percent of the opera company, Kahn never controlled so much as a single brick of the house itself. The ill-starred old "malt-house" was the property of the original boxholders, the seventy families who had built it in 1883. The vehicle of their ownership was the Metropolitan Opera Real Estate Company, whose relationship to Kahn's Metropolitan Opera Company was strictly nominal. From 1908 nearly to the end of his life, Otto Kahn produced operas for the pleasure of what one of his biographers called the "feudal barons clinging to their castles and patents of nobility"—their boxes in the Diamond Horseshoe. He put on the shows; they owned the building.

For a time in the early 1920s, Kahn began to make some progress on a plan for a new house. But that effort died in 1925 with George C. Haven, the head of the Real Estate Company, with whom Kahn had worked since taking over the producing company in 1908. Haven's replacement as the representative of the boxholder/owners was R. Fulton Cutting. If, as at least one historian suggests, Kahn was immediately discouraged by the prospect of negotiating with Cutting, then Kahn knew his man well: over the next six years, the two would become so enmeshed in agreements, arguments, threats, appeasements, feints, and parries that had it all been set to, say, Puccini, it could have satisfied the neck-craning riffraff way up in the Opera House's cheap seats. After all, what entertainment could be juicier than a prolonged catfight between aristocrats?

There, on one side of the stage, stood Kahn, a modern Maecenas: America's leading patron of the arts, sponsor of promising talent, ubiquitous symbol of the cultural life of New York—"a town frequently mentioned in connection with the name of Otto Kahn," wrote one ironist. By 1926 he had put millions of his own dollars into placing musicians in the pit and singers on the stage of the yellow-brick brewery. The house was by then even less adequate than it had been when he recruited Gatti and Toscanini eighteen years earlier, the signs of age compounding the inadequate seating and the cramped performing areas. The Met's storage capacity was so abysmally small that scenery was stacked against the side of the building along 39th Street. By day, people traveling to work picked their way past Parisian garrets, ancient Roman arches, lacquered Chinese thrones. Kahn no doubt agreed with Frederick Goetze's harsh appraisal of the neighborhood, the glamorous shops, restaurants, and hotels of an earlier era now supplanted by . . . the garment industry.

One would think that on this, at least, Kahn would have been able to find common ground with the other figure on this stage, R. Fulton Cutting. His genealogy could be a translator's key to old New York. He was a Fulton and a Cutting, of course, but also a Bayard and a Livingston. It was in the summer home of Cutting's great-grandfather, William Bayard, that Bayard's friend Alexander Hamilton died, David Hosack at his bedside. His family had a box at the old Academy of Music, and occupied a new one in the Horseshoe when the Met opened in 1883. The Cuttings had been there ever since.

If the triumph of good government could be measured by the number of groups devoted to its propagation, Fulton Cutting would have reigned as undefeated champion: he was a founder of the Citizens' Union, founder and chairman of the progressive Bureau of Municipal Research, president for nearly thirty years of the Association for Improving the Condition of the Poor, president for almost twenty of the tuition-free Cooper Union. He also belonged to the National Citizens Union of a Thousand, whose members included John D. Rockefeller Jr. and 998 other gentlemen who wanted the government to enforce the prohibition laws. He emerged from his limestone mansion on East 67th Street each day in the tall silk hat, cutaway coat, and striped trousers of the Victorian era, his beard trimmed in such a way that he bore an improbable resemblance to Cardinal Richelieu. His professional life was limited to "private banking"—a discreet euphemism for "owning things," in his case sizeable pieces of real estate and various commercial enterprises. He also found the time and energy to serve as ranking lord among the society of peers that controlled the Metropolitan Opera Real Estate Company. As such, R. Fulton Cutting was Otto Kahn's landlord, and for all of Otto Kahn's experience, the role of tenant was not a familiar one.

On Memorial Day in 1913, nine-year-old George Hearst, dressed in a crisp white sailor suit and accompanied by a twenty-one-gun salute from a battery of warships in the Hudson, pulled the cord that unveiled a lavish monument to the battleship *Maine* in Columbus Circle, at the southwest corner of Central Park. Now the gilded figures in the monument's heroic sculptural group could sail eternally forward from the idea that launched them: the creation, fifteen years earlier, of the slogan "Remember the *Maine!*," concocted and popularized by young George's father, William Randolph Hearst.

The Maine Monument made its landing in Columbus Circle because that was the epicenter of the real estate empire the senior Hearst had begun to assemble in a corridor running east from the Hudson River on both sides of 57th Street. Over the next decade and a half Hearst acquired so much of this 57th Street corridor that there had to be more to his ambitions in the area than simple monomania.

There was. Shortly after 1920, Hearst's colleague, the editor Arthur Brisbane, convinced him that the time was right for a trans-Hudson automobile bridge, and that 57th Street was perfect for its eastern terminus. Hearst's acquisition of property in the area accelerated rapidly. At Park Avenue he bought all four corners, including the Ritz Towers. At Eighth Avenue he landed the spot for the headquarters of his publishing empire. Along Sixth and Seventh Avenues, Hearst and Brisbane together purchased whole blockfronts of low-rise, low-rent buildings. But the potential flood of traffic emerging from a trans-Hudson bridge held little appeal for most New Yorkers. By 1923 opposition to so large an intrusion on an increasingly congested midtown pushed the proposed bridge six miles north to 178th Street, far from the Duchy of Hearst-Brisbane. Thus did a piece of land become available on the block that ran west from the plot Hearst had reserved for his headquarters. Otto Kahn thought it would make a nice spot for a new opera house.

In late 1925, Kahn paid $2.67 million for the property, a parcel that ran 325 feet along West 57th Street toward Ninth Avenue, all the way through to 56th Street. Deed in hand, he sent a twelve-page letter to Fulton Cutting, a comprehensive catalog of the Metropolitan Opera House's deficiencies onstage, backstage, in the wings. He specified the inadequacy of the ventilation system, the insufficient storage capacity, the vexing traffic problems in the auto-clogged streets of the garment district. And, making very clear who suffered most in this profoundly ill-conceived building, he addressed the front of the house as well. "The accommodations for those patrons of the opera who cannot afford to buy the more expensive seats," Kahn wrote, "is inadequate as to quantity and wholly unsatisfactory as to quality. . . . It is really an act of unfairness to take money for some of [the worst seats]—especially from people of small means."

Within days, word of Kahn's challenge to the Real Estate Company was out. So, in the last week of January, was Cutting's public reply: "If the music lovers of New York want a new opera house they are entitled to have one," his statement said. But the owners of the current opera house, he continued, "are not . . . of the opinion that the present house is antiquated or that its site is undesirable. . . . No doubt several of its characteristics could be improved and its superiority to other similar institutions still further enhanced. If it is desirable that the building should be replaced by one larger and more scientifically equipped, I presume the company of which Mr. Kahn is the chairman will undertake the project." Put simply, if Kahn wants a new house, let Kahn pay for it.*

Apparently, most of New York thought he might do just that. Kahn's announcement brought forth waves of supplicants who saw their own interests enhanced by the prospect of a new house. Writing from the Hotel d'Hermitage in Monte Carlo, Mrs. Florence S. Bache virtually begged for two Monday night subscriptions. Mrs. Roland Harriman made an earnest pitch for seats, and financier John Jacob Raskob pulled Kahn aside at a dinner to stake his claim on a new box every bit as prominent as his old one. Thomas Lamb, the architect whose fevered fantasies had created many of

---

*Not that Cutting and his colleagues couldn't have handled it: just a few weeks earlier, they had turned down a $7 million offer for the site of the old house on Broadway and 40th, insisting on a highly unlikely $10 million.

the lavishly overdone movie palaces of the era, applied for the job of designing the new Met; his rivals, the Rapp Brothers of Chicago, offered to do preliminary sketches for free. Theatrical impresario Lee Shubert commended to Kahn an acoustician who would be perfect for the job. Among the mob of tile manufacturers, ironworks fabricators, plumbing suppliers, and other contractors throwing themselves at Kahn, one of the most persistent petitioners was an architect/politician/World War I veteran whose name would live on in New York through the century: Major William F. Deegan, eventually to be immortalized by an expressway in the Bronx.

It took Kahn a year to line up enough support to allow him to reveal his plans. With the backing of such men of means as George Eastman, Marshall Field, Clarence H. Mackay, Vincent Astor, and Robert Goelet, he announced in January 1927 that they would, as a group, "be in a position themselves to make the necessary arrangements to finance a new Opera House" if the Real Estate Company continued its resistance to the idea. Part of the group's power was more than financial: in Goelet and Astor, Kahn had allies on Cutting's board, which in February formally approved Kahn's plans to build on the Hearst property. Shortly thereafter Kahn set sail for his semiannual trip to Europe, no doubt buoyed by visions of the new house that the architect Benjamin Wistar Morris and the designer Joseph Urban would soon be devising.

If any player in the saga of Rockefeller Center had a genealogy as plush as R. Fulton Cutting's, it had to be Ben Morris, whose long line of forebears was studded with Revolutionary War heroes, Episcopal bishops, and other certified members of the patriciate. He looked the part, too: tall and angular, he had the appearance, wrote one contemporary, of "a cultured rail-splitter."

Ignore the fact that Morris was born and raised in Portland, Oregon, a continent away from his family's Philadelphia roots; forget, too, that he had pursued a career selling insurance before packing off for Paris to study at the Ecole des Beaux-Arts: no society architect came so naturally to the position as Morris, and his client list confirmed it. After an apprenticeship in the office of Carrère & Hastings while that firm built the magnificent New York Public Library on Fifth Avenue and 42nd Street, Morris moved through a series of jobs that might have been booked through a well-thumbed edition of the *Social Register*. He assisted his partner Grant La Farge on the Cathedral Church of Saint John the Divine; married to a Morgan cousin, he designed the J. P. Morgan Memorial in Hartford, an addition to the Morgan

Library on 36th Street, and a Morgan country palace on Long Island. His neo-Georgian Union League Club on 37th and Park is probably as close as one can get to the architectural equivalent of a stuffed shirt. (The contextual equivalent was his store for Brooks Brothers on Madison Avenue.) Morris's finest commercial building was crafted for the one business entity that people in his social ambit were most likely to patronize: the Cunard Lines, whose stately headquarters near Bowling Green sat directly across the street from the Rockefeller family offices at 26 Broadway.

Kahn's other candidates for the opera house job included some of New York's most distinguished firms, including Warren & Wetmore, which had designed Grand Central Terminal, and the legendary McKim, Mead & White, which had designed nearly everything else. In Morris, however, Kahn found someone not only competent but, better still, highly unlikely to ruffle Real Estate Company feathers. When, in February 1927, Kahn wrote to Cutting to inform him of his choice of architect, Cutting responded immediately: not only did he think highly of Morris, but he was delighted to point out that fellow Real Estate Company board members J. P. Morgan Jr. and Robert S. Brewster "very well heartily approve" the selection as well. Kahn had reached Cutting during his—and Morgan's and Brewster's—winter holiday at the Jekyll Island Club, a members-only retreat in coastal Georgia that each February was as thick with New York patricians as the Opera House on a November Monday.

But approving Morris did not mean that Cutting and his colleagues approved the task Kahn had assigned him. They may have formally accepted the idea of a new house in February, but while Kahn enjoyed his European trip, his opponents on the board of the Real Estate Company began a counterattack. Nearly every aspect of Kahn's plan came under assault: its requirement that the boxholders put up some of the cash for the new house; its reduction in the number of boxes; its insistence that the boxholders control their seats only on Monday nights, and not for other performances. Some board members expressed their disapproval of the 57th Street site itself, so far west, so unstylish, so close to the Ninth Avenue Elevated and its unappealing crowds. At an April 12 meeting of the board, when the formidable Mrs. Cornelius Vanderbilt III expressed her displeasure and either elicited or commanded the support of her nephew Robert Goelet—a Kahn ally just months before—Kahn's plan was severely wounded.

At least one commentator attributed the Vanderbilt opposition to the family's interest in development on the East Side, where most of their holdings lay; others saw in it the knife of anti-Semitism. But the stated reason was a euphemism of exquisite banality: the board of the Real Estate Company thought it undignified for its Opera House to be situated in the center of a block, not on a corner.

When the White Star liner *Majestic* docked at Manhattan's West Side piers on June 2, 1927, the presence on board of Mr. and Mrs. Otto Kahn was itself news. Returning from three months of "conferences with statesmen and financiers," the *New York Times* reported (failing to mention some pleasure cruising in the Mediterranean with *Vanity Fair* editor Frank Crowninshield), Kahn announced that he was no less committed to the 57th Street site than he had been before Cutting and colleagues reneged on their February agreement.

During Kahn's time abroad, the men he had hired to design the new house set to work. Opera politics may have dictated his selection of Morris, but opera experience led Kahn to yoke the architect into an involuntary partnership with Joseph Urban. "As well commission Brangwyn and Picasso to do a joint mural as set Benjamin Wistar Morris and Joseph Urban designing a single opera house," commented a disbelieving writer in *The New Yorker*. (In fact, the unimaginable yoking of Picasso with the British academic painter Frank Brangwyn nearly came true six years later in Rockefeller Center.) Urban, a Viennese émigré, had designed many opera productions for Kahn's company over the preceding decade, his renown expanding so greatly that he would, in time, receive equal billing with composers. He was perhaps even better known for his work for Florenz Ziegfeld. Not only did Urban design the impresario's eponymous theater on West 54th Street, but every visual aspect of the annual Ziegfeld Follies was his. He designed the sets, the costumes, the gigantic hats of feathers and plumes and spangles assembled into towers reaching several feet above Ziegfeld's gorgeous showgirls (who wore far more above their heads than on their bodies). All this theater experience and much of this lavish imagination were just what Ben Morris lacked. Urban, did, however, share one qualification with his new collaborator: as art director for William Randolph Hearst's Cosmopolitan Studios (where he worked on eleven different films starring Hearst's inamorata, Marion Davies), and as architect of Mar-a-Lago, Marjorie Meriwether Post's ripe 118-room Palm Beach playhouse, Urban had learned how to work for the rich.

For months the two men labored at cross-purposes. Morris remained vigilantly loyal to the need for a reborn Diamond Horseshoe (he could hardly do otherwise: the keystone of the horseshoe, Box 35, belonged to his sort-of-cousin and primary patron, J. P. Morgan Jr.). Urban, meanwhile, pushed various schemes for what he called "a democratic house." But in July Kahn sent Morris on a two-month tour of opera houses and other theaters in France, Italy, and Germany, and his creative imagination was at last ignited. He met with architects, set designers, and opera directors everywhere he went. Whenever he could, Morris would pause with his drawing pad, fashioning page after page of sketches in the same fine hand that distinguished his student work at the Beaux-Arts, where he had spent hours depicting the classical vocabulary of columns and pediments and grand symmetry.

In New York, Urban applied his fecund imagination and his astonishing productivity to the opera house project. He also continued the robust eating and drinking and partying that was so congenial an accompaniment to his large and jovial personality, most especially the weekly Friday afternoon marathon lunch sessions with the architects Ralph Walker, Ely Jacques Kahn (no relation to Otto), and Raymond Hood. Urban was Ray Hood's closest friend, and though his tenure on the opera house project would last less than eight months, it would have a critical, and permanent, impact on at least one of Hood's most important projects. From the nine different plans Urban created for Otto Kahn in his first two months on the job came the basic configuration of the revolutionary auditorium in Radio City Music Hall.

Ben Morris, on the other hand, merely came up with the idea for Rockefeller Center.

While Urban worked and partied, and while Morris traveled and sketched, Kahn began looking for a new site. He kept a brave public face on the original plan, if for no other reason than to prop up the value of the land he had acquired at such a high price. But over the ensuing months the array of options brought to him indicated that in real estate circles, at least, everyone knew the 57th Street plan was dead. The suggestions poured in: the site of the Century Theater, on Central Park West in the 60s. Central Park South and Sixth Avenue. Park Avenue and 96th Street. (After examining some drawings for the 96th Street site, Metropolitan general manager Giulio Gatti-Casazza asked, "And where is Broadway?") A downtown group proposed a site in the western reaches of Greenwich Village, "not congested at either matinee time or in the evening," but not terribly far from the reek of the wholesale meat district. Visions of operatic dollars entranced the developers and landowners of New York to such a degree that a representative of Charles Schwab even suggested the site of his employer's enormous full-block limestone chateau on Riverside Drive and 73rd Street, which the steel magnate had built only twenty-one years earlier. Kahn's search for a site was so public and so futile that it soon provided comic material for the Marx Brothers: in *Animal Crackers,* Captain Spaulding—Groucho—tells a character based on Kahn, "Why not put it in the [Central Park] reservoir and get the whole thing over with?"

More surprising than Kahn's willingness to shift away from 57th Street was the evolution of his relationships with his two architects. Kahn came to feel ever more comfortable with the earnest, accommodating, and surprisingly resourceful Morris. In October 1927, Kahn fired Urban, not because of the quality or quantity of his work but because he published some of his preliminary opera house drawings in *Musical America.* At a luncheon meeting at the downtown Mid Day Club, Kahn told a group that included, notably, both Cutting and Morris that Urban had "succumb[ed] to a stress of artistic temperament, had acted most unwisely, unethically and in an unfortunate matter" when he allowed the plans to be published, and that Kahn had accepted his resignation. Morris would now work alone.

However much Cutting might have appreciated Kahn's including him in what the latter called "a family affair," however much Kahn might have hoped that casting his lot with Morris might be construed as a cooperative gesture by the architect's friends among the boxholders, any thaw between the two sides was only momentary. Several weeks later, continuing conflict between Kahn and Cutting's boxholders led to a war council at the home of banker George F. Baker which failed so completely that Morris was told to suspend his work. And then, a few days into the new year, R. Fulton Cutting received a caller who had an interesting idea.

When a sixty-four-year-old man named John L. Tonnelé dropped dead of a heart attack in a Manhattan taxicab in 1949, his passing received respectful, if slight, notice—about what one might expect for a fifth-generation New Yorker who had done fairly well in the real estate business. But embedded in one obituary was the provocative assertion that, twenty-one years earlier, Tonnelé "woke up one morning and announced to his wife" that he had an idea that would solve the Metropolitan Opera's problematic search for a new home, and speed the development of midtown in the process.

It doesn't diminish Tonnelé's contribution to the creation of Rockefeller Center to note that, although he did have a very good idea, it hardly arose from a concern for either the Met's housing problem or the development of central Manhattan. Tonnelé's employer in January 1928, the long-established real estate agency William A. White & Sons, was on assignment for a client that wanted nothing more than a prepaid escape route from midtown's increasingly commercial streets. That client was Columbia University.

For at least fifteen years, the ill-used Upper Estate had nagged at Nicholas Murray Butler. On occasion he'd ask treasurer Frederick Goetze to bring him up to date on real estate values in the area. At times he even devised his own proposals to enhance university income, including a clever—and prescient—plan to grant the city "sufficient property" to build a north-south street running from 48th to 51st Street, roughly halfway between Fifth and Sixth Avenues. Columbia would thus own "twelve new corners," Butler said, with the increased rental income that corner lots could command—"the easiest way within our power to make a literally stupendous addition to our productive capital," he told the trustees.

But nothing came of Butler's schemes, and by late 1927 Goetze, inspired by the realization that a large number of Upper Estate leases would expire the following year, had actively begun to explore alternative means of boosting the puny stream of cash trickling from the Upper Estate to Morningside Heights. He turned to Harry Hall, president of William A. White & Sons (Hall happened to teach a course in real estate management at Columbia) and asked him to consider the disposition of the university's midtown holdings. It was an obvious course of action; around the same time, as Manhattan real estate values pushed to new peaks, the trustees of the Cooper Union were arranging to lease their land on Lexington Avenue and 42nd Street to Walter P. Chrysler, who would build his headquarters on it.

Hall and his firm, which had been among the first to assemble large parcels of land for skyscrapers in lower Manhattan, were by this point confirmed believers in the future of midtown; in the winter of 1927–28 they had even decided to move their own offices from the financial district to Madison Avenue and 45th Street. Like other real estate operators, Hall and his colleagues had seen the boom of the twenties reconfigure the economic shape of the city, the retail stores that had pushed the mansion-owning wealthy northward now joined by office towers spiking the midtown sky. In 1920, advertisements placed by the Astor interests had promoted the sale of some midtown holdings with the elaborately capitalized assertion that

"The Heart of This Great City Is Now Settled for All Time. It is the district from 34th to 59th Sts., 3rd to 10th Avenues." By the time John Tonnelé called on Fulton Cutting, nearly eight years later, Columbia's blocks of dreary brownstones looked like a severely neglected patch in midtown's lush commercial garden.

In introducing himself to Cutting, Tonnelé, a youthful-looking forty-three, might have cited their shared academic roots: he was Class of '06, Cutting was '71—Columbia, of course. He certainly invoked what he had been reading in the papers, that Kahn's Ninth Avenue dreams had been waylaid by Cutting and his Real Estate Company board. Perceiving a match between his client's needs and Cutting's interests, he proposed that the Opera build a new home on Columbia land, specifically at the western end of the block between 48th and 49th Street, backing up to Sixth Avenue and facing a new north-south street cut into midblock. "It was I who conceived the idea [of] Rockefeller Center when it was thought that the Opera might be part of the development," Tonnelé wrote in 1943, and in a way he was right.

Within days Cutting handed a rope, a boat, and several weeks' fuel to a drowning man: he passed Tonnelé's idea on to Ben Morris. The architect had invested so heavily in Kahn's plan, and had become so familiar with the Real Estate Company's clear unwillingness to back it, that he must have recognized that his opportunity to design a new opera house—a commission that would render insignificant everything else he had done before—was rapidly evaporating. Tonnelé's scheme, wrote Morris to Cutting, wasn't financially sound, "but it fathered my thought that if carried further it might show a way out of our difficulties." Morris didn't merely carry Tonnelé's plan further; he grabbed it, expanded it, reshaped it, and at every step pulled it closer to reality. In the process, he made it his own.

Employing impressive political skills and unceasing effort, Morris initiated a single-handed blitz along three different fronts: without alienating Kahn, who was still paying his bills, he had to move ownership of the very notion of a new house from Kahn's domain to Cutting's; he had to persuade Columbia at least to entertain the idea of an opera house on its midtown land; and he had to commit to paper a plan for the site that made both aesthetic and financial sense.

On the first front, Morris managed to position himself as the link between Cutting and Kahn, whose distaste for each other was growing ever more intense. He met with Kahn's real estate advisor, William H. Wheelock, to persuade him of the virtues of the 49th Street site, and even after Wheelock pronounced it a rotten idea, Morris wisely continued to include him in all phases of his planning. If Kahn was going to abandon Morris, it wouldn't be because Morris had aligned himself strictly with Cutting.

At the same time, Morris ramped up his efforts with Cutting and his board. Less than two weeks after John Tonnelé called on Fulton Cutting, Morris was speeding south to the Jekyll Island Club. His bloodlines provided access to the world's "richest, most exclusive . . . most inaccessible" club, where for two weeks Morris could enjoy the private racetrack, the expansive beaches, the streams and fields stocked with fish and game—and the company of J. P. Morgan Jr., George Baker, and other Real Estate Company board members who used the place as a winter playground.

To Kahn, Morris burbled with enthusiasm for the 49th Street site; to Cutting, he argued the inadequacies of a plot on Central Park West that had come into play. With Tonnelé he devised strategies that might thaw the icy resistance of Frederick Goetze, who believed that an opera house would have a negative impact on the university's midtown holdings.*

Something must have worked: when Goetze airily asserted to Tonnelé that the proposed opera house site was not for sale, he appended a coy postscript—not for sale, that is, unless the price was right, and how does five million dollars sound? That was just for the western end of the block bounded by 48th and 49th Streets, and it was a staggering sum even in the overheated Manhattan real estate market of early 1928. To Morris, though, it was not remotely discouraging, for it was around this time that he began to develop the idea that, as he had told Cutting, would "show a way out of our difficulties." An opera house on its own, Morris believed, could never be self-supporting without income from adjacent properties. This called for something far grander than anything he or Kahn, much less the blinkered Cutting, had yet envisioned.

On March 10, Ben Morris committed to paper the first real articulation of what would evolve into Rockefeller Center. He wrote of a "monumental arcade" threading from Fifth Avenue to midblock, where it would open onto a large square fronting the opera house. The arcade would make the opera house visible from—and give it an address on—Fifth Avenue; under the terms of the New York zoning law, the open space of the square would

---

*Once the old Met at 40th Street was torn down, Goetze predicted, "the property contiguous to it will flourish like the proverbial green bay tree"—as if it were the opera that had depressed that part of town.

allow adjacent, income-producing office towers to rise substantially higher than any others in the neighborhood. Retail stores on the ground floor of the buildings lining the square completed the picture, and from the entire development, which he soon expanded to encompass all three blocks of the Upper Estate, Columbia would receive, Morris wrote, a "permanency of income."

If the elaborate network of bridges and ramps and elevated porte cocheres that Morris envisioned never came to pass, if the hours he had spent sketching the Place Vendôme and the Vatican Piazza on his 1927 Kahn-financed European trip turned out to have no bearing on what would evolve, it really didn't matter: by mid-April, Morris had identified all the essentials of what would evolve over the next four years into Rockefeller Center. It was missing only one thing: a Rockefeller.

On April 24, 1928, Morris was handed a note informing him that "Mr. R. Fulton Cutting called up to advise that he is endeavoring to arrange a dinner for 25 to 30 prominent men which would be given at the Metropolitan Club. . . . Mr. Cutting would like [Morris] to attend the dinner and to be prepared to submit the proposed plans to the best possible advantage and suggests that it might be advisable to have a paste board model made." The note concluded with genteel delicacy: "It is Mr. Cutting's plan that this dinner shall mark the beginning of an effort to interest the prominent men he has in mind."

By now, at last, Kahn and Cutting had begun to cooperate. In early April, fed up with the Real Estate Company's unwillingness to pick up a meaningful share of the cost of a new house, Otto Kahn had told his friend, the eminent lawyer Paul Cravath, "Pulling teeth is a delectable diversion as compared to getting anything out of these people." But once the Real Estate Company indicated it was prepared to underwrite construction costs (provided, of course, that boxholders could retain the traditional privileges Kahn had sought to dilute), Kahn agreed to collaborate with Cutting in the search for money to acquire the land. Together they drew up the list of people they would invite to a dinner at the Metropolitan Club. Two and a half weeks before the event, Kahn told Cutting that he wished to invite one more person, someone whose wealth could be more readily measured in influence than in money: the self-described "family physician to big business," Ivy Ledbetter Lee.

Others may lay claim to having first uttered the term "public relations," but Ivy Lee was the first to practice this gray art with such galloping success. Tall and dignified, with steel-blue eyes that could nail a man in place, the Georgia-born Lee was never his clients' factotum; they saw him as an equal or, in some instances, as a sort of superior being possessed of wisdom beyond the reach of mortals. As a young man he coined the phrase "enlightened self-interest" to describe why it was sometimes good to do well, and vice versa—exactly the sort of nostrum that could enable a Progressive Era businessman to make a buck and feel noble at the same time. George Washington Hill, the irrepressibly flamboyant buccaneer who ran the American Tobacco Company, said he paid the firm of Lee, Harris & Lee $40,000 a year: $10,000 for publicity, and $30,000 for the privilege of talking to Ivy Lee. Nothing better served Lee's primary task—explaining the behavior of the powerful to the rest of the world—than his ability to embrace two conflicting ideas at once. This skill was most vividly demonstrated during the years he was the leading American exponent of diplomatic recognition of the Soviet Union while simultaneously meeting with Adolf Hitler to discuss Lee's representation of the German chemical trust I. G. Farben. At the peak of his success, Lee operated out of an enormous office at 15 Broad Street in lower Manhattan, tending to a client list that ran from Otto Kahn and Walter P. Chrysler to Princeton University and the government of Poland. And to an institution every bit as exalted (and a great deal richer) than any of those: John D. Rockefeller Jr.

The two men met in 1914, when a lethal anti-union effort at the Rockefeller-owned Colorado Fuel & Iron Company in Ludlow, Colorado, turned a coal field into a killing field. Among the dead were thirteen women and children asphyxiated in the cellar of a dwelling that had been torched by the state militia. Ludlow was the fulcrum of the junior Rockefeller's life. Even the labor organizer Mary Harris Jones—the legendary "Mother Jones"—recognized that he was neither culpable for the murderous tactics of the anti-union forces nor without honestly felt horror at their outcome, but the newspaper-reading nation thought otherwise. The Rockefeller son, having none of the confidence of his father, that unmistakable buoyancy that holds the self-made aloft, flinched from the hail of opprobrium and sought the shelter of an expert. When Lee, recommended to him by his friend Arthur Brisbane, told the younger Rockefeller that he should simply tell the truth, openly and frankly, a bond was struck for life. "This is the first advice I have had that does not involve deviousness of one kind or another," Rockefeller said.

Of course, not everyone considered Lee's counsel a distillate of the Ten

Commandments. Not even Lee: telling the truth, he argued, was worth doing not because it was a moral good but because it was good for business; in many instances, he felt, saying nothing at all was even better. He often withheld his facts strategically, and in the process earned from Upton Sinclair the nickname "Poison Ivy," and from Carl Sandburg the epithet "Paid Liar." Robert Benchley was a lot more playful: Lee, he wrote, "has devoted his energies to proving, by insidious leaflets and gentle epistles, that the present capitalistic system is really a branch of the Quaker Church, carrying on the work begun by St. Francis of Assisi." Take away "insidious" and you have a description of a worldview that approximated John D. Rockefeller Jr.'s most earnest imaginings.

Otto Kahn would have had a more sophisticated view of the capitalist system that had made him so wealthy, but his sense of Lee's indispensability matched Rockefeller's. Lee began representing Kahn's public persona in 1918, and for most of the years they worked together every letter to the editor, every speech, every public utterance Kahn wished to make ("The Problem of Leisure," "The Motion Picture," "A Plain Statement of Presidential Preference") would be sent to Lee for clearance. With uncharacteristic intimacy, Kahn addressed his scores of letters to Lee "My dear Ivy"; Lee, eschewing the formality that scented most of his own correspondence, invariably opened his letters to Kahn with a spirited "Dear Boss." The one that arrived at Kahn's office on May 5, 1928, connected the circuit between Lee's two most important clients: "I cannot come to any other conclusion than the one I suggested as the best way to approach Mr. Rockefeller" about Morris's "thrilling" idea, Lee said. "I am sure he will be interested."

As Ben Morris addressed the assembled decimillionaires on that May Monday in the Metropolitan Club's Stanford White–designed palazzo, a stranger could not have guessed the peculiar circumstances. Morris's audience was a group of men either already committed to his plan (Kahn, Lee, a few Real Estate Company board members) or almost irrelevant (everyone else). His real audience was the man who wasn't present, who would learn of the evening's details only when Lee reported on them.

If Morris knew this, he didn't let on. He directed the group's attention to his model, detailed down to the tiny clay cars cruising Fifth Avenue. His slides showed a formal plaza fronting a rather severe opera house, its auditorium bracketed by private lobbies for the boxholders. Office buildings rose on the south and north sides of the plaza in symmetrical lockstep, and a long arcade stretched from Fifth, passing between two more buildings and across the plaza to the opera house doors. The slide indicating the development's location in the grid of midtown Manhattan identified nearby landmarks: the subway and elevated lines, adjacent hotels, and—Morris knew the men he was talking to—the Racquet Club, the Union Club, the University Club, the Harvard Club, the Yale Club.

"The whole thing stands or falls on the . . . increase in revenue obtainable due to the creation of an open square," Morris said. He explained how the presence of the plaza would, under the zoning laws, allow taller buildings at its flanks; how the additional height would make up for the revenue lost to the plaza itself; and how premium rents could be had for those office suites that benefited from the open views outside their windows. The income from the office towers would cover continuing costs at the opera. All that was needed was the money to buy the land for the plaza.

Ivy Lee was now ready to take care of that. Four days later his report landed on John D. Rockefeller Jr.'s massive Queen Anne desk in the family offices at 26 Broadway, near the southern tip of Manhattan. After duly reporting the essentials of Morris's plan, Lee made his pitch. "The key to the whole situation," he wrote, "is the raising of two and one-half million dollars . . . to purchase the grounds from Columbia University."

CHAPTER TWO

The name by which the world identified him was itself diminishing: Junior. It signified that he was young, which was all right when he was a child but by the time he reached his fifties, in his professional and personal prime, it

*A plain, simple, earnest, sincere, honest, well-meaning, **commonplace person,** destitute of originality or any suggestion of it.*

—MARK TWAIN
ON JOHN D. ROCKEFELLER JR.

could only imply a sort of inadequacy. Junior as in junior partner, which is to say not quite fully fledged; junior as in subordinate to; junior as in, worst of all, son of. In his own offices, where he presided over dozens of family employees—investment strategists, legal experts, property managers, security guards—even here he was Junior, although business etiquette, post-Edwardian manners, and the nature of service elevated him slightly: to the clerical staff and many others, he was always "Mr. Junior."

The word also suggested self-effacement, and John Davison Rockefeller Jr. was by all reasonable standards self-effacing. Senior—his father, the first John D., the one who built the immeasurable fortune—Senior may have been a dutiful son, a religious man, at times something of a prig, but he was also larger than life, vivid, a man snugly comfortable in his fortune, in his skin, in his name. Junior knew guilt and doubt, and though he never expressed anything but earnest respect in his thousands of letters to his father, he knew the chill of living in the dark recess of another's shadow. In Junior there was, for much of his life, a profound, inescapable juniorness.

In time, with a determination that eventually overwhelmed the doubts and fears and emotional breakdowns that would sometimes paralyze him, Junior found a role that suited him—the exaltation of his father and by extension of the family name. Smiling slightly, his gray-blue eyes taking on as much twinkle as his clenched psyche would allow, he would sometimes say, "You know, I didn't choose this job," but his devotion to it, expressed through philanthropy, public citizenship, and religious commitment, became his life's definition. Only once did he engage in a meaningful business venture of his own, and even this, it turned out, reflected benignly on the father. Ask people which Rockefeller built Rockefeller Center, and even if they don't know a Sr. from a Jr. from a III, most will conjure up the shriveled old oil monopolist who gave dimes to children. Even the cover illustration of *Titan,* Ron Chernow's masterful 1998 biography of Senior, incorporates a photograph of Rockefeller Center. Not only did Senior have absolutely nothing to do with the creation of this cynosure of the family's success, there isn't any evidence that he even once set foot there. Rockefeller Center was Junior's one great claim to business success, but it is a claim that the popular imagination does not honor.

Junior served his father. There was nothing cynical about this service; a man less cynical than Junior would be a biological impossibility. So would a creature less rebellious, or less calculating. His mother once admonished him, "You can never forget that you are a prince, the Son of the King of kings, and so you can never do what will dishonor your Father or be disloyal to the King." Never mind the alarming conflation of the two Rockefeller men with God and Christ; so accepting was Junior of his role on the planet that had his mother compared him to a plow horse in service to a farmer, it would have been just as effective.

In fact, the mother was a stronger influence on Junior than was Senior. The father spent the son's formative years building the Standard Oil Trust and its various appendages, offshoots, tendrils, and tributaries; "it was his mother who developed [Junior]," Senior acknowledged. Laura Celestia Spelman Rockefeller, called Cettie, was a passionate creature with a core moral commitment to charity and to a sort of evangelical progressivism, particularly in the area of race relations, which would mark the Rockefellers for generations. She also was determined that her children—Junior had four sisters—would never grow too comfortable in the embrace of their money (which, Junior said, was always "there, like air or food or any other element"). It was a difficult challenge, but Cettie rose to it with tests that might have been drawn from Greek myth: she once told a neighbor, "I am glad my son has told me what he wants for Christmas so now it can be denied him."

This wasn't fun. Cettie and Senior may have given Junior strong moral lessons and a sturdy Baptist faith, but they also endowed him with a disabling emotional fragility. After the family moved permanently to New York in 1884, when Junior was ten, the boy was twice shipped back to the Rockefeller estate in Cleveland—once for a full year—in the care of family retainers charged with supervising his recovery from debilitating bouts of "nervous collapse," precursors of the crippling headaches and other neurasthenic symptoms that gripped him most of his life.

Tentative, overly cautious, by his own description "shy [and] ill-adjusted," the Junior who matriculated at Brown in 1893 would have stood apart from his classmates even if he hadn't carried the name Rockefeller on his unrobust shoulders. Simply picking a college scared him: to one family adviser he wrote, with heartbreaking self-knowledge, "I do not make friends readily, and some of those interested in my welfare fear that if I go to Yale in a class wholly strange to me, I will be 'lost in the crowd' . . . and remain much by myself, instead of getting the social contact I so greatly need." Though at Brown he struggled to escape from the prison of his shyness— he did take up dancing, a pastime he would enjoy the rest of his life— Junior nonetheless could not loose the knots of habit or the chafing bonds of family expectation. His Baptist mores constrained him, and his instinct for frugality struck others as penury. It did not help that he continued to record every expenditure, even of pennies, in the little accounts book he carried with him at all times, or that he once was seen struggling to separate a pair of stamps that had been glued together. "Old Smokestacks," as some of his classmates called him, could not win: a Rockefeller peeling stamps apart may have been cause for sniggering, but a Rockefeller blithely tossing the ruined stamps in the trash would have fulfilled the most obvious caricature of the wasteful wealthy. A phrase from the speech Junior gave at his class's fiftieth reunion, in 1947, underscores the agony of the years before he attended college and the leaden burden that he carried with him in the long years after; in a more general sense, it illustrates the need of the chronically unhappy to recall moments that were merely uncomfortable as if they had been blissful: Only at Brown, the seventy-three-year-old Junior said, "did I enjoy a completely independent personality."

Imagine, then, the small, timid twenty-three-year-old who stepped off the elevator onto the mustard yellow carpets of 26 Broadway's ninth floor on an October morning in 1897, his first day of work. He was there, really, because he had nowhere else to go. The momentum of great wealth and the dictates of dynastic logic had propelled him to this place, with nothing specific to do, no responsibilities to assume, not even any particular ambitions whose roots might be fortified here. Senior, not yet sixty years old, had already retired, but he had turned over management of his vast enterprises to the first generation of the professional family retainers who would come to be known collectively as the Rockefeller "associates." Twenty-three-year-old Junior sat at his ninth-floor desk and lost himself in minutiae, floating an order for something as trivial as office wallpaper upon a sea of memoranda, letters, confirmations, acknowledgments. "He could spend a half-hour on the wording of a telegram," wrote one family biographer, solely to "reduce its length to the minimal charge." An unlikely regular visitor to 26 Broadway was Mark Twain, whose description of the Junior he came to know was, unsurprisingly, a bull's-eye: "a plain, simple, earnest, sincere, honest, well-meaning, commonplace person, destitute of originality or any suggestion of it."

In time, however, Junior found a direction for himself through the advice of the man who dominated the four-room office. Frederick T. Gates, an outspoken former clergyman who was Senior's closest advisor in matters both financial and spiritual, unfurled Junior's future for him. They were an unlikely pairing, the faint-hearted Junior now in the care of a man who once described himself as "eager, impetuous, insistent, and withal exacting and irritable." But Gates, to whose professional tutelage Senior had entrusted his only son, was endlessly tolerant as he not only schooled Junior in the language of business but also sang to him the more compelling choruses of philanthropy. Gates provided Junior with "a postgraduate degree in business and benevolence," he said, but with a clear emphasis on the latter.

Washed in Baptist piety, Junior saw the Kingdom of God embedded in good works done on Earth; no doubt intimidated by the fact that he bore the same name as the world's most successful capitalist, he could find no safe haven in the byways of business. No success, either: in a first, fumbling foray into stock speculation, Junior lost several hundred thousand dollars and had to turn to Senior for cash to cover his losses. In 1904 a devastating bout of depression kept him away from the office for six months. He was propelled further from the world his father had made by a bribery scandal involving the president of the Standard Oil Trust, an event, said Junior, that "sickened" him. After representing Senior on numerous corporate boards— Standard Oil, of course, as well as U.S. Steel, National City Bank, and more than a dozen others—by 1910 he had resigned from all but two.

A letter Junior sent to his father in 1902 expressed the agonizing dichotomy he had to negotiate. You can almost sense in its syntax the emotional pressure he bore: "Of my ability I have always had a very poor opinion," Junior wrote, "but I [am] wholly and absolutely devoted to your interests." Philanthropy was the vehicle that enabled him to sublimate the first impulse and allow the fullest expression of the latter. It was as if he took literally the famous admonition Gates directed at Senior in 1906. Summoning all the rhetorical power that he had once brought to the pulpit, the millennial thunder of his words vibrating on the page, Gates virtually roared: "Your fortune is rolling up, rolling up like an avalanche! You must keep up with it! You must distribute it faster than it grows! If you do not, it will crush you and your children and your children's children."

The 1902 letter in which Junior expressed his devotion to Senior's interests was written in gratitude: the father had just bestowed upon the son a salary increase, to ten thousand dollars a year. It was not idly given. Junior had gotten married the year before.

As easy as it is to understand why John Davison Rockefeller Jr. wished to marry Abby Green Aldrich, why she wished to marry him is far less clear. The cynic's explanation—access to the luscious Rockefeller fortune—just didn't apply: she had quite a lot of money, and even more strength of character. Junior himself once said, wonderingly, that she "was so gay and young and so in love with everything that [I don't know] why she ever consented to marry a man like me." Perhaps it was this wonderment that had led him, by his own admission, to pray daily for four years, seeking the guidance that would eventually lead him to propose to her.

As vivacious as Junior was tremulous, as confident as he was shy, Abby had met her future husband in 1894, when he was at Brown. She was Providence royalty; her father, Senator Nelson Aldrich, was one of the most powerful men in the nation, so effective as the political representative of the late-nineteenth-century plutocracy that he was called the "Boss of the United States." Like Senior, Aldrich was self-made; unlike Senior, his act of construction made use of such fine materials as art and culture. Where Senior was a prayerful Baptist, Aldrich was a confirmed nonbeliever. "I don't think too much church agrees with the Aldrich family," wrote one of Abby's sisters, referencing the Rockefeller family's religious fervor. "Wasn't it Elsie who put a bone out in her spine while she was kneeling in prayer?" The senator had "a zest for everything of the senses," wrote Abby's biographer Bernice Kert, and his daughter was no different.

Junior's most endearing quality, in fact, may have been the depth of his infatuation with Abby, who gave him access to his smothered emotions. A teetotaler and a Bible-school teacher who would never profane the Lord's day, he seemed to find all his earthly pleasures in his wife. He loved to dance with Abby, and their extensive travels often seemed tailored more to her cosmopolitan tastes than to his relatively narrow outlook. At home this formal, old-fashioned man, who would still be wearing high-buttoned shoes as late as 1952, would pinch her legs from behind as he followed her upstairs. When they were apart he wrote to her daily, letters often bereft of any meaningful news but brimming with genuine love and tenderness. Once, in the summer of 1922, he wrote, "Miss you . . . so sadly . . . need you so much . . . it seems as though you have been away from home for months." She had been gone for a day. For Abby, he was even willing to abide her enthusiasm for the twentieth century. Only after her death in 1948 did he finally ask the Museum of Modern Art, which owed its very existence to Abby's energies and her charity, to remove his name from its mailing list.

The philanthropic campaign that Junior embarked on in the first decade of the twentieth century and maintained for the rest of his long life has had no parallel in American history—in world history, probably. The mythology that maintains that he engaged in it strictly to cleanse his father's oil-stained reputation is no more accurate than the mythology that attributes World War I only to the assassination of Franz Ferdinand in Sarajevo.

For one thing there was Junior's heritage. His socially progressive mother had not married an ungenerous man: as an impecunious produce clerk, the teenaged Senior was already setting aside 6 percent of his wages for charity. In 1859, when he was twenty, Senior sent money to a black man in Cincinnati who was trying to buy his wife out of slavery. Junior's discomfort with (and lack of ability in) the business world, Gates's fiery convictions and charismatic manner, and Abby's instinctive generosity all propelled Junior toward a life of philanthropy. But so did his passionate Christianity, by which he genuinely attempted to live, and his inescapable conviction that the money that had been amassed in the Rockefeller name had a purpose, almost as if that purpose had been attached to it as a precondition.

And then there was Ludlow. After he had quit all the others, the only corporate board on which Junior continued to sit was the one that presided over Colorado Fuel & Iron. The Rockefeller family held a controlling interest in the money-losing enterprise, and Junior vainly hoped he could help it toward success. Instead he found himself singled out in 1914 as the villain of the murderous conflagration provoked by the militiamen who had been pressed into service by the company's local management. In the public mind it was easy enough, and not altogether wrong, to equate "CF&I" with "Rockefeller." Even the *Cleveland Press,* in the city where the family arose, said "the charred bodies of two dozen [*sic*] women and children show that *Rockefeller knows how to win.*"

Against his father's better judgment, Junior traveled to the literal and figurative minefields of southern Colorado. His very presence meant that he accepted responsibility, and his willingness to make himself accessible marked him as different from other industrialists of the age. Unaccompanied by bodyguards, he spoke with workers and their families, and at one point, at a dance in a local hall, he even made several turns around the floor with miners' wives. He removed the man responsible for CF&I's labor policies from his job, and he allowed the workers to organize a union. It may have been a company union, independent of other miners' unions, but it was a union nonetheless.

Years later, Junior characterized Ludlow as "one of the most important things that ever happened to the family." He probably said this because it led him to understand that each stock certificate in the Rockefeller vault represented not just ownership in a company but responsibility for the lives of thousands of men and women as well. He also might have cited the beginning of his association with Ivy Lee, or with the Canadian industrial relations expert—and later prime minister—W. L. Mackenzie King, who became one of his closest advisers and friends, or with Mother Jones, introduced to him by King (ten years later, Junior referred to Jones in a public address as the "marvelous, vigorous, courageous organizer of the United Mine Workers of America"). Ludlow also marked a rupture in Junior's relationship with Gates, who didn't think Christ would have "adopted any spirit of conciliation toward those who came to him in the spirit of these unionists." But the truly important result of Ludlow was this: for the first time in his life, Junior had taken an independent step. He was forty.

After Ludlow, Junior was the Rockefeller who mattered. His father was seventy-five in 1914, long retired, more a symbol than a meaningful presence in American life. Reporters and photographers pursued Senior for pictures of the old man handing out a dime, or playing golf, or celebrating yet another birthday in the long skein that would eventually stretch nearly to his hundredth. But now they went to Junior for opinions on the state of the economy or the behavior of giant corporations (even if, as H. L. Mencken argued, "he has never said anything . . . that was beyond the talents of a Rotary Club orator"). In Junior's philanthropic activities the press found material far more compelling. The chronicling of his charitable acts became a newspaper staple, his bland, unlined face the inevitable photographic accompaniment.

The Rockefeller Foundation, its charter nothing less than "to promote the well-being of man-kind throughout the world," had opened for business in 1913, with Frederick Gates in charge and Junior not far from his side. Following Cettie's death in 1916, Senior accelerated a series of gifts to his son that would total $465 million over the next six years, a huge portion of which filtered directly into Junior's personal benefactions. These included grants to study prostitution and its effects on the women involved; to preserve ancient artifacts in Palestine; to restore Versailles, Fontainebleau, and the cathedral at Reims; to underwrite the pioneering birth control activities of Margaret Sanger; to support the efforts of black colleges (as much as he may have loved Brown, Junior gave only $715,000 to his alma mater—and $3,500,000 to Tuskegee Institute and Hampton Institute). Later in his life, he would acquire and give to the nation much of the land that became Grand Teton National Park, large stretches of the Great Smoky Mountain and Shenandoah National Parks, Palisades Interstate Park in New Jersey, and nearly a third of Acadia National Park in Maine. Colonial Williamsburg, in Virginia, was Junior's idea, executed entirely with Junior's money.

In New York, his gifts were so ubiquitous that critics could claim that any civic institution that did *not* have Rockefeller support was severely stigmatized and not likely to get support from others. Such institutions were few. Junior built the interdenominational Riverside Church on a low bluff over the Hudson, and the nearby International House for foreign students. Across town on the East River, he expanded the Rockefeller Institute for Medical Research (now Rockefeller University) and, across the street, built what became the Memorial Sloan-Kettering Cancer Center. Farther downtown, he would in 1946 acquire a large tract of low-lying real estate and immediately donate it to the United Nations as the site of its new home. Up in Harlem he built the Paul Laurence Dunbar apartments and opened on the same site the Dunbar National Bank, the first black-managed bank in New York. Way uptown, near Manhattan's northern tip, he bought the land for Fort Tryon Park, gave it to the city, and then upon its highest point decreed into being the Cloisters, imported stone by stone from five different French monasteries and, after a renovation paid for by Junior, turned into a home for the medieval collections of the Metropolitan Museum of Art. The Cloisters' most famous holdings were the late-fifteenth-century Unicorn

Tapestries—relocated from 10 West 54th Street, the home of Mr. and Mrs. John Davison Rockefeller Jr.

As a label, "10 West 54th" never became the universal signifier that "26 Broadway" did ("the world's most famous business address," Ron Chernow called the latter, "shorthand for the oil trust itself"). But in the New York of the 1920s, the home Junior and Abby had moved into in 1908 was a familiar, if imposing, beacon. The tallest private residence in the city, its nine stories of stately limestone towered over Senior's mansion just across the open garden on number 10's eastern flank. Once given, what Junior gave away was rarely associated with him; of the New York institutions he created or supported, only the Rockefeller Institute for Medical Research bore the family name. But everyone knew whose house this was.

Even though it was patrolled by a private guard, 10 West 54th was the most accessible manifestation of the Rockefeller fortune. The 765 separate buildings on the 3,300 acres of the family compound at Pocantico Hills, rising above the Hudson in Westchester County (more than three times the size of Central Park, and with much better views) were beyond public access; the Eyrie, Junior's 107-room summer home in Seal Harbor, Maine, with its forty-four fireplaces, twenty-two bathrooms, and fifty-seven miles of exquisitely landscaped carriage roads, was beyond public imagining.

His ability to enjoy the luxuries offered by his great wealth was a sign that, by the mid-1920s, Junior was fully formed; he had grown not only into his self and his name, but also into the privilege that had so discomfited him as a young man. The headaches may still have afflicted him, but he was more than willing to leave his responsibilities to his associates for months at a time and recuperate in Florida, in the south of France, at Dr. Kellogg's sanatorium in Battle Creek. His occasional fits of penury, when he would squeeze nickels until they wept, may have seemed inexplicable to others, but he understood his behavior perfectly: "It was rather expected of me that having inherited money I would waste it," he once said, so "I made up my mind that I wouldn't do it." Several years later, when Junior was looking for someone to write Senior's biography, no less a figure than Winston Churchill offered his services. To Junior, turning Churchill down because his price was too high had nothing to do with whether he could afford it; it had to do only with who Junior was and how he wished to think of himself. The builder Louis Horowitz said that Junior's concern with small things and small amounts was the result of his "defending himself . . .

against being drawn into an unreal world where [the Rockefellers] would dwell alone."

In 1928, Junior at middle age may at last have known who he was, but that did not make him any less solitary a figure. No matter how fast he gave the family money away, he still controlled the nation's largest fortune. He ran no companies, nor did he supervise any. He sat alone atop a massive pile of capital that would soon be characterized as "a potential power which hangs, a vast charge of static electricity, over the world of U.S. industry, a power which is [his] to direct if he cares."

CHAPTER THREE

Know some men by their clothes, but know this one by his office: quiet, stately, reverent not to a specific past—not this collection of French, Spanish, and English pieces—but to the very idea of the past. Here, while the twentieth century accelerated past him, Junior could plant himself in the comfort of centuries long departed.

*In view of the possible development of the Columbia property, all of **these properties will be greatly increased in value.***

—CHARLES HEYDT TO JOHN D. ROCKEFELLER JR., JUNE 25, 1928

In 1923, after a three-week stay in the sanatorium at Battle Creek (where his headaches were diagnosed as "auto-intoxication brought on by strain") and several months more in Florida recuperating from debilitating flu, Junior had ordered up a new office for himself. Behind the gently curving limestone facade of 26 Broadway, up on the twentieth floor, he would preside over a museum's worth of European artifacts installed by the society decorator Charles of London (who was actually Charles of 57th Street, but no one seemed to mind). Five brass chandeliers hung above Junior's Queen Anne desk, his Louis XIII armchair, his Jacobean refectory table. Sixteenth-century Tudor paneling from a manor house in the Cotswolds surrounded a Moorish prayer rug, velvet-covered Charles II armchairs, and recessed oak bookcases. One of these last was filled with sham books, their finely wrought—if empty—bindings handsomely arrayed behind the leaded-glass cabinet fronts.

This was where Junior conducted his business for the decade that he would remain at 26 Broadway, and long after that, too: when he moved into Rockefeller Center in 1933, he took the entire room with him. Dismantled piece by precious piece, it was reinstalled in the southwest corner of the 56th floor of the RCA Building, a custom chimney flue venting smoke from his carved-stone fireplace into the midtown sky. (After Junior's death in 1960, the room remained unchanged for several more years, then was once again disassembled, eventually to be reconstituted in the Rockefeller Archive Center on the grounds of the family estate in Pocantico Hills.)

If there was a certain fortresslike quality to the dark and heavy furnishings, that, too, was revealing. He was not the most accessible of men. His native shyness was compounded by an entirely understandable reluctance to make himself too available: when you are not only the world's richest man but also by the most quantifiable standard its most generous one, the line of applicants, supplicants, and mendicants will be a very long one.

Junior did not often see visitors or venture out to the business quarters of others. His weekdays, which began with his arrival at the office at precisely 9:30 A.M., were largely devoted to correspondence. He dictated letters by the score to his secretaries. He wrote nearly daily to his father, as often as not conveying expressions of filial obligation and gratitude; at times, he was weirdly formal in his attention to matters that one could barely imagine concerning any other father and son on the planet: "In line with our recent correspondence," Junior wrote in 1929, "I am happy to enclose herewith, as a present on your ninetieth birthday, my check for $19,000, being the cost of a Rolls Royce car which I offered you, and instead of which you said you would prefer to have cash."

His interoffice correspondence was simultaneously mountainous and filigreed with detail. The same obsessive care led him to fill the small, black, cardboard-bound diaries he carried in his pocket with notes to himself, quotes he liked ("When the sunset comes, it will find us"), medication schedules, lists of things he could eat safely in restaurants ("cream soups: asparagus mushroom spinach tomato pea"). Like his father before him and his sons after him, he seemingly never threw out a piece of paper. He maintained a growing archive devoted not just to business and philanthropic matters or family finances, but also, under the heading "Reference files," a collection of articles, aphorisms, poems, and inspirational writings, all carefully alphabetized from "Advice" and "Age" to "Women, Influence of" and "Youth."

This wall of paper was, in a way, a form of insulation that helped him keep the world at arm's length. Similarly, he used the small circle of men *Fortune* called his "cabinet" to navigate the currents of commerce flowing outside the walls of 26 Broadway. They understood, above all else, what their roles were: service to Junior and, through Junior, to the entire Rockefeller family. His most intimate associate was Thomas M. Debevoise. Junior and Debevoise had met as young men in the 1890s, when they belonged to the same fraternity, Junior at Brown and Debevoise at Yale. The longevity of their relationship and the daunting force of Debevoise's personality led him to become known in the office as the "Prime Minister." A lawyer of exceptional skills and insuperable confidence, Debevoise actually addressed his employer not as "Mr. Rockefeller" or "Mr. Junior" but, alone among his associates, as "John." He also had unparalleled access: a secret door cut into the ancient oak paneling of Junior's office opened directly into his own.

The other members of Junior's inner circle included Bertram Cutler, who joined the staff as a bookkeeper in 1901 and rose to manage all the family investments, in the process becoming known on Wall Street as "the man who votes the Rockefeller stock." Arthur Woods, a "rotogravurish figure" who was married to Alexander Hamilton's great-great-granddaughter and had been a famously honest New York City police commissioner, took on the role of general adviser and administrator. At least once Woods was called upon to use his law enforcement connections to try to close down an especially noisome speakeasy on the block behind 10 West 54th; one colleague recalled Junior's "occasional remark, 'Your barrel is full. Let's put this in Arthur Woods's barrel.'" Not far from 26 Broadway were Ivy Lee, of course, and Abby's brother Winthrop Aldrich, a mandarin of the New York legal establishment.

If you were to extend *Fortune*'s cabinet metaphor, Charles O. Heydt would at best be an assistant secretary, or even a senior civil servant. This would have been partly because of background, partly because of his function. Heydt had entered the business world in 1891 as a fourteen-year-old office boy. On October 2, 1897, he joined the Frederick Gates–dominated Rockefeller office as a stenographer. In time he became a real estate specialist, a capable negotiator of leases and terms of sale; it was Heydt who assembled in Junior's behalf the land and buildings that became Colonial Williamsburg. In the thirty-third year of his service to the family, wishing to take some long weekends away from the office, Heydt, by then fifty-two, felt compelled to ask Debevoise's permission, adding helpfully and hopefully that "I would have office papers with me every time so that I would not be neglecting things here." When he retired in 1941, after forty-four years on the Rockefeller payroll, Junior and his five sons gave "C. O.," as he was known, an engraved watch.

What none of this revealed was that Junior extended to Heydt a degree of trust he may have withheld even from Debevoise. The day before Heydt had become the eleventh member of the family office in 1897, Junior had become the tenth. Professionally, and in the eyes of the family, they grew up together. While working as a confidential secretary to Cettie and Senior, the genial Heydt was assigned by Cettie—who "thought of [him] as an adopted son"—to accompany Junior on a tour of the family's timberlands and mines in the Pacific Northwest. By 1905, Heydt had become Junior's personal secretary and after that, in some ways, his closest business associate. If there was one moment that cemented their relationship, it occurred in 1915 when Heydt, alone among the family staff, accompanied Junior during his epiphany at Ludlow. Any doubt about the degree of comfort Junior felt in Heydt's company was dispelled in 1922, when he asked C. O. to join him for the three weeks of his medical confinement at Battle Creek. In 1936, when two members of the office tried to get him to shove Heydt into retirement, Junior lashed out at them, challenging their assertions and questioning their motives. The targets of Junior's anger were his own sons, John and Nelson. Heydt stayed.

In the early spring of 1928, Charles Heydt had much to discuss with Junior, and until very late in May none of it had to do with the Metropolitan Opera Company, Columbia University, or Otto Kahn. Heydt's concern was about something of far greater and importance to Junior: West 54th Street between Fifth and Sixth Avenues, where Junior had grown up and where he still lived with Abby, was threatened.

In 1923 the slow, northward migration of the wealthy from midtown to upper Fifth Avenue turned into a stampede. The trigger was a successful lawsuit, brought against the city by an architect named J. E. R. Carpenter, that overturned height restrictions on upper Fifth and thus allowed the development of apartment houses north of 60th Street. In 1925 the *Times* published a lengthy article that confirmed the residential supremacy of the apartment house, in part because most of the better buildings have "a service department from which servants can be procured by the hour . . . about as easily as taxicabs can be picked up on Broadway." For everyone but the superrich, the single-family house was becoming a dinosaur.

More than sixty years after Senior moved his family into the Huntington mansion, his son would still be able to rattle off the names of his West 54th Street neighbors in the 1880s. "Chauncey Depew was at Number 17," he reminisced to his biographer. "The Gurnees . . . B. Altman . . . William K. Vanderbilt and his sister, Mrs. Shepherd . . ." Now, in the middle of the 1920s, it was stores to the east, the increasingly decrepit el to the west, in the neglected Columbia blocks to the south an irruption of speakeasies— *speakeasies, only two blocks away!*—and to the north, an inevitable beach-head for more commerce. In 1922, even the Fifth Avenue Baptist Church, where Junior had taught Bible school for eight years, abandoned West 46th Street for Park Avenue. But Junior held fast, doing whatever he could to protect the Rockefeller properties: his own house; the annex next door at number 12 (acquired in part to hang the Unicorn Tapestries, which just didn't seem to fit in the nine stories of number 10); his father's house, the old Huntington mansion, at number 4; the family gardens at numbers 6 and 8; and, backing onto those, numbers 5 and 7 West 53rd Street, the double mansion that was the winter home of Junior's sister, Alma Rockefeller Prentice.

Junior's field general in the various Battles of 54th Street was Heydt, who directed an effort that "only a Rockefeller can afford," said the real estate executive Peter Grimm—fundamentally, the assembly of a moat made of buildings. From 1924 forward, whenever an adjacent property went on the market, it was Heydt's job to take it off the market—to buy it. By the end of the decade the Rockefeller family owned fifteen separate lots (and their buildings) at the Fifth Avenue end of West 54th Street, thirteen more on the adjacent stretch of West 53rd, another six on West 55th, and a stately row of parcels marching up the west side of Fifth between 52nd and 55th Street.

This frenzy of acquisition was only part of Junior's campaign. At the same time, according to the civic reformer William H. Allen, his representatives used political and economic muscle to keep tax appraisals substantially below market value. And now, in early May 1928, Heydt's attention was turned toward a skirmish taking place in the regulatory labyrinths of the city's zoning laws. Property owners on 53rd and 54th Streets who were not Rockefellers had petitioned the city to rezone the streets for business, arguing that without such a change they'd go broke. On May 11, when the *Times* reported the remarkable outcome, the story ran across two columns at the very top of page one. Even though thirty-eight of forty-five non-Rockefeller property owners supported the rezoning, Junior prevailed. In the block west of Fifth, from 42nd Street all the way up to 59th, 53rd and 54th would remain the only streets closed to business.

In 1911, when the Rockefellers took control of the Equitable Trust Company—the foundation of what would become the Chase Manhattan Bank—they had the essential assistance of Kuhn, Loeb & Company, which in turn designated Otto Kahn to join the Equitable board. In the years following, Kahn's firm and the Rockefeller interests continued their productive relationship, and Kahn and Junior shared a variety of personal communications. In February of 1928, Kahn took the time to commend Junior on his testimony before a Senate committee, saluting him as the representative of "that large majority of business men who are decent and right-thinking." But in Junior's office, custom still took precedence over personal history. Four days after Ben Morris's May 21 presentation at the Metropolitan Club, Kahn wrote Junior to request "ten minutes of your time." Like all business or philanthropic propositions directed to Junior, this one would not penetrate the ramparts. He asked Kahn to meet with Heydt.

It was a meeting Heydt had been anticipating for six months. Just as Ivy Lee had maneuvered Junior into a position that made him susceptible to Kahn's entreaties, so had Heydt been waiting to engage himself (and thus Junior) in a plan to develop the Upper Estate. In late December 1927, even before John Tonnelé first called on Fulton Cutting, Heydt was already discussing with Thomas Debevoise the development potential of the Columbia land. Further, his intimacy with every vibration in the midtown real estate market had doubtless been heightened by both the zoning battle and his vigilant attention to protecting Fortress Rockefeller on 54th Street.

Consequently, before Heydt met with Kahn on Friday, June 1, to discuss the opera house project, a long list of virtues would already have been apparent to him: here was a worthwhile civic undertaking; an opportunity to play a role in the demolition of the speakeasy culture so alien to Junior; a chance to create not just a buffer to protect 54th Street but a bulwark; and, incidental but no less appealing, the chance to turn a handsome profit in the process. Three weeks after he saw Kahn, Heydt suggested that Junior buy ten properties on 53rd and 54th Streets. He said such an action would block the planned development of a sixteen-story apartment hotel on 53rd Street "which would be very noticeable from the rear of your own house." He also said it would likely forestall another rezoning effort he expected in the fall. And, he concluded, "In view of the possible development of the Columbia property, all of these properties will be greatly increased in value and the whole area within three or four blocks of [the Upper Estate] will take on new life."

It is not entirely far-fetched to suggest that Junior was pulled into developing Rockefeller Center because a member of his staff wanted to enhance the value of the family's holdings in the neighborhood. Not once in his voluminous, nearly daily correspondence with his father in 1928 did Junior mention the opera company, the Columbia land, or any plans for engaging in a major development effort. His mammoth restoration of Versailles was not yet completed, and the recolonizing of Colonial Williamsburg was just getting up to speed. The first residents would soon be moving into Junior's Dunbar Apartments in Harlem (W. E. B. Du Bois and Paul Robeson among them), with the Dunbar National Bank scheduled to open in September. He was also preparing to begin an extended and painfully public proxy fight—a crusade, really—to remove from the chairmanship of Standard of Indiana Colonel Robert M. Stewart, whose involvement in the Teapot Dome scandals of the Harding administration was only now coming fully to light.

Heydt, however, was not distracted by any of Junior's other activities; he was the office real estate specialist in an office barely concerned with real estate (the Dunbar complex was Junior's first meaningful foray into development). He took to the opera house project in much the same manner Ben Morris did (even if much more comfortably: unlike Morris, he knew he'd still have a job if the project didn't proceed). For Heydt—for any real estate man, including all those in the growing contingent sniffing around the Upper Estate, making the pilgrimage up to Morningside Heights, or dropping off their cards at 26 Broadway—this was catnip. Less than three weeks after his meeting with Kahn, Heydt had transformed what had begun as a possible contribution toward the purchase of land for the square fronting the opera house into a scheme to lease the entire three blocks of the Upper Estate for up to eighty-seven years. He knew that Columbia's income from the land was ridiculously low, and knew as well the delightful fact that nearly all of the land leases held by current tenants would expire within three years. This was like buying an apple tree the day before it burst into fruit. On June 22, Heydt asked Junior for permission to begin formal discussions with Columbia.

The university's interests and Junior's were moving into alignment, abetted by the involvement of William A. White & Sons. The firm had first been involved in the Upper Estate as Columbia's representative, but it had also handled the Rockefeller family's New York real estate business ever since two friends from Cleveland, White and the first John D. Rockefeller, had arrived in the city in the nineteenth century. After the late July withdrawal of an offer from a competing syndicate led by the First National Bank, W. A. White president Harry Hall (who was rewarded for his efforts with a $250,000 commission) brokered a basic agreement between Heydt and Columbia's Frederick Goetze: Junior would buy the land for the square *and* the opera house for $6 million, and also pay $3.3 million annual rent for the rest of the Upper Estate for a minimum of twenty-four years, with potential options for sixty-three years more.

It was an indication of Junior's faith in Heydt that, eventually, he not only signed a lease along terms reasonably similar to these, but he did so without having in place a plan for the land's development. Heydt had taken an incremental approach, gently bringing Junior along throughout the summer of 1928, keeping him informed but not drawing him into the details of the undertaking. Late in the summer Heydt invited a variety of Manhattan real estate operators to recommend a course of development, asking each of them to estimate the potential rental income from the land (all along, Heydt had presumed that Junior would sublet the buildable property to developers). After collating the results, he wired the vacationing Junior on September 6 informing him that "not a single dissenting voice from the half a dozen experts consulted" challenged the wisdom of the project. At no point did he feel compelled to tell Junior that one of the experts questioned "whether the opera is an important factor in developing the property." Neither did he mention that another, a sharp-eyed buccaneer named John R. Todd, had closeted two of his own architects in their office over the cool, drizzly Labor Day weekend and had them craft a plan that acknowledged the opera's central place in the development but, even more, vivified the site's commercial possibilities.

In the telegram Heydt did tell Junior that Columbia had demanded a commitment in principle no later than noon the next day. Hours later, Junior wired back. Yes, he said, Heydt should proceed, even though he did think it "rather unfriendly" for Columbia to demand an answer on such short notice.

If Charles O. Heydt had been the sort of man to leap up from his desk, punch the air, and let loose a whoop of triumph, this would have been the moment for it. Two days later, though, he chose a more circumspect form of expression, a letter to Junior. Through this project, Heydt wrote, "I feel sure you will not only do a remarkable thing for the city, but a very profitable one for yourself."

The subject, the sentiments, even the very cadence of the words—the letter that landed on Junior's desk on September 28, 1928, could have been written by only one man: "Some time when occasion serves," it read, "I shall outline to you the history of this Upper Estate. That history reads like a romance. Had it not been for the sturdy common sense, the vision and the courage of those who managed the affairs of old Columbia College two and three generations ago . . ."

Throughout Goetze's negotiations, Nicholas Murray Butler had stayed offstage. He had, of course, remained in constant touch with his treasurer but had kept his distance from Junior, whom he would sometimes refer to as "the principal from the other side." Now, just before the Columbia board's formal acceptance of the Rockefeller offer, Butler was expansively Butlerian. After dispensing with the formalities, the congratulations, and the hymns to Columbia's past, he got to the point of his letter to Junior: there was one house on the Upper Estate that "I had hoped to be able to preserve," he wrote. "But the fates are against me." This was the McKim, Mead & White–designed mansion of Mrs. John Innes Kane at 1 West 49th, which he had intended to "take . . . down stone by stone" and rebuild on Morningside Heights. But "to my surprise," Butler concluded, "I found that the lowest estimate I could get for doing this work was so far beyond our capacity that I had reluctantly to yield my hopes." Obviously, he concluded, the house, "beautiful as it is," will have to be torn down.

The sound of Butler's sighs could not obscure the image that the letter provoked: the college president, hat in hand, trying to wheedle a gift. It was an astounding act of nerve. Here, on the brink of signing a lease that would instantly transform Columbia's financial situation, Butler was cruising for cash. Still more astonishing, he was zeroing in on the very agent of the university's transformation. Junior's lease commitment exceeded $3 million a year, for a piece of real estate that was generating barely one-tenth that much under Columbia's direct management. Even if Junior or his heirs chose not to exercise their renewal options, the Rockefellers would be pouring more than $75 million into Columbia's treasury. In 1928 the Rockefeller rent would have covered more than 25 percent of Columbia's entire operating budget. Unsurprisingly, Junior did not offer to save Mrs. Kane's house.

Yet it would have been easier, and more in character, for Butler to boogie down Broadway than to be content with this geyser of cash. In fact, the money terrified him: he was preoccupied all fall with a desperate wish to manage the release of the news in such a way that, as he wrote to Goetze in September, "it encourages several large donors and does not give them the impression that we do not really need their gifts." It was the essential conundrum of any college president's life: if you claim you need a certain amount of money for your institution's survival and growth, what do you do after someone has actually given it to you? When Goetze told Butler that rumors of the deal were already out, and enclosed recent clippings from the *Herald Tribune* and the *American* as evidence, Butler refused to believe it, asserting that "detailed as they are, [the news reports] have made no impression on the general public consciousness." To arrive at this conclusion, Butler had probably placed his thumb on the pulse of seven or eight members of the Union League Club; as one longtime Columbia faculty member said shortly after Butler's death two decades later, "whenever Butler pronounced on what the American people thought, I always came to the conclusion that the American people were thinking the other way." This applied equally well to the citizens of New York.

Butler did know, though, that the newspapers would matter, at least in their cumulative effect, and to that end he was determined to manage the news of the deal. In anticipation of the inevitable questions, he created a "Special Committee" that would bear responsibility for the disposition of income from the Upper Estate. He tried to get Goetze to persuade the Rockefeller office to allow Columbia to make a preemptive announcement even before the deal was signed; Goetze, who had just been awarded a $25,000 bonus from the Columbia trustees for his role in the negotiations, calmly resisted. Butler told one trustee, "I know perfectly well that the reporters, when they get hold of the rental, will multiply it by the years of the lease and create a desperate misconception." Multiply it they would: the *American* compounded the value of the Rockefeller lease payments for the initial term as if they would be invested—a not unreasonable approach for a university seeking to build its endowment—and came up with a gross sum of $112,516,000.

As the date of signing approached, after the original fifty-four-page lease document was barnacled with the customary layers of amendments, revisions, codicils, and covenants, Butler's anxiety about false impressions turned to panic over the possibility of being upstaged: King George V was gravely ill with pneumonia and septicemia. "Were he to die," Butler wrote to Harry Hall, now urging a postponement of the announcement, "our newspapers for the next few days would give little attention to anything else." For the anglophiliac Butler, sitting in his library in the President's House on Morningside Drive, not far from his copies of *Burke's Landed Gentry* and *Whitaker's Peerage, Baronetage, Knightage and Companionage,* it must have been painful even to write these words. However great his concern for the king's health, his fear of being bumped off the front page by the king's death was far greater.

The king, it turned out, lived another seven years. As for the agreement, the newspapers continued to report rumors, speculation, the whisperings of reliable sources. Ivy Lee told them nothing, following his principle of never commenting on possible Rockefeller investments in deference to "the stability of the market." A grumpy Butler held on to his formal statement until the deal was done.

On January 22, 1929, at eleven in the morning, a distinguished group gathered in the conference room in Columbia's downtown office, on William Street. On one side of the table sat Goetze and a few Columbia associates; opposite them sat a delegation led by Junior's brother-in-law, Winthrop Aldrich. After a brief round of greetings, Arthur Woods asked, "Is it ready for us to sign, Aldrich?" According to Harrison Dimmitt, a young associate in Aldrich's law firm,* "Mr. Aldrich drew his lips together into a severe oval, released them, and said, 'It is, Colonel Woods.'" In his capacity as president of the newly formed Metropolitan Square Corporation—named for the plaza Morris planned to put in front of the new Metropolitan Opera House—Woods committed his signature to paper and his corporation's sole stockholder, John D. Rockefeller Jr., to a minimum of twenty-four years of rent payments. For its part, as a writer in the *Herald Tribune* put it, "Columbia . . . has nothing to do but to receive its annual check."

The terms of the lease Woods and Goetze signed on that wintry Tuesday were somewhat different from those Junior had first approved and the Columbia trustees had agreed to in October. The principal change arose from Junior's decision not to purchase the sites for the plaza and the opera house but simply to add them to the acreage covered by the lease, a change that, the trustees agreed, was "to the mutual advantage of both parties," and that

---

*Dimmitt would be "severely censured" by the firm for writing about the event in *The New Yorker;* he later found redemption as the longtime secretary of Harvard Law School.

lifted the initial annual rent to $3.6 million. Junior held three renewal options on the twenty-four-year lease, each potentially extending the term an additional twenty-one years.

The renewal options were critical, for whether Junior were to develop the land himself or sublet it to others, the value of any investment in new buildings would accrue only during the maximum eighty-seven years of the leasehold. Not only would the land remain Columbia's, but at the end of the lease, as early as 1953 if Junior chose not to exercise his first option, ownership of any buildings erected on the site would revert to Columbia. If this potential cap on his return would seem to limit the appetite for enormous investment in improvements, the countervailing inflation hedge written into the deal was enormously valuable to Junior: the lease's complex option provisions would enable Junior and his successors to avoid any meaningful rent increases through 1973.

Junior's heirs consequently enjoyed enormous leverage when, in the early seventies, they considered buying the land from Columbia; the $3.8 million annual rent they were then paying was worth only 40 percent of its 1929 value. Butler and Goetze were, of course, long dead by then, but they were present in spirit, almost as if each had become an incubus inhabiting the body of his lineal successor. When Alton Marshall, the president of Rockefeller Center in 1973, broached the possibility of purchasing the land outright, Columbia president William McGill expressed interest—whereupon treasurer William Bloor told him, "No, we're not going to sell; if we did, you would just go spend it all."

Of course: that's what college presidents do, and that's why college treasurers devote so much effort to pruning their presidents' more profligate fantasies. In 1929, though, with the Rockefeller money on the way, Goetze could barely suppress the fountain of projects Butler had in mind: money for better pensions and disability payments, money for buildings and grounds and maintenance, money for improved salaries for junior faculty. He needed $250,000 to buy the "invaluable" library on economic subjects that belonged to Professor E. R. A. Seligman, and $40,000 more for "an expedition to Africa . . . in order to procure material to study from an entirely new point of new . . . the relation of the other primates to man." And, in case he had forgotten anything, he wanted an annual $100,000 "for unexpected and unforeseen but highly important purposes"—the "president's oil can," as he would call it.

To a copy of the very same memo in which he made these requests Butler attached a note to one of the trustees, complaining of "the persistent belief which confronts me at every turn in my search for new funds, that Columbia is so rich that it does not need the help for which I am asking." Butler couldn't lose for winning.

New York's newspapers received news of the consummated deal as if puffs of signifying white smoke had finally emerged from the chimney of 10 West 54th. After months and months of speculation, rumor, and misinformation, the papers could now report what the *World* called "the most important real estate transaction New York has ever seen." The *Herald Tribune* made reference to the "commercial paradise" expected to rise on the site. The *Times* bluntly called the news "huge" and made it the lead story on page one.* Within days, though, reporters began to peer around the edges of the deal and find a story within the story: that Junior had been motivated to make the deal because he wished to enhance the value of all those lots and buildings near his home on West 54th Street that he had been buying up in recent years. If so, he would not be the only one hoping to benefit: before the week was out, an independent group of speculators had bought three properties on the north side of 51st Street, facing the Upper Estate, the shot of a starter's pistol that began the next phase of the midtown land rush.

It was difficult to imagine the race getting any faster. Beginning in the middle twenties, Manhattan property values had begun to leap beyond any previously imagined levels. In 1925 the *Times* reported that "the pressure of population . . . has made land so expensive that even the fabulously rich are moved to economize in the use of it." The peculiar New York institution of Moving Day (through most of the 1920s, residential leases throughout the city expired simultaneously on October 1) clogged the streets on that 1928 Monday with the household goods of more than 100,000 families making the shift from one home to another. Two months later President Coolidge was telling Congress that "the requirements of existence have passed the standard of necessity into the region of luxury." And the morning after the Rockefeller-Columbia agreement hit the papers, Arthur Brisbane, whose own ventures with William Randolph Hearst in the West 50s had already made him a very rich man, codified for his readers in the *American* the lesson of the Upper Estate deal: "Select your real estate CAREFULLY," Brisbane wrote, "but GET SOME."

---

*It also made available eighteen column inches for the formal statement Butler had written while waiting for King George to die.

Junior, through Heydt, had selected his: an eleven-acre tract of speak-easies, rooming houses, and scruffy retail shops. The next steps would require painstaking, systematic effort. The Rockefeller organization or its designees would have to purchase leases on 203 different lots in the tract or wait out their expiration; pay several score subtenants to give up their dwellings; tear down 228 buildings; cart away massive piles of rubble; and build something on the site that would yield at least $3.6 million net rent, plus enough additional revenue to profitably amortize the cost of building.

All that was needed was an architect. And a builder. And a financial plan—in fact, *any* kind of plan. Just in case anyone in Junior's office had embraced the notion that there was a persistent logic behind the entire venture, Fulton Cutting wrote to Debevoise the day before the lease signing to let him know that the Metropolitan Opera Real Estate Company would probably not be able to finance a new house after all.

CHAPTER FOUR

It was clear that there were only two courses open to me. One was to abandon the entire development. The other to go forward with it in the definite knowledge that I myself would have to build it and finance it alone . . .

I chose the latter course.

—JOHN D. ROCKEFELLER JR.

In the long architectural careers of L. Andrew Reinhard and Henry Hofmeister, nothing they did distinguished them more than the productive sacrifice of their Labor Day weekend in 1928. Hofmeister had already left their office on Friday afternoon when Reinhard tracked him down and told him that the man to whom they owed their livelihoods, John R. Todd, had an urgent task for them. Up to this point of their careers, neither Reinhard nor Hofmeister, both in their late thirties, had made a notable contribution to the built world of New York; in the years following—both men lived past seventy—they did decent work, but little that was distinguished. The only Reinhard & Hofmeister creation cited in the fourth edition of the comprehensive, 1,056-page *AIA Guide to New York City* is the Federal Building at Kennedy Airport, which the authors describe with a single, unelaborated hyphenate: "neo-frumpy." Their largely anonymous careers, though, could be attributed neither to lack of talent nor to inadequacy of personality. It was simply this: the binary division of classes that has long characterized the architecture profession defined the two men—there are designers, and there is everyone else. Reinhard and Hofmeister were not designers.

Designers imagine buildings as we will eventually see them: their shape, their volume, the decoration on their surfaces, the entire vocabulary of appearance. These are the architects whose signatures are palpable in their creations—a Frank Lloyd Wright house, a Stanford White museum, a Cass

Gilbert office tower. They are studied in universities, celebrated (or condemned) in the critical press. To some degree they are even known to the public, for designers play the glamour positions, architecture's equivalents of quarterback or running back. As such, they are dependent on teammates who do the blocking, the heavy lifting, the grunt work: any cliché will do. Generally unknown outside their offices, these supporting players are responsible for the placement of heating ducts, the disposition of elevators, the specification of nuts and bolts and brackets and sills. They also make sure, working with structural engineers, that the buildings their colleagues design don't fall down. As essential as they are invisible, they are very much like Andy Reinhard and Harry Hofmeister, the interior columns of support for the architects who would design Rockefeller Center.

In the late summer of 1928, the recently formed partnership of Reinhard & Hofmeister worked out of offices in the Graybar Building, on Lexington Avenue. They did most of their work for the man who developed the Graybar, John R. Todd, acting chiefly as "rental architects," limning the floor plans for the hundreds of office suites arrayed within the building's twenty-six stories. Todd's son and collaborator, Webster Todd, called them "good, prompt, reliable workhorses." Theirs wasn't glamorous work but it was remunerative, and connected to the prolific Todd, it was certainly reliable.

A week before Labor Day, Todd had received a solicitation from Charles Heydt. Todd, Robertson & Todd, which had done some work for Junior's Williamsburg restoration, was one of the five firms Heydt had chosen to poll on the development potential of the Upper Estate. This was the last i-dotting and t-crossing that Heydt needed to complete before recommending that Junior commit to a deal with Columbia. Heydt wanted to know what sort of development each firm would suggest, and he also wanted an estimate of the rental income the development would generate. The other firms wrote about their ideas ("a combination of many of the best retail centers in the world outdoing in its uniqueness the Rue de la Paix, Regent Street, Bond Street or any other high class shopping center known today"), and they estimated annual income between $3.156 million and $3.75 million. Todd tactically, if incautiously, estimated the income at a staggering $5 million. And instead of unreeling his ideas in wishful prose, he locked up Hofmeister and Reinhard for three grueling days and had them produce a detailed plan for the site.

It was a foul late-summer weekend, temperatures dropping into the fifties, the skies spitting intermittent rain. Sequestered in their Graybar offices, the two men spun variations on the scheme Ben Morris had presented at the Metropolitan Club in May. Had Morris known, it likely would have galled him. Hofmeister was a quiet, self-taught high school dropout with an earnest affinity for ventilation and plumbing systems; the dominant partner, Reinhard, whose chief professional credential was the eight years' labor he had largely devoted to sketching tenant floor plans for Todd, had in fact begun his career, at fourteen, as an errand boy in Morris's office.

But Reinhard, whose exquisitely waxed mustache, knife-edge trouser creases, and impeccable pocket squares would have had him played onstage by a young Adolphe Menjou, had both confidence in himself and an intimate knowledge of his client's predilections. Years later, after Rockefeller Center was an established success, he told a reporter that "in a big operation like this the first principle to consider is not appearance. Sorry, but that's true. First comes cost, second comes time, third comes looks." Or, as Todd himself once put it, "Romance is the greatest thing in the world, outside of bread and butter."

Actually, John Reynard Todd said many things, for many purposes. Sometimes he even meant precisely what he said. Usually, though, he opted for the allusively aphoristic, the sly, or the intentionally provocative, as if intent on fulfilling the vulpine connotations of his middle name. Explaining how he and his brother David, after being expelled from their small church college in Missouri, found their way to a school that would have them, he said, "We had heard of Princeton, so we went there." He said he considered life to consist of four elements: "selling, romance, dog fights, and horse trades." At another time, he reduced the elements to two: "Life," he declared, "is made up of music and work." He once told a man working on a Todd project, "For an architect, you show almost human intelligence." The slim notebooks he carried with him at all times were filled not just with mundane reminders to himself but with aphorisms he might use to inflict a sharp (if temporary) verbal wound on a recalcitrant underling. Todd's method could be explained simply, one collaborator felt: "He was a master at the art of the kindly and productive insult."

He might have added that Todd was a master at false humility. In a life that encompassed teaching Latin, English, and mathematics in Beirut; practicing law; making a fortune in Manhattan real estate; setting records as a Republican Party fundraiser (and as a GOP breeder, too—his son Webster Todd became party chairman in New Jersey, his granddaughter Christine Todd Whitman the state's governor); and writing one book about camellias and another on the history of Prince William's Parish in South Carolina, Todd said his greatest accomplishment was "Changing from a left-handed golfer to a right-handed golfer." He accomplished this at fifty, bragged about it at sixty-four, said at sixty-nine that he wanted it on his tombstone. It was a joke wrapped in a tease inside a boast. Like Todd himself, it was coy, but it was also, on its own terms, pretty damn impressive.

To everyone who knew him, he was "John R."—not grandly, as in "Elizabeth R," but still implying both singularity and familiarity, like "Cecil B." or even "Franklin D.": no last name needed. The other Todd in the name of his firm was his older brother James, a surgeon who had somehow been lured by John R. into the development business. Doc Todd tended to the details—colleagues called his part of the operation "the obstruction department"—while John R. painted the broad and vivid strokes. The third partner was Hugh Robertson, like the Todd brothers a minister's son, but unlike them a man whose focus on the task at hand allowed no jokes, no provocations, no theatrical self-deprecation. In time, after John R. allowed his immense success to draw him ever more frequently to the enjoyment of its fruit, and after he allowed his vanity to spill out on the pages of a misbegotten profile in *The New Yorker,* Robertson would take over as the executive manager of Rockefeller Center.

But that was after the development had survived a dreadful beginning to become a proven success, after most of its buildings were completed and occupied, and after Junior had become—surely to his astonishment—not just the heir to the world's largest fortune but, as *Life* characterized him, one of New York's leading restaurateurs and nightclub operators; its most successful commercial landlord; the owner of the world's biggest motion picture theater; and the man behind "the largest tourist business in the United States." Yet without John R. Todd, Rockefeller Center would have been no more than a collection of buildings in midtown.

Todd and Junior really had only two things in common. They were both teetotalers, which was incidental to their relationship, and they both knew Tom Debevoise, which was not.

It's somewhat odd that a friendship would form between Debevoise and Todd. Debevoise was as severe as Todd was prankish, revealing his lighter aspects only in long, discursive anecdotes he would tell close friends, the humor underscored by the dour style of the telling. Usually he employed his detached, appraising manner to evaluate the deeds and ideas of others, such examination followed by one unvarying response: definitive judgment. The aristocratic Debevoise would have been as likely to start chanting in Yiddish as utter the words "I'm not sure." He despised overstatement, eschewed anything resembling publicity, and established "no" as the most effective word in his vocabulary. Junior's five sons were the first to refer to Debevoise as the "Prime Minister," which was accurate enough but maybe not quite as close to the mark as "Lord High Executioner." There was no appeal, really, from a Debevoise decision, and certainly no pleasure in being the target of his frequently negative judgments.

Todd, of course, had just as much confidence in his own judgment, but at least he had fun (even if, at times, somewhat malicious fun) exercising his "benevolent acerbity." But the friendship between the two men was genuine, and it was longstanding. They had first met in 1901 in the late-Victorian splendor of Summit, New Jersey, where both had established country residences. In time Debevoise's firm would handle much of the legal work for Todd's various development enterprises, affording Debevoise an intimate view of his neighbor's rise in the boom years of the skyscraper business.

Todd got into it, he would always insist, by accident. He had just been admitted to the New York bar in 1894 when Henry Clay Irons, a fellow resident of his Brooklyn rooming house, needed help: a client had defaulted on an apartment house he was building, and Irons was stuck with the project. Together the two young lawyers finished the building, filled it with tenants, and sold it for a profit. It was so easy that Todd immediately forgot about practicing law. "It was simply one building after another," he said.

Nearly overnight Todd went from the Brooklyn rooming house to a thirteen-room apartment on Morningside Heights to the place in Summit. Soon he had a plantation and a hunting lodge in South Carolina as well, and after that tacked on an estate in Easthampton, on Long Island. He managed to work a six-month traveling vacation—the Mediterranean, Paris, the Middle East—into his schedule every few years, each trip a perfect restorative after one or another of his successes: the Architects Building at Park and 40th; the Ritz Towers; the American Woolen Building; the Barclay Hotel. For the first of these, Todd devised a birds-of-a-feather rental scheme that he would use with great success at Rockefeller Center. From single practitioners operating out of virtual garrets in the upper floors to the mammoth main office of McKim, Mead & White, where nearly a hundred draftsmen labored on plans devised by the firm's celebrated partners, Todd gathered virtually an entire industry under one roof. The Architects Building marked his leap from projects that were entirely speculative—if highly lucrative—to those that were contractual, committed in advance, and even more lucrative. He held an equity share in every property he developed, and long after the Barclay was completed, his firm retained a leading role in its management. Todd himself maintained an apartment there, several floors above the gilded birdcage—a very Toddian touch—that adorned its lobby.

The successes that propelled Todd into the highest ranks of the development business, and qualified him for the job that would lead to the Rockefeller Center engagement, were the Cunard Building and the Graybar Building. The first—designed by Ben Morris—was a handsome triumph of large-scale architecture and corporate identity. The domed, mural-bedecked hall on the ground floor (large enough to hold half a block of six-story brownstones) was not just a ticketing space but a declaration of sorts, an announcement that Cunard liners were no mere conveyances. As Todd might have said, the great hall was a demonstration that music, even if only a figurative kind, had a place in architecture. Externally, the Cunard hummed another felicitous tune, its handsome facade harmonizing with the stately building across the street—26 Broadway.

But to Todd and those who admired his style of development, the aesthetic charms of the Cunard were trumped by something much more characteristic: the economic wonder that was the Graybar. If there was any music in the Graybar, which opened in 1926, it was music to count money by. Attached to the eastern flank of Grand Central Terminal, its 1.2 million square feet of office space mammoth confirmation of the midtown office boom, the Graybar was the apotheosis of cost/benefit architecture. In its creation, no architectural notion was transferred to steel and stone unless it passed the simplest of analyses: would it more than pay for itself in increased income? This did not mean that Todd asked his architects to eschew aesthetic enhancements, some of which could elevate the rents Todd was able to charge. The bronzed cables supporting the building's entrance canopy are fashioned as hawsers leading up to the side of a ship; seabirds and other maritime creatures etched into the frieze above the doorway elaborate the nautical motif. But Todd barred the architects from extending the design to the upper floors; the only people who would see ornamentation up there would be the occupants of *other* buildings. A junior architect who worked on Rockefeller Center summarized the logic that underpinned Todd's entire career: "If the Graybar Building was a financial success, then everything else about it must [have been] perfect." This was not the sort of reasoning that would send either Charles Heydt or Thomas Debevoise screaming in the other direction.

In May of 1929, Otto Kahn sent this cable to his office on William Street: "I AM NOW PLAETTBAR SCHIZZANDO MY NELITRIS PORISME." Kahn had neither lost his mind nor been sabotaged by an inebriated teletypist; he was simply using the peculiar code he had devised to keep his wishes and intentions secret. The employee who decoded it inscribed his translation in the telegram's margins: "I am now in a position to sell my 57th Street property." The price, Kahn said, was "MITIGHERAI MITIGACAO"—$3.85 million.

A year had passed since Kahn had plotted with Ivy Lee to draw Junior's interest to the Upper Estate. Ben Morris had migrated from Kahn's payroll to Junior's, and if Kahn hadn't entirely ended his feud with the board of the Metropolitan Opera Real Estate Company, he had at least passed along to Junior and his associates the burden of putting up with Fulton Cutting's high-hatting, foot-dragging, and poor-mouthing.

By the summer of 1929, Junior was finally compelled to engage himself personally in his Manhattan real estate venture. He had committed to $3.6 million in annual rent while collecting barely $300,000 from the tenants in the 228 row houses of the Upper Estate. The slow pace of lease acquisition had pushed back the projected start date for demolition. At his first meeting with Morris, Junior expressed his disappointment in the progress of the architectural planning. An irritable Junior called in Heydt one morning and said, "I wish you'd figure out what my carrying charges are on the property we have acquired, and multiply the figure by three, and go down in the vaults and put aside that sum of money in securities to one side—just put in a box that says 'To be opened three years from this date.' In the meantime, we'll forget altogether about the property we own up there."

Junior's logic may have been hard to parse, but his mood was not. In August, ensconced in his seaside palace in Maine, he exploded in response to a letter in which Heydt enumerated a new set of problems that were costing $10,000 a day: "WHAT IS CAUSING DELAY AND DAILY FINANCIAL LOSS OF WHICH YOU SPEAK," he wired back. "WHY WAS THIS MATTER NOT PRESENTED LAST WEEK IN OFFICE."

It could not have been an accident that Heydt had included the latest litany of difficulties in a missive that also contained these words: "It does not seem . . . that [these problems] can be handled by a committee." The project "must have a strong personality at its head, in other words a man competent to take full charge and work at it rapidly and decisively so as to bring us matured plans for development. Such a man we have in Mr. John R. Todd."

From the moment he lashed Reinhard and Hofmeister to their desks on Labor Day weekend in 1928, Todd was the project's heir presumptive. Heydt turned to him regularly in the ensuing months for advice. Todd provided space in the Graybar both for midtown meetings and for the storage of the financial records of the Metropolitan Square Corporation and he took a seat on the Metropolitan Square board. He visited Morris's office to examine the developing plans, and he actually commented on them with a civil tongue.

But in the late summer of 1929, Todd finally won the development contract for the Metropolitan Square job the way a prince wins the hand of a fair maiden: by making certain to call on the king. On a late August Monday, accompanied by Heydt, he arrived on Mount Desert Island, on the Down East coast of Maine. Even for a man like Todd, who had considerable firsthand experience with large buildings and elegant resorts, his first encounter with Junior's summer home must have caused a little slackness in the jaw. None of the other Gilded Age "cottages" on Mount Desert was quite like this one. When Junior bought the Eyrie in 1910 it had sixty-five rooms; over the ensuing years, in the process of making it his own, he had added another forty-two. Perched on the lip of the Atlantic, with handsome mountains arrayed behind it, the Eyrie offered views from 2,280 separate windows. The chinoiserie and other Asian elements in its decoration were complemented by Abby's spectacular Beatrix Farrand–designed garden; the tiles atop the brick walls that enclosed it came from the old city wall of Beijing.

Junior and Todd worked out most of the details of their nascent professional relationship behind a pair of handsome black horses pulling a carriage through the Mount Desert forest. They had met before, on matters relating to Williamsburg, but this was their first extended exposure to each other. Todd, who had been a director of the National Horse Show Association for years, was delighted by the opportunity to course through Junior's eleven thousand acres behind this pair of equine beauties. Snaking for fifty-seven miles through the woodlands and along the rocky coast, the Rockefeller roads, closed to motorized vehicles, were surfaced in granite gravel taken from local quarries. Transplanted wild blueberries and native ferns lined the roadside in an artful improvement on nature's work, a feat executed by Farrand in collaboration with the sons of Frederick Law Olmsted. No wilderness had ever been tamed more graciously.

Nor was it likely that any plutocrat had ever been so thoroughly seduced by a potential employee. Todd, sixty-two at the time (Junior was fifty-five), was an impressive man, tall and thin, with admirable posture and daunting self-possession. Over three days and two evenings, he deployed his "caressing, almost hypnotic voice" to illustrate the complexities of large-scale development and to demonstrate his mastery of them. He also said he required a quarter-million-dollar annual fee. And a one-third share of the profits. And a five-million-dollar investment by Junior in a new Todd project planned for the East Side of Manhattan.

And one last thing: he demanded operating control over every single aspect of the venture. Todd and his associates would contract for and supervise design, construction, promotion, renting, management. Final decisions, of course, would remain Junior's. But the responsibility for getting it all done, and getting it done both well and profitably, would have to be Todd's alone.

To Junior, whose greatest professional skill was his ability to delegate responsibility while simultaneously retaining authority, Todd may have seemed a gift from heaven. He was clearly competent (as Heydt had told Junior, "Mr. Todd . . . has never made a failure of any of his undertakings"). His undiluted confidence must have impressed Junior as well. Consider Todd's daring reply when Junior asked how much of his personal time he intended to devote to the project: "All of my time," Todd answered. "One-half on the job and one-half as far away from the job as trains and steamers can carry me, to places where I can get the hair out of my eyes and a clearer and better view of things."

These words were Todd's own recollection of the conversation, committed to paper some fifteen years after the fact, and they are characteristically Toddian in their grandiosity and self-regard. But there can be little doubt that Todd did not exactly present himself as an obedient servant while riding along with Junior behind those fine black horses. The very fact that he was insisting on a five-million-dollar investment in a wholly unrelated project demonstrated a degree of nerve that impressed Junior even if the sum itself, and the terms under which it would be granted, irritated him. Less than two months earlier, Junior—the world's wealthiest man but hardly its most openhanded one—had asked Ben Morris to discount his fee because of the visibility and prestige the architect would derive from the project. Now, Todd's insistence on substantial financial concessions struck Junior as "a great disappointment" and, Junior told Debevoise, did not conform to his "sense of the appropriate."

Yet such was the power of Todd's presentation that Junior agreed to every demand the developer made, over the objections of valued associates. Some were simply irritated that Todd had met privately with Junior, and had even begun to negotiate with him—an unheard-of breach of protocol. Arthur Woods, who carried the title of president of Metropolitan Square Corporation, objected to the size of Todd's fee.* Junior's brother-in-law, the lawyer Winthrop Aldrich, didn't like the ten-year commitment Todd was demanding and thought it would be wiser for Junior to develop an in-house "executive organization which would be capable of handling not only . . . Metropolitan Square" but other projects as well. Besides, Aldrich concluded, Todd's expectation of one-third of the profits "borders on absurdity."

Then Todd and Aldrich met. It is unclear whether Todd needed to invoke one of the life principles he would later inscribe in his pocket diary: "Defend high salaries." Somehow, though, in the course of a three-hour lunch Aldrich's concerns were "largely dissipated" by a combination of Todd's charm, persuasiveness, and sheer life-force. After his session with Todd, Aldrich told Debevoise, "I am frank to say that he has . . . convinced me."

Thus did Todd finally sign on as, in effect, chief executive officer. Getting Todd on the team also procured the services of Todd's brother, James, and their exceptionally effective partner, Hugh Robertson. There was more: Todd brought along the firm of Todd & Brown, an engineering/construction management business run by his son, Webster, and Joseph Brown, a former construction superintendent on Todd projects. He also carried one final piece of freight to Metropolitan Square: an absolute determination to make certain no opera house would ever rise on the site.

Outwardly, Winthrop Williams Aldrich, son of a senator and brother-in-law of a billionaire, was as austere and as dignified as his high-WASP name. The pince-nez, the stout but meticulously trimmed mustache, the hand-

---

*Woods may also have had a problem with Todd's prairie origins. In a memo to Debevoise, he had said they needed a project manager with the proper cultural background—"Harvard, of course, preferable."

made Lobb shoes he ordered from London by the dozen were all brush-strokes in a handsome and propitious portrait. When he assumed the presidency of the Chase National Bank—the "Rockefeller bank"—in his late forties, he won a place in the business world that matched his exalted social standing. Years later he attained comparable heights in the public arena, appointed ambassador to Great Britain by Dwight Eisenhower. If Aldrich had wished to calculate a life path, he could not have crafted a glossier one. Of course, he never really had to: his were the positions and privileges that arise when inheritance is conjoined with talent.

Aldrich helped his brother-in-law any way he could, including advising him on the selection of Debevoise as his personal attorney. But the two men were hardly similar. Aldrich was as comfortable in his public role as Junior was at times uncomfortable in his. Where Junior liked to drive his carriage over the fine roads of Mount Desert, Aldrich enjoyed the stiffer (if no less aristocratic) challenges of ocean sailing, most notably when he served as navigator on the J-class sloop *Enterprise,* winner of the America's Cup in 1930. His other pastimes, and the way he pursued them, marked even greater differences: in 1953 "he arrived at the Court of St. James," it was said, "with a closed mind and an open fly." Aldrich knew who he was, but he also knew what the world wanted him to be. He once joked to a friend that, to maintain the right bankerly reputation, "I never smile south of Canal Street."

But that was later, after the Rockefeller family took control of the Chase and installed Aldrich as president. Until his migration to the banking world, Aldrich made his mark as a lawyer, his work at Murray, Aldrich & Webb filling the legal interstices in the web of Rockefeller connections, interests, and activities. This inevitably meant maintaining links with moneyed New York, into which Rockefeller interests necessarily extended. Aldrich was the obvious man to carry out the last, excruciating negotiations with the impossible Fulton Cutting.

Well into the fall of 1929, Rockefeller negotiations with the Real Estate Company had been moving slower than three acts of Wagner. In the months since Cutting had informed Debevoise that he and his board would not finance the new house on their own, the Real Estate Company had sought a buyer for the old opera house on 40th Street, hoping the sale proceeds would cover construction costs of a new one. Through the summer, Cutting still had not formally committed to building on the Upper Estate. Along the way, Heydt told Junior that no one had "contemplated that the Opera Group would be given all this time to make up their minds whether to come into the development." A low rumble of complaint—utterly out of character for the loyal Heydt—followed: "Just why we should be so tender and considerate of them [I] cannot understand."

But Heydt was being somewhat disingenuous. He knew that Aldrich, Debevoise, and especially Woods (who only two days later would privately dismiss Heydt as being "way beyond his powers") were still counseling patience in the opera negotiations, and he certainly knew that the elaborate scaffolding of social relations that supported the New York aristocracy would likely keep any of the three from forcing the Real Estate Company's hand. But by midfall, two events would change everything.

The first was Todd's formal assumption of responsibility. To Todd, an opera house in Metropolitan Square would guarantee failure. "The Opera House would be a dead spot and greatly reduce shopping values in all property facing it," he argued; closed during the daytime, it would loom over the square like a gigantic mausoleum. Even at night it wouldn't be much better: the opera season was not particularly lengthy, and an opera house "can't be used for anything else." He told at least one friend, "if [I] could only stick the Opera House on Ninth Avenue or in Harlem, [I] could make real money for Mr. Rockefeller." And that, of course, was his job.

But it was the second event that finally rushed the long final act to its conclusion: the stock market crash. When Wall Street imploded in October 1929, it scattered its shrapnel everywhere wealth resided. It also emboldened the men of the Real Estate Company board to exercise what Rockefeller family historians would call "genteel blackmail." Suggesting they were strapped for cash, unable (or unwilling) to sell the old house for an adequate sum, they said they wanted Junior to pick up the tab not just for the land but for half the opera house, too.

On an early-December afternoon Junior was dining privately with his associate Kenneth Chorley, no doubt discussing aspects of the ongoing Williamsburg restoration, which was one of the most gratifying of Junior's projects and was now under Chorley's direction. As Chorley remembered it, a knock on the door preceded Aldrich's entrance. "John," Aldrich said, "I've just come from a meeting of the directors of the [Real Estate Company] and their whole attitude is, 'You've got the money and therefore there's no reason why you shouldn't do this' "—assume half the cost of construction.

Junior's response was instantaneous: "Winthrop," he said, "go back and tell them that I am no longer interested."

Four years had passed since Otto Kahn had first made the public case for a new opera house. Now, the day after Junior's announcement that there would be no opera house in Metropolitan Square, Kahn and his wife received Benjamin Morris in their enormous Italianate palazzo on upper Fifth and began planning how to get Junior to reconsider. But just one week later, Kahn and Morris gave up and turned their attention to the search for a new site. It proved fruitless. In 1931 Kahn resigned after nearly a quarter century as chairman, principal owner, and, essentially, godfather of the Metropolitan Opera. Before his death in 1934, Kahn told the critic Olin Downes that "the primary cause, he believed, of the [Real Estate Company board's] coolness to him was the fact he was a Jew. . . . As a result of this feeling, he continued, he had to work almost entirely alone." According to Kahn's biographer, Theresa M. Collins, he "no longer found much dignity in being the exceptional Jew among genteel Gentiles."

Cutting and company had compiled a humiliating record: they had chased away, in Kahn, New York's most ardent supporter of opera; they had failed in their attempted shakedown of Junior; and they'd done nothing to improve conditions on 40th Street. "The board of directors," said Peter Grimm, who replaced Harry Hall as president of William A. White & Sons, "was very dumb."* By 1954 the land under the old house, for which they had turned down a $7 million offer in 1925, was appraised at $4 million. The Met didn't get the new house it had so desperately needed in the 1920s until 1966, when a replacement for the yellow-brick brewery opened at Lincoln Center—John D. Rockefeller 3rd, Junior's eldest son, chairman.

Junior himself moved rather more quickly after deputizing his brother-in-law to terminate negotiations with Cutting. Francis T. Christy, a thirty-two-year-old lawyer at Murray, Aldrich & Webb, remembered how his wife had "pressed the least shiny of my suits, had selected my best shirt with matching tie, and had polished my other pair of shoes"—he had been asked by Aldrich to accompany him to a meeting in Junior's office. On the four-block walk to 26 Broadway, Aldrich pointedly told Christy the story of the

---

*Cornelius Vanderbilt Jr., a renegade from his family and his social class—he was both a journalist and a Democrat—was harsher. He maintained that the Depression's impact on High Society's regard for opera was summed up by a dowager who said, "Now that we don't dare to display our jewelry in public, why should we continue to support these wops?"

young lawyer who had casually mentioned in an elevator that he was working on Rockefeller business and by the next morning had been taken off the case.

But a nervous Christy found Junior to be more than cordial, listening attentively as Aldrich, Debevoise, Todd, and others presented alternative courses of action now that there was to be no opera house. The proposals ranged from buying his way out of the Columbia lease (which Junior declared "unthinkable") to proceeding on a staggering $125 million investment—Todd's estimate—to develop the land on his own. As Christy would recall, "Mr. Rockefeller lost no time in making his decision, from which he never thereafter faltered."

This is how Junior himself described it almost ten years later, as he stood at the podium in the employee gymnasium in the tenth of Rockefeller Center's buildings: After the opera people withdrew, he said, "it came about that . . . with the depression under way and [real estate] values falling rapidly, I found myself committed to Columbia for a long term lease, wholly without the support of the enterprise by which and around which the whole development had been planned. . . .

"It was clear that there were only two courses open to me. One was to abandon the entire development. The other to go forward with it in the definite knowledge that I myself would have to build it and finance it alone. . . .

"I chose the latter course."

CHAPTER FIVE

In the early mornings of 1929, before dawn burned off the fog and the city started to emerge in front of him, Hugh Ferriss felt

Architecture never lies. Architecture *invariably expresses its Age correctly.*

—HUGH FERRISS

he stood poised not on the parapet outside his midtown office but on the deck of an ocean liner. As the buildings slowly began to take shape, it was almost as if Ferriss were personally willing the cityscape into existence. In a way, he had already tried that: a few years earlier, Ferriss had produced a fanciful series of architectural studies called "Future City." Some of his drawings almost look like set designs for Fritz Lang's *Metropolis,* with planes zipping between office towers and viaducts arching over miles of buildings. But "Future City" also contained such embellishments as rooftop gardens, depressed roadways, and other urban enhancements that Ferriss and Harvey Wiley Corbett, his collaborator, imagined might actually exist by 1975. Their guess turned out to be too conservative—by more than forty years.

Ferriss had come to New York from St. Louis, and soon after found his way to an apprentice draftsman's desk in the office of architect Cass Gilbert. Over the ensuing years he made his living as an "architectural delineator," turning the plans and blueprints of designers into handsome drawings of what the imagined building would look like when finished. But he had made his reputation as a visionary. In 1929, just shy of forty, he was conceivably the most important architect in the city—according to Ada Louise Huxtable "catalytic to the twenties," and ready to leave his mark on the thirties. Ferriss never designed a single noteworthy building, but after his death a colleague said he "influenced my generation of architects" more than any other man.

He was a wonderful speaker (he had overcome a youthful stutter), a witty host, and an indefatigable polemicist whose coruscating prose could emit sparks capable of both igniting his followers and incinerating those he criticized. But Ferriss's authority came from neither his popularity nor his prose; it resided where his visionary imagination and his graphic skills merged on paper. In pencil, crayon, and charcoal—especially charcoal, with which he could break black into an astonishing palette of lights and darks—Ferriss drew skyscrapers past, skyscrapers present, and skyscrapers future. In 1929, when he wrote about the early morning view from his office atop the Architects Building (the one John R. Todd had built), he saw a "city of closely juxtaposed verticals" that might have leapt from those exploratory drawings he had crafted earlier in the decade, at the moment when law, fashion, and commerce jointly conspired to launch the Second Skyscraper Era. That was the epoch that made the American city look the way it looked until after World War II; that confirmed the physical habits of American business; and that spawned Rockefeller Center, the era's last and greatest accomplishment.

In 1890, when the Pulitzer Building at the corner of Park Row and Frankfort Street in downtown Manhattan reached its full eighteen stories and opened for business, a visitor alighting from an elevator on the top floor paused to ask, "Is God in?" It was not an entirely inappropriate question, for the Pulitzer was the first secular building in New York to surpass in height the steeple on Trinity Church, half a mile away. It was also a metaphor well suited to the advent of Skyscraper New York: in Manhattan, wrote Lincoln Steffens in *Scribner's* magazine just a few years later, "the enterprise of business has surpassed the aspiration of religion."

By the time the new century began New York was a city in the process not simply of change but nearly of alchemy. The vertical style of architecture that for centuries had belonged exclusively to the exaltation of the church could now be adapted to the needs of commerce by the transformative power of technology. Elisha Otis's elevator brake introduced in 1853 and the steel-framed construction method developed in Chicago in the 1880s were the most obvious propellants, but architects were assisted in their struggle against gravity even by inventions as apparently trivial as the revolving door: patented by a Philadelphian named Theophilus Van Kannel in 1888 as a device intended to keep inclement weather outside busy buildings, it happened as well to solve the problem caused by the buildup of air pressure in a very tall building, which could make it nearly impossible to open a conventional entry door.

Technology had created possibility, but for the New York skyline of the early years of the twentieth century, it was a possibility the city's architects were not prepared for. The men whose designs dominated this First Sky-scraper Era looked at Manhattan but could see only Paris, not because of pretensions to European cultivation (although there was plenty of that, too) but because Paris was where they had learned their craft. Until 1868 there wasn't a single school of architecture in the United States, and the conventional apprentice system proved of little utility when the first skyscrapers began to sprout. Ever since the 1850s, when Richard Morris Hunt arrived in New York fresh from his studies in Paris "like an ambassador of the arts," the most ambitious architects in the East emulated his example. Hunt had been the first American to study at the Ecole des Beaux-Arts, where he had learned the skills—and adopted the tastes—that three generations of architects applied to the face of New York.

For Hunt, that meant great chateaus like those he designed for the Vanderbilts. For those who followed him to Paris, it meant as many variations on the Beaux-Arts themes as their wealthiest clients could afford. The Ecole des Beaux-Arts was itself a government supported institution, but it flourished in a time (and a country) in which government's self-image was reflected in broad boulevards, heroic statuary, and an architectural style that fostered what one critic called "a palatial urbanism." In the various ateliers that emanated from the Ecole, students were inculcated in a design ideology that mandated buildings light in color, generally symmetrical in disposition, and historicized in their design vocabulary. Sculptural decoration, as often as not allegorical and mythic, decorated the lush facades of these buildings like jewels on the bosom of a duchess. Not for nothing was the style often called *Le Pompier.*

The Beaux-Arts graduates who came home to "dominate the field of architecture in the United States" were propelled from the salons of the upper classes onto a wider stage by the World's Columbian Exposition in 1893. After the vast "white city" torn right out of the Beaux-Arts sketchbook arose on the Chicago lakefront, a barely Americanized version of the style clothed almost every courthouse, capital building, university library, or city hall built in the United States over the next several years. In New York the Beaux-Arts approach spread from the Millionaires' Mile of Fifth Avenue to the entire array of public and semipublic buildings that decorated Manhattan. They were—they are—some of the finest edifices ever built in New York: Cass Gilbert's Customs House. Carrère & Hastings's New York Public Library. Warren & Wetmore's Grand Central Terminal. Blossoming forth from the phenomenally successful firm of McKim, Mead & White, a splendiferous garden of buildings: churches, men's clubs, museums, the Columbia campus on Morningside Heights. Even Hunt, the progenitor, got into the public act with his noble Fifth Avenue facade for the Metropolitan Museum of Art.

But nineteen centuries of necessarily horizontal architecture between the time Vitruvius wrote his *De architectura* and Elisha Otis unveiled his new elevator had little relevance in a suddenly vertical world. Only ecclesiastical architecture (and just a subset of that) aspired to the vertical. And of what relevance was Chartres in the canyons of Manhattan, where even Trinity Church now looked like an out-of-place runt?

By the end of the twentieth century's first decade, a style euphemistically called "modern French" had taken hold—bad Beaux-Arts elongated in a funhouse mirror. It could not prettify the frightful forests of stone and steel germinating in Manhattan, especially downtown in the Wall Street area, where narrow byways laid out in precolonial times were now shrunken and shadowed by parallel rows of towers thrusting ever upward. Poor Leroy Buffington, the architect who had patented skyscraper (he called it "cloud-scraper") design in 1888. Had Buffington prevailed in court when he tried to win a 5 percent royalty on every skyscraper erected, New York in the early part of the twentieth century might have made him as rich as Junior. "It is as if some mighty force were astir beneath the ground," marveled a writer in *Harper's Weekly,* "hour by hour, pushing up structures that a dozen years ago would have been inconceivable." The skyscraper, said one cold-eyed architect, was nothing more than "a machine that makes the land pay."

Oddly, the man who said this was the one New York architect of the era who successfully managed to exalt a building's commercial role by making it gorgeous as well. On April 24, 1913, moments after Woodrow Wilson pushed a button on his desk in Washington, light washed over Cass Gilbert's Woolworth Building and revealed its sixty soaring stories of Gothic splendor sheathed in a lacy cloak of terra cotta. Its sponsor, Frank W. Woolworth, had conceived the building as "a giant signboard to advertise around the world" his chain of five-and-ten-cent stores. Gilbert's tower was engraved on each piece of the company's stationery and emblazoned on many of the products sold out of the stores that had financed it. Situated right across Broadway from City Hall Park and the wide square formed by the angled intersection of Park Row and Broadway, it could be perceived from top to bottom in one sweeping look, whether from across the street or nearly anywhere else along the length of lower Broadway. On the day of its opening, a dedicatory clergyman anointed the Woolworth the "Cathedral of Commerce," ascribing to it a sacred quality that would be elevated to a form of divinity several years later by Ayn Rand. Aboard a ship steaming into New York Harbor in the 1920s, the immigrant Rand saw the Woolworth thrust boldly into the Manhattan sky and proclaimed it nothing less than "the finger of God," an anthropomorphized benediction on the capitalism practiced within its walls.

But after the achievement of divine grace, there's nowhere else to go. The Woolworth turned out to be not only the apogee of the First Skyscraper Era, but also the herald of its end. For, just six blocks down Broadway, developers who quivered with joy at the now-proven economics of super-scaled buildings took the most obvious lesson of the Woolworth sermon (that Big is Good), ignored the less obvious (that Beauty has a role, too), and created a hulking skyscraper that would force a radical alteration in the very appearance of large buildings in New York, and as a consequence in all of urban America. The Equitable Building was a far more efficient—if less glamorous—economic machine than the Woolworth. Engulfing virtually every inch of its plot of land, its forty block-sized stories rising straight up from the lot lines, its brooding shadow darkening seven adjacent acres of lower Manhattan, the Equitable eschewed the Woolworth's aspirations to filigreed beauty (or to any sort of divinity) and sought only bang for the buck: what was the most building that could be erected for the least cost?

It was an architecture of brutality.* When it opened in 1916, the Equitable loomed over Broadway—over all of lower Manhattan—like an ominous warning before a deadly hurricane. Reformers searching for the disappearing sky above the financial district could all too easily envision a city cast into perpetual twilight by malproportioned excrescences closing in on sunless streets. At the end of the workday, the Equitable disgorged the 16,000 people who labored within its 1.25 million square feet of rentable space into those dark canyons, as if seeking to prove Louis Sullivan's declaration that the architecture of lower Manhattan was "hopelessly degraded in its pessimistic denial of our . . . civilization." Years later, the man who developed it, Louis Horowitz, called the Equitable "a monster office building," but when he was building it his attitude was somewhat different; with the airy confidence of a poker player holding four aces, he told his critics, no-

---

*Bizarrely, the Equitable's designer, Ernest R. Graham, was the protégé of and heir to Daniel Burnham, the Chicago architect whose immortal gift to New York, the Flatiron Building, was as pleasing as Graham's Equitable was thuggish.

ble citizens all, that if they wanted to turn the Equitable block into parkland, they were free to buy it.

Horowitz and his partners got to keep their building, of course, but there would never again be another one like it. (In fact, although far taller buildings soon followed the Equitable's construction, none would surpass it in square footage until the Empire State Building opened in 1931.) What stopped the creation of more Equitables was the enactment of a body of laws as crucial to the development of twentieth-century America as any other reformist product of the Progressive Era: zoning.

Seven decades after America's first zoning law ushered in the Second Skyscraper Era, long after its eventual encrustation with more than 2,500 amendments and its ultimate replacement in 1961, a character in a novel best explained the look of the New York that zoning had shaped. In Milan Kundera's *The Unbearable Lightness of Being,* the protagonist's mistress draws a contrast between the European ideal of civic beauty and the New York version. In Europe, where a Haussmann backed by imperial decree could lay out the *grands boulevards* of Paris, or where an arm of the church could invest an entire century in the building of a single God-glorifying cathedral, beauty was the conscious object; the distinctive profile of the New York skyline, on the other hand, was a triumph, the character says, of "beauty by mistake." Twentieth-century New York, she concludes, represents "the final phase in the history of beauty."

The concept of a zoning law had been burbling along for a decade or so before the erection of the Equitable Building, primarily in the fantasies of the small group of men who gathered in 1907 to form the Fifth Avenue Association. The FAA was dedicated to the proposition that while all else might change in the subway-digging, immigrant-absorbing, capitalism-unleashing New York of the early twentieth century, Fifth Avenue would not. The merchants and property owners of the FAA really didn't fear another Equitable Building, because in 1915 a building that size would have been about as likely to rise in an Indiana cornfield as in the residential/retail midtown of the era. What made them tremble was the prospect of the loft buildings of the booming garment industry migrating northward. As this was hardly the sort of issue around which they could mobilize public opinion, the gentlemen of the FAA instead latched onto more general concerns. "If the present tendency toward scraping the sky continues," warned an FAA official in 1911, "we may yet live to see the seemingly absurd spectacle of men groping their way with lanterns each afternoon at the bottom of deep canyons." When the controversy over the Equitable exploded downtown a few years later, the FAA speedily harnessed the resulting energy and turned it toward its own political uses, namely the enactment in 1916 of the New York City Building Zoning Resolution. For the first time in American history, the right of property owners to build as they wished was constrained by law.

The keystone of the zoning ordinance—the "mistake" that by the 1930s made New York look like New York—was a complex series of restrictions that forbade the uninterrupted vertical rise of a building from its lot line. Provoked by the example of the Equitable, the men who wrote the law made verticality a function of street width. A building fronting a street eighty feet wide, for instance, might be allowed to rise two and a half times that width—two hundred feet—before a setback was required; the depth of the setback in turn determined the height of the next vertical segment. When the setbacks had taken so many bites out of the building's footprint that just one-quarter of that footprint remained to accommodate additional vertical rise, the height of a building's slender tower was restricted only by gravity and cash.

But what had begun as a reformist political doctrine (or, more cynically, the expression of the interests of a propertied elite) necessarily morphed into an aesthetic prescription. One of the truisms of urban commercial design holds that architecture begins with the establishment of limits. To Hugh Ferriss, the zoning law was the "crude clay" from which the city would be fashioned. In 1922, when Ferriss collaborated with Harvey Corbett on a polemic addressing the architectural consequences of the zoning law, the *World* hailed his "remarkable drawings depicting the evolution of the 'envelope'"—the potential shapes into which an architect could stuff the maximum volume of a particular building in a particular location.

The concept of the envelope and the ways a building could fit into it formed a puzzle not immediately solved. At first architects and builders followed the easiest paths. When the firm of Warren & Wetmore designed the Heckscher Building for a lot at the southwest corner of 57th Street and Fifth Avenue, New York's first post-1916 skyscraper was made to conform with the zoning requirements essentially by planting its narrow tower on top of a broad pedestal: a Woolworth without style. But for the Shelton Hotel on Lexington Avenue and 48th Street, architect Arthur Loomis Harmon came up with something both entirely appropriate and entirely revolutionary. The Shelton was the first building that used the zoning-compelled setbacks as an integral part of its design, its thirty-four stories composed in stair-step fashion, a carefully calibrated pattern of vertical-horizontal-vertical-horizontal-vertical. It was a concept for a tall building that seemed to be the expression in masonry of Hugh Ferriss's explorations in charcoal and paper, and sufficiently cutting edge to attract sensibilities as artistic as those of Georgia O'Keeffe and her husband, Alfred Stieglitz. She painted the building (*The Shelton with Sunspots*), they both lived in it, and both used the open views from their thirtieth floor apartment to render the city around them through avenues of light framed by the setbacks.

According to Ferriss, in his landmark book *The Metropolis of Tomorrow*, "lilliputian critics" originally called the Shelton "uncouth" and "uncivilized," and complained that it "lacked 'style,' 'scale' and 'taste.'" But he also noted that "yesterday's critics have now persuaded themselves that they liked it from the start." For by 1929, when *The Metropolis of Tomorrow* was published, the Shelton's innovations had been completely absorbed into the urban bloodstream. Zoning laws had been enacted in more than three hundred U.S. cities, and stepwise, "wedding cake" buildings became the visual vocabulary of the modern American downtown. New York itself, from the Battery to midtown to the avenues framing Central Park, provided the stage for scores upon scores of ziggurats in brick and limestone. Pyramiding upward, their rectangular sections like so many building blocks placed strategically atop larger ones below, they were the collective expression of a "a compulsory cubism," as one scholar called it, that had been imposed upon the city's architects and builders not by tastemakers or architectural theorists but by the men who wrote the zoning laws: "beauty by mistake."

"Architecture never lies," Hugh Ferriss once wrote. "Architecture invariably expresses its Age correctly." He was right, but in the Manhattan of the 1920s the age took a while to define itself. Instead of spawning new styles, the overwhelming propulsive force of the decade's economic boom left innovation gasping for air: who would bother to come up with anything new when you could throw a decorative cornice on top of a graceless pile and call it a day? Around the same time the Astor family made 141 plots of land available for development in 1920, a popular guidebook of the day asserted that a new building of some sort was rising in New York every fifty-one minutes. As Ferriss said many years later, when you didn't have any work you had time to think. But everyone had work in the middle of the twenties, so historical references, sculptural details, and symmetrical massing continued to keep New York office building architecture hopelessly earthbound. Even the innovative cubism of the Shelton Hotel was marred by the non-sequiturial Romanesque details (an arch here, a column there) that stuck to its skin like bad makeup. The society architect John Russell Pope took the prize for loopiest attempt to apply a classical architectural vocabulary to the skyscraper, proposing for a lot on Fifth Avenue between 54th and 55th Streets a fifty-story obelisk—a chubby Washington Monument with windows.

The new idea that finally broke through all this came from the 1925 Exposition Internationale des Arts Décoratifs et Industriels Modernes. It helped that the show that spawned the name Art Deco and the style it signified took place in Paris, where so much else in art, literature, and music was defining modernity. But so radical in the mainstream design world was the very *concept* of modernism that Secretary of Commerce Herbert Hoover sheepishly declined an invitation for formal American participation in the show—America had nothing modern to display, he said. To learn what the United States had been missing, Hoover sent an official commission to Paris to report back to him. However unlikely it may seem that a bugle call to American artists and designers should bear the name "Herbert Hoover Report," the delegation members who issued it strongly urged "a parallel effort of our own upon lines calculated to appeal to the American consumer."

The time that elapses between inspiration and execution in, say, furniture design can be a matter of weeks; in architecture, especially large-scale architecture, years will pass. Architect Ralph Walker's headquarters building for the New York Telephone Company was well under way at the time of the Art Deco show, but at least a few Deco elements could be incorporated into its design and any classical ornaments that had been planned could be banished. "Trivial reminiscences of the Gothic have fallen away" in Walker's building, said one approving commentator, his choice of adjective signaling the sudden shift from the past. In 1927 a wide range of Deco motifs showed up on Ely Jacques Kahn's 2 Park Avenue. But it wasn't until 1929, when Sloan & Robertson's Chanin Building opened on 42nd Street, that New York saw its first building not only born after the 1925 show but conceived after it as well. The Chanin was a riot of Deco, its bronze grillework, its streamlined massing, its celebration of the new oozing from every inch. Here and at other buildings sprouting in the overheated economy of 1929, the three-dimensional Beaux-Arts style was elbowed aside by the flat ornamentation of Art Deco. Zigzags and chevrons in glistening bronze and steel replaced Corinthian capitals and Second Empire garlands rendered in implacable stone. Rosemarie Haag Bletter and Cervin Robinson, in *Skyscraper Style: Art Deco New York,* point out that the completion in 1929 of this first true Art Deco skyscraper marked the beginning of an era that ended barely two years later, with the opening of the last pure Deco monument in New York, the Empire State Building. But what came next, rising from the bedrock of Columbia's Upper Estate, would have Art Deco—along with the aspirational commercial architecture of the Woolworth Building and the imposed rules of the 1916 Zoning Ordinance—embedded in its DNA.

Return, then, to Hugh Ferriss, standing on his parapet at dawn, looking out at Beaux-Arts New York, and Equitable Building New York, and Shelton and Chanin New York; over there, just rising into the sky, the framework of the Chrysler Building; in between, everywhere, the low rows of nineteenth-century buildings that a visiting Maxim Gorky had once described as "a jaw load of rotting teeth and mere stumps." This skyscraper-strewn landscape resembled nothing the world had ever seen. By decade's end there were 188 structures in New York more than twenty stories tall—fully half the total in the entire country—and it was necessary to find new ways of looking at Manhattan.

Ferriss, who had envisioned this startling efflorescence of skyscraper architecture even if he didn't much care for it, said, "as a whole, it is not a work of conscious design." As obvious as this may seem, it was for the architects who still clung to the Beaux-Arts ideal an acknowledgment of defeat. But although D. Everett Waid, a former president of the American Institute of Architects, mournfully predicted that "American cities [are] in danger of growing faster than architects could be trained to design their buildings," Ferriss took note of something else: in mid-June of every year the streets around the Architects Building were thronged by hundreds of young men just out of architecture school and looking for the chance to add their signatures in stone and steel to the map of Manhattan—and in the process to glorify a new ideology that one later theorist described as the "hedonistic Urbanism of Congestion."

At the time most established architects, lost in their reveries of broad boulevards and heroic white buildings, saw congestion as a scourge. They found unlikely allies among the rising generation of theorists who may have attacked the class-based pretensions of Beaux-Arts style but saw salvation in the new theology of city planning. The most articulate of these was Lewis Mumford, an urbanist Savonarola whose impressive literary gifts and capacity for outrage catapulted him to the movement's front, where he led the assault on the "disease of growth." For Mumford, who considered even Art Deco style "a kind of mechanized romanticism" whose "financial motives" had been "popularized and disguised" by Hugh Ferriss, New York itself was suspect. A phrase he would use later summed up his view of the city: it was nothing but "reckless, romantic chaos."

But the young men crowding the streets around the Architects Building had their own polemicists and heroes. Among the former was Ferriss's collaborator on Future City, Harvey Wiley Corbett, who said, "people swarm to the city *because* they like congestion." Among the latter, the brightest light was Raymond Hood, like Corbett a product of Beaux-Arts training but now the city's leading practitioner of skyscraper architecture. Said Hood with characteristic frankness and economy, "Congestion is good."

He would soon have the chance to prove this in the creation of Rockefeller Center, where Hood would join Junior and Todd as the project's chief designer and its third, and final, co-author. Was it remarkable that Junior and Todd would bring in as primary architect a man who was celebrated for his irreverence and notorious for his drinking? Who fewer than ten years earlier, already past forty and with no clients and no prospects, had been on the brink of giving up architecture in New York altogether? Whose manners and habits were antithetical to those of the wealthy and aristocratic men who were the natural companions of Metropolitan Square's architect of record, Ben Morris?

Yes, yes, and yes. But in February of 1929, when Metropolitan Square announced the creation of an advisory board of architects "to assure an appropriate and artistic environment, ample and convenient approaches and circulation, and dignity and harmony of architectural composition," the board's membership (with the exception of Corbett) was so reactionary they might have come from the personal atelier of Louis XVI. Their collective inappropriateness for the project was so nearly ruinous that, in the end, Ray Hood was really the only antidote. Hood was a joker, a provocateur, a scamp—but also, in the words of historian and critic Vincent Scully, "our greatest skyscraper architect."

CHAPTER SIX

In January of 1929, one week before the ceremonial signing of the Columbia-Rockefeller lease in the university's business office downtown on William Street, Frederick Goetze appended his name to a form letter that went out to every

If there is one thing calculated to bring ***tears of joy to*** *the eyes of* ***a small business man,*** *it is to hold a lease in a piece of property which is being assembled by John D. Rockefeller, Jr.*

—FREDERICK LEWIS ALLEN

leaseholder in the three blocks of the Upper Estate. For Columbia, Goetze's role in shepherding the deal to this point was not unlike Charles Heydt's on the Rockefeller side. Heydt's painstaking labor in behalf of the diffident and somewhat distracted Junior had surely been frustrating at times, but there was never any question about who was serving whom. This was, of course, precisely the relationship that enabled Junior's associates to be so effective and explained as well the length of their tenure: each came to work every morning knowing exactly why he was there.

It was different for Goetze. First, there was Butler—irrepressible and unstoppable, intolerant and intolerable, with an answer for every question and an insistence on being the one who does the asking. It was not for nothing that *Vanity Fair* called him "the most diligent man in America." It was often the sort of diligence that can drive a subordinate to harbor unpleasant thoughts. His badgering of Goetze on every aspect of the finances, uses, and potential disposition of the Upper Estate had been going on, at levels of ever greater intensity, for years. And Butler wasn't even Goetze's boss; his masters were the trustees of Columbia, members of a self-perpetuating body of New York aristocrats and moguls, and, as such, men who had other things on their minds. Consequently, they employed a Frederick Goetze to tend to the details and to Butler.

For Goetze, unloading the burdens of the Upper Estate may have been nearly as important as the fountain of money that would soon pour forth from it. Landlording was neither his interest nor his métier. There were special irritants as well: for instance, maintaining the secret of the New Yorker "of great prominence and wealth . . . with a high reputation for moral rectitude" who had assigned his lease for a luxurious apartment to a young and gorgeous "beautician." The assignment was never recorded, never made public, payments made under it bore a bogus name, and the details remained known only to Goetze himself.

But the letter the treasurer signed in the trustees' behalf on January 15, 1929, must have given him special pleasure to cross off his list of obligations. It informed each leaseholder that "from and after the date of this notification you should deal with said Met. Sq. Corp. as your Landlord." If Columbia was not exactly getting out of the real estate business—it still owned the land, of course—at least it was no longer responsible for conjuring with a cloud of gnatlike lessees or subjecting itself to the decades-long humiliation of mismanaging some of the most valuable land in the world.

These chores now fell to John D. Rockefeller Jr., or more accurately to those men who came to work each morning knowing precisely why they did so. In this case, their first obligation couldn't have been clearer. Under the terms of the lease, Junior would be paying Columbia $3.6 million each year, and in exchange would be entitled to all the income the land produced—at last count, for 1928, that would be $300,000. However much it would cost to demolish 228 buildings and erect something wonderful to replace them, it was almost certainly more expensive *not* to build.

Thus began a sprint that turned into a marathon: the effort to acquire, dissolve, or otherwise negate every one of the leases then in effect on the Upper Estate, and simultaneously to purchase and similarly disencumber the Sixth Avenue frontage not owned by Columbia but deemed necessary to the development of Metropolitan Square. This required the dissolution not only of all the ground leases (203 on the Columbia property alone), but the entire series of contracts attached to them—all those subordinate leases covering the buildings erected on the land, the occupants of the buildings, the subtenants of the occupants. This was not necessarily bad news for many of these people. As Frederick Lewis Allen wrote a few years later, "If there is one thing calculated to bring tears of joy to the eyes of a small business man, it is to hold a lease in a piece of property which is being assembled by John D. Rockefeller, Jr."

The leaseholders of 1929, like the roughly five thousand tenants and subtenants who lived in their buildings, were a fair reflection of the city New York had become: for every Helen M. Ryan there was a Francesco A. Petronio, for every G. Willett Van Nest a Hyman Glassman. But economically and socially they were a somewhat more surprising crew. At the eastern end of the property, on or near Fifth Avenue, the leaseholders included such eminences as the distinguished lawyer William Nelson Cromwell, whose four-story limestone mansion at 12 West 49th was sufficient for himself and his wife, while the neighboring houses at numbers 10 and 14 provided him with protection against development from the east and, to his west, a place to store his books and paintings. Behind Cromwell's garden stood 13 West 48th, a house belonging to William G. McAdoo, Woodrow Wilson's son-in-law (and his secretary of the treasury as well). Moving westward one passed the homes of solid New Yorkers like Dr. Arthur Lyman Fisk, various members of the Schermerhorn clan, and even Peter Grimm, the new president of William A. White & Sons. The White firm was now charged with negotiating all the lease buyouts, including those on the four properties Grimm controlled on the north side of West 49th Street, one of them his own residence.

But these were exceptions. The visiting French journalist who rhapsodized about the neighborhood, calling it "a sort of Montmartre [populated by] artists, writers, journalists, that is, men of vivid imagination, little money, and great optimism," got his Parisian districts confused: this was more like Pigalle. Though some artists and writers did indeed live in the Upper Estate—the painter Charles Sheeler, for one, sublet rooms in one of Grimm's houses—the Frenchman had likely encountered them in somewhat less domestic premises. When he was police commissioner, Grover Whalen estimated that there were thirty-two thousand speakeasies in the five boroughs, and as another commentator said, Columbia had "sold Rockefeller a thousand" of them.

To many, this was a real thigh-slapper: America's most famous prohibitionist, a teetotaler who was the son of teetotalers, who at one time was the single largest contributor to the Anti-Saloon League, and who at the age of eighty, three decades after repeal, would threaten to close down a beach club he had supported if it ever served a drop of alcohol—now this man had become landlord to what may have been the greatest density of liquored-up lawbreakers in America. Even more comic was the attitude of the Fifth Avenue Association, which hated booze and its purveyors just as much as Junior did, and on top of that had managed to ban "pool rooms, funeral parlors, dance halls, gasoline stations, bowling alleys, [and] motion picture theaters" from the avenue, not to mention neon lights, projecting signs, and "the bare-faced use of the word 'sale.'" For a man prone to headaches, Junior must have contracted a doozy when he received a horrified letter from Captain William A. Pedrick, executive vice president of the FAA, expressing the association's "considerable uneasiness" arising from "press statements intimating that a gigantic theatrical undertaking, or some equally undesirable enterprise, is to be established on your property." All those speakeasies—which Junior was of course going to tear down, along with the rest of the three blocks of semislum that lay just to the west of Fifth—were apparently less offensive than a big movie theater.

The "thousand speakeasies" Junior had acquired may have been more than writerly hyperbole. By Grover Whalen's definition, "All you need is two bottles and a room and you have a speakeasy." There were plenty of these in the three blocks, where divided and redivided brownstones, many in dreary disrepair, harbored hundreds of down-at-heels rooms that could accommodate the bottles and those who might wish to drink from them. But there were several far more substantial establishments that made the Upper Estate one of the wettest neighborhoods in America. Years before John Perona founded the swank nightclub El Morocco, he operated a speak at 39 West 49th. The celebrated saloonkeeper Tony Soma—later "a highly respectable restaurant owner," and later still the father-in-law of John Huston and grandfather of Anjelica—controlled a batch of moist properties on the south side of 51st. The most notable of the speaks, which had begun operating in 1927 in a nondescript brownstone at 42 West 49th, was initially called the Iron Gate, after the heavy black fixture that separated the property from the sidewalk. Over the next two years it changed its name to the Grotto, then 42, then Jack and Charlie's, and finally the Puncheon Club. The eponymous Charlie, a graduate of NYU Law School named Charles Berns who was not nearly as cherubic as he looked, said he and his partner, Jack Kriendler, changed the name so often "in order to avoid continuity in the IRS records." After accepting an $11,000 lease buyout from the Rockefeller agents, Berns and Kriendler reinstalled the gate in front of their new establishment on 52nd Street, the "21" Club.

That deal took much less strain than some of the negotiations with the demi-mondaines of the Upper Estate. Just as you could have a speakeasy with two bottles and a room, all you really needed for a brothel was a woman and a bed, and the three blocks harbored more than their share. Rockefeller lawyer Francis Christy, in his unpublished memoirs, said that evicting the hookers and pimps from the old houses by serving legal process "resembled a battle front" with "a serious risk of casualties." The two men detailed to this particular task, a legal clerk named Bill Graham and "his body-guard, Bob Reilley, who resembled an ex-cop, ex-marine and ex-prizefighter rolled into one," wore reinforced derbies to protect themselves from bombardment by flowerpots, crockery, and other missiles hurled from the upper windows of buildings. This was a tactic the girls resorted to after the offer of fleshly enticements to Graham and Reilley proved ineffective.

But to a large extent the simple threat of eviction proceedings enabled the Rockefeller representatives to bounce the lowest of the lowlifes from the Upper Estate. A different strategy was reserved for holders of ground leases, each of whom anticipated a delicious Rockefeller-funded payday, the sooner the better. The effort to acquire the leases at favorable prices—and any operation involving Junior required nearly as much attention to the pennies as to the dollars—was consequently planned like a military campaign.

Shortly after the Columbia-Rockefeller lease was signed in January of 1929, Grimm's firm prepared a multicolored map indicating the order of battle: leases on the red lots had either already expired or had less than a year to run; leases expiring in 1929 were signified by blue; 1930 expirations by yellow, and so on. The closer a lease was to expiration, the less Junior would have to pay; conversely, the longer Grimm's men bluffed and stalled, the longer demolition, excavation, construction, and, finally, rental income would have to wait. Working under the financial oversight of Heydt and the legal supervision of Christy (and, starting in late 1929, with John R. Todd hovering above both), William A. White strategists set both a first-offer price and a deal price for each property. From the start they sought to conclude fairly generous agreements with the largest leaseholders, hoping these men could sway their more reluctant neighbors. Among the most influential was the unlikely Solomon Kalvin, "a character straight out of the Old Testament" who in the spring of 1929 sold thirteen ground leases to Junior for $1,150,000. Kalvin and his son Nathan, who had started with nothing, were so highly regarded for their success in the real estate business that their action, Francis Christy recalled, was "instrumental in inducing [others] to sell their leases."

Even the paperwork went forward with choreographic precision. Once a deal was struck, the leaseholder would be scheduled for an appointment downtown at the offices of Murray, Aldrich & Webb. Douglas S. Gibbs, a young associate, would greet the leaseholder at the door, introduce him to a closing agent from the Title Guarantee and Trust Company, offer a seat at a desk, and indicate on the fully prepared papers where the leaseholder should sign. The closing agent would take the acknowledgment and Gibbs would hand over the check—sometimes made out for more than a million dollars—stand up, shake hands, and usher the newly enriched leaseholder out the door. The entire procedure, once Gibbs perfected it, took exactly two minutes.

Early on in the lease acquisition campaign, *The New Yorker* told its readers about "a boom trading in the [Upper Estate] leases; they are changing hands back and forth on telephonic deals. Before it is over some tailors, hairdressers, speakeasy owners, and others will retire for life." Harry Hall complained to Heydt that "unscrupulous speculators" had been buying up leases "with the purpose of holding us up for large amounts." The deus ex machina that saved Junior from what Hall called "substantial extortion" was Fulton Cutting's unwillingness to make a formal commitment: in the summer of 1929, whispers concerning the Metropolitan Opera's possible withdrawal from the project induced a certain dread among the leaseholders. Like everyone else in New York—including, at that point, Junior—they believed that an opera house was essential to any development. A more foresightful Heydt told Junior that "if, by any chance, the whole Opera House scheme falls down, these people will become panicky and sell at very much lower prices than they are [currently] asking." He added that he wanted to start demolishing the buildings on leaseholds they had already acquired so they could simultaneously stop paying taxes on those houses, prepare for construction, and "create conditions which will make it desirable for the remaining owners to come to terms with us." So much for Arthur Woods's belief that Heydt was in over his head.

But demolition didn't begin that summer, nor would it for nearly a year. With the larger leaseholders already signed on and paid off, the plodding work of lease acquisition became a campaign of attrition, progressing building by building. The Misses Addie and Babette Liveright amiably agreed to relocate their 49th Street bookstore to 51st, where Junior would become a regular customer ("He was crazy over light fiction . . . and books about trees," Babette said). Charles Sheeler gave up his parlor-floor space in one of Peter Grimm's houses in exchange for eight months of rent-free tenancy in another Upper Estate building scheduled for later demolition. Mrs. Daisy Bright of 39 West 49th Street agreed to a $60,000 buyout so long as she could remove the building's oak paneling and take it with her. The lease

to a front parlor in a house on 50th Street went for $6,400; an entire build-
ing across the street made its owner richer by $280,000. Fortunately for
Grimm, Christy, Heydt, et al., the gambler Arnold Rothstein—the man
who had fixed the 1919 World Series—had been murdered in the Park
Central Hotel just two months before Junior acquired the master lease to
the Upper Estate. Rothstein owned the house at 26 West 51st, and the
Rockefeller agents were able to acquire the rights to its ground lease at an
estate auction instead of a poker game.

The Upper Estate was not the only land that had to be cleared for development. If Junior wanted to control the entire three blocks from 48th to 51st,
from Fifth to Sixth, his representatives had to acquire two parcels Columbia did not own. The university had sold the smaller one, along Fifth Avenue between 48th and 49th, to the Dutch Reformed Church in the 1850s;
the church in turn sold off a portion to Robert Goelet, the Vanderbilt son-
in-law who had been Otto Kahn's faithless ally in the battle with Fulton
Cutting. Neither Goelet nor the church wanted to sell.

Along Sixth Avenue, though, all three blocks were lined with a collection of buildings as dreary as the el tracks above and as ripe for development
as the entire Upper Estate. It was Charles Heydt, so influential in every
stage of Rockefeller Center's prenatal life, who had first suggested the acquisition back in December 1928, a month before the Columbia lease was
executed. Ben Morris subsequently included the Sixth Avenue lots in his
"Plan B," developed in May 1929. Morris reasoned that ownership of so
much frontage along an avenue the width of Sixth would increase the zoning envelope substantially, which in turn would increase potential rental
income. It would also provide marquee space near the Broadway entertainment district for the project's planned theaters. And it enabled Morris to
transform his original plan into a prototypical piece of Beaux-Arts site design, so exquisitely symmetrical that if you tapped it on one end it would
vibrate for days.

By the end of the summer of 1929, a strategy had developed. A new vehicle, the Underel Holding Corporation, was established for the sole purpose of acquiring the land that was, appropriately, under the el. It began as
a beard for Junior, who had gotten used to this sort of subterfuge when he
took on the pseudonym "Mr. David" (after his youngest son) in matters
pertaining to the acquisition of Williamsburg. Underel negotiations were
conducted not by William A. White & Sons but by a variety of brokers.

Underel lawyering fell not to Murray, Aldrich & Webb but to an unrelated firm. An independent property manager was brought in to collect the rents and maintain the buildings once they were acquired, and the word "Rockefeller" was banned from all documents. Not that any of the disguises fooled the Sixth Avenue property owners, who proved quite a bit more difficult to dislodge than the denizens of the Upper Estate. Not until September 18, 1931, three months after excavation had begun and one week after the foundation was poured for the first building in Rockefeller Center, were Metropolitan Square officials able to formalize the ongoing site assembly campaign by delivering 383 separate legal documents to the New York County Register's office. It was the largest single filing in New York history.

Importantly, these papers included an assignment to Underel of the ground lease for 70 West 51st Street, which belonged to Ella Wendel, the last surviving member of one of the richest, and oddest, families in New York. Just as importantly, the filing did *not* include documents concerning the property at the southeast corner of Sixth Avenue and 50th Street, nor a row of buildings on Sixth between 48th and 49th owned by the movie mogul William Fox, nor any connected to William Nelson Cromwell's properties at 10, 12, and 14 West 49th. The problem of the southeast corner was mooted by architecture, and Fox was outmaneuvered by Junior's agents. But the Cromwell predicament was so sticky that it led Frederick Goetze to go to Nicholas Murray Butler and tell him that "you are . . . the one man" who could "settle the matter with Cromwell on a friendly basis." Goetze was right, too—even if it took another eighteen years to prove it.

About half a mile south of the Upper Estate, at the corner of 39th Street and Fifth Avenue, stood a broad, four-story house that dated back to the 1850s, once home to John Gottlieb Wendel and his seven sisters. As each of the Wendel siblings died, another room was closed off. By the fall of 1930, 442 Fifth had but two occupants: the seventy-seven-year-old Ella Virginia von Echtzel Wendel and her white poodle, Tobey. Not just any Tobey: this was the seventh or eighth in a long line of Tobeys, each of them white, each of them a poodle, each of them Ella Wendel's only companion. There were servants in the house, too, but not much else: no electricity, no telephone, virtually nothing that hadn't been there when the house was new. It was four stories tall, as wide as two conventional brownstones, but now as decrepit as it once was grand. With the land it sat on and that extended back toward Sixth, 442 Fifth was assessed in 1928 for $3.69 million—$3.684

million for the land, $6,000 for the house. The wrecker who eventually razed it in 1934 said its total salvage value amounted to $500.

Ella Wendel was the granddaughter of Johann G. Wendel, who emigrated to the United States from Germany late in the eighteenth century, went into the fur business with his countryman John Jacob Astor, and married Astor's half-sister. When Astor began to invest his profits from the fur trade in Manhattan real estate, so did Wendel. After his death the family holdings were increased by Johann's son John D. Wendel, and yet further by John D.'s son John G., until the family owned 111 different properties in Manhattan alone, plus scores more in the outer boroughs, Long Island, and Westchester County. The Wendels were no more interested in improving their land than they were in selling it, and on much of it stood structures little distinguished and poorly maintained. One such building, a plain five-story brownstone on the south side of West 51st Street just east of Sixth Avenue, was on Underel's shopping list.

Except, as everyone in New York knew, "the Wendels never sell." Apparently a paraphrase of a deathbed declaration uttered by Johann, the patriarch, it became so identified with the family that it would have been the perfect motto for a Wendel coat of arms. Mervin Rosenman, in *Perjury, Forgery, and an Enormous Fortune,* his book on the bizarre battle over Ella Wendel's will, suggested an equally apt alternative, from a phrase that appeared in every lease the Wendel family issued: "Tenant shall make his own repairs." Another ironclad Wendel rule dictated that the family would issue leases to its land for no term other than three years.

The first two male Wendels in the United States were exceptionally capable businessmen. The third, Ella's brother John G., was that and something of a monster as well. (Also something of a paranoid: fearful that disease could enter his body through his feet, he stomped around in a custom-made, mutant form of platform shoes, their inch-thick gutta percha soles extended by fenders reaching another full inch in each direction.) The eldest and only male among John D.'s children, John G. subjugated his sisters in the name of the family patrimony. He forbade them to marry, for marriage would dilute the ownership of the Wendel holdings. All wore black high-necked dresses that John required them to sew themselves, and none could own jewelry. When the second youngest, Georgiana, broke free from his grip at the age of fifty, he had her pronounced insane by a sheriff's jury and committed to a sanatorium; she eventually won her freedom by lawsuit—and then returned to the gloomy mansion on Fifth and 39th. Only one escaped. After sixty-one-year-old Rebecca, the third oldest, married a man she had met at Trinity Church, John responded with a tyrant's logic: now the other Wendel women were no longer allowed to attend church.

Besides Rebecca, three other sisters survived John's death in 1914, and by then there was little likelihood that any would break free from the prison in which they had been raised and to which they had grown accustomed. Rebecca, who became de facto head of the family, was able to cope reasonably well with that responsibility until she went blind at seventy-eight. Retainers and lawyers ran the Wendel affairs after that, well enough that by the time Rebecca died ten years later in 1930, leaving her seventy-seven-year-old sister Ella the last Wendel on earth, the rental income from the family properties ran to $1.2 million each year, all of it to the benefit of Ella and whichever Tobey it was who now occupied her lap.

For the Underel agents assigned responsibility for purchasing the Sixth Avenue frontage, it could not have been a happy day when they learned that 70 West 51st was not only not part of the Upper Estate, but that it was Wendel property (John G. had acquired it in 1884). There is no evidence that Ella, who had never been meaningfully involved in the family's business affairs, was party to or even aware of any negotiations. Still, "the Wendels never sell"; it was clear there could be no purchase. However, a subsidiary family commandment—John G.'s insistence on signing no lease that ran longer than three years—worked to Junior's benefit: the current version expired during the site assembly period, and on January 28, 1931, Underel assumed control of the land.*

Not six weeks later, on Monday, March 9, 1931, Ella Wendel suffered a stroke. On Wednesday the 11th a telephone was finally installed at 442 Fifth so nurses attending Ella could reach her doctor in an emergency. On Friday the 13th the last of the Wendels died, leaving small sums of money to her servants and the bulk of her enormous estate to various charities that her sister Rebecca had enumerated in her own will. This did not keep 2,303 individuals across the country and in much of German-speaking Europe from asserting their claims to Ella's millions. Surrogate Judge James A. Foley declared at a hearing, "From abroad we have claims filed by whole villages whose inhabitants only bear the name of Wendel." Executors

---

*The Wendel lease was coterminous, in original term and extensions, with the Columbia lease. However, an especially Wendelesque clause required Underel, upon the lease's expiration, to demolish and remove anything it might have built on the site. Additionally, just in case Junior or his heirs got into financial trouble, Underel was required to place the estimated cost of demolition in escrow.

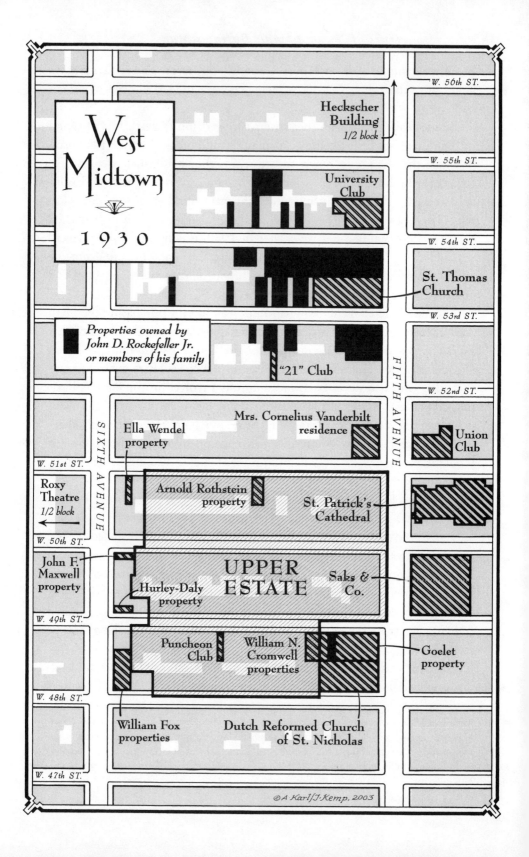

West Midtown

1930

Heckscher Building
1/2 block

W. 56th ST.

W. 55th ST.

University Club

W. 54th ST.

St. Thomas Church

W. 53rd ST.

Properties owned by
John D. Rockefeller Jr.
or members of his family

"21" Club

W. 52nd ST.

Mrs. Cornelius Vanderbilt
residence

Union Club

Ella Wendel
property

SIXTH AVENUE

FIFTH AVENUE

W. 51st ST.

Roxy
Theatre
1/2 block

Arnold Rothstein
property

St. Patrick's
Cathedral

W. 50th ST.

John F.
Maxwell
property

UPPER
ESTATE

Saks &
Co.

Hurley-Daly
property

W. 49th ST.

Puncheon
Club

William N.
Cromwell
properties

Goelet
property

W. 48th ST.

William Fox
properties

Dutch Reformed Church
of St. Nicholas

W. 47th ST.

©A Karl/J.Kemp, 2003

commissioned map publisher Andrew Hagstrom to lay out a family tree that would presumably help them sort things out; Hagstrom's tree measured five by eighteen feet. Surrogate Foley presided over nearly two years of claims and counterclaims filed by more than two hundred lawyers.

And when it was all over, and it was established that there were no more Wendels to invoke Johann's deathbed declaration, on March 6, 1935, Underel Holdings Corporation purchased the lot at 70 West 51st Street from the Estate of Ella Wendel for $120,000, plus $2,800 in well-earned broker's fees.

In 1852, six years before Dagger John Hughes set the New York archdiocese to work raising money to build St. Patrick's Cathedral, a grocer named John F. Boronowsky bought a twenty-five-by-sixty-six-foot lot at the southeast corner of 50th Street and Sixth Avenue for $1,600. Three quarters of a century later Boronowsky's grandson, John F. Maxwell, was contentedly collecting $16,000 a year in rent from the United Cigar Company, whose subtenants in the three-story redbrick building included, among others, a shoeshine shop, a beauty parlor, a women's tailor: just the sort of businesses that commuters alighting from the 50th Street el station might patronize.

"The . . . southeast corner of 50th Street we cannot buy," Heydt told Junior in June of 1931, because its owner "refuses to sell at any price." This was not quite accurate: Maxwell wanted a nice, even million for the lot. Francis Christy pointedly noted that Maxwell was "a Scotsman," as if that explained everything. Maxwell told reporters that the Rockefellers never made an offer for the property. Heydt got Junior's approval to acquire a seventeen-year lease, but it proved futile.

Or, as it turned out, unnecessary. For less than a block south, on the northeast corner of 49th Street, a four-story building under long-term lease to Daniel Hurley and Patrick Daly happened to occupy a lot roughly the same size as Maxwell's property. Hurley and Daly, whose families had operated a saloon on the premises from 1892 until the passage of the Eighteenth Amendment, had been reduced by prohibition to hiding their bar just inside an unmarked entrance on 49th and subletting the rest of their space to a barbershop, a luggage store, a fruit stand, a flower shop, a pool room, and a Mrs. Shea, who rented out "furnished rooms." Hurley and Daly were definitely not Scotsmen, and by late 1931 they knew that prohibition was on its last legs. Their request for a 250-*million*-dollar lease buyout suggested nonnegotiability. Underel bought the building, but had to allow Hurley and Daly (who reopened their saloon on the advent of repeal) to stay until their lease expired in early 1942. Rarely had the Scots and the Irish worked in so comfortable a collaboration. The two little buildings survived to become matching bookends for the RCA Building, which in early 1932 began to rise, with graceful symmetry, between and behind them.

The Rockefeller willingness to build around holdouts was a last warning to the few remaining recalcitrants: ask too much and you'll get nothing.* After construction began, even so hardened a negotiator as William Fox, founder of the Twentieth Century–Fox studio, had to capitulate. Fox owned the row of six small buildings along the east side of Sixth running north from 48th Street, and more than two and a half unavailing years had passed since Underel had first approached him. By late 1932, though, the box office and foyer of one of Rockefeller Center's first buildings, the RKO Roxy Theater, had been completed just to the Fox row's north. The bulk of the L-shaped building wrapped behind the row and down to 48th Street. Fox's six little buildings were dwarfed by the 3,500-seat theater structure, and isolated as well.

When Fox finally gave in, just three weeks before the RKO Roxy's opening night, the process of assembling the site for Rockefeller Center was at last completed. The press release announcing this milestone was magnanimous, or maybe smug. Fox sold the six lots, it said, because he "was motivated by a desire to contribute to the complete fulfillment of the largest building project ever undertaken by private capital."

Now the numbers could be totaled. The original $6 million Heydt had budgeted for the Sixth Avenue acquisitions had ballooned to more than $10 million, in addition to the $3 million spent on buying out Upper Estate leases. But if Junior was irritated by the overrun, he left no record of his dismay in his voluminous papers. This was out of character for a man who was by nature offended by the waste of a nickel and who could ask associates to devote hours to the proper allocation of a dollar. Late in his working life he had a functionary arrive at how much he and each of his sons should

---

*A softer attitude prevailed when the lease on the Hurley-Daly building expired in 1942, and Rockefeller Center agreed to renew it; the bar the two men reopened when Prohibition was repealed had become popular with the NBC employees working in the giant tower into whose massive form it was so daintily tucked. Rockefeller Center eventually took over the lease in 1975, five years after purchasing the Maxwell property.

contribute to a Christmas fund for their office employees by determining what portion of the office's total square footage each was using; shares ranged from Junior's $431.16 to David's $7.52. But counting pennies at this point in the project was less fruitful than counting days: the sooner buildings could go up, the sooner they could be producing revenue. Those who wanted to build—Junior and his associates—cared deeply about this. So did those who got their leverage from Junior's urgent itch to begin—the Wendel Estate, the two Kalvins, nearly everybody who had sold land or lease to Junior before demolition began. Even the immovable holdouts, Maxwell, Hurley, and Daly, hungered for the profits they knew would come from the project's upward lift on foot traffic and property values.

William Nelson Cromwell, however, couldn't have cared less—about money (of which he had plenty), about being terribly cooperative (it wasn't really his way), or even about the desperate situation in which he had placed his alma mater, dear Columbia, whose officers had been getting nicer and nicer to him as he got older and older. It wasn't a bad bet: Cromwell was extremely wealthy, demonstratively philanthropic, rapidly aging (he turned seventy-five in 1929), and conveniently childless. To Nicholas Murray Butler, these were four splendid attributes. They were, however, potentially made moot by Columbia's obligations to deliver to Junior control of all property in the Upper Estate that was no longer under lease to a third party. Cromwell's leases on 12 West 49th and 14 West 49th had expired in 1927, which was good for Columbia, but his refusal to acknowledge this legal nicety was not.

Cromwell was no William Fox, flattering himself into thinking he could run a bluff on the Rockefellers. He was the real thing, a titanic figure in New York legal circles whose career was nearly unmatched in its length—he had co-founded Sullivan & Cromwell in 1879—and in its accomplishments. His clients included E. H. Harriman, whom he helped win control of the Wells-Fargo Company; J. P. Morgan, for whom he did the legal work establishing U.S. Steel; and Ethel Barrymore, whom he would address as "my fair Portia" when kneeling to kiss her hand. His greatest fame came from the job he did for the Panama Canal Company at the turn of the century, when his mastery of the complexities surrounding the transfer of the Canal Zone to U.S. sovereignty earned him a fee in excess of one million dollars. He doubtless made quite a lot more from the specialty he developed after the passage of the Clayton Antitrust Act in 1914: reorganizing companies so their activities would conform at least to the letter of the law. It was not surprising that Columbia flinched when Cromwell threatened to

"devote the entire efforts of eighty lawyers in his office to defending his position"—whatever that position happened to be. Cromwell based his claim
on oral assurances he claimed had been made to him by various members
of Columbia's board, but had he chosen to, he likely would have been able
to build a plausible case that he was entitled to indefinite lease extensions
because Mars was in a particular alignment with Neptune.

Did anyone notice that one of the Cromwell houses was empty and that
he hardly lived in the other one? That number 14 was used almost entirely
for storage and number 12 (the one with the racks of vintage champagne in
the basement, the tapestries on the walls, the statuettes and paintings nearly
everywhere) was essentially a pied-à-terre? (To say nothing of number 10,
which was not part of the Upper Estate and which Cromwell owned outright, strictly to buffer him from whatever might be going on to the east at
number 8.) Although he had long used number 12 as both his residence
and his personal place of business, and had from time to time opened its
enormous dining room for elaborate, white-tie dinners for his partners, as
he got richer and older Cromwell spent more of his time in France. There,
where his benefactions included construction of a monument to the Lafayette
Escadrille outside Paris and the postwar rehabilitation of the lace industry
in the northern town of Valenciennes, he indulged an avid Francophilia
that was memorialized when he was awarded the Legion of Honor. This
medal made a handsome addition to the entire Cromwell package: an un-
ruly mop of silver hair, an equally silvery and impressively thick Mark
Twain–style mustache, a glittering watch fob spanning his buttoned waist-
coat. His aspect was as notable as his accomplishments.

The Cromwell of the gold-plated resumé and the Kentucky Colonel appearance must have been daunting to John Godfrey Saxe, the Columbia
lawyer assigned this unpleasant piece of work. At a dinner party in 1929,
Saxe found himself seated next to a rampant Cromwell, who denounced
"the university's want of honor" and, with an especially bizarre flourish,
threatened to "take [my] pants off and fight" if Columbia so much as
sought an appraisal on the property. Fortunately for Saxe, who was reporting regularly to Goetze on his lack of progress and might otherwise have
had his reportorial skills questioned, an extremely reliable witness was
seated on the other side of Cromwell: Columbia trustee Benjamin N. Cardozo. Three years later, when Cardozo was named to the U.S. Supreme
Court, he joined on the high court the former Columbia law school dean,
Harlan Fiske Stone, whom another trustee had once suggested would be an
appropriate consultant to Goetze on the Cromwell mess. What issue of con-

stitutionality could possibly be as important as unknotting the Columbia-Cromwell tangle?

Complications multiplied. Robert Goelet, planning to develop his corner lot and the adjacent properties at 2, 4, and 6 West 48th, could not build without a release from an easement that Cromwell controlled and now held hostage in the war with Columbia (another agony for Butler: Goelet's "interest and friendship are also matters of large concern to us," he reminded Goetze). Cromwell retained former New York governor Nathan Miller as his lawyer and stopped paying rent on number 14. At the same time, the Rockefeller forces prepared to initiate legal action of their own against Columbia (because Cromwell's leases had already expired, the university was obligated, under the terms of the contract with Junior, to deliver the land). Not only were they insisting that Columbia deliver immediate possession of the Cromwell properties, but by early 1930 they were claiming "a loss of income from the inability to construct a building" on the site and an "impairment of the aesthetic arrangement of the development." By year's end, with Cromwell "steadfastly refus[ing] to relinquish possession" of the two buildings, Rockefeller lawyers were urging Columbia to commence formal eviction proceedings against him and demanding that the university deliver his two lots to Metropolitan Square no later than January 31, 1931.

Saxe was lawyer enough to know that a lawsuit could lead to no solution at all and persuasive enough to convince Junior's associates to pursue milder means of dislodging Cromwell. Architects were asked to explore ways to build around the two properties. John R. Todd's partner, Hugh Robertson, suggested the possibility of offering Cromwell "something fine in exchange" for his leasehold rights. Visions of two large bequests (Goelet's as well as Cromwell's) growing fainter and fainter, Butler could only grumble that "our good friend, Mr. Cromwell, has pretty much lost his wits." Which is to say, Cromwell had outsmarted, and outlasted, the combined forces of Columbia University and the Rockefeller family.

In the years ahead, while the rest of the neighborhood was demolished and a new city of skyscrapers rose in its place, the houses at 12 West 49th and 14 West 49th slept. In a misreading of the situation that nonetheless became to some degree accepted wisdom, *Fortune* said that Junior had decided to build around the two properties because of "Lawyer Cromwell's eloquent plea." Cromwell's legal blackmail was no more an eloquent plea than horseflies are pleasant dinner guests.

But the Rockefeller forces adapted, and not just by postponing development of the south block or rejiggering the master plan (both of which they did) on the apparent assumption that Cromwell (a) would never give in as long as he lived, and (b) might live forever. Early on, back when they couldn't believe that Cromwell would really keep this up, Todd, Heydt, and the other men planning the property's future expected the Rockefeller holdings in the southern block to reach all the way to Fifth, as was the case in the central and northern blocks. Goelet prevented that, but Junior's men still wanted to go as far toward Fifth as they could. Once Cromwell agreed to convey the leases on numbers 12 and 14, they reasoned, he'd of course sell number 10 as well. Consequently, an offer was made to purchase number 8, just east of the Cromwell threesome, to complete the Metropolitan Square holdings.

In March of 1932, after construction had started and steel had begun to rise north of 49th Street, Heydt acknowledged that "I should have cancelled that [offer] as soon as it became evident we would not get the Cromwell Houses." And now, he told Thomas Debevoise, Junior was "very much averse to buying the house at the present time but is willing to leave the final decision to you and me."

Debevoise had bad news: the offer, by his reading, was ethically irrevocable. Junior had to pay $200,000 for the five-story house at 8 West 49th Street, with its dress shop on the second floor and the six apartments scattered above it, even though none of his associates or counselors had any idea what could be done with either the building or its motley tenants. For another four years, until the bell rang for Round Two in the heavyweight battle of Columbia versus Cromwell, the only event of interest at 8 West 49th Street was the arrest in her third-floor bedroom of Ada Payne, legal tenant of John D. Rockefeller Jr., on a charge of prostitution.

CHAPTER SEVEN

In the optimistic April of 1929, at the same time that Arthur Woods was recruiting architects for Junior's advisory board, surprisingly long lines formed for an exhibition at the Metropolitan Museum of Art on upper Fifth Avenue. The crowds—

I like having a lot of people against me, because the more there are, the more they get balled up and start talking at cross-purposes, giving me ammunition to use effectively against them.

—JOHN R. TODD

15,000 on opening night, 10,000 the first Sunday—had been seduced not by the show's shop-class title, *The Architect and the Industrial Arts,* but by its glamorous content: Art Deco furniture designed by the nation's leading modern architects, an all-star lineup that included Raymond Hood, Eliel Saarinen, Ralph Walker, and Ely Jacques Kahn.

These men were a vanguard leading a dispirited army—the legions of designers and architects who avidly recited the modernist creed but whose clients were unheeding. "The contemporary designer," architect Edwin Avery Park had written just a few years earlier, "will dance and dine to jazz, read *Ulysses,* have himself psychoanalyzed, listen to Debussy, appreciate Cezanne, and ride in an aeroplane. But he will be installing an Empire suite in some wealthy lady's apartment." The crowds who kept the Met show running for months beyond its originally scheduled closing date were passionate, but they were not the commissioning class.

In fact, neither was Junior; his wealth, his renown, and his eleven acres in midtown made him a member of no class but his own. It's unlikely that he would have been aware of the ideological divide in the New York architecture community, but if it managed to capture a corner of his attention there's no question where he would have lined up. His wife, busily establishing the Museum of Modern Art with two other women at the same time Junior's office was preparing to build Rockefeller Center, had all the modernist credentials in the world, but this made Junior even more hostile to modernism and the aesthetic ideology behind it. According to their son Laurance, Junior considered the modern pieces Abby was buying "strange, irresponsible objects [and] he did not approve of them." If mere paintings and prints (which didn't really interest him as art forms) could provoke such a scowling response, his tolerance for experimentation in architecture risked something far more intense. He actually cared about architecture.

More precisely, Junior cared about buildings. Rarely was he as happy as when he was building something, when he could lose himself in blueprints and elevations and the hidden marvels of the construction process, almost like a boy with a set of toy trains. Early in the century he had persuaded his father to let him supervise the design and construction of Kykuit, Senior's (and later Junior's) mansion at Pocantico Hills. It was back then that he began to carry a collapsible wooden ruler in his pocket, a habit—a delight— he would indulge the rest of his life.

But as much as Junior loved the details of building, the big picture— what makes a particular design work, even what makes it appropriate— eluded him. Kykuit is an ungainly, ill-proportioned mess, a mix of styles and nonstyles only its creator could possibly love. Riverside Church, the pan-Christian monument near the Columbia campus that Junior willed into existence, is the confused child of an uneasy marriage between thirteenth-century French Gothic and 1920s Skyscraper Style, adorned with exceptionally bad stone carvings of such modern saints as Booker T. Washington and Albert Einstein. (At least the guidebooks identify it as Einstein; the piece actually looks like Sam Jaffe in *Lost Horizon*.)

Like nearly everything in the world around him, Junior's view of architecture and architects was obscured by the unbreachable wall of his vast wealth. Despite his ecumenical spirit, his sincere attentions to the plight of the poor, and his unprepossessing manner, he lived in a gilded bubble. Abby forged friendships with the artists she met; Junior spent his time with lawyers, bankers, and clergymen. The architects he knew were either aristocrats themselves (like Abby's brother William T. Aldrich, who practiced in Boston, and Ben Morris) or they had entered the upper reaches of society through that sometimes convenient door, salubrious professional affiliation, or that even more welcoming one, fortunate marriage.

One such was John Russell Pope, son-in-law of the Baltimore art collector Henry Walters and protégé of Charles Follen McKim, the lion of

McKim, Mead & White. While Morris continued to labor in Otto Kahn's behalf during the last months of the fractious Rockefeller–Metropolitan Opera relationship, and before John R. Todd had come aboard and arrogated the entire project to his imperial self, Junior turned to Pope to help him figure out what to do not just with the opera house plot, but with the entire three blocks that were now his to mold.

This was the same Pope who had proposed the fifty-story obelisk for Fifth Avenue, not a hundred yards from where Junior lived. Although he did design a few fine buildings in his career, notably the National Gallery of Art in Washington, Pope worshipped so fervently at the altar of the Beaux-Arts it's a wonder he could straighten his knees. Invited to design a new facade for the American Museum of Natural History, on Central Park West, Pope suggested that it serve as the focal point of a statue-studded and grandiose "Boulevard of Art" slicing right through Central Park from Fifth Avenue. Two things survive from this scheme. One is the overblown, column-framed facade that adorns the museum's main entrance. The other is Central Park itself, fortunately spared the vivisection Pope had proposed.

Junior didn't hire Pope to design Metropolitan Square but to oversee selection of the architects who would. Pope, aided by two colleagues, was asked to solicit proposals from seven more architects, then recommend the best plan. The other members of Pope's panel were the Philadelphian Milton B. Medary and the redoubtable Cass Gilbert. Gilbert was now seventy years old, collaborating with the engineer Othmar Ammann on the design of the George Washington Bridge (only a Depression-induced cash shortage saved the GWB from the ponderous stone cladding Gilbert desired) and turning over management of his office to his son, Cass Jr. As fine an architect as he was, Gilbert was not the most open-minded of men: he urged Cass Jr. in 1929 to hire only "gentlemen—not 'kikes'" as draftsmen.

The process evolved into a case of the bland leading the bland. Raymond Hood wasn't invited, nor were his two fellow modernist renegades, Ralph Walker and Ely Jacques Kahn. As Allene Talmey wrote in *The New Yorker* in 1931, "The blue book of architecture and the Social Register are still one." Hood, Walker, and Kahn, Talmey continued, "are only in the telephone book."* Six of the seven contributors whom Pope, Medary, and

---

*Hood once complained that competing against some of the blue book/*Social Register* firms was like "fighting spooks, wraiths and ghosts," for when the firm still known as McKim, Mead & White went after a job, they were trading on the work of men who had been dead for two decades.

Gilbert selected for the "Symposium," as it came to be known in the Rock-efeller offices, were as bound to the Beaux-Arts as the three supervisors. Morris was among them, as was Abby Rockefeller's brother William Aldrich, a Boston architect who had no meaningful experience with skyscrapers (or with New York) but whose bloodlines were just swell (to give Aldrich his due, his judgment was excellent: he had earlier made a futile effort to get his brother-in-law to hire Raymond Hood). Four more reputable if unexceptional firms nearly completed this roster of traditionalists. The nonconforming participant was Harvey Corbett, whom Pope urged on Junior because he "has had to do with many municipal problems." Pope's spelling ("Corbitt") was as shaky as his syntax, but the point was made: nothing Corbett had designed on this scale had ever been built—nothing *anyone* had designed on this scale had ever been built—but for several years, often in collaboration with Hugh Ferriss, he'd been thinking and writing about the future of the city and all the issues of zoning and traffic and congestion connected to the developing discipline of "urbanism." And could it possibly hurt that one of his partners, a young comer named Wallace Harrison, was a Rockefeller relative by marriage?

In February of 1929, each of the seven was asked to submit a development plan for the Upper Estate, including "a possible treatment of an open square and underground garage suggested by Mr. Morris." All ten, including the supervising trio, would be paid five thousand dollars apiece. (Corbett funneled a portion of his fee to Hugh Ferriss, who executed the renderings for him.) The commissioning letter, over the signature of Arthur Woods, stated this was "in no sense a competition." But it was a competition. How could it not be? Charles Heydt's mailbox was filling up with letters from the uninvited begging to be given a chance—important firms like Walker and Gillette, and single practitioners like the self-described "former architect and decorator to the Czar of Russia," a theater designer named Roman Melzer. For all of New York's architects, but especially for the fortunate few invited to take part in the Symposium, Metropolitan Square was the pot of gold at the end of the 1920s rainbow.

The various plans submitted in May were appropriately ambitious, encompassing anywhere from four to five million square feet of rentable space in several tall buildings. (The proposed Empire State Building, itself about to enter the design process, was to have 2.1 million rentable square feet.) But the submissions were so far off the mark in other respects that on May 22, 1929, exactly one year and one day after Ben Morris had presented his initial plans to the gathered multimillionaires at the Metropolitan Club,

Pope, Medary, and Gilbert categorically recommended that none be adopted. After examining the Symposium submissions, Junior agreed. The firm of Cross & Cross had submitted a plan featuring an enormous, round, almost phallic structure rising from the lot line along Fifth Avenue. Behind a similar dominant structure William Aldrich had placed ten skyscrapers around the perimeter of the plot in rigid symmetry, then connected them with an improbable series of bridges at the thirtieth-story level. One plan actually had the entire three-block area girdled by a high, fortlike wall separating the development from the neighboring streets as forbiddingly as if there had been a moat dug along the surrounding sidewalks.

But the Symposium served its purposes. For one thing, it underscored the need to hire a John R. Todd, someone who wouldn't need a double-layered committee structure to make a decision. Valuable ideas came from the Symposium as well, some of which would eventually become part of the completed project: low buildings along Fifth Avenue in the central block; a "focal tall building" at that block's western end; a belowground mall connecting to the planned Sixth Avenue subway. And from the man who had been there all along, Ben Morris, came several ideas to add to his "open square and underground garage" that had already been institutionalized in the commissioning letter from Woods. In his May submissions, Morris called for planted terraces on some of the buildings and the acquisition of the non-Columbia land underneath the Sixth Avenue El.

After the Pope committee acknowledged its failure to find a workable plan, Morris's firm stood alone as the only architectural office connected to Metropolitan Square. For much of the summer of 1929, while ground leases were being purchased and Todd was pitching for the management job and Junior's associates were squabbling with Cutting and his opera colleagues, Morris pushed forward. Several times he met with Arthur Woods and Heydt, and on occasion with Junior himself—who, Morris was pleased to note, made clear that "a conservative type of architecture should be used rather than any extravagant expression of modernistic tendencies." Woods at one point acknowledged how unusual it was that the client had no firm idea of what kind of buildings he wanted to build and had to turn to the architect to get a plausible answer. In August the William A. White firm analyzed Morris's most recent plans and pronounced them sound financially "and of great architectural interest." A grateful Nicholas Murray Butler, surely mindful of the lovely phrase Morris had used to describe the benefits accruing to Columbia from his plans—"permanency of income"—granted the architect an honorary doctorate.

Nevertheless, before the year was out Ben Morris was fired. Worse, he wasn't paid. Even though John R. Todd praised Morris's work at a press conference and indicated that "the final plans will not differ radically from those [he] prepared," the architect had to put in nine months of pleading, argument, and legal saber rattling to get Junior to hand over even a portion of his fee.

Late in life, long after the success of Rockefeller Center had conferred on Todd great wealth (if not great renown), he welcomed a man named William P. Vogel Jr. to his suite in the Barclay Hotel. Todd had concluded his nearly five-decade career in the construction and development game and was now engaged in the sort of victory lap that elderly men of accomplishment (and vanity) afford themselves: a memoir. Vogel had been recruited to serve as Todd's ghostwriter, and the "tall, spare, erect" seventy-seven-year-old greeted him in classic John R. fashion: "Hm. So you're the writer," he said to Vogel. "I'm a better writer than you."

Todd was right; Vogel produced for him a rambling, genial graduation speech of a book festooned with tiresome homilies, false humility, and advice to the young. Todd's private writing was usually brisk, vivid, and appealingly honest in its unashamed self-regard—the same self-regard he displayed in the rude welcome he gave his collaborator. You could measure Todd's confidence in miles. He felt he was a better writer than the writers, a better lawyer than the lawyers, and a better architect than the architects. Except he wasn't an architect—didn't have the training, didn't have the technical knowledge, didn't have the professional license. Architects were simply a necessary nuisance: "For an architect, you show almost human intelligence."

An admirer once observed that Todd was "slow to hire, and slow to fire, but after people have been with him a reasonable length of time, he gets to love them." (The admirer was Todd himself, in a memo to a journalist writing a piece about him.) But no amount of time could repair the relationship between Todd and Ben Morris, strained before their simultaneous (if brief) association on Rockefeller Center and entirely obliterated afterward. In later years, when the two men encountered each other in the Union League Club, they would not speak.

They had known each other for years and had worked together more than once. Their most recent collaboration had concluded in 1924 with the opening of the handsome Cunard Building, a modern (and greatly enlarged) version of a Renaissance palace directly across the street from 26 Broadway. The Cunard's enormous Great Hall had quickly become one of New York's most celebrated spaces and the credit had gone, as it should have, to Morris. The architect's partisans claimed that envy had gotten the best of Todd and inspired him to denigrate Morris to potential clients. If so, Morris turned the other cheek: in 1927, shortly after he had begun his two-and-a-half-year involvement with the opera house project, he told Otto Kahn that engaging either of two distinguished builders would assure Kahn and his colleagues "comfort and satisfaction." One of them was Todd, Robertson & Todd.

But by 1929 there was enough ill will between Morris and Todd that Morris stopped working the instant he learned from Woods that his old collaborator had taken over the development of Metropolitan Square, pending further word from Todd himself. When it came, it was not encouraging: Todd sent Morris a contract indicating, among other things, that Morris would be just one of a group of architects, and that his work— all the architects' work—would proceed under Todd's personal direction. And Morris knew that personal direction couldn't get more personal than in the grip of the imperious Todd.

The ill feeling between the two men was now palpable; a Metropolitan Opera bureaucrat still involved in the planning at this point witnessed "violent disagreements" between Todd and Morris. But one suspects Todd would have rebuffed Brunelleschi if the great Florentine had been available. After paying public lip service to Morris's contributions over the previous two-plus years, Todd struck. On October 28, 1929, with the whole New York architectural world watching, he announced that the unknown Reinhard & Hofmeister—*tenant* architects, for God's sake, men who knew how to put dividing walls between rectangular offices!—would be the lead architects for what *Fortune* would later call "the largest single [architectural] opportunity of [a] generation."

Three days later, at a Metropolitan Square board meeting, Todd plunged a knife through the hearts of Morris's latest plan and another put forth by Harvey Corbett. And then the man who wasn't an architect pinned his own plan to the wall, declared it the winner, ordered Hofmeister and Reinhard to work, and began a conversation with Raymond M. Hood.

By 1929 the south side of West 40th Street between Fifth and Sixth Avenues had probably enjoyed as great a variety of views as any street in New

York. When it was first laid out, the land immediately to its north was a potter's field. By 1845 a gigantic stone wall on the plot's eastern end enclosed the four-acre Croton Reservoir, the city's primary water supply, and eight years later the thrilling iron-and-glass Crystal Palace exhibition hall, home to the first world's fair held in New York, rose to the reservoir's immediate west. Advertised as fireproof, the Crystal Palace demonstrated the reliability of both nineteenth-century fireproofing and nineteenth-century advertising when it burned to the ground five years after it opened. The reservoir was drained and its enclosure demolished toward the end of the nineteenth century to make way for the New York Public Library and Bryant Park. This was at roughly the same time that the south side of 40th Street was evolving into a row of stately club buildings and the like, a parade of Renaissance- and Beaux-Arts–inspired palazzos.

In 1924, though, a startling exclamation point suddenly punctuated the classical vocabulary of West 40th Street. The new headquarters of the American Radiator Company was an imposing twenty-one stories, but it differed from its neighbors in more than size. It was sheathed in jet-black bricks. At its top, gilded terra-cotta flourishes, lit by night, made it appear as if the building were some sort of enormous candle, and until taller buildings intervened the Radiator Building's glow could be seen from Staten Island. Georgia O'Keeffe painted it. Several years after it opened Heywood Broun, in the *New York World,* called it "a happy combination of the art of the architect with that of the pastry cook." This was not a unanimous opinion. Hugh Ferriss said the Radiator Building "has undoubtedly provoked more arguments among laymen on the subject of architectural values than any other structure in the country."

On the building's fourteenth floor in the fall of 1929, you could find the man who had started those arguments sitting in his Windsor chair, his tiny feet propped up on a high stool before him. On his desk rested a plasticine model of an idealized New York skyline. If it was midafternoon, Ray Hood might be enjoying his daily snack of milk and ginger cookies; if it was late in the evening, which was not an uncommon work hour in the offices of Raymond Hood, Godley & Fouilhoux, the liquid in the glass was probably applejack. At any hour, Hood might be writing an article lampooning architectural pretenses, or sharing a joke with one of his colleagues, or sometimes even attacking a particular design problem with a 6B pencil on a pad of drafting paper. Or, if no drafting paper was near to hand, on the back of a menu, a stretch of table linen, a scrap of stationery or, at home in Stamford, Connecticut, on the pillars that framed his handsome waterfront house.

Not ten years earlier Hood had been unemployed, in debt, and ready to give up architecture for an office job at a Rhode Island bank. Now, at forty-eight, the designer of the thrilling American Radiator Building was so successful that he and his partners—Frederick A. Godley, who ran the business side of the firm, and J. André Fouilhoux, the French-born engineer who made Hood's designs buildable—might have worried whether they could handle all the new business flooding in. When one of the young associates despaired that there wasn't an inch of space for another drafting table even though the volume of work demanded at least one addition to the staff, Hood was unabashed. "Hire another man anyway," he said. "There is always one guy on the can."

Small of stature, his bristling brush of gray-brown hair a futile gesture toward height, Hood was impish in mien as well as in personality. His eyebrows, twin circumflexes, assumed an attitude that made him usually appear surprised and often delighted. He wore his sleeves rolled up and his professional stature lightly. Wandering around the office, he'd stop by one or another drafting table to talk with the fanatically devoted young men who considered themselves lucky not just to work for him but simply to be able to share his glowing presence. On one such foray he visited the table of Walter Kilham Jr., a recent Harvard product who had been putting in very long hours. Hood asked after his well-being and told Kilham "this working all day and night doesn't pay. You'd better cut it out from now on.'" Hood paused briefly, then added an afterthought. "By the way," he said, "I have a scheme here for a three block development in New York. You don't think you could have something worked out by morning, do you?'"

That was a lot to ask, but Hood's staff had much to give. Kilham didn't solve the problem of Rockefeller Center overnight, but at another point he did manage to produce eight completely different plans in one intense, four-day burst. That was in December 1929, right after Junior broke off talks with the Opera people and decided to go it alone, and Todd determined that Andy Reinhard and Harry Hofmeister were going to need more than just a little help.

Six weeks earlier, when he had put the two young architects nominally in charge of planning for Metropolitan Square, Todd had hedged his bets a bit. He had also retained, as consultants on "architectural style and grouping," Hood, Morris, and Harvey Corbett. Morris was already on his way out the door. The charismatic Corbett served a purpose, but more as a presence than as a designer. Reinhard and Hofmeister were capable, but limited. And Hood? If one were to enumerate Hood's ten outstanding characteristics, they would practically be antonyms for a similar list compiled for Todd.

Yet there was one trait that Todd and Hood could not have shared more fully had they been genetically matched. Decades later, Todd's son Webster was asked why his status-conscious, authoritarian, teetotaling father had hired the thoroughly unaffected and nearly libertine Hood. "Because he had *ideas*," Todd replied.

"I like having a lot of people against me," John R. Todd once said, "because the more there are, the more they get balled up and start talking at cross-purposes, giving me ammunition to use effectively against them." No wonder he ended up hiring eight architects. From their Babel he would distill one voice, the only voice, that Junior would hear. He even specified that among the scores of people who would in time be working on various phases of the project, only he would speak directly to Junior. (Though an exception was eventually made for Francis Christy, who supervised the legal staff, even that waiver required the intervention of Debevoise.)

The legal document commissioning the architectural design for Rockefeller Center was, formally, a contract with three separate firms. Reinhard & Hofmeister, of course, had been there from the beginning and continued to be treated somewhat separately from the others because of its responsibilities for tenant office layout and related work. Raymond Hood, Godley & Fouilhoux was engaged, according to the contract, specifically to guarantee the services of Hood; André Fouilhoux did become an important contributor to the solution of various engineering problems, but Frederick Godley soon retired to a professorship at the Yale School of Architecture. As for Corbett, Harrison & MacMurray, William A. MacMurray never became involved in Rockefeller Center; he was a business-affairs man whose contributions would have been redundant in an office dominated by Todd, Robertson & Todd and its affiliated firm, Todd & Brown. The celebrated Corbett was there for—in ascending order of importance—his reputation, his ideas, and his ability to translate architectural terminology into ripe and impressive statements that could be dangled before the press and potential tenants.

The eighth member of the Associated Architects, as Todd's recruits would become known, was Corbett's talented partner Wallace K. Harrison, a young man who only a few years before had completed the prestigious traveling fellowship he had won at the Ecole des Beaux-Arts. All Harrison's academic and professional effort had culminated in a partnership with the much older Corbett; all his social effort had reached a peak when he wed Ellen Milton, whose brother David was married to Babs Rockefeller, Junior's only daughter.

The names of all eight men appeared on the contract with Metropolitan Square. Hood, one eyebrow probably shooting skyward, noted that the contract devoted twenty-nine pages to the rights of the owner and the obligations of the architects, and one page to the rights of the architects and the obligations of the owner. Yet if any of the eight, especially the five principals (Reinhard, Hofmeister, Hood, Corbett, and Harrison), were reluctant to leap into this unprecedented project they did not reveal it. Hood's young draftsman, Walter Kilham, advised his boss not to take on the job, as "this time he wasn't an architect dealing directly with his client, but was reduced to dealing with his agent"—Todd—and, based on what Kilham knew, "that might not be so easy." The contract was specific: the architects would be "subject at all times . . . to the control, direction and supervision of the Owners and/or Todd, Robertson, Todd Engineering Corporation and Todd & Brown, Inc." That was a long way of saying "John R. Todd."

Still, the only architects who said they disapproved of Todd's manner were those he didn't select. Given the rapidly deteriorating economic circumstances in the winter of 1929–30, every architect in town could use a little work, and it was only going to get worse; by 1934, six out of seven American architects were unemployed. The orgy of building that had marked the twenties was ended by the cold shower of financial catastrophe. In Rem Koolhaas's phrase, "the sound of the riveting machines had died upon the air." It didn't take long for the once skeptical Kilham to note that he was lucky to have a job, no matter what he had heard about Todd.

The architectural firms involved in this one project, compensated at 4 percent of the total cost of construction, might see a payday unlike any they had ever imagined,* conjoined with an opportunity that *Fortune* described as "the redesigning of the very heart of the greatest city in the world." They would have to put up with Todd, and at close quarters, too: the architectural team was to be lodged, rent-free, in the Graybar Building, within

---

*The customary 6 percent fee was reduced because Todd's firm had responsibility for construction supervision.

shouting distance—or insult distance—of Todd's office, where the camellia-filled greenhouse on the adjacent setback could provide him only so much distraction. But all the architects would have Hood running interference in behalf of their designs, and no one did that better, or with clearer purpose, than he. "For the client," Hood once said, building a skyscraper "is a chance to get a return on his money, for the manufacturer a chance to sell his products, for the contractor a chance to make a profit.

"There remains the architect," he concluded, "the building's only friend."

CHAPTER EIGHT

Ray Hood's life, said his friend Thomas E. Tallmadge shortly after the architect's much too early death, "was a joy ride in

Anyone who could eat so much must be a genius.

—PLACIDO MORI, ON RAYMOND HOOD

which everybody got a thrill." He may have been speaking literally: driving through the Connecticut countryside, Hood had the disconcerting habit of speeding up whenever he came to an intersection. "Intersections are where the danger lies," Hood once explained to an unnerved friend, "and you want to get through them as fast as you can."

How like Hood this was—the headlong rush through life; the nose-thumbing at conventional logic; the winking joke at his own expense. It was also like Hood to put himself in harm's way while in an automobile. Not two months before John R. Todd first drew him into the Metropolitan Square project, he suffered a broken arm when his car rudely skidded into a telephone pole. No problem: his "designing arm is going to be better now," he told a friend, because it would have "more bone in it." That made about as much sense as everything else in Hood's career, which followed no known form of logic. And why should it? He was "Little Ray Riding Hood," whose motto was "Never decide today what you're going to do tomorrow" and whose "patron saint in architecture [is] one whose name is Whim."

Hood was born in Rhode Island in 1881, the son of a well-off box manufacturer who like Senior raised his son as a pious Baptist. He started on the path to an architecture career at the Massachusetts Institute of Technology and after graduating went to work for the Boston firm of Cram, Goodhue and Ferguson. Ralph Adams Cram was a devout believer in both the theological tenets of the Episcopal church and the incorruptible glory of Gothic architecture—notions that made him, as architectural historian Alan Balfour

wrote, a "custodian of nineteenth-century values and eleventh-century principles." Cram's partner, Bertram Grosvenor Goodhue, was an atheist who
thought that someday, somewhere, an architectural form would emerge and
forever replace the effete and tedious Gothic. Goodhue and Cram did not
stay partners for very long.

However, they did catapult the young Hood toward Paris, where his first
attempt to enroll at the Ecole des Beaux-Arts was rebuffed because of a perceived deficiency in his ability to draw freehand. He was twenty-three, alone
abroad, and so much a product of his Baptist upbringing that he refused
even to step inside Notre Dame. His abhorrence of Catholicism was as intense as his disapproval of alcohol and rendered irrelevant just as quickly.
For Hood, Paris became a party. After finally gaining admission to the
Beaux-Arts, he came to enjoy a life that might have been modeled on the
scene at the Café Momus in *La Bohème.* Buoyant by nature and intoxicated
by the seductions that surrounded him, he flourished. He developed excellent French, and even his graphic skills improved. The vivid nude studies
Hood drew at the Beaux-Arts shimmered with life, and the architectural
sketches that filled his notebooks were somehow both grand and subtle—
they had a sweeping quality to them, but the way he was able to use a few
lines of a single detail to suggest *all* the details was evidence of uncommon
skill. At the Beaux-Arts he was that most admired of students, "a second-
place man." First place in academic competitions belonged to the highly capable and absolutely conventional; the truly brilliant, whose innovative
work made the masters at the Ecole uneasy, learned to be content with second. Unless, that is, they wished to prove the premise of Charles-Edouard
Jeanneret, the bomb-throwing Swiss architectural theorist who called himself Le Corbusier: "The instruction of the Ecole des Beaux-Arts," he wrote,
"allows the intelligent students to escape."

As capable as he was, Hood wouldn't really escape from the ranks of the
Beaux-Arts for more than a decade. Paris may have radically transformed
his taste for living, but his architectural ideas remained conventional, even
if brilliantly expressed. Concepts that may have been considered radical on
the Rue Bonaparte were so tame that when Hood returned to the States in
1906, Goodhue, his mentor, fired him, disappointed that he had inhaled so
much of the Beaux-Arts aroma. In a series of disconsolate letters that autumn to a friend in Paris, Hood confessed his financial difficulties and his
professional disappointments, and revealed as well a distaste for the burgeoning Skyscraper New York. "Downtown, where you pass the day," he

wrote, "is a place in which the sun never penetrates except by reflection. . . . The whole existence here is a sort of coffee existence—you live on your nerves, which are . . . pulled together by black coffee at every meal. You may have gathered from this hemorrhage that I do not like New York." His only solace, he reported, was gathering occasionally with friends "in some dirty but eminently Italian joint . . . to drink Chianti wine."

New York didn't take. Soon Hood was back in Paris, where he ended up devoting nearly six years to studying architecture, traveling through western Europe, and worshipping the fruit of the vine. His *diplôme* project for the Beaux-Arts was a City Hall for his hometown of Pawtucket. A broad stair-case led to a monumental arched entrance, and on either side a framing pair of columned and pedimented Greek temples seemed to complete the com-position. But rising above the archway, reaching for something that Hood himself probably couldn't yet explain, was a tower. The tower was extrava-gantly ornamented at its top, but on the way up, climbing like the future it-self from the temples below, sleek and straight and virtually unadorned, it looked like the very definition of verticality.

Hood returned from Europe to stay in 1911—not to New York, but to Pittsburgh, where he found a position as a designer in the office of Henry Hornbostel. For three years he worked steadily and successfully for "Horny," as Hood inevitably called him. But as Hornbostel's son remembered years later, Hood wanted to be "the greatest architect in New York," and in 1914 he came back to the city that had defeated him eight years earlier.

This time it was even worse. Hooking up with the protobohemian crowd beginning to gather in Greenwich Village, Hood now loved the city, but the affection wasn't returned in paying work. The office he opened up-town with his friend Rayne Adams in a West 42nd Street brownstone might as well have been in Pittsburgh, or even Pawtucket. The two men were so undisturbed by callers that they eventually hung a sign on the door that read "Adams & Hood, Fumeurs." Hood was not entirely without clients, but those who somehow found their way up the stairs to his two-room suite—one for an office, one for living in—didn't want much from him. His most reliable patron may have been Mrs. Whitelaw Reid, widow of the newspaper publisher who had been Theodore Roosevelt's ambassador to Great Britain. Their relationship began when she asked Hood to redo a bathroom at Ophir Farm, her Westchester County estate. After he gave Mrs. Reid a fine bathroom, she set him to work on a series of comparable tasks—changing the doorknobs, fixing the roof, presiding over the transfer of eight crumbling Reids from one family mausoleum to another. Hood's other outstanding client was someone who didn't pay him at all. Placido Mori, who owned a restaurant on Bleecker Street in the Village, kept Hood in food and drink in exchange for his doing some work on the building, and Hood ate and drank quite a lot. Mori believed in Hood, he said, because "anyone who could eat so much must be a genius."

By the time he turned forty, in 1921, this graduate of MIT and the Ecole des Beaux-Arts, acknowledged by many of his contemporaries as the most talented architect of his generation, was making his living designing radiator covers. It may have been demeaning but at least it was steady, and it brought him $500 a month. This enabled Hood and his wife, Elsie (who was also his secretary), to move into an apartment of their own in a house on Washington Square. But on the day their first child was born, in 1921, Hood was fired from the radiator job. He was $10,000 in debt and had already replaced every discolored brick and repaired every cracked walkway on Mrs. Reid's estate. He diddled away some time contributing "A Vocabulary of Atelier French" to an architecture magazine (including not just the words for "gargoyle," "charcoal," "loft," and other terms of the trade, but also translations for "cheap restaurant," "working girl," and "sumptuous repast"). And then he got lucky—so unexpectedly, blessedly, and surpassingly lucky that upon learning his money worries were over, Hood sat stock-still for two hours, too stunned to move, too stunned even to speak.

In 1931, writing about some of his plans for what was by then known as Radio City, Hood described what had become the single greatest challenge and inspiration to skyscraper architects: from the accelerating technologies that enabled buildings to rise higher and higher (and, he could have added, from the promulgation of the 1916 zoning law) had come the need for design skills that went beyond the articulation of a facade. Previously, the "designed" part of a large urban building was little more than a false front glued onto the street-facing wall, while the hidden rear and the adjacent sides, flush against neighboring buildings, were, in Hood's phrase, "left raw." But now, Hood continued, "the builder, having four visible faces to deal with, realized the need of the architect. And the architect grasped his opportunity."

Hood's path to this insight, and to the Rockefeller Center job that would be its apotheosis, began nine years earlier, when Robert Rutherford McCormick and Joseph Medill Patterson, first cousins whose family controlled the *Chicago Tribune,* realized they needed to put on a promotional event to upstage their chief rival in the Chicago newspaper wars, William Randolph Hearst. At the same time, they wished to build a new headquarters building on a lot they owned on Michigan Avenue just north of the Chicago River, and it couldn't hurt if the neighborhood's real estate values were fertilized in the process. On June 10, 1922, McCormick and Patterson gave over a column on their front page to the announcement of an international competition for the design of their new building. Though critics would question their intentions and, when the contest was over, lampoon—and in some cases vilify—the choice of a winner, in the annals of newspaper promotional contests this was a relatively noble effort.

In fact, hedging their bets against the unpredictable nature of open competitions, Patterson and McCormick commissioned ten leading American architects to submit designs, offering each of them a two-thousand-dollar retainer plus an obvious edge in the race against volunteer contestants for the unprecedented hundred thousand dollars in prize money, half of it for the winner. Ray Hood had neither a shot at being invited nor the resources to invest in a speculative entry. Among those who did make the short list (including Bertram Goodhue and Benjamin Morris) was John Mead Howells, son of the celebrated author and editor William Dean Howells. A New York architect whose best-known (if highly derivative) work adorned college campuses in the northeast, Howells happened to have married into a family that was among the *Tribune's* ownership group. But Howells was either too busy or too keenly aware of his own professional shortcomings to take on a project like this one by himself. One story has him running into the impecunious Hood in Grand Central Terminal and, after an exchange of niceties, deigning to invite him to collaborate, almost as an afterthought. A more credible one, without the violins sighing in the background, suggests that Howells wanted to enter the competition, knew he needed a talented man to head up the effort while his office pursued more certain commissions, and considered himself lucky that Hood was available.

With less than six months to complete a design, both men set to work immediately. Hood ran the operation, with Howells consulting and several others, including the young Wallace Harrison, pitching in at the drafting table. Howells's one surviving drawing shows a building that bears only the faintest familial relationship to the finished design; once in Hood's hand, its form evolves quickly from the Howells version to the final product—a tall, graceful, carefully articulated and somewhat rounded shaft gradually dissolving into a tower, complete with flying buttresses at the top, that might have adorned a Gothic cathedral. The buttresses, which truly fly but buttress nothing at all, were pure decoration, and Hood knew that decoration wasn't likely to offend a jury consisting of five midwestern newspaper executives plus one lone architect dependent on the newspapermen for his paycheck.

Not that Hood had by this point reached much beyond a faintly modernized Gothic style in his architectural thinking. What he was good at, and what the completed design showed, was what his friend Ely Jacques Kahn would call "clarity and logic in plan and mass." In their submission (by "John Mead Howells in association with Raymond Hood") the two architects, pointedly noting the difference between their design and recent buildings erected in Chicago and New York, said, "It is not a tower or top, placed on a building—it is all one building. . . . It climbs into the air naturally."

Standing magisterially alone, its "four visible faces" the intoxicant that brought out his best, the thirty-six-story building Hood created was not remotely revolutionary. But it was a winner, and as much as the vestigial buttresses provoked criticism verging on ridicule (even one of the building's most prominent fans called them "illogical"), they added an undeniable charm to the tower. Writing nearly eighty years later, architecture critic Blair Kamin said they "put the sky within the skyscraper."

There is no record of Howells's reaction when he received the telegram from Robert McCormick revealing the jury's decision and requesting both architects' attendance at the announcement of the winners two days later. Hood, emerging from the stupefaction that immobilized him following receipt of the news, turned to the abidingly tolerant Placido Mori for one last loan, to cover the fare to Chicago for the ceremony and the clothing he would wear to it. And then he embarked on a twenty-four-hour toot one admirer would memorialize as "his finest spree."

Hood's wife, no less gratified by this reversal of fortune, waited until Hood's prize money arrived before beginning her own celebration. Check in hand, Elsie Hood got in a cab and instructed the driver to take her to the offices and stores of everyone to whom the Hoods owed money. She didn't take the time to cash the check first: she was happy simply to be able to show it to each one of them, to prove that there was at last a reward for their patience—and for hers as well.

Howells kept $40,000 of the first-prize money for himself and gave Hood the remaining $10,000. Hood didn't object; Howells had been the one invited to enter, and he had provided the office resources that enabled Hood to complete his work. Howells also insisted that Hood receive fair credit, and less than three weeks after the prize was announced he wrote to the *Tribune*—for publication—to insist that mention of his own name alone in connection with the design "must absolutely be stopped. . . . I must say to you personally that I regard the credit to be really due as much or more to Mr. Hood as to myself." In the months after Hood lost his radiator-design job, he had been earning at a rate of $3,000 a year. Ten thousand dollars for six months' work was just fine.

But even that sum—nearly $110,000 in 2003 dollars—was nothing compared to what soon followed. First, there was one grand reward: Hood would share in the 7 percent architects' commission on the total cost of the building (the $50,000 in prize money was applied against it, but still . . .). There were also some tasty smaller benefits, such as the McCormick-financed grand tour of European architectural sites Hood took with Howells so they could bone up on the proper sort of detailing for the Tribune Tower's decorative elements.* The greatest reward, however, was incalculable, enduring, and life-changing: publicity.

As Katherine Solomonson wrote in her excellent history of the competition, "the *Tribune* [had] cast itself as the hero of its own narrative," and when you call yourself "the World's Greatest Newspaper," as the *Tribune* did on its front page every day, you do whatever you can to prove it to the world. Consequently, the *Tribune* took its act on the road, in the first half of 1923 sponsoring museum exhibitions of the winning entry and the more interesting losers in twenty-seven North American cities. At one architecture school, "students 'literally camped in the Exhibition room.'" Museum directors unable to adapt to the *Tribune* schedule were devastated. A nearly complete collection of the entries—*The International Competition for a New Administration Building for the Chicago Tribune*—was in bookstores by the following summer. Only months before, Ray Hood was an unemployed radiator-cover designer. Now he was one of the most famous architects in America.

By all accounts the Hood who emerged from the Tribune Tower competition and the ballyhoo rattling along behind it was in most respects the same Ray Hood as before—garrulous, playful, in the words of his friend Ralph

---

*This trip inspired the decision to portray themselves symbolically in a carved stone screen for the building's lobby. Howells appears in the form of a howling dog, Hood as Robin Hood, and Hood's engineering associate, the French-born J. André Fouilhoux, as a frog.

Walker "a flea [who] bit, jumped and left no wound." He just wasn't the same architect. The agent of Hood's transformation was the entry granted second place by the Tribune jury, a late-arriving submission from the Finnish architect Eliel Saarinen. No Gothic fantasies were inscribed on the surfaces of this powerful structure; at its top, the building not only had no ornamental tower, it didn't even have a decorative cornice. Unlike the uninterrupted shaft of the Hood-Howells design, Saarinen's culminated in a series of subtle setbacks that lightened the mass of the upper floors while simultaneously enhancing the feeling of height. Reporting on its arrival, the *Tribune* said Saarinen's entry "smote [the jury] with its message of silent majesty." It was not so powerful a blow that it changed the jury's decision—they had clearly already settled on a winner—but its reverberations were potent. Louis Sullivan, the Moses of Chicago architecture, called the Saarinen entry "a priceless pearl" that had been rejected in favor of a design that had come from "a mind unaccustomed to distinguish between architecture and scene painting."

Sullivan was not alone; architects and architectural critics hailed the Saarinen design at the time it was unveiled, and in the decades following celebrated it as the first expression of a truly modern solution to the design problems posed by the skyscraper. Almost from the time the Saarinen entry was published, the best architects stopped trying to stand Beaux-Arts ideas on end and make them stretch skyward. No longer were they reaching back to medieval times to retrieve the cathedral towers that had been their only vertical reference points. By the late 1920s devotees of Deco would use broad, smooth surfaces derived from Saarinen on which to etch their triangles and chevrons and lightning bolts.

No one, however, embraced Saarinen's ideas as eagerly—and as agreeably—as Hood, who even told Ralph Walker that he believed Saarinen deserved the victory. And it wasn't just Saarinen's lessons that he lapped up; it was as if Hood picked up the book of competition entries and ravenously consumed the best ideas in its pages, particularly the daring modern ventures by the German entrants Max Taut, Walter Gropius, and Adolf Meyer. He did it gracefully, too, always ready to credit others and to diminish his own work (he put flying buttresses on the Tribune Tower, he said later, because "embroidery was in vogue" when he designed them). Saarinen, wrote Norval White, "gathered such praise and admiration that he moved to America to enjoy it," but it was Hood who successfully championed the best ideas from the Tribune competition, and with them forged the newborn art of modern skyscraper design.

Pausing only to pay back Placido Mori by completely remodeling his loyal patron's restaurant on Bleecker Street, Hood capitalized on his new eminence. Right after his Chicago triumph, the American Radiator and Standard Sanitary Company determined that the radiator-cover designer they had dismissed a few years earlier was just the man to design their new headquarters building. Like a telescope standing on end with its eyepiece in the air, Hood's Radiator Building would rise in the same novel pattern of shrinking setbacks that Saarinen had deployed in his Tribune entry. The gold-painted terra-cotta decorative elements at the top were Hood's lagniappe; the black brick in which the building was cloaked was Hood's first, strong stride toward modernity as well as a conscious effort to obviate "the unpleasant effect" of a light-hued surface "with black holes punched in it for windows." (A crude contemporary judgment likened the effect of gilded terra-cotta and jet-black brick to "a negro prizefighter who had an eminent supply of gold fillings.") The setbacks gave the tower four full faces, and when floodlit it articulated an even bolder advertisement for itself than the Tribune Tower did. As critic Paul Goldberger has written, the Radiator Building was nothing less than "the first- and second-prize winners of the Tribune competition joined in a single building."

Hood was now launched for good, and his office in the Radiator Building vibrated with his rocketing success. He made a constantly shifting (yet always congenial) series of partnerships with collaborators, gave the young men on his staff free rein to proceed however they wished on the projects they were responsible for, and on Friday afternoons he'd confidently leave it all behind for a visit to the "Four-Hour Lunch Club," the all-talking, all-drinking weekly revel he shared with architect buddies like Ely Jacques Kahn, Ralph Walker, and Joseph Urban. Dream buildings scribbled in soft pencil competed for space with gin stains on the tablecloths at Mori's or their other hangouts. Weekends in Connecticut were an extension of Hood's never-ending joyride, his frequent social gatherings spiked with his favorite pranks (he was inordinately fond of firecrackers), his favorite cocktail (an explosive combination of applejack, lemon juice, and absinthe), and more architecture talk, architecture argument, architecture scribbling. "My tablecloths are all covered with pencil marks," a despairing Elsie Hood told the *New York Times.* "It is impossible to keep a laundress."

The Stamford house, which Hood had designed himself and moved his family into in 1925, seemed at odds with his growing reputation as a modernist: a large and handsome structure of fieldstone and stucco in a vaguely French style, with a broad lawn, a tennis court (he was an excellent player), and a dock for the cabin cruiser he would eventually acquire, it could have belonged to any wealthy New York executive who wanted to rusticate within commuting distance. Hood was less interested in making statements than in making what he called "honest" architecture—architecture well adapted to its use. As Hood saw it, "Utility produced beauty."

That was about as far as he would allow himself to go as a theorist. He did embrace Le Corbusier's *Toward a New Architecture,* and at times he would publish a piece offering provocative, futurist ideas: a Manhattan connected to the mainland by a series of bridges that had apartment buildings suspended from the cables, or a "City Under a Single Roof," with offices, factories, shops, and residences gathered in one enormous building. But Hood never festooned his work with ideology. "The Tribune and Radiator buildings are both in the 'vertical' style . . . simply because I happened to make them so," he said. "If at the time of designing them I had been under the spell of Italian campaniles or Chinese pagodas, I suppose the resulting compositions would have been 'horizontal.'" While Harvey Corbett sang the anthems of skyscraper theology and Hugh Ferriss provided visual accompaniment in his powerful essays in charcoal, Hood advanced the art in brick and steel and stone.

The Tribune Tower made Hood's reputation, but it was a radically different building that led Todd to bring him onto the Rockefeller Center team. As different as this new landmark would prove to be, its nominal purpose couldn't have been more similar—a newspaper headquarters—and the client couldn't have been closer to the owners of the *Tribune.* Not long after the Tribune Tower was completed, one of the men who commissioned it moved out. Joseph M. Patterson and Robert R. McCormick had little in common but a pair of grandparents, a lot of money, and an itch for newspapering. McCormick was a polo-playing archconservative of aristocratic mien; though equally wealthy, Patterson, his cousin, was an ex-socialist (he had even managed Eugene V. Debs's presidential campaign in 1908) who prided himself on his empathy for the common man. It wasn't exactly a natural partnership, and in 1925 Patterson left for New York to devote himself full-time to the tabloid *Daily News,* which in the six years since its founding had become the largest-circulation daily in the United States—a success so immediate and so huge that it proved Patterson's assertions about his understanding of the tastes of people who had none of his breeding, his education, or his mountains of cash.

No architect ever had a better patron. When Hood defined his favorite clients as "sane enthusiasts, interested in the building as a problem to be solved seriously as much as in the building itself" he was undoubtedly thinking of Patterson. Before embarking on the *Daily News* project, Hood created a nine-story apartment building for the publisher at 3 East 84th Street just off Fifth Avenue; a few years later he designed a country house for Patterson in the Westchester County town of Ossining. From Hood's perspective the problems posed by the 84th Street project would immediately have been apparent: it had to fit in among the mansions that lined the block, and it had to do so without sinking back into the Beaux-Arts past from which Hood was still struggling to free himself. For the country house, Patterson elucidated the problem himself. "Make it look as if I didn't have any money," he said.

The country house was too large to satisfy the publisher's implausible request, but Hood's solution, a series of unadorned cubes painted in camouflage, couldn't have made a louder declaration of his break from the architectural past had he built it of Bakelite. For the city apartment building Hood's strategy sounds simple: he accommodated the other structures on the block by using classical limestone for the vertical elements; and he acknowledged the present by making the spandrels—the portions of the exterior walls that separate one floor's windows from those immediately above and below—out of metal, imprinted with a Deco design. Seventy-five years after he designed it, 3 East 84th still looks both fitting and fresh. It also looks familiar: the limestone piers and the metal spandrels are a miniaturized trial run for the buildings of Rockefeller Center.

Patterson wasn't Hood's only client in the late 1920s; he was just the most bountiful one, the "sane enthusiast" whose idiosyncratic provocations led to Hood's most innovative work. In the time between the Radiator Building and the Daily News Building, Hood designed the New York studios of the National Broadcasting Company; offices for the Metropolitan Museum's Division of Contemporary Art; the Masonic Temple in Scranton, Pennsylvania; another American Radiator office building, this time in London. He was well paid, and his clients were by all indications pleased with what he did. One, a speakeasy owner who got Hood to reconfigure his establishment, rewarded his architect by regularly driving out to Stamford to deliver a supply of booze. Joseph Patterson rewarded Hood by financing the skyscraper that enabled him to transform himself from an excellent craftsman into an architectural pioneer.

The publisher didn't want an advertisement in stone like the one that he and his cousin had decreed for the *Tribune;* in New York, he wished only to build a factory. For a man who could be pretty ostentatious in his repudiation of ostentation, Patterson had chosen a conspicuous spot for a factory, East 42nd Street and Second Avenue. But his reasoning was unassailable: in a nine-newspaper town speed of distribution was critical to success, and a location smack in the heart of the city, on two major thoroughfares, was a bull's-eye. Having told Hood he wanted a printing plant and some simple offices, Patterson was stunned when Hood presented him ten weeks later with plans for a thirty-six-story office tower and an adjoining nine-story printing plant hunkering inconspicuously behind it on 41st Street. Hood abjured an aesthetic justification—he never rooted his arguments in theory or what he later called "beauty stuff"—and instead told Patterson how rent collected from office tenants would boost the paper's profits. Unconvinced, Patterson resisted—until he saw a devastated Hood sag like a punctured tire. According to an eyewitness, "After waiting till the effect of his blow was complete, [Patterson] put his arm around Mr. Hood and said, 'Listen, Ray, if you want to build your god damn tower, go ahead and do it.'"

It was characteristic Hood. Clients were so fond of him, and so willing to be charmed, that he almost always got what he wanted—according to another architect, "things which [the client] in his right mind . . . never would have done otherwise." But when he couldn't sway the client he speedily adapted, and from these adaptations came some of his greatest innovations. When Patterson would not spring for limestone cladding and insisted on less expensive brick, Hood surrendered to his own vast talent. Taking a carving knife to the clay model that stood in his office, Hood began "do[ing] a little zoning myself," whittling away at the model until he settled on a scheme he liked: a spike of a tower, unadorned on top and unprecedented in its decoration: broad stripes of color made of red-and-black-brick spandrels (and complementary russet window shades) alternating with stripes of white brick, a declaration of verticality stretching uninterrupted from the building's base to its very top.

What he had created, Hood explained, was a building in which "the first and almost dominant consideration was utility." The tower was pragmatic, as he had argued to Patterson, for it provided the rental income that justified the construction of a printing plant on a swath of prime real estate. He went on to say that he preferred a functional simplicity to buildings in which "plans, exteriors and mass have been made to jump through hoops, turn somersaults, roll over, sit up and beg, all in the attempt to arrive at the goal of architectural composition and beauty." The animal trainers at one of the architectural magazines, groping for an intellectual justification for the building's stripes, maintained that "unrolled newsprint [suggested the] exterior design." But the stripes, insisted one of Hood's cronies, were really inspired by nothing more than "a pair of red and white striped BVD's in a haberdasher's shop on Third Avenue," and Hood's wish to disguise the windows.

For Hood, it was simpler than simple. "If a man asks for a fork," he wrote in 1929, "he isn't offered a spoon. If he wants a work bench, he isn't given an Italian altar piece." Patterson got his factory, and he got it cheaply—according to *The New Yorker,* "a factory at factory price." But the Daily News Building was more than that. Today it may seem unexceptional; where once it stood virtually alone on the East Side skyline, crowds of adjacent skyscrapers have since ganged up on it, jostling it into indistinction. But at the time of its construction the building was so sleek, so spare, so utterly radical that, as the architectural historian William H. Jordy wrote, it was "as though a shining new world had popped from the crust of the old."

In the eyes of his fellow members of the Four-Hour Lunch Club and all the other modernists in town, Hood had created a beacon. To those architects intrigued by the building's silhouette and looking for a theory to explain why he hadn't attached any sculptural ornamentation to its surface, Hood replied, "Why not try nothing?" And to detractors like Royal Cortissoz, the powerful conservative critic for the *Herald Tribune* who proclaimed of the Daily News Building, "That's not architecture," Hood shrugged and said only, "So much the better."

Hood's indifference to—even distaste for—architectural ideology so closely resembled John R. Todd's attitude that, had Todd heard Hood's reply to Cortissoz, he undoubtedly would have inscribed the exchange in one of his notebooks, storing it for the next time he might need to insult an architect. From his Graybar Building office two blocks away, Todd could see the Daily News Building. Even better, from his plugged-in position at the center of the New York development world, he could also see that Hood had in Patterson a strong-willed, well-pleased client; that Patterson hated spending needless money; and that the kind of publicity a building might get from an architect like this one could help rent an awful lot of space, at very appealing prices. To a man who believed that "romance is the greatest thing in the world, outside of bread and butter," the prospect of working with Ray Hood must have seemed delicious.

CHAPTER NINE

In the winter of 1929–30, the magazine editor Eric Hodgins recalled more than a decade later, "the whole economy of the United States clapped a hand over

*Mr. Rockefeller told me that he would rather have **a hundred lawsuits** than pay more than $50,000.*

—RAYMOND FOSDICK

its heart, uttered a piercing scream, and slipped on the largest banana peel since Adam Smith wrote *The Wealth of Nations*." Thirty billion dollars of market value—double the national debt—had evaporated almost overnight. In New York many of the newly unemployed soon became homeless as well. Francis Christy, who had been processing the legal documents that memorialized the lease buyouts in the Upper Estate, suggested to Thomas Debevoise that the empty buildings, not yet scheduled for demolition, be turned into shelters "to relieve the suffering." Debevoise replied in character: "There is no housing shortage for the unemployed at the present," he growled; acting on an idea like Christy's would, he concluded, be "borrowing trouble."

Francis Christy's generous instinct notwithstanding, it was startling how insulated from economic events the Rockefeller office could seem. Although Junior would see his net worth sliced in half during the first four years of the Depression, the pain was relative: late in 1932 he could still count $475 million in assets, and they were so productive that his income tax bill for a typical year could exceed $8 million. (Good lawyering enabled him to keep his New York state personal property tax south of $13,000.) As Eddie Cantor said when Junior and his father announced their patriotic intention to invest in common stocks immediately after the Crash, "Sure—who else had any money left?"

Junior probably had little idea (and Senior would have had absolutely none) how much of the family money would need to be committed to the nascent Metropolitan Square project. The architects had just been signed up, and the first real drawings hadn't yet been made. The lease buyouts were proceeding, but it was still too early to know exactly how much it would cost to clear out those motley tenants. Even the corporate structure of the organization created to do whatever it was that was going to be done here—Metropolitan Square Corporation—was only now taking shape. The contract with John R. Todd and his associates having been concluded, Todd on November 24, 1929, formally took up his role as executive manager of the project and simultaneously resigned from the Met Square board.

That same day the board of directors welcomed his replacement, a twenty-one-year-old Dartmouth College senior whose interest in business may still have been developing but whose sense of self was ripe. "Just to work my way up in a business that another man has built," he wrote to his father around that time, "stepping into the shoes of another, making a few minor changes here and there and then finally, perhaps at the age of sixty, getting to the top where I would have control for a few years . . . isn't my idea of having a real life."

Getting in on the ground floor was. Even at twenty-one, Nelson Aldrich Rockefeller possessed appetites that were virtually his self-definition, a definition drawn not necessarily from the specific objects of those appetites (for art, for people, for power) but rather from their unremitting intensity. His sister Abby (known to her family as "Babs" and to the readers of the *New York Times* as "the wealthiest young woman in America") wasn't interested in much more than having a good time and disregarding her father's wishes. Nelson's older brother John D. Rockefeller 3rd—"Johnny"—had been awarded the honored patronym but was nearly broken by its terrible weight. Nelson, however, was Nelson, and that was plenty.

To the three youngest Rockefeller siblings bouncing around 10 West 54th—in descending order of age Laurance, Winthrop, and David—the disparate personalities of the three oldest must have made a lively show. Babs defied her father by smoking, driving too fast, avoiding church, and kissing off school. When she married the lawyer who represented her in a widely publicized traffic case (the family's Westchester neighbor David M. Milton) she handed the *Times*'s page one headline writers some wonderful material: "ABBY ROCKEFELLER WEDS DAVID MILTON IN HOME CEREMONY / 'Obey' is Omitted at Her Request from Simple Service." According to a family member, Babs both feared her father and hated him. But even had she been as pious, sober, and dutiful as Johnny, Babs would not have had a role in the family business. Like her father's three sisters, she undoubtedly would have been pushed to the sidelines of the persistent Rockefeller patriarchy.

Johnny was the anti-Babs. Shy, diffident, by his youngest brother's description "uncomfortable with himself," he sought to please his father by doing everything he asked but rarely satisfied Junior's chilly standards. He struggled earnestly to navigate the intricacies of each institution or company his father asked him to become involved with, but when he tried to assert himself his recommendations were in most instances ignored. Inevitably, the assertions stopped. From the time he joined the office staff at 26 Broadway in December of 1929 until he went off to the navy in 1942, a friend would recall, Johnny "had not done much of anything. He was just sitting around his family's office." When he had to declare an occupation to get his marriage license in 1932, he wrote "associated with father."

Many years later, Johnny's wife, Blanchette, told a reporter that "He suffered from being outstripped and outrun in adventure and naughtiness." It was an odd pair of nouns, as if his suffering (which is palpable, if not addressed directly, in Johnny's detailed diaries) arose directly from his cautious and obedient nature. In a family that included a young woman as angry and occasionally as reckless as Babs, such a nature might have been considered a virtue. But in a family that also contained a Nelson—actually, "contained" juxtaposed with "Nelson" is oxymoronic—it was a white flag of surrender. Johnny hesitated; Nelson grabbed.

On West 54th Street in late 1929, while Johnny placed a tentative toe into affairs downtown at 26 Broadway (starting salary $2,400 a year) and Nelson revved his engines up in Hanover (despite severe dyslexia, he managed to graduate cum laude), their mother was finding her own path. With two other women, she had decided to create a new museum devoted to the collection, display, and study of modern art. "Art is one of the great resources of my life," Abby had written the year before. "I believe that it not only enriches the spiritual life, but that it makes one more sane and sympathetic, more observant and understanding, regardless of whatever age it springs from, whatever subject it represents."

As a statement of principle, this would seem unimpeachable. In practice, it represented the single greatest point of contention in Junior's and Abby's marriage. Simply put, he hated her taste in art. What the Museum of Modern Art's first director, Alfred Barr, characterized as Junior's "granite indifference" to Abby's passionate enthusiasm wounded her greatly. He extended no direct financial support to the museum; even before its founding he had set a specific limit on the amount of money she could spend on art. (When he informed Abby that he was willing to pick up the bill for no more than $25,000 in purchases each year, Junior chose to do so in a formal, typed letter sent from 26 Broadway to the house on 54th Street, signed "Affectionately, John.") Early in the museum's life, when it was housed in a few rooms in the Heckscher Building at 57th and Fifth, Abby did get up the courage to give her husband a tour, but the result was baleful. "I showed Papa the pictures and the gallery today," she wrote in May of 1929, "and he thinks that they are terrible beyond words, so I am somewhat depressed tonight." The correspondent to whom she had chosen to unburden herself was twenty-year-old Nelson.

He was the obvious choice. Of all Abby's children, the one she and Junior had named after Abby's father was the one who most nearly reflected her exuberant personality and most thoroughly shared her aesthetic enthusiasms. Nelson's biographer, Cary Reich, speculated that he might have pursued the visual arts because of the reading problems caused by his dyslexia. Although this may have helped make his empathetic connection with his mother comfortable, their affinity was grounded in something else—a shared appetite for as much adventure as a Rockefeller dared allow himself to enjoy. Nowhere was this opportunity more readily available to them than in the collecting of modern art and, just as much, of artists. As Abby immersed herself in the invigorating affairs of the fledgling Museum of Modern Art, Nelson accompanied her, before his Dartmouth graduation joining a "Junior Advisory Committee" whose other members, including George Gershwin, Lincoln Kirstein, and Philip Johnson, he soon dominated. Not long after Abby became interested in contemporary Mexican art, Nelson picked up the beat, eagerly reporting back to his mother about "a wonderful trip to Boston" where "we went to visit the exhibition of Modern Mexican painters shown by the Harvard Modern Art Society." Their shared enthusiasm led Abby and Nelson to engage in some highly un-Rockefellerian pursuits that might have offended Junior had his "granite indifference" to his wife's interest in contemporary art not absented him so fully from her activities in this area. Junior probably wouldn't have objected when Abby commissioned the Mexican communist Diego Rivera to paint a portrait of Babs, and he might even have tolerated Abby's purchase (from her $25,000 stipend) of Rivera's sketchbook of May Day in Red Square. It's doubtful, though, that he would have remained passive had he known that his wife had asked Rivera to make her a copy of *Night of the Rich*, a mural he had completed in Mexico City depicting an ancient, shriveled John D. Rockefeller Sr. dining with his fellow plutocrats J. P. Morgan and Henry Ford, their table, festooned with ticker tape, set up in a bank vault.

Nelson? It had been a long time since Junior had been able to control Nelson. Years earlier, Junior had managed to condition his left-handed son to adapt to right-handedness by tying a string around the wrist of the offending hand and yanking hard whenever the boy used it to lift a fork. By now, though, iron chains could not have compelled the adult Nelson to curtail his enthusiasms—including a new and vigorous friendship with Rivera, and an active role in the promotion of the painter's very interesting career.

For all the differences between Junior and Abby, or Junior and Nelson, all three shared one critical trait: an absolute dedication to whatever task lay before them. The roots of this dedication, however, were individual and distinctive. Abby's sense of commitment arose from her passions, from an enthusiast's belief in the value of her efforts. Though it was her friend Lizzie Bliss who gave the Modern Art museum its first important gifts (twenty-one Cézannes, a few Seurats, a handful of Picassos, Matisses, and Modiglianis), it was Abby's commitment that marked the museum's growth into a Museum, through the benefactions of her time, her money, eventually the very land on which the museum was built.

Nelson's dedication arose, it seemed, from birthright, from an absolute sense of entitlement conjoined with a congenital can-do disposition, as if he were half royalty, half Rotarian. If Nelson wanted it, he got it, and he never seemed to doubt that he deserved it. When he married the Philadelphia debutante Mary Todhunter Clark in the summer of 1930, Nelson enjoyed a honeymoon of staggering indulgence, beginning with two weeks at Junior's 107-room house in Seal Harbor, the newlyweds roughing it alone—save for the twenty-four servants. Possibly no other twenty-one-year-old could have embarked on the ensuing nine-month world tour without either a small flush of embarrassment or a little woozy nervousness. Although Cary Reich aptly called the honeymoon trip "a grand state visit by a Rockefeller crown prince to the many outposts of the family's empire," for Nelson it was a stroll in the park. Standard Oil officials lined up meetings and social events with political figures, business leaders, royalty; they even arranged an audience with Mohandas Gandhi, who confided in Nelson and his wife details of recent private meetings with the viceroy. Nelson would later note that Gandhi "showed no interest in me whatever."

Junior's motivations came neither from passion nor entitlement. He was moved first by obligation—here is something I must do—and by the ensuing responsibility to complete what he had begun. This emotional double whammy he absorbed alone. In none of his various projects—Riverside Church, Williamsburg, the Dunbar Apartments, Rockefeller Center—did he have a partner, no one to whom he could assign responsibility for a difficult decision. To Junior the threat inherent in collaboration wasn't the fear of compromise; it was that far more intolerable consequence, the abrogation of final responsibility.

Despite the tiers of assistants, advisors, and attendants who surrounded him, he needed to see himself as one man, alone, bearing a world of responsibilities with stoic endurance. When Herbert Hoover asked Arthur Woods to head a national effort against unemployment, Junior, traveling in Spain, cabled his office, "HE MUST DO WHAT HE THINKS BEST I WILL GET ON." When negotiations with the uncooperative—like Fulton Cutting—eroded his patience, a steely Junior would in effect rise from the table, walk away, and move on to an alternative that may have been less appealing but that did not offend his paramount convictions, namely, obligation and responsibility. And when that opportunity did not exist, when a challenge to his sense of rectitude could not be parried by a principled withdrawal, Junior's determination not to give in caused him to vibrate with something very close to rage.

At times Junior could channel this choler into productive action, as when he led the proxy fight to remove the morally offensive Colonel Stewart from the chairmanship of Standard of Indiana. This was so public and so sustained a campaign that it, probably more than any other single act, changed the meaning of the word "Rockefeller" in the popular mind. Said the *Chicago Tribune*, "No one would have believed that a Rockefeller would be engaged in such a struggle and fighting on the side of a more scrupulous business morality." Newspaper cartoonists around the country portrayed Junior as a hero, a knight, a crusader in behalf of the average man. In New York, the *Times* reported the stirrings of an improbable movement to draft Junior as a fusion candidate for mayor.

When there was no productive outlet for Junior's anger, however, he could simply turn mean, in both of the word's adjectival senses. Nowhere was this clearer than in his needless, misguided, and in the end mutually unsatisfactory battle with the least likely of enemies: Ben Morris.

By the time Junior and Morris first met in the early summer of 1929, the architect had been working on plans for one or another version of Metropolitan Square for more than two years—before, in fact, Metropolitan Square was even an idea. In the beginning he was the opera house's architect, working for Kahn, tending to Cutting, and persevering in his squirrelly partnership with Joseph Urban.

That, of course, changed on May 21, 1928, when Morris's presentation at the Metropolitan Club proved to be the lure in the benign trap set for Junior by Ivy Lee and Charles Heydt. From that moment forward, the one constant had been Morris. The various plans—for the Kahn site on 57th Street, for a freestanding building in the southern block of the Upper Estate, for an opera house fronting an open plaza at the center of a symmetrical three-block development—that emerged from his office in the Architects Building did so with such regularity that it was as if he'd been publishing a periodical. Even after Reinhard & Hofmeister had produced Todd's Labor Day plan of September 1928, and after Kahn and the opera interests had withdrawn from the project, Morris proceeded with adaptations. Retained by Arthur Woods to participate in the Symposium competition, Morris soon took on the assignment of incorporating the few good ideas that the Symposium had produced into yet another master plan for the site.

Had he indeed been publishing a periodical, it might have been called *Labor in Vain*. When John R. Todd signed on, Morris was out. By all accounts he was graceful in defeat. One of his replacements, Wallace Harrison, recalled that Morris was "very much of a gent, who handled himself just about the best of any of us. He refused to get into any kind of a snap." At least not until he learned that, except for the $5,000 he had earned for contributing to the Symposium, he would not be paid for any of the work he had done since Kahn bowed out, nor for the ideas he had developed along the way and that Todd had since incorporated into his own preferred plans. Todd himself said in his October 25, 1929, press conference, that these plans "will not differ radically from those prepared by Mr. Morris." It wasn't a slip of the tongue; a more formal Metropolitan Square announcement released three days later hailed Morris as "the first architect to propose the placing of the Opera House, with the plaza in front of it, in the centre of the three blocks." Also the first architect to suggest a promenade leading from Fifth Avenue, the acquisition of the Sixth Avenue frontage, roof gardens on the setbacks, covered arcades, and a number of other elements soon prominent in Todd's vision.

In December of 1929 Morris sent Arthur Woods a nine-page, single-spaced letter detailing every bit of work he had done on Metropolitan Square since leaving Kahn's payroll and every conversation he had had with Junior ("Mr. Rockefeller," Morris reminded Woods, "felt that a conservative type of architecture should be used"), with his associates (Woods himself had told Morris it was unusual for the client to come to the architect to ask "what buildings to build"), and with his agents (William A. White & Sons had found Morris's ideas to be "sound financially and of great architectural interest"). The only disingenuous note in the document came near the end: "Should Mr. Rockefeller feel that my authorship of the idea of the Square . . . and the surrounding development on which lease has been made, has any value to him not yet compensated for, I should be very happy—it is of course understood that no financial claim whatever is made by me in this respect." Nevertheless, this elaborate curtsy was attached to a bill for $234,156.29, a sum based not on his "authorship of the idea" but on a highly technical analysis of conventional architectural fees relative to the construction cost of three of the planned buildings. Even so, Morris added, he thought $175,000 would be more than fair.

Though it was Todd who had elbowed Morris off the stage, it was an inflamed Junior who refused to pay up. Negotiations that began politely deteriorated when Woods offered $5,000 in full settlement. A bruised Morris, convinced he could persuade Junior if only they could talk face to face, found himself straight-armed by Junior's secretary, Robert Gumbel. Lawyers were rolled out onto the battlefield, and the two sides dug in. In August of 1930 Junior finally said he was willing to settle with Morris for $50,000, but that he would "rather have a hundred lawsuits than pay" a penny more.

In a reconstruction of the Morris–Metropolitan Square relationship prepared for Junior, Heydt included a letter from Morris dating from the previous summer that became the fulcrum of Junior's position. Asked by Junior to propose terms for an architect-client relationship, Morris had written, "I suggest no charge for the actual authorship of the idea of the Square . . . which was exclusively mine and was developed at my expense . . . for Mr. Cutting's dinner at the Metropolitan Club in May 1928." Yet Heydt failed to tell Junior that the rest of Morris's terms—the usual architect's percentages— would have earned Morris millions of dollars in fees had he been selected as supervising architect, the job on which Junior had asked him to put a price.

But that was an extenuating circumstance, and in Junior's world circumstances did not extenuate. It was his greatest failing as a businessman, as a philanthropist, even as a father. In Junior's view, consistency was an essential component of honor; hidden from his view but embedded within his psyche was an unimaginative man's need to cling to consistency as if to a life raft. As generally compliant as they were, Junior's associates outdid themselves in yesmanship when Junior found himself in a contest like the one with Morris. Gumbel, Heydt, Woods, and the lawyer Raymond Fosdick formed a chorus chanting Junior's justifications—not just to Morris, but to Junior as well. Harry Hall, of William A. White & Son, played the bass note: Hall thought Junior should pay Morris no more than $2,250, for "the few sketches . . . he presented in July and August."

Eventually Morris settled for Junior's final $50,000 offer. Many of his ideas would become critical to the success of Rockefeller Center, and not long after actual construction got under way Raymond Hood publicly acknowledged Morris's "earliest" plan and noted how its "similarity to the present scheme is remarkable." But Todd, whose hiring had made Morris's dismissal inevitable, tried to cleanse himself of any responsibility for Morris's forced exile by pretending it had never happened. Having told a reporter in 1936 that "Morris put away his plans and declined [my] offer that he come in and be one of the consulting architects," Todd later sealed his version of events tightly. "Ben Morris declined to serve with us," he wrote in his autobiography, and "stayed loyal to the Opera, his original client, as he should have done."

Morris was not quite sixty when he was fired from Metropolitan Square, and his career was drawing to a close; his largest assignment in his later years was the design of some of the public rooms on the *Queen Mary* for his old client, the Cunard Lines. But in 1935 and 1936 he was still working on plans for a "Proposed Music Center for the City of New York" at Columbus Circle, including a hall for the Metropolitan Opera. And in 1943 the seventy-three-year-old architect signed his name to a drawing he had just prepared. The legend read "Metropolitan Sq. Site, 5th to 6th Ave. 48th to 51st Sts." A year later, Morris was dead.

CHAPTER TEN

In the New York City social-business world of 1930, John D. Rockefeller Jr. stood apart not just because of his wealth. There was also the persistent shyness and social discomfort that had plagued him since his boyhood and an innate formality that he simply could not overcome. "He did not

*This country . . . has developed the habit of saying, "**Let Owen Young do it.**" No business man in America's whole history has shouldered as many appalling, public-spirited responsibilities.*

—FORBES MAGAZINE, 1932

have intimate friendships," his son David recalled. "He found it difficult to let down and just chat." He joined a few clubs, and summers on Mount Desert Island gave him the opportunity for some reasonably relaxed socializing with such neighbors as Edsel Ford and the Philadelphia investment banker Edward T. Stotesbury. His closest friend was probably W. L. Mackenzie King, the Canadian social-reformer-turned-prime-minister who had helped Junior find his way through the agonies of Ludlow. It reveals much about Junior's social comportment to know that, for the full thirty-five years of their friendship, the two men addressed each other only as "Mr. King" and "Mr. Rockefeller."

Still, the behavioral barriers that enclosed Junior did not cut him off entirely from New York's interlocking directorate of the wealthy and the well connected. Some of his closest advisors, notably Winthrop Aldrich, were members of the city's social and business nobility. His wife and his children, even the recessive Johnny, lived outside the isolating infrastructure of 26 Broadway; school, charitable activities, and their own social appetites necessarily engaged them with a widening world of friends and acquaintances. Someone knew someone who knew someone who knew a Rockefeller, and through this tidy relay, real business could be conducted. Take, for instance, the unlikely Julian Street Jr., who was poised at the fulcrum of an elaborate set of social and familial connections that would bring the Radio Corporation of America to Metropolitan Square.

Here's how it worked: the son of a novelist who was as successful in the first quarter of the twentieth century as he has been forgotten ever since, Julian Street was launched out of Princeton in 1925 to a job at the *Herald Tribune.* Soon he married Narcissa Vanderlip, with whom he joined the regular rotation of bright and shining couples smiling out at the readers of New York's society pages. Mrs. Street was the daughter of Frank Vanderlip, a blacksmith's son who had been, in sequence, financial editor of the *Chicago Tribune,* assistant secretary of the treasury, and president of the National City Bank, at the time (and today, as Citibank) the largest bank in the country. Vanderlip's boss was James Stillman, the widely feared chairman of National City known on Wall Street as "the Man in the Iron Mask."* Stillman had two daughters, Isabel and Elsie, who obligingly married the two sons of their father's dear friend and fellow stock market manipulator William Rockefeller. (If you're still following this, you're getting the idea; if you're not following it, you're *really* getting the idea.) This Rockefeller† was brother of Senior, uncle of Junior, and great-uncle of the rebellious and occasionally impudent Babs, who was something less of a problem to her father now that she was married to David Milton, whose sister Ellen was married to Wallace Harrison, who not only knew Julian and Narcissa Street from the party circuit of sparkling young couples but knew as well that Narcissa's uncle Edward Harden, who in 1895 succeeded Frank Vanderlip as financial editor of the *Chicago Tribune* and later married Vanderlip's sister Ruth, was chairman of the Real Estate Committee . . . of the board of directors . . . of the Radio Corporation of America.

The reader can exhale now. In late 1929, Wally Harrison, newly recruited as one of the architects chosen to replace Ben Morris, inhaled, and on what appear to have been instructions from John R. Todd called his good friend Julian, Harden's nephew by marriage, and arranged a lunch date. The handoff of the idea—that Junior could use a major tenant for the opera house site—went from Todd to Harrison to the Streets to Uncle Edward in no time

---

*Stillman's forbidding reputation was underscored by his penchant for elaborate and inexplicable code names—Senator Nelson Aldrich, for instance, was "Zivil"; E. H. Harriman was "Zoosperm."

†Stillman referred to him as "Tumacar."

at all. Just after Christmas, Junior wrote Todd to say that his friend Edward Harden had called to raise the possibility of RCA "making this new site the centre for their entire broadcasting and radio operations and offices." This was a lead, Junior added with genuine enthusiasm, that "seemed to me to be well worth looking into." Once again he had been led to the precise spot his associates had wished him to reach.

A few weeks later Harden wrote to Junior from Los Angeles that he was ready to return on a moment's notice to help consummate the RCA-Rockefeller marriage. Lest the nineteenth-century man to whom he was writing doubt this bold assertion, Harden gave Junior assurance. "As you know," he concluded, "one can fly from Los Angeles to New York in 48 hours." Actually, Junior might *not* have known. In 1930 he had not yet been on a plane. By 1960, when Junior died at eighty-six after a lifetime of nearly annual European trips and equally frequent visits to the American West, he had *still* not been on a plane.

As Julian Street remembered it, when Edward Harden suggested to Owen D. Young that RCA had the opportunity to replace the opera at Metropolitan Square, Young called it "the most marvelous thing he'd ever heard about." The level of confidence suggested by this assessment might have surprised anyone who knew that RCA's stock had lost three-quarters of its value in the previous few months, that its profits were dropping nearly as quickly, and that Young was chairman—creator, in fact—of RCA. He was also chairman of General Electric, out of whose loins RCA had sprung; co-chairman of the recently concluded second international conference on war reparations, for which exertions *Time* had named him Man of the Year; proud owner of Charles Dickens's personal tea caddy; a future honorary officer of the Balzac Society of America; and almost universally acclaimed as American industry's greatest hero. When Ida Tarbell, the muckraker who had indelibly etched the first John D. Rockefeller as a predatory monster, published a book entitled *Owen D. Young: A New Type of Industrial Leader,* one reviewer was impelled to ask, "This man Owen D. Young—hasn't he any weaknesses?"

"No" would have been a plausible answer. Encountered in his cramped and musty office downtown at 120 Broadway or sitting alone in the restaurant downstairs where he ate every day, Young would hardly have seemed, as *Fortune* would call him, the "miracle man of American business." But one miracle that qualified Young for the epithet was, in fact, how much he differed from other businessmen of the age.

At least he looked the part—tall, lean, his hair parted neatly in the middle, his confidence apparent in his stance. Young's passage from a farm in upstate New York to a legal career in Boston to a vice presidency at General Electric was conventional in a Horatio Alger sort of way, but once established at GE he followed a script theretofore unknown in American industry and not terribly common thereafter. He first made his mark with the amicable resolution of a strike at GE's plant in Lynn, Massachusetts, inaugurating a period of labor relations at the company so serene that once he was installed as GE's chairman in 1922, Young actually invited the American Federation of Labor to organize his company's workers.

The AFL declined, ostensibly because of its pettish belief that craft unions were noble and trade unions contemptible. But one could understand how simple disbelief might have motivated the federation's leader, William Green, to stare so suspiciously into the gift horse's mouth that he forgot about GE's workers. This did not deter Young. He did more for the company's labor force than any union could have dreamed, establishing pensions, profit sharing, mortgage loans, and company-paid life insurance as worker benefits. Having consulted with Mackenzie King at the time of the Lynn strike, Young and his enlightened labor attitudes inevitably attracted the attention of Mr. King's friend Mr. Rockefeller. In 1925, Junior asked Young to become a trustee of the General Education Board, the Rockefeller charity formed to foster increased educational opportunities for southern blacks. Young accepted this invitation but declined another: no, he said, he'd rather not address Junior's Bible class.

Young's public activities, culminating in his service at the 1929 reparations conference, led *Forbes* to exclaim, "Instead of saying 'Let George do it,' this country—and even Europe—has developed the habit of saying, 'Let Owen Young do it.' No business man in America's whole history has shouldered as many appalling, public-spirited responsibilities." Wrote *Time,* "He has never refused Herbert Hoover anything except, in 1928, his vote." Young was thoroughly a Democrat—so progressive, wrote Frank Kent in the Baltimore *Sun,* that he "makes Governor Roosevelt . . . look like a reactionary." Had he not resisted calls to enter the race, Young would have been a serious contender for the party's 1932 presidential nomination.

Young's single greatest accomplishment as a businessman—the formation of RCA—was itself rooted in the perceived national interest. At the same time in 1919 that Woodrow Wilson's postwar peace plan was rendered unrecognizable by the nibbling and gnawing of the British and the French at Versailles, Wilson's assistant secretary of the navy, thirty-seven-year-old Franklin D. Roosevelt, asked Young to receive a secret delegation of naval officers in his New York office. President Wilson feared that the new science of wireless communications—radio—would be controlled by the British, and he wanted General Electric, the nation's leading technology company, to find a way to prevent this.

Young's solution even had a ringingly patriotic name: the Radio Corporation of America. By creating a corporation jointly controlled by five separate companies, Young pooled the complex array of patents held by competitors and welded the interests of the many into a common mission. GE's new collaborators were Western Electric, American Telephone and Telegraph, Westinghouse—and the ringer in the group, the United Fruit Company, which had been so reliant on wireless communication between its boats and bases in Central America that it had acquired some interesting patents on a certain kind of loop antenna. For a 4.1 percent piece of the new company, United Fruit was happy to get out of the antenna game and back to the business of shipping bananas and undermining Latin American governments.

Was it logical that an industrial colossus would grow out of a quasi-military imperative? Not nearly. Yet in retrospect it was almost inevitable. As Tom Lewis points out in his history of the radio industry, *Empire of the Air,* radio had barely made an impression on Young until the government came calling. But once the technology was free to develop in the rich soil of a virtual monopoly, fertilized by the encouragement of the federal government, RCA's "lien on science," as *Fortune* called it, yielded exceptional returns. One development led inexorably to another, and each one suggested two more. If you could transmit signals wirelessly, why not words and music? And once you began to transmit music and words, wouldn't it be wise to manufacture the receivers on which people might hear them? And to make the records that the broadcasts would popularize, and manage the careers of the artists who made the records, and make the movies the artists would appear in, and . . .

All this activity was wonderful to behold, but Owen Young thought it would be yet more wonderful if only it had a place to call home.

The delight Junior had expressed to Todd after Edward Harden called to assert RCA's interest in Metropolitan Square soon provoked action. For Junior, though, "action" was a relative thing. Not for him the blatant and sometimes grubby gymnastics of negotiation. On January 13, 1930, he dispatched Raymond Fosdick (later head of the Rockefeller Foundation, and eventually Junior's authorized biographer) "to discuss the radio's educational possibilities" with Young.*

To Young, this was sweet music. He had his share of technological dreams, including an obsessive conviction that people all over the world would eventually be connected by something very close to e-mail. But the near-to-hand aspirations he most cherished arose from radio's potential for social and cultural uplift. Radio, he told an associate, "can no longer be considered apart from opera, from symphony and education." To Fosdick he translated his vision into a single, enticing, and immediate image: Metropolitan Square, Young told Junior's emissary, should include an opera house, a concert hall, a Shakespeare theater—and both broadcast studios and office space for RCA and its affiliated companies.

Junior may have been delighted with Fosdick's report of the meeting but John R. Todd must have been ecstatic: RCA would require nearly one-third of all the space called for in the most recent plan Reinhard and Hofmeister had drawn up, and under these circumstances even he could abide Young's invocation of those dreaded words "opera" and "house." Although Young had just stepped down from the chairmanship of RCA he retained his position at GE, and GE effectively controlled the radio company. If Young's enthusiasm could be made tangible in the form of his signature across the bottom of a lease, the towers of Metropolitan Square might soon replace the weary brownstones and dilapidated storefronts of the Upper Estate. But it wasn't Young's signature that mattered. As soon as negotiations began he turned over responsibility for their conduct to the man he had just made president of RCA, David Sarnoff.

In the upper reaches of New York society in the 1920s, anti-Semitism was as much a behavior as an attitude, an almost ritualized expression of community. "Excluding Jews," wrote Theresa Collins in her biography of Otto Kahn, enabled the existing elites "to secure their own sense of class distinction." And nowhere did the behavior of existing elites establish the tone for an entire community more than in the business world.† You didn't

---

*The medium's other virtues interested him less. Junior was "adamantly opposed" to installing a radio at 10 West 54th, relenting only when he was assured it would be played quietly, and never in the main parlor.

†Except, perhaps, the educational world. Horrified by a surge of Jewish enrollment at Columbia, Nicholas Murray Butler in 1917 had instituted a quota that within four years reduced the school's Jewish population from 40 percent to 22 percent of the student body. His strong support for the expansion of the public City College was based, wrote the scholar Thomas Bender, on his "hope to divert immigrant students there."

have to dislike Jews or think them inferior (although there were plenty who did both); you just had to regard them, and treat them, as the Other.

If any financial titan could be expected to eschew anti-Semitic behavior, it would have to be John D. Rockefeller Jr., immunized by a singular and lofty status that generally put him beyond infection by the attitudes of others. He also could not have avoided the influence of his wife, who deplored the conventions of caste. "I want to make an appeal to your sense of fair play," Abby wrote to her three oldest sons in 1923. ". . . The social ostracism of the Jews . . . causes cruel injustice." She wanted, she said, "to have our family stand firmly for what is *best* and *highest* in life. . . . If you older boys will do it the younger will follow."

Junior was fundamentally free of anti-Semitism, and maintained throughout his life social, professional, and philanthropic bonds with a number of Jews. But even he could lapse into the ugly clichés of bigotry, as when he referred to a real estate operator he felt was trying to shake him down as a "slippery Jew speculator." Some of the men around him went quite a bit further, acting on the prevailing habits of mind in the milieu in which they operated. In 1936 Debevoise urged John D. Rockefeller 3rd—Johnny—not to join a certain corporate board unless "it is to be larger and there is in it a good mixture of prominent men who are not of the Jewish persuasion." Joseph O. Brown, of Todd & Brown, once engineered the demotion of a Rockefeller Center personnel manager ("extremely competent," according to her supervisor) because her "references . . . are all people of the chosen race." Brown also felt "it would be a serious mistake to have [a Jew] in a position" where she "interviews or in any way sorts applications for positions." The woman's chastened supervisor promised he would hire "no more 'strange brothers.'"

So it may not have been out of the ordinary for Winthrop Aldrich to tell Owen Young that the Rockefeller interests "preferred dealing with [Young] rather than RCA's abrasive president," Sarnoff. Nor was it exceptional for some of RCA's own executives and clients to make similar requests of Young—or for Young to rebuff every one of them, as he did Aldrich. As a consequence, the negotiations that would bring Rockefeller Center its largest tenant; that would, astonishingly, soon yank a displeased Junior into the movie business; and that would create a relationship destined to nettle Rockefeller associates for more than four decades—these critical negotiations were placed in the hands of a man who famously, and accurately, said, "I don't get ulcers—I give them."

To suggest that Owen Young and David Sarnoff made an odd couple would be like saying Junior was well-to-do. Young was tall and thin, Sarnoff short and stubby. Young was as American as the hops farm on which he grew up in Van Hornesville, New York, while Sarnoff at the beginning of his career was every bit as exotic as the tiny Russian shtetl where he was born in 1891. Young enjoyed the invigorating distractions of physical labor; Sarnoff thought exercise of any kind a foolish indulgence. Young's wide-ranging interests were exemplified by his fervent bibliophilia, which led him to assemble a 15,000-volume collection that became the foundation of the New York Public Library's celebrated rare book holdings. Sarnoff's only real interest was business, and he was so good at it that Young embraced him virtually as a father would a son. Six years after *Fortune* called Young "the miracle man of American business," the magazine anointed Sarnoff "U.S. industry's No. 1 Boy Wonder."

Back when Miracle Man met Boy Wonder in 1919, the David Sarnoff yet to come—vain, officious, a man whom music historian George Marek would call "a communist's idea of a capitalist"—had not even begun to show himself. The Sarnoff that Young first encountered was a hard-working young man of twenty-eight who spoke with earnest passion about the future of radio. He was just twelve years removed from the immigrant boy who had dropped out of school in the eighth grade to support his fatherless family, and who one year after that found work for $5.50 a week as a junior wireless operator at the American Marconi Wireless Telegraph Company.

Here the legend of David Sarnoff accelerates. Never mind his exaggerated claims about being the first to receive and disseminate news of the sinking of the *Titanic,* for the facts are impressive enough. On a visit to New York, Guglielmo Marconi discovered this bright and industrious young man and helped propel his career. In 1916, working as an assistant traffic manager at American Marconi, Sarnoff sent a staggeringly insightful memorandum to the firm's head in which he asserted that wireless frequencies—at this point still a cacophony of dots and dashes—were capable of carrying music into the American home. This "simple 'Radio Music Box' . . . placed on a table in the parlor or the living room," Sarnoff wrote, could disseminate not only music but baseball scores, educational lectures, "national events." If only 7 percent of the nation's households "thought well of the idea" and were willing to commit $75 to the purchase of the music box, Sarnoff figured, American Marconi could anticipate $75 million in revenue.

It was one thing for Sarnoff to recognize the medium's possibilities, quite another to bring them to fruition. But his business skills—management, negotiation, recognition of talent and the good ideas talent could produce—proved as powerful as his technological insight, sufficient even to overcome the relentless anti-Semitic torment handed out by his competitors within RCA. In 1921 Young brought this harassment to an expeditious end: he named Sarnoff general manager of the entire company, with full authority to hire and fire, and, effectively, to run the company as he saw fit.

Thus began a decade of RCA's expansion, diversification and innovation in an exploding industry, one that wouldn't find a true analog until the advent of the personal computer more than half a century later. RCA remained in the international wireless messaging business—the one Woodrow Wilson had first charged it to enter—but also developed patents enabling it to collect a royalty on 90 percent of the radios sold in the United States (average price by decade's end $135, or more than a month's wage for the average American worker); entered (and soon dominated) the recorded music business; and assembled the first, and for decades preeminent, broadcasting network. RCA, wrote one commentator, "merchandised one miracle [and] had a dozen more up its scientific sleeves." There was not a sector of the fastest-growing business in America that the company did not command.

Yet Sarnoff, who believed absolutely in the transformative power of communications technology, saw RCA as more than a radio company. It was a vision that would circuitously lead to his developing both an interest in Junior's midtown property and a claim on the lead role in the negotiations. Around the same time that Western Electric devised the first mechanism that would bring sound to the movies, RCA was developing its own version, called the Photophone. Western (one of RCA's owners but contractually free to develop new technologies unrelated to wireless communications) struck an exclusive agreement for use of its Vitaphone with Warner Brothers, and the creators of another entrant, the Movietone, hooked up with the Fox studios. Sarnoff, dressed up for the party but not asked to dance, had no guaranteed market for RCA's Photophone.

He solved his problem with characteristic directness: he bought—created, really—a movie company. In partnership with a real estate operator and bootlegger who had insinuated himself into the motion picture business a few years earlier, Sarnoff in 1928 quickly executed a series of purchases and mergers that culminated in the creation of Radio-Keith-Orpheum, or RKO. The partner, Joseph P. Kennedy, stuck around the movie business just long enough to begin his famous affair with Gloria

Swanson and to score a profit of more than $2 million on RKO stock, bailing out before it took a fatal nosedive in 1931. Sarnoff was left with a controlling interest in a film studio that had many assets but was missing a critical one: unlike its more established "Big Five" motion picture competitors, RKO didn't own a major theater in New York, and at the apogee of the first American Age of Publicity, if you didn't own a major theater in New York in which to launch your releases with suitable noise, you were nowhere.

Sarnoff took control of the RCA/Metropolitan Square negotiations in a series of meetings conducted largely at the Lotos Club, on West 57th Street, in the winter and spring of 1930. They proceeded so smoothly that by mid-March, Todd, visions of enormous rent checks dancing in his head, felt confident enough to suggest to Junior that he purchase the land from Columbia outright. Junior, only four months removed from his risky decision to proceed without the opera, declined the opportunity, leaving it to his heirs to spring for $411 million half a century later.

Sarnoff and Todd worked out the lease details alone, without the assistance or impediments provided by brokers or lawyers. The two men got along well, and as long as Todd remained involved in Rockefeller Center he would continue to handle relations with the increasingly stubborn Sarnoff. Despite their radically different backgrounds, they were in some ways very much alike—disciplined, direct, and when not engaged in the self-glorifying mythmaking in which they both indulged, utterly unsentimental. Sarnoff had purged himself of any trace of an accent, and his spoken English, polished to a high gloss through sheer diligence, came forth in shapely paragraphs, free of ums and ahs and the meandering uncertainty that Todd deplored. "Thinking out loud isn't thinking at all," Todd once said. "It is simply a lazy man's way of stating a problem in the presence of others to clear the fog out of his own mind."

Not a wisp of fog clouded David Sarnoff's mind. Midway through the negotiations, on May 13, 1930, the Department of Justice filed suit in federal district court, seeking the break-up of the Radio Trust that controlled RCA—seeking to undo what the federal government had itself created back in 1919. Sarnoff, working with Todd, stuck to the task in front of him, and by the end of May they had a deal. They wrote the basic terms on two sheets of paper, signed them, and agreed not to show the document to their lawyers. For an annual payment of $4.25 million, RCA and its affiliated companies—NBC, RKO, RCA Victor, Photophone—would take control of one million square feet of office and studio space; four broadcasting-equipped theaters; and naming rights to this entire, western part of the development.

Todd cheated on the no-lawyers pledge and had Francis Christy review the handwritten agreement. Troubled by a particular clause, Christy redrafted it. Sarnoff was inclined to accept the rephrasing but objected to one element: the new sentence, he said, contained a split infinitive.

In the middle of June 1930, Junior had a characteristically full plate of projects and concerns. Construction was progressing on Riverside Church, an effort that so engaged him he even got involved in selecting materials for the baseboards. The just-completed merger of the Rockefeller-controlled Equitable Trust Company with the Chase National Bank had made him the largest stockholder in what had just become the world's largest bank, which enabled him to install his brother-in-law Winthrop as president. Early in the month, he had announced that he was giving the sixty-six acres of wooded Manhattan uplands that would become Fort Tryon Park to the city, along with the Cloisters (whose views across the Hudson would remain forever pristine, as Junior had already preserved nearly eleven miles of the opposite shoreline for the Palisades Interstate Park). Just ahead lay Nelson's wedding, scheduled for June 23, a pleasant prospect mitigated only by the bride's parents' apparent intention to serve champagne. It wasn't clear which upset Junior more, the alcohol or the disregard for the law that its presence announced.

Amid all this activity, Junior could open his *Times* on June 14 to read this front-page headline: "ROCKEFELLER PLANS HUGE CULTURE CENTRE; 4 THEATRES IN $350,000,000 5TH AV. PROJECT." Secrecy had been of such concern during the RCA negotiations that all names had been removed from copies of the leases distributed to lawyers and others, and the signed originals were placed in a safe at the Chase. Most of the newspaper's details were right, however, and whoever had fed them to the *Times* was clearly intimate with the project. Still, this number—*three hundred fifty million dollars*—was something new not only to the rest of the *Times*'s readers, but to Junior himself.

No one—not Junior, not even Todd—had any meaningful notion of what the project would cost. Three days later, when the official Todd- and Sarnoff-approved version appeared on the paper's front page, the number had been modulated down to $250,000,000, a milder figure but every bit as arbitrary. The architects had only two weeks earlier completed a new plan accommodating the four new theaters as well as two department stores and four other buildings, the whole development encompassing more than 120 million cubic feet of enclosed, heated, wired, plumbed, and elevator-equipped space. No one—anywhere on earth, at any point in history—had ever tried to build anything like this, much less attempt to put a price tag on it.

The Upper Estate, 1931, looking southeast from the corner of Sixth Avenue and 51st Street. Midtown had already grown up around the three decrepit blocks; buildings in the background, reading left to right, include St. Patrick's Cathedral, Saks Fifth Avenue, the New York Central Building (in the distance, with pyramidal top), and the 38-story Fred F. French Building.

The Metropolitan Opera House that Ben
Morris, below left, never got to build.

Right: Nicholas Murray Butler—university
president, Nobel Prize winner, politician,
antiprohibition crusader, and (said Theodore
Roosevelt) "an aggressive and violent ass."

Otto Kahn, left, said, "Pulling teeth is a delectable diversion as compared to getting [cooperation]" from Fulton Cutting, below, and his colleagues.

Clockwise across spread, from left: Junior—as a young man, with banker Stephen Baker; with his omnipresent ruler in his antique office in the RCA Building; with Abby on a 1931 trip to the Grand Tetons. He said he could never understand why the spirited Abby, below, at 10 West 54th Street, "consented to marry a man like me."

Junior relied on Ivy Lee, above left, to tend his public image; on Abby's brother, banker-lawyer Winthrop Aldrich, above right, for counsel on a variety of business matters; and on his old friend Thomas M. Debevoise, below—the "Prime Minister" of Room 5600—for nearly everything else.

According to *Fortune*, "there is more to say about Nelson than any of his brothers." That was in 1931, just after Junior's second son joined the family office. Nelson would assume complete authority over Rockefeller Center before his thirtieth birthday, succeeding Arthur Woods, below right, as president, and ousting the Center's "co-author," John R. Todd, below left.

The Rockefellers may have wished that William Nelson Cromwell, right, was a character out of someone's imagination, but no one could have dreamed him up.

Below, to the left of the row houses, the Goelet Building. Next to it, in order, 8 West 49th, the house Junior got stuck with; 10 West 49th, the empty dwelling Cromwell maintained as a buffer; 12 West 49th, the house Cromwell occupied until 1948; and the original Time & Life Building, reduced in size by Cromwell's two-decade holdout.

The men who made Rockefeller Center, in a staged publicity photo: seated, left to right, Harvey Wiley Corbett, Raymond M. Hood, John R. Todd, L. Andrew Reinhard, and James M. Todd; behind them, Joseph O. Brown, Webster B. Todd, Henry Hofmeister, and Hugh S. Robertson.

As a student in Paris, Raymond
Hood quickly went from Baptist
to bohemian; two decades later he
moved nearly as suddenly from the
trappings of failure to the house
he built on Southfield Point in
Stamford, Connecticut.

Rough plasticine models, above, made in the Graybar suite evolved into the ill-received and short-lived "hatbox" plan, below. As the models were refined, one designer carved an alternative name into the vertical marquee for the RKO Roxy: "Racketeer Cinema," right.

For a chairman of a major industrial corporation, Owen D. Young of General Electric, above, was progressive, even radical; his protégé, David Sarnoff, "was a Communist's idea of a capitalist."

No one hated Rockefeller Center more than Lewis Mumford, below left; no one boosted it more than Merle Crowell (left, with Mrs. Crowell; they called each other "Toad"). Hartley Burr Alexander, below right, wanted to put Corn Maidens on the buildings' walls.

When the site was cleared, it provided a home for the first Rockefeller Center Christmas tree; when excavation was completed, it yielded enough Manhattan schist—556,000 cubic yards of it—to build roads, support piers, and fill reservoirs throughout the five boroughs.

The caption on the news release read, "What would mean heart-failure to most of us street-bound mortals is just a happy hiatus in the day's job to these two workmen." The photographers charged with documenting such press-friendly stunts, like Thomas Kelley, had to have fairly strong hearts as well.

Topping off the RCA Building, April 26, 1932—a rare triumph in Depression New York.

CHAPTER ELEVEN

Let Wallace Harrison, who was there at the beginning and stayed with it the longest, have the first crack at describing the unlikely collaboration John R. Todd set in place on the twenty-fifth and twenty-sixth floors

*People are always asking **who designed Rockefeller Center.** Each of us answers, "I did."*

—WALLACE HARRISON, 1937

of the Graybar Building in 1930: "The architects cooperated on Rockefeller Center not because they wanted to," Harrison recalled, "but because they were paid by Mr. Rockefeller."

They all knew each other at least a little. The world of New York architecture was small and it was a rare architect who didn't find himself collaborating with or employing others during the boom years of the mid-twenties. Harrison and Andrew Reinhard had both worked on Ray Hood projects. Hood and Harvey Corbett had been two of the stars of the floating debating society that dominated the stages of architecture conferences—Corbett the theorist, Hood his practical foil—and commandeered the pages of the architectural press. All five of Todd's architects had been baptized in the tenets of the Beaux-Arts: Hood, Corbett, and Harrison were graduates of the Ecole itself; Reinhard had studied at its New York avatar, the Beaux-Arts Society of Design; even Reinhard's partner Henry Hofmeister, who would be far more engaged by engineering problems and administrative details than design challenges, had spent the first seventeen years of his career at that bastion of Beaux-Arts theology Warren & Wetmore, the firm that put the enormous Doric columns and the effulgent sculpture of Mercury rampant on the facade of Grand Central Terminal.

But if the architects' common genealogy suggested that Todd intended to garnish Junior's buildings with pendulous garlands, posed nymphs, and Grecian friezes, he had executed a characteristically adept act of misdirection. Each of the architects he selected, unlike the discarded Ben Morris, had already to a large extent separated himself from the church of the Beaux-Arts. To various degrees they had even moved beyond the lightning bolts and zigzags of Art Deco, and Harrison could have embraced the three-word credo of the German modernist architect Adolf Loos, "Ornament is crime." Hood's last job before signing on at Metropolitan Square was the shining McGraw-Hill Building on West 42nd Street, a muscular slab decked out in steel and blue-green terra-cotta.

Todd had no architectural ideology. His philosophy had been expressed in its entirety in the statement he made to his architects the day Junior had decided to proceed without the Metropolitan Opera: "From now on," Todd told them in a memorandum on December 6, 1929, "this square will be based on [a] commercial center as beautiful as possible and consistent with the maximum income that could be developed." He had specified the fundamental form of that center at the November 1, 1929, Metropolitan Square board meeting held just after he had dispatched Ben Morris: retail along the Fifth Avenue frontage, department stores midway to Sixth, office buildings flanking the opera house at the western end, and new streets cut through the center of the plot on a north-south axis. When negotiations with RCA began, he ordered Reinhard and Hofmeister to replace the opera house with an indeterminate "major building." From that point forward, the offices in the Graybar Building began to take on the atmosphere of what architect Harold Buttrick called a "six-year charrette," invoking the term architects use to describe the last, frantic period before a project is completed.

It was a process Todd orchestrated through a carefully articulated series of procedures and mechanisms, not least among them his own physical presence just down the hall from the architects' space. Here in his own building—where an elevator always waited in the lobby whenever Todd was out, and always waited on the twenty-sixth floor when he was in—he had already provided space to Metropolitan Square's financial staff and a satellite office for Murray, Aldrich & Webb, permanent outside counsel to the project. John R.'s son Webster shared a two-man desk with his partner Joseph O. Brown. With the opening of the architects' offices, the Metropolitan Square colony inside the Graybar Building became an occupying army. In 1937, when Henry Luce hired the real estate firm Webb & Knapp to find new premises for his burgeoning Time Inc. publishing empire—a mission that would lead the company to settle in Rockefeller Center—the Graybar was one of the buildings under consideration. The Webb & Knapp consultants who dismissed it because "it has almost a factory like atmo-

sphere" must have visited when the Associated Architects were still en-
camped on the premises.

On the twenty-fifth floor, one enormous drafting room contained forty-
two identical drawing boards, each the size of a six-seat dining room table;
another room harbored twelve more, and an additional fourteen stood just
outside the principals' offices at the top of the circular iron staircase connecting 25 to 26. From the tiered steps just inside the entrance to the main
room, the tables ran two by two for 130 feet to a distant wall, a T-square on
the center of each one, an ashtray fixed to every upper right-hand corner.
Lamps suspended from the ceiling on long chains brought light, if not exactly joy, to the premises.

Walter Kilham, who had known something very different in Raymond
Hood's office in the Radiator Building, was struck by the "order and the efficiency," how everything was "run by the clock." Harrison called it "gang
planning." Groups of designers were divided into teams, each captained by
someone who attended the weekly meetings that enabled the left brain of
engineering and finance to keep track of what the right brain of design was
up to, and vice versa. A Dictograph system, forerunner of the office intercom, connected all the offices to each other and to a master switchboard
that was in turn hardwired to the blueprint companies and other suppliers
upon whom the office was dependent. The filing system for three different
classes of drawings (originals, blueprints, shop drawings) was so finely
tuned that one clerk was stationed permanently at a master file that was an
index to all the other files.

As part of an extraordinary, ten-part series of articles published in *Architectural Forum* because of the readership's "unusual interest" in the project, both Harrison and Reinhard wrote pieces elucidating a work flow as
complex as a labyrinth yet as efficient as a waterfall. On any given day as
many as a hundred draftsmen and designers signed in at exactly 8:30 in the
morning and, save for a lunch break, stayed at their tables until precisely
5:30 in the evening. Anything beyond that required formal approval by a
management representative, usually the parsimonious Joe Brown, who was
as careful with words as he was with nickels: "You are hereby authorized to
work overtime on Saturday, November 28th, to check the structural steel
drawings of the basement and first floor [RCA], submitted by Mr. H. G.
Balcom. This is in addition to our contract with you for Architectural Services dated July 1st, 1930." That contract was the document that spelled
out the relationship between the Associated Architects and Metropolitan
Square, Incorporated; the "you" was anyone working under the architects'

supervision, down to the greenest file clerk. Nothing less buttoned-up was tolerated during working hours: "If the drawing you wanted" from the long row of file cabinets "didn't pop out of the file in seconds . . . ," Kilham recalled, "the office boys found there was hell to pay." One of the senior designers was tongue-lashed when he stayed away from the office for the birth of his son.

Designers who wished to dodge the formalities hid a key in the men's room and returned to work after Todd's men had left for their homes in Westchester or New Jersey. After-work trips to nearby speakeasies like the Old Cedar on East 43rd Street or the Architects' Club on East 46th could put an exclamation point on the end of a grueling day, just as a midafternoon blast on Walter Kilham's whistle would occasionally enliven the long afternoons. But this was not an environment easily vivified, disrupted, or modified in any other fashion. The draftsman who carved the words "Racketeer Cinema" into the clay marquee of one of the theater models expressed as much rebellion as the office could abide. After another designer, a short man who felt uncomfortable working on a standard-issue drafting table, arranged to have his stool and table legs cut down to a more congenial height, it was as if the room's rigid uniformity had been fatally corrupted. That afternoon, management had every other table and chair in the vast room cut down as well.

Still, for all the formality and the military-style organization—natural products of the job's complexity and Todd's unbending devotion to order— there were aspects of the architects' task that even the Prussian general staff could not have organized. Six years earlier, working on the Radiator Building, Hood had contended with a schedule that had him designing the top of the building while the masons were about to complete the brickwork only six floors below him. Now he and his colleagues had to conjure not just one office building but four theaters, two department stores, at least three skyscrapers, two low-rise buildings on the Fifth Avenue frontage, an enormous broadcasting facility (something that had never been designed before, anywhere on the planet) somewhere near Sixth, and the entire site all these buildings would inhabit—the elements of Todd's plan as amended by the requirements of the Sarnoff lease, all to be created under just the sort of deadline pressure you might expect from agents of a man who was losing three million dollars a year on three blocks' worth of speakeasies and flophouses.

Back when Hood felt the hot breath of the masons on the Radiator Building, he hadn't hesitated to use the circumstances as an excuse: "I merely [mention] this to ask for a little indulgence on the part of people who might otherwise be inclined to be very critical of the result." But compared to what Hood and his colleagues would encounter designing Rockefeller Center, the Radiator Building entailed no pressure at all, and all the indulgence in the world couldn't have salved the criticism Hood and the others would soon endure.

Anyone encountering the five lead architects in a lineup would have mistakenly picked Harvey Corbett as their leader. Towering over the rumpled Hood, sleek and elegant from the round-rimmed tortoiseshell glasses on his strong face to the shiny spats six feet below, the fifty-seven-year-old Corbett was a living Bachrach portrait; he looked like he carried his own lights with him. By the time he took up occasional residence in the Graybar offices, his excursions into architectural speechifying and theorizing had apparently proved more gratifying than his adventures in design. It was unclear whether Corbett's buildings were the product of his theories or his theories the children of his buildings. His finest creation, the supremely elongated Bush Tower, rising 480 feet above West 42nd Street from a base only 50 feet wide, was the apotheosis of his belief in verticality, the gesture with which he divorced himself from his training at the Beaux-Arts. "We have vertical stripes on our clothes because we think they add to our appearance," Corbett once wrote. Conversely, he added, in the sort of deliciously phrased formulation so appealing to journalists and others who would spread Corbett's fame, "the uniforms of convicts . . . have broad horizontal stripes."

The theory that established Corbett's reputation as a design polemicist emerged in 1923, during his service on the Regional Plan Association's panel on traffic, when he articulated his concept of a multilevel city: local auto traffic at street level, long-distance highways one level up, pedestrian traffic on promenades above that—a configuration of thoroughfares he likened to "basket weaving." He had elaborated that theme ever since, and made it yet more appealing for newspaper citation by appending the rubric "Venice in New York" to one version of it, likening Manhattan's traffic-ridden streets to the Italian city's canals, his imagined pedestrian promenades to its bridges and piazzas.

At Metropolitan Square, Corbett largely confined his efforts to the role of kibitzer. No doubt daunted by Hood's mastery and his alliance with the arch-antitheorist Todd, Corbett attended meetings, offered opinions, and stayed on the payroll throughout Rockefeller Center's formative years but did little actual work. It was during this period that Corbett was sliced up by a magazine writer who did not hear the sound of trumpets in the Great Man's voice. "Seven or eight years ago, the name of Harvey Wiley Corbett could not have been omitted from a list of the five greatest, or even the three greatest American architects," John Fistere wrote in *Vanity Fair.* Then came the knife: "Once a shining apostle of the new school, he is now an interesting lecturer."

The other three principals were much younger than Corbett and Hood, at different points in their careers and in the grip of different ambitions. Hofmeister, quiet and deliberate, for the most part applied his architectural talents to mechanical and structural issues, rising to visibility only in his methodical supervision of the entire drafting and specification process—he was "the man who got the work out." Much more a presence in the office, by dint of both personality and Todd's sponsorship, was the gregarious and puckish Reinhard, who seemed to derive his style from Corbett, his humor from Hood, and his aspirations from the youngest (and after Hood the most important) of the five architects, Harrison.

Nearly fifty years after Wally Harrison met the man who would shape his life ("Can I be of any help pinning up the drawings?" the young Nelson Rockefeller had asked); about forty years after Harrison left the offices of the Associated Architects; some twenty years after he led the international panel of designers that created the United Nations headquarters; and less than a decade after he stepped down as chairman of the board of architects at Lincoln Center, he told an interviewer that he didn't really like the idea of architecture by committee: "You and the building lose personal contact" when you have to explain and justify everything to a group, he said. But what a friend called Harrison's "equable, accommodating presence" had served him well in his long career. Those same qualities, seasoned with large portions of charm, had also buoyed his well-favored social life. Of course, equanimity, accommodation, and charm will earn a man detractors as well, and he had his share of those.

There was something of the nineteenth-century French novel in the arc of Harrison's life, beginning as it did in provincial pathos, passing through the glittering chambers of the wealthy and the powerful, and concluding in disillusion and disappointment. Late in his life, after his moment in architectural fashion had faded like the last echo of a brilliant bell, Harrison began to spend more time in the past than in the present. A parade of architectural historians, documentary filmmakers, and other interviewers provided him the opportunity to look back; a sputtering rage over what had happened to him provided his motivation. The critical vituperation that greeted his last major work was humiliation enough; now the patron—the *friend*—for whom he had worked and with whom he had collaborated for more than four decades cast him aside. Spurned by Nelson Rockefeller, Harrison actually wept. In a spidery hand, he scrawled across the bottom of a page of questions from an interviewer an aphorism, from Georges Clemenceau, that had nothing to do with the subject under discussion but everything to do with his state of mind: "America," Harrison wrote, "is the only country to pass from barbarism to degeneration without passing through civilization."

This was an immensely bitter statement for someone who had spent his life as the fortunate recipient of America's beneficence. His mother died when Harrison was fourteen, and his alcoholic father almost immediately deserted him. There was little comfort for a teenaged orphan in the unpaved streets on the south side of Worcester, Massachusetts, in 1909; Harrison quit school in the ninth grade and found a job as an office boy with a large construction firm. He eventually learned draftsmanship, taking to it so well that in 1916 he felt able to leave Worcester for New York. Six feet three, good-looking, his posture "like a column," possessed of an easy smile and a saleable skill, Harrison was one of those characters who, as E. B. White put it, were "born somewhere else and came to New York in quest of something." They were, said White, the people who made the city what it was.

By his own description the young Harrison was "like a clear glass bowl into which nothing had yet been put." During the day he was one of the scores of men seated at the long rows of drafting tables in the offices of McKim, Mead & White in the Architects Building on 40th Street; evenings he'd walk over to Keen's Chop House on West 36th, not to engage with the politicians, businessmen, and entertainment figures who thronged the place but to climb three flights above the restaurant to the atelier of Harvey Wiley Corbett.

Harrison's association with Corbett ignited his career. His talent quickened it. The scholarship he won to the Beaux-Arts both confirmed and refined his skills, and the time he spent in the early 1920s in Paris and then traveling through Europe and Egypt further buffed the polish he had acquired since leaving Worcester. Back in New York, he met and married Babs Rockefeller Milton's sister-in-law Ellen, who was bowled over by his impressive appearance and his comfortable manner. Though he failed to build a successful practice of his own (he spent a full year on one small commission while searching vainly for a second), he kept busy through the mid-twenties freelancing for prominent architects—in Herbert Warren Wind's phrase, "taking in architectural washing." In 1927 Harrison's career as a laundryman ended when his old mentor Corbett brought him into his firm as a partner. And just two years after that, the Corbett-Harrison office was tapped by John R. Todd for Metropolitan Square because, said Webster Todd, "Harrison was half related" to the Rockefellers.

For his entire career, Wally Harrison endured more than his share of scorn from those who saw him only as "a compliant servant of the rich," specifically the Rockefeller family. He designed houses for Nelson in Maine and at Pocantico Hills, a Nelson-backed cultural center for Dartmouth, and a Nelson-conceived apartment complex in midtown Manhattan. For Nelson's brother Johnny, the Rockefeller who would finally provide a new home for the Metropolitan Opera, Harrison was both director of the board of architects responsible for Lincoln Center and designer of the opera house itself. David Rockefeller recruited him to design the Morningside Gardens housing complex on upper Broadway. When Junior bought a stretch of land on the East River and gave it to the United Nations, which in turn hired an international committee of architects to design its headquarters, Harrison slid comfortably into the seat at the head of the table.

Finally, after his work in the 1960s and 1970s on the brutal row of sky-scrapers marching joylessly down the west side of Sixth Avenue from 50th Street to 46th—all of them Rockefeller commissions—Harrison's career concluded with one of the most egregious acts of architecture ever committed in the United States. The Governor Nelson A. Rockefeller Empire State Plaza in Albany, a Stalinoid Stonehenge rising out of nowhere and signifying nothing but the enormity of the ego that willed it into being, represented more than the final act in the four-decade saga of Nelson Rockefeller and Wallace Harrison; it was the living incarnation of one of the architect's aptest epigrams: "When all is said and done," Harrison said, "an architect is a designer with a client."

"It is needless to say that every [architect] associated with Rockefeller City"—as it was briefly known—"knows that he is risking his reputation, his professional future."

"The approach to the problem . . . may be summed up briefly . . . 'cost' and 'return.'"

An economic model for construction and design allows "the cobwebs of whimsy, taste, fashion and vanity [to be] brushed aside."

These statements may sound like extracts from the collected epigrams of John R. Todd, but their author was Raymond Hood, in an article he wrote for *Architectural Forum.* It was a sign of the development's importance to the architectural profession that the magazine would run a ten-month series describing every aspect of its design and its planned construction. It was a sign of Hood's role in the project that he led off the series and that he could sound so much like Todd. One could say that this was wily old Ray Hood lulling his client into a contentedness that would get the architect what he wanted without the client even knowing it. Except Hood believed everything he said in the *Architectural Forum* piece. He never made grand assertions for architecture as art; he referred to his buildings as "jobs."

Todd loved him. At the weekly design meetings, where Todd generally presided with the patience of a cranky judge in night court, he'd allow Hood freedom of the floor. Early on, Todd loaded the five architects and several other key men from the Graybar offices into a motorcade of open cars for a tour of Manhattan architecture, from Bowling Green on the harbor to Spuyten Duyvil at the island's northern tip. He wanted to show them everything he didn't like about skyscraper architecture, and found plenty. When he concluded the tour with a predictably Toddian pronouncement— "If you men were responsible for what has been built, you ought to be shot"—Hood replied, "Don't shoot us. Just take us somewhere and get us half-shot." What's remarkable about this story is not Hood's characteristic jokiness, but the fact that it was the teetotaling Todd who approvingly repeated it.

Among the other architects—both the principals in their private offices on the twenty-sixth floor and the worker bees at the endless rows of tables on 25—it quickly became obvious that Hood, who described himself as "spokesman for my associates in a great adventure," was first among not-remotely-equals. Harrison admired Hood professionally and personally, and his famous equanimity would have led him to accommodation in any case. Corbett was present more during the early days of chin-scratching and hypothetical-raising than when the actual work was getting done, and the drafting room men imported from his office, described by a colleague as "too timid for their own good," soon found themselves out of work. Reinhard and Hofmeister were junior figures, their position—and Hood's— made concrete in the very first press release issued by the Rockefeller

Center publicity department: the initial draft listed their firm first, followed by Corbett and Harrison's, and finally Hood's. The master version from which copies were made a few days later was hand-patched to reverse the order.

During the long months of the Symposium and Morris's last stand, and Todd's putsch and subsequent appointment of the Associated Architects; while the market crashed and Fulton Cutting equivocated and David Sarnoff began to negotiate; while the project's financial losses grew larger with each successful buyout of a ground lease or a subtenancy on the Upper Estate—during all this time, Junior was increasingly unsettled by his associates' inching progress and burdened by his own failure of imagination. So much was happening, but the only thing Junior could actually see was a desolate three blocks of condemned buildings that he now owned, buildings that no longer produced even the piddling rents of the year before. As Francis Christy put it, "How could [Junior] look at a scullery maid and visualize Cinderella?"

The opening of the architects' office changed that. Two years after Ivy Lee had reported to him on the meeting at the Metropolitan Club, Junior became, for the first time, truly engaged by the emergence of palpable evidence that buildings might actually rise from his eleven acres of midtown. Riverside Church (including the meeting room set aside for Junior's men's Bible class) was scheduled to open in the fall, the restoration of Colonial Williamsburg was well under way, and if there was a vacuum in the life of this man who "loved projects," he now found on the twenty-fifth floor of the Graybar Building material to fill it.

Unlike most architects, Raymond Hood developed his plans not through progressive iterations of sketches but from small-scale clay or plasticine models that evolved with his ideas. The translator who gave dimension and volume to Hood's vision was René Chambellan, a sculptor (born in New Jersey but trained—of course—at the Beaux-Arts) who had worked with Hood since the architect's hand-to-mouth days more than a decade earlier. Among connoisseurs of decorative sculpture, Chambellan would become known for the stone gargoyles he suspended from the walls of Princeton, Yale, and other universities; the commemorative hardware he designed, including the Caldecott and Newbery Medals for children's literature; and even for some of the work that would add gloss to the finished Rockefeller Center, notably the tritons and dolphins and other bronze creatures cavorting in the fountains of the Channel Gardens. Among Hood's generation of architects, however, Chambellan was cherished for his models, like those in the urbanist toyland of towers and shops and promenades rising on the drafting rooms' tables.

Hood's communication with Chambellan seemed telepathic. The architect could describe an idea and with a few swipes of his modeler's knife Chambellan would articulate it in clay. One historian, noting that Chambellan was paid an hourly wage, dismissed him as "an artistic handyman," which was about as accurate as calling Todd a construction worker. Many of the Rockefeller Center models emerged from his studio on East 39th Street, where Chambellan and his employees sometimes cleared enough space to set out a bountiful and bibulous lunch for the grateful architects, who would return to the office in midafternoon lubricated for cooperation. At the daily Graybar meetings, Chambellan's early models provided focus and discipline, every idea rendered at a scale of ¼₄ of an inch to a foot, evaluated by the group, then left to stand or be erased by another Chambellan knife stroke. Some were rough versions of the envelope, others (at larger scale) so detailed you could pick out prospective shades in suppositional windows, or tiny, lifelike figures crossing speculative streets. In the main drafting room there proliferated a veritable city of Chambellan models, simultaneously templates for the draftsmen and a standing record of the design process.

Junior's newfound engagement with the real estate business found traction in Room 2626, just down the hall from the architects' private offices, at the weekly meetings attended by delegates from every part of the burgeoning operation, finance and renting and construction and the like taking their seats alongside the designers. Until the completion of the RCA Building in 1933, he never missed a meeting if he was in town, his collapsible four-foot ruler at the ready. "He was an ideal client," Harrison remembered, "keeping close watch on every aspect of the project . . . and rejecting almost every opportunity to impose his personal notions of good design upon his architects." Good thing: early on, returning from a trip to the Middle East, he had suggested a group of buildings in "Egyptian" style.

But with Todd firmly in place, Junior deferred both to his manager's judgment and to the power of his personality. Reinhard liked to refer to the Associated Architects as "a guild of master builders," but anyone attending the weekly meetings—including Junior—recognized that the only attendee meriting the appellation "master" was Todd. Presiding from the head of the table, flanked on one side by his genial, diplomatic brother, James, and on the other by his chief enforcer, the nickel-squeezing Joe Brown, John R. would solicit opinions on a particular design issue from nearly everyone— the renting expert estimating its appeal to prospective tenants, the construction specialist offering a way to cut costs, the engineer pointing out its effect on elevator placement. Once he'd made up his mind, though, Todd's tolerance for discussion evaporated. Persisting in an argument after its Todd-mandated conclusion "was like jumping into a bull ring with a maddened bull."

Only two things seemed to abate John R.'s temper. One was the intervention of "Doc" Todd, who had given up his career as a surgeon thirty-five years earlier to join his younger brother in the development business but could still deploy a bedside manner capable of calming both the maddened bull and the victims of his stampeding temper. The other was that irresistible combination of attributes that invariably soothed John R. and delighted him: charm and common sense, as conjoined in the singular Ray Hood. Said Hood's first business partner, Rayne Adams, "His whims are reasonable and his reasons are whimsical." Who could resist that?

Nearly all architectural projects begin with what the trade calls a "program," the systematic delineation of the project's intent and its requirements. In a private home the program might be "large living room, eat-in-kitchen, three bedrooms, central courtyard." In an office building not built for a specific business, a program could conceivably be boiled down to something as simple as "25 floors with 30,000 square feet of rentable space on each one." For a project as complex and as superscaled as Rockefeller Center, any program would obviously have to be far more detailed, specifying how many buildings, of which type, for which uses, arrayed across what landscape features. It would likely be posited in terms of a budget, and would also set forth the particular requirements of tenants already committed to the project.

The Metropolitan Square program articulated by Todd in November 1929 became a moving target. The first major change occurred when the opera house was dropped, but even the advent of RCA and its million-plus square feet of theaters, studios, and offices didn't stabilize matters. Todd and his architects would alter their course with each perceived change in the economy; with the appearance on the horizon of each potential major tenant; and with each explosion of imagination that detonated in the Graybar offices. These last events, generally but not exclusively sited somewhere in the skull of either Hood or Todd, confirmed a wise variation on a famous dictum. Louis Sullivan said, "Form follows function." Architectural historian Carol Willis's version: "Form follows finance."

Todd looked at buildings as investments and tenants as paying customers. The relationship between the two was the sole determinant of a project's success or failure, and Todd never had a failure. But Hood's ability—eagerness, even—to speak the same language of cost and return should not suggest that the designer was faking it to endear himself to his boss, or that Todd was unappreciative of his architect's creative gifts. For Todd recognized that within the context of tenant desires, the better a building, the higher the rents. Hood not only knew how to make buildings better, but how to make them better in ways that might gratify the customers.

This was underscored in the development of the plan to put gardens on the roofs of the Center's low buildings and on the setbacks of its towers. Although Ben Morris had included roof gardens on the setbacks of the opera house in his post-Symposium plan, the idea was vastly expanded by Hood, who believed that the view *from* Manhattan buildings was more important to the typical New Yorker than the view *of* those buildings, which were rarely discernible more than a few floors above the hemmed-in streets. "The view from the tower windows . . . will look down not upon the dirty-brown cluttered waste of unrelieved ugliness which is the roof view of New York," Hood wrote, "but upon a . . . picture to which art and nature have contributed color and design with a note of gayety." Todd figured these enhanced views would translate into as much as a dollar a square foot in additional rents—justification, Hood argued successfully, "to landscape those roofs like the hanging gardens of Babylon." Even more than his eminence in the profession or his congenial nature, it was Hood's fertile symbiosis with Todd that made him the planet around which the other Associated Architects spun.

Harrison's contributions to the discussion came in the form of passionate enthusiasms engagingly presented. His talent, his lively mind, and his innate good nature were manifest not only in the daily workings of the architects but also in the actual limestone and steel of Rockefeller Center. The bitterness that gripped Harrison late in life revealed no antecedents in the "very charming and serious person" who inhabited the Graybar offices. Harrison was the office diplomat, in Norval White's phrase "the Benign Compromiser" who could smooth out the thorniest disagreements. More, he was the advocate who could challenge his patron: when Junior expressed his preference for Gothic ornamentation Harrison yowled, "Goddamn it Mr. Rockefeller, you can't do that! You'll ruin the building if you cover up its lines with all that classical gingerbread."

Those two brief sentences contained three strikes—temper, profanity, and insult—yet Junior didn't call him out. When a man as calm as Harrison expressed such passion you had to listen. (This was long before Harrison "alarmed" his friend Brendan Gill: the trouble, said Gill, "was not that Harrison and his colleagues [at Lincoln Center] had produced so great a number of alternative designs as that he seemed to be about equally pleased to champion each of them." According to a close friend, Harrison explained that he "just tried to get things accomplished as best he could amid diverse pressures.") Among the men in the Graybar Building, Harrison was the architectural progressive, embracing the latest design ideologies, enjoying friendships with such fellow modernists as Fernand Léger and Alexander Calder, and carrying the banner of the New in all the architects' deliberations. He was the embodiment of those modern architects who, wrote Susannah Lessard, "looked in the direction of characteristics that were physically the opposite of the Beaux-Arts style—flatness, simplicity, straight lines, abstract forms—and came to associate these qualities with virtue as closely as they associated the old style with vice."

In 1932, when a twenty-six-year-old aesthete from Cleveland persuaded his wealthy father to help underwrite the cost of a museum show the young man wished to stage, Harrison and his fellow modernists were handed a flag to march behind. Philip Johnson, just two years out of college, was the first director of the new department of architecture at the Museum of Modern Art (although not yet an architect himself: that was more than a decade in the future). The show he put on with co-curator Henry-Russell Hitchcock, *Modern Architecture: International Exhibition,* celebrated the functionalist movement emanating from Germany and the Netherlands, conclusively ended the brief reign of Art Deco, cut off the oxygen to the still gasping classical styles, and established the primacy of a new architectural aesthetic.

Today, the International Style needs little more introduction than do the television set, transatlantic air travel, Velcro, or any other twentieth-century technological marvel rendered commonplace by its ubiquity. Johnson, Hitchcock, and partisans like Harrison, clutching Louis Sullivan's "Form follows function" as their "In the beginning . . . ," now added the exegeses that comprised the movement's New Testament. They spoke of a building's volume rather than its mass, of design predicated on regularity rather than symmetry, of the superfluity of "arbitrary decoration." Detractors may have dismissed the products of the style as soulless boxes of glass and steel, but the International Style dominated American architecture for half a century, in forms ranging from the elegantly detailed masterpieces of Ludwig Mies van der Rohe (such as the Seagram Building in New York) and Gordon Bunshaft (his Lever House, catty-corner across Park Avenue from the Seagram) to the thousands of landscape-deadening office buildings scarring the shoulders of every suburban ring road circling an American city.

The first avatar of the International Style in the United States was George Howe and William Lescaze's Philadelphia Savings Fund Society Building, which opened in 1932. A nearly contemporary example, one of the few New York buildings Johnson and Hitchcock included in their show, was Hood's McGraw-Hill Building on West 42nd Street, whose color and graphics evoke Deco but whose massing is unmistakably International. True to form, Hood wasn't particularly interested in belonging to the modernists' club. Speaking to a symposium organized by MOMA, he all but asked to be excluded from the exhibition: "I was told, 'We do not use ornament.' 'Who are you?', I asked, 'to say "Thou shalt not; thou shalt not"'?" Hood was genuinely angry. "I wish we could all work with our own sense of discipline and be free as the devil," he told the audience. "For the moment we put a cast iron frame on this international style, this fine, marvelous movement will turn into a tight, hard, unimaginative formula."

For all the noise the Internationalists made about form and function, it was really an idea as old as the act of making buildings. Architectural form has always followed function, if you consider function at its core levels. Back when the function of a building was the exaltation of a monarch or the glorification of a deity, architects gave their clients palaces and cathedrals, soaring spires and imposing entrances, acres of glistening marble and triumphant legions of heroic statues. When the industrial revolution turned the attention of the commissioning classes to a new function—sheltering and circumscribing the means of production—solid and stolid walls enclosed vast, undecorated factory rooms. And when the seats of production became factories not just for workers but for owners and managers, too, architects—at the behest of their clients—invented the office building.

With the RCA Building Raymond Hood perfected the form. It is one of those expressions of architecture that, after seven decades, seems so natural it's hard to comprehend how revolutionary it was. Critics at first repelled by the RCA's very existence would in time acknowledge both its innovation and its beauty, and the most vituperative among them, like Lewis Mumford, ended up contrite if not exactly apologetic. In a 1937 speech Harrison said, "People are always asking who designed Rockefeller Center. Each of us answers, 'I did.'" But even Harrison, who lobbied hard and long for International Style principles in the Graybar debates, eventually acknowledged that Hood's concept for the RCA Building was more daring and more effective than his own. Harrison would in time be chief designer on more Rockefeller Center buildings than Hood. But the RCA was so dominant in its sheer size, so clearly the Center's focal point, and so determinative in its influence on the Center's other buildings (and every other aspect of its layout and appearance) that each of the Associated Architects who answered the "who designed" question with "I did" was mistaken. Ray Hood, who did not live long enough to have the question asked of him, designed Rockefeller Center.

What he began with was a piece of land. During the summer of 1930, at the same time that Junior's lawyers and real estate operatives were trying to conclude the acquisition of ground leases on the site and the first demolition crews were mobilizing, the architects began to refine—or, perhaps more accurately, noodle with—the plan. Hood played with a scheme entailing bridges over 49th and 50th Streets and various auto ramps, a seeming adaptation of Corbett's "Venice in New York." The most extreme idea called for a single building, like a massive pyramid, covering the entire three blocks. Another version placed a much smaller pyramid as a sort of signature building at the center of the Fifth Avenue frontage; Hood, aware that a pyramid suffers from ever-decreasing floor space as it rises to its apex (or requires ridiculously large floor space at its base), replaced it with a low building shaped like an oval hatbox.

In July, Hood and Corbett together argued for making the RCA headquarters building more than just the tallest building on the plot. Envisioning something monumental and "impressive," they initiated the "Fling" project (so called for the "fling of imagination" all the designers were asked to attempt). This intensive midsummer charrette yielded scores of plans—plans ringed by circular walkways, plans crosshatched by arcades and galleries, one plan incorporating a version of Hood's hatbox bisected by a ribbon of arcade running right through it. Still, every one of them balanced on the fulcrum of a towering building near the Sixth Avenue end of the plot.

This was a placement dictated by Todd. It was obvious that the Fifth Avenue frontage was the best spot for retail businesses, which would ideally be contained in low buildings; no one liked to take elevators to do their shopping. Besides, Todd reasoned, fronting the entire development directly on Fifth would have created a dead zone in the western half of the site, where the Sixth Avenue El still rumbled and wheezed. Set back near Sixth but with its front facing Fifth, the RCA Building would pull the center of gravity westward (abetted by the eventual opening of the Sixth Avenue subway line) while maintaining a Fifth Avenue aspect, "draw[ing] the public interest and with it the value into the Square," as Corbett explained, and thus "increas[ing] the area of high retail values," as Todd told Junior. All of this would additionally enable the architects to capitalize on the zoning laws, which allowed the transfer of the low buildings' "tower rights" to other portions of the site. Consequently, the RCA Building could borrow from the Fifth Avenue buildings and the open plaza to soar to the sky without the burden of broad-shouldered setbacks; it could be whatever the architects wanted it to be. An excited Harrison saw in this the opportunity for a "plain, beautiful slab" consonant with his modernist design ideology, and Reinhard drew an early version of one. But as Hood developed his ideas over the ensuing weeks, an ingeniously modified "slat," as he called it, would merge function with beauty in a way the modernists could not have imagined, much less achieved.

The key to Hood's approach was no less mundane than a number—to be exact, twenty-seven. That was the maximum number of feet natural light could travel from a standard-size window to a desk inside a building constructed at New York's latitude. Especially before the advent of fluorescent lighting (not to mention air conditioning), what windows brought into offices included not just light and fresh air but money as well. "I have never collected an extra dollar of rent for space more than thirty feet from a window," Todd once said. Builders called anything that couldn't be reached by natural light "deep space"; Hood, never indirect, called it "bad space." Now he resolved to design a building that had none.

The technique he used was a version of what Todd called designing "from the inside out"—planning the interior space for efficiency of construction and tenant-friendly operation and only later designing the exterior. This was why, in his memoir, Todd called his space planners, Reinhard and Hofmeister, "our chief architects." In fact, the inside-out approach was consistent with the manifestoes of the modernists (even if Todd was driven by visions of profits rather than aesthetic ideology). Harrison, for one, was captivated by it. Building tall, he felt, was an obvious reflection of man's wish to "expand his ego." But all the functional stuff—distance from desks to windows, how many elevators per tenant, traveling at what speed—involved "the needs of man as ant," he said, and those were more interesting than ego.

The vehicle that carried Hood to a solution of the window/light issue—and as a consequence the essential determinant of the RCA Building's eventual appearance—was an elevator cab, or more accurately the forty-two elevators in five separate banks necessary to the efficient distribution of tenants and visitors to the building's sixty-six floors. "As each elevator shaft ended," Hood explained in *Architectural Forum*, "we cut the building back to maintain the same 27 feet from the core of the building to the exterior walls. By so doing we have eliminated every dark corner." By so doing Hood also created the building's distinctive look, particularly the dramatic sculptural effect of its facade, narrowing and also drawing back as it climbs, an exaggerated upthrust of receding perspective terminating not in a spire or a radio tower but in what Hood's friend Ralph Walker described as "an abrupt climax [followed by] complete silence." It was an effect that led a critic to call it "the largest frozen fountain ever built" and that prompted an early visitor—Alice B. Toklas—to observe, "It is not the way [it goes] into the air but the way [it comes] out of the ground that is the thing."

Finally, following the outside-in procedure mandated by Todd, attention turned to details of the exterior. Harrison advocated a polychromatic brick treatment that would lend the building "a tapestry effect." Others presented drawings that arrayed the windows in thin horizontal bands with expanded courses of brickwork every dozen floors, or that created elaborate patterns of mixed horizontals and verticals. Hood favored a rough-faced form of limestone with thin striations in its surface that lent an appealing texture (and a surprising name to the Todd & Brown spec sheets: "Buff Indiana Limestone in promiscuous scabbled blocks"). When John R. balked at the cost, Hood proposed cladding the building in painted sheets of corrugated iron. Thus tweaked, Todd immediately relented, the limestone stayed in the design, and Hood completed the suit of clothes he had always had in mind by perforating the building's walls with 5,817 windows laid out to accent its verticality—"mere lineations like the ribbing in the texture of a fabric," wrote architectural historian Sigfried Giedion.

Hood's final brushstroke connected one floor's windows to the next with dark aluminum spandrels, a variation on those he'd used on Joseph Patterson's apartment building on East 84th Street. The skin was as simple as the mass was daring, and really all that was needed for a building so massive: its 2.3 million square feet of rentable space exceeded even the 2 million feet about to be enclosed in the much taller Empire State Building, at that moment rising on 34th Street and Fifth Avenue. Worrying about the details on something as huge as a modern office building, Hood said, was like "wondering what sort of lace shawl you should hang on an elephant."

Seventy years later, critic Paul Goldberger had another animal in mind. Speaking of the collaborative design effort, Goldberger said, "a camel should have been produced. Instead, they got a racehorse." Another commentator put it differently. On the same 1935 visit that led Alice B. Toklas to marvel at the RCA Building, her companion considered it from the head of the Channel Gardens on the Center's eastern edge. "The view of Rockefeller Center from Fifth Avenue," said Gertrude Stein in her Gertrude Steinish fashion, "is the most beautiful thing I have ever seen ever seen ever seen."

CHAPTER TWELVE

On December 31, 1929, Doris Kenyon emerged from a bathroom in the house at 42 West 49th Street wearing a smile on her pretty face and a toilet seat around her elegant neck. This would have been at least a little puzzling to anyone who'd seen Kenyon play Betsy Ross opposite Francis X. Bushman's George Washington, maybe less so to those who'd seen the actress a few years earlier in the somewhat less edifying lead role of a silent film called *Loose Ankles.* But to any of her fellow New Year's Eve celebrants in the old brownstone who bothered to take notice, it was perfectly clear what Kenyon was up to: she'd assumed personal responsibility for demolishing the ladies' room, and the seat was proof of her success.

*I feel all right, but I don't sleep so well. I walk the floor nights, **wondering where I'm going to get the money** to build these buildings.*

—JOHN D. ROCKEFELLER JR.

Still, who would bother to take note of Kenyon when there was so much else to grab a person's attention in the city's most glamorous speakeasy that night? Charlie Berns had armed everyone—Robert Benchley and Beatrice Lillie, Hollywood producers and Park Avenue bluebloods, friendly cops and even friendlier chorus girls—with crowbars and pickaxes and various other implements of demolition and invited them all to have a go at the premises Berns and Jack Kriendler were turning over to the Rockefeller interests that night. The sound of floorboards being ripped up and wall panels crashing down made a lively accompaniment for the strolling Hawaiian musicians hired for the occasion, and all that hard physical labor created a healthy thirst for the Major Baileys—mint juleps made with gin—the bartenders were pouring so generously for the invitation-only crowd.

At midnight the year of the market crash was over, the twenties were over, and the Puncheon Club was over, too. Eleven thousand dollars of

Rockefeller buyout money in their pockets, Berns and Kriendler led a cara-
van through the snowy streets, their staff and their guests pushing wheeled
carts loaded with dishes, glasses, knickknacks, and illegal booze three blocks
north to West 52nd Street and their new place of business, the "21" Club.

The two saloonkeepers were solicitous of their neighbors. "We considered several houses on West 53rd and West 54th," Berns told an interviewer. "But there were Rockefellers living on both of those streets, and
they didn't like speakeasies." The New Year's Eve demolition party was a
courtesy, too: the razing of the houses on the Upper Estate would soon begin, and Berns and Kriendler had given the wrecking crews a head start.

"In New York," wrote Edna St. Vincent Millay in a letter to her family, "you
can *see* the noise." In the city's passage from nineteenth-century port to
twentieth-century metropolis, clatter and shout had turned into pounding
and roar. On their own, the elevated tracks over Sixth Avenue emitted an
infernal clamor so overpowering, wrote William Dean Howells, that "No
experience of noise can enable you to conceive of the furious din that bursts
upon the sense." From 1924 to 1932, the number of cars coming into
Manhattan increased by 47 percent. With the concurrent construction
boom, Walter Lippmann said, this created "a dissonance comprised of a
thousand noises."

And then came the wreckers. The actions of the New Year's amateurs at
Jack and Charlie's place on 49th Street notwithstanding, the wholesale demolition of three blocks of midtown began in earnest on May 17, 1930,
when crews from the Albert A. Volk Company began dismantling the north
side of 48th Street and the south side of 49th. While lawyers were still acquiring leases and architects were still completing plans, the growl of bulldozers and the crash of tumbling walls provided a basso continuo that
would run for nearly three full years, amplified along the way by the percussive dynamite blasts of the excavation crews and the full-orchestra roar
of actual construction. Mrs. Cornelius Vanderbilt III, still resident in the
mansion at 640 Fifth, on the northwest corner of 51st, more than once had
her lawyer register complaints with Todd's office.

Mrs. Vanderbilt was yearning for a serenity that could never be recap-
tured, the Fifth Avenue of gaslight and coaches and, in this last surviving
Vanderbilt palace, the four roses in four silver vases her staff continued to
place in the window to let passersby know that the great lady was At Home.
She knew her time was past. "I feel deeply for poor, dear Marie Antoinette,"

she said, "for if the Revolution came to America, I should be the first to go." Next in line might be the members of the Union Club, directly across Fifth Avenue from Mrs. Vanderbilt. As demolition on the Upper Estate began, the "Mother of Clubs" was preparing to decamp for new quarters at Park and 69th, leaving behind not just its grand Italianate clubhouse (designed, in part, by Cass Gilbert) but also the game its members loved to play while looking out at Fifth: betting on "the number of Negroes who will pass in a given time."

At the opposite end of Junior's leasehold—"Stretching," wrote Robert Sherwood in a lengthy piece of doggerel, "from old St. Pat's to older El,/ Bounded, in fact, by heaven and hell"—demolition promised opportunity. "MUST VACATE/BUILDING COMING DOWN," read the sign in the window of Mike Appel, Haberdashers, on Sixth Avenue. "TAKE ADVANTAGE OF THESE MARVELOUS BARGAINS." Owners of adjacent properties hoped the efforts of the Rockefeller wreckers might speed the arrival of crews charged with dismantling the loathed el tracks, a deliverance promised them six years earlier. Colonel Clement Jenkins, general manager of the Sixth Avenue Association, announced his organization's intent to "fight this destroyer of life, limb, health, nerves, peace, happiness, beauty, prosperity and progress . . . until it is vanquished and removed." Jenkins had only eight more years to wait before Fiorello La Guardia touched a ceremonial acetylene torch to the platform at Sixth and 53rd.

Midblock, between the screeching of the el and the noises that kept Mrs. Vanderbilt awake and her lawyers busy, a new voice joined the chorus: the gasp of surprise that greeted each discovery of a salvageable wonder that had somehow survived the neighborhood's long decades of decline. One house in the northern block yielded a hand-carved oak mantelpiece, a sunken marble-and-tile bath "of Turkish design," and "plush tapestry" on the parlor walls. Junior himself arranged to have a bathtub transported to Pocantico Hills, there to be used as a horse trough. Fourteen months after demolition began, more than two hundred buildings, most of them barely fifty years old, had been reduced to rubble.

A shopper on one of the upper floors of the Saks Fifth Avenue building on the east side of Fifth Avenue could have looked out a window around then and seen a new desert forming in the heart of midtown. A few buildings in the eastern end of the southern block remained standing, thanks to William Nelson Cromwell's Last Stand, and though the northern block was only half cleared, the remaining empty brownstones looked no more alive than the debris surrounding them. But it was in the central block, due west of the Saks building, that the effect was most striking. A moonscape of dirt, dust, and stone stretched all the way to two buildings standing on either corner of Sixth, bracketing the empty block—Hurley and Daly's old saloon to the south, John F. Maxwell's three-story building to the north. The abutting brownstones had been cleared away, and from the east all one could see of the two lonesome survivors were their windowless rear walls. Architects and builders call these "blind walls"—in this case, blind to the new world about to rise behind them.

Colonel Jenkins of the Sixth Avenue Association might have outranked Captain Pedrick of the Fifth Avenue Association, but there was no question who had the better job. Pedrick, who was never any farther from the invocation of his World War I military rank than he was from his own skin, had impressive assets: strong connections to the Tammany Hall leaders who still controlled the New York Democratic Party; the interests of the city's most powerful merchants and some of its wealthiest landowners; and most of all, the gold-backed security that was Fifth Avenue itself, the "synonym for luxury and good taste." Colonel Jenkins (who on occasion responded to "Mister") was like a criminal lawyer with a confessed murderer for a client.

What both men had in common was an impressive capacity to annoy Junior and the men who worked for him. Jenkins was a jackhammer, endlessly pounding on a single issue: the elimination of the el. First he made a vain effort to get Junior to become a member of the "Committee of Five Hundred for the Removal of the Sixth Avenue Elevated." Then he tried the direct appeal: "You are going to benefit by this change," he wrote to Junior, adding (in a display of nerve if not tact), "Ask yourself what you have done to cooperate and do your share in this important work we are doing." Switching course, Jenkins made a public appeal on broader social grounds through a publication he began called *The Boulevard* (the name with which Jenkins hoped to rechristen Sixth once the el was gone). He claimed that removal of the elevated would all but solve unemployment in New York, creating one hundred thousand new jobs in "over a hundred new buildings" that would rise when the "steel footed cumbersome dragon" was slain. (King Kong took a crack at it in 1933, but that was just the movies.) Junior wanted the Elevated gone, too—replacing it with a Sixth Avenue subway line was a critical part of Todd's plan—but would rely on other means to achieve this goal. He did have one piece of advice for Jenkins: "Boulevard" was an inappropriate name for a business thoroughfare, and something incorporating "Avenue" would be preferable.

Unlike the one-issue Jenkins, Pedrick maintained a catalog of complaint. He was like a high-strung terrier scurrying around the Rockefeller ankles, yipping and biting and never running out of the energy necessary to do either. The threat of "a gigantic theatrical undertaking, or some equally undesirable enterprise" was what most exercised him, but Pedrick could be provoked by a pinprick. He griped about the temporary parking lot Todd installed on the lower block. He fretted about the "alarming rumors" concerning Rockefeller plans for the Fifth Avenue frontage. In order to protect the avenue's reputation, Pedrick told Junior, the association had tried "to repulse the invasion" of an odd assortment of transgressions by an unlikely collection of infidels. His list lumped together "charitable and philanthropic organizations" with "cigarette testimonial exhibits, live animal exhibits, . . . mechanical window displays," and anything else that "might be construed to be garish, bizarre, freakish, or sensational," including "auctions [and] lectures."

Although Junior found Pedrick "altogether too officious," he essentially sympathized with the general goals of the Fifth Avenue Association. But he had bigger problems as Metropolitan Square inched its way from concept to concrete, ranging from the exasperating to the nettlesome to the truly consequential. The first was the sudden reappearance of emissaries from the Metropolitan Opera. The aftershocks of the stock market crash, plus the imminent (and offended) withdrawal of Otto Kahn from his role as the opera's patron, put Fulton Cutting and his colleagues in a very deep hole. The performance fees demanded by the leading singers and conductors had ridden the wave of the 1920s, peaking in the 1929–30 season; at that same moment, revenue took a swan dive. The following year loomed as the first in two decades to produce a substantial loss, and the possibility of bankruptcy soon arose. Apparently believing that RCA's ambitious plans for four theaters might create room for opera, the Met effectively petitioned for readmission. In Junior's behalf Todd, carefully negotiating the rocks of public relations, told the press that his office was "working in perfect harmony" with Cutting's people to provide space for "the kind of a home opera deserves." He didn't tell the papers that he was asking for a rental price that all but guaranteed that the opera would say no. The Met's putative interest kept looming into view for the next few years, almost like a bad dream— and just as ephemeral.

More troubling to the men in the Rockefeller office was what they perceived to be a sophisticated shakedown by Martin E. Greenhouse, the man an angered Junior rashly described (repeating, it must be noted, someone else's phrase) as "a slippery Jew speculator." In the summer of 1930, Greenhouse, a Philadelphia real estate developer, appeared with an offer to "take the Columbia Tract off of Mr. Rockefeller's hands" and leave Junior with a $4.2 million profit for his troubles. Debevoise and Heydt straight-armed him for a while—Debevoise told an associate that "we could not in good faith to the Radio people consider his proposition"—but Greenhouse reappeared several months later, this time sending Junior a detailed critique of the portion of the architects' plans that had been made public and appending to it a cleverly modified plan of his own. When another Greenhouse letter arrived at the Eyrie in August, the calm of a Seal Harbor summer was broken. Debevoise, himself rusticating in the Adirondacks, immediately issued a tread-lightly warning to everyone in the Rockefeller and Todd offices. Todd, for his part, tried to persuade one of Junior's secretaries not to show him the Greenhouse letter, as "it would only bother him and do no good."

It was in this context that Greenhouse, who had immigrated to the United States from Russia as an eighteen-year-old, actually showed up in what must have been the fairly alien precincts of Mount Desert Island, not at the impregnable ramparts of the Eyrie in Seal Harbor but at the home of Junior's friend, investment banker Edward Townsend Stotesbury, in nearby Bar Harbor. Stotesbury, reputed to be the richest man in Philadelphia, was the reigning nabob of Drexel & Company, a J. P. Morgan partner, and bearer of a most unbankerly nickname, "Little Sunshine." His report on Greenhouse's mission to Maine was less than sunny. This is how Junior related it to Debevoise: Stotesbury, Junior wrote,

> telephoned me yesterday to say that a Mr. Greenhouse of Philadelphia had just been to see him, seeking an introduction to me. Mr. Stotesbury went on to say that Greenhouse is a very shrewd, slippery Jew speculator, who makes real estate suggestions to people, seeks to draw forth letters from them and to establish the appearance of their having received and acquiesced in his suggestions, whereupon he demands large compensation for the adoption of his ideas and sues if such compensation is not voluntarily given. Mr. Stotesbury told Greenhouse that he would not give him an introduction to me and advised him to go back to Philadelphia.

Whether or not Greenhouse (or "Greenhaus," as he was occasionally identified by Rockefeller associates) was intentionally setting a trap cannot be known, but Junior and his closest advisers were convinced he was. Though Greenhouse would continue to make occasional and seemingly innocent approaches for another two years, by Debevoise's order Junior's office stopped responding altogether. In 1948 a high-ranking Rockefeller Center official said that "Greenfield" (they always did have trouble with that name!) may have been unsavory but that did not suggest that either the offer, or Greenhouse himself, was illegitimate.

"I feel all right," Junior told Wallace Harrison one day during Rockefeller Center's planning phase, "but I don't sleep so well. I walk the floor nights, wondering where I'm going to get the money to build these buildings." It's an admittedly odd image, the world's richest man worrying about his bills as if he were a homeowner who'd taken on too much mortgage. Junior's contemporaries would have grasped the severity of the post-Crash context, but they would have had difficulty comprehending how even an economic calamity of this magnitude could threaten the sleep of a man whose personal income, even in the bleakest days of the Depression, still exceeded $15 million a year.

But like so many other Americans, Junior had been suckered by the twenties. When you've gotten used to earning more than $40 million per annum, which Junior did in the decade's most overheated years; when your very essence is defined by your charitable efforts, which led Junior to make enormous future commitments to a wide range of beneficiaries; and when one of the more modest of these philanthropies—a donation of land to the Metropolitan Opera—has metastasized into something no longer either modest or philanthropic, you worry and you pace. Even worse for one as conservative as Junior, you are forced to learn to eat your losses. The value of the stock Junior and his father had bought in their well-publicized effort to buoy the market after the Crash had plunged in the months since, and financial exigencies forced Junior to switch from buyer to seller. Standard of New Jersey, its annual profits shaved from a pre-Crash $100 million to less than $300,000 in 1932, had fallen from $83 a share in 1929 to $20 in 1932. Standard of New York had dropped even further, from a pre-Crash peak of $48 to $5.25 a share. A *New Yorker* writer's acute characterization of the Ford Foundation—"A large body of money surrounded by people who want some"—could just as well have defined Junior, but by 1931 the pumps that had always filled the basin had stopped working. Junior was not only compelled to sell stock at the market's all-time bottom, he at one point even had to borrow $8 million to meet obligations. This did not help him sleep.

His father reacted rather differently. Dividing his time now between his estates in Ormond Beach, Florida, and Lakewood, New Jersey, long removed from affairs of philanthropy and even longer from those of business, Senior enjoyed himself about as much as a nonagenarian teetotaler could. He played a lot of golf, and did it well enough to be able to send his son a telegram one month after his ninety-first birthday announcing that he'd just played six holes on his Lakewood course in twenty-five strokes. He toyed with his carefully cultivated public image, winkingly acknowledging the Depression by replacing the dimes he'd long given to strangers with nickels. And he played the stock market.

It drove Junior nuts. "There has been no financial and industrial crisis in the world's history so colossal in its magnitude, so far-reaching in its extent and so serious in its character as the present one," he wrote to his father in 1931. "What calls may be made upon people of means before the situation improves, both for urgent philanthropy to relieve actual distress on the part of millions [and for other purposes], no one can predict." But Senior wasn't listening for such calls; he was too busy scanning the market for bargains and borrowing money from his daughter Alta, among others, to finance a gluttonous orgy of bottom-feeding. "Is it worthwhile," Junior pleaded, "in the face of the unknown future so pregnant with dangerous possibilities, to sail so close to the wind?"

Senior was not immediately convinced; in fact, it took the better part of eighteen months for him to emerge from his indebtedness, right around his ninety-fourth birthday. But along the way, a heightened interest in his financial circumstances seems to have led Senior to provoke his son in a fashion unprecedented in their adult relationship. At a meeting in Lakewood with three of Junior's ranking advisers, including Debevoise, the elder Rockefeller declared that an "equitable adjustment" of his and Junior's relative responsibility for the operation of the family office, plus a congruent reallocation of the family's tax indebtedness to the state of New York, required Junior to pay him $3.5 million.

Junior reacted as if he had been violated. After a lifetime's devotion to his father, his father's interests, and his father's reputation, this was a blow beyond measure. "For my own self-respect, for the sake of my standing with my wife and children," he wrote to Debevoise, "I cannot . . . recognize any such claim or the existence" of the grounds on which it was made. He would "be unwilling," he continued, "to consider the payment of one cent on the basis of an adjustment." Near the letter's end, still addressing De-bevoise, Junior nonetheless sounded as if he were speaking to himself, try-ing perhaps to measure by articulation the extent of his grievance. "I have never sought anything for myself," Junior wrote. "I have striven always to serve his interests. Perhaps you can understand, then, how deeply wounded I have been by the criticism which Father's request implies. Nothing in all my life has hurt me as much."

It was a variation on the theme that Junior had played his entire adult life, namely the painful effort to determine his place in the solar system rel-ative to the blinding sun that was his father. This time it had mutated into a rage previously unexpressed. Yet in a matter of days Junior reverted to the more familiar voice of his fifty-eight years. He once again embroidered his daily correspondence with Senior with filial love and respect. Nevertheless, he also took the time to forward to Ivy Lee a two-sentence declaration he had originally embedded in his letter about Senior's $3.5 million invoice:* "I did not seek nor choose to be the recipient of great wealth, with the stag-gering responsibilities inevitably coupled with its marvelous opportuni-ties," Junior wrote. "It has not meant the greatest happiness."

It was a declaration that could have described his efforts on the Upper Es-tate. He had not chosen to be a modern pharaoh erecting the twentieth-century version of the pyramids in midtown Manhattan; yes, it was an opportunity, but not necessarily a pleasant one; and do not think for a mo-ment that success would necessarily bring joy. As late as September 1930, even as Hood was carving a model of the RCA Building out of Chambel-lan's clay, Junior was still expecting that at least some portions of the three blocks would be leased to tenants who would erect their own buildings. As he himself would remember it seven years later, he was facing "immense capital outlays" that he had "never contemplated"—by Todd's "rock bot-tom" estimate, $126 million. In a word, Junior needed a mortgage.

In September 1929, just before John R. Todd disposed of Benjamin Morris and brought in his own design team to execute his program for Metropoli-tan Square, a syndicate nominally headed by former New York governor Al Smith and bankrolled by the financiers Pierre S. du Pont and John J. Raskob hired some architects of its own. Two days later demolition began on the old Waldorf-Astoria Hotel on Fifth Avenue and 34th Street, and just

---

*As it happened, Senior forgot about his request almost immediately after issuing it.

twenty months after that the world's tallest building opened for business on the site.

The process of erecting it may have been dazzling in its efficiency and unprecedented in its speed, but even as it rose, the Empire State Building was already a bust. Depression conditions had so severely wounded the Manhattan office rental business that the vacancy rate reached 14 percent even before the Empire State's 2.1 million square feet—that's *forty acres*—of rentable space were added to the market. Although one of the men responsible for its design said "the production of income . . . is the primary purpose of building," you wouldn't have known it from an examination of the Empire State's operating statements. The owner-developers set rental prices 30 percent lower than the going rate in the Grand Central area, and still the building would open with less than 25 percent of its space leased. During construction the decision was made to leave fifty-six of its eighty-five stories as raw, unfinished space. If you couldn't find tenants willing to move in, why bother with walls?

Raskob, du Pont, and the other members of their syndicate weren't the only ones on the hook for the cost of this fiasco. The Metropolitan Life Insurance Company had granted them a world-record $27.5-million mortgage, a decision that must have looked pretty horrible by the time Met Life's president, Frederick H. Ecker, ran into Tom Debevoise in March of 1931. This time, the venue for one of those fortuitous social/commercial encounters tidily knit into the fabric of upper-class New York was Yeamans Hall, a couple hundred miles up the Atlantic coast from Jekyll Island. Carved out of an old South Carolina plantation, Yeamans Hall provided its members with a lovely setting for the pursuit of golf and what a later age would call networking. The vacationing Debevoise, ever mindful of Junior's financial predicament, sought the counsel of his Yeamans clubmate Albert H. Wiggin, who by virtue of his position as chairman of the Chase Bank was a de facto financial adviser to the Rockefellers.* Wiggin's houseguest in his Yeamans Hall cottage was Ecker, like Debevoise a Chase director.

Ecker was happy to help. Although Todd, who had known him for years, had suggested Ecker as a potential lender early on, Debevoise had another idea—that Junior's development could be financed by selling bonds directly to the public. This plan had little to recommend it except for the rather piquant prospect of Mr. and Mrs. America extending credit to

---

*It was a relationship that would end two years later when it became known that Wiggin had made a bundle off the Depression by short-selling Chase stock.

John D. Rockefeller Jr. Ecker quickly began nudging Debevoise in another direction. Junior could save $650,000 in distribution costs by placing the entire mortgage with a single lender, Ecker said, and his company might well be interested in the role. With $27.5 million of Met Life's money tied up in the Empire State Building debacle and with economic conditions worsening, Ecker's enthusiasm might have been considered rash were it not for two conditions he attached to his offer. His first proviso was that no other debt could be attached to the project, so that he alone could decide how to dispose of the buildings in the event of a default. This was inconsequential, though, compared to his second requirement: that Junior personally guarantee the entire loan.

Junior fretted. His chronically fragile nervous system had already been tested to the point that he had left New York on doctors' orders for a two-week rest in Florida; returning to New York as the mortgage negotiations began, he was back barely a month when he again sought respite, this time in Arizona. Ecker was willing to lend Metropolitan Square $65 million at 5 percent interest, but even this unprecedented sum would cover barely half of Todd's "rock bottom" estimate of the project's cost, and Junior would have to open his own checkbook for the rest. After Debevoise returned to New York from Yeamans Hall, a group of Junior's advisers convened in Wiggin's private dining room at Chase headquarters to determine how to pay for the development of Metropolitan Square. In addition to Wiggin himself, this all-star lineup of legal and financial wizards included Debevoise, Todd, and Todd's partner Hugh Robertson; from Winthrop Aldrich's old firm, the "prototypical 'white shoe'" lawyers Albert G. Milbank and Morris Hadley; and from 26 Broadway, the man who supervised all of the Rockefeller family investments, Bertram Cutler. The solemn gathering mulled possibilities, considered alternatives, and consequently determined that there was no other obvious source for the kind of money Junior was seeking. They agreed to accept Ecker's terms.

For Junior, the mortgage was a sort of certifying event: Ecker's commitment, even if buoyed up by Junior's personal guarantee, served in some fashion to confirm that this enormous endeavor might in fact make financial sense. For Metropolitan Life, it turned out to be a fine investment— "very satisfactory," one of the firm's officials said in 1940, especially in light of the insurer's Empire State adventure; Met Life was eventually compelled to cut its interest rate in half and forgive more than $4 million of that unhappy loan. For Todd, who had first identified Ecker as a candidate, it enabled him to take credit for arranging the record-breaking mortgage, which he did insistently for the rest of his life. For the lawyers, who had to draft, negotiate, and vet a hundred legal documents (half to be signed by the officers of Metropolitan Square Corporation as mortgagor, the other half requiring Junior's personal signature as guarantor), it was a spectacular payday, their fees based on traditional fixed percentages of the mortgage principal. The Charles P. Young Company, legal printers, had reason to be especially grateful: the firm's owner later told Francis Christy that all the documents emanating from the project were "the only thing that kept him out of bankruptcy during the Depression."

The mortgage also gave enduring employment to a functionary in the Rockefeller family offices named Rudolph A. Travers. Travers's duties included combing the *Patent Office Gazette* each week in search of "infringements on our name" and forwarding purchasing requests to various Rockefellers for their consent (to Nelson, August 1934, for the Rainbow Room: approval requested for "Cocktail Caddie $75.00 . . . Pot Rack $50.00 . . . Ice Cream Molds $42.70"). But Travers's permanent responsibility required him to travel once a month for the next nineteen years to the offices of Metropolitan Life Insurance, on Madison Square, to deliver the mortgage payment by hand.

CHAPTER THIRTEEN

If there was any hint of the trouble to come, Nicholas Murray Butler was its carrier: few barometers were more accurate than Butler's unfailingly bad judgment, a counterindicator to set your watch by.

*If Radio City is the best **our architects** can do with freedom, they **deserve to remain in chains**.*

—LEWIS MUMFORD, 1931

After visiting the Graybar offices in February 1931, just weeks before a planned public unveiling of Chambellan's finished models, Butler reported to Junior his "delight and deep satisfaction at the dignity and distinction of the plans. They seem to me to combine in a very exceptional fashion the meeting of practical needs with a development that will be of significance in the life of Manhattan Island."

Had Raymond Hood and the other architects read the letter, they would likely have been troubled by Butler's endorsement; what they were about to show the world may not have been revolutionary, but it was definitely modern enough and functional enough to warrant at least a squeak of complaint from someone as culturally conservative as the Columbia president. Either Butler had allowed his sycophancy toward Junior to triumph over his aesthetic judgment, or he was simply relieved that there was at last something to see.

In the nearly nine months since the Graybar offices had opened, the architects had been tugged toward functionalist shapes by Hood, toward unadorned surfaces by Harrison, and toward the bottom line by Todd. Early on, when a few colonnades and cornices still adhered to the walls of the models and a superfluity of fountains still decorated the renderings, "details of the Rockefeller Art and Amusement Center project" were about to be published in a New York real estate magazine when it was suddenly announced that they had been "temporarily withheld" because of "proposed changes." For the next eight months nothing emerged from the Graybar for public viewing except the crowd of draftsmen, delineators, and modelers exiting the building every afternoon at precisely 5:30. The *Times,* which had published eight separate articles on the progress of the design during a single week in June 1930, went all but silent on the subject until the following March. The one exception was an October 16 item asserting that the plans were being rearranged to accommodate the Metropolitan Opera, a story as indestructible as it was persistently inaccurate well into the second half of the decade.

Over the fall and into the winter of 1930–31, after the various "fling" plans were assimilated and the shape and size of the RCA Building was firmly established, the remaining elements of the plan fell into place. The theaters—reduced to two by now—and broadcast facilities were all pinned to the western edge of the property along Sixth Avenue as firmly as the retail elements were planted along Fifth. The department stores had been replaced by additional office buildings. A "sunken plaza" ringed with shops was sited in front of the RCA Building, with two means of egress: you could go back up the steps on the eastern, Fifth Avenue side, or exit through a western set of doors into an underground concourse terminating at a proposed Sixth Avenue subway station. Pedestrians never liked to retrace their steps, the thinking went, so anyone lured into the plaza by its showy fountain, its elaborate floral arrangements, and its stylish stores would inevitably be guided toward the western exit, there to run a gauntlet of retail enticements in the concourse.

One design element that emerged around this time was Hood's "hatbox," the oval building planned on Fifth Avenue directly in front of the sunken plaza. From the very first of Reinhard and Hofmeister's site plans—the one Todd extracted from the two young architects over Labor Day weekend in 1928—this prime real estate had been reserved for two low, rectangular buildings, but the Chase Bank's interest in a single structure for a headquarters sent the architects back to Chambellan's modeling table. Although Hood would later boast that the overall design process had been dignified by "a marked absence of architectural whimsies," the fourteen-story hatbox indicated that even he could not avoid the sort of self-indulgence "of which most of us architects are guilty from time to time." The curved walls, he argued to a dubious Junior, would draw pedestrians from Fifth Avenue toward the sunken plaza. Harrison disagreed: "You'd never have drawn people down there," he said years later, "because you [couldn't] see around it." By early 1931 the hatbox was forgotten but not yet gone. It remained in place on the plans and in the models being prepared for public display, for Todd knew it would be controversial, and controversy yielded publicity, and it was time for the fanfare to begin.

When Andrew Reinhard and Henry Hofmeister started their practice in 1928, John R. Todd quickly became their most important client, but he wasn't their first. Shortly after they opened for business Walter P. Chrysler hired them to design a hunting lodge on Maryland's Eastern Shore. Just as Todd had earlier employed him to do tenant work on various projects, Reinhard had been engaged by Chrysler in the planning stages of the industrialist's eponymous tower directly across Lexington Avenue from the Graybar. This most effusive embodiment of the Deco aesthetic, which opened in 1930, couldn't have been more unlike the stolid Graybar, chiefly because it had been built for a different purpose. Designer William Van Alen ("No old stuff for me!" he once exclaimed. "Me, I'm new!") utilized the hood-ornament gargoyles lunging from the corners of the sixty-first floor, the frieze of hubcaps wrapped around the thirtieth floor, the lavish appointments of the Chrysler's onyx-trimmed lobby, and the lustrous gleam of its stainless steel tower for one purpose: to sell cars. On the ground floor, the company's latest products rotated on a turntable set up in a showroom window. When the completed design for Metropolitan Square was finally ready for its closeup, Reinhard and Hofmeister went across the street to borrow the turntable from their former client.

The press representatives invited to the design's debut were primed for the event. The Depression, more than a year old by now, had pushed most upbeat stories—expansive stories, optimistic stories—out of the newspapers. But in the three years since it had first popped into print, in May of 1928, the saga of John D. Rockefeller Jr. and Columbia's midtown land had never been far from the city's front pages. Even during those quiet months in the second half of 1930 when the *Times* had nothing to say about the design plans, its pages regularly featured speculation on subjects as varied as the prospects for television broadcasting from the new studios or whether Leopold Stokowski was really ready to abandon the Philadelphia Orchestra for a new podium in Radio City, the name by which the whole project was now generally known. On March 2, 1931, the paper of record announced that the plans for Radio City would be revealed three days later, and if that wasn't an adequate introductory drumroll, a longer story ran on the designated day itself, this one informing readers that the design "will be disclosed tonight when a model of the project will be shown for the first time in the office of Todd, Robertson & Todd."

The cavernous drafting room on the twenty-fifth floor of the Graybar had been transformed for the event. So had the calendar, in a way; it was as if the Depression had never happened. The long tables where designers and draftsman labored by day now supported tureens of lobster Newburgh, bowls of caviar, platters of chicken in aspic. On the walls hung gorgeous watercolors of "lofty exteriors and . . . lavish interiors" executed by John C. Wenrich, an architectural delineator of exceptional talent whom Hood had brought in to translate the architects' imaginings into something that the layman would find enticing. Crowds of newspapermen and magazine writers mingled with Todd, the architects, and various RCA officials, and unquestioningly swallowed their assertions that the whole development would cost $250 million (double Todd's actual estimate); that it would be completed by the end of the following year; and that television programs would be broadcast from its studios immediately thereafter. But the apparition at the far end of the drafting room was even more provocative than the most grandiose publicity claims. Slowly revolving on the turntable in front of a backdrop of velvet drapes, by the *Times*'s account "glisten[ing] like a mirage," stood a five-foot-high model of what the *Herald Tribune* called "the new acropolis of entertainment." This was Radio City, rendered precisely to scale by René Chambellan, from plans created by Raymond Hood and in fulfillment of the vision of John R. Todd.

Every detail was in place, down to the glowing lamps in the buildings' pillared doorways. Front and center belonged to Hood's oval *folie,* likened by the *Tribune* to "a jewel box" and by a more expansive (if no more imaginative) *Times* to a "jeweled powder box on a dressing table." Behind it a plaza shaped like an inverted U to mimic the rear wall of the oval building served as the center segment on a north-south street running from 48th to 51st Streets. This private thoroughfare was bracketed at either end by tall archways carved out of the lower floors of twin forty-five-story office buildings straddling the north and south blocks. Behind them to the west were, respectively, an "unassigned" space and, clinging like a burr to a cuff, a rather modestly proportioned, plainly decorated and, one suspects, cynically included opera house. Along the model's Sixth Avenue side stood the entrance to an "RKO Picture Theatre" on the north block and an "RKO Vaudeville Theatre" anchoring the south flank. A skyscraper intended to house RKO's corporate offices towered above the Picture Theatre, and though plain in aspect it was nonetheless in one way the most remarkable of all the aforementioned structures: it actually got built.

As did the exquisite sculpture at the display's center. The five-foot-tall RCA Building, imposing even at these radically reduced dimensions, was the hub around which the turntable, the model, and the entire conception of Radio City revolved. "It is of severe simplicity, like a gigantic slab set on end," wrote an unnamed *Times* reporter, who also likened it to a cliff, an obelisk, and something "Egyptian or Saracen." It was the nicest thing anyone would say for quite a while.

Of all the people who hated the plans for Radio City—and almost everyone did—none hated them more than Lewis Mumford. In one sense this was odd, as Mumford believed that the twentieth-century city could survive only if a process of careful planning were allowed to take precedence over the odious forces of the open marketplace. Developing three central blocks in midtown as a unit instead of allowing them to be chewed up by individual speculators was an idea straight from the Mumfordian catechism. In 1923 he was one of the founders of the Regional Plan Association, a year after he published *The Story of Utopias,* his first book. Utopias and centralized planning were appropriate subjects for the twenty-seven-year-old Mumford, a self-taught polymath who would spend the rest of his long and productive life searching for an idealized twentieth-century civilization. He eventually "addressed himself on a large scale to every social problem with the confidence of a Victorian prophet," wrote Alfred Kazin, but Mumford first made his reputation writing about architecture, specifically the architecture of New York. Actually, "Victorian prophet" didn't quite do it, insofar as Mumford's architectural polemics were concerned. He was Dante, searching for abominations in the hell that was twentieth-century New York.

Mumford and Ray Hood met at least once, when they served on a Museum of Modern Art panel connected to Philip Johnson's International Style exhibition. One suspects they disliked each other. The congestion that Hood loved, that he thought gave cities their very pulse, was to Mumford a plague. Hood was joky, informal, and never took himself seriously; Mumford was relentlessly serious, even capable of comparing himself to Petrarch, whose disillusion with the Provence of his youth, Mumford felt, matched his own growing abhorrence for the New York he once cherished. By the mid-1930s Mumford so despised the city that he abandoned it permanently for a small town in upstate New York.

Judging by his reaction to the model revolving on Walter Chrysler's turntable, Mumford was sent into exile specifically by Rockefeller Center. In a piece published in the *New Republic* shortly after the press presentation, he warmed up on the just completed Chrysler Building ("inane romanticism . . . meaningless voluptuousness . . . void symbolism"), then let loose on what Hood and his associates had wrought: "The weakly conceived, reckless, romantic chaos that has been projected for this development . . . is the New York Style with a vengeance." He assaulted its "absence of scale," its promotion of "super-congestion," even a perceived moral turpitude evidenced by its "failure to recognize civic obligations." He attacked Junior for "wantonly" wasting the opportunity to do something valuable, then concluded his rant with a roar: "If Radio City is the best our architects can do with freedom," Mumford thundered, "they deserve to remain in chains."

Ouch. Tempered criticism had begun to appear right after the press showing—a *Times* editorial was exquisitely balanced, applauding the effort while questioning its aptness—but Mumford's attack seemed to provide intellectual justification for the blizzard of criticism that soon filled the air. An emboldened *Herald Tribune* said that this "affair of bald cubes assembled in expressionless order" compelled the paper to "protest against a set of buildings typifying . . . the negation of style" and to conclude with a four-word summary: "Radio City is ugly." Architects as varied as the visionary Frank Lloyd Wright and the archconservative Ralph Adams Cram jumped in, the former calling the development "the last atrocity committed upon a people already about to revolt" and the latter all but anticipating architectural Armageddon: "By all means let us see Radio City built as quickly as possible," Cram declared, "for the sooner we accomplish the destiny it so perfectly foreshadows, the sooner we shall be able to clear the ground and begin again."

The lay response was no kinder. The plans "aroused the public as no architectural undertaking has ever done," said a surprised writer at one of the architecture magazines. Newspaper letters columns featured such phrases as "ugliest conglomeration of buildings in New York," "hopeless hodgepodge," "disgraceful symbol of a generation". A member of the Union Club who had previously opposed the club's move uptown from Fifth and 51st wrote to the *Times* to announce that the Radio City designs, "so lacking in imagination, in fertility, in taste, in beauty," compelled him to urge his clubmates to move "as quickly as possible. The sooner the better." The *Herald Tribune,* house organ of the city's Republican establishment, turned to that establishment's most respected member for salvation, noting that his "adventures among buildings have hitherto been governed above all by his faith in architectural monuments as forming 'the patrimony of all nations'. We believe that he will continue in that faith and demand in Radio City what it so sorely needs, the 'inspiration' that he loves."

The paper's wished-for savior, of course, was Junior, and it was direct about its desires, calling on him to "intervene before it is too late." The *Trib's* editors evidently hoped he'd just not been paying attention—as if Junior ever failed to pay attention—and that now, confronted by universal condemnation, he would sweep in and dismiss the miscreants preparing to commit this act of "high-power commercial vandalism" in his name.

But that would have required Junior to listen to this chorus of complaint. When Wallace Harrison worried that he and the other architects would be fired in the aftermath of the furor, Junior put him at ease. During the Ludlow strike, he told Harrison, he had learned that "I should avoid reading about the things that would be too painful to read."

Junior's most important associates in this venture were press-hardened, too. Both Todd and Hood had the confidence—and, in Hood's case, the magnanimity—to withstand the most carefully aimed slings and the sharpest arrows. Just weeks after Mumford's ambush, a relaxed and genial Hood gave a speech at the University of Pennsylvania, where a delighted audience appreciated his "smiling countenance" and his modest assertion that he and his associates in the Graybar offices had designed Radio City to be functional—"but," he winked, "with a wee bit of art." And if the art went unappreciated, he could live with that, too. Criticism, Hood believed, was the public's prerogative: "It may be my building," he once said, "but it's their skyline."

Todd felt comfortable enough with the project's direction to plan a trip to Europe (devoted Republican that he was, Todd claimed he wanted to "fact find" on the state of the continent and report back to Herbert Hoover). Nelson Rockefeller returned from his nine-month, round-the-world honeymoon and jumped gleefully into the thick of things, taking a seat next to his brother Johnny at planning meetings. As a group, the architects began modifying their plans, and if they claimed that the revisions had little to do with public criticism, they protested too much: if you believed, as at least

Hood and Reinhard certainly did, that a project's architectural success could be measured by its financial success, then paying attention to public criticism made sense. The summer of 1931 was given over to modifications: Hood's gardens were added to the buildings' roofs; the sunken plaza was enlarged; the forerunner of Radio City Music Hall was drawn in on its eventual site; and the notorious hatbox was finally replaced by a gesture copied directly from the Beaux-Arts script: two low, rectangular buildings on either side of a formally planted promenade leading to the sunken plaza.*

With the original shock out of the way, reaction to the modifications was mild, at times even approving, and Joseph Patterson's *Daily News* ("We're all for Hood and his crowd") was no longer Radio City's only booster. By August, Hood could say that some of the most vociferous critics had begun to discern "a certain magic—even a touch of romance" in the evolving plans. By midautumn both Hood and Todd came to believe that additional visual amenities would, like the gardens, enhance the development's popular appeal and consequently its rentability. Junior agreed to set aside $150,000 to commission original sculptures and paintings for the various buildings and outdoor spaces. And as final assurance of the project's nobility, an expert was brought in to conjure up a suitably inspiring "thematic synopsis" to guide the commissioned artists.

There is little hard evidence that Raymond Hood alone was responsible for hiring Hartley Burr Alexander to promulgate a theme for the decoration of Rockefeller Center. But everything points to his responsibility for what was possibly the worst hiring decision in the Center's history—everything, that is, except logic. According to the eminent anthropologist Clyde Kluckhohn, Alexander was "a figure from classical Athens or Renaissance Italy or Elizabethan England strangely appearing on the twentieth-century American scene." According to Hood, Alexander was "a famous California philosopher," which was true as far as it went—he did teach at Scripps College in southern California, and he did hold a Ph.D. in philosophy from Columbia. But he was also a popular lecturer, a specialist in American Indian folklore, a mystic poet, an opera librettist, an expert on Latin American mythology, and for a brief period in the 1920s and 1930s, America's most successful "thematic engineer." Possibly the only one, too.

Alexander was teaching at the University of Nebraska in the early twenties when Bertram Goodhue, Hood's first employer, was commissioned to

---

*In 1986, the hatbox enjoyed a form of resurrection as the inspiration for Philip Johnson's "Lipstick Building" on Third Avenue.

design a new state capitol. While Goodhue was working on his plans, Alexander offered to develop appropriate texts to be carved into the capitol's walls, a virtual requisite for monumental public buildings of the era. His words, he told Goodhue, would demonstrate a "rejuvenated provincialism" as a bulwark against "the present chaos of European and world ideals." The man had a knack, of sorts: "Honour to Pioneers Who Broke the Sods That Men to Come Might Live," reads one Alexanderism etched into the capitol building's stone. For the university's football stadium he devised "Not the victory but the action; not the goal but the game; in the deed the glory." And from Nebraska he went national, with major commissions in Los Angeles, Philadelphia, New York, and Chicago, the last of these under the aegis of Hood, who in 1930 had joined the committee overseeing the design for the 1933 Century of Progress world's fair.

It's difficult to know what attracted the worldly Hood to Alexander, but it's possible that Hood recognized in this guileless Nebraskan a sensibility that would mesh well with Junior's. (At one point Junior "expressed considerable interest in the thought of James M. Barrie"—the author of *Peter Pan*—as the basis for a decorative theme.) On his own, and certainly in tandem with Todd, Hood could confidently sell Junior on the general shape, size, and placement of the Rockefeller Center buildings, but when it got down to the decorative fillips and cosmetic gestures a building's tenants (or its owner) might encounter every day, Hood hadn't the same persuasive mastery, nor did he have all that much interest. Hartley Alexander not only had a head crammed full of aphorisms, homilies, and exhortatory declarations suitable for execution in stone (or, better, needlepoint), he had also developed a sense of what he deemed appropriate visual accompaniments for his epigrams. Alexander, whose books included a goofily earnest item called *How to Make Friends with Art,* didn't just write the captions; he visualized the pictures themselves.

Thus did his "Rockefeller City: Thematic Synopsis" become the initial blueprint for the entire decorative program of sculpture, painting, mosaic, and other plastic arts that Junior had agreed to finance. Alexander's prescriptive report began blandly enough ("The Symbolism should follow a consistent plan and theme . . . The Decoration should be splendid without being flamboyant, stimulating without being tiring"), picked up steam with the announcement of the dominant subject matter ("Homo Faber, or Man the Builder"), and then rocketed straight into a tone more Martian than human. An almost random selection from the lengthy document is really the only honest way to represent it:

"The Plaza entrance of Building No. 1 [RCA] is the most important entrance in the group," Alexander wrote.

> Its general theme: the <u>VOICE SPEAKING THROUGH TIME AND SPACE</u>, or more figuratively, <u>A VOICE SPEAKING FROM THE CLOUDS</u>. . . . The tremendous upward sweep of Building No. 1 . . . invites symbolic elements. Obviously only massive engaged forms could be used, these to be treated with utter abstraction . . . : <u>EXPERIENCE</u>, flanked by <u>HISTORY</u> and <u>SCIENCE</u>. . . . <u>UNDERSTANDING</u>, flanked by <u>REASON</u> and <u>SYMPATHY</u>. . . . These great symbols should be like silver crests rising above one another in a challenging sweep. . . . Cinema Theatre: First Foyer: the <u>STEALING OF THE CORN MAIDENS</u> [who are] lured away by the Flute Musician to the Cavern of Mist and Cloud, the entrance to which is a Rainbow arch. There they are concealed beneath the wings of flying birds until the Sun Hero darts his rays through the mists, discovers and frees them, to return dancing to the fields. . . .

And on it went, slogging along in a fashion somehow both solemn and breathless, for thirty-two lunatic pages. When he brought his opus to Todd, Alexander told Hood, "He practically threw me out of his office." Hood tried to comfort Alexander by enumerating how many of his own ideas John R. had summarily rejected. Yet within weeks the "famous California philosopher" was gone, and responsibility for the development of an art theme was turned over to the metaphysicians and phenomenologists in the Rockefeller Center publicity office. They came up with "New Frontiers," which accommodated just about anything.

In *The New Yorker*'s June 20, 1931, issue, the magazine's new architecture critic made his debut in a froth of rage. "People willfully, unfairly, unreasonably thought that they could expect a touch or two of public spirit from Mr. Rockefeller," wrote Lewis Mumford, who had just moved over to Harold Ross's magazine from the *New Republic*. Mumford concluded that "It was by the canons of Cloudcuckooland that Radio City was designed." Two weeks later *The New Yorker* institutionalized Mumford's position as its own: "this frightened magazine," wrote E. B. White in an unsigned note, ". . . share[s] his dread of the organized chaos of the Rockefellian dream."

By late 1933, after many of the paintings and sculptures subsumed under the "New Frontiers" theme had been unveiled (a few of them based on some of Alexander's remnant ideas), Mumford was uncontainable. "I cannot find a word of even faint praise for any of the sculptural or graphic decorations now visible on any of the buildings," he wrote. He continued to hammer Junior and the architects as if they had not merely introduced bad architecture to the streets of New York, but had brought in the smallpox virus along with it. From reading Mumford, you would think he had nothing else to write about—which, it could be argued, he in fact didn't: while Rockefeller Center rose, virtually the only other architectural action taking place in Depression New York was in the Hooverville of shanties and lean-tos huddled together in Central Park. Mumford called the RCA Building's dramatic vertical setbacks "the little scratchy tooth marks the mice have left in their cheese." The Center's entire decoration scheme was "bad with an almost juvenile badness." The gardens on the roofs gave "the effect, from the street, of inverted mustaches." Overall, "bad guesses, blind stabs, and grandiose inanities" had produced "mediocrity—seen through a magnifying glass."

Even that wasn't the last word, as a new Mumford polemic seemed to pop up in *The New Yorker* with the opening of each new Rockefeller Center building. Even when he found something to praise, Mumford couldn't quit pounding on the same themes. In 1935, while lauding the forecourt of the newly opened International Building, he paused to dismiss once more the gardens and the art, calling them "not architectural features but newspaper features, the last ironic note in paper architecture." At last, as the 1930s concluded and the project was nearly complete, when it had established itself as the heart of Manhattan and had vaulted past both the Statue of Liberty and the Empire State Building to become the most popular tourist destination in the city, when the RCA Building's chiseled silhouette had become a virtual symbol for New York itself, Mumford delivered his semifinal judgment: "This group of buildings has turned out so well" as a "visual contribution to the midtown section," he said, that he could pronounce it "a serene eyeful." A little more than a year later came the definitive thunderbolt: "architecturally," Mumford wrote, Rockefeller Center was "the most exciting mass of buildings in the city."

For some reason he declined not only to tell his readers why he had changed his mind, but that he had ever thought anything else.

CHAPTER FOURTEEN

Destroying old brownstones was an act of unbuilding. Building began on July 22, 1931, when spade first touched earth and excavation started. By the following week eight steam shov-

You can't even begin to realize how **desperate** *we were* **for business.**

—JAMES A. FARRELL, PRESIDENT OF U.S. STEEL, CA. 1938

els, one hundred trucks, and more than two hundred men were assaulting the crust of Manhattan. It was perfect digging territory. *The Topographical Atlas of the City of New York,* created in 1874 by the spectacularly named Egbert Ludovicus Viele and still the unchallenged authority in 1931 (and in 2003) revealed that the Upper Estate sat above none of the reclaimed marshland or subterranean streams that crosshatched so much of Manhattan. Dr. Hosack had planted his garden in topsoil that lay just above an ancient variety of pure rock known as Manhattan schist, and over the next seven years excavation crews would remove 556,000 cubic yards of it. This was used to fill the South Reservoir in Central Park (thereby forming the foundation of the grassy plain now known as the Great Lawn), with enough left over to build a few piers near Canal Street, an extension to Riverside Drive in upper Manhattan, some landfill in Queens, and a portion of the Shore Road in outermost Brooklyn.

It was some scene. That first summer of excavation, an army of shirtless workers hammered holes in the rock with pneumatic drills, the holes in turn stuffed with sand-packed dynamite unloaded from fearsome red trucks bearing the legend "Du Pont Explosives," the dynamite-studded rock then covered by enormous blankets of woven steel. Youthful apprentices scurried about gathering discarded bolts and other loose scraps of metal until the blast signal was sounded. After each explosion huge cranes lifted away the steel blankets and then, wrote Frederick Lewis Allen in *Harper's,* the steam shovels moved in to "gobble up mouthfuls of stone" dislodged from "the rocky backbone of Manhattan," a feast of rubble carted away in more than 100,000 truckloads.

Pedestrians flinched at the detonation of each dynamite charge, and despite the introduction of a new device called the Dust Eliminator a powdery mist hovered over the site like the shadow of an unseen giant. Mrs. Vanderbilt wasn't the only neighbor who complained about the ceaseless noise. The reluctant operator of a neighboring rooming house, whose owner had lost it to repossession, wrote pleadingly to John R. Todd, "We are having an awful time keeping tenants in the building on account of your building operation—and in a nut-shell, would say that we are taking it on the chin pretty hard." Before passing the letter on to his field supervisors, Todd scribbled a note across the bottom that he would have done well to have run off on a printing press and handed out as needed over the next seven years. "Let the men on the job show some interest and an effort to be neighborly," Todd wrote, "even if they cannot do very much."

The progenitor of the world's most famous Christmas tree was a relatively modest balsam rising out of a rock floor near the eastern end of the central block. On December 24, 1931, some very fortunate men dressed the tree in strings of cranberries, garlands of paper, and even a few tin cans, then took places in a line beside it. The men didn't *look* fortunate, shuffling forward in their dust-caked work boots and grimy overalls, but as the line reached the clerk standing beside an upended wooden crate next to the tree, each man was handed proof of his luck: a paycheck.

The nation was in horrible shape. A year earlier, the International Apple Shippers' Association had figured out how to unload its surplus by selling it—on credit—to the unemployed men who now seemed to be offering apples for sale on every street corner in every American business district. In August of 1931 the Ford Motor Company virtually closed down its Detroit operation, throwing 75,000 men out of work. Two months later U.S. Steel, Bethlehem Steel, and Alcoa cut the wages of the employees they hadn't already laid off by 10 percent.

There is no comfort in comparative misery, but New York was worse off than most of the country. Unpaid and often uncollectible taxes reached 15 percent of total revenues, plunging a desperate city government so deeply into debt that it owed nearly as much as the governments of all forty-eight states combined. More than a third of the city's manufacturing firms had gone out of business, and *Fortune* estimated that there were three-quarters of a million unemployed in the city, "160,000 of them at the end of their tether." Many learned how to put together the facsimile of a free meal at the Automat, fashioning a pathetic "tomato soup" out of ketchup and hot water.

In the construction business . . . well, there really wasn't any construction business left, at least not until the New Deal began providing federal dollars for various bridges, tunnels, post offices, and other public projects. But that was still more than two years off, and in December 1931 parts of New York looked as if God had gotten bored with the Creation business in the middle of the sixth day and simply walked off the job. Work had stopped on the new West Side Highway, which consequently ran much of the length of Manhattan but without benefit of any exit or entrance ramps. Over in the East River seventeen massive columns rose through the water and into the sky vainly waiting to support the Triborough Bridge, a project that had become more notional than real. The president of the American Institute of Architects urged recent graduates not to come to New York—there weren't any jobs. In the trial issue of a projected architecture magazine prepared by the editors of *Time* and *Fortune,* a columnist wrote, "We wonder if there will ever be any building again." Sixty-four percent of the city's construction workers were unemployed.

Late in 1930, Junior had addressed the employment crisis in his accustomed manner—philanthropically. His check for one million dollars immediately increased the sum collected by a private New York charity called the Emergency Employment Committee by more than 30 percent; the committee's chairman estimated that this single act would create four thousand jobs and support four thousand families. Far more effective than philanthropy, however, was Junior's massive building project in midtown Manhattan. This hadn't been his intention, of course—as he recalled several years later, Junior's original interest had merely been the sponsorship of a "civic improvement" in which he had intended to "participate" with the Metropolitan Opera. But it had transmuted into something as close to Junior's bone as his most dearly held values.

This example of private enterprise promoting public welfare was knit from the warp of Junior's Protestant beliefs and the woof of his Republican principles. At every point along his journey from pietistic Baptist to liberal ecumenicist, Junior embraced no biblical verse more fervently than "Unto he who much is given, much shall be required." Politically, he adhered to a form of Republicanism at odds with the prevailing Darwinian attitude famously expressed by Treasury Secretary Andrew Mellon, a man whose wealth rivaled Junior's but whose spirit did not: "Liquidate labor, liquidate stocks, liquidate the farmers, liquidate real estate . . ." Mellon told Herbert Hoover when the tides of the Depression threatened to swamp the nation. "People will work harder, live a more moral life. Values will be adjusted, and enterprising people will pick up the wrecks from less competent people." Junior's solution to the economic catastrophe was several degrees warmer. "The practical answer to the problem of unemployment," he said at one point, "is to find jobs for men who want to work."

Junior also said that "Idle capital means idle labor," a pretty broad hint about how he felt capital should be occupying itself during hard times and, given the state of the nation's economy, an expression of profound faith in the American future. There is no way of knowing exactly how many people found employment during the Depression through the creation of Rockefeller Center, but it may have been a number exceeded only by the federal government's various job creation programs. Estimates emerging from the Center's press office over the years hovered in the range of 40,000 to 60,000, with occasional spikes to 75,000 and, in the unlikely version presented in Raymond Fosdick's worshipful biography of Junior, a meter-busting 225,000. But even Fosdick began with a reasonable formula, figuring that for every man laboring on-site, two more "worked elsewhere preparing material." A passage from an early press release counted an "army of supply" of 46,000 men, identifying them in cadences that might have come from a *March of Time* newsreel: Here were "miners of iron ore in Alabama and Michigan; of copper in Arizona; of lead in Colorado; of asbestos in Quebec; of asphalt in Trinidad, and of coal in Pennsylvania and West Virginia." There were "lumberjacks, log-rollers and millmen in the great timber areas of the South and the Pacific northwest, and in the mahogany forests of the Philippines and South America." On and on the catalog rolled, alighting on rubber plantations in the Amazon, brick kilns on the Hudson, marble quarries in Italy.

In New York alone, the job creation was enormous. Imagine the size of the work crew required to erect a skyscraper today, multiply by the nine major buildings and two smaller structures in the original Rockefeller Center, and then increase that figure by however many additional hands would have been required to perform the thousands of tasks since rendered superfluous by seven decades of technological innovation (in 1931, for instance, it took four men to seat a single rivet in a beam or girder, and these were the highest paid laborers in the entire project). During the bank holiday that Franklin Roosevelt declared shortly after his inauguration in 1933, "most of the business done by the merchants in town on Saturday was due to 'Todd & Brown currency'"—scrip—that Rockefeller Center had issued the previous day to pay its workers. As president of the American Federation of Labor in the nineteen fifties, George Meany, who had been a rising figure in the New York State union movement in the thirties, said he "could never forget what [Rockefeller Center] meant to the workingman in the depression" and considered the project "a real act of patriotism on [Junior's] part." Two officers of the Sheet Metal Workers International Association wrote to Junior in 1932, "In behalf of Humanity, our Government and our Industry, we desire as a committee to thank you. . . . In this bitter work day world, expecially [*sic*] now, your action stands out as a beacon light to those who earn their livelihood by the sweat of their brow." To know what the union men were grateful for is to know just how bad the Depression was for the construction industry in New York: while other employers were demanding larger cuts, Junior was being thanked by the union officers for "the magnanimous spirit you displayed in favoring only a 15% reduction in our wages."

For Rockefeller Center, this was the other, salutary side of the Depression equation: sellers can get extremely cooperative when there's only one buyer in sight. Junior's concern for the working public was genuine, and his satisfaction in providing jobs was merited. But the delight of those who were spending his money and building his buildings was boundless. For them—particularly for Todd & Brown, the construction management firm run by John R. Todd's son Webster and his associate Joseph O. Brown—the Depression was a lever that saved tens of millions of dollars, accelerated work schedules by months, and made the Rockefeller Center buildings the finest, hardiest, and eventually most valuable office buildings in New York.

As excavation proceeded and foundation work got under way in the autumn of 1931, the three blocks began to resemble a rectangular body of water. In addition to the Hurley and Maxwell properties in the central block, a few other buildings still stood, chiefly some old brownstones in the upper block waiting for the wrecker's ball and in the lower block William Nelson Cromwell's houses waiting for the cranky old coot to give up, move away, or die. But the gaping holes carved by jackhammer and dynamite—in some places as deep as eighty feet—made 49th and 50th, the crosstown streets that trisected the site, look like causeways skimming the surface of a lake.

Soon a field office went up on Fifth Avenue, in the central block. The plaster model put on display was an accurate representation of the planned first flight of buildings: at its center, the RCA Building; in the northern block, facing Sixth Avenue, the thirty-one-story RKO Building; in the southern block, also on Sixth, a large motion picture theater; on Fifth, the two buildings that had replaced the hatbox, designated the British Empire Building and La Maison Française; and east of the RKO, an enormous "vaudeville theater" identified on plans and in the press as the "International Music Hall." Although both Hood and Corbett had been to some extent distracted by their participation in planning the Century of Progress world's fair scheduled to open in Chicago in 1933, the architects remained busy working extended variations on the Center's established theme, particularly on the six buildings of this first flight, which were scheduled to begin receiving tenants late in 1932. In that economy, if you wanted any tenants at all, you had to be prepared to accommodate their wishes, and architects who worked for John R. Todd were accommodating to a fault.

Unless you were one of these architects, it was a horrible time to be an architect in New York. In 1932, Wallace Harrison brought in a salary of $7,929; that same year, just 1 percent of employed Americans earned more than $5,000, and the take-home pay for the average worker was less than $25 a week. Nelson Rockefeller later noted that "what with the Depression and all" many of the men working in the Graybar suite "weren't in any hurry" to finish their work, but he acknowledged that "you couldn't blame them in a way [because] after that job there was nothing ahead for them." Andy Reinhard, in behalf of the entire Graybar team, pledged one hour of salary from each man each week to aid New York's unemployed architects. Even the stingiest must have been glad to pony up; there but for the grace of Junior went every one of them.

As busy as the architects remained, the center of gravity in the Graybar offices was shifting to the men responsible for executing the architects' plans—the 1,860 separate blueprints filed with the city's Department of Buildings—within the bounds of Todd's timetable and his budget. John R.'s organization had evolved into a command center, with various offices arranged by function reporting to him and, more and more, to his younger partner Hugh Robertson. These functional groups included architecture, finance, legal, renting, publicity, and the one now stepping onto center stage, construction.

In other words, Todd & Brown. Corporately separate from Todd, Robertson & Todd, it was nonetheless attached to it as if by an umbilical cord. The two firms shared office space, contracts, and bloodlines. Web Todd and Joseph O. Brown had been put in business by John R., who in the winter of 1927–28, fabulously enriched by the building boom of the twenties, had begun to wind down the affairs of his own firm. Wanting, he said, to enjoy "a time of relaxation after years of hard, driving business," he set up his son with Brown, TRT's chief construction superintendent. Web Todd, who had been working for TRT since his Princeton graduation in 1922 while attending law school by night, was an able administrator, with much of his father's charm but little of his cantankerousness and none of his megalomania. Like his father he successfully married his social life to his business life. In 1930 a developer friend asked him to be general contractor on a sixteen-story cooperative apartment building at One Beekman Place. The project soon became a virtual Rockefeller colony, its residents including not just Webster Todd himself but also John D. Rockefeller 3rd, Thomas Debevoise, Arthur Woods, and the developer, Babs Rockefeller's husband, David Milton, who had launched the project with a million-dollar loan from his father-in-law securely in hand.

Web Todd hadn't the devotion to business that had so forcefully postponed his father's "time of relaxation" in 1929. Shortly after his fiftieth birthday, long after Rockefeller Center was complete, the younger Todd retired and turned his attention to his two great passions, his farm in the New Jersey hunt country and the Republican Party. In 1952, while running Dwight Eisenhower's campaign in New Jersey, he took the time to get in touch with his old school friend Adlai Stevenson. "It does give one a good feeling to know that no matter who wins in November," wrote Todd, "someone of the character of yourself or General Eisenhower will be the next President." Web Todd's manner was congenial, his approach to conflict conciliatory, his style that of the enlightened patriciate to which the Todd family had been elevated through John R.'s great success.

On one side of the two-man desk he shared with Brown, Web Todd's mild disposition enabled him to work calmly through the mountain of details, the scores of contractors and suppliers, the hundreds of daily decisions a project the size of Rockefeller Center demanded. On the other side of the desk the anti-Todd ruled. His lively eyes behind round-framed glasses and a boyish cowlick popping up from the back of his head made Joe Brown look pleasant enough, but he was about as soft as sandpaper. If every organization needs someone to play the brute, the Todd office was well equipped. The opportunity to say no seemed to make Brown quiver with delight, and he never wanted for ways to say it, rolling from abrupt to sarcastic to cruel with the self-absorbed pleasure of a mean little boy torturing a small animal.

Brown criticized unacceptable work from a contractor as "absolutely disgraceful and would not be expected in a garment center job," and easily found himself "convinced that there is nothing for us to do but to clean house." He had no problem at all excoriating the most experienced of the Graybar draftsmen for using an unacceptable typeface on something as inconsequential as the drawing for a cornerstone. Brown refused a man's request for a brief leave to work on Fiorello La Guardia's fusion campaign for mayor in 1933 because, he snarled, La Guardia was no better than Tammany Hall (this was, of course, before Junior's youngest son, David, went to work for La Guardia). One turndown that Brown used over and over again, often as not typed on the back of a piece of already used paper, foreclosed all argument: "what we have is good enough." He knew where every penny of the enormous construction budget went, and he followed each one until it landed with a *chink* on the bottom line. Five years into the project, by which time seven buildings were open and occupied, and Rockefeller Center was clearly on the way to success, he challenged the decision to use a certain typeface for the sign over a trucking ramp. If the general Rockefeller Center font were used instead of the specific International Building font, Brown argued, it would save $89.

Nothing made Brown's fists tighten like the argument over paint colors. "Whether the scheme [of a room] was based on red, white or blue," wrote Walter Kilham, "Brown would explain the first rule: 'It shouldn't show the dirt.' The second rule was that the color be one that would be stocked in the building supply room." "I think brown should be used," he'd type on the back of a torn-up floor plan. "This is what you're trying for," he would bark at the architects, jabbing a well-worn page in a sample book. It was always brown, always exactly the same brown, a color the designers eventually tagged with a name. Not "dirt brown" or "mud brown" or "chocolate brown," they decided. The perfect name was "joe brown."

Brown's willingness to be the bad guy suited him to supervision of the bidding and purchasing processes, and the novel structure John R. Todd had set in place abetted Brown's ability to squeeze suppliers. Three firms of general contractors—one, in essence, for each of the three blocks—were chosen after a bogus bidding process; according to Francis Christy, Todd selected firms he could count on to follow his orders. The name partners of one of the three firms, Barr, Lane & Irons, consisted of two Todd, Robert-

son & Todd alumni (Barr and Lane) and the sons of John R.'s original part-
ner and rooming-house neighbor, Henry Clay Irons. Another of the firms,
Hegeman-Harris Company, was clearly favored by Hood: they had built the
Tribune Tower, the American Radiator Building, and the Daily News
Building.

Each of the winning firms was relieved of the contractor's usual responsibility for purchasing materials and selecting subcontractors. That fell to
Todd & Brown, and mostly Brown. He played the Depression economy
like a virtuoso, and handled the competing bidders the way a tyrannical
conductor treats his musicians. It wasn't enough that the bidders had all
been rendered desperate by the collapse of the construction industry. The
scheme John R. assigned his son and Brown to execute placed potential
suppliers in a panic: all the purchasing for all the planned buildings would
be done at one time. Not only could the size of an order save a faltering supplier from bankruptcy, but failure to land the order would foreclose any future participation in the only major construction project in view. Take, for
instance, the nation's major plumbing contractors. All but idled for more
than a year by the swooning economy, they were now presented with a shot
at a job so huge that the *addendum* to the specifications prepared by Todd &
Brown for the RCA Building alone ran to sixty-six pages. Every one of them
was desperate for the business.

The one-chance-only bidding scheme was like inviting a starving man
to a bountiful banquet and then asking him to sign over his soul if he
wanted to eat so much as a crumb. Web Todd wrote, "I doubt if anyone has
ever experienced a more constant fire" than the assault launched by the
subcontractors, manufacturers, shippers, formulators, and other desperate
suppliers who stormed the Graybar offices daily. The movie theater in the
southern block alone required forty-five different subcontractors or suppliers, from the company that poured the foundation to those that provided
mail chutes and "chair leg ventilators" to another that furnished the theater's organ. Many suppliers tried flanking maneuvers. A brick manufacturer enlisted his boyhood friend, Senator Robert F. Wagner, to make an
approach in his behalf. A cement contractor dispatched William H. Walker,
nephew of Mayor Jimmy Walker, to 26 Broadway, where Charles Heydt
received all supplicants and passed them on, usually without comment,
to Brown. The Minneapolis-Honeywell Regulator Company tried a relay
approach: it asked the president of the American Express Company to lean
on Winthrop Aldrich in the hope that he would in turn intervene with
Todd & Brown. As important to the Chase Bank as American Express

might have been, Aldrich demurred. He had already forwarded so many people to the Todd office, he said, that he just couldn't do it again.

To Web Todd fell the responsibility for being "gracious" to bidders when it was "necessary for political or social reasons." Todd deployed his excellent manners to mollify such potent entities as a division of the Socony-Vacuum Corporation, a Standard Oil spinoff that wanted to sell the developers a few tankers of lubricating oil. Heydt, concerned that any inkling of rigged bidding or other unfair advantage would be damaging to Junior's reputation, generally deflected Rockefeller neighbors, friends, associates, friends of associates, and other hangers-on who were after the stone-carving contract or the varnish-supply contract or the laundry-service contract or some other piece of this luscious pie. Sometimes, though, the courtier was so influential that Heydt, Brown, Todd, and everyone else involved in the process had to step aside and wave the privileged bidder through. Thus did Todd arrange to shift some of the enormous Rockefeller Center freight business—six thousand carloads of structural steel alone—to the Baltimore & Ohio, the Lackawanna, and two other rail lines, "provided [they] make satisfactory arrangements for the purchase of coal from the Consolidation Coal Co." The petitioner who stipulated the quid pro quo, demonstrating a previously unknown affinity for the sort of vertical integration upon which the family fortune was built, was Junior himself: Consolidation Coal was a Rockefeller holding.

Several suppliers received favorable treatment in exchange for renting office space in the development, a state of affairs that would turn into a saga in its own right. But everyone else who wanted to play on this field had to do it Joe Brown's way. The last time anyone had used negotiating muscle so effectively might have been when John D. Rockefeller Sr. consolidated the oil industry. By agreeing to use their product exclusively, Brown got the American Radiator Company to provide all its heating and plumbing goods at a price 10 percent below the lowest price they had ever granted a *wholesaler*. He compelled the Atlas Portland Cement Company to agree to a contract guaranteeing that "if the price of cement goes up, the lowest price at which Atlas has sold cement to us will be maintained until the finish of the job or until a lower price is again quoted." It was a hedge against the possibility of an economic recovery, yet with no risk whatsoever attached to it. The gigantic order of limestone for the buildings' exterior walls came especially cheap because the largest U.S. supplier had been shoved into receivership by the nationwide halt in construction. The banks to whom the Indiana Limestone

Company was indebted (including the Chase) had no choice but to accept the price offered by the only buyer in sight.

Even the largest industrial companies were no match for the deadly combination of a drowning economy and a rampaging Joe Brown. He brought the predecessor of Consolidated Edison to its knees by letting its negotiators know that his engineers were working on plans to include an electric generating plant on the premises. This was a literal truth but not much more: mechanical engineer Clyde R. Place determined that such a facility could in fact be constructed on the site, but that it would cost $2.5 million to build and $146,000 a year to operate. When Con Ed came in at a price of $154,000 a year—with zero capital expense—Brown had himself a very nice deal.

His greatest success came in negotiating the mammoth steel contract. The order for 154,000 tons of structural steel was not only the largest steel purchase ever made, it alone was expected to account for 13 percent of the cost of building Rockefeller Center. A hungry Bethlehem Steel and a famished U.S. Steel engaged in a desperate bidding war, each one dropping its price almost daily. "You can't even begin to realize how desperate we were for business," James A. Farrell, U.S. Steel's president, said later. Actually, anyone watching Farrell's behavior at the time of this reverse auction would have seen a virtual definition of desperation. When Brown finally indicated he was happy with U.S. Steel's price, an anxious Farrell called the young Rockefeller lawyer preparing the contract and begged him to have the complicated agreement ready the next day. The most powerful man in the steel industry arrived at the Graybar offices the following afternoon without lawyers, but with his corporate secretary at his side. The papers were signed and sealed on the spot.

Although Farrell and U.S. Steel lost money on the Rockefeller Center deal, the company did manage to keep two plants open and more than 8,000 men employed. And so it went, for the 1,000,000 square feet of window glass, the 200 miles of brass pipe, the 20 acres of wire mesh; for the 3,000,000 pounds of aluminum, the 12,250,000 feet of copper wire, the 245,700 tons of sand; for every other inch, ounce, or teaspoon of animal, vegetable, or mineral product, and every minute of human sweat and toil, that went into building what a CBS radio commentator called John D. Rockefeller Jr.'s "expression of faith in the future of America."

The Depression's effect on costs was like a slow leak's effect on a tire. John R. Todd's initial $126 million "rock bottom" price tag for the first group of buildings dropped to $115 million by 1932 and to $102 million once all the bills were in at the end of 1935. Even adding in the cost of the four additional large buildings erected between 1936 and 1940, Junior never had to draw down more than 70 percent of the Metropolitan Life loan.

He could have saved more, yet Todd chose to capitalize on the bargain prices through a form of investment—overbuilding. The prospect of renting more than three million square feet of office space in a glutted market provoked him to abandon the just-good-enough standard he had established while developing the utilitarian Graybar Building. As the budget effectively expanded because of the plunging cost of labor and materials, each new expenditure enhanced Rockefeller Center's eventual profitability, either by extending its useful life, ensuring its operating efficiency, or heightening its appeal to tenants. Utility conduits were made larger than normal, the better to accommodate later improvements. A contract may have been concluded with the New York Steam Corporation to provide heat from its 106-mile network of tunnels beneath the streets of Manhattan, but an enormous boiler was nonetheless installed 53 feet below street level, its stack rising 900 feet to the roof of the RCA Building. Soundproofing devices engineered by Hiram Percy Maxim, the man who invented the pistol silencer, were placed near every air intake. Hood's fanciful "hanging gardens" required extensive reinforcement in the steelwork, Todd said, "to carry the tremendous load of the necessary soil." Nowhere were the dollars saved by Depression economies put to more effective use than on the most visible part of the whole project, its exterior walls. Had Hood and Corbett not persuaded Todd to cover those vast surfaces with limestone—"the accepted badge of dignified gentility," said builder William Starrett—Rockefeller Center would have been dressed in brick.

Still, for all the savings and all the upgrades the Depression made possible, Todd and his partners could not resist hedging their bets. In 1940 a visiting insurance man noticed sprinkler heads poking out of the ceiling on each floor of the British Empire Building and the Maison Française. This may have been uncharacteristic or even inappropriate for the high-end retail shops and importing concerns in the building, but it was not accidental. During construction someone had realized that the New York City Building Code mandated that any edifice used for manufacturing had to be completely sprinklered. If the renting hadn't gone as well as anticipated and the Depression had lasted longer than expected, the reasoning went, you could knock down a wall here, open an archway there, and have yourself a couple of nice little factories.

For much of the decade construction was managed by an organizational structure that could have been created by Bismarck, in a setting that might have been painted by Bosch. The tumult of the site, an anthill of workmen and machinery, piles of materials and convoys of trucks, battalions of security guards and regiments of newspapermen and photographers, could probably not be parsed by anyone but Web Todd and Joe Brown. Each building had its own staff superintendent, who attended a daily coordinating meeting and a weekly planning meeting, bringing details from the field to Todd and Brown and carrying back their decisions and instructions to the three construction firms. These contractors, freed from their conventional responsibility to pay for and schedule materials and labor, could focus on the details of building instead of management. Six structural engineers roamed the site inspecting concrete and steel as they were set in place. Four mechanical engineers monitored progress on the various utility systems and the network of wires and pipes—red for hot water, white for refrigeration, yellow for steam, and so on—that spread like capillaries from a sub-subbasement sixty-eight feet below street level. Two architects on the Metropolitan Life payroll wandered ceaselessly around the site to watch the mortgage money being spent.

Todd's ruthless schedule allowed no time for serial construction. While masons finished the brickwork on the RKO Building in the north block, steel rose on the motion picture theater in the south block and the foundation of the RCA Building neared completion in between. Soon the 3,200 carloads of limestone began to arrive from Bedford, Indiana, along with the 50,000 cubic feet of Deer Island granite from Stonington, Maine, for the street-level exterior trim, the 25,000 metal doors from Jamestown, New York, the 23 acres of window glass from Pittsburgh—a never-ending chain of supply that seemed to keep the American railroad industry in business, the traffic around Rockefeller Center in a permanent knot, and the activity on the site in a constant frenzy.

In 1935 a Rockefeller Center press release boasted that "only 50,000 man-hours of labor" had been lost to accidents in the first four years of construction. This may have been a number to be proud of (it represented about one-half of 1 percent of the labor expended in that period), but it only underscored the immensity of the enterprise. It took a full-time insurance office on-site to process claims and seven physicians supported by a regiment of nurses to staff the field hospital in one of the last old brownstones still standing on the north side of 50th Street. Much of the work was dangerous, especially the high-steel acrobatics performed by the riveting gangs and the men responsible for pushing hand trucks bearing several hundred pounds of limestone along unprotected girders spanning large swatches of Manhattan sky. Even more at risk, perhaps, were the men working directly below these aerialists. In this pre-walkie-talkie era, crews on different levels could communicate only by ringing bells attached to long ropes, a signal that it was time, say, to hoist a beam into place. With several tons of metal swinging your way, it was wise to pay close attention to the bells.

To a large degree the labor force was divided along parallel lines of trade and nationality. The brickworkers came chiefly from English stock, the stoneworkers from Scottish. Artisans of French origin applied the finish paint to walls plastered by Germans and Italians. There were no black workers on the site, and Joe Brown was not about to upset that apple cart. When a Harlem-based group called the Cooperative Committee on Employment sought redress, Brown asserted that the Rockefeller Center contractors did not discriminate and "will not bar a colored person who applies" if he meets "the contractors' requirements." These requirements, he added, included union membership. He did not point out that for a black man seeking work in the building trades in the 1930s, union membership was not much more accessible than an apartment on Fifth Avenue.

One non-European ethnic group prospered because of Rockefeller Center: many, if not most, of the high-steel workers were Caughnawaga Mohawks from upstate New York. The Caughnawagas had first displayed their affinity for this sort of work during the construction of a railroad bridge near their tribal lands on the St. Lawrence River in 1886. Praised by a construction superintendent on that job who considered them "as agile as goats," the Caughnawagas soon began to show up high in the girders of projects all over the country. Drawn to New York by the 1920s building boom, previously itinerant work gangs established a permanent colony near the Gowanus Canal in Brooklyn. Now they swarmed to Rockefeller Center, scurrying over the towering steel lattices to be rewarded as "the aristocrats of the site" everyone knew they were: a typical high-steel worker earned $13.20 a day before overtime, which went a long way in mid-Depression Brooklyn.

The iconic photograph of Rockefeller Center workmen eating their lunches as they sit on a beam suspended over thin air doesn't even hint at the audacious dexterity these men demonstrated each day. In every four-man riveting gang, one man used a portable forge to heat rivets to the glowing point, pulled each one from the fire with tongs and threw it across open space to a crewmember who would catch the burning metal in a can. He, in turn, set the rivet in a hole in a beam, there to be held in position with a special tool by the third man while the fourth pounded it into place with a portable jackhammer. Wallace Harrison, fearfully pushing himself ten yards across a high beam on his butt in order to inspect some work on the sixty-fifth floor of the RCA Building, marveled at Mohawks jumping from one beam to another across four-foot gaps, more than eight hundred feet above street level. Photographer William Leftwich was rewarded for his nervy visit to the uppermost reaches of the RCA's steel frame when two workers standing fifteen feet apart on a single beam began to toss a football back and forth.

But when the photographers weren't around, it was all work. In the south block immense grading machines began manicuring the cleared land, preparing it for the construction that would come when Junior, Todd, and Nicholas Murray Butler finally figured out how to dislodge William Nelson Cromwell. In the central block, the excavation directly in front of the RCA Building began to fill at its western end with what looked like a subterranean building—a four-story structure, sixty feet wide, running from 49th to 50th Street. The "ceiling" of this structure was a welded steel platform topped with a layer of asphalt: Rockefeller Plaza, a north-south street resting like a piecrust atop three stories of underground corridors that would be used for shops, maintenance, and storage. The north block saw the rise of the steel skeleton of the thirty-one-story RKO Building, growing a stunning three floors each week and culminating in Rockefeller Center's first "topping-off" ceremony, on February 8, 1932. Smaller and less complicated than the RCA, it actually looked like a building by April, the exterior completed save for the window glass.

In many ways the RKO appeared to be the least distinguished in the first group of buildings, handsome enough in its limestone cloak but standard in its massing. What was not readily visible was a neat trick of puzzle-solving accomplished by Andrew Reinhard's partner, Henry Hofmeister. New York law at the time forbade construction of anything directly above a theater space, but Hofmeister determined that some appendages—entranceway, ticket booths, lobby—of the immense theater rising just to the east could be tucked under the RKO. This was an exceptionally efficient use of ground space, and at the same time would allow the theater, once the el came down, to show its face on Sixth Avenue while resting its vast bulk on less conspicuous land to the east.

If the man who presided over the creation of the Music Hall ever gave credit to Hofmeister for this clever piece of design, there's no record of it. But it's not likely that S. L. Rothapfel, aka S. L. Rothafel, aka Roxy, would have done so, for the impresario behind the creation of Radio City Music Hall would have preferred to have you believe that the whole thing grew directly from his lush imagination. In a way, he was right. The rest of Rockefeller Center was the product of careful planning spiked with some imaginative dreaming, while the most famous theater in the world was, from the beginning, pure hallucination.

CHAPTER FIFTEEN

Peculiarly, William Fox called him "the greatest genius of motion picture production"—peculiar because Samuel Lionel Rothapfel

Don't "give the people what they want"—give 'em something better.

—ROXY

never produced a single film. What he accomplished was far more distinctive than that, had far greater impact on the movie industry, and reached its apotheosis as well as its nadir in Rockefeller Center, at Radio City Music Hall.

He arose from the unlikely soil of Stillwater, Minnesota, a small town on the St. Croix River whose lumbermen had their shoes repaired by a German-Jewish immigrant named Gustave Rothapfel. That Gustave would move his family to New York in 1895, when his son Samuel was twelve, was nearly a historic inevitability: the boy and the city needed each other the way a drum major needs a band—and vice versa.

S. L. Rothafel, who dropped the tongue-tying *p* along the way, took several years to become "Roxy"—both the person bearing the name and the self-invented icon of 1920s America, when the claim that he was the most famous individual in the nation might have been challenged by Babe Ruth and maybe Jack Dempsey, but by few others. By 1932 he could be the subject of a five-page piece in *The New Yorker* that not once referred to him as anything but "Roxy," that never paused to identify him, to invoke a portion of his resumé, or to categorize him with a job description or title: he was as much of a given in American life as the president himself. He got to that point via stints as a "cash boy" on 14th Street, a bootblack, a messenger, a U.S. marine (not, as he claimed, seeing action in the Boxer Rebellion but spending most of his time on a gunboat in U.S. waters). When he mustered out of the Marine Corps in 1905, he may or may not have played semiprofessional baseball in northeastern Pennsylvania but he definitely found his way there somehow and discovered the work—and the style—that would become his life.

The scene is the sort of sentimental tableau that in a few years one could encounter in one of Rothafel's movie palaces. A young man trying to find his way in the world arrives in Forest City, Pennsylvania, peddling encyclopedias. He wanders into a small, family-run restaurant and bar, and while he extols the virtues of his encyclopedia he notices the comely daughter of the proprietor. The music swells, he marries Rosa Freedman, he starts working behind the bar and, in time, opens Rothapfel's Family Theater in the back room.

For the coal-mining families of Forest City, any entertainment was an unexpected gift. For the encyclopedia salesman, it was a transfiguration. Borrowing chairs from the local funeral director (and consequently closing down the show when someone died), hand-cranking a rudimentary projector stocked with Vitagraphs—"living pictures"—that were passed for modest rental fees from small-town theater to small-town theater, augmenting the show first with his own lectures on how it all worked and then with a brief piano recital by Mabel Rennie, a spinster who lived with the Freedmans, Rothafel created the model that would serve him his entire career: don't give the public what they want—give them *more* than what they want. Is there any reason for a dull spot while Rothafel changed reels? Never—that's what Miss Rennie's unlikely presence forestalled. If you're showing a short on the Tournament of Roses Parade, is there any reason not to dip some sponges in rose water, tie them to a fan, and then turn on the fan when the roses appear on-screen?

The spinster pianist, the scented air, the solemn lectures from this earnest young man—soon enough, word of the "high-toned little theater" and the coal-mining families who were nightly filling the funeral home seats traveled beyond Forest City. Benjamin F. Keith, who had started in the business the year Rothafel was born, was the nation's leading operator of vaudeville houses, viceroy of the chain that would in time be signified by the "K" in RKO. He put the young impresario on the road, charging him with bringing his innovations to Keith Circuit houses.

Rothafel became a Johnny Appleseed of the movies, spreading his notions of motion picture presentation across the country. After traveling the nation for Keith he set out on his own, hooking up in each new city with a theater operator whose business needed a strong dose of Rothafel. Milwaukee, 1910, the Alhambra: he installs a baby-sitting nursery, puts the orchestra on the stage, introduces movies where there had been only vaudeville. Minneapolis, 1911, the Lyric: melding motion pictures with an elaborate stage show, he himself becomes news. "Mr. Rothapfel . . . who is directing the destinies of the Lyric, is only a young man," intones the Minneapolis *Journal.* "But he has made for himself a national reputation." Chicago, 1912, another Lyric: now all the elements of a Rothafel show are in place. On June 6, an ad in the *Chicago Tribune* promises "Revue de Luxe: Increased Concert Orchestra, Melodious Pipe Organ & La Basque Grand Opera Quartette—Ten Days with the U.S Battle Ship Fleet–Niagara Falls—Cavalry Test Marches in Belgium—Life Among the Savage Tribes of Borneo—'The Lady of the Lake,' in three parts." The final element, at the bottom of the advertisement but set off just enough to stand out: "Direction S. L. ROTHAPFEL." He was still a month shy of thirty.

Had Todd or Junior or any of the others involved in choosing Rothafel to run the theaters at Rockefeller Center looked carefully at his career, they would quickly have realized that his way with a dollar was not theirs even with a dime. From Forest City onward, there's no evidence that Rothafel ever spent a penny less than whatever was available to him in concocting his hyperromantic vision of entertainment. If all he could afford was Miss Rennie at the keyboard, he went with Miss Rennie; if the owners of the Chicago Lyric had the dollars to support an "increased concert orchestra," then the orchestra would keep increasing, with La Basque Grand Opera Quartette thrown in to boot. Rothafel kept his eye on the gross receipts. He counted the house first and let others add up the expenses later. By then, though, he was usually gone to the next place. And after Chicago, the next place was New York.

"It matters not how humble your theater is, or where it is situated. Try and have an air of refinement prevail throughout." Such was the advice the former marine from Minnesota, who never got past grammar school, who virtually boasted that "my ancestors were peasants [who] never did anything," would soon be giving to the motion picture industry. The industry would listen, too: barely four months after Rothafel responded to a summons to take over the Regent Theatre on 116th Street, in Harlem, *Motion Picture News* proclaimed that he had created "an environment so pleasing, so perfect in artistic detail, that it seemed as if the setting were a prerequisite to the picture." He was already the most admired motion picture operator in the nation.

The first deluxe picture palace in New York, the Regent was a hybrid of the northern Italian Renaissance and the upper Manhattan version of the

Edwardian Age. Few of the era's two-reelers compelled enough of the German Jews who populated lower Harlem's stolid brownstones to fill the Regent's seats. But when Rothafel introduced a sixteen-piece orchestra to play on every bill—and particularly to play, for the first time in any theater, music that was thematically connected to the action on the screen—the neighborhood responded. So did an audience that mattered even more to Rothafel's future: the big-time exhibitors downtown in the burgeoning entertainment district around Times Square. Rothafel had turned around the Regent overnight, and by morning he was gone. Less than six months into the job, he leapt into the very heart of Broadway to take over operation of the new Strand Theatre. After the Strand he soon conquered the Rialto, after the Rialto the Rivoli, after the Rivoli the Capitol, all in the space of six years. Every one of the great Broadway movie palaces, except for the Paramount, became a glittering step on Rothafel's starry ladder.

The word he used to describe himself, and which he bestowed as if a knighthood on a very few others, was "showman." That audiences might attend his theaters simply to see the current picture was, to Rothafel, immaterial. Years later, the critic Gilbert Seldes wrote, "Nothing he ever said or did gave the slightest indication that he had an interest in the moving picture . . . except as an element in [larger pageants]. For a long time I considered him the greatest enemy of the moving picture in America."

Perhaps he was. But he did run motion picture houses, and he did know how to do it with a flair that guaranteed press coverage, gossip, and envy—all of which, of course, sold tickets. When the Strand was held up by three men who tied up the night watchman and blew the safe, Second Deputy Police Commissioner John Robert Rubin refused to begin an investigation until Rothafel signed an affidavit swearing it wasn't a publicity stunt. At the Rialto, Rothafel saw to it that the theater's owners, among them Otto Kahn's brother Felix, bought him what the *Times* obligingly called "the largest life insurance policy ever written on the life of a moving picture theatre director." He understood that the showman himself could be part of the show. By 1917, when he was installed at the Rivoli, he had a suitably grand office and an even grander salary, and also the sine qua non of the mogul: a Japanese body servant, albeit one he trained to skillet-fry hot dogs "Forest City–style."

By the time he reached the Capitol, the 5,300-seat "White Elephant of Fifty-First Street" that was the flagship of the nationwide Goldwyn Pictures chain, the Rothafel approach (and, finally, the *p*-less spelling) was indelibly established. The June 4, 1920, reopening of the huge theater was advertised as the "Newest, Latest Rothafel Motion Picture-and-Music Entertainment." All the houses on the Goldwyn/Capitol circuit, for which he had also assumed presentational responsibility, trumpeted "Presentations by S. L. Rothafel, Originator of this Form of Divertissement."

"Divertissement" doesn't begin to describe it. Brooks Atkinson called Rothafel's presentational style "a cultural orgy." In two hours the Capitol audience might get a concert from the house orchestra, a ballet number, some interpolated singers, a newsreel, a short (such as the immortal *Hagopian, the Rug Maker*), perhaps a historical recitation with accompanying staged tableaux, and then the feature film—all this in a palace of marble and mahogany, silver leaf and rock crystal, an architectural concoction (designed by Thomas Lamb, the Rothafel of theater designers) fully as over-the-top as the show itself. The customer got all this for as little as thirty cents at a matinee, and the orchestra alone might have justified the ticket: 110 pieces under the baton of Erno Rapee, a Hungarian immigrant of substantial skill and sharp commercial instinct who would soon publish the *Encyclopedia of Music for Films,* a collection of some three hundred orchestral snippets appropriate to every possible screen situation. His orchestra was no collection of hacks. The concertmaster was Eugene Ormandy, on his way to the podium of the Philadelphia Orchestra; when Ormandy became Rapee's associate conductor, he was succeeded as concertmaster by Frederic Fradkin, who had previously held the same position with the Boston Symphony.

Rothafel saw orchestral music as the essence of his cherished "refinement." He couldn't read a note himself, but with the innocent zeal of a passionate amateur he genuinely loved the music Rapee and his men created. He even allowed the conductor to introduce Debussy, Stravinsky, and Schoenberg to the Capitol audience, as accompaniments to the theater's showing of *The Cabinet of Doctor Caligari.* Once, at the Rialto, Rothafel actually tried his hand at conducting, the musicians feeling their own way through Tchaikovsky's *1812 Overture* while up in front the stocky man in the maroon velvet jacket flailed blithely away. Rothafel finished four beats ahead of the orchestra—as one observer put it, "somewhere in 1808."

On a Sunday night in November of 1922, Rapee was in his accustomed place in the Capitol pit, this time conducting Richard Strauss's tone poem *Ein Heldenleben*—conducting, in fact, its American premiere. But what marked the evening was happening offstage, and in houses and apartments

far removed from Broadway and 51st Street. Samuel L. Rothafel was introducing himself to a radio audience over station WEAF. "My friends call me
by my nickname, Roxy," he said, with his characteristic, thudding earnestness, "and when you write you can call me that, too, if you want to." Such
were the inauspicious beginnings of three landscape-shifting innovations in
American entertainment history: the birth of commercial broadcasting; the
creation of the variety-show format presided over by a host who was not a
performer; and the transposition of a four-letter nickname into a word fully
part of the language. Roxy—let's call him nothing else from this moment
forward—had arrived.

The first broadcast stations were barely two years old in 1922, and like
any new industry radio was groping toward the rules, the conventions, the
very vocabulary of its future. In New York, WEAF—owned by American
Telephone and Telegraph, and soon to become the keystone of the first network, NBC—had begun to broadcast sponsored programs, although "sponsorship" at the time merely prefigured the public radio model that would
develop in the latter half of the century. Gimbel's or Macy's would be announced at a program's outset, but what they sold and what price they sold
it for went unmentioned.

Until Roxy. Working that November evening in a style closer to that of
a sportscaster than of a theatrical announcer, he described to the radio audience what was onstage. They could hear the music, but the sets, the costumes, even the plot of the feature became visible—sort of—via Roxy's
play-by-play. When, in all ad-libbed innocence, he encouraged his listeners
to come down to the Capitol and see it for themselves, the radio advertisement was born. And when the lines the next morning reached halfway
down the block, four abreast, the radio advertisement was on its way to
commercial beatification.

The following Sunday, November 26, Roxy was back. This time he
opened with, "Hello, everybody—this is Roxy speaking"; at the program's
end, stumbling for a sign-off, he stammered out, "Good night . . . pleasant
dreams . . . God bless you." Within weeks both opener and closer were national catchphrases. Bags of mail filled the Capitol offices as previously unconnected individuals within the signal's reach had been forged into
something resembling a community by what one correspondent called
Roxy's "benediction."

The show was huge, radio's first genuine hit. Because Roxy knew the
novelty of his play-by-play movie descriptions would soon pale, he installed
a studio deep in the caverns of the Capitol and began to produce a weekly

two-hour casserole of symphonic music, pop and classical singing, and merry chitchat. From his stage show he plucked performers who had broadcast personalities, including concertmaster Ormandy and the giggly ballerina Maria "Gamby" Gambarelli, and called the ensuing melange "Roxy and His Gang." Talent from other sources he presented with the same goofy enthusiasm: "Hello everybody," he'd begin. "Now you're going to hear the greatest little girl . . . ," and the little girl would turn out to be the sixty-nine-year-old contralto Ernestine Schumann-Heink. Every Sunday night at 7:20, America listened. Nearly fifteen years later, in the heart of radio's heyday, Aaron Stein wrote in the *New York Post,* "It is difficult to conceive any idea of what American broadcasting might be today if Roxy had not pioneered in . . . transforming radio from an instrument of communication into a form of entertainment."

Roxy being Roxy, one suspects he would have preferred this description: "When science shot lilting melodies through the air and called it radio," the *American Business Record* intoned in 1925, "Roxy was born in the first pink blush of radio's morning. . . . They placed a microphone before his lips, he spoke into it, and his words clutched a million hearts though the miles between were many."

Three-quarters of a century later, you could find traces of Roxy in virtually any telephone directory: the Rockin' Roxy DJ Service in Toronto; Roxy Drug Company in Irvington, New Jersey; Pop Roxy, an all-female rock group in Murfreesboro, Tennessee. There was Roxy Rider the porn star, roxy.com offering "Digital Products for the Digital Age," Roxy nightclubs, unrelated to one another, in Austin, in New York, in Cologne, Germany. Plenty of theaters, of course, and restaurants—but also the Centro Cultural Roxy in Guadalajara, Mexico; a line of Roxy furniture out of Sydney, Australia; the Quiksilver Roxy Pro Women's Surfing Championship at Sunset Beach, Hawaii; the Roxy Hotel in a converted warehouse in Atlanta. And, sublimely, the Roxy Zipper Company in Los Angeles. In 1961, Ben M. Hall, in his superb history of the old motion picture palaces, *The Best Remaining Seats,* compiled a similar list, and asked a question still cogent four decades later: do the proprietors, much less the patrons, of all these establishments have any idea of their eponymous forebear?

The actual Roxy was a man of medium height and placid expression, his most memorable feature heavy-lidded gray eyes that would spark to fire whenever he was crossed. He smoked cigars and a pipe, carried a walking stick, commanded some attention by his bearing but had to demand most of it through solipsistic exhibitionism. After rehearsals of his onstage extravaganzas, he'd gather the company and go over what was good and what was bad. If you did your part well, he could be very complimentary. If not, he would explode in a high-pitched whine, shouting, "Why do you do this to me? Why do you do this to me?" over and over, a martyr in falsetto. He displayed the egoist's trait of overcompensation, affecting lavishly overdrawn manners to neutralize his inherent monomania. "When Roxy thanks a friend," Allene Talmey wrote in 1927, "God and Love and the Sermon on the Mount are all inextricably mixed."

Roxy's wife, Rosa, there when it all began in Forest City, stayed in the background with the children, Arthur and Beta, in their apartment on Riverside Drive. How thoroughly her own personality was subsumed by the force of nature who sat across the breakfast table was revealed by the name she (and everyone else) commonly used. "I'm just Mrs. Roxy," she told a reporter in the first newspaper interview she ever gave, in 1931. "What could you say about me? I'm not important."

There were those—many, in fact—who loved him, chiefly the New York press. Hyperactive and desperately needful of attention, he was a newsman's dream, and he had no problem receiving reporters at home, in bed, in his pajamas. Members of his "Gang" couldn't help but enjoy his public jollity, and both his staff and his performers were nonplussed by the sunny aura that suffused those days when everything was going well. For favored artists, upon whom he lavished the attention of any alert producer, the generosity, the sweetness, and the thoughtful consideration combined powerfully: the great ballerina Patricia Bowman, première danseuse at two Roxy theaters, fifty years after the fact admitted that "I fell desperately in love with Mr. Rothafel." Other members of the company were convinced that Roxy had affairs with Bowman and, before her, Gambarelli.

But no one's fondness for Roxy could possibly match his own. Late in the evening of March 11, 1927, concluding what had to be the happiest day of his life, he stood on the balcony of a modern Xanadu on Seventh Avenue and 50th Street that bore his name. The Roxy Theatre was the apogee of its excessive era. "Take a look at this stupendous theatre," he said to his wife and children. "It's the Roxy and I'm Roxy." What's more, he concluded, "I'd rather be Roxy than John D. Rockefeller or Henry Ford."

Rockefeller—more precisely Rockefeller Junior—wouldn't likely have traded places with Roxy either. While Roxy's mammoth new theater was being readied, Junior was caught up in a rather different project. He had

just agreed to finance construction of his first great New York City benefaction, Riverside Church. The man H. L. Mencken liked to call "John the
Baptist" had over the years shed his narrow creed for a broad ecumenicism
that he wished to nurture on Morningside Heights, just a few blocks from
the Columbia campus. "A shipwrecked man doesn't quarrel about which
lifeboat picks him up," he told his son Laurance. Riverside was meant to be
an enormous ark, nondenominational in creed and biracial in congrega-
tion. Junior did more than write the checks for this particular charity; he
took over active management of the church's construction, serving as chairman of the building committee.

While Junior was tentatively testing his aptitude for the role of Master
Builder, Roxy, his future collaborator, was finishing his motion picture
palace. Film historian Terry Ramsaye, who worked with Roxy for several
years, said of this project, "It was bigger. It was louder. It was more magnificent. It was tremendous. It was the biggest in the world. It was, in other
words, a Roxy." The investors who financed the Roxy Theatre—it would
end up costing roughly four times as much as the hyperlavish Capitol—got
their man pretty easily. They promised Roxy part ownership, control over
design and decoration, and his name on the door. Actually, his name appeared in a galaxy of lights over the door, on the front of every program, at
the top of every advertisement, and in monogram form on nearly every surface, inside and out. Even on the ceiling: shortly before the Roxy opened
Gloria Swanson came by to visit. As plasterers were finishing their work on
the theater's great dome, Roxy and Swanson came out on a catwalk to join
them. She asked to borrow a mason's trowel, and scratched "Dear Roxy—I
Love You—Gloria" into the wet plaster of the ceiling. Roxy ordered that her
words be left there forever.

The Roxy was half theater, half fever dream. Roxy mixed his metaphors
when he christened the place "The Cathedral of the Motion Picture," for in
decorative style it looked more like the world's biggest and fanciest whore-
house. Patrons bought tickets at six box offices, entered a vast rotunda
through six sets of bronze-trimmed doors, and milled about in a grand,
arching lobby where two pianists in tails played twin Steinways. Tall, handsome ushers trained to military precision by an ex-marine named Charles
Griswold wore uniforms that led women to swoon and Cole Porter to rhap-
sodize, "You're the top, you're the steppes of Russia / You're the pants on a
Roxy usher." The 6,200-seat auditorium, in a style Roxy called "Spanish
Renaissance," was a boundless cavern of gold and red. Stalactites of crystal
dripped from coffered arches. Medallions and dadoes, niches crammed

with statuary, fluted columns and scalloped ogives—if this was Spanish Renaissance, then woe unto Spain. When Roxy gave the theatrical producer
Arthur Hopkins a tour, Hopkins looked down into the enormous orchestra
pit and said, "Be careful. Shuberts will want to build a theater there." Roxy
told the *Times* that the theater infirmary was equipped to handle major operations. The whole place, he said in purest Roxyese, was "the largest similar theater in the world."

As extravagant as the public areas were, family didn't hold back—Roxy's
own domain was yet more extreme. His penthouse suite above the rotunda
harbored a massage room, a sauna, immense cedar closets, a dining room
seating fourteen, and a private staircase and tunnel leading directly to his
private box, where gold columns supporting a red canopy framed the regal
splendor in which Roxy and his guests could watch the show. Before or after, Roxy entertained visitors in his penthouse by sitting at his grand piano
and, wrote Ben M. Hall, "playing an intricate bit of Chopin or Liszt with a
great deal of shoulder dipping and body English, then get up and light a
cigar while the music continued to play." It was an Aeolian Duo-Art electric player piano, and given Roxy's general lack of humor, not a bad joke at
all. It all fit a man the *Times* was now, in front-page stories, calling "a world
figure," and whose ushers, on the theater's first anniversary, serenaded him
with a choral tribute:

> Let us tell you, Roxy, now, before we go,
> Let us tell you Roxy, so that you may know:
> We're glad of our places and glad of the chance
> To watch the Roxy make an advance.

Inevitably, the song would come to be called the Roxology.

In Junior's long passage from the arms of the regal Otto Kahn into the
somewhat coarser embrace of Roxy Rothafel, the jilted party—or at least
the one that felt misused—was Columbia University. Shortly after Todd
struck his deal with David Sarnoff and RCA in the summer of 1930, members of the Columbia board of trustees began to grumble that the "general
plan of development," which they had the right to approve, had been sig-
nificantly altered. Hadn't Junior always represented his midtown intentions
as a civic-minded beneficence? How had theaters for vaudeville, plays, and
movies found their way into the scheme? Columbia treasurer Frederick A.

Goetze wrote Arthur Woods that some of the trustees felt the new plans would "tend to give our property the atmosphere of a theatrical district, with its attendant employment agencies and hangers on. . . . In our opinion it appears to fall short of the high type of development which we had expected and hoped for." The trustees decided to accept balm for their wounds in Junior's monthly rent check, and on September 30, 1930, signed off on the theater plan.

Four months later the Roxy Theatre announced that its manager had quit. Despite his assertion to the *Times* when the Roxy opened—"I'll make a bet that in my time or yours you are never going to see this theatre equaled"—he had never let his own millennial hyperbole stand in the way of the next opportunity. He didn't say where he was going, but within days of his resignation the papers began to mention his name in connection with Radio City.

Roxy began working for Junior on April 1, 1931, just two days after returning from a "Roxy and His Gang" vaudeville tour of sixty cities in two months, including a sentimental mid-March stop at his Minnesota birthplace. He was given full responsibility for the enormous vaudeville house planned for the Sixth Avenue side of the northern block, and for a large movie theater—first called the Photoplay, then the RKO Roxy, eventually the Center Theater—in a similar position on the southern block. "The Mayor of Radio City," as he was referred to almost immediately in the press, told the *Times* that he envisioned an "elevated esplanade" bridging the entire Sixth Avenue frontage through twenty-five-foot arches. "This esplanade would be the common foyer of the theatres," the paper reported. "In this way, between the acts, the crowds . . . will be mingled together in a great open space, and the crowd psychology will be raised to the nth power." It was a confirmation of Roxy's belief that "the audience is . . . as much a part of the show as the aggregation on the stage."

Roxy's esplanade never appeared in any plans, and like two additional theaters he talked about (one intended, for some reason, specifically for comedy, the other for drama) it was soon forgotten. But the roof of the Music Hall did provide the architects with the opportunity to provide an appealing space for mingling. Because no structure could be built over the auditorium, this expanse eventually became the site of a fabulous playground for the Music Hall's staff, a wonderland of courts for handball, volleyball, and paddle tennis, deck chairs for lounging, and other recreational facilities, all ringed by an instant orchard of cherry trees and hawthorns. Back when Raymond Hood persuaded Todd to invest in roof gardens because they would justify higher rents for the offices that overlooked them, he didn't figure in the "tenant appeal," as *Architectural Forum* phrased it, of planting some of the gardens not just with trees and flowers but with a gamboling herd of off-duty Rockettes and Music Hall ballerinas.*

Roxy had nothing to do with the Music Hall's roof. (It was one of his successors who instructed the dancers relaxing on the rooftop to "not at any time or under any circumstances remove the tops of your suits.") But from the first moment of his involvement, the interior of the enormous theater was necessarily a collaboration with the Associated Architects. It was quite a match. On one side, a man whose mode of architectural expression was a loony amalgam of styles, eras, nations, and schools—if you had to give it a name, it would be something like Greco-Persian-Portuguese-Alhambra-Rococo-Gothic-Provincial-Pagoda-Traditional. On the other, men under the influence of the burgeoning modern movement.

So off they went to look at theater architecture together. While the bulldozers and steam shovels prepared their site, Roxy and Wallace Harrison led a four-week tour of European theater capitals that was quite a bit grander than the trip Ben Morris had taken under Otto Kahn's sponsorship in the summer of 1927. Joining them were Reinhard and Hofmeister (Corbett and Hood were too busy); O. B. Hanson, RCA's top radio engineer; his colleague Gerald Chatfield; Webster Todd, whom his father had assigned to be Roxy's handler; Harrison's wife, Ellen, Babs Rockefeller's sister-in-law; and Peter B. Clark, one of "the colossal anonymities," as the *World-Telegram* would later eulogize him with rueful irony, "unknown to the public except for a line in fine print on the program."

In fact, without Peter Clark, the American theater might not have developed the way it did. Trained as an engineer, Clark early in his career tilted his efforts toward the mechanical solution of theatrical problems. Before his thirtieth birthday he was an essential part of every show produced by Florenz Ziegfeld. He made possible theater effects that even the motion picture business would grow dependent upon, inventing the system of counterweights that replaced the cumbersome and dangerous sandbags that had been used to pull off scenic changes and building the first hydraulic stage elevator. One neat trick of Clark's devising must have been particularly appealing to Roxy: for the Hippodrome, on Sixth Avenue and 43rd

---

*The magazine never commented on whether increased rents were collected from those offices in the RCA Building directly opposite the dancers' changing rooms, where in the late 1940s the staff of Walter Winchell's Sunday night radio show spent much of their time contemplating exactly what it was that made a Music Hall girl so appealing.

Street, he had concocted the famous "mushroom tank," which enabled a phalanx of chorines to disappear into a pool of water. It was a practical—well, sort of practical—elaboration on the effect you get when you thrust an upturned glass into a bowl of water and a large volume of air gets trapped inside it. At the Hippodrome, when a score of bathing beauties stepped into the tank and vanished, it was a dazzler.

Clark and Roxy had known each other for years, and alone among the traveling party Clark was able to tease Roxy out of some of his more grandiose poses. It turned out to be a four-week gala of lavish meals, expensive wines, and luxurious accommodations. Roxy was the constant host, except when he was the honoree: 150 "theater notables" turned out to salute him at a luncheon in Berlin, and when the party would arrive in one city or another, Harrison recalled, "You might be met by a parade from the RKO of France or something." In Berlin the impresario Max Reinhardt took them to the enormous Grosses Schauspielhaus; in Russia they visited the Constructivist theater clubs that had begun to pop up in the 1920s. Roxy also took time to deliver a radio broadcast in Moscow, signing on—ready for immediate translation—with a hearty "Hello, everybody!"

As it turned out, Peter Clark's innovations were so far ahead of what the Europeans were doing that the trip turned out to be more boondoggle than benefit (and left Clark ticked off that he was expected to cover his own expenses). But the single best-known account of Radio City Music Hall's origins arose from the European adventure. They still talk about it today in the tour of the grand old theater that more than 100,000 people take each year: aboard the SS *Europa*, Roxy found himself one evening on the B deck, gazing out to sea. And there in the sky was a sunset of great beauty, a breathtaking display of light and color cast symmetrically across the ocean sky. That's what the ceiling and the proscenium of the Music Hall would look like, he said to himself: a magnificent sunset of his own manufacture.

In fact, it was a configuration from Rockefeller Center's prehistory, part of Joseph Urban's original designs for Otto Kahn's opera house. But who could get ink—or a myth—out of a story like that?

Had the junketeers really picked up any good ideas in Europe, it would have been a little late to implement them. By the time the *Europa* docked in New York, excavation was nearly complete and crews were finishing the foundation of the RKO Building, to which the Music Hall would be immovably linked by Henry Hofmeister's clever positioning of the theater's lobby beneath the RKO tower. All the architects had to do was agree on a design for the place.

It sorted out fairly easily. Hood was deep into the planning for the RCA Building, Corbett was off giving speeches and issuing manifestoes, and Reinhard and Hofmeister, the maestros of the floor plan, largely remained involved in tenant layouts, elevator siting, and the like. This is not to suggest that responsibility for the Music Hall fell to Harrison by default; on the contrary, his theater work with Corbett on the Bushnell Memorial Hall in Hartford was one of his foremost accomplishments before he was brought in on the Rockefeller Center job. Although he did little actual pencil work on the Music Hall, to Harrison must go much of the credit for the theater's radical break with the recent history of American theater architecture. In the design of Radio City Music Hall, European models gave way to American invention, complexity yielded to simplicity, and the overstuffed stepped aside for the sleek. Two men, working under Harrison's direction, engineered the revolution, one of them a drunk, the other an egomaniac. If the abstemious and self-effacing Junior had ever seen Edward Durell Stone or Donald Deskey at work, it would likely have been their last day on the job.

When Stone first hit New York in 1929, he was many years away from becoming the creator of some of midcentury America's best-known (if not best-liked) buildings. He had first come north from Arkansas to attend architecture school at Harvard, where he dazzled his classmates with his skill and his profligacy. "Ed Stone," it was said in Cambridge, "could draw anything except a sober breath." Walter Kilham, who was his classmate at Harvard and his closest colleague on the Rockefeller Center job, said Stone was the "soul of the school," at once a heavy-duty party guy and a brilliant designer.

From Harvard Stone went to Europe on the same traveling scholarship that Harrison had won earlier in the decade. When he came back to the States in November of 1929, he had only twelve dollars in his pocket but the promise of a gig as a draftsman on the new Waldorf-Astoria Hotel. From the Waldorf job he migrated to the Associated Architects suite in the Graybar at a time, he would remember, when "architects who hoped to work on [the Rockefeller project] could be numbered in battalions." But his talent was clear, at least to Harrison, who had seen Stone's work on the Waldorf interiors and hired him at $125 a week—spectacular pay for a young architect in the Depression.

With his Harvard pal Kilham, Stone alternated bursts of work with explosions of play, and sometimes tried to accomplish both at the same time. Later in the decade, after he had designed the celebrated Mandel House in Mount Kisco, New York, and the Museum of Modern Art on West 53rd Street (Abby Aldrich Rockefeller, primary sponsor), Stone could be found nearly every day at the bar at the "21" Club. (He would stop drinking altogether several years later, but in the early thirties, while working on the Music Hall, he would take his drink wherever he could find it.) Just as he would for all the other buildings, René Chambellan fashioned a mock-up of the Music Hall; for the theater's auditorium, however, he outdid himself and made his model to one-inch scale, a square twelve-by-twelve room whose ceiling was high enough to accommodate a big man standing up beneath it. Stone preferred to do his work in Chambellan's model on his back, a battered derby on his head, by his own admission "pretty heavily laced with homemade wine." As Stone and the other architects corrected the curves in the ceiling or instructed Chambellan to move an organ grille from *here* to *there,* the world's greatest theater resolved into its final conformation under the influence of rotgut.

The Music Hall's mezzanines were Roxy's contribution. He had made it clear to the architects that he didn't want the traditional big balcony hanging over the loge, believing it would divide the house in half, nor did he have any patience for the opera house format, in which boxholders on either side of the orchestra would find it easier to look at each other than at what was on stage. In either configuration, he told Harrison, "Nobody's going to be enthusiastic. They'll forget to clap. They forget everything." To Walter Kilham, he said unless you have a place where the people "laugh and cry together," you haven't got a theater. Thus did the three shallow tiers come into being, cantilevered off the back wall, leaving most of the main-floor audience—more than 3,400 people—with nothing above their heads except Roxy's spreading sunset. The architectural historian William H. Jordy wrote, "The picture of thousands slumped in upholstered ecstasy beneath this mechanical heaven is possibly more disturbing than enthralling." But it worked, and nearly seven decades later it still does.

There were two other things Roxy insisted upon: the seats had to be red ("He didn't know of one theater that was a success that didn't have red seats," wrote Kilham, "and that was that"), and there had to be at least 6,201 of them—more, in other words, than in the 6,200-seat Roxy. With his shallow mezzanines, this wasn't an easy task; in fact, the finished auditorium accommodated only 5,960, but Roxy got his number up to the required

6,201 by counting the seats in the orchestra pit, the operators' stools in the elevators, the chairs in front of the makeup mirrors in the powder rooms.

The building's exterior was a fairly undistinguished effort in the same Indiana limestone as all the other buildings, but Stone innovated by hiding the fire escapes along the 50th and 51st Street flanks behind the sort of metal screens that would years later become his design trademark. He also devised three ninety-foot vertical signs visible all the way over to Broadway and the six horizontal marquees beneath them. Inside the building he was responsible for all the public spaces that give the Music Hall its grandeur. The most notable of these was the Grand Foyer, a room that, wrote William Jordy, "calls for Packards, tuxedos, and evening gowns." This 165-foot-long, three-story space, a paradise of gigantic mirrors and mammoth vertical chandeliers and a sweeping grand stairway and undulating balcony railings, is a design masterpiece—if you can find a way to ignore the gigantic Ezra Winter mural on the north wall, or if you've got Junior's taste in art. The painting, a 2,400-square-foot refugee from Hartley Burr Alexander's "thematic synopsis," was based on a vague Oregon Indian myth about the Fountain of Youth and other foolish human vanities.* "Words fail me with which to express adequately my delight with the Ezra Winters [sic] painting," Junior wrote to Roxy after his first tour of the almost completed Music Hall. Words didn't fail critic Manuel Komroff. He likened the timidly academic mural to "a great wormy intestine floating in a muddy cloud."

Donald Deskey hated the mural. Most of the time Donald Deskey didn't like anything he hadn't either designed himself or anointed by commissioning. About the Winter painting, though, both Deskey and Komroff were right. It was—it is—in Deskey's favorite term of opprobrium, "God-awful." But Deskey cried God-awful too often: Stone's exterior for the Music Hall was God-awful, he said, and his interior spaces weren't much better, and the auditorium was much too ornate, and if only he had gotten involved earlier. . . . To listen to Deskey tell it, late in his long, successful, and phenomenally self-involved life, whatever the other guy did was God-awful, whereas what he himself did was merely engineer the complete reinvention of American furniture design and interior decoration.

---

*Alan Balfour wrote that "Only by reading Alexander can one understand such elements as the awkward gray lumps surrounding the foreground cliff. They are 'the first people, the ancients of mankind.'"

Which was true. The Machine Age designer and theorist Walter Dorwin Teague once said that his generation of designers—men like Deskey, Norman Bel Geddes, and Henry Dreyfuss—could design anything, "from a pen to a city." Deskey would eventually build an international business with more than a hundred employees in six countries, chiefly in product design; his most familiar "pen," as it were, was the Crest toothpaste tube, still unchanged nearly half a century after its introduction in the 1950s. But his "city" was the Music Hall, in whose interiors he fashioned a revolution.

The pre-Rockefeller Donald Deskey was pretty characteristic of his fellow modernists (Harrison, Hood, Stone) except in one critical fashion. While he was sowing artistic oats in Paris (naturally) in the early 1920s and otherwise emerging from the damp chrysalis of his Edwardian-era childhood in rural Minnesota, he was also developing a genuine aptitude for business—for marketing, for promotion, for office management, and for all those other things that Hood, for one, never bothered to master. Stage designer Lee Simonson put it succinctly: Deskey was "an artist," he said, "with a good sense of double-entry bookkeeping."

In 1925, Deskey made a second trip to Paris, this time to attend the Exposition Internationale des Arts Décoratifs et Industriels Modernes, the event that launched the Art Deco movement. This gala of aluminum and steel and plastic, of straight lines and sharp edges, was a life-changing event for him. Shortly after returning from Paris and a German pilgrimage to the Bauhaus in Dessau, he was hired by the Franklin Simon store to decorate its Fifth Avenue display windows. A commission from Saks Fifth Avenue followed, and the Braque-like abstract shapes he concocted woke up the Manhattan art world. Soon he was part of a group brought together by the furniture designer Paul Frankl to discuss and promote modern design and architecture; other members included Hood, Harrison, and William Lescaze, the last of whom at that point "had only designed an ashtray," said Deskey, but soon would create one of the first great modern skyscrapers, the Philadelphia Savings Fund Society Building. While Lescaze fiddled with ashtrays, Deskey introduced mass-produced tubular metal furniture based on designs by Marcel Breuer and Ludwig Mies van der Rohe that he had seen in Dessau.

The critical stop on Deskey's path to Sixth Avenue and 50th Street was at 10 West 54th Street, where in 1929 he designed and installed galleries for prints, paintings, and ceramics on the seventh floor of Junior's townhouse. The client, of course, was Abby, not Junior; Deskey had come to her attention through the windows he'd designed a few blocks away at Saks. She recognized that what Deskey was designing was a faultless match for the modern works she was collecting: a sleek, stark repudiation of the romantic and the classical, an essay in stainless steel and Bakelite and other modern materials. To Junior, Deskey's decoration would likely be profound insult piled atop severe injury, but Abby may have figured that her husband would never enter the gallery rooms anyway, so why hold back? Two years later, while Junior was traveling in the far west, she wrote to him, "On Monday I got the pictures hung in my gallery. I hate to say 'my gallery' but I know you object to my saying 'our gallery.'"

It is difficult to conjure at least one aspect of that spring morning in 1932 when Deskey, through Harrison and Hood, was given his chance to pitch for the Music Hall interior design job. Can one possibly imagine Junior's reaction to a man who had not only designed that odious gallery of Abby's on 54th Street, but could also describe himself in one of his press releases as "a prototype of the cosmopolitan man. . . . A modern man of multiple interests . . . world traveller . . . cosmopolite and cognoscente"? Deskey wore gray spats, well-tailored dark blue suits, and a pocket-handkerchief so crisply folded it might have cut bread. An exquisitely trimmed mustache accented his lively eyes, and he brought it all off with an air of exceptional confidence.

The notion of staging a competition to pick a designer for the Music Hall's interior probably came from the architects, who felt that trying to marry their divergent ideas into something coherent was hopeless. But one senses Junior's hand in the list of competitors: Wanamaker's, Marshall Field & Company, Lord & Taylor, W. & J. Sloane (who, said Deskey, "had never had a piece of modern furniture or accessory in the place"). But also on the slate were Eugene Schoen, a modernist on the faculty of New York University, and Deskey.

Rather than present a statement of intent accompanied by a series of sketches, as was customary in such instances, Deskey decided to overwhelm the selection committee. Exhausting his savings and setting aside all his other work, he brought in a team of draftsmen to execute forty detailed renderings of various rooms and more than a hundred scale drawings of furniture he'd designed specifically for this job. He mounted the drawings on placards, each one accompanied by fabric swatches, upholstery samples, materials for covering floors and walls.

On the day of his presentation, scheduled for 9 A.M. in a large room in the Graybar suite, Deskey drove into the city from his home in Mount Kisco, stopping at a deli on East 57th Street for coffee and a Danish. On biting into the pastry, he felt his mouth begin to swell. It was, he knew immediately, a reaction to Brazil nuts, to which he was severely—and, in medical circles, somewhat famously—allergic. The counterman found a physician to give Deskey a shot of adrenaline. "Oh, you're the famous Brazil nut case," the doctor said. "Do you mind if I told my wife? She's specializing in allergies and I'd like to have her observe this."

Deskey declined the opportunity, got the shot, and went to his corkwalled apartment on 51st Street to get ready. The adrenaline made his hand shake as he shaved, but it also stoked him up for the task ahead. Presenting to Junior, the architects, the managers, Roxy, the RKO brass—to thirty-five people in all—he charged through three and a half hours of nonstop demonstration, elaboration, and persuasion. Two days later Ed Stone called to say he'd won.

Roxy had his own ideas and chose to convey them to Deskey directly. "Portuguese rococo," he said. Deskey, thinking fast, convinced him that what he really meant was "modern rococo." Roxy seemed to like the sound of that, and went away happy.

Oxymoron that it was, "modern rococo" was not entirely inaccurate, insofar as Deskey was concerned. He would later blame his friend Stone for making the Music Hall "more rococo and ornate than if I had been on my own," but that was long after the event, and may have had more to do with burnishing a reputation than correcting the historical record. This was pure Deskey; hidden inside his dismissal of Stone's excesses was a license he was issuing to himself, allowing him to take credit for whatever someone liked about the place while simultaneously creating a goat to take the blame for any perceived missteps.

Whatever his self-justifications might have been, there's no denying the impact of Deskey's interiors. What Deskey knew, and what the men who selected him for the job knew, was that a historical line had been crossed between the opening of the Roxy in 1927 and the design of the Music Hall in 1932. "The introduction of sound motion pictures," Bosley Crowther wrote, "brought a certain realism to the screen that changed the quality of illusion provided by the silent film." And, implicitly, the desire for illusion in the theaters they were shown in. The Rialtos and Rivolis and Roxys had been built for an era of fantasy and mirage, when the screen was filled with sheiks charging across desert sands and pirates sweeping maidens into their muscular arms. The Music Hall would belong to an era of Fred and Ginger, well-cut tuxes, and sparkling martini shakers—also a fantasy for most Americans, but a fantasy grounded in the moment. That was logical; what was shocking was how Deskey (along with runner-up Eugene Schoen, who had been chosen to design the RKO Roxy, in the southern block) moved theater design, and with it interior design, from the oxcart to the airplane without any intermediate steps along the way.

On a warm, muggy Monday, June 27, 1932, the most ferocious bear market in New York Stock Exchange history was about ready to bottom out; the Dow Jones Industrial Average lay only 1.71 points and eleven days away from its all-time low, a drop of nearly 90 percent from its pre-Crash peak. Even graver evidence of economic disaster was presented in the *Times,* which reported that a slump in the speakeasy business compelled "116 petty offenders in prohibition cases"—bartenders, mostly—"to go to jail for two days each instead of paying the customary $25 fine." A petition circulating among New York businessmen called for the removal of the rogue mayor Jimmy Walker, whose financial malfeasance was even greater than his passion for his city. "I would rather be a lamppost in New York than mayor of Chicago," Walker once said, but on this June day Chicago was where he was, along with the rest of the Democratic Party luminaries and functionaries who were about to nominate New York's governor, Franklin D. Roosevelt, as their candidate for president.

On the site of Dr. Hosack's ancient botanical gardens, the vast excavations were rapidly filling up. Temporary seats and a dais were being put into place for the coming Saturday's dedication of the cornerstone for the British Empire Building at Fifth and 50th. On the Sixth Avenue frontage, the brickwork for the RKO Roxy was being readied for the superimposition of the theater's granite and limestone facade.

The International Music Hall, soon to become Radio City Music Hall, had begun to look like a building. The steelwork had been completed, including the installation of a gargantuan, three-hundred-ton truss to support the great ceiling/sunset in the auditorium: one more "world's largest" for the Rockefeller Center publicists, permanently afloat in their self-made sea of superlatives. The contract for the design and installation of stage equipment by Peter Clark's firm was announced, a document that called for not only the creation of the real thing but a half-inch scale model of the stage as well, roughly the size of a kitchen oven. Music Hall set designers and directors would work out their scenery and their stage directions on Clark's model—complete with working elevators, turntables, flies, and motorized curtain—for the next half century.

That same day, Rockefeller Center formally proclaimed Donald Deskey the winner of its design competition and allowed Deskey to issue his first statement revealing his intentions. In an uncharacteristically jaunty play on words, the release characterized the garish school of theater design as "gilt-ridden." The *Times* introduced Deskey as "the noted modernist," and Deskey introduced himself as an advocate of "sane modern design as differentiated from modernistic design. I use the term 'modernistic' in a derogatory sense to cover the multitude of interiors which take as their starting point mere deviation from established form." Novel materials continued to be his trademark, and the Rockefeller Center press release promised "bas-reliefs in cork, murals of inlaid linoleum, bakelite and aluminum, pyroxalin-coated fabrics of rare design . . . hairhide upholstery . . . and pigskin wall-coverings."

Revolutionary stuff, but a little arcane: who knew from pyroxalin, or whether it worked with pigskin? What caught the most attention in the announcement of Deskey's appointment was the list of artists he intended to commission to execute original works for the Music Hall. Earlier in the year, rumors that the Rockefellers would be contracting with foreign artists to decorate the Center had roiled the art world. Now Deskey rattled off an American all-star team: painters Stuart Davis and Georgia O'Keeffe, sculptors William Zorach and Robert Laurent, ceramicist Henry Varnum Poor. (Those were some of the contributors he eventually landed; he also promised Maurice Sterne, Walt Kuhn, and Max Weber, but those commissions were never consummated.)

One name was conspicuously missing from Deskey's roll call. At the end of the press release that had detailed Deskey's plans in direct quotation came this unattributed disclaimer: "Ezra Winter's mural, the largest in the world . . . , was undertaken before Deskey assumed charge of the interior decoration of the big theater." Deskey had made it clear to the publicity office: separate me from that piece of crap.

Because Stone's plans for the Grand Foyer were complete and Winter's mural was already well under way, the announcement of Deskey's appointment had a deflating little phrase built into it: he would be responsible, the press release said, for the interior furnishings of the Music Hall and its "31 auxiliary rooms"—for the most part, its bathrooms and lounges. Though critics would inevitably have their fun with the notion ("American Art has been used only to glorify American plumbing," Manuel Komroff wrote in

Creative Art), the artists themselves weren't remotely insulted. "It was an opportunity to get a work out in public," Stuart Davis said, "even in a men's room."

Until the advent in 1935 of the Works Progress Administration and its ample schedule of public projects, the Depression was as dreadful a time for artists as it was for architects, contractors, bricklayers, and everyone else. Even as important a figure as Davis, who had lost his teaching job at the Art Students League to a budgetary axe, was dependent on a fifty-dollar monthly stipend from art dealer Edith Halpert. In April 1932, shortly before Deskey started handing out commissions, the annual exhibition of the Society of Independent Artists devolved into something resembling a peasant market in some backward country; more than forty paintings, including works by such artists as Chaim Gross and Alfred Maurer, were bartered for "everything from zoology lessons to 88 pounds of coffee," said *Art Digest.* It was a very hungry art community that was complaining so loudly about the rumors that the Rockefeller interests were planning to hire foreign artists.

Less than a month after the Society of Independent Artists fiasco, the Museum of Modern Art, now situated in a five-story limestone row house at 11 West 53rd Street that Abby had somehow cajoled from Junior, mounted *Murals by American Painters and Photographers,* an exhibition put together by a young Lincoln Kirstein. It was a show, Kirstein said with appealing candor, "made urgent by the problem confronting the architects" of Rockefeller Center. "While the Museum does not take sides in this controversy, it does believe that American artists of less academic characteristics have not had a fair opportunity to display their possibilities."

One can sense in the show's provenance the fine hand of Nelson Rockefeller, displaying the mastery of intrafamilial tactics that had already made him primus inter pares in the third Rockefeller generation and had him rapidly gaining on the second. Nelson and Kirstein were charter member of the museum's Junior Advisory Committee and frequent lunch companions as well. Nelson had also been making his presence felt more and more in the Graybar Building, which might explain how it was that John R. Todd was seduced into underwriting the mural show's catalog. He had also become very friendly with Roxy, and was developing a growing interest in the Music Hall.*

---

*Part of this interest was connected to his effort to find jobs for numerous Dartmouth classmates and their relatives. Included among these was the future film director Joseph Losey, whom Roxy hired as assistant stage manager. Years later, a less than grateful Losey referred to Roxy as "a grotesque little man."

It's impossible to imagine how John R. must have reacted to the show. It was one thing for the critics to lay waste to the choices the twenty-four-year-old Kirstein had made ("In sheer, dismal ineptitude the exhibition touches bottom," said the *Herald Tribune*), but Junior and other wealthy and powerful men had to endure the arrows contained in the works themselves. Hugo Gellert's piece, entitled *Us Fellas Gotta Stick Together,* showed Rockefeller Senior, J. P. Morgan Jr., Herbert Hoover, Henry Ford, and Al Capone (to whom the title quote was attributed) camped behind a wall made of moneybags. William Gropper produced an aggressively offensive joint portrait of Morgan and Andrew Mellon. Ben Shahn was somewhat less provocative; he showed the anarchist martyrs Sacco and Vanzetti laid out in their coffins.

Somehow, Nelson managed to soothe a furious museum board, sheepishly apologizing "for the unpleasant situation which has arisen in connection with the present exhibition." He also called personally on Morgan, who, Wallace Harrison said, "couldn't have been a better sport" about the way he was pictured. For dealing with Junior, Nelson had the most potent of allies: his mother. According to Shahn, Abby once told him genially that "come the Revolution, they will find I have some Groppers and Ben Shahn's pictures of Sacco and Vanzetti in my house, and they will perhaps spare me." She apparently didn't mention Diego Rivera's sketchbook of May Day in Red Square, which she purchased in 1931, around the same time that Nelson bought his first piece from the Mexican painter.

The MOMA show may have been intended, as one commentator wrote, "as 'first aid' to the Radio City commissioners in deciding upon their decorators," but the critical reaction and the political fireworks were certainly no balm. Yet if Donald Deskey was disturbed by any of the noise, he didn't let it discourage him in his choice of artists. Stuart Davis, Louis Bouché, Henry Varnum Poor, Henry Billings, and Georgia O'Keeffe all had works in Kirstein's exhibition, and each was among the first group of artists commissioned by Deskey to execute pieces for the Music Hall. The managers and the architects imposed no aesthetic or political limitations.

For Deskey, more valuable than the MOMA show was the unstoppable Edith Halpert. If anyone could take credit for helping Abby become "the outstanding individual patron of living artists in the U.S.," as *Time* called her, it was Halpert, who was her adviser, her buyer, her friend. Halpert also was the go-between who provided the introduction to Deskey when Abby saw the designer's windows at Saks, and the roster of her Downtown Gallery became the shopping list for Deskey's Music Hall art program. Stuart Davis was a Halpert artist, and so were the sculptors William Zorach and Robert Laurent and the painter Yasuo Kuniyoshi. Halpert also brought to Deskey's attention the work of some artists she didn't represent, notably the little-known young sculptor Gwen Lux.

With Deskey in charge, Halpert whispering in his ear, and especially with Robert Edmond Jones, the outstanding theatrical set designer of the era, brought in as the Music Hall's staff art director, the New York art community began to believe that something positive might be happening at 50th and Sixth. Jones spoke ardently of "a potential art-loving audience numbering 12,000 people a day who before and after the performance can see and discuss . . . the work of contemporary artists." Deskey raised a protofeminist banner: "We have long since overcome the mid-Victorian notion that women can never be artists of merit," he said, and in addition to O'Keeffe and Lux, he brought into the project textile artist Ruth Reeves and, as his own top aide, designer Marguerita Mergentime.

Even though Deskey was sympathetic to the financial plight of the artists, he soon learned to use the Depression economy as effectively as Joe Brown did. A magazine report said that "One of the artists recently calculated the amount of labor it took to do the walls of the room assigned him. Had he been a scene-painter, working at the union scale of wages, he would have fared a great deal better." When Deskey started lowballing her client Robert Laurent for his two-piece sculpture *Goose Girl,* Edith Halpert was dumbfounded. "Donald's chest expansion is increasing hourly," she wrote to Laurent, lamenting the influence of "the elegant gents of the fifties" with whom Deskey was collaborating. "The whole outfit," she continued, "is about the craziest bunch of gazooks I have encountered."

For Halpert, that was pretty harsh: Abby was her good friend and her best customer, and she was comfortable enough with Junior to address him as "John." But the nickel-and-dime parsimony she was battling in behalf of Laurent and, equally, William Zorach, eventually wore her down. "Deskey is more slippery than I had imagined," she wrote to Laurent, who, like Zorach, would receive $850 for the large aluminum nudes each of them had been commissioned to create. "The price is ridiculous, and I shall leave it to you entirely." To Deskey's credit, he did manage to persuade Alcoa to cast both pieces, as well as Gwen Lux's, for free. It's possible that the quid pro quo was the aluminum-foil wallpaper he created for the men's smoking lounge—a design idea whose time would never come, alas for Alcoa—but the result was that Deskey presumably had a few more dollars available for the artworks themselves.

If you're among the hundreds of millions who have visited Radio City Music Hall and looked beyond the stage extravaganza to the other wonders the hall contains, you've seen a collection of artworks and design ideas that range from the stunning to the pedestrian, from true invention to pale cliché. Deskey's own designs are uniformly superb: the witty stenciled aluminum-foil wallpaper he called "Nicotine"; his lively, Cubist-derived carpet pattern, "Singing Women," on the auditorium floor; most of all, his several score bold, glossy chairs, tables, and other furniture pieces in the downstairs lounge that are the brilliant apotheosis of the Machine Age aesthetic. René Chambellan, given a reprieve from his modeling duties, executed a charming series of six brass plaques for the Sixth Avenue doors, each of them portraying a different musical act. Stuart Davis's *Men without Women* (removed from the Music Hall in the hard days of the mid-1970s, returned to it in 1999) is an outstanding work, so vital in composition that Picasso used a newspaper photograph of it to help him position the forms for his monumental *Guernica.*

At the other end of the scale, Louis Bouché rightly considered his own *Phantasmagoria of the Theater* in the downstairs lounge "very bad"; late in his life he wrote that "the last time I saw my mural, I noticed that someone had placed a huge vending machine in front of it . . . a blessing in disguise." Witold Gordon's *History of Cosmetics* in one of the ladies' rooms is a wan, lifeless dud. Deskey may be blameless for Ezra Winter's mural, but it's there, it's huge, and it's dreadful.

One thing the visitor doesn't find in this singular collection is a painting by one of the first people Deskey commissioned, Georgia O'Keeffe. "I have such a desire to paint something for a particular place," O'Keeffe wrote to a friend in 1929, "and paint it *big.*" She was forty-two years old, one of the best-known painters in the country, an artist whose works were already selling for more than $5,000 apiece—this at a time when one could buy an original Picasso for as little as $310. Two years later, when Kirstein began soliciting submissions for his MOMA show, O'Keeffe leapt at the opportunity. Her mural, a mix of fantasy and pictorialism—large flowers suspended in the night sky over Manhattan—was one of the few pieces in the show to get positive notices. If the Kirstein exhibition was in fact an audition for Deskey, it helped win O'Keeffe a part in the Radio City Music Hall extravaganza.

Deskey wanted O'Keeffe to paint all four walls and the slightly domed ceiling of an eighteen-by-twenty-foot ladies' powder room on the second mezzanine, her work to frame, wrap around, and otherwise provide a setting for the nine makeup mirrors Deskey had designed for the walls. When he offered her his top fee of $1,500, she accepted. Her husband, the sixty-eight-year-old photographic pioneer Alfred Stieglitz, exploded. On one level, Stieglitz had a point. As one of O'Keeffe's biographers wrote, he "had devoted the past sixteen years to raising the price of a single O'Keeffe oil to several times the fee being offered for the entire mural." Partly because of the vigilant Halpert, every artist on the job knew what every other artist was earning. Soon, so would every gallery, critic, and collector in town. Stieglitz immediately recognized the damage Deskey's puny check might do to the prices for his wife's other work.

But Stieglitz, whose controlling urges—and skills—were brutal and unremitting, had other agendas as well. He hated "the Mexican disease called murals," and accepting commissions from the likes of the Rockefellers, he felt, was a form of whoring. He was also clearly enraged by the plain fact that O'Keeffe had accepted the job without his approval, a gesture of independence that set him on a course that would have disastrous results.

He began with an assault on Deskey, whom he telephoned, apparently without O'Keeffe's knowledge, to say she could not do the room for less than $5,000. As Deskey would remember it, he pointed out to Stieglitz that his wife had already signed a contract, and the fee in the contract was $1,500. Stieglitz sputtered that his wife was "a child not responsible for her actions," a comment that may have horrified even the self-regarding Deskey. Then Stieglitz "came back a few days later and said . . . 'she's very anxious to do this,'" Deskey recalled. "'Except she won't do it for $1,500. She's going to do it without cost, except for her materials.'" And then he said that the materials would cost $5,000. Deskey once again cited the contract and didn't budge on the price.

As she prepared to do the mural, O'Keeffe had to contend with a smug and wary paymaster on the job and a volatile brute pounding away at her at home. All summer and into the fall Stieglitz hectored her constantly, even accusing her of betrayal. "No one in my world wants me to do" the Radio City painting, O'Keeffe wrote to a friend, "but I want to do it." And to another, she wrote, "I'll get Hell [from Stieglitz] if I fail." Around this time the painter Peggy Bacon described Stieglitz as "charged with some high explosive which seems about to shake [his aging body] to bits." O'Keeffe stood right in the path of the shrapnel.

On September 24 she came into the city from her upstate home in Lake George to study the room, still under construction; she envisioned a garden of camellias climbing up the walls and arching across the ceiling. The hall's scheduled opening was confirmed for late December, and now O'Keeffe began to worry about time. She wrote her friend Dorothy Brett, "I can't paint a room that isnt [*sic*] built and if the time between the building and the opening isn't long enough I cant [*sic*] do it either." When she visited again in October, the room was still not done, the canvas for the walls not yet in place, and when she expressed her scheduling concerns to Deskey, he was unsympathetic. He told her that the contractors "will put the canvas up. You'll have plenty of time to do your damn flowers on the wall."

On November 16, O'Keeffe came back to New York again, this time ready to paint. She had thought she'd need ten weeks to complete the work; she had fewer than six. Stieglitz was spending more and more time—more and more publicly, too—with his young mistress, Dorothy Norman, and his verbal abuse of O'Keeffe for her acceptance of the Radio City commission had not ceased. The tumult of the construction process proceeding around them, Deskey, his assistant, and O'Keeffe went to the room, where workmen had hung the canvas on which she would paint. As they sat there, a ripping sound came from one of the walls; the canvas was separating from the plaster. O'Keeffe left in tears, and the next day Stieglitz called Deskey to say she had suffered a nervous breakdown, and would be unable to fulfill her contract. Soon, nearly broken by the events of 1932, she began a two-month hospitalization.

Deskey, who had little time before the scheduled December 27 opening, brought in Edith Halpert's client Yasuo Kuniyoshi to do the room—an odd choice given his well-known slow work pace. But Kuniyoshi pulled it off, a lovely, sensual garden of tulips and anemones, delicate grasses, and broad, Rousseau-like greenery. It was one of the finest works in all of Rockefeller Center until it was defaced in a phenomenally misguided renovation in the early 1980s.*

Writing in late 1932, Lewis Mumford grudgingly admitted that he sort of liked the powder rooms that Kuniyoshi and others had created for the Music Hall—but, he complained, "half the human race is barred" from them. So it was when O'Keeffe, four years later, finally got the chance to do

---

*A subsequent restoration, in 1999, salvaged much of its original charm.

her first mural: it went up on a wall just a few blocks away, at Elizabeth Arden's famous Fifth Avenue beauty salon.

In the latter part of 1932, a pedestrian walking along the south side of 50th Street toward Sixth Avenue could look about forty feet up on the wall of the nearly completed Music Hall and see the first works of art installed in Rockefeller Center: three allegorical roundels memorializing the performing arts, each of them eighteen feet in diameter, crafted from copper, bronze, aluminum, and chrome-nickel steel, the metals painted in bright vitreous enamels. Deskey no doubt thought them "God-awful," but Deskey had no say over the building's exterior decoration. Conceived as part of Alexander's "Homo Faber" theme and likely positioned by Edward Durell Stone, they were executed by Hildreth Meiere, a ceramicist and decorative sculptor whose work had earlier adorned Manhattan's Temple Emanu-El and St. Bartholomew's Church, as well as the Goodhue-designed, Alexander-themed state capitol in Lincoln, Nebraska. "Proto-WPA," her style has been called, approvingly; the product of "some giant [who] had spat on a pure space," according to a grumpier conservative critic circa 1932.

Even an admirer of the Meiere medallions, though, finds a hint of a far greater work of art farther up that same mammoth wall. At the very top sits the lip of a balcony. Just beyond the balcony, tucked beneath the giant three-hundred-ton truss resides Donald Deskey's masterwork, an exquisite group of rooms known as the Roxy Suite. If Nick and Nora Charles had lived above a theater, this is what their apartment would have looked like. The cherrywood walls of the living room terminated in a ceiling twenty feet high. ("I'm smothering," Roxy had complained to Wallace Harrison when he first saw the room. "Cceiling's too low." Harrison cut through the beams and started again.) The round dining room was topped by a parabolic dome; beneath it, eighteen people could be seated and served around a black table, the opaque panel at its center suffused with glowing light cast from below. There were two kitchens conveniently outfitted to function as broadcast studios as well, and a pair of bedrooms. "Carpet so thick it suggests snowshoes" ran beneath furnishings that comprised a dazzling, Deskeyan flourish of rare lacquered veneers, polished metals, and glossy plastics. He loved exotic woods with names like macassar ebony, thuya burl, and palisander almost as much as he cherished Transite, Bakelite, and Permatex. Light fixtures and lamps, each one of modern—not modernistic!—

design, were placed low on tables and along the walls, providing an oblique luminosity Deskey found particularly flattering to women.

According to Francis Christy, Roxy used his suite to "nap or spend the night or engage in a frolic if he so desired," but he never lived there. Even if he'd wanted to, the law made it impossible: New York's building code said only janitors could reside in office buildings or theaters. Edwin Goodman, proprietor of the Bergdorf Goodman store on Fifth and 57th, who lived with his family in a penthouse above the store, had himself listed in city directories as the building's janitor, but that was the sort of playing-outside-the-rules that the rectitudinous Rockefellers would never have tolerated. It also implied a sense of humor and a lack of pretense utterly alien to Roxy.

Roxy had learned to love Deskey's "modern rococo," and even began to suggest that the idea for the design scheme was, of course, his own. "I didn't conceive the idea," he said. "I dreamed it. . . . The picture of the Radio City theatres was complete and practically perfect in my mind before artists and architects put pen to drawing paper."* To Walter Gutman, whose "News and Gossip" column in *Creative Art* was the diary of the New York art world, this must have been quite a surprise. Roxy, Gutman's sources had told him, originally wanted all the murals to cleave to the theme "Motherhood and Childhood," including one particular piece that would feature a clown shedding a tear. When told it was trite, wrote Gutman, "Roxy's electrons raised his body to its full dignity as he replied, 'A broken heart is never trite.'" Instead of mothers and children and clowns, he got Stuart Davis, who claimed quite a different set of inspirations: "gasoline stations; chain-store fronts and taxicabs; synthetic chemistry . . . Earl Hines's hot piano and Negro jazz music in general." Davis also published a little magazine named, in a most un-Roxyish fashion, *Shit.*

But Roxy was adaptable, and he had plenty of things other than brushstrokes to worry about. He quarreled with his former partners over the use of his name at the RKO Roxy; he attended to the installation of Peter Clark's elaborate stage mechanicals; he supervised the setup of a lighting scheme designed by Professor S. R. McCandless of the Yale Drama School (no white lights, McCandless mandated, only ivory, because of their salutary effect on "feminine makeup"). Presumably, Roxy also began to figure

---

*At another point he gave credit to his adoring fans, asserting that the Music Hall's design was the product of "experience gained from a study of 6,000,000 letters" from the public. This would have required him, during his twenty years in the theatrical business, to have studied 300,000 letters a year, or 821 a day, or—factoring in his typical twelve-hour workdays—68 an hour.

out what sort of entertainment he would present in the Music Hall, but he declined to reveal his thoughts. It was almost as if he were imagining something so grand, so new, that to discuss it would somehow diminish it.

In August, four months before the Music Hall's scheduled opening, the drumbeat of publicity began to intensify. Deskey welcomed the *Chicago Tribune* into his office on 57th Street, where the paper's correspondent found "a young, very busy man [sitting] in an office . . . among the sketches and blueprints [evaluating] the offerings of his assistants." What Chicago wanted to know was what kind of clothing a woman should wear to the Music Hall. "Modern clothes," said Deskey. "Exactly the clothes women are wearing today." In October art critic Louise Cross was invited in to gush over Rockefeller Center, calling it as "the most important single step that has been taken so far" in the development of modern sculpture, including Deskey's "stroke of genius" in the selection of the young "and extremely significant" Gwen Lux to execute a large, nude Eve. In November, Roxy grabbed the spotlight for himself: *Roxy and His Gang* went out over NBC on Sunday afternoon, November 13, the first broadcast from anywhere in Rockefeller Center. Same network, same day of the week, same emcee as the first Roxy show, which had aired almost precisely ten years earlier.

Now the Winter mural went up in the Grand Foyer, affixed to the concrete wall with an indestructible compound made from white lead. Touring journalists from the popular press were shepherded through the unfinished Music Hall and the RKO Roxy, dazzled with details of the lavish spending, enticed with glimpses of the vast auditorium spaces, regaled with assertions of grand accomplishments; Henry McBride of the *New York Sun* was assured by someone from the architectural staff that "we have solved the problem of acoustics. We now guarantee acoustics." Writers from the specialized trade press were given angles of their own: the awestruck man from *Plastics and Molded Products* was led to proclaim, "It is not difficult to believe that this theater contains more plastic uses than any other building in the world."

Roxy was now operating in three modes: publicist, producer, and construction foreman. He was superb in the first capacity, unmatched in the second, and—well, whatever common touch he had was now long past, and his communications with the workmen were at best strained. While his friend Nelson Rockefeller, son of the world's richest man, could spend a lunch hour sharing sandwiches with carpenters or electricians sitting on a beam out in the sun, Roxy had attained a grandiosity that threatened to separate him from the very people who comprised his audience. To the world he was always Roxy; to his staff he was only Mr. Rothafel. Doris Pallet, his longtime rehearsal pianist, said, "No one ever turned his back [on Roxy] in his office; you backed out." He might still know the name of everybody who worked for him, but he expected them to hold the door for him whenever he passed by. Inspecting the construction, he'd pick his way through oceans of plaster and forests of scaffolding, his chauffeur following at a "respectful distance," remembered Louis Bouché, "carrying [Roxy's] lap robe."

In the best of times Roxy's workday was a broken-backed impossibility: in the office noon to five, home for dinner, nap till ten, back to work until three or four in the morning. As the December 27 opening neared, time for naps and visits to his new apartment in the Majestic, on Central Park West, began to evaporate. The previous year Roxy had been hospitalized with what he had thought was indigestion but turned out to be a mild heart attack. Now he was beset by acute prostatitis, and a private nurse accompanied him all his waking hours as he raced toward the opening night he knew would be his finest hour.

It would not, of course, be his alone. Designer Robert Edmond Jones had been part of the Music Hall team since nearly the beginning, and Roxy had arranged to bring back to the orchestra podium his old comrade from their days at the Capitol, Erno Rapee, who had decamped to Hollywood two years earlier to serve Warner Brothers as music director. Now a battalion of key personnel from the Roxy Theatre began its eastward march along 50th Street. Charles Griswold, the General Pershing of the usher corps, and Sydney Goldman, assistant theater manager, came over to take care of the front of the house, and brought a platoon of ushers with them. On the creative side, almost the entire core of the Roxy Theatre's staff jumped to the Music Hall: associate producer Leon Leonidoff; ballet mistress Florence Rogge; Rogge's sister, Hattie, who headed the costume department; associate conductor Charles Previn; lighting engineer Eugene Braun. So complete was Roxy's raid on his old operation that even Anna Beckerle, the nurse who had run the Roxy infirmary, came over to the Music Hall, where she would preside over cuts and sprains and fainting spells for the next thirty-five years.

Rapee was acknowledged to be the very best in his profession, as was Jones in his. Leonidoff would become the Music Hall's most successful producer, and Florence Rogge is a major figure in the history of American ballet. A young costume designer named Vincente Minnelli, who joined the Music Hall staff that fall, would do pretty well in motion pictures. If you measure an executive by the quality of the people he hires, Roxy was nonpareil. But of all the people he brought over from the Roxy or recruited from other places, none was more important to the Music Hall's future success than a slight, sandy-haired former financial clerk from Westfield, New Jersey, who loved to dress in light blue, wore a thin, exquisitely trimmed mustache, lived in an apartment on Riverside Drive with his mother and sister, and was rarely happier than when he could stand in the wings of the Music Hall's vast stage and shout, "Shake it up for daddy, girls!"

Russell Markert first got the idea for a line of loose- and long-limbed precision dancers while watching the John Tiller Girls, a twelve-member English act tucked into an edition of the Ziegfeld Follies in 1922. He had already become an assistant dance master on Broadway, and now he had the notion of assembling an act similar to the Tiller Girls, but American, taller ("with longer legs," he said), and more numerous. Three years later, transplanted to St. Louis, where he mounted shows for the theater-owning Skouras brothers, he presented his first troupe of sixteen Missouri Rockets—none shorter than five feet three," none taller than five seven.

Performing Markert's complex tap routines in exact formation, kicking chin high, locking arms all the way down the dazzling line (right arm over, left arm under), the Rockets were an immediate hit. Soon Markert took them on the road as the American Rockets, and in 1928 they found their way to New York, where they were to join the cast of a Broadway revue, *Rain or Shine*. Markert's girls were getting ready for the show at Bryant Hall, a rehearsal space on 42nd Street, when the *Rain or Shine* producers, postponing the opening because of book problems, laid them off. A girl in the line who had been with Markert since St. Louis knew Charles Previn, who had conducted the orchestra at the Missouri Theater before joining Roxy's staff. Stranded in New York with no gig in sight, Markert and his girls returned to Bryant Hall to audition for Roxy, tapping their way around postcelebratory debris from a Hungarian wedding the previous evening. Roxy, accompanied by Leon Leonidoff and Previn, needed to watch for only a brief time: the American Rockets were now the Roxyettes.

But only when they played the Roxy. As successful as his dancers were in the mammoth movie palace, Markert had the entrepreneurial and managerial skills to turn his troupe into a big business. He soon had ninety-six young women working a variety of stages. One detachment of Rockets traveled with the national company of the finally launched *Rain or Shine,* another appeared with the Marx Brothers in *Animal Crackers,* a third contingent worked the "subway circuit" of New York–area theaters beyond Manhattan, and the best of the bunch—now up to thirty-two in the line—decorated the stage at the Roxy. Markert scoured the country looking for girls to add to his roster; in Boston he would occasionally raid one dance school for sixteen at a time. He liked to say that wherever he traveled, the cry went up, "Hide your daughters, Markert's coming to town!"

But even the Roxyettes/Rockets couldn't withstand the trends working against them. By 1932, retreating from the cultural and economic tides that had swamped vaudeville and reduced his Rockets to a single contingent, Markert found high ground at Rockefeller Center. He announced in November of 1932 that he would be terminating his arrangement with the Roxy Theatre at month's end. Just two weeks later, Markert and his girls showed up for work at the Music Hall; rehearsals for opening night were about to begin.

By the time the Roxyettes came on board, other members of the Music Hall company were polishing their opening night acts in the Palace Theater, where Roxy and his staff had rented office and rehearsal space. The show that had existed only in Roxy's mind began to take shape. Rapee and his ninety-piece orchestra, joined by the new Radio City Music Hall Glee Club, worked on the accompaniments to the enormous variety of musical acts Roxy had signed up for the opening. Florence Rogge, leading what would be the first full-time, resident ballet company in the United States, drilled her twenty-eight ballerinas in the dances she had created for the star, Roxy's favorite, Patricia Bowman. As soon as Peter Clark's incredible stage was ready to perform its tricks at the Music Hall, Roxy and his associates set out to see what it could do.

Even Ziegfeld could never have imagined a stage like this one. Three gigantic pistons fifty-seven feet deep and twenty feet in diameter operated three separate elevators topped by a three-piece revolving turntable fifty feet wide, the whole array of mechanicals able to make the stage look like a wedding cake, an amphitheater, a landscape in high relief—or all three in sequence. Thirteen different motors controlled cables sewn into the three-ton, satin-faced, asbestos-lined stage curtain, the motors programmable to open up the entire 144-foot-wide proscenium or to close down like a camera shutter to a single man-sized opening. An eight-thousand-gallon water tank lodged beneath the stage provided the hydraulics for the elevators, and a separate mechanism governed the movements of Clark's most impressive creation: a bandwagon that rolled along railroad tracks from just outside the musicians' dressing room to the top of the orchestra pit elevator, where it would rise to stage level. After completing the overture, the orchestra could then sink back down, perhaps to travel all the way beneath the stage to the rear elevator, which would lift the musicians back into audience view, this time behind the dancers or other performers. For Roxy, this was candy. For the opening night show he was putting together, he wanted a confectioner's factory full of the stuff.

With four weeks until the premiere, Roxy immersed himself in the planning. The list of acts grew daily, among them the young comic dancer Ray Bolger; the monologist DeWolf Hopper, whose declamations of Ernest Thayer's "Casey at the Bat" had kept him working well into his seventies; and, still early in her career, the future empress of modern dance, Martha Graham. Squadrons of seamstresses at every costume shop in the city set to work cutting and stitching the 1,117 different outfits, changes included, that the evening would require. At one point Roxy ordered a redesign of the uniforms for his ushers, complaining that "they are beginning to look like full admirals"; his sudden change of preference, wrote Hugh Blake in *The New Yorker,* threatened to "ruin . . . the epaulette, gold-braid and frogging industries of the country." He presided, with Harvey Corbett and Nelson, over a ceremony in which twenty-five mechanics were given certificates and gold buttons for outstanding craftsmanship in the hall's construction. At rehearsals, sitting in the middle of the theater "surrounded by confusion, secretaries, yes-men, busboys with food," he imposed a whim of iron on the evolving show.

The *Herald Tribune* provided a vivid sense of Roxy at one rehearsal: "'Take those tables out of there,' cried Mr. Rothafel into the loud speakers, superfluously. 'Take 'em out! They make it look cheap and common!'" It's a great scene, and you can imagine Roxy being played by, say, Warner Baxter. A few minutes after the offending tables have been removed, Roxy, sitting at the desk he'd rigged up in the middle of Row MM of the loge, complains about a chill on the back of his neck—"Get the house manager and stop that draft," he shouts; then he's overruling Leonidoff, who has told singer Jeannie Lang, one of Roxy's Gang, not to laugh at a particular point in her song. "Of course she'll laugh there," Roxy cries. "That laugh of hers is famous! Go ahead and laugh, Jeannie!" Sometimes, though, he's a little less precise in his instructions; another journalist caught Roxy shouting, "That's ordinary! I want it done differently!"

Of course, doing things differently, to Roxy, might simply mean doing them in a fashion that could draw press attention. Thus, on Tuesday, December 13, just two weeks before opening night, he played his ace: announcing that he believed them to be "somewhat in advance of popular appreciation," he ordered the cast-aluminum nudes that William Zorach, Robert Laurent, and Gwen Lux had executed for Donald Deskey removed from the Music Hall. "I found myself unable to endorse the selection of these subjects with my personal appreciation," Roxy said, and if he couldn't appreciate them, "it seemed that my own reaction, wholly honest and sincere, would be repeated in the reaction of the audiences who would frequent this building."

Laurent, whose *Goose Girl* was one of Deskey's first commissions, pointed out that Roxy had long ago seen drawings of the work; photographs of all three pieces had, in fact, already been featured in official Music Hall press releases, which boasted of the "175,000 office workers [who would] view daily the work of a distinguished group of American artists." (Several laborers in the hall had been amusing themselves by pinning brassieres to the statues and placing cigarettes between their fingers.) Even John S. Sumner of the Society for the Suppression of Vice, who on most days could locate depravity before he had his morning coffee, said he had "no moral objection" to the sculptures, even though he did allow that they seemed a little out of proportion—"but," he apologized, "maybe that's because I don't know much about modern art." Anyone paying attention could reasonably have wondered, if these straightforward, representational pieces were, as Roxy insisted, "somewhat in advance of popular appreciation," then why had he picked them for banishment rather than Stuart Davis's highly abstract, decidedly modernist painting?

By the time Zorach had announced he would put the plaster cast for his piece on public display elsewhere, and Lux had threatened legal action, and the American Society of Painters, Sculptors, and Engravers had issued statements condemning Roxy, and word had leaked out that Nelson and Abby were dismayed by Roxy's philistinism, the controversy had provided New Yorkers with nearly ten days of prominently displayed stories and pictures. One, in the *Daily News,* showed four society women thoughtfully examining Laurent's banished *Goose Girl,* a tableau that had been obligingly made available to the photographer by the publicity department. By the time this artificial storm had blown past, the most memorable comment—maybe the most serious one—on the three offending nudes had been attributed to De-Wolf Hopper: "I've had six wives," he said, "and none of them looked as bad as that."

On December 18 the *Times* published a special "Rotogravure Picture Section" on the forthcoming opening, its elaborately printed pages touting "the first completed unit of Rockefeller Center ready to open its doors to the public." A *New Yorker* writer who had just toured the Music Hall announced the dawn of a new era in theater design. Sensing a good thing, Markert and Roxy had increased the Roxyette line to forty-eight dancers. Rehearsals for various parts of the program (there never was a complete, full-cast run-through) lasted most nights until 4:00 A.M.; on Christmas Eve work ceased at 3:00, but first call for Christmas Day was still 8:00 A.M. "The last six days and nights were all one rehearsal," recalled dancer Margaret Dunne, "and some of the girls didn't even get to bed at night." Roxy announced that his office had received 60,000 requests for the 6,000 opening night seats. Nelson alone wanted 44 in the first mezzanine and Roxy dashed back a note: "Will take care of the seats for you, of course, and you are going to have the front row—what do you think of that?"

Addressing a luncheon at the St. Moritz Hotel, Roxy finally made a public announcement describing his entertainment policy and what was in store for the carefully primed, thoroughly stoked, ready-to-be-ravished public. "I stand here in almost abject humility," he said. "This is the first time in my career that I have attempted to do anything without moving pictures. We will not have movies in the Music Hall. We have traveled all over the world to secure talent for it." He spoke with particular pride about Martha Graham and Robert Edmond Jones and some of the other high-toned types he had added to his team. He didn't say that the members of Graham's troupe—in their dark, severe costumes, always walking as a group escorted by their rehearsal pianist, speaking to no one else and leaving the building the moment their rehearsals were done—were perceived as such an oddity by everyone else that the Roxyettes and the Glee Club singers and all the rest called them the "Graham Crackers." Graham herself was told that the rest of the company thought "[we] were Greek and could speak no English."

In one of his last public pronouncements before December 27 Roxy said, "This thing will make theatrical history." And did it ever.

Opening night of what the advertisements called "The Supreme Stage Entertainment of All Time!" began with a dancing curtain. But that was after everyone was seated, after they had marveled at the stunning design of the Grand Foyer, after they had responded to the buglers who had summoned them inside the huge auditorium, where the gilded ceiling, unobstructed by balconies, made a visitor feel "as though one were a Lilliputian standing inside an old-fashioned collapsible drinking cup." There were two shows that night: the one made of music and dance and light on the stage, and the one shaped of limestone and glass and silk and steel, augmented by large quantities of daring, vision, and cash.

Across town, in his sister Babs's apartment at One Beekman Place, Nelson began the evening playing host to the forty-three guests he'd asked Roxy to save prime seats for—the architects, designers, key office staff, and other principal figures in the Rockefeller Center saga. Deskey was there (it was a double bill of Deskey that evening; he'd recently remodeled much of Babs's apartment) but the Music Hall's two other primary progenitors were not. Roxy, as one would expect, was frantically dotting the building's last *i*'s, such as having Henry Varnum Poor's vases and ashtrays in the lounge downstairs screwed into place in order to thwart the worst instincts of souvenir collectors. The other missing figure was Edward Durell Stone. Not long before, his work on the Music Hall all but completed, Stone had gone on vacation to Bermuda and while there discussed designing a home for a personal client. When the managers found out that he was working for someone else while collecting a salary from Rockefeller Center, he was fired—on Christmas Eve. Had he been any less self-involved, Roxy (the man who claimed to believe that "a broken heart is never trite") might have wept at Stone's circumstances: the thirty-year-old architect, a new father, alone at what should have been his greatest moment, wandering through the crowd on the rainy opening night in rented white tie and tails. The Little Match Girl herself, imagining the wonders she'd never see, couldn't have made a sadder tableau. "Then," recalled his first wife, Orlean Stone, many years later, "our Depression began." It was more than a year before Stone would again have a regular job—working with Deskey, for forty dollars a week, on the Mandel House in Mount Kisco.

The opening night crowd, smiling through the unrelenting rain, emerged from a long, slow-moving line of cabs and limousines creeping beneath the elevated tracks on Sixth Avenue, where traffic cops had been placed at every intersection from 43rd Street all the way up to 55th. They arrived beneath the magnificent marquee designed by Mortimer Norden, the lighting specialist who had made Broadway into the Great White Way and had here arrayed 6,000 feet of neon tubing along the edges of Ed Stone's vertical signs—creating, Norden said, "a Maxfield Parrish sky." Doormen (none, by Roxy's edict, shorter than six feet) helped the arriving audience thread their way through the mob of press photographers and newsreel cameramen crowded beneath the marquee.

It was a society columnist's feast day. "Never," wrote one, "were so many top hats, so many furs and lorgnettes seen at a music hall." Here, in a collar of white ermine atop a silver gown, was Amelia Earhart, with Bernard Gimbel and Mrs. William Randolph Hearst; over there, Barbara Hutton, Prince Matchabelli, Mr. and Mrs. Walter P. Chrysler. Nicholas Murray Butler, counting the rent money, came with his daughter, Sarah. Edward G. Robinson was there, and Ethel Barrymore; so were Leopold Stokowski, Fannie Hurst, and Mrs. August Belmont. Junior smiled politely as he passed the photographers but didn't pause for even a moment. Nelson arrived from the party at his sister's place with Raymond Hood's wife on one arm and Mrs. Roxy on the other. Newsreel footage shows him looking a little ill at ease, nervous, almost shy—unfamiliar attitudes for the most comfortably public of all the Rockefellers, yet somewhat understandable when one remembers that he was only twenty-four.

Retired heavyweight champion Gene Tunney, silk scarf draped around the Ionic column of his neck, talked briefly to the newsreel cameras; so did pudgy little David Sarnoff, of course, and the elegant Merlin Aylesworth of NBC, who spoke of "that great genius, Roxy." Walter Lippmann arrived in a party that included Mr. and Mrs. Gerald Swope (he was Owen Young's successor as president of General Electric), Rose Kennedy, and Al Smith. The former governor was virtually the only man in the place who wasn't wearing a silk topper: "Sure, it's my brown derby," he said. "Why not?" In London, the BBC journal *The Radio Times* would summarize the evening with Anglocentric economy: "Six thousand famous people, including Noël Coward, attended."

As the crowd began to move toward their seats, Roxy left his position in the foyer, where he had spent thirty minutes greeting important guests, and disappeared into an elevator that took him to the topmost point in the auditorium. There, in a room built into the back wall of the third mezzanine, he settled into a reclining chair, his nurse, his doctor, and a stenographer beside him. An intercom system connected him directly to the light booth, the sound booth, the orchestra pit, backstage, to every position occupied by his army of aides. At 8:45 the intercom carried the voice of the commander of the ushers, Charles Griswold: "Roxy, the theater is ready."

Came the cue from the distant booth high above the auditorium, and the show began. Not with Graham or Bolger or even a Rapee overture, but with the curtain. Sure, it was a pretty nifty curtain, thirteen motors and all, but . . . a dancing curtain? No, not just a dancing curtain: this, the first act in what Roxy had promised would be "the finest entertainment . . . that the world has ever known," was "The Symphony of the Curtains," a piece for full orchestra, soloist Caroline Anderson (singing Rimsky-Korsakov's "Hymn to the Sun"), and two thousand yards of cloth.

So began an evening of overweening pretension, overdrawn ambition, and overwhelming length. This was no mere flop of an opening night; it was a catastrophe. The dancing curtain was followed by a dedicatory incantation ("And thus it rose to Heaven, stone on stone . . .") drafted by one of Roxy's publicists and declaimed by an actor whose words "seemed to get lost in the static of [his] long, white beard." Thereupon unrolled a stupefying series of acts that adhered to no known logic, no unifying theme, not even a particular standard of quality. A "Radio City Overture" by Ferde Grofé was followed by the Flying Wallendas on the high wire and an "Oriental Risley Act." A pair of vaudeville comics named Eddie and Ralph enacted "The Pulling Scene" from "The Dentist of Seville," only to be followed by Patricia Bowman and the first-rate ballet corps. Now came the London music hall dancers Kirkwhite and Addison, preceding the celebrated choir from Tuskegee Institute brought to New York from Alabama for the first time, singing the spiritual "Beautiful City"; just in case, the 101 Tuskegee voices were augmented by another 60 from the Radio City Glee Club. A German soprano sang some Strauss, Ray Bolger did his comic dance, the *danseur noble* Harald Kreutzberg led the ballet corps through a dance-drama called "The Angel of Fate." ("I want more light!" a relentless Roxy howled into the intercom during the act. "Give me a number seven on Kreutzberg!") The Roxyettes kicked an accompaniment to the singing of Jeannie Lang (who laughed just where Roxy wanted her to laugh), a comic billed as Doctor Rockwell delivered an oration, and then a boffo number called "Night Club Revels"—featuring Bowman, Bolger, the Roxyettes, the chorus, the corps de ballet, and four other acts including the lyricist Dorothy Fields in her stage debut—brought down the curtain.

For intermission.

What were they thinking? If you knew Roxy, you knew what he was thinking—his association with the Rockefellers had inflated his already healthy sense of self to a point of bloated grandiosity, and this grandiosity had obliterated what had once been his superb judgment of public tastes. During the intermission he came down from his eyrie to congratulate his "children": "I'm proud of you all. You were marvelous," he told cast and crew, seemingly unaware of the audience's numb dismay. Given the world's largest stage and a budget equal to its size, he had tried to cram it with whatever in the world was available to him, a more-is-more amalgam that proved to be far, far less than the sum of its parts. As critic Percy Hammond said in the *Herald Tribune,* "The mountain labored and gave forth a mouse."

For its part, the audience knew early on what it was in for. Leaning over to read their programs in the light cast by the small lamps on the back of each seat, they saw there was no way this straining locomotive could possibly reach its destination at a reasonable hour. "If the seating capacity of the Radio City Music Hall is precisely 6,200," wrote Roxy's old colleague Terry Ramsaye, "then just exactly 6,199 persons must have been aware [that] it was the unveiling of the world's best 'bust.'" One audience member felt Roxy's "notion of perfect entertainment is to place everything as far away as possible and then throw a mist of steam in front of it." M. R. Werner, in the *Atlantic Monthly,* said, "only when forty-five girls all placed their toes in one direction was there any slight enthusiasm" from the audience. Fred Allen said he "mistook, in the great distances of the theater, white stage horses for mice."

So deadening was the show that many in the audience wandered out into the lobby areas as the evening proceeded—including Junior, who agreed to pose for pictures as he took a constitutional on the great staircase. (Asked earlier in the evening for his view of the theater, he said, "I shall let the place speak for itself.") In newspaper reports the next day, some reviewers who had been compelled by their deadlines to leave early commented on the show's length, but because they weren't there for the ending they had to guess: one moaned that the show had continued to midnight, not knowing that it lasted until well past two. The writer probably underestimated because he saw there were only four acts listed in the program after intermission. Had he had the energy left to read the fine print, he would have seen that one—"Excerpts from *Carmen*"—included six full scenes from the opera, and that the closer, called "Minstrelsy," could have made a full-fledged evening on its own, with DeWolf Hopper, in addition to thundering through all the verses of "Casey at the Bat," serving as Interlocutor for fully thirteen acts (including the tenor "John Pierce," born Jacob Pincus Perelmuth and soon to be renamed Jan Peerce*). The last performers in Hopper's roster were the ancient vaudevillians Weber and Fields, who had been around since before the Flood; they had opened their own music hall, on Broadway and 29th, on a gala evening in 1896. Louis Bouché, who had included their portraits in the mural he had painted downstairs in the lounge, was succinct in his judgment: "They were terrible."

The most controversial act of the evening, though, was the penultimate one: Martha Graham and her troupe performing her "Choric Dance for an Antique Greek Tragedy." Anyone not in the front of the loge saw only a small group of tiny figures running around on the revolving turntable on a totally bare stage. Graham had, as she had always done, choreographed a piece for a normal-sized stage in a normal-sized theater. In the yawning proscenium of the Music Hall—which, according to *The New Yorker,* looked like "the mouth of a cannon" from just halfway back in the loge—the effect was somewhat different. "They went around on the revolve and it looked like they were going faster and faster," remembered assistant art director James Stewart Morcom. "Then they turned around and went against the revolve and it looked like they hardly moved at all." The celebrated Graham, whom Roxy had been so proud to sign up for his theater, "looked like a mouse being chased by a lot of other mice."

To Mary Watkins of the *Herald Tribune,* it really didn't make any difference: those still in the audience by the time Graham reached the stage "found themselves satiated to the point of indifference as to whether the performer were Miss Graham or Ray Bolger, or both together in a pas de deux."

By 10:00 P.M. a specially installed telegraph in the Music Hall office had logged 5,700 congratulatory wires from well-wishers unable to be present on the glorious night. Less than five hours later, a pale, exhausted Roxy told an acquaintance, "It's the greatest moment of my life," but admitted he was

---

*Born and raised on the Lower East Side, Peerce was discovered and renamed by Roxy, who inspired the diminutive tenor when he "banged his fist on the desk and shouted at me 'You're the tallest man in the world! You're the handsomest man in the world! All you have to do is believe that and it's so!'"

"pretty tired." His close colleagues knew it was worse than that; he was, said Sydney Goldman, "broken-hearted." There were no parties; the exhausted cast simply limped home. Staff arranger Earle Moss walked into the Grand Foyer after the show with his wife and was stunned by the quiet, so unlike most first nights. Roxy held himself together for two more days—he had to preside over the opening of the RKO Roxy, down the street, on the twenty-ninth—and then he collapsed. On December 30 he was admitted to Post-Graduate Hospital.

Robert Edmond Jones, whose style of set design did not travel well from the relative intimacy of the Broadway stage to the oceanic reaches of the Music Hall, had left the building during the show, "disappointed with himself and disgusted with the production"; his resignation was accepted in the morning. Martha Graham and her company were fired, too. The reviews ranged from pitying to enraged. John Mason Brown, in the *Post,* said the show bore Roxy's "unmistakable stamp as surely as Italy reflects the character of Mussolini." Terry Ramsaye used his influential column in the *Motion Picture Herald* to label it "a negative triumph beyond compare in the history of the amusement industry." In the *Times,* art critic Edward Alden Jewell went after the decoration: the Winter mural was "far less effective than the . . . mirrors," he said, and the lower lounge "degenerates into cheap gloom." He was glad Zorach's banished nude wasn't there, for it was too fine a piece of art for such surroundings.

But it fell to Walter Lippmann, who like any good columnist managed to turn a social evening into a professional one, to provide a devastating assault that encompassed the building, the art, the show—and, most vividly, the entire concept of Rockefeller Center. Lippmann wrote of "a theater which is so long that from the back rows the performers look like pygmies and is so wide that from the nearer seats the eye cannot encompass the whole stage." The men behind Rockefeller Center, he said, "had built a pedestal to sustain a peanut. . . . The esthetic aimlessness of [Rockefeller Center] is exceeded only by its social irresponsibility. . . . Either the existing theaters and existing office buildings must be gutted to provide audiences and tenants for Radio City or Rockefeller Center will have deficits to meet commensurate with its own pretentiousness."

The only thing worse than the lashing suffered at the hands of the nation's most respected columnist was an unsigned parody of Roxy's hyperventilations published in the *New York Sun.* "I never saw anything like it," the piece began. "It seats 6,200 people, who if placed end to end would form a girdle twice around the acoustics at a cost of $350,000 and be visible from all parts of DeWolf Aylesworth! There is an orchestra of 200 hollow-tiled musicians, with henna-colored brocatelle over porcelain. . . . There are more than 3,500 rivets driven into the conductor alone! . . . The Roxy usherettes, designed by Ezra Winter after Johann Strauss's 'Wiener Blut' are semi-circular in shape with nine overlapping arches."

Radio City Music Hall was worse than a failure; it was a joke.

CHAPTER SIXTEEN

In terms of its national impact, the dinner John D. Rockefeller Jr. convened at the University Club in May of 1932 may have been the most momentous such evening in his adult life. The invitation asked

*We were criticized for our **ruthlessness** which **was just another word for good business** ability to go out and get tenants.*

—JOHN R. TODD

twelve of his closest associates, all of them "leaders in various walks of life," to consider "in confidence" what he identified only as "a problem of great national importance." For more than five hours Junior and his guests (including Thomas Debevoise and Winthrop Aldrich, as well as Nelson and Johnny) discussed "the prohibition experiment." They no doubt did it by the book, too: Junior allowed neither cocktails nor wine to be served at his dinners, a policy Debevoise, a "two-martini man," had learned to accommodate. Three days after the dinner Junior conferred with a man whose involvement in this issue was almost as unlikely as the document that would emerge from their meeting.

On Monday, June 6, 1932, an open letter from Junior to Nicholas Murray Butler appeared on the front page of the *Times,* a placement repeated the following day in scores of papers across the nation. The committee that had awarded Butler the Nobel Peace Prize the previous year cited the wrong accomplishment: Butler played as large a role in the anti-Prohibition movement as he had in the creation of the Kellogg-Briand Pact, and—more to the point—it actually had a real effect on the real world. Even his most acid critics gave him grudging respect: "honestly convinced of the evils of Prohibition," wrote Dorothy Dunbar Bromley in an otherwise blistering "Portrait of a Reactionary" in the *American Mercury,* Butler "seized upon repeal as a God-given opportunity for leadership." Over much of the previous decade, wrote Alva Johnston in *The New Yorker,* Butler had "made the wet cause respectable"—even if, he added, Butler had also "contrived to make himself a little obnoxious" by asserting "that he personally obeys the Volstead Act" (this was not only obnoxious, but false). Now Butler had converted to the cause John D. Rockefeller Jr., who truly did abstain, and who had the credibility to push repeal over the top.

"My position may surprise you," Junior wrote in his open letter to Butler, "as it will many of my friends. I was born a teetotaler; all my life I have been a teetotaler in principle. Neither my father nor his father ever tasted a drop of intoxicating liquor, nor have I." He continued, "My mother and her mother were among the dauntless women of their day . . . praying on their knees in the saloons." But, he said, "drinking has generally increased" since the enactment of Prohibition. Still worse, "a vast army of law-breakers has been recruited and financed on a colossal scale" and "many of our best citizens . . . have openly and unabashedly disregarded the Eighteenth Amendment." As a result, he concluded, "respect for all laws has been greatly lessened to an unprecedented degree."

"If any single public statement sounded Prohibition's death-knell," wrote one historian of the period, this was it. Alva Johnston said Junior "broke the deadlock between wets and drys," causing "an astonishing stampede of wavering citizens." A syndicated newspaper cartoon showed "Young Rockefeller" (he was fifty-eight at the time, but still his father's son) in the prow of a dory hurling a harpoon at a sea beast labeled "Prohibition"; the harpoon bore the legend "Rockefeller Letter." The *New York American,* flagship of the Hearst chain, said Junior "has done the country an inestimable service which no other man occupied a position to render." Will Rogers urged him to run for president.

Junior was now a living symbol of integrity as well as generosity, public spiritedness as well as private rectitude.* His long, deliberate campaign to change the word "Rockefeller" from the signifier of rapacious greed to a symbol of enlightened citizenship had been predicated not on cynical manipulation of public opinion but on his deeds. Junior guarded his name even more than his fortune. His associates vetted potential projects first for

---

*And confident enough to indulge in a little humor: "Now that you and Tom have got me to work on the repeal of the Eighteenth Amendment," he wrote Aldrich, "I presume you will have some plan with reference to the legalization of betting."

their propriety, and only then for viability or appeal. As a young man he had nearly been crippled by his lack of confidence; now he wore the cloak of "America's most useful citizen" with poise, even assurance.

Consequently, while there might have been some unease among the small audience whom Junior addressed one afternoon in the spring of 1933, none could have been surprised by what this famous moral leader had to say. "You are a fine looking group of young men, and look as if you could do a job," he told the thirty rental agents Hugh Robertson supervised. "But I want you to understand that it will not serve my best interests if you sell anyone anything they cannot use properly and afford to pay for."

As if their task wasn't hard enough already! A veteran New York rental agent familiar with the glut of space choking the office market would have had to try hard not to kick his dog when he got home that night. But fortunately for Junior—and, as it would turn out, somewhat uncomfortably for him as well—Robertson had hired a staff that was almost totally void of experience (including twenty-five-year-old Nelson Rockefeller, who came on as a rental consultant at eight hundred dollars per month). Although this was Robertson's long-established modus operandi, Frederick Lewis Allen found it appropriate to Rockefeller Center's historical moment. "Experienced men," wrote Allen, "would know they were attempting the impossible."

Back in the summer of 1929, when John R. Todd was auditioning for Junior on the carriage roads of Mount Desert Island, he chose not to represent himself as anything other than what he was: a blunt and arrogant (if brilliant) egomaniac. Debevoise, who arranged the meeting and was Todd's biggest booster, had written to warn Junior, "It is true that Todd is sometimes dominating and arbitrary." When Todd boasted that if Junior hired him he intended to spend half his time on the job and the other half "as far away . . . as trains and steamers can carry me," it was a fine demonstration of his blustery vainglory. Forewarned, and maybe a little bit amused, Junior didn't flinch.

Todd wasn't kidding. Ever since he had made his first fortune, he had assiduously (and often ostentatiously) cultivated his away-from-work life. Trips to Paris (where he stayed in suitably grand style at either the Crillon or the Meurice) were frequent, as were the London "furniture-buying binges" he and his wife indulged in. His home in New Jersey was filled with fine rugs collected in the various capitals of the Middle East, and the place in Easthampton, on Long Island, made an ideal summer retreat. The house

Todd cherished most was his winter seat, a colonnaded plantation manor on 1,291 acres along the Combahee River near Beaufort, South Carolina, where he cultivated his collection of rare camellias and his pretensions to gentryhood. He even published a lavish, oversized volume of local history, in a hand-numbered edition of a thousand copies, each bearing his emphatic signature just above (and quite a bit larger than) the names of the book's actual authors. Tracing the history of the land from colonial times up to its annexation by the far-flung Commonwealth of Todd, *Prince William's Parish and Plantations* was for this Wisconsin-born, Kansas-raised son of an itinerant preacher a confirming document, a sort of genealogy-by-purchase.

When he did find himself in New York, Todd lived in his apartment in the Barclay, the elegant hotel he built in 1927 on 48th Street, just up Lexington Avenue from the Graybar Building. He would begin most days with a breakfast with one of his colleagues, arrive at his office sometime before nine, and immediately plunge into a self-renewing cycle of meetings with his partners, the heads of the various operating departments, the architects, the lawyers, the accountants, and the delegations of Junior's associates from 26 Broadway. With his brother and Robertson he had divided up oversight responsibilities for specific components of the huge Rockefeller Center operation, reserving for himself public relations, architecture, art, and liaison with both Metropolitan Life and David Sarnoff. But not for a moment in his nine-year engagement with Rockefeller Center did Todd ever think of himself as—or act as—anything except supreme commander of the vast enterprise. "I'm glad to take responsibility for every bit of trouble, failure, and delay," he once wrote to Wallace Harrison and Andrew Reinhard. "That is my job. But I have found out after several years of business experience that the man who takes the blame for all those things always gets the credit, the successes, and everything that is good." He was chiding his young colleagues for attempting to pin responsibility for a construction delay on someone else, but he was also setting out the expansive boundaries of his self-regard.

In the creation of Rockefeller Center, Todd was the man at the head of the table. Once a month this was literally true, when he interrupted the infinite relay of meetings to host a lunch at the Barclay for about thirty key associates and department heads. "Business is not discussed," he said. "The seating order is changed every time. The Luncheon is good. The time is short. . . . It works awfully well." Although the lunches may have been designed as casual events, Todd came prepared. His secretary would provide him in advance with the seating chart and a crib sheet containing data that enabled John R. to engage each of his guests while reminding himself where each fit in the Toddian universe. For every man he had at hand salary, age, place of birth, colleges attended, and previous job. Knowing that lawyer Francis Christy, for instance, was born in Scranton, attended Dartmouth and Harvard Law, previously worked at Murray, Aldrich & Webb, was born in 1897, and earned $27,500 a year enabled Todd to . . . well, to be Todd.

Apart from his brother, his son, and Robertson, Todd was probably more intimately acquainted with Lawrence A. Kirkland than with anyone else present. According to a lunch seating chart from 1936, Kirkland was forty-four years old, earned $30,000 a year (the 2003 equivalent of roughly $380,000), graduated from Davidson College and the University of South Carolina Law School, and practiced law in Camden, South Carolina, before joining Todd, Robertson & Todd in 1930. The specificity of Todd's instructions likely compelled his secretary to provide this information, but he hardly needed it. Todd had first met Kirkland while working on the Williamsburg project, when the young lawyer had been assigned the un-lawyerly task of traveling throughout the South purchasing boxwood plants to enhance the restoration. After he moved north Kirkland worked briefly as Todd's personal assistant and then was elevated to a position of such importance that he became John R.'s primary breakfast companion. Having proved himself expert at shrub acquisition, Kirkland, who barely knew how to get around New York, was put in charge of all the other inexperienced men charged with renting 4 million square feet of new office space at a moment when more than 3.5 million feet in midtown lay as empty as a Herbert Hoover campaign promise.

Between 1925 and 1931 the inventory of Manhattan office space had increased by 92 percent; in the next two years the Empire State Building and Rockefeller Center would together goose that by another 56 percent. At the same time, businesses were closing, cutting back, or at the very least postponing nonessential expenditures, which surely included relocation to new quarters. At Ray Hood's spanking-new McGraw-Hill Building, children who came to visit Daddy in the office were treated to roller-skating parties on the empty floors. The large complex of buildings on the East Side developed more than a decade earlier in conjunction with Grand Central Terminal would have been justified in reassuming its original name, but with a different meaning: Terminal City. Journalists chronicled "crushing vacancy rates, falling rents, unpaid taxes, and interminable bankruptcy proceedings." Many mortgage holders refrained from foreclosing out of the conviction that taking possession of empty buildings would only push them into their own bankruptcies. Even so, ownership of some mighty towers fell to the auctioneer's hammer. The fifty-three-story Lincoln Building on 42nd Street, built in 1929 and 1930 at a cost of $30 million, passed to its bondholders in the summer of 1933 for $4.75 million. When the Bank of Manhattan Building at 40 Wall Street teetered into default in 1935, the mortgage holder put it up for sale for $1.2 million—less than the original cost, five years earlier, of the building's forty-three elevators.

Like any epidemic, the economic woe ravaging the New York office rental market in the early 1930s knew no boundaries and spared no class of citizens: Robert Goelet, a Vanderbilt on one side and the heir to his family's Manhattan real estate empire on the other, developed the southwest corner of Fifth and 48th, just east of William Nelson Cromwell's holdout houses, in 1932, and two years later the handsome, modernist building still didn't have a single tenant. Rockefeller Center suffered from the common disease, but also had to endure a plague of its own. The bankruptcy of the RCA-controlled RKO—over a three-month period in 1931 the film studio's share price plunged from $50 to less than $1—led Sarnoff to demand a lease revision. When these negotiations were concluded, Junior owned 100,000 shares of RKO common stock, 100,000 shares of RCA preferred stock (worth about $4 million), and two new headaches: Sarnoff had reduced his lease commitment by half a million square feet, and Junior suddenly found himself in the movie business.

The Rockefellers didn't have much to do with the film company apart from batting away supplicants who wanted them to underwrite their pictures. They did find themselves onstage, though, on September, 30, 1933, when the Irving Berlin–Moss Hart revue *As Thousands Cheer* opened at the Music Box Theatre five months after the RCA Building was completed. In one sketch, an audience that included Al Smith, D. W. Griffith, Dashiell Hammett, and Helen Hayes watched Clifton Webb portray Senior, celebrating his ninety-fourth birthday. When Helen Broderick as Abby and Leslie Adams as Junior presented the old man with a cake in the shape of Rockefeller Center, Webb shouted, "That's no birthday present, that's a dirty trick!" and chased Adams and Broderick off the stage with a carving knife. For the first two hundred performances of *As Thousands Cheer* there wasn't an empty seat in the house, and everyone got the joke.

During Rockefeller Center's gestation and early infancy, it sometimes seemed that *The New Yorker* had appointed itself the official chronicler of its every misstep. Editor Harold Ross wasn't content simply to grouse about having "to look at that damn thing every day of my life" from his office on 43rd Street; he used his magazine to underscore his complaint. Lewis Mumford, of course, repeatedly savaged the development's conception, its design, and its execution, and probably would have impugned its parentage if given the chance. E. B. White, in his unsigned "Notes and Comment" pieces, was belittling: "we would trade the whole project of Radio City for two fairly comfortable beer gardens in Central Park." The eminent playwright Robert Sherwood took up two full pages with his comic poem about "the Citadel of Static." But it was a little-known poet named Leslie Nelson Jennings who got to the crux of things in a slender piece of light verse: "What I should like to know is this: / Who's going to fill that edifice?"

The answer, in three words, was Hugh Sterling Robertson. When Todd and his partners divided up responsibilities at the outset of the project, Robertson's claim on the renting department was as firm as Caesar's on Gaul. Though he first made his bones with John R. as a construction superintendent a quarter century before ground was broken for Rockefeller Center, he was managing rental operations soon after Todd made him a partner in 1919. Robertson had his own way of doing things, and his preference for inexperienced agents eager to accept his dictates always paid off. Bernard Wakefield, a young property manager whom Robertson had hired to help populate the Cunard Building in 1921, later saw his partnership with his brother-in-law, a shrewd businessman with the not-quite-credible name J. Clydesdale Cushman, grow into the city's largest real estate firm. Rentals in the vast reaches of the Graybar were handled by Andy Reinhard, who suspended his architectural career until he could marry it to these new skills during the planning for Rockefeller Center.

Robertson had come by his knowledge of commercial real estate entirely on the job. Like the Todd brothers the son of a clergyman, he was born in Cleveland, came east for boarding school, bypassed college, and except for a few years as a bookkeeper for the New York Central Railroad had spent his entire professional life with John R. Apart from their fruitful partnership and the South Carolina low-country plantations they had both acquired from its profits, the Todd of the grand gesture and the Robertson of careful calculation had little in common. As a professional team, though, they were well matched—Todd the visionary, Robertson the tactician and manager; Todd often outrageous, Robertson always composed. Steely eyes and a long, narrow nose, an abrupt mustache atop thin lips that rarely curled up at the corners, clothing as dour as his expression—Robertson could have been, say, head bookkeeper in a Victorian insurance office examining rows of numbers, and rows of other men examining yet more rows of numbers.

Inside the crusty exterior lay a crusty interior. Robertson had the guts of a poker player running a bluff with nothing but a pair and the implacable calm of someone sitting on a straight flush. When members of a Democratic Party clubhouse on West 49th Street wanted to get out of their lease and turn the building over to Metropolitan Square, Robertson declined; he didn't need the property until the end of the lease. Charles Heydt warned him that the request had come through the mayor's office, but Robertson was unmoved: he wanted to collect a few more months' rent, thank you.

Robertson also knew when to spread his bets around, as when he conceived the notion of dedicating the two small buildings on Fifth Avenue to foreign businesses and then found British and French syndicates to take responsibility for renting them. This was a Depression-defying feat abetted by Junior, whom Robertson had managed to enlist in the effort apparently by invoking virtues more noble than commerce. In a letter to the titled Englishman whom Robertson had recruited to lead the British syndicate, Junior apotheosized the British Empire Building and the "Palais de France," as he called it, as "symbols in stone and steel of the common interests . . . and good will of three great powers." His earnest belief in international amity led him to assert that "No other single feature of this enterprise affords me keener satisfaction than what may be termed the spiritual significance of these two buildings." All this harp music no doubt pleased Robertson but it isn't likely that it moved him, for with Robertson sentiment never had a chance when it wrestled with practicality. In the late thirties, after enduring the first sustained labor stoppage in the Center's history, Robertson—who had as much love for unions as you might expect—summarily dismissed the chief electrician because he couldn't get along with the men who had been on strike.

Robertson's tilt toward the practical, toward whatever tactic would work to produce the desired result, could be looked at as "an uncanny ability to overcome obstacles as they arose," as Francis Christy wrote. It could also be considered cold amorality. This could be trivial, as when he endorsed subsidizing an advertising program for the Center's retail shops not because it would draw business, as the retailers hoped, but because it might draw more shops. It could also be ugly: despite the Rockefeller family's enlightened racial attitudes and even the direct pressure of Nelson and his brothers Johnny and Winthrop, Robertson managed to keep the staff of Rockefeller Center, save for porters and cleaning women, lily-white until the late 1940s. If you put black people into meet-the-public jobs—elevator operator, doorman, and the like—it might cost you a tenant, and it was Robertson's duty to round up tenants, do whatever was necessary to get their names on a lease, and never let them go.

An unsigned, undated memorandum from the files of Todd, Robertson & Todd, but clearly drafted sometime in 1930 or '31 when the firm was trying to determine a construction budget, hypothesized levels of income for various stages of the project. Apart from the RCA commitment, the memo said, the intended reader or readers should "figure balance of space as follows: 50% rented Oct. 1, 1932 to May 1, 1933. 75% rented May 1, 1933 to Oct 1, 1933. 97½% rented thereafter." By the time those dates rolled around it was clear that whoever had written the document might have saved his job by failing to sign it. Even the first flight of buildings in Rockefeller Center wasn't 75 percent rented until the middle of the decade, and 97½ percent was so far in the future that only a world war and its ensuing peacetime boom could make it come to pass.

"The battle of the leases," as John R. Todd called it, was more like a protracted war. Yet however slowly Kirkland's staff got up to speed, however brutal the wintry economic conditions in which they labored, however desperate, unpopular, and even amoral some of the tactics they employed, the plan laid out by Robertson appeared to be a model of strategic and tactical brilliance. Kirkland's men—whose "zeal," said *Time,* "became proverbial"—assembled detailed dossiers (current lease terms, lease expiration dates, estimated future requirements) on more than 1,700 New York businesses deemed to be prospects, and by the end of 1933 had initiated conversation with nearly 1,200 of them. The legal department was ordered to prepare an encyclopedia of lease clauses, riders, and codicils anticipating every conceivable tenant requirement and every consequent quid pro quo. Rental agents were armed with sales materials of unprecedented lavishness.

One sales piece in particular revealed in its packaging and content the image Robertson and Kirkland wished to project. Rolled out in 1932, during the construction phase, it was an eleven-by-fourteen-inch folio bound in hard covers that bore an embossed image of the planned buildings. Nine of John Wenrich's breathtaking watercolor renderings decorated forty pages of text, none of the paintings done to scale but each representing something far more arresting than dimensional exactitude: they depicted a dream. Wenrich, whose work was first exhibited in New York through the influence of Ezra Winter (the painter of the "wormy intestine" in the Music Hall's foyer), had just completed a stint as architectural illustrator for the upcoming Chicago world's fair when Hood brought him to the Graybar suite. Wenrich worked as an architectural illustrator in Rochester his entire life, except for the five years he wielded his red-sable brush to cast washes of sunlight across lush green gardens on Rockefeller Center's roofs and set-backs. It's not likely that even Hood imagined gardens and paths and fountains as rich and as inviting as those conjured by Wenrich, who longed for his upstate cabin in the woods but for a time had to make do with the more artful version of nature he interpolated into midtown Manhattan.

The sales piece's luxuriant physicality denoted the wonders a tenant would enjoy, but in case you didn't make the connection the rhapsodic prose didn't hold back. "Rockefeller Center is not Greek," it read in part, "but it suggests the balance of Greek architecture. It is not Babylonian, but it retains the flavor of Babylon's magnificence. It is not Roman, yet it has Rome's enduring qualities of mass and strength." And, it might have continued, it was not Macedonian, but the campaign to fill up what real estate specialists called the "carpet space"—the rentable square footage—would have done justice to Alexander the Great.

For Robertson, image and tactics occupied two different realms. The first component of his strategy was the use of what politely might be called leverage but more accurately would be labeled muscle. It worked like this: while Joe Brown tortured a potential supplier on the rack, Larry Kirkland would come by with a pen in his hand. It's the middle of the Depression, Brown is squeezing you tighter and tighter on a materials or services contract you desperately need to land, and along comes this courtly southerner with a simple proposition: sign a lease and you get the contract. Robbed of his chance at another money-saving conquest, Brown would grumble, but he would learn to live with it. When Charles Heydt called him to account on his apparent resistance, Brown bowed immediately. "Where there is a possibility of obtaining tenants" by waiving our procurement policies, Brown told Heydt, "you may be assured that we would not let [our policies] come first."

Robertson of course treasured every nickel Brown could save in construction costs, but he knew as well that filling the buildings with tenants was, in the long run, more important. Success begat success, and each new lease—trumpeted to the newspapers, brandished before fence-sitters—would have a geometric impact on the entire rental program. Penn Dixie was contemplating a major lease? Brown started using Penn Dixie cement. General Cable Company was in talks with the rental staff? Maybe it was time to buy some wire from General. The company that won the contract for twenty-five thousand office doors, the company that supplied structural glass, the company that excavated the site and poured the foundations all wandered into Kirkland's web, and onto Brown's approved supplier list as well.*

The most auspicious of these deals involved the purchase of elevators for the RCA Building. It would be decades before anyone else placed an elevator order the size of this one, and although that couldn't be known at the time, for the two main contenders, Westinghouse and Otis, this was clearly an elevator job to beat all elevator jobs. Not only was it huge but it was epochal in other ways. Rockefeller political influence brought to bear in City Hall in 1931 had already led to a change in the building code, increasing the maximum allowable elevator speed from 700 to 1,200 feet per minute and setting up a publicity coup for the winning bidder (for someone working on the sixty-fifth floor, it was calculated, the increased speed would reduce travel time by thirty seconds per trip, or more than eight hours over the course of a year). The RCA Building might also be one of the first major sites for elevators equipped with the newly perfected photoelectric-cell technology, or "electric eyes." The company that won this contract would collect not just many millions of dollars but acclaim, credibility, and ego rewards worth nearly as much.

The elevator decision was no less critical to Todd and Robertson. In a building this size, elevators were nearly as important as the floor beneath a tenant's feet and the ceiling over his head. When the cubist painter Fernand Léger called on the architects in the Graybar suite, Harvey Corbett told him that "accommodating 20,000 people living in one building" was his current work, and that the most vexing part of it was figuring out how to get them to and from their offices; ten engineers, Corbett said, had already put in six months on the problem. In the overall Rockefeller Center budget elevators were, after structural steel, the second largest single line item, accounting for 13 percent of the total cost of construction. Architectural historian Carol Willis has written that "the greatest price of height lies in the

---

*The office staff was expected to remain loyal even after a lease was signed. When the American Pencil Company took space in the RCA Building, Webster Todd requested that all Rockefeller Center departments "give preference to their products when buying pencils."

requirements of efficient vertical circulation"; if the elevator system didn't work as efficiently as possible, if it didn't get the tenant down to the lobby from the fiftieth floor without undue waiting, the cost could be incalculable. Someone figured that the RCA elevators would collectively travel 2,100 miles every working day, and each one of those miles mattered.

J. H. Van Alstyne, the president of Otis, was undoubtedly aware of this calculus and its ramifications when he called on Todd, but John R. had another equation in mind. "We told him that we needed leases just as much as we needed elevators," Todd wrote in his memoirs. "What did he think? He thought nothing of the idea." Web Todd remembered his father putting the question like this: "OK, you want to sell elevators? Where are your offices located?"

In 1932, Otis's rival bidder answered "460 West 34th Street" and "150 Broadway." But a year later, a Westinghouse executive told his company's employees that, in the building they would soon move into, "you will feel at home [because] you will be transported to and from your offices by Westinghouse elevators. . . . Your power will be brought in through the medium of Westinghouse transformers. Your lighting will come from Westinghouse luminaires. Your power will be metered through Westinghouse metering panels and distributed through Westinghouse switchboards and panelboards." Seventy-seven thousand square feet of carpet space on floors 14 through 17 of the RCA Building were now spoken for.

Floors 23 through 29, much of 33, most of 54 through 56, a large chunk of 64, and various suites scattered throughout the building fell to a much simpler part of Robertson's strategy. It was the real estate variation on the way theatrical producers papered the house when they needed to create the illusion of success. If you can't get the paying public to show up, pack all those empty seats with friends and family. The Empire State Building, lifeless and teetering near bankruptcy, was a constant reminder of how failure begat more failure; once it had been hung with the nickname "Empty State Building" there was no saving the place. Whatever rental difficulties Rockefeller Center endured, it had an asset that came with the deal: it had the Rockefellers, in name and flesh.

The name wasn't an automatic. The idea of having his own surname "plastered on a real estate development" had never occurred to Junior, and when it was first broached it appalled him. Metropolitan Square had the virtue of bland anonymity and, at the same time, a descriptive connection

to the opera company. Radio City came from the RCA lease, which entitled
Sarnoff to designate a name for the western, entertainment-oriented part of
the development. But Metropolitan Square had become an atavism, and
Radio City would not do for the whole development, tainted as the words
were by the scent of showbiz. Nicholas Murray Butler, needless to say, was
appalled by any connection to the entertainment industry, and the threat of
Radio City becoming the official name by default—the newspapers were
using it regularly—detonated a characteristic splutter of vanity. He wanted
to "substitute a phrase that is more becoming and on a higher plane," Butler told Harvey Corbett, and even invoked the phantom chorus he kept on
standby whenever he was about to run out of arguments: "At least half a
dozen men," all of them unnamed, of course, but "some of them prominent
in real estate circles" agreed with him. This was not, on its own, persuasive.
A few months later, more composed, Butler reaffirmed his preference for
the unapt Metropolitan Square, boasted that "The newspapers will do almost anything which I ask of them," and forthwith assigned Frederick
Goetze to break the news to Debevoise.

Fortunately for Butler, men who carried more influence with Junior also
wanted an alternative to Radio City. Although many would claim credit for
the idea, including Ivy Lee's main competitor in the public relations racket,
Edward Bernays, it was Lee who first suggested "Rockefeller Center" to Junior, in the summer of 1931. John R. Todd endorsed it with a pitch no one
else would have dared to offer: "It's your money," he told Junior. "Why not
use the name?" Nothing would draw tenants more effectively, and everyone
agreed that drawing tenants was a good thing. Junior still thought it "flamboyant and distasteful," but the prospect of empty buildings was distasteful, too.

A younger Junior, less comfortable with himself, never would have
agreed to the commercialization of the family name. But that same younger
Junior, uncertain and a little obsessive, might well have sought refuge by
disappearing into the rabbit hole that now presented itself: *Center,* or *Centre?* This was a problem you could lose yourself in for weeks. In his correspondence Junior preferred *Centre,* which was also the way the *Times*
spelled it when the paper announced the name change. But others were sure
Center was the right spelling, and it was soon apparent that this was something that could be resolved only by importing that always purchasable
commodity, expertise.

Enter Frank H. Vizetelly, who was armed with enough expertise to impress even Nicholas Murray Butler. It was Vizetelly who had famously dis-

covered that in seventy-five speeches delivered between 1913 and 1918, Woodrow Wilson had used exactly 6,221 different words. It was Vizetelly who had forcefully argued that a proper English alphabet would have sixty-two different characters. It was Vizetelly who claimed to know fifty synonyms for "money." And it was Vizetelly who, as editor of the *New Standard Dictionary* and author of *Words We Misspell in Business,* was the right man to referee the match between *center* and *centre.* After taking the question under advisement, he emerged with the learned conclusion that *centre* had Norman French roots, while *center* was the spelling preferred by Shakespeare and Milton and Burns, and therefore by Vizetelly. He did acknowledge that Milton was actually a little unsure, using *center* in *Paradise Lost,* and *centre* in *Paradise Regained.* Consequently he might have forgiven the *Herald Tribune,* whose respectful obituary in 1938 listed Vizetelly's many accomplishments, but spelled his name with an *s* instead of a *z.*

Todd was thrilled to have the name on the door; Robertson cared more that the men and institutions who either bore it or marched behind it soon followed, if possible with parades and fireworks. In fact, they populated the place like mushrooms after a rainstorm. Junior of course committed to move his offices uptown from 26 Broadway, replacing that fabled address with a new one that would attain comparable renown: Room 5600. This was a synecdoche for the entire fifty-sixth floor of the RCA Building, where the family enterprises—for decades identified in the building directory as "Rockefeller, Office of the Messrs."—would root themselves in 1933 and remain through the remainder of the twentieth century and into the twenty-first. It was in the southwest corner of this suite that Junior had his antique office reassembled, from the baronial sixteenth-century paneling on the walls to the ancient bookcases paned in leaded glass. The rest of 5600 accommodated his sons, his associates, clerks and messengers, and other functionaries of the family empire.

But that was just a fraction of what Junior brought with him. The Rockefeller Foundation took the entire fifty-fifth floor, half the fifty-fourth, and a dining room and lounge on the sixty-fourth. Three other family philanthropies, the Spelman Fund of New York, the General Education Board, and the China Medical Board, came along as well. The Consolidation Coal Company—the Rockefeller enterprise the railroads were required to buy coal from if they wanted the Center's freight business—took 17,000 square feet on the thirty-third floor. The extended family pitched in, too: brother-in-law Winthrop Aldrich brought along the American Society for the Control of Cancer (he sat on its board) as well as an especially ritzy branch of the Chase that occupied the southeast corner of the RCA's ground floor, second floor, and first basement, its walnut paneling and furniture, its crystal chandeliers, and its fresh-cut flowers broadly hinting at the sort of clientele the bank expected to bring to this august address.* Transit Advertisers, Incorporated (David M. Milton, Babs's husband, vice president), moved into a suite on 7.

All these enterprises gathered in the RCA Building not just out of a family herding instinct or because the other buildings were inferior, but because Robertson and Kirkland knew that this was the building on which attention was focused and thus where critics and competitors would look for signs of failure. And while in many instances—certainly in the case of Room 5600—the rent money was being transferred from one Rockefeller account to another, for the Rockefeller Center, Incorporated, operating statement it was income nonetheless. Late in the 1930s, a clerk noted that the apparent lateness of Junior's monthly rent check for $5,652 should cause no alarm: "tenant usually pays between 6th and 7th of every month," he wrote.

The most useful contribution from a family-associated business arose from the Rockefeller past, and it dovetailed with another part of Robertson's strategy. Years earlier, Todd had been one of the pioneers of the concept of grouping component parts of a single industry in a single location when he developed the Architects Building on Park Avenue. Now Robertson directed Kirkland and his staff to throw out the printed list of rental rates and negotiate whatever price was necessary to land the anchor tenants whose presence would draw others in the same industry. He also threw out the real estate man's article of faith first expressed in 1895 by the pioneering Chicago developer Owen F. Aldis as one of the seven key principles of building design: "A large number of small tenants is more desirable than large space for large tenants," Aldis said. "They do not move in a body and leave the building with a large vacant space when hard times hit." (And, he added, "they do not swamp your elevators by coming and going by the clock.") But this project was suffering hard times at its inception. If Robertson could sell big space, the little space would follow.

---

*The final details of the Chase–Rockefeller Center lease were negotiated in a private exchange of letters between Junior and Aldrich. The annual rental was set at .5 percent of the branch's first $20 million of deposits.

With the Sperry Corporation and Curtiss-Wright in hand, Kirkland's agents could line up enterprises in the airplane business as large as Fairchild, as small as the Casey Jones School of Aeronautics, and as useful to all of them as the Information Division of the Aeronautical Chamber of Commerce, which leased space in the RCA Building for "the largest collection of aeronautical books in this country." After American Cyanamid moved five hundred people into Rockefeller Center, a range of other chemical concerns from Dow to U.S. Gypsum followed. NBC's presence alone justified the occupying army that settled in across the street in the RKO Building· film companies (Republic Pictures, Walt Disney), talent agencies (William Morris), musicians (the Casa Loma Orchestra), theater figures (Katharine Cornell, Noël Coward), and other entertainment industry types (producer Mike Todd, publicist Irving Mansfield) flocked to the place. From the lunch counter at the Pennsylvania Drug Store in the lobby to the miniature theater in the offices of the William Morris Agency near the top of the building, the RKO was so steeped in show business that you might think Broadway had been rerouted and Tin Pin Alley dropped here intact. In the mornings the elevators were filled with song pluggers calling on the orchestra leaders and show producers headquartered in the building. Early afternoons saw the elevators jammed with actors, most of whom seemed to feel compelled to visit their agents immediately after lunch. This was, of course, the living nightmare that Captain Pedrick of the Fifth Avenue Association had feared, but the sinful precincts of the RKO Building were perhaps exalted by the presence of the Code Authority of the Motion Picture Industry—the famous "Hays Office" of industry censors who installed twin beds in every movie bedroom.

The piece of the Rockefeller past that reappeared on West 50th Street was the heaviest anchor of them all, the Standard Oil Company of New Jersey, known within the family and the industry as "the Jersey Company," and to the rest of the world as Esso, later Exxon. After the breakup of the Standard Oil Trust in 1911 the descendant companies went their own ways. Though the Rockefeller name remained associated with them in the public imagination, no Rockefeller played a role in the management of any of the Standard companies; neither Junior nor his sons sat on any of their boards; and the only member of the family who ever even worked for one was the fourth son, Winthrop, who labored as a roughneck in the oil fields of West Texas following his expulsion from Yale.

But even after selling off quite a bit of his stock to meet expenses in the early thirties, Junior remained the Jersey Company's largest shareholder.

When Charles Heydt suggested to Thomas Debevoise that "we should use every influence" to lure the Jersey Company to Rockefeller Center, he might as well have been urging a fish to swim. With 175,000 square feet spread through eight floors of the RCA Building—two and a half times the size of the Westinghouse commitment—as well as an Esso Touring Center in the building's lobby, the world's largest oil company instantly became the Center's second largest tenant, after RCA itself. And as Jersey went, so went the entire industry. Over the next two years there was an oil rush in midtown: Harry F. Sinclair's Consolidated Oil signed up for seven full floors in the International Building; Shell Union Oil colonized five floors of the RCA; Standard Oil of California planted its New York stake just upstairs from Shell. Trailing the giants came camp followers by the score: the Asiatic Petroleum Corporation and the Venezuelan Petroleum Corporation; the American Petroleum Institute and the Oil Well Supply Company; the *National Petroleum News* and the Atlantic Refining Company. The Estate of Walter Jennings, a former Jersey Company director and son of one of Senior's associates in the creation of the Standard Oil trust, hopped aboard, too, as if even in death old Walter just couldn't bear to miss this marvelous reunion of the oil clan.

By almost all accounts Robertson's grand design was working brilliantly. An average of two press releases went out to the real estate editors of the New York papers daily, each announcing the acquisition of another tenant ("Yardley & Co. Ltd., perfumery and soap makers of London, have taken a long term lease"; "The Leisure League of America . . . has leased extensive offices"). Judging by what one could read in the *Times,* the place would soon be sold out. Even Junior seemed pleased: "Things at Rockefeller Center are moving along splendidly," he reported to his father.

The problem with grand designs, however, is the way their magnificence can divert attention from more mundane details—details like what *Time* called "desolate acres of unrented space." All the Rockefeller enterprises in the world, all the whipsawed suppliers, and all the carefully recruited industry groupings did not suffice. Despite the impressive results the rental staff achieved, the men behind Rockefeller Center knew they had been trying to fill an enormous hole by using teaspoons for shovels. These buildings—accounting for only 60 percent of the area designated for eventual development—simply contained too much space. In March of 1933, with tenants already moved into the RKO Building, the Maison Française and the British Empire buildings nearing completion, and the RCA Building's opening just weeks away, a lugubrious Lawrence Kirkland told Todd and Robertson, "We are very close to exhausting our supply of leases in hand"— the stockpile of unannounced agreements that the publicity department fed to the papers each day. By late fall, after the first four office buildings had been open for months, just 59 percent of the carpet space was rented. The original plan had been predicated on a 97.5 percent occupancy rate by then. "The progress of the leasing," said Kirkland, "has been very slow."

The rental agents, who had earlier tried to lure tenants by touting features like the "broad dining terraces" on either side of the RCA Building or the Venetian-style bridges spanning 49th and 50th Streets, now saw such costly plums dropped from the plans. By early 1934 they began to concentrate on a radically different sort of inducement, offering space previously priced at $4 per square foot for as little as $1. (By way of comparison, Junior's old lease on his space at 26 Broadway called for $5.58 per square foot.) By late 1934 there was no longer even a printed rate schedule at Rockefeller Center; the stated policy had become "find[ing] the proper space for the tenant at the proper price." The situation made staff members so jumpy that one functionary worried that the famous view into the Music Hall's dressing rooms from certain offices on the third through ninth floors of the RCA Building would make those offices *harder* to rent: tenants, he feared, "will object to having the attention of employees taken up by the exposures of the actresses in the dressing rooms."

However upbeat Junior might appear—for him—at his occasional public appearances, however cheery he had willed himself to be in his communications to Senior, he suffered private agonies. The debilitating headaches that had come and gone his entire life now arrived in waves. Migraines that his family attributed to stress led him to seek an hour of undisturbed rest each day when he came home; he soon submitted to a series of inoculations in his desperate quest for relief. Some of the emergency tactics Robertson deployed angered him. "Conditions over which we have apparently had no control . . . ," he wrote Debevoise on March 21, 1933, "have constantly been forcing me to make investments in the Rockefeller Center project and in tenant enterprises of the project that I never would have dreamed of investing in under other circumstances. That this has been very distasteful to me, and to you as well, goes without saying. I feel there is a limit to which we can wisely go along this path, in order to rent space." Several months later these "investments . . . in tenant enterprises," as he euphemistically called them, put Junior and his development on the front pages not for fiscal daring, or for architectural innovation, or for a noble expression of faith in the ravaged national economy. Let a few of the words that appeared on page one of the *Times* on January 11, 1934, suggest the nature of this newfound notoriety: "Coercion . . . unfair . . . monopoly . . . unlawful acts . . . special privilege . . . destructive competition," all under a headline that began with the words "ROCKEFELLER GROUP." It was as if a time machine had dragged the family name back to the era when Americans had first gotten to know it, and to hate it.

"In real estate circles we were criticized for our ruthlessness," wrote John R. Todd shortly before his death, in 1945, "which was just another word for good business ability to go out and get tenants." From the beginning Robertson, Kirkland, and their agents—among them a sizeable contingent of former college football stars*—had been a little sharp of elbow. According to *Architectural Forum,* competitive brokers found them "uncordial." An internal Rockefeller Center document warned, "The high powered methods that created success in 1928 create resentment and resistance today. . . . Tolerance and generosity must replace the hard-boiled formulas of aggressive competition. . . . Avoid all hard business, or appearance of it. Buy close but do not chisel. We need friends." The writer of the unsigned memo was not persuasive. At Debevoise's insistent urging, William A. White & Sons, the firm Junior had first retained in 1929 and that had been handling Rockefeller real estate transactions in New York for decades, had its commissions cut off. On one page of a lengthy letter Todd sent Junior late in 1933, detailing progress and difficulties relating to every aspect of the development, one of the very few comments Junior inserted in the margins came at that point where Todd noted a savings of more than $800,000 derived from working "without outside brokers and the attendant brokers' commissions." Considering the difficulty of renting all that space, someone else might have found this a foolish economy. Junior did not. In his tiny, careful hand, just above Todd's comment, he wrote one word: "good."

There was no impropriety in working around the city's established real estate brokers; if anything, their you-scratch-my-back-I'll-scratch-yours way of doing business could use a jog or two. But the stratagems that placed the headline "ROCKEFELLER GROUP SUED FOR $10,000,000" on the front page

---

*One, a former Notre Dame captain named John Law, kept up his competitive edge during his spare time by coaching the football team at Sing Sing prison.

of the *Times,* with all those unpleasant characterizations trailing below it, were far rougher and had more meaningful repercussions. And though Junior did not conceive these tactics, it wasn't an accident that they evoked the unpleasant aroma that scented the Rockefeller name before Junior scrubbed it clean: this was a way of doing business right out of Senior's Standard Oil hymnal, utterly legal, utterly deadly to the competition, and, enhanced by large quantities of cash, utterly irresistible to those who could make it succeed. In a word, Robertson was paying businesses to skip out on their existing leases and decamp to Rockefeller Center.

The man who brought the lawsuit against Junior, Todd, Robertson, Winthrop Aldrich, Nelson Rockefeller, and virtually anyone else whose name would fit onto the first page of the court papers was, according to a contemporary characterization, one of "The 100 Men Who Make New York What It Is Today." August Heckscher had arrived in the United States shortly after the Civil War, a nineteen-year-old émigré from Germany. He made his fortune mining zinc, and thereupon transformed it into gold by exposing it to the alchemical properties of the Manhattan real estate market. He was an incongruous sort, a dapper little man with a white goatee who would show up at one moment donating Long Island parkland to the state of New York or providing the funds for one of the first playgrounds in Central Park;* at the next, in a theatrical gesture ordered up by the Democratic Party, he'd make a point of publicly "pleading" with the corrupt Jimmy Walker to run for reelection. Heckscher famously maintained his excellent physical condition through a regime that "consisted largely of thumping himself vigorously, pounding his head and chest and the heavy muscles of his legs and arms." He owned the thirty-story Adams Express Building on lower Broadway; he owned a variety of glamorous apartment buildings on the Upper East Side; he owned, obviously, the Heckscher Building on the southwest corner of Fifth and 57th. This was not only the first office tower erected under the 1916 Zoning Law but also the first home of the Museum of Modern Art, consisting of five rooms on the twelfth floor Heckscher made available to Abby Rockefeller and her co-founders in 1929 at the eleemosynary rate of barely twenty cents per square foot per year. Heckscher had another pre-1930 Rockefeller connection: he owned a handsome six-story house on the west side of Fifth Avenue between 49th and 50th Streets.

---

*Two generations later, Heckscher's grandson, also named August, served as the city's famously active parks commissioner.

But it was neither his threat to evict the museum (the noise from the unexpected crowds was irritating other tenants), nor the loss of his house to the Rockefeller Center wreckers, nor the fact that he was a board member of the syndicate that had taken such a beating on the Empire State Building that put Heckscher crosswise with Junior. The apartment houses uptown and the hulking Adams Express Building downtown were nice things to own, but Heckscher's biggest bet was a midtown parlay of eight office towers between 40th and 57th Streets, and Hugh Robertson's tactics threatened the balance sheet of every one of them.

To coax Universal Pictures out of a Heckscher property and into three floors in the RCA Building, Robertson's twin tools of seduction were predatory pricing and the outright purchase of the company's Heckscher Building lease. The latter was an example of the "investment [in] tenant enterprises" that angered Junior. To acquire tenants, Robertson was enabling them to skip out on their leases; a new entity, Centroc, Incorporated, was created for the specific purpose of managing the space Robertson was gobbling up. For him, subletting it at below-market rates was less troublesome than carrying empty space in Rockefeller Center. For the owners of the midtown buildings that were the natural competition, it was a triple whammy: first, Rockefeller Center was underpricing them; second, their buildings were taking on the sickly air that emanates from suddenly empty space; and third, Centroc could now offer this empty square footage for less than the building's owner might be charging for identical space just down the hall.

The process of depopulating a building was cumulative; as tenants left, the establishments that depended on them—barbershops, restaurants, shoeshine stands, newsstands—would be strangled as well. With a building's support services gone, office space was far less attractive, and that sickly air could soon become fatal. If Robertson was troubled by the consequences of his raiding parties, he did not reveal it. His only goal was to fill up Junior's buildings, and profitability didn't figure in it; profitability would come later. Heckscher's goal was to make a buck on the buildings he already owned. In the piquant language of his complaint papers, Rockefeller Center was "this modern Frankenstein [stepping] through the door of special privilege into the realm of destructive competition."

Frederick Lewis Allen, whose 1932 article in *Harper's* was the most acute analysis of Rockefeller Center in its infancy, had called it exactly right: "Where will [the Center's] tenants come from?" Allen had asked. "Not out of the dauntless expansion of business—not to-day, at least. They will mostly come . . . out of other buildings." Before Monsanto and the other chemical companies followed American Cyanamid into the Center, Robertson lured Cyanamid itself out of its twenty-three floors at 535 Fifth with a huge lease buyout. Shell Union Oil was interested in joining the Jersey Company in the RCA Building, but no one ordered up the moving vans until Centroc agreed to assume the leases Shell held in five Manhattan buildings. Robertson considered the lease buyouts "common practices," as he told the *Chicago Tribune* a few years later, but he nonetheless objected "to the word 'inducements.'" He told the paper, "We have carried on absolutely clean competition with higher prices and better goods," a sentence in which one of three assertions was true.

Robertson may have stonewalled, but the Heckscher suit and its lowering cloud of publicity did provoke defensive action. Friendly newspapers allowed Junior to provide canned statements drafted by Todd, who dressed them in curlicues of Edwardian syntax ("If no new and improved buildings were to be constructed . . . because the existing buildings contain more than enough space for the existing tenantry, would not the curtain be rung down on progress?"). In the rental offices, heightened sensitivities led Lawrence Kirkland to provide his bosses "details of all leases which affected other landlords in any way." And Rockefeller lawyers took their battle stations armed with enough writs, motions, and other legal parries to stall the case for seven full years, until it was dismissed on stipulation after Heckscher's death, at 92, in 1941. The *Times's* obituary for the "philanthropist, real estate and steel operator" ran on page one, and an editorial eulogized his "individuality and personal charm." Nowhere did the paper mention his lawsuit or recall the bank foreclosure brought against the Heckscher Building in 1934.

But long before the Heckscher suit was permanently placed on a shelf in some back room in the New York County Supreme Court building, the "canny Scotchman," as one newspaper called Robertson, had deployed his canniness—and his available resources—in devising a new way to attract major tenants without alienating other landlords. When he set his cap for the notorious oil baron Harry F. Sinclair, Robertson demonstrated that this venture was all business: Sinclair, who had served six months in federal prison on contempt charges arising out of his involvement in the Teapot Dome scandal, was not exactly Junior's kind of guy. But his company was large, and Rockefeller Center's need was great. To induce Sinclair to move his Consolidated Oil Company from its own thirty-story headquarters building at Liberty and Nassau Streets in the financial district, Centroc simply purchased the entire edifice.

This was something Junior could not tolerate. Already exercised over the "investments" he had been making in barely fungible leases, he stiffened at the notion of buying buildings outright. At Debevoise's suggestion he insisted "absolutely and unqualifiedly" that his prior consent must be obtained before the managers could ever "buy or take over" another building in behalf of the rental effort. This consent was not necessarily unobtainable. The record indicates that Junior gave his approval at least once, when the U.S. Rubber Company was lured to Rockefeller Center by the purchase in 1939 of its opulent, marble-sheathed headquarters (designed by Carrère & Hastings) at Broadway and 58th Street. The language Charles Heydt employed to tell Debevoise about the deal makes one wonder whether the stiff-backed Debevoise hadn't bent a bit to make the transaction possible. One element of the U.S. Rubber seduction, Heydt said, included "$250,000 when they move in next April, half of it for so-called moving expenses."

One doubts that the so-called Prime Minister mentioned this lagniappe to his client, but it's possible Junior wouldn't have objected had Debevoise done so. By 1939, Robertson had been doing his job so well for so long that he'd been made Rockefeller Center's sole "executive manager," supplanting Todd as the highest-ranking man in the organization whose last name wasn't Rockefeller. Robertson managed so deftly, in fact, that he even made it possible for Rockefeller Center and the family for which it was named to emerge with their reputations intact after the deal he made with Benito Mussolini and the one he very nearly made with Nazi Germany.

CHAPTER SEVENTEEN

Merle Crowell initiated the flood of words with a couple of mundane droplets. "Excavation work," as his Press Release #1 began, would not normally inspire the typical newspaper editor to read the rest of the sentence. But in the Man-

All the Finns in Helsingfors, the Mexicans in Guadalajara or the Scots in Dundee do not equal in numbers the daily population of Rockefeller Center.

—PRESS RELEASE, JULY 23, 1933

hattan summer of 1931 *any* work was news, and so was any document emanating from the Todd, Robertson & Todd offices in the Graybar Building. Just in case the editors he wished to influence were unimpressed, Crowell backloaded his opening phrase with dynamite. This was "excavation work," he wrote with insouciant immodesty, for nothing less than "the largest building project of all time." And—well, what the hell, why stop there?— here was a price tag for literalists who wanted their hyperbole buttered with statistics: the project was, Crowell proclaimed, a "$1,000,000,000 undertaking."

Soon enough, the man hired to tell the world about Junior's development dialed back his official estimate to a modest $250,000,000, which itself was a gross exaggeration but at least within the realm of human arithmetic. It may have been the only compromise with reality Crowell would ever make in his tenure as Rockefeller Center's head cheerleader, drumbeater, minnesinger, and mythmaker. It wasn't that Crowell lied—although he did that often enough—as that he just couldn't shut up. Once the words began to flow, they would continue in a thundering cataract for the thirteen years Crowell presided over a publicity effort that ranks as one of the most effective campaigns since the evangelists wrote their gospels. If you listened to Crowell (and if you lived on the North American continent, you couldn't help but hear him), the saga of Rockefeller Center had to be the Second Greatest Story Ever Told.

A farm boy from Maine, Crowell had come to New York hoping to become a lawyer or a newspaperman. He would have done splendidly in the first profession as, say, a litigator specializing in the kind of lurid murder cases painted across the front pages of the tabloids of the 1920s. His cavalier manner, his powerful build, and his vivid red hair would have harmonized well with the peculiarly hypnotic carny-barker eloquence that seemed to be his native tongue. The attraction of seeing his name in print, however, pulled Crowell toward journalism. By his late twenties he found his way into the developing mass market at *American Magazine,* where he soon rose to editor in chief by mastering the art of making mountains out of speed bumps and heroes out of the humblest clay.

When Todd and Robertson brought him in, Crowell assumed responsibilities that had belonged to the inevitable Ivy Lee. But by the early 1930s, Lee's practice had become so exalted that he was largely devoting his talents to keeping the names and deeds of his clients *out* of the newspapers. "If it is a question that cannot be answered," he told the editor Stanley Walker, "I say that we have no comment to make." When you're negotiating with both Columbia University and the Metropolitan Opera Real Estate Company, and preparing to acquire hundreds of leases from their suspicious holders, there are many questions you may not wish to answer. But when you're trying to line up occupants for four million square feet of office space, you'll talk to anyone, and Crowell was the designated talker.

That first press release was issued on July 25, 1931, as the steam shovels arrived on the site. In this three-page document he set out the notes of the chord he would play for his entire tenure: "largest . . . mammoth . . . greatest . . . impressive . . . largest . . . largest . . . largest ever executed." The nouns scattered between them mattered less than the percussive boom of his repeated superlatives. The catchall locution Crowell eventually settled into was "the largest building project ever undertaken by private capital," those last three words an acknowledgment of the existence of, say, the Pyramids or the Great Wall of China. (The phrase first showed up in 1932 and was still being used by Rockefeller Center tour guides in the 1960s.) When superlatives didn't suffice, Crowell turned to lists: "All the Finns in Helsingfors, the Mexicans in Guadalajara or the Scots in Dundee do not equal in numbers the daily population of Rockefeller Center. The entire population of the island of Tasmania or the republic of Turkestan is not so great as that of the development." Other favorite Crowellian tropes included the

Stunning Visualization ("If the 1,000,000 square feet of glass called for by the contract were spread out flat, it would cover completely an area of nearly twenty-three acres"; "If all 14 buildings were piled on top of one another they would reach 3,890 ft., almost ¾ mile") and its variant, the Preposterous Calculation ("If one man were to do all the work, it would take him 33,330 years"). There was also the Audacious Fabrication, as in his decision, sometime after May of 1932, to stretch limestone, steel, and the truth, asserting that the sixty-six-story RCA Building was seventy stories tall ("for publicity purposes," he said), a measure still accepted by reference books and architectural historians nearly three-quarters of a century later. In almost every Crowell release, numbers told the story, numbers that danced, numbers that dazzled, numbers that piled atop one another so precariously that they occasionally collapsed into an unintelligible heap. One release about the elevator contract for the RCA Building contained twenty different numbers, quantifying everything from weight to speed to capacity to the distance traveled each day ("2,100 miles . . . or about 760,000 miles a year—more than thirty times the distance around the world").

Neither public ridicule nor forces as influential as Thomas Debevoise and Ivy Lee could restrain Crowell. A *Fortune* writer moaned that "after reading about . . . an annual steam consumption of 298,000 pounds, or about the blaze produced by 39,200,000 annual kilowatt hours of electricity, your impulse may be to fly home and try to climb inside the attic of your five-year-old daughter's two-by-four dollhouse." Debevoise criticized "the most rampant boasting about size," and because he feared the public would conclude that "Mr. Rockefeller and his people have the biggest heads in the world," he asked Lee to "use your benign influence to stop this."

But the publicity effort was going so well that Junior had already begun to ease Lee out. "Now that the Rockefeller Centre [*sic*] has employed at a high salary a publicity representative who gives all his time to its requirements," Junior wrote to the man who had been one of his closest advisers for sixteen years, "it ought not to be necessary for that enterprise to call on you except for occasional consultation and advice." He also cut Lee's annual retainer by 20 percent, prelude to a further cut of 25 percent less than two years later.

Junior obviously recognized that Crowell's trumpets made irresistible music. Crowell never failed to remind his client of his effectiveness, even in the pages of the house organ he published. In 1934 the *Rockefeller Center Weekly* paused to assert that Rockefeller Center had appeared in newspapers and magazines more than a hundred thousand times in the preceding three years. By the end of the Center's first decade, Junior had become so pleased by and comfortable with Crowell's efforts that he became a willing participant in some of them: for a *March of Time* segment he allowed newsreel cameras to film him as he stagily measured blueprints with his folding yardstick; a few years later he agreed to a thirty-minute session with a photographer from *Life,* who had Junior walk back and forth in Rockefeller Plaza until he had the shot he was looking for.

From the beginning, coverage was constant. Over the three months just before construction began, the *Times* averaged more than three-quarters of a column about the development each day. Pictures taken by the squadrons of photographers Crowell sent crawling over the steelwork, scuttling through the excavation, or dogging the heels of visiting celebrities were staples in all the city's papers. One photograph of two workmen high in the beams of the RCA Building revealed the marvelous, sweeping southerly view, including, read the caption, "another mid-city skyscraper" in the background. Touché: from the photographer's perspective, and from a publicist's as well, the Empire State Building seemed insignificant, even irrelevant.

Outside New York, Crowell was, if anything, more effective. Newspapers across the country and overseas were happy to rely entirely on his version of Rockefeller Center, and Crowell obliged. He was peddling a story that couldn't miss: something expansive and optimistic at a time of enduring gloom, direct from the nation's commercial capital, and frosted with the glitter of the Rockefeller name. When the story of the buildings, their construction, and the publicity department's inventory of 6,355,782 factoids—if each one was a cantaloupe, you could fill Yankee Stadium!—could bear no more fanfare, Crowell began staging events that were news (feature news, at least) in and of themselves: an exhibition of English old master paintings at the British Empire Building; a tribute to "Famous Women in French History" in the Maison Française (featuring portraits by Ingres and David, and a butter mold that had once belonged to George Sand); the debut of the Ford Motor Company's new line of cars in the plaza in front of the RCA Building. Frequently the event was a pretext for appearances by celebrities whose presence might guarantee coverage: in 1935 cases of fruit (moderately interesting kumquats and tangelos as well as boring old oranges and grapefruits) were auctioned off for charity by Elsa Maxwell, Jimmy Durante, Sophie Tucker, and Ozzie Nelson.

Sometimes the event didn't even take place on Rockefeller property. When news occurred nearby, Crowell made terraces, setbacks, and other vantage points on the Center's buildings available to press photographers,

On West 54th Street, two Rockefeller houses: Senior's, left, and Junior's. In the background, three blocks south, three Rockefeller Center buildings: International, left, RCA, and RKO. The houses were razed in 1937, in part to make room for the Museum of Modern Art sculpture garden.

Roxy. He said "a broken heart is never trite," and also seemed to think that a nude sculpture was always inappropriate. He consequently tried to banish from the Music Hall works, below, from left, by William Zorach, Robert Laurent, and Gwen Lux.

Donald Deskey, in the Music Hall smoking lounge he decorated with aluminum foil wallpaper of his own design; below, the Roxy Suite, which was Deskey's most influential work—at least until he designed another icon, the Crest toothpaste tube.

Peter Clark, who created the Music Hall's mechanicals. He also devised this fully operational miniature version of the mammoth stage, which set designers and choreographers would use for decades as they worked out details of the Hall's live shows.

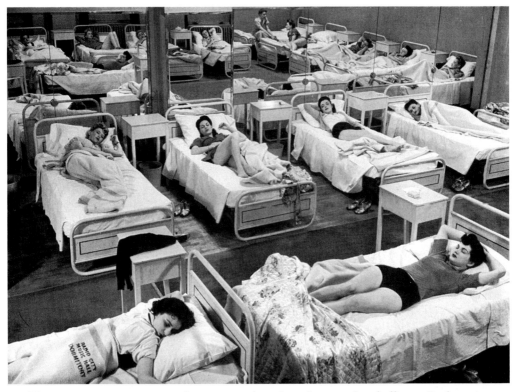

There was no surer guarantee of newspaper space than photographs of off-stage Rockettes (here in their Music Hall dormitory) casually baring some leg. They were certain to be more elaborately clothed when posing with Junior (accompanied in this instance by Music Hall director W. G. Van Schmus). Junior likened them to "the young ladies at Southampton."

The scale model of Rockefeller Center made its foreign debut when presented to Benito Mussolini, far left, in Rome. Hugh Robertson, next to Mussolini, and two aides secured the Fascist leader's cooperation in the development of the Palazzo d'Italia. Opposite page: The 250 Pyrex bricks of Attilio Piccirilli's panel for the building's facade were boarded up after the United States entered World War II, and disappeared from storage some years after that.

Diego Rivera in April 1933, at work on the "wailing wall";
weeks later it was covered in tar paper, which remained in place
until the mural's destruction in February 1934.

Rivera's mural, as reconstituted in Mexico City. Lenin appears between the two ellipses on the right; on the left, beneath the venereal germs in the upper ellipse, Junior enjoys a martini.

Junior found Leo Friedlander's figures above the north and south entrances to the RCA Building "gross and unbeautiful." Frank Brangwyn's cartoonish lobby murals won his approval, even though the artist had located the model for the nursing mother—"a fine, strapping wench from Brighton"—through a somewhat leering newspaper campaign.

The Gardens in the Sky were a triumph of both aesthetics and engineering (the RCA Building's heavily reinforced steelwork had to support 3,000 tons of earth), but a commercial flop.

The contest between Nelson (above, at his desk between portraits of his grandfathers Aldrich and Rockefeller) and Johnny was no contest at all; Nelson manipulated his older brother cruelly, and successfully.

In the 1930s, one elevator to the Rainbow Room was reserved for customers in formal dress, meaning white tie; men dressed more casually in tuxedos had to travel second-class. Off-season requirements were relaxed to allow "the type of summer dress accepted as formal at most country clubs, i.e., white jackets or white trousers for men, and summer evening frocks for women."

William Steig with the winter-frolicking "Small Fry" he painted
on the walls of the English Grill. Like James Thurber's chalk
drawings on the walls of the Café Francais just beyond the
skating rink, Steig's work proved temporary. So did the
magnificent Center Theater, demolished in 1954.

The Rockefeller Center maintenance staff at attention, in 1942; the next year, a Channel Gardens display sought to dramatize "The Nature of the Enemy."

Junior drives the Last Rivet, 1939. Rockefeller Center's formal completion did not come, however, until 1948, when he deeded it over to his sons. The following year, the clan gathered for a formal portrait. Seated left to right (and identified here by the ritualized nomenclature of Room 5600), Mrs. Winthrop, Mrs. David, Babs, Mrs. Nelson, Mrs. Laurance, and Mrs. John; standing, David; Winthrop; Babs's second husband, Irving Pardee; John; Junior; and Nelson. (Laurance was not present.)

who were gently informed that "we would, of course, appreciate mention in the caption of the fact that the photographs were made from Rockefeller Center"—not really germane for a shot of Cardinal Hayes's funeral cortege pausing outside the doors to St. Patrick's, but how could it hurt? Sometimes the event wasn't even an event: what paper could resist the story of the death of "Oscar . . . the world's most pampered pigeon," even if no one had ever heard of Oscar while he was alive—if, in fact, he had actually ever lived?

Another phenomenally effective device at Crowell's disposal was, in essence, a gigantic set of amplifiers. If "Every informed man in the world knows about Rockefeller Center," as one journalist wrote in 1939, the collaboration of the nation's preeminent radio network helped make it possible. NBC, which had its own stake in the Center's success, almost always announced its broadcasts' place of origin ("Direct from Rockefeller Center in New York"), and the network obligingly provided live coverage of Crowell-produced groundbreakings, cornerstone layings, and other events (and nonevents—the president emeritus of Bryn Mawr got fifteen minutes of network airtime out of an alumnae party in one of the rooftop gardens). After Arturo Toscanini and the NBC Symphony had been on the air for a few years, Studio 8H in the RCA Building was undoubtedly more famous across the nation than Carnegie Hall. And NBC wasn't Crowell's only influential collaborator: *News-Week* (as it was then spelled) was the very first tenant in the first-to-open RKO Building, and before the Center was ten years old Henry Luce's *Time, Fortune,* and *Life;* the New York office of *U.S. News;* and the headquarters of the Associated Press were all located in Rockefeller Center. All those writers, editors, and photographers could hardly ignore the wondrous occurrences taking place right outside their doors. More than half a century later, the Center's role as host to the disseminators of the nation's news continued to have its powerful effect. As a surgeon from Alabama standing outside the street-level *Today* show studio told a *Times* reporter in 1997, "All these people are smiling, 'Hey, Mom! I'm here in New York! And everyone is having a wonderful time!'"

"Mr. Chairman," Nelson Rockefeller began, standing on a rostrum in a tent thrown up on Fifth Avenue just north of 50th Street in the summer of 1933, "ladies and gentlemen. It gives me great . . . ," and he was off to the races. Although he had just turned twenty-five he had the comfortable manner of a pro. His speech celebrating the groundbreaking for the Palazzo d'Italia, just north of the British Empire Building, elucidated his father's interest in international amity, stressed the opportunities that Rockefeller Center presented for "better understanding" between nations, and proudly affirmed that thousands of men would be employed by this next phase in the Center's construction. When he was through, the applause was earnest but not particularly loud: his audience had consisted of two men operating newsreel cameras, a guy with a microphone, and a few dogsbodies whose assignment was to clap so loud their hands hurt.

Nelson had delivered the same speech just a few minutes before to a real audience of distinguished guests, local dignitaries, and several dozen men chanting ardently in Italian. The ruckus from the chanters led the camera guys to ask for a retake, and Nelson was happy to oblige. Call it publicity, or public relations, or spreading good will, if it involved interaction with crowds or cameras, Nelson was ready. His was an "easygoing charm," wrote Geoffrey Hellman in 1942, that "made him the logical man . . . to open bunny gardens in the Sunken Plaza, dedicate wisteria exhibits and skating rinks, present certificates and gold buttons to outstanding construction workers, and so on. On these occasions he made graceful little speeches with the manner of a particularly articulate and successful basketball coach."

What was striking about the slogans chanted at the ceremony for the Italian building was that several of the dignitaries arrayed on the podium behind Nelson joined the chorus. The intruders had come not to herald a new building at Rockefeller Center but to cheer the good health and long life of Benito Mussolini, who had personally endorsed this addition to Fifth Avenue. Il Duce's delegates on the purple-draped dais included Senator Antonio Mosconi, according to Crowell's release "a permanent Secretary of State of the Italian government [and] one of the foremost exponents of Italian economics," these last two words comprising a sly euphemism for fascism. If Nelson had been looking for an opportunity to prove his willingness to cut every available ribbon, shake every hand, and seduce every camera with a knowing wink, his encounter with the blackshirts sufficed. Then again, if Hugh Robertson and, to a degree, Nelson's brother Johnny had had their way, the political career of the future governor and vice president would have been snuffed before it was born: even Merle Crowell wouldn't have been able to explain away a public flirtation with the Nazi party and Adolf Hitler.

The Rockefeller family's entanglement with Mussolini and the near-miss with Hitler began in benign collaboration with the British and the French.

Robertson had cooked up the idea on a European trip in the summer of 1931, and Junior signed on immediately. To Robertson, the notion of dedicating specific buildings to the trade of specific countries was a way to lure tenants who might not have realized they needed prominent space in midtown Manhattan. It was that to Junior, but it was also a vivid demonstration of his committed internationalism. He told Debevoise that these were tenants "which we very much want," and was prepared to subsidize 40 percent of their costs for the first two years. The six-story structure planned for the southwest corner of Fifth and 50th was named the British Empire Building, its twin immediately to the south La Maison Française. Everyone liked the names except Nicholas Murray Butler, who found the second one undignified. He wrote to Junior—at his home address on 54th Street, perhaps to avoid the intercession of one of Junior's associates—to tell him it really ought to be called the "Palais de la République de Française."

Robertson brought in British and French syndicates, created especially for the task, to take on leasing responsibility in exchange for a handsome share of the rental income. While these groups went tenant hunting in London and Paris, looking for businesses that might benefit from a stylish presence in New York, they were represented by a couple of spotless front men. With Junior's name on his letterhead Robertson quickly recruited a sitting member of the French senate, Jean Philip, and the former head of the British Board of Trade, Sir Francis John Stephens Hopwood, First Baron Southborough, P.C., G.C.B., G.C.M.G., G.C.V.O., G.B.E., K.C.S.I. Lord Southborough told Junior that King George V and Queen Mary, to whom he had shown pictures of the planned buildings, "were much interested." He otherwise didn't do a lot for the project except deliver a speech and pose for pictures at the cornerstone ceremony in the summer of 1932, a grand event—broadcast nationally by NBC—that kicked off a three-day junket for the distinguished British visitors that concluded with a tea hosted by Junior and Abby at Pocantico Hills. For the cornerstone ceremony someone had installed a portable toilet, which was fortunate both for those who had to sit through the speeches and for a bemused Andy Reinhard. It was very thoughtful to have a toilet at hand, the architect said, because "Lord Southborough [is] one of the foremost peers of England."

To aid his effort to populate the foreign buildings, Robertson turned to the federal government. Lester Abberley, a well-connected real estate lawyer and professional schmoozer long associated with Todd and Robertson, looked like Winston Churchill but could play politics like a Tammany ward captain. Abberley went to Washington and came back with a priceless gift:

he got Senator Robert F. Wagner to introduce (and lobbied the rest of Congress to pass) the 1932 Exhibition Act, which provided "for the entry under bond of exhibits of arts, sciences, and industries, and products of the soil, mine, and sea," but only at Rockefeller Center. Fundamentally, the legislation turned a warehouse beneath the foreign buildings into a free port, where goods imported by Center tenants could be displayed or stored duty-free until they were sold. As August Heckscher described it in his futile lawsuit, this enabled a select group of importers to "carry on the practice of trade without the requirement of capital with which to pay duty."

The foreign syndicates proved unsuited to the rental task and were eventually eased out, but Kirkland's staff (including two men who set up offices in London and Paris) rounded up a respectable number of tenants, abetted by a law far more important to their effort than the Exhibition Act. The latter might have helped Kirkland land Les Parfums de Molyneux and Baccarat crystal, *Encyclopaedia Britannica* and the Librairie de France, the French Consulate and Alfred Dunhill of London. But only the repeal of Prohibition, enacted just as the two buildings were about to open, made it possible for the importers of Mumm's champagne, Marie Brizard liqueurs, Gordon's gin, three different scotches, and a wide variety of burgundies and clarets to plant their roots upstairs in the British Empire Building and La Maison Française and simultaneously take the lion's share of space in the warehouse that lay thirty-five feet below.

For Comte Charles de Ferry de Fontnouvelle, most mornings would begin with a ritualistic announcement of his presence as French consul-general in New York. After completing the ten-block journey from his apartment at Pierre's—that's what its clientele called the three-year-old Hotel Pierre, on Fifth and 61st—the Count would arrive at his office in La Maison Française and within minutes run his personal flag up the pole near his window over Fifth Avenue. Protocol required the U.S. flag to be raised at the same time on an adjacent standard, so a tipster—maybe one of the Maison's elevator operators, who all spoke French but were understandably loyal to their employers—would always alert a Rockefeller Center custodian.

The United Kingdom's consulate remained downtown in the Cunard Building, but the British Empire Building bore its national affiliation proudly. When Rockefeller Center ended its arrangement with the British syndicate, John R. Todd went to London and promised Lord Southborough that 620 Fifth Avenue would "at all times be maintained as a British building to be occupied by British tenants." If some unimaginable circumstance prompted a change in that policy, Todd added, the stone coat of arms above the main doorway and the four heraldic figures carved into the limestone of the top floor by René Chambellan would thenceforth be removed from the building.

Together, the two buildings and the broad passage that separated them were Rockefeller Center's first great success, if not commercially (the six floors of the British building would not be fully rented until 1937, the French even later), then at least aesthetically. Viewed from Saks Fifth Avenue across the way, with the blade of the RCA Building slicing the sky between them, it was a Beaux-Arts composition culminating in a Machine Age fortissimo. The formally planted promenade that fixed its axis was "a 200 foot long steeply banked corridor which led pedestrians, virtually by gravity," past the shop windows and into the heart of the Center. The slope concluded at the stairs that led into the so-called sunken plaza, where more shops and elaborate gardens awaited. The Café Henri Charpentier, its proprietor the celebrated chef who had invented crêpes suzette for King Edward VII of Great Britain, opened onto the plaza as well, at least for a while. "To have landed Crepes Suzette for Rockefeller Center is, we think, Mr. Rockefeller's most notable achievement to date," wrote E. B. White in *The New Yorker.*

The name Junior approved for the promenade was perfect: the Channel Gardens, dividing the British Empire Building from La Maison Française just as the English Channel divided the two countries in whose honor the buildings were named. No objections emanated from the Columbia campus, but that may have been due to Butler's continuing obsession with La Maison Française, a name he considered suitable for a restaurant or a drugstore but an embarrassment for a building as dignified as this one. He gave up on "Palais de la République de Française" and campaigned instead for "Maison de France." To Todd and Robertson this was a distinction without a difference, and despite a series of polite rebuffs Butler continued to badger Junior, Todd, and Robertson for nearly two and a half years. As often as not he cited his omnipresent if invisible chorus: the name "has been criticized time and again to me in France," he told Todd. At another point he cited "the constant scoffing which is the result of the present name." Todd politely reminded him that the French consul-general had been consulted early on and had approved the name, as had Senator Philip of the French syndicate, and that the former French premier Edouard Herriot had not objected when he spoke at the building's dedication ceremonies in April of 1933. Butler may not have picked up on this last fact, for during Herriot's speech the seventy-one-year-old Columbia president sat behind the French-man on the dais, arms folded, chin on chest, apparently fast asleep.

By 1934, Robertson knew that however much the rental effort was im-proving in the first group of office buildings—RCA, RKO, British, and French—it could never keep pace with costs. Lease payments to Columbia, mortgage payments to Metropolitan Life, and tax remittances to the city of New York needed to be amortized across a broader base of income, he said, "and therefore it will be necessary to go ahead with buildings on some of the vacant areas." Further, the construction and materials contracts for the first group of buildings, the ones Joe Brown had negotiated with the assis-tance of thumbscrews, water torture, and the rack, were still in place; Charles Heydt noted that if development of the eastern end of the north block proceeded, "the saving . . . under these [original] contracts would amount to approximately $2,000,000" relative to current prices.

The sort-of-success of the British and French buildings motivated Robertson to extend the international theme northward. After Ray Hood modified the original architectural plans, construction began on a thirty-eight-story tower directly opposite St. Patrick's, with two six-story exten-sions flanking the tower's forecourt on Fifth Avenue, where Lee Lawrie's heroic statue of Atlas would eventually reside. The need to cram as much rentable space as possible into the north block precluded the more capa-cious disposition granted the French and British buildings, but Hood de-signed the extensions—one called the Palazzo d'Italia, the name of the other very much up in the air—to match them, forming a harmonious quartet stretching from 49th to 51st Streets. Brown pushed the construc-tion schedule of the International Building so vigorously that only 136 working days elapsed between the placement of the first steel in the excava-tion and the day it was ready for occupancy.*

The hurry-up schedule was justified, as this new phase of the develop-ment marked the Center's first great commercial success. The tricolor and the Union Jack snapping in the Fifth Avenue breeze had signaled the first meaningful presence of international trading firms in the neighborhood;

---

*The only real construction delay was caused by a dogged search for the right metallic color for the four-story-high ceiling in the building's lobby. Andrew Reinhard finally discovered the per-fect hue in a bronze ashtray his fifteen-year-old daughter had made in school; the workmen bur-nishing the ceiling placed Ruth Reinhard's precious creation on a silken pillow and installed it in a place of honor on their scaffolding.

the duty-free warehouse in the basement offered such firms exactly the hedge against costs that August Heckscher's lawsuit had identified. The development of midtown had led to an efflorescence of first-class hotels in the area (the enormous Waldorf-Astoria opened on Park and 50th in 1931), and importers needed to be near the out-of-town buyers when they came to New York. Even better for Robertson, the steamship companies needed to be near the importers. When the Italian Line signed its lease for space in the Palazzo d'Italia (ticket offices and entrance lounge for first class and tourist passengers at street level, for third class passengers in the basement), an unsigned internal memo noted, "This lease is of the utmost importance inasmuch as it marks the beginning of the migration of the big steamship lines from the downtown section." The French Line, the Grace Line, the United Fruit Company, Matson Navigation, the Swedish-American Line and several others ("The armada of vessels operated by these companies totals nearly 500," read the press release) proved the writer's point, as all of them committed to space in the International Building and its annexes before they opened in the spring of 1935.

The steamship lines ferried in the operation that guaranteed the International Building's success—a U.S. Passport Office, relocated from the historic Subtreasury Building at the corner of Broad and Wall Streets, in the same neighborhood the shipping companies had just abandoned. It was the first time the State Department had located such an office in a privately owned building, but as the head of the Passport Division explained, "since most of the major steamship lines have moved their booking offices into this neighborhood," the relocation was necessary. The Passport Office was a mighty magnet. Soon Rockefeller Center was home to twenty-three travel agencies. New consular offices (China, Greece, and Latvia joined France in the first wave). Luggage stores. Foreign-language schools. And, glued to the Passport Office like a barnacle to a boat, the Passport Acme photography company, eventually churning out head shots for a thousand people on an average day, as many as eighteen hundred on a really good one.

Charging the government only a dollar a year for its space, Robertson was Tom Sawyer whitewashing his fence. There's no record of how much he might have been willing to pay the Passport Office to do the job for him, but apparently no one ever asked.

"Your Excellency," Junior's letter began, "I take great pleasure in submitting for your consideration the project of a Royal Italian Palace in Rockefeller

Center. It would afford me the utmost satisfaction if your great nation were to be represented." Three paragraphs later, it ended with this: "It would be my hope that through the years to come these buildings might bear silent testimony to the common purpose of our nations to promote friendly relations among the peoples of the world."

Within weeks Hugh Robertson was in Rome to present an in-person proposal to Junior's pen pal, Benito Mussolini, who obligingly posed for pictures next to the elaborate model of the Center that Robertson had brought along. (To indicate scale, and perhaps to appeal to Mussolini's imperial sense of himself, the architects flanked the composition with models of the Pantheon and the Column of Marcus Aurelius.) The Italian dictator had not yet invaded Ethiopia or pledged his troth to Hitler. He was a surprisingly popular figure in the United States, his political strength seen as a bulwark against communism, his economic policies as a potential tonic for the Depression. Franklin Roosevelt's National Recovery Act and the Agricultural Adjustment Act, in one scholar's phrase, "attempted to cartelize the American economy just as Mussolini had cartelized Italy's." As late as the summer of 1934, *Fortune* could devote an entire issue to Mussolini's Italy, not without admiration. While the magazine rued the fact that Italian "democracy . . . is dead" it also acknowledged that the impartial observer "must recognize certain ancient virtues" at fascism's core, notably "Discipline, Duty, Courage, Glory, Sacrifice." Those are all qualities Junior would have admired, so at one level it's possible to imagine that he really expected Mussolini to join "in common purpose" to "promote friendly relations," as he had said in his letter. On the other hand, he must have known that his potential partner had declared a police state eight years earlier, abolished parliament two years after that, and generally shown himself to be a not very nice man.

Yet the United States and Italy were not belligerents in 1932, and the list of nations Robertson engaged in negotiations was assembled without ideological bias. It even included the government of Joseph Stalin, whose potential involvement in Rockefeller Center was publicly acknowledged by no less a figure than Foreign Minister Maxim Litvinov only days after Roosevelt granted diplomatic recognition to the Soviet Union. It was as if there were no better way for a totalitarian nation to score propaganda points than to participate in this most visible of capitalist ventures. The fascist minister of state who led the Italian syndicate gathered support by describing how Junior, a man "more powerful than any monarch," was building "an international center where hundreds of thousands of people" from all over the world "will meet every day." Robertson, who managed to secure commitments for more than half the space in the Palazzo d'Italia before ground was broken, knew a good thing when he saw one, and for Rockefeller Center few things could be better than a nation that had reason to preen and pose in the heart of New York.

The twenty-three-year-old man who showed up for his first day of work at 26 Broadway in December 1929 was a taller, thinner, and possibly even less confident version of the twenty-three-year-old who had walked through the same door thirty-two years earlier. Launching his career at the height of the Age of Publicity, the third John Davison Rockefeller was greeted by headlines. Dozens of stories ran in newspapers across the country. The *Times* headline read, "ROCKEFELLER 3RD GOES TO WORK WITH FATHER; GUESS OF $5,000 SALARY CALLED 'WAY TOO' HIGH.'" He would have no specific responsibilities, his father said, but would begin by poking around the office and looking for something that caught his fancy. "I am not going to urge him to do any work that is not interesting to him," Junior said, "for I think a man succeeds best in what interests him." This was either delusional or disingenuous; his brother David believed John was "smothered by the number of boards Father put him on."

For his part, John told reporters, he thought that even working in the oil fields would be "darned interesting." Asked about his hobbies, he said he liked reading fiction and had just completed John Galsworthy's *The Forsyte Saga,* which he found "very interesting." His choice of words was automatic. John D. Rockefeller 3rd, whose most creative act in the first thirty-five years of his life might have been fastening an Arabic 3 instead of a Roman III to his famous name, found nearly everything "very interesting." This was more a function of the bankruptcy of his descriptive powers than of the intensity of his curiosity. In his voluminous diaries, the young John reported on his encounters with some of the most notable figures of the era with what would appear to be an oxymoron but can really be described no other way: stunning blandness. If a time machine had enabled John to attend a dinner party with, say, Martin Luther, Vincent van Gogh, Eva Perón, and Joe Louis, he would no doubt have proclaimed the evening "very interesting." And if he liked any of them especially, he would probably append his most enthusiastic form of endorsement: Luther, he might have written, was "an awfully nice fellow."

Junior "was like a sun and the boys like the planets," said John Lockwood, Debevoise's eventual replacement as the family's ranking Wise Man. "If one of them got too close, he got burned; if he got too far away, he spun into space." This applied to none of them as much as it did to John, who, despite frequent misgivings, agreed to do whatever Junior asked of him and then excoriated himself for his all but inevitable failures. In later life, freed from his father's expectations and his brother Nelson's manipulations, John demonstrated genuine skill and quite a lot of imagination in his full-time role as a philanthropist, particularly in the areas of population control and United States–Asian relations. As a young man, though, he found it difficult to form an opinion much less to express one. A sentence from his 1934 diary describing (after a fashion) an event at which he presided captures his essence: "Several post office officials were there and numerous photographs were taken," John wrote, as if standing entirely outside even this innocuous action. His was a life lived in the passive voice.

But in 1933, a few years before Nelson swatted him out of the way with a cruel carelessness, John engaged in an effort that could have had enormous impact on the future of Rockefeller Center. This was when he became the bewildered tool of Hugh Robertson in his campaign to complete the Fifth Avenue suite of La Maison Française, the British Empire Building, and the Palazzo d'Italia with what would have been called Das Deutsches Haus.

The idea of a German presence in Rockefeller Center began to percolate at about the same time that the Italian effort was getting under way. Crowell mentioned it in a press release, and the *Times* featured it prominently: "TWIN BUILDINGS FOR ITALIAN AND GERMAN INTERESTS TO FRONT ON 5TH AV. IN NORTH BLOCK." It was June of 1932; the next month a Rockefeller operative in Berlin wrote Robertson about his efforts to recruit someone to lead a German syndicate. He was getting assistance from the executive director of the Federation of German Industries, with whom Robertson had already met, as well as from local representatives of the Chase bank. The German political situation was uncertain because of the upcoming elections, but the present government—"mostly men of very high grade [from] aristocratic families"—was "in good favor." Well, not exactly: two weeks later, the Nazi party captured a plurality in the Reichstag.

Looking back from the twenty-first century, we might be left with a more savory impression if planning, negotiations, tenant recruitment, and other activities relating to a potential German building continued apace in the months before the Nazis took control of the government, then dissipated thereafter. In fact the opposite was true. Hitler became chancellor at the end of January 1933, the Reichstag was incinerated one month later, and in March the Enabling Act granted Hitler absolute power. By that point he had outlawed all political parties other than the National Socialists; jailed thousands of Communists and other anti-Nazis; shut down the opposition press; and required all civil servants to prove they had no Jewish blood. The same month, Ellery C. Huntington Jr., whom Robertson had sent to Europe to survey developments in Paris, Rome, and Berlin, affirmed "the belief . . . prevalent on the Continent that, for better or worse, Germany has at last a government which will have a better opportunity for stabilizing conditions there than has any other regime since the war." If Rockefeller Center Incorporated followed the same course it was pursuing with the Italians, it would be this government—specifically, "the official head" of this government—whom it would ask to "express publicly his approval [of the German Building] and give it his moral support and sponsorship."

In the months that followed Huntington's report, the pro-German (or at least pro-German Building) faction in Junior's circle asserted itself. Its leading members were Winthrop Aldrich, Ivy Lee, and Hugh Robertson. As president of the largest U.S. lender to Germany—in 1931, 3.5 percent of the Chase's total assets were in German credits—Aldrich had a special interest in fostering close ties with the German government, so he encouraged his office in Berlin to abet the project while "urging" Junior "at length" to proceed with it. Shortly after Hitler came to power, Lee had been hired by the German chemical giant I. G. Farben "for his aid in smoothing German-American relations," as the *Wall Street Journal* described it, and had already taken steps toward that end in meetings with Hitler and his propaganda minister, Joseph Goebbels. Although the Germans paid him more money than Junior ever had, Lee's interests were nonetheless conflicted. He advised Junior to go ahead with a German building, but suggested that he postpone announcement "until Hitler is better understood" in the United States. Only Robertson's interest was unalloyed: he had space to rent.

Enter Leon von Transehe, a fallen German nobleman who had befriended John D. Rockefeller 3rd. Transehe had been working in a filling station just a few years earlier, but the rising economic tide caused by the gravitational pull of Rockefeller Center lifted his boat, too. Robertson hired him to help find tenants for the German building, but appears to have recognized that Transehe's most effective work would turn out to be his attempt to manipulate the credulous John, and through him, Junior. Reading his meticulously detailed diaries, you get the sense that John never read a newspaper, listened to a radio broadcast, or discussed the political situation in Germany with a single disinterested party. At the same time Hitler was opening his first concentration camp, at Dachau, John was giving tours of Rockefeller Center to German dignitaries Transehe had brought his way and faithfully recording in his diary whatever line Transehe was feeding him: at one time or another Transehe said Rockefeller Center would serve the cause of international trade by including a German building; he said it would be an immediate financial success; and, in the words of the German consul in New York, whom Transehe brought by for lunch, "Jewish agitation" that "kept things stirred up" was but a bump in the development road.

Lee and Robertson joined the chorus. Lee told John the future of Europe depended on this new Germany. "[Lee] has complete confidence that Germany will succeed," John wrote, "and feels that Hitler is doing much to bring this about. A war in which Germany would be involved was unthinkable." Robertson avoided endorsement of Hitler or his policies, characteristically keeping his arguments on a practical plane. Although some Jews were threatening to withhold patronage of Rockefeller Center and its theaters if Germany won a place in the development, Robertson assured John he had talked to "several . . . Jews about the possibility of a Jewish boycott, and that they all had felt the danger was negligible."

John reprised the arguments of the pro-German party to his father, but on Labor Day, September 4, 1933, Junior was exposed to a profoundly different reading of German politics. Near the end of his annual summer sojourn at the Eyrie, in Seal Harbor, Junior, accompanied by John and John's wife Blanchette, called at the home of another rusticating New Yorker just up the road in Bar Harbor. Their host was financier Henry Morgenthau Sr., former ambassador to Turkey, father of Franklin Roosevelt's secretary of the treasury, and one of the "prominent Jews" someone like Junior would choose to consult in a situation like this one. Morgenthau's assertions were unambiguous and breathtakingly prescient. While Ivy Lee considered Hitler the herald of a bright new European morning, Morgenthau saw only darkest night. His "misgivings about the future of Germany" led him to tell the visiting Rockefellers that not only was war inevitable, but that "Germany would be dismembered" and "what would be left would not . . . be a world power for many years to come."

Barely a week later John recommended that Junior postpone a decision, while "mak[ing] no statements denying that we are contemplating the rental of this building to German interests . . . as this would put us in an embarrassing position with the Germans with whom we have been in touch." For Robertson and his allies, the door remained open. In late September, Robertson renewed an agreement with a German trade group that had been retained to solicit German tenants. In December, Transehe arranged for Hans Luther, the German ambassador to the United States, to call on Junior. Three months later another German friend was working on John, telling him that "one of the main purposes of the Storm Troopers was to break down class distinction and party lines." It was a pitch that Ivy Lee himself might have fashioned, tailored to appeal to Rockefellerian sentiments.

Even a year later, several months after Junior had issued his final, definitive no and after Leon von Transehe had disappeared into the anonymity from which he had arisen (abetted, perhaps, by his occasional use of a different name, Leon von Rosneck), and after Nazi depredations had escalated horribly, Robertson could not stop scratching the itch. At a meeting of the Rockefeller Center executive committee on October 25, 1934, he said he had commitments in hand from German concerns for 65 percent of the space in what was now referred to as "the unnamed building." In the unedited draft minutes of the meeting, he had this to say as well: "various people, recently consulted, seemed to feel there would be less opposition now to a German building."

Finally, though, Robertson was compelled to give it up. Even Todd, so supportive of his partner in most circumstances, had turned his attention elsewhere. To a surprising place, in fact: in a letter to Debevoise, he reported on a meeting with representatives of the Soviet government. They were keenly interested in the orphaned building, Todd wrote, "and we were decidedly in favor of giving them pretty much all they wanted and help[ing] them in every way we could."

The Soviets never got a building in Rockefeller Center; the last of the four foreign units was eventually named the International Building North and opened to anyone who could pay the rent, an inert solution to a combustible problem. And the closest Nazi Germany ever got to the place was in a series of propaganda displays the U.S. Office of War Information mounted in the Channel Gardens during World War II, such as the one featuring cutouts of goose-stepping German children wearing gas masks, bayoneted rifles slung over their shoulders: very patriotic, and very much in keeping with the sort of internationalist spirit that would pervade the Center for its entire history. In 1976 Wallace Harrison said, "I never heard anybody mention a German Building for Rockefeller Center." When "that monkey [Hitler] was operating, how could you think of putting up a monument to him in Rockefeller Center? We never thought of it."

CHAPTER EIGHTEEN

It was probably unavoidable that the biggest building in the complex, Rockefeller Center's symbol as well as its anchor, would cause the biggest headaches. Although Junior had once been capable of disappearing into mazes built of inconsequential details, the matchless efficiency of Hugh Robertson, Joe Brown, and others had largely freed him from distraction. But you can't ignore a lightning rod during an electrical storm, and for Junior the RCA Building served as one figuratively, much as its incised silhouette, viewed from the east, suggested one physically.

"What do you paint, when you paint on a wall?"
Said John D.'s grandson Nelson.
"Do you paint just anything there at all?
"Will there be any doves, or a tree in fall?
"Or a hunting scene, like an English hall?"

"I paint what I see," said Rivera.

—E. B. WHITE

He never really liked it in the first place, especially its jagged profile. Seen from his house on 54th Street, he said, the building "lack[s] symmetry or balance."* Ray Hood tried to explain that the RCA's exterior was "a frank expression of the interior," but he might as well have been speaking Urdu to an Eskimo. Junior thought the architects might at the very least even out the roofline by adding "a colonnade with arches and glass French windows" to its western end, and then capping the entire structure with . . . a pergola.

He was serious. Other important skyscrapers, he told John R. Todd, "are

---

*Some of his neighbors were more troubled by the shadow the 850-foot building cast over the West 50s for six months of the year; *The New Yorker* called March 13, the day when the sun finally reached the south-facing windows on 53rd Street, "the Rockefeller Equinox."

symmetrically designed and have a pleasing profile each in itself," and he couldn't understand why this one had to be different. Couldn't Todd drive down Fifth Avenue "from Mrs. Carnegie's house at Ninetieth Street . . . so that you may see the [RCA] Building from that viewpoint down?" He asked Todd to herd the architects onto a bus and have them do the same. It was the spring of 1933, and Junior's attention was focused by the calendar: the building was scheduled to open in less than a month.

Todd obliged Junior, but he stood up to him, too. "I sat in the front seat, as suggested," he reported two days later. But the view from Mrs. Carnegie's house or any other point did not change his opinion of the building:."I love it—am crazy about it," he told Junior. "I think it is the best thing in New York, or any other place." Todd agreed to have the architects work on some drawings, but no colonnades, French windows, pergolas, or other romantic fungi ever sprouted atop Hood's clifflike walls. Though the architects did agree to add small metal arches of unmistakably Gothic origin to the trim on some of the uppermost floors, you had to be next to them to see them. Unable to appreciate the building's appearance from the outside, Junior had to learn to enjoy it from within, gazing from his windows in the southwest corner of the fifty-sixth floor over these implausible throwbacks to the Middle Ages.

But Junior did have to enter the building from the ground floor, and there he would have to deal with a pair of twentieth-century scourges. One was modern art, in the form of some sculptural pieces he so despised that he couldn't bear to use the entrances they adorned. Seventy years later, Leo Friedlander's high-relief *Radio* and *Television,* represented in the form of allegorical nudes Junior found "gross and unbeautiful," are still in place over the building's north and south doors, even if largely unnoticed. The other scourge was modern ideology, as expressed in a battle that would echo off the lobby's marble columns forever. No episode in the Center's history has been more thoroughly (if inaccurately) chronicled, dramatized, or apotheosized than the encounter between the Rockefeller family and Diego María Concepción Juan Nepomuceno Estanislao de la Rivera y Barrientos Acosta y Rodríguez de Valpuesta, whose legend was as large as his name. It couldn't have been otherwise: in one corner, wearing the colors of capitalism and Protestant rectitude, the royal family of the free market; in the other, drenched in vivid Marxist red, an extravagantly flamboyant provocateur whose aptitude for publicity was nearly as acute as his skill as a painter. Junior may not have recognized the latter attribute, but from the very beginning he was mindful of the former. "Although I do not personally care for much of his work," he told Ray Hood, Diego Rivera "seems to have become very popular just now and will probably be a good drawing card." And wouldn't he just.

Rockefeller Center did not come by the sculpture and paintings that grace its walls, doorways, courtyards, and lobby ceilings because the men who built it were aesthetes. "It has been decided to decorate . . . the various buildings with the works of decorative painters," Webster Todd wrote to his construction manager, Ernest L. Smith, in February of 1932. "The work [is] to cost approximately $10 per square foot, plus cost of canvas and placing same on wall." A few months later his partner, Joe Brown, sent Smith a clipping from the *Herald Tribune* containing a fairly accurate list of artists who had been offered commissions at Rockefeller Center. Brown characterized it as "a list of artists of whom I have never heard." He commanded Smith to "please find out where in the world they expect to get the money for some of this work." James Todd, John R.'s brother, genially endorsed the idea of covering lobby walls with murals "as long as they are cheaper than plaster."

John R. had incorporated the cost of art in the budget from the beginning, but only minimally. The $150,000 he initially planned to spend wouldn't have covered much beyond the works Donald Deskey had commissioned for the Music Hall. Taking it further required the consent, and the enthusiasm, of a patron. Years later Wallace Harrison recalled that a million Depression-era dollars were pumped into the art program, and while this seems high it's unquestionably closer to the actual outlay. The Todd-ordained process of design and construction might have been, as Andy Reinhard described it, "a constant study of finance and form with ornament a last consideration," but Junior bent the process to accommodate his lofty aspirations.

Satisfying Junior's cultural wishes demanded more than a trained eye or an informed aesthetic—his inclinations required the pedantic march of exposition, justification, *meaning*. The men around him may have had tastes ranging from the daring and modern (Wallace Harrison) to the purely decorative (Todd), but only Junior seemed to take seriously a thematic approach to art. True to form, he decided to replace the unfortunate Hartley Alexander, whose Corn Maidens in the Cavern of Mist and Cloud had disappeared with him, with one of his customary Rockefeller committees of elderly eminences, asking the members to apply their worldly experience to the act of conjuring up a new theme. One committee member, George Vincent, the retired president of the Rockefeller Foundation, took a stab at it but struck only air. In a cover letter accompanying his outline of a theme, Vincent told Arthur Woods about "the futility into which I was plunged" by the assignment. "I sincerely wish I could be of some real value, but the unpleasant truth is that it is not in me."

Not that Junior recognized this, or even acknowledged it. He thought Vincent's memo "one of the most carefully thought out and helpful suggestions we have had," and seemed not to recognize how the theme Vincent had been embarrassed to suggest—"The Contemporary World"—was so broad as to be meaningless. So was the equally anodyne "New Frontiers," which Merle Crowell eventually plucked from a list of possibilities distinguished only by its indistinction ("The New World, New Frontiers, Newer Frontiers, Frontiers—Old and New"). Individual works were burdened with such titles as *The Abolition of the Painful Labor of Former Ages by the Creative Intelligence of the Machine,* or *Art, Science, Industry—Attributes of Civilization.* By comparison, Michelangelo had had it easy; at least *The Creation* connotes something specific.

A knot of committees and consultants, interwoven with layers of architects, managers, and Rockefellers, selected the artists and gave them direction. Most ideas originated with the architects, and final say of course resided with Junior, but John R. Todd guarded the gates, rejecting the architects' more outré ideas and, if Junior raised objections, stoutly defending those he favored. (One notion that didn't survive Todd's scrutiny was Fernand Léger's "moving mural," which the artist and Wallace Harrison had cooked up for the International Building, its projected cubist images—to be animated by Walt Disney—traveling up the lobby wall at exactly the same speed as the adjacent escalator.) When the architects gathered to discuss an artist, Junior often sent as his representative Florence Beresford, a devotee of chintz, satin, and plaid horsehair upholstery moonlighting from her interior decorating practice on the Upper East Side.

Yet another blue-ribbon committee, this one made up of distinguished curators and museum directors, was assembled, ostensibly to advise on aesthetic decisions. Some of its members, notably the director of the Philadelphia Museum of Art, Fiske Kimball, a specialist in eighteenth-century design and architecture, and Herbert E. Winlock, the Egyptologist who ran the Metropolitan Museum, seemed engaged by their unaccustomed foray into the art of the 1930s, and offered their opinions freely and frequently. But the great trainer of curators Paul J. Sachs, who had abandoned the family business, Goldman Sachs, to devote himself to a life of connoisseurship, hardly showed up at all, perhaps heeding the words he once uttered in a different context: "Let us be ever watchful to resist pressure to vulgarize and cheapen our work through the mistaken idea that in such a fashion a broad public may be reached effectively."

The sheer number of locations to decorate, the variety of media to be used, the varying tastes of the men doing the commissioning, and the innate vacuity of the "New Frontiers" theme all precluded any consistency of quality, much less style, in the scores of pieces that would adorn all those walls, ceilings, entryways, and plazas.

Some of the artists recruited to the task were among America's best known and most accomplished, foremost among them Gaston Lachaise. In 1918, twelve years after emigrating from France, Lachaise astonished the art world with the first of his huge, frankly erotic female nudes, *Standing Woman.* Four years later his work brought the highest price at the first major American auction of modern art. His renderings of women with giant breasts, enormous hips, and a powerfully expressed sexuality revealed both his gift and his obsession. At the very moment he was discussing what he might do for John D. Rockefeller Jr.—probably through the intercession of Nelson, who was one of the sculptor's foremost supporters—Lachaise was working on a bronze entitled *Breasts with Female Organ in Between,* a reductionist abstraction with a precisely descriptive title. It was the sort of work that led curator Holger Cahill to say that Lachaise had a "twisted temperament" that made him "look upon himself as a vaginal bacteria."

Lachaise would produce nothing gynecological, erotic, or even remotely radical for Rockefeller Center, nor would one have expected him to; his temperament wasn't so twisted that he couldn't understand the nature of the client or the commission. The four bas-reliefs he made for the Sixth Avenue facade of the RCA Building, and the two he carved directly into the stone at the base of the International Building's western side, are handsome works, the first a set of allegorical panels (*Gifts to Earth of Mankind,* and so on), the others representational tributes to the workmen who built the Center. They are hardly among Lachaise's best work, but they do what they are meant to do: add a little grace and a little inspiration to a public space. In fact, Lachaise served Rockefeller Center better than Rockefeller Center served him. His Sixth Avenue panels were obscured by the el tracks until 1939, and are situated so high on the building's wall—at the third-floor level—that they can really only be apprehended from across the avenue, which is simply too far away.

Paul Manship got a far better position for his work. The urbane Manship, whose career choice of sculpture instead of painting was ordained by his color blindness, was America's most celebrated sculptor, capable of earning as much as $75,000 from a single commission. He owned three attached townhouses on East 72nd Street, where a staff of assistants (Lachaise himself had been one for eight years) helped him issue a profusion of pieces—large figures, small medals, and objects of every size in between. His 1918 bust of John D. Rockefeller Sr. (to whom he had been recommended by John Singer Sargent) displeased its subject, who never wanted it shown ("Father feels so strongly that the bust gives an impression of weakness," Junior wrote). Frank Crowninshield, however, considered it nothing less than "the finest work of portraiture in sculpture of modern times," and in a rare father-son disagreement, Junior vowed, "If I were contemplating having a bust made myself, I should be inclined to select Mr. Manship." He also thought Manship "a delightful man personally."

Given Junior's regard for him (as well as the enthusiastic backing of Paul Sachs, who had not yet absented himself from art committee deliberations), it's little wonder that Manship was granted the most prominent outdoor spot for his piece, a fountain to be placed at the western end of the sunken plaza, down the long axis of the Channel Gardens where the eye stops before racing up the facade of the RCA Building. His subject was Prometheus, the god who gave fire to mankind, and, in this incarnation, punch lines to a generation of cartoonists and other wise guys. From the day of its unveiling, the eighteen-foot-long bronze, coated in gold leaf and weighing in at eight tons, was considered more an amusement than a work of art. Robert Day drew a cartoon for *The New Yorker* depicting two matronly women and a guard standing near the statue, one of the ladies asking, "Pardon me, but is this meant to be permanent?" For Rockefeller Center's house organ, Abner Dean showed one man saying to a friend as they gaze upon the statue, "Let's tie up the rights to radiator caps." A critic said Prometheus "look[s] like he [has] just sprung out of a bowl of hot soup." Many felt its unfortunate horizontal posture at the base of the starkly vertical RCA Building was all wrong; it looked as if it had fallen from the roof. Shortly after the piece's installation, the sculptor acknowledged that while working on it he had imagined the RCA Building would be "much wider than it actually turned out to be." Prometheus quickly acquired a nickname and a variety of bemused characterizations: he was "Leaping Louie," who looked like the Daring Young Man on the Flying Trapeze, or maybe a "young man escaping from his marriage ties."

Still, Prometheus became arguably the fourth most famous piece of sculpture in America, trailing only contenders of more substantial proportions—the Statue of Liberty, Mount Rushmore, and Daniel Chester French's seated Lincoln in Washington. In time the ridicule evolved into a sort of fondness. "There is . . . something innocent and endearing about a Prometheus who looks . . . like an idealized Western Union boy perhaps practising for the Olympics," wrote architectural critic Douglas Haskell in the 1960s. Manship, however, was less fond. Asked point-blank what he thought of it twenty-five years after its installation, he said, "I don't like it too well, no. I don't think too well of it."

On the Sixth Avenue side of the RCA Building a covered entrance, abutting the lot line and consigned to reside, at least for several years, in the shadowy pall of the el tracks, offered little opportunity for great art. This may be why the space was assigned to painter Barry Faulkner, who was Paul Manship's closest friend but miles beneath him in talent. Faulkner, who had worked for Todd on the decoration of the Cunard Building, persuaded the architects to let him make a mural in mosaic. Nineteen artisans at the Ravenna Mosaic Company in Long Island City glued nearly a million tiny tesserae to Faulkner's design, an allegorical porridge so opaque that every figure in it bears a label ("Thought," "Publicity," "Cruelty," "Hygiene") lest anyone mistake them for the ill-formed caricatures they are. One of Faulkner's friends who served as a model, the McKim, Mead & White partner James Kellum Smith, is rendered standing up, wearing a pair of lime-green overalls, his palms turned beseechingly upward; Smith is so badly modeled that it's no surprise to learn that Faulkner had him pose lying down, as if he were *trying* to make him look uncomfortable. When Faulkner's piece was unveiled in the entranceway, the Rockefeller Center press office announced that it "strikes a new note in exterior building ornamentation." *Times* art critic Edward Alden Jewell agreed, in a way: "I have been trying to decide where, in the wide, wide world, this acre of mosaic might make a nice spot, but for the life of me I can't. . . . As a work of art it is one of the most inept, graceless, empty pieces of mural decoration I have ever seen." Jewell did admit that "the little cubes seem to be correctly cemented, side by side."

Things couldn't have been more different at the opposite end of the building. Seen from the east, down the long telescope of the Channel Gardens, beyond and above the sunken plaza and golden Prometheus, right where the great upthrust of Hood's dynamic facade shoots toward the sky, the RCA's main entrance provided an operatic, even Wagnerian, opportunity for decoration. This job went to Lee Lawrie, whose total of fourteen pieces scattered through the three blocks made him Rockefeller Center's most prolific artistic contributor. Lawrie's best-known work inside the Center is the mammoth bronze Atlas that dominates the forecourt of the International Building; outside the Center, it would have to be his rendering of Franklin D. Roosevelt that several hundred million Americans of succeeding generations would carry in their pockets, on the face of the dime.

Although Hartley Alexander could rev up his engines to describe Lawrie as a representative "of the Renaissance, filled with the exuberance of a Cellini and rising into the visions of an Angelo," he was in fact a mild and unassuming man who considered his life, he said, "no more exciting than a grocer's." But Lawrie believed passionately that architectural decoration was the noblest expression of the sculptor's art, and constantly urged his fellow sculptors to leave the galleries and museums behind and get their work "up on the walls of buildings." Rockefeller Center provided him with walls and courtyards, lintels and spandrels, and, in one case, on the southern flank of the International Building facing the sunken plaza, a fine expanse of limestone that he converted into a giant pierced-stone screen. For the RCA Building entrance Lawrie fashioned a dramatic thirty-seven-foot-high representation of "Wisdom," in the form of a giant, godlike figure holding a draftsman's compass—an unattributed borrowing, as it turned out, from a William Blake frontispiece dating from the 1790s.

The Lawrie piece was a headache for Junior. His problem arose, it first appeared, from his never-ending search for Meaning, from wanting to make sure the words attached to the Lawrie piece were right. Sustaining an argument with the sculptor, the architects, and Todd for well over a year, he rejected at least fifty-six iterations, ranging from Lawrie's innocuous "Guided by Light, Heralded by Sound, Time Marches on Through the Ages," to the bizarre choice from the Book of Psalms that emerged from a meeting of the architects, "Day unto Day Uttereth Speech and Night unto Night Sheweth Knowledge." As each new idea for the inscription reached Junior's desk, his ill temper seemed to increase. He declared at one point that he "would prefer to have the space for the inscription left blank rather than to have something there that [has] no real meaning." But this wasn't adequate explanation for the intensity and duration of his displeasure. He eventually ended up accepting a quotation from Isaiah ("Wisdom and

Knowledge Shall Be the Stability of Thy Times"), but before he did, Junior revealed to Todd the reason for his persistent choler: he cared so much about the disposition of this entrance because "I shall not be able with complete satisfaction and pleasure to enter my new office building by either the north or the south entrance because of the Friedlander sculpture[s]." Those would be the severely elongated, "gross and unbeautiful" nudes perched over the 49th and 50th Street doors, which Todd had approved and which Junior just could not bring himself to order destroyed.

In an odd confluence of cultural opposites, the 1920s and early 1930s saw the same sort of heroic imagery that had begun to characterize Soviet art permeate the work of the most conservative artists of the West. The Armory Show, cubism, German expressionism—none of the early twentieth century's signifying art movements manifested themselves in the citadels of communism or the temples of capitalism. The same image might not have been able to adorn a wall in the Kremlin and one in the Hoover White House, but if his or her name were disguised, the works of the same painter could. It was a time of "convergence," wrote Rem Koolhaas, when "the style of Communism and the style of Capitalism—two parallel lines that might be expected to meet in infinity, if ever—suddenly intersect."

A signal moment in this convergence took place on a Thursday afternoon in January of 1932, at 10 West 54th Street. The occasion was a luncheon given by Abby Rockefeller. The guests included four architects; Abby's friend and adviser Frances Flynn Paine; the twenty-three-year-old Nelson Rockefeller, who was never far away when the subject was art; and Abby's new friend, Diego Rivera, the man photographer Edward Weston had named "the Lenin of Mexico." Wrote Abby afterward, "We had an amusing and I hope worthwhile discussion," mostly about the walls of Rockefeller Center and who might be asked to paint them (among the candidates: *New Yorker* cartoonist Peter Arno). Of course the discussion was amusing; Rivera's charm was nearly as legendary as his political beliefs, and in some ways equally opaque. "I have never known anyone with more perfect poise," wrote the sculptor Clifford Wight, who worked for a time as Rivera's assistant. "And I don't think anyone really knows what his bland smile conceals."

Certainly not Abby Rockefeller, or even the somewhat more worldly Nelson. Imagine: there in the parlor of New York's largest private home was this astonishing prodigal, six feet tall, weighing nearly three hundred pounds, in the concise phrase of his friend and biographer Bertram Wolfe "a monster of nature." At forty-five Rivera was midway through a career of extraordinary artistic accomplishment periodically debased by a propensity either to compromise the principles he claimed to cherish or to overdramatize them. Pete Hamill wrote that as a painter, Rivera "created a vision of the future," but as an individual he "was a liar, a mythomaniac, an artificer." His politics veered from one cell of sectarian Marxism to the next, and the further he fell out of favor with a segment of the left, the more he seemed to desire its acceptance. He rarely bathed, but this did not keep him from assembling a long and spectacularly varied list of lovers, among them Tina Modotti, Paulette Goddard, Helen Wills Moody, a young Louise Nevelson, and (most famously and most raucously) Frida Kahlo, as well as Kahlo's sister and, by Rivera's own assertion, the sister of another one of his wives. Rivera's "attractive ugliness"—Bertram Wolfe's apt term—was apparently not compromised by his dubious moral code any more than it was by his dubious hygiene. His friends and patrons included the J. P. Morgan partner Dwight Morrow and Leon Trotsky, Edsel Ford and Pablo Picasso. And Abby Rockefeller, who suggested that a mural by Rivera would be a wonderful addition to Rockefeller Center.

They had met through Rivera's New York agent, Frances Paine, the well-connected daughter of an American official in Mexico. It was from Paine that Abby had started buying Rivera pieces, including his sketchbook of scenes from May Day in Moscow, and through Paine that the Museum of Modern Art had arranged its popular show of Rivera murals in the winter of 1931–32. Between the completion of the May Day sketchbook and the debut at the MOMA show of *Frozen Assets,* his harshly critical portrait of a New York brutalized by capitalism, he had been expelled from the Communist Party. This was not a prerequisite for entrance into the Rockefeller social circle—the broad-minded Abby didn't operate that way—but it could not have hurt.

In early 1932, in the months immediately following the enormously successful MOMA show, Rivera was a regular guest at West 54th Street, frequently in the company of his twenty-five-year-old wife, Frieda Kahlo (who had not yet removed the Teutonic *e* from her first name in one of the era's more peculiar protests against Nazism). The entire Rockefeller family was captivated by the impish and impious Rivera. Nelson and his wife began collecting his work and seeing him socially, and David, the youngest of the brothers, who considered Rivera "great fun, charming and interesting," proudly hung one of the artist's May Day watercolors on the wall of his room at Harvard.

Abby developed a particular bond with "Frieda Rivera," as Kahlo signed her tender and touching letters to her new friend. Kahlo contained herself around Abby. She may have remained her excitable self—Abby's sister, Lucy Aldrich, said Kahlo reminded her of "a monkey who might climb up a curtain at any moment"—but at least she forsook the bilingual sailor's vocabulary that usually spiked her speech, presenting herself with demure gentility. Abby was almost motherly to her, especially after Kahlo miscarried in the summer of 1932. Frieda responded with equal warmth: "I can not forget the sweet little face of Nelson's baby," she wrote, "and the photograph you sent me is hanging now on the wall of my bedroom." A few days later, even Rivera (who had abandoned at least one of his own children) was drawn into this familial hug: "[Diego] misses very much your daughter's little baby and he told me that he loves her more than me. . . . He is very glad that you and Mr. Rockefeller liked [the drawing of Babs they had commissioned] and he thanks you."

Not only the greatest muralist of the day, but a quasi uncle, too! How could Rivera *not* have a wall to paint in Rockefeller Center?

It was indicative of Rivera's renown and the esteem in which he was held by the art world that he would be granted the indoor equivalent of Manship's prime location, the sixty-three-foot-long, seventeen-foot-high wall facing the main entrance to the RCA Building. And if that wasn't flattering enough, consider the names of the men asked to create subsidiary pieces in the corridors on either side of the Rivera wall: Henri Matisse and Pablo Picasso. Matisse, who would later take on other commissions from the Rockefeller family, declined politely, citing obligations to the Barnes Foundation in Philadelphia (where he would produce some of his greatest work). Picasso, who never responded to the invitation, at least had a good excuse for his bad manners: Webster Todd had addressed the wire requesting a meeting to "Pierre Picasso."

The replacement of Matisse and Picasso by the Catalonian muralist José Maria Sert and England's Frank Brangwyn did nothing to relieve the anxiety that had begun to gnaw at the New York art community when word of the mural commissions leaked out. Sert was best known in America for the murals he had painted in the new Waldorf-Astoria Hotel, on Park Avenue. In Europe he was known as a "society artist" whose work was "geared to the fashion world, the rich, and the vaguely talented," and whose fondness for cocaine and morphine did not deflect the patronage of the Spanish royal family and, later, Francisco Franco. Brangwyn was a decorative painter and illustrator who had apprenticed to William Morris as a young man, and his tastes and style remained forever buried in the nineteenth century even though he lived through half of the twentieth.

New York's artists got in a twist over the Sert and Brangwyn commissions not due to the quality of their work but because of Depression- and unemployment-stoked xenophobia. Fifty art students from the New School for Social Research demanded that Junior "give preference to native painters," and artists throughout the city and beyond saw Europeanist pretension robbing them of the patronage of the only patrons in sight. In response, Lincoln Kirstein's Todd- and Rockefeller-sponsored group mural show at the Museum of Modern Art provided an audition stage for American painters. Merle Crowell, writing in *Architectural Forum,* put on his dancing shoes and tapped his way across the head of a pin: it was an "unfounded rumor" that Rivera and Sert had signed contracts ("signed" was the operative word here) but "it seems logical that some of the work should be done by foreign artists." Still, Crowell proclaimed without even grazing the truth, "the most important work . . . will be done by American artists." Crowell would have been fine if he had elided the word *important;* the important work, at least insofar as painting was concerned, was the RCA Building work. But, pestered by the protesters and discouraged, no doubt, by their clumsy pursuit of Picasso and Matisse, the architects and managers turned to the home team. The only foreign national who received a Rockefeller Center commission outside the RCA Building was the sculptor Alfred Janniot, who landed his gig because the tenants of La Maison Française insisted that the building's main doorway be decorated by a Frenchman.

Janniot's superbly modeled representation in bronze of the friendship of Paris and New York bears scarcely a hint of the era that produced it. In this it was anomalous. Although from the very beginning critics assaulted a selection process conducted, as H. L. Brock wrote in the *Times,* "so as to suit everybody and to offend nobody," the architects, the managers, the bean counters, the old men of the art committee, and two generations of Rockefellers did a fine job. Taken as a whole, the art of Rockefeller Center does one of the noblest things art can do: it expresses the age that created it.

In one instance, this was true to the point of discomfort. To decorate the facade of the Italian Building, the architects commissioned sculptor Attilio Piccirilli. Born in Italy, virtually atop the rich veins of marble near the Tuscan town of Carrara, he had been working in New York for more than four decades, issuing from a studio complex on East 142nd Street in the Bronx (shared with his five stone-carving brothers) a body of work that decorated buildings and cenotaphs all over the city, notably the stirring Maine Monument at Columbus Circle.

Piccirilli was perhaps the closest friend of New York's primo Italian-American, Fiorello La Guardia, with whom he shared an aesthetic philosophy as well as an ethnic heritage. "I think art should be pretty," the mayor declared. In less delicate fashion, he once said of a sculpture by William Zorach, "If that's a bird, I'm Hitler." You could never misread the content of a work by the aesthetically conservative "Uncle Peach," as La Guardia called his dear friend. Zorach, creator of one of the nudes Roxy briefly banished from the Music Hall, once said that "architectural sculpture is essentially design—not expression," and most of Piccirilli's career proved him right. But what no one factored into Piccirilli's commission to create a ten-by-sixteen-foot glass sculpture for the facade of the Palazzo d'Italia was that in 1935, a literal-minded (and politically complaisant) Italian-born artist very well might produce a fascist icon.

It was a marvelous piece of work; during its incubation, when Junior learned on a visit to the artist's studio that Piccirilli's costs were running higher than the original estimate, he was nonetheless so excited by what the sculptor showed him that he arranged for a five-thousand-dollar check to be delivered to the Bronx the next morning. It was a backlit panel made of some 250 individually molded Pyrex bricks forming the heroic nude figure of a muscled workman digging with a spade. The legends carved into the Pyrex on either side read "ARTE E LAVORO" and "LAVORO E ARTE"—"art is labor, labor is art." Above the central figure, in large, bold characters, appeared the Italian for "Advance Forever, Eternal Youth," a puzzling title for the image but nonetheless imbued with the sound of bugles. Whether or not Junior—or even Piccirilli—perceived the piece as fascist imagery, the context made such an assumption inescapable to any sentient observer. Compounding the symbolism and the sloganeering, four spandrels by the sculptor Leo Lentelli at the building's roofline, corresponding to similar sets on the British and French buildings, celebrated the four ages of Italian greatness: the Roman Empire, the Renaissance, Unification, and Fascism. The last of these was represented by the party's logo of bundled ax and rods, inscribed with a bold "AXII" in commemoration of Mussolini's triumphant march on Rome on August 12, 1922. Suspended between the spandrels and the Pyrex panel, a huge stone carving of the Italian coat of arms bound the suite of images together.

This was powerful iconography; you could almost envision Mussolini himself, fists on hips, legs set wide, medals and ribbons bursting from his breast, standing atop the Palazzo a few floors above Piccirilli's dramatic screen to survey a parade of blackshirts marching up Fifth Avenue. It made Lee Lawrie change his plan for a carving he had been asked to execute over the Palazzo d'Italia's 50th Street entrance. "An ancient war galley would be the appropriate symbol . . . ," Lawrie said, "but I should like to do just the opposite thing—a St. Francis of Assisi Feeding Birds. . . . Although it may seem incongruous in the light of present events, it is a symbol of Italy that connotes Giotto, Dante, and all of the humanities."

As oblique as it was, this was the only recorded demurrer concerning Piccirilli's work—at least until the chilly day when workmen fixed sheets of wood over the front of the Palazzo d'Italia, entirely covering the stone coat of arms, the slogans, and the musclebound nude. This happened on December 12, 1941, when someone determined that celebrating the ideology of a country with which America was at war was not a very good idea.

Today, just a few yards north of where the laboring artist (or, if you prefer, artistic laborer) once toiled, a Piccirilli glass panel still in place on the front of the International Building North depicts a heroic young man pointing the way for a charging charioteer and his horses. When this three-ton beauty was unveiled in the spring of 1936, it clarified the mystifying title atop Piccirilli's piece for the Italian building, which had made its Fifth Avenue debut ten months earlier: *here* was that eternal (if elusive) youth, preparing to advance forever. Obviously conceived as a companion to the first panel, this one nonetheless survived World War II, apparently because no fascist catchphrase corrupted its surface. The fate of the two Piccirilli panels characterizes the odd convergence of public art styles in the 1930s. One piece was condemned by its context, while its ideologically fraternal twin was allowed to survive.

Diego Rivera carried his context with him. "All his paintings are conscious expositions of Communism," a critic wrote in 1931, two years before Rivera began mixing his paints in the lobby of the RCA Building. "The ultimate object of the paintings is . . . to expound the lesson of Communism, just as that of the mediaeval artist was to expound the lesson of Christianity." (This was no condemnation; the critic was the twenty-four-year-old art historian—and, it would turn out, Soviet spy—Anthony Blunt.) If Rivera painted a nude workman thrusting his spade into the earth and framed it with "Art Is Labor" and "Labor Is Art," it would have been read as an extract from communist scripture. No one in the Rockefeller or Todd offices who was even half-awake to the prevailing culture of the period could have been surprised when Rivera chose to use his RCA Building wall as a political placard. Rivera and publicity were well-matched mates. He was a world figure, "a tireless giant, a prodigy of fecundity," an artist whose accomplishments were as great as his appetites and whose appetites were immense. He was intoxicated by controversy, and controversy thought well of him, too.

Born in central Mexico in 1886, Rivera came to his artistic maturity in Paris, where he lived from 1909 until 1921. Those years also saw the emergence of a political identity that Bertram Wolfe characterized as "an undigested mixture of Spanish anarchism, Russian terrorism, Soviet Marxism-Leninism [and] Mexican agrarianism." After returning to Mexico he quickly established himself as one of the world's great muralists but eventually ran afoul of communist apparatchiks who attacked him for "trading with the enemy"— accepting commissions from the Mexican federal government. Following an eight-month stay in Russia (where he completed the watercolor sketchbook that Abby Rockefeller would purchase) and a few ideological skirmishes with Marxist sectarians, his expulsion from the Communist Party was made official.

"I continued to regard myself as a Communist in spite of my expulsion," Rivera wrote near the end of his life. You wouldn't have known it from the company he kept. Late in 1929, he accepted a commission to paint a series of murals in Cuernavaca; his patron was U.S. ambassador Dwight Morrow, the former Morgan partner whose daughter, Anne, would soon marry Charles Lindbergh (and whose murdered baby Rivera would paint into one of his murals a few years later). After completing his work for this capitalist general, Rivera went to work for an entire army, agreeing to create a mural for the wall of the members' dining room at the Pacific Stock Exchange in San Francisco. And then, in early 1932, right on the heels of those cozy social afternoons and evenings at 10 West 54th Street, Rivera was off to Detroit, at the invitation and under the sponsorship of the one American family that might rival the Rockefellers as the embodiment of the American economic system, the Fords.

None of this endeared him to the Communists, nor even to the Trotskyites with whom he had aligned himself, or to members of the other Marxist fragments floating loose in the body of the left. Rivera tried to justify his apparent alignment with the rich by saying he was using the pulpits they provided him to spread the Marxian gospel; describing his mural for the Pacific Stock Exchange, he claimed that he "painted the fruits of the earth which enrich and nourish because of the productive labor of workers and farmers." It would have taken a docent reading from a transcript of Rivera's description to make this clear to the brokers and bankers who paid him, or to anyone else who happened upon the handsome mural. They probably would have focused instead on the mural's large central image, a likeness of Rivera's lover of the moment, the tennis champion Helen Wills Moody, who was a dubious allegory for "the productive labor of workers." In his justifications Rivera really reached the far edge of plausibility when he underscored the revolutionary aspects of the painting by enumerating what he *didn't* include: "I painted no mortgage-holding bankers, or industrial overlords, or parasitic exploiters"—or, he might as well have said, no trapeze artists, dry goods salesmen, or scuba divers.

During the months he worked on the Ford commission, executing in the Garden Court of the Detroit Institute of Arts an exceptional series of murals meant to represent "Detroit Industry," Rivera negotiated with the Rockefellers. Money wasn't the problem; the $21,000 offer (which was also expected to cover his expenses, including salaries for his assistants) was $9,000 more than Dwight Morrow had paid him for the Cuernavaca mural and slightly more than double the original sum in his contract with Ford. But he didn't like Hood's idea that all the murals in the RCA lobby should be executed entirely in shades of black, white, and gray. He refused to take part in a precommission competitition. And when Hood and John R. Todd returned from their Parisian Picasso- and Matisse-hunting trip in the fall of 1932 without landing either painter and announced that they would be replaced by the vastly inferior Brangwyn and Sert, Rivera wanted to withdraw.

But eventually Rivera accepted the assignment. Buoyed by his work in Detroit, where Edsel Ford was nothing but supportive and encouraging (Rivera called it "the best and most fruitful period of my life"), he agreed to come to Rockefeller Center when he received the assurance that Abby and Nelson supported his appointment, and that Nelson had persuaded Hood to drop the black-white-gray idea (and a pretty bad idea it was, given how Rivera's work derived so much of its power from the brilliance of his palette). Rivera would even be allowed to paint his wall in true fresco, the paints embedded in the plaster itself. In mid-October 1932, with work on the RCA mural scheduled to begin in just three months, Nelson wrote Rivera, "May I take this opportunity to again tell you how much my mother and I appreciate your spirit in doing this mural under the existing circumstances."

If Diego Rivera ever read the standard contract extended to the Rockefeller Center artists, he would have noticed that in exchange for an agreed sum of money Rockefeller Center would hold full ownership over the art produced and would retain complete discretion over whether or not the work would be exhibited. But Rivera signed his contract without reading it and brushed aside Hood's suggestion that he show it to a lawyer. "You signed my sketch without looking it over," Rivera told Hood, who had come to visit him in Detroit. "You trust me, I trust you."

This account, provided by Rivera's young assistant Lucienne Bloch, who kept a detailed diary of the events of 1933, rings true at least insofar as their lack of concern for details and legalisms was characteristic of both men. (Hood had been thrown into the odd position of lead negotiator because the Mexican painter's second language was French, and Hood's French was superb.) It also seems accurate because at this point Hood knew that his opinion of Rivera's sketch was immaterial. An earlier version had already been approved by "two members of the owners' family," Rivera later wrote, "[who] were interested—or so they assured me—in having at least one true mural in the building."

And so it had. Not just a sketch but a textual elaboration of it as well, both of them in keeping with the ponderous theme Rivera had been given: "Man at the Crossroads Looking with Hope and High Vision to the Choosing of a New and Better Future." On November 2, 1932, Rivera traveled to New York to show Abby the sketch, a minutely detailed pencil rendering drawn on a thirty-one-by-seventy-one-inch sheet of brown paper and signed "Avec mes hommages tres respectueux et affectueux à Madame Abby Aldrich de Rockefeller, Diego Rivera, 11/32." Three days later he mailed her two copies of his synopsis, one for her, one for Nelson. His cover letter read, in part, "I assure you that . . . I shall try to do for Rockefeller Center, and especially for you Madame, the best of all the work I have done up to this time."

A year earlier, Hartley Alexander's "thematic synopsis" had suggested that "if a whole population, such as Rockefeller City will possess, can be lifted into a finer life in their working hours, then the economic democracy of America will have begun its answer to the Bolshevist challenge." Not if the Bolshevists got there first. Rivera's synopsis sounded like a less melodious version of the Communist Internationale, framed in the form of a very long caption: "My panel will show the Workers arriving at a true understanding of their rights regarding the means of production," he wrote. "It will also show the Workers of the Cities and the Country inheriting the Earth." In one segment of the fresco, "The Worker gives his right hand to the Peasant . . . and with his left hand takes the hand of the sick and wounded Soldier . . . leading him to the New Road." The text explained where Rivera intended to situate "methods of production," where he'd place "images of War" and so on; it just didn't say exactly what those images would *be*.

For that, Nelson and Abby had to look at the sketch itself, where there was no mistaking what Rivera intended. Most vividly, he placed in the upper left a mass of troops in gas masks marching in threatening ranks; in the upper right, in evident opposition, heroic ranks of workers rallied in front of the walls of the Kremlin, with Lenin's Tomb clearly visible. This was not a Boy Scout rally, nor was it rendered as the sort of vague allegory that Piccirilli would create for the Palazzo d'Italia. It was what one bought when one bought Diego Rivera. But in neither this sketch nor the more fully worked-out version that Hood waved off in January, did there appear a portrait of V. I. Lenin, anyone remotely similar to V. I. Lenin, or the variety of other provocations that Rivera had either not yet dreamed up or had simply decided to withhold from his sponsors. On November 7, Hood sent a telegram to the painter in Detroit: "SKETCH APPROVED BY NELSON ROCKEFELLER."

"Great murals are the product of three things," said *Fortune* magazine in a February 1933 article about Rivera. "An artist, a patron and a clean white wall." As that winter began, Rockefeller Center could claim only two of the three. The space where Rivera was to create his fresco was "a mighty clutter and stir of machine and workman, trucks snorting in and out, slings and hoists going aloft with stone, bricks, mortar, radiators, window frames, what not," wrote H. L. Brock in the *Times*. "It looks more like a gallery in a mine than the lobby of the biggest modern office building." A member of the advance company Rivera dispatched from Detroit to prepare his wall described how they had to pick their way through the showering dust and the clangorous din to "the main lobby, strewn with debris, scaffolds, stacks of metal pipes and rolls of wire."

As the Detroit project neared its conclusion more assistants relocated to the new site. A large, movable scaffolding capable of supporting a thousand-pound load went up near the wall, and one of the assistants built a shack on the lobby mezzanine that would function as a sort of headquarters. Telephone lines, work tables, a two-by-four-foot white marble slab for grinding colors, a supply of distilled water—all the requisites for the job were now in place, including a large sign one of Rivera's people felt compelled to post near the plastering area for the benefit of the unmannerly construction workers still toiling in the building: PLEASE DO NOT PISS HERE!

Thirty-five-year-old Ben Shahn, who wanted to learn fresco technique, joined the crew, an international bunch that included a Bulgarian, a Texan, a Japanese, a couple of Mexicans (including Rivera's personal chemist), and diarist Lucienne Bloch, twenty-two-year-old daughter of the eminent Swiss composer Ernst Bloch. One assistant, Clifford Wight, quit in midjob reputedly under orders from the Communist Party, which had begun to accelerate its attacks on Rivera for his growing intimacy with the rich. Others found themselves negotiating with the Plasterers Union, which announced it would not allow any of Rivera's assistants—Marxists, perhaps, but not union members—to continue working on the wall without joining up, which required payment of a very large initiation fee. The solution—the Rivera crew's agreement to hire a union man to sit by idly while they worked the walls—was probably not anyone's idea of a revolutionary act.

Rivera arrived from Detroit on March 20, 1933, and with Kahlo moved into a two-bedroom suite in the Barbizon-Plaza Hotel on Central Park South. Kahlo was as eager as a child to see her friend "Madame Rockefeller" again; Rivera was eager to paint. His assistants had enlarged the detailed sketch he had completed while working in Detroit, each half-inch square translated onto a one-foot-square piece of tracing paper and then stenciled in blue chalk on top of the third coat of plaster. Now Rivera paced back and forth in front of the wall, examining the blue tracery, experiencing the faint outlines of his composition from the same perspective as the thousands who would soon be walking each day through the building's vaulting lobby.

When Rivera worked, he was like some unstoppable train, fueled by little but the vision in his head. In Mexico he had once collapsed from exhaustion, fallen from his scaffolding, and lain unconscious for twenty minutes, unaided by the superstitious workmen who were convinced he had been pushed by the huge hands he had been painting on the wall. Here he painted mostly at night, hour after hour, rarely stopping to eat the food Frieda prepared. Between his ferocious bouts of work he played entertainer, rascal, raconteur. Shortly after arriving in New York, he amused his assistants with tales of the near-scandal he had provoked in Detroit, where the newspapers, some churchmen, and various other guardians of civic virtue had called for the destruction of the murals he had just completed. The pictures did not shrink from portraying the cold brutality of factory life.

Rivera was pleased that his sponsor, Edsel Ford, had remained steadfast in his support, and ecstatic that a number of blue-collar laborers had stepped forward to guard the murals from defacement. That, he said, was "the realization of my life's dream."

Now he readied himself to paint the Rockefeller wall. While Brangwyn and Sert worked in their own studios on canvas that would later be glued to the walls, in the not-yet-completed lobby of the RCA Building Rivera plunged into this most complex and arduous of artistic processes. Fresco requires both great speed and great care—"a race against drying," as *The New Yorker* put it in 1931. Right before the painter assaulted each new section of the mural, perhaps two square yards at a time, assistants applied a fine coat of fresh plaster, troweling and smoothing it to a shine. Then Rivera had about eighteen hours to conjure the world he had created in sketch and commit it to the wall before the plaster began to set. He used colors made from powdered clay and from metal oxides, the cobalt blues and Venetian reds and other vivid hues that gave all his work its extraordinary, vibrating life. "No fixative or protective covering is applied over the painting," said a press release announcing the start of work. "It will last, however, as long as the wall on which it is executed."

Rivera did not confine his New York labors to the Rockefeller wall. Asked by a reporter what her husband did in his spare time, Kahlo said, "Make love." This was true up to a point. But he also pursued additional research, striving for the exactitude of detail that combined so effectively with his grander, more mythic images. In Detroit he had spent a month studying the men and machines of the Ford Motor Company's gigantic Rouge plant in nearby Dearborn, and the verisimilitude of the assembly lines and blast furnaces and scores of other auto manufacturing components he incorporated into the work made his vast murals hum with life. For the New York fresco he pursued details invisible to the naked eye, traveling to hospitals and research laboratories in Manhattan and Brooklyn to study the shapes and forms of the "infinitesimal organisms connecting atoms and cells with the astral system" that he had indicated, in his synopsis, would occupy a portion of the mural's center. He did not want for top-shelf advice: Nobel Prize–winning surgeon Alexis Carrel, who was on the staff of the Rockefeller Institute of Medical Research, became his guide to the world as seen through a microscope, and at times even joined Rivera on his scaffold late at night, "lending me his biological skill and knowledge to be made plastic on the wall."

"Have you seen the final sketches of the work proposed by Diego Rivera?" Web Todd asked the architects late in March of 1933. "As you know, Rivera is now at work on the building and I think it very important that we see exactly what he proposes to install." His query was likely provoked by the events in Detroit. Eleven days later a frustrated Todd addressed the architects again: "could we at this time call your attention to our memorandum sent to you on March 27th, 1933, asking whether his final sketches have been approved by your office." No written answer survives, but on April 10, Todd told a colleague that "Diego Rivera is now working at the building and coming along very smoothly."

If anyone else was worried, they didn't let on. In a lengthy article about him in the *Times,* Rivera was at his provocative best. He seemed to be speaking directly to the party commissars who had expelled him and simultaneously provoking his employers for the CP's benefit. Asked whether he had painted "the philosophy of Moscow" on the walls of the Detroit museum, he replied, "Of course, because it is the only ultimate form of social life among civilized people." He said he painted to please the working classes, and considered "hostility and attack from the enemies of the workers" the highest of compliments. "The greater the attack, for me, the greater the success."

But no one bit. His former comrades in the CP, rejecting Rivera's obvious effort to reestablish his revolutionary credibility, continued their campaign of vilification. For its part, the Rockefeller camp was so little abashed by Rivera's statements to the *Times* that Merle Crowell actually boasted to Nelson that he was responsible for the article's appearance. And Nelson himself wrote to Rivera, promising to come by soon and look at the mural as it unfolded but in the meantime letting him know that "We all felt so badly about the discussion which followed the opening to the public of your murals in Detroit." If that was encouraging to Rivera, imagine how this sentence in Nelson's letter struck him: "As you know, the building opens the first of May and it will be tremendously effective to have your mural there to greet the people as they come in for the opening."

May 1! This was like offering a match to an arsonist. The idea of unveiling a work celebrating "the philosophy of Moscow" on the holiest day of the communist calendar inspired Rivera to work at a pace and with an energy remarkable even for him. He spent less time bantering with the gaggle of admirers, as many as a hundred at a time, who had been buying tickets to watch him paint. His assistants might enjoy moments of fun—on April 11, the day Repeal took effect, Rockefeller Center witnessed its first beer bash—but Rivera kept pushing himself, May 1 looming ever closer. To complete the thirty square feet of mural he now averaged each day, Rivera was frequently at work for sixteen, eighteen, sometimes twenty-four hours straight. Even after finishing the allotted thirty feet, he would go to the temporary shack on the mezzanine and examine his working sketch for hours at a time. One evening, taking a rare break to join his assistants for a meal at the Waldorf Cafeteria, under the thundering racket of the Sixth Avenue El trains, he was barely coherent and seemed in a daze, spilling six spoonsful of salt into his cereal, staring blankly ahead.

But when he worked, the images seemed to pour right out of Rivera's brushes. He always began his murals in the upper left, and now he filled the composition's first corner with the malevolent marching troops from his sketch, reinforced by baleful warplanes droning overhead. Below them policemen clubbed protesting workers, one of whom carried a placard reading "DOWN WITH IMPERIALISTIC WARS AGAINST SOVIET RUSSIA." Not far away, bejeweled women (their faces based on two Vassar students he had persuaded to pose for him) idly played cards and sipped cocktails. By Rivera's own description, these women represented "the debauched rich." An ellipse over their heads contained vastly enlarged amoebae and other microscopic life-forms that Rivera had studied so assiduously with Alexis Carrel and other scientific advisors, but the point they were meant to illustrate was not immediately clear.

This was not the case on the other side of the fresco, past the eight-and-a-half-foot figure ("Man at the Crossroads") Rivera drew from life, his model a Rockefeller Center construction worker.* On this side of the composition Rivera portrayed what was obviously the alternative to the simultaneously effete and brutal capitalism he had limned in the mural's other half. His version of "life in a socialist country" began with a parade of singing women in kerchiefs of deepest red marching valiantly forward, near athletic young people brimming with health. Sometime around the middle of April, Rivera drew in the first rough of a trio of workmen of different races clasping hands. Wrote Lucienne Bloch in her diary, "It is to prove to

---

*It actually required two models. The first one Rivera selected turned out to be the grandnephew of Tammany Hall leader John F. Curry; Rivera scraped his likeness off the wall when he learned he wasn't a genuine workingman, and started over with a new subject.

[the Communist Party] that he is not afraid of any capitalists that he paints the Moscow May Day with gusto and with plenty of Venetian red."

Certainly Rivera had not been given any reason to fear the capitalists he had been working for, not the members of the Pacific Stock Exchange, not Edsel Ford, and not Nelson Rockefeller, whom he considered his current employer. Though Rivera may have met Junior on one of his and Frieda's visits with Abby, it was Nelson who had recruited him, persuaded him, run interference for him with Hood, and, as executive vice president of Rocke-feller Center, had signed the letter commissioning him. It was Nelson who had been sending his friends to the RCA lobby to look at the mural-in-progress, and whose wife had at least once joined Rivera up on his scaffold, sitting there with the great collector Gertrude Vanderbilt Whitney for several hours, chatting with Rivera and watching him work. And it was Nelson who provoked the ecstatic entry Bloch inscribed in her diary on April 19: "Nelson R. called on Diego, is crazy about the frescoes!"

About a year earlier, before Rivera had been commissioned, Nelson Rockefeller had tossed a challenge at the august members of Junior's art committee and the architects they had been asked to advise. The men had all gathered in a private dining room at the University Club to pick an artist to create the first of the Center's murals, a sixteen-foot panel for the lobby of the RKO Building. It was a formal competition: five candidates had each been paid $150 to submit the sketches that were now posted around the dining room. No clear winner had emerged. The discussion that followed dinner degenerated into torpor, then cranky impatience. The deliberants couldn't even agree whether to select an established figure (John Sloan and Reginald Marsh were among the contestants) or to encourage New York's younger artists by choosing one of the lesser-knowns. Nelson, not yet twenty-four years old, rose to his feet. "Gentlemen," he began, "we seem to have reached an impasse in the judgment and the time is getting late." He had a way out: "If you select the work of the well known artist and it turns out badly, then it is his fault. If, on the other hand, you choose the work of the unknown artist and it turns out badly, then it is your fault."

Diego Rivera might have substituted a different adverb for "badly," but he definitely would have agreed with the first part of Nelson's formulation: this may have been the Rockefellers' wall, but it was his painting. In the hectic days before the fresco's scheduled completion date, he decided to make this known through Joseph Lilly of the *New York World-Telegram.*

When Lilly returned from his pleasant visit with the "very polite" Rivera, the paper's editors knew they had a delicious scoop. On Monday, April 24, they slapped it on the front page, beneath one of those headlines that editors concoct when they think they've got a chance to launch a controversy: "RIVERA PERPETUATES SCENES OF COMMUNIST ACTIVITY FOR R.C.A. WALLS— AND ROCKEFELLER, JR., FOOTS THE BILL." Rivera had given Lilly an inch-by-inch tour of the mural, now hidden from general view behind a large canvas suspended from the ceiling, spelling out every provocation he had embedded in it, including the information that among the microscopic creatures floating above the card-playing women were the organisms that caused syphilis and gonorrhea. In return for his scoop, the reporter supplied Rivera with a platform from which he could address his detractors and, suiting both the paper and the painter, thereby ignite a scandal. "I am a worker. I am painting for my class—the working class," Rivera told Lilly. "To be useful [to that class] is my object." The reporter understood the context perfectly well. Noting Rivera's expulsion from the CP and the accusation that he had abandoned communist principles, Lilly explained that "those close to [Rivera] say that he has seized this occasion to nail to the mast his personal colors."

And *still* there was no sign of alarm, or even concern, from the Rockefellers. Nelson met with the Art Committee on April 26; if they discussed Rivera, the painting, or the press coverage, which had now been kindled by the city's seven other newspapers, they left no record of it. (Nothing Lilly wrote could have surprised them; when Nelson visited Rivera on the scaffolding just a week before, he had seen everything Lilly described.) Rivera seems to have found the silence discouraging. On April 28 he sent his assistants out to find a portrait of Lenin, who had not appeared anywhere in the sketches, in the stencil, in the blue chalk outline, or in the red ocher adjustments to the outline Rivera had been making as he prepared to assault each new stretch of wall. The addition of Lenin, wrote Bloch in her diary, was "an afterthought."

As was the way it was discovered. Some Rockefeller Center workmen hurrying to apply a final coat of paint to the ceiling adjacent to the fresco got sloppy, and a little of their paint dripped onto Rivera's mural. Complaints to the Todd & Brown man on the job went unanswered, so Rivera's assistants turned to the usually available and always affable Ray Hood. While he was up on the scaffold to examine the drip marks, Hood noticed a new face in the lower right quadrant of the fresco. He looked at the bald man with the dark *V* of a goatee below his mouth and the circumflex of mustache above it, the slightly Asiatic eyes, the workingman's buttoned-up tunic, and asked Ben Shahn, "Who's that, Trotsky?"

And then, as Shahn remembered it, "the fun began."

In the entire humid jungle of correspondence, memoranda, posters, newspaper articles, ideological pamphlets, and other paper that grew out of the encounter between Rockefeller Center and Diego Rivera in May and June of 1933 there is not a single scrap that reveals the thoughts of the man to whom the wall belonged. Junior just went about his business. He let it be known that he thought it advisable to use artificial grass for the roof gardens. He recommended a decorator "willing to do work for us on an actual cost and ten per cent basis" for the office space he and his sons would soon occupy on the fifty-sixth floor. With Abby he took one of his restorative vacations at the Homestead resort in Hot Springs, West Virginia, and in mid-May he traveled alone to Dartmouth College. "While in Hanover I saw the murals of the other Mexican painter—Oresco or some such name," he wrote to Abby. "All I can say is that I am glad they are not on the walls of Rockefeller Center."

The man who painted the Dartmouth murals was José Clemente Orozco, a contemporary of Rivera's who, with David Alfaro Siqueiros, completed the era's triumvirate of aesthetically and ideologically revolutionary Mexican mural painters. Junior's lack of interest in Orozco's name and lack of respect for his art suggest how far removed he was from the fire of controversy crackling around Rivera's painting. So do the blandness of his tone, the brevity of his comment, and the unconcern he demonstrated by absenting himself from New York during the days when the flames burned hottest. For Junior it just didn't register.

It did, though, for Nelson. He had brought Rivera in, and in time he would see to it that he was ushered out. First, though, he tried conciliation. The May Day unveiling had been postponed, and on May 4 Nelson sent a fateful letter to his good friend Diego. While "viewing the progress of your thrilling mural," Nelson wrote, "I noticed that in the most recent portion of the painting you had included a portrait of Lenin." It was a beautifully painted portrait, he said, and "if it were in a private house" it would be acceptable. "But this mural is in a public building and the situation is therefore quite different. As much as I dislike to do so, I am afraid we must ask you to substitute the face of some unknown man where Lenin's face now appears.

"You know how enthusiastic I am about the work which you have been doing and to date we have in no way restricted you in either subject or treatment," he concluded. "I am sure you will understand our feeling in this situation and we will greatly appreciate your making the suggested substitution." Nelson may not have noticed the hammer and sickle Rivera had painted on a matchbox on the society ladies' card table, or the much larger one in the night sky at the painting's center. But he could not have missed all the other provocations he ignored in his letter. He said nothing about the rampaging police, nothing about the May Day parade, nothing about the syphilitic spirochetes and gonorrheal bacteria swirling over the heads of the card-playing socialites. Lenin alone was the offense.

In 1974, Nelson told an interviewer that when he first learned of Lenin's presence in the mural, he went to see Rivera at the Barbizon-Plaza. Rivera agreed to change the painting, as Nelson recalled it, but Kahlo later turned him around. Certainly Rivera's assistants, all of them committed leftists, pushed him to resist; Ben Shahn drafted a statement that the rest of the assistants signed, threatening to go on strike against Rivera if he dared to remove the head of Lenin. "It was not hard for them to persuade Diego," wrote Bertram Wolfe; as Rivera said to Wolfe, "What would the party say about my being a painter for millionaires?"

So Rivera declined, in a letter every bit as polite as Nelson's ("In reply to your kind letter . . ."). He offered to add a portrait of Lincoln to "balance" Lenin, and to insert as well a few other heroic Americans, such as John Brown, Nat Turner, or Harriet Beecher Stowe. He even indicated that he would replace "the sector which shows society people playing bridge and dancing" with these new portraits. But in one portion of the letter the placatory and largely nonideological language was stiffened by a brief spasm of rhetoric: "I am sure that the class of person who is capable of being offended by the portrait of a deceased great man, would feel offended, given such a mentality, by the entire conception of my painting. Therefore, rather than mutilate the conception, I should prefer the physical destruction of the conception in its entirety, but preserving, at least, its integrity."

Rivera signed the letter, and in his memoirs took direct credit for it. But he had not written it. His English was precarious, and it's possible that his resolve was as well. He told one friend that "it was [Kahlo] who prompted him to put all of those things into the mural," and told another that he "would have been glad to remove the head of Lenin . . . if only the painting would not be destroyed." But the letter, drafted in a strong and declarative hand on a series of small slips of unlined paper, was written by Ben Shahn, the most ideologically adamant of his assistants. Shahn likely didn't realize what a powerful weapon he was handing the people he perceived to be Rivera's enemies, but surely he intended to turn up the ideological heat.

After Lenin pitched his tent on the lobby's wall, security suddenly increased. A photographer Rivera hired to document his threatened work was denied entrance. Lucienne Bloch hid her Leica in her dress and snapped away at the Lenin portrait while another Rivera assistant distracted the guards by noisily adding a layer of plaster to an unfinished part of the fresco. The bantering art students and other Rivera fans who had been coming to watch him work had now been replaced by "Communists who made no pretense at art," but who very much wanted to defend Rivera and his painting from Rockefeller assault. On the morning of May 9, Frances Paine, the friend of Abby's who served as the painter's New York agent, handed Rivera the reply to the letter he had sent Nelson three days earlier.

Except it wasn't from Nelson. Nelson had left town. The letter, signed by Hugh Robertson, stated that Rivera had misled Rockefeller Center, Incorporated, with his November sketch and synopsis; that he had "taken advantage of the situation to do things which were never contemplated by either of us when the contract was made"; and "therefore . . . there should be no hesitation on your part to make such changes as are necessary to conform the mural to the understanding we had with you."

Robertson's first two statements were undeniable; Rivera had deceived the Rockefellers, and he had exploited the situation for his own purposes, namely the rehabilitation of his reputation with the communists who shunned and attacked him. The third statement is arguable. Under both the explicit and implicit terms of the commission, both the painting and the wall were Rockefeller Center's property; on the other hand, it's hard to imagine how anyone who knew Rivera and had watched the mural take shape could have been surprised by what the painter had done.

The one phrase in Robertson's letter that was patently untrue was the last one: "We know that . . . you will receive this letter in the friendly spirit in which it is written." After reading the letter Rivera went back to his painting. At 6:00 P.M. Robertson entered the Saturday evening gloom of the RCA lobby accompanied by a dozen uniformed guards and ordered Rivera to stop working. He handed him a check for the full amount he was owed for the painting ($14,000, added to the $7,000 he had been paid at the outset) and a letter telling him he was fired. Half an hour later, the scaffolding was wheeled away and workmen covered "Man at the Crossroads" in a funeral shroud of tar paper and wood.

A tale this epic cannot end so neatly. In fact, it could be argued that it still has not ended, seventy years later. It provided material for poets (Archibald MacLeish issued a chapbook entitled *Frescoes for Mr. Rockefeller's City*), commentators (Will Rogers: "You should never try to fool a Rockefeller in oils"), and wits (E. B. White's "I Paint What I See: A Ballad of Artistic Integrity" ran for forty-eight lines in *The New Yorker* just one week after the event).* Each new book about one of the major figures adds a new fact to the story, or at least a provocative interpretation. Hayden Herrera's fine biography, *Frida,* reveals that even the militant Kahlo felt that "in the case of the Rockefellers," as she wrote to a friend, "one could fight against them without being stabbed in the back." Cary Reich, in his cold-eyed but in many ways admiring *The Life of Nelson Rockefeller: Worlds to Conquer 1908–1958,* pointed out how Robertson's role on the night of May 9 arose from the "princely tendency—exhibited by Nelson over and over in his young life—to have surrogates handle his dirty work." Movies, like Tim Robbins's *Cradle Will Rock* and Julie Taymor's engrossing *Frida,* simultaneously burnish the story and blur it, inserting fictional details for the understandable purpose of advancing the plot but at some real cost to historical understanding. Yet they all keep the story alive: spend three or four hours at the eastern end of the RCA Building's lobby, and you are guaranteed to hear someone ask, "Where was the Diego Rivera painting?" Or, in the case of those who haven't been reading the papers for the past several decades, "Where is the Diego Rivera painting?"

It isn't there, of course, having been smashed into dust nine months after the tarpaper went up. Nelson, supported by John R. Todd, tried to get the trustees of the Museum of Modern Art to ask Rockefeller Center to donate the mural, cloaked by late 1933 in a canvas sheath, to the museum. He even thought MOMA could charge twenty-five cents admission to "cover the expense involved in taking it from its present location and setting it up somewhere else," and Todd went so far as to suggest that Rivera be invited to "touch up and finish the work." Either the trustees were unresponsive, or the act of removing a fresco was every bit as difficult as the press release announcing Rivera's arrival in New York had suggested ("It will last . . . as long as the wall on which it is executed"). Not long after a huge holiday wreath affixed to the canvas came down in early 1934, a phalanx of work-

---

*The entire poem is reprinted on pages 457–58.

men pushing an armada of wheelbarrows arrived in the RCA Building late on a Saturday night. Some accounts say they tried to remove the painted plaster, which by one calculation weighed nearly eleven tons, in large pieces; others suggest the fresco's destruction was brutal and swift. Rivera, in Mexico City, expressed sardonic thanks "for its destruction because it will advance the cause of the labor revolution." Rockefeller Center issued a press release that said, in its entirety, "The Rivera mural has been removed from the walls of the RCA Building and the space replastered. The removal involved the destruction of the mural."

Outrage ensued, particularly from artists preparing to take part—and now determined to boycott—a city-sponsored, Rockefeller-hosted art show in a new three-level gallery space elsewhere in the RCA Building. But many of the artists soon dropped their protest when Robertson authorized the release of another few words—those contained in the rhetorical fanfare written in Rivera's behalf by Ben Shahn months before: "Rather than mutilate the conception, I should prefer the physical destruction of the conception in its entirety." This was the argument-ending explanation cited by Rockefeller Center spokesmen in 1934; by Raymond Fosdick in his 1956 biography of Junior; and by Rockefeller Center public relations people for decades after the event.

Every major actor in the "Man at the Crossroads" drama played a long-running part; epics are like that. Even the mural itself survived, after a fashion, in an amended version painted by Rivera on a large wall in the Palacio de Bellas Artes in Mexico City. In this one a saintly light shines on Lenin, who has been put into a suit and tie instead of the worker's tunic he wore on 50th Street. Less prominently but more pointedly, a new portrait appears near the card players: John D. Rockefeller Jr., one hand clutching the elegant hand of an unseen woman, the other grasping a martini glass. "Junior's head," wrote a proud Rivera, was "but a short distance away from the venereal disease germs."

Only briefly had Rivera lost his poise. He was deeply shaken the night he was fired, and even the large crowds of protesters who had gathered outside the RCA Building by 9 P.M. couldn't lift his spirits. Police dispersed Rivera's supporters before they could disrupt the crowds about to emerge from Radio City Music Hall. "Riot cars hooted through the side streets and up aristocratic Fifth Avenue," said *Newsweek,* whose writers could watch the events from their windows in the RKO Building. Rivera himself went to his lawyer's office on 40th Street. Three days later he received a telegram from the Detroit architect Albert Kahn, who had earlier commissioned him to paint a mural in the General Motors Building at the Chicago world's fair. "HAVE INSTRUCTIONS FROM GENERAL MOTORS EXECUTIVES DISCONTINUE CHICAGO MURAL," the wire read. Wrote Bertram Wolfe, "All the promised walls in America vanished with that telegram." In the words of architectural historian Alan Balfour, "class solidarity cuts both ways."

Yet within days Rivera was the main attraction in a crowded schedule of marches, rallies, protests, and other meetings. Writers, painters, and a mixed assortment of strange bedfellows, including Lewis Mumford and Hugh Ferriss, signed protest letters. "In order to get here I had to do as a man does in war," Rivera told one audience before a week was out. "Sometimes in times of war a man disguises himself as a tree," he added, by way of explaining his subtle infiltration of the capitalist classes. The next day, addressing a crowd of fifteen hundred students gathered in front of Low Library on the Columbia campus to protest the firing of a communist faculty member, he took the opportunity to strike at an enemy-by-association, urging the crowd—in French—to "wrest control of the university from Dr. Nicholas Murray Butler." Though some communists, including party spokesman Sid Bloomfield, attacked Rivera for having offered to compromise with the Rockefellers, others now rose to his defense, one proclaiming that "Bloomfield is answered by the head of Lenin." Living on what he called "the money extorted from the workers by the Rockefeller exploiters," Rivera stayed in New York another several months, then returned to Mexico. As the events receded, his version of the entire affair got bolder and less accurate; soon he began to assert that he had given the Rockefellers a detailed description of absolutely everything that would appear in the mural. In 1954, following his fifth formal application, he was finally allowed back into the Communist Party. Two years later Diego Rivera had a new revelation for the journalists he had served so well and for so long: *"Soy Católico!"* the old man announced, just a year before his death: "I am a Catholic!"

At one point during the early weeks of rallies and protests, a day "that included an address by the painter before the Art Students League, a mass meeting in Columbus Circle, a radio address and a protest meeting . . . at the John Reed Club" came to a rowdy conclusion on West 54th Street, right in front of the Rockefeller house. Abby was in Providence visiting her sister, so she did not have to look out her window and see signs bearing such slogans as "HITLER AND ROCKEFELLER STIFLE CULTURE." Before leaving town Abby had sent Hugh Robertson a photocopy of the original sketch that she and Nelson had approved. "This is most important for our records," Robertson replied, for it resembled the finished mural about as much as Rivera resembled a Rockefeller. Two years later Abby made an anonymous gift of the sketch to the Museum of Modern Art, and gave a Rivera watercolor she owned to her son John. She felt Rivera had betrayed her, and so far as it is known she never saw him again.*

Nelson, however, did. Having persuaded himself that Kahlo was the culprit of the affair, Nelson continued to collect Rivera paintings, loaned some out for museum shows, and rarely had anything but good things to say about Rivera. Late in life he remembered with fondness an evening he had spent with both Rivera and Kahlo in Mexico City. Hayden Herrera later uncovered a photograph of Nelson and Kahlo sitting together amiably at a luncheon buffet in 1939. *Ars brevis, vita longa.*

Junior? Well, as Junior had never had much use for Rivera in the first place, it wasn't surprising that he stayed clear of the whole affair. Within hours of Rivera's dismissal Junior decided that any query made of him, Abby, or Nelson, from any source, regarding any aspect of the controversy, would be answered like this: "Your letter of [date] has been referred to the Managing Directors of Rockefeller Center." The managers, in turn, rose to the task. Robertson handled everything, from the firing of Rivera to the destruction of the fresco to the press manipulation he orchestrated with the baton handed him by Ben Shahn. John R. Todd was more John R.-like than ever: "The incident attracted even more attention to the Center," he would remember, "and again gave us reams of free advertising, not only throughout the country but in the world press as well."

It's possible that the offending presence of Lenin was exactly what Junior had expected all along, the obvious consequence of Abby's and Nelson's flirtations with artists of Rivera's stripe, yet by the evidence, it didn't bother him unduly. Until the very last act of the Rivera saga, Junior remained far more exercised by the continued presence of Leo Friedlander's nudes over the RCA doors on 49th and 50th Streets—two sets of allegorical figures, all of them distorted in shape, vague in content, and so unabashedly naked you could imagine them shivering in the New York winter. After several months of negotiation through the Todds and the suggestion that Friedlander

---

*Shortly after the fresco was destroyed Abby learned that Nelson had made an anonymous donation of $100,000 to the Museum of Modern Art to help it over a financial hump. She wrote him to say how glad she was that their common interest in art "brought us particularly near to each other." His interest in "the cause I most care about," she added, "fills my heart with a joy and gratitude such as I have never known before."

meet directly with Junior, the sculptor finally refused to make any alterations. The elongated, almost Mannerist disposition of his figures, Friedlander explained, was dictated by the three-quarters view from which most pedestrians would encounter them. As for the nudity, he would not even discuss it. (Friedlander may have been warned off such a dialogue by Lee Lawrie, who proposed for the Italian Building a carving of the nursing Romulus and Remus that Junior discouraged because it would have to include "too many teats.") Friedlander's obstinacy displeased Junior enormously. "I shall never be happy until this sculpture is either modified or replaced," he told Todd. This would seem to be a dispositive verdict, but Junior held back. "Since you gentlemen feel that this is not the time to go further with the matter," he added, with what was either reluctant grace or peevish resentment, "I of course acquiesce in your judgment."

However, when the judgment of the professionals reflected his own sensitivities, Junior could readily approve radical action. He did not order the Robertson-engineered annihilation of Rivera's fresco, but there is no question that it was an act he strongly endorsed. In that most private of venues, his intimate correspondence with his father, he told Senior the mural had been destroyed because of "a fact which has never been made public before, namely, that the picture was obscene and . . . an offense to good taste." He could only have been referring to the venereal microbes circling over the heads of the women. Curator Holger Cahill, who worked for both the Museum of Modern Art and the Rockefeller family at various times, supported the theory that the Rockefellers generally, but Junior implicitly, "were outraged by the vulgarity" suggested by the "syphilis and gonorrhea germs." If Junior couldn't bear Friedlander's callipygian muses, how could he possibly have tolerated this?

In the event, of course, he never had to. And from the summer of 1933 forward, art did not reach the walls, ceilings, or floors of Rockefeller Center without Junior's prior consultation and, often, explicit consent. Press releases announced that sketches for new works "have been officially approved." René Chambellan could not even craft the fountain nozzles for the pools in the Channel Gardens until Junior signed off on the designs. Believing religious representations to be out of place in a commercial building, Junior even made life difficult for the hapless Frank Brangwyn, who told the *Herald Tribune* "he had encountered the greatest puzzle of his artistic career because the Rockefeller Center authorities had asked him to depict the Sermon on the Mount . . . but to leave Christ out of the picture." In Brangwyn's finished canvas a hooded figure, seen only from behind, looms like some sort of pre-Christian Darth Vader.*

It took four years to come up with a replacement to adorn "the Wailing Wall," as the Rivera space became known in the Rockefeller offices. Junior and his advisers rejected N. C. Wyeth, they rejected Carl Milles, they rejected someone who wanted to put up a map, someone else who wanted to do something with mirrors, and Junior's own preference for that twentieth-century cliché, a series of clocks showing the time in different cities (Todd dissuaded him, explaining that somebody might "try to catch a train by the time in Singapore, and that wouldn't be so good"). Shockingly, they came close to hiring Pablo Picasso—the shock being not that Junior would consider hiring him but that Picasso would consider working for the Rockefellers. Less than three months after Rivera's firing, Picasso entered into negotiations, said Todd, to "do the job in one of his earlier styles, preferably the neo-classic." But he would budge neither from his stated price of $32,000 nor his refusal to show a sketch in advance. Finally Junior agreed to hand over Rivera's wall to that partisan of cocaine, morphine, and Francisco Franco, José Sert, who had delivered his side-hall pieces on time, on budget, and on subject, and whose sketches Junior insisted on approving personally.

Sert labored long and faithfully to produce the puzzling sepia mural that has held the RCA Building's place of honor ever since its installation. "The mural painter must give himself to the wall," Sert said around the time the Rivera storm began. It was a phrase every bit as vapid as *Labor Collaborating with Art,* as his painting was called, with its standing Abe Lincoln

---

*This was the least of the paintings' problems. Brangwyn's murals for the north corridor were so poorly conceived and dully executed they looked like cartoons. The ludicrous text blocks painted into the compositions, written by a British hack novelist named Philip Macer-Wright ("it has no human interest whatsoever," the *Times* said of one of his books) made Hartley Alexander's overheated panegyrics sound like late Hemingway. On a panel filled with naked (but discreetly posed) men rooting about in what appears to be a jungle while a dumbfounded woman nurses a baby, Macer-Wright's oversized caption read, "Man Labouring Painfully with His Own Hands; Living Precariously and Adventurously with Courage Fortitude and the Indomitable Will to Survive." The elderly painter recruited the model for his nursing mother by telling London's *Daily Mail* that he could not find women "of full and splendid figure, strong and supple of limb, children of nature grown up in nature's way." His needs thus advertised to all of England, his Sussex studio was within days overrun not by "flat-chested and narrow-hipped products of modernity" but by "women symbolic of their sex, as Eve must have been"; he ended up picking, he said, "a fine, strapping wench from Brighton."

leaning on the shoulder of a seated (and unrecognizable) Ralph Waldo Emerson; with a representation of the RCA Building looming in the background; with a lot of people climbing things on the left and sitting on things on the right; with its central image of what Frederick Lewis Allen called "a man on a scaffold throwing a tree at another man on another scaffold."

But did anyone ever look at Sert's panel just around the corner to the right, at the beginning of the north corridor? In April of 1943, as allied troops battled the Nazi army in North Africa, the *World-Telegram* did. Peering hard at the shadowy image of some tiny figures waving from a platform near a speeding locomotive in the upper part of the composition, maybe eighteen feet from the floor, reporter Helen Worden saw this: "Five characters in a José Maria Sert mural . . . are giving an unmistakable Fascist salute! With arms raised, palms outstretched and fingers held together in the regular Hitler-Mussolini manner, the five men stand on the platform of a racing train. . . . It is said that Rockefeller employees have been trying to hush the news of the 'Heil' salutes."

Oh my. If Junior read Worden's story, maybe he sought comfort by reaching into a file and pulling out the telegram his father had sent him ten years before, when the Rivera mess reached its messy climax. Even from the grave Senior's wisdom might have been comforting: "TAKE THINGS EASY DON'T WORRY BLESS YOU ALL."

CHAPTER NINETEEN

Nelson Rockefeller always believed he had assumed his exalted place in the family hierarchy in 1908, on a rainy summer Wednesday in Seal Harbor, Maine, at the instant of his birth. A third child would not normally arrogate to himself special rank or privilege, but Nelson perceived that the date of his birth was, as Ron Chernow wrote, "an omen, if not outright proof, that he was destined to lead the next generation of Rockefellers." For July 8 was also Senior's birthday, and Nelson grew to worship the old man and to emulate him, too. His energies were as prodigious as Senior's, his appetites as large. But what Senior had hungered for—money and dominance—Nelson inherited. Having no need of those things, Nelson wanted everything else.

I did not want to go on any boards— **I was not interested in sitting and listening** *to other people talk about what they were going to do. I wanted to do my own thing.*

—NELSON A. ROCKEFELLER

Like his grandfather, Nelson demonstrated a sense of purpose at an early age. Senior expressed his in the columns of numbers he entered in his famous "Ledger A." Compiled when he was a teenager and containing a record of every penny he spent or earned, cherished for the rest of his life as if it were a talisman, Ledger A explained who Senior was: careful, orderly, self-motivated. The precocious Nelson, at seven, revealed his own nature when he wrote in a notebook, "I would like to have the Sistine Madonna. I would hang it in my dining room. I would not sell it for all the money in the world. I would not give it to the Museum." Nelson was acquisitive, he was determined, and his sense of entitlement was boundless. Most of all, though, he was *certain.* Doubt did not cloud his days, nor did it disturb his dreams.

Whatever precocity Nelson demonstrated as a child may have arisen directly from his disability. His dyslexia was severe, and the struggle to overcome this impairment seemed to harden him, to make him tougher than his brothers—tougher in the face of adversity, and tougher on those who crossed him. Even in the exclusive fraternity that was the Rockefeller home when the boys were young, Nelson was head boy. He easily elbowed his way past the timorous Johnny, and built a permanent alliance with Laurance, his closest intimate for his entire life. Early on, Nelson and "Bill" (as Nelson would call Laurance for more than six decades*) created a mutual-offense alliance for the purpose of torturing their younger brother Winthrop, whom Nelson ceaselessly enraged with the taunting nickname "Wissy-Wissy" (Winthrop forgave but did not forget, in the 1950s pointing out to a visitor the tree in the Seal Harbor woods "where Nelson and Laurance used to kick me and tie me up and leave me"). The dyslexia made Nelson so weak a student that he could not attend Princeton, where Johnny was enrolled (and where, one would think, administrators would have been happy to take in a chimpanzee if his last name was Rockefeller). But after matriculating at Dartmouth, Nelson embarked on a systematic self-improvement campaign, carefully underlining words whose spelling eluded him, rising each morning at seven to study, and in time graduating with distinction.

Once launched into the business world, Nelson tried to devise ways to overcome his trouble with words—for instance, if he received a handwritten letter, a secretary would type it out for him before it reached his desk. "I have a terrible time," he once told an associate. "I can't see a whole word. I have to go through it syllable by syllable. If I just glance at something I get it mixed up. I have no confidence in reading." Nor in writing—his appointment diaries contain references to meetings at the "Harver Club," and he could not even master Wallace Harrison's name, though Harrison became one of his closest friends through their collaborations at Rockefeller Center. In his diaries Nelson frequently spelled it "Harryson."

Is it possible that Nelson's enduring battle with dyslexia convinced him that not everything had been handed to him, that he had faced a roadblock and vaulted past it on the springs of his own determination? There's no question that he somehow found a way to cast aside the muddled legacy of guilt and obligation that enclosed Junior; something other than genetic ac-

---

*Laurance—the spelling came from his grandmother Laura's name—had become "Bill" and Nelson had become "Dick" when they were children and determined that their given names were unmanly.

cident must have enabled him to shed the mantle of humility donned nightly at Junior's dinner table. Once asked how he would have pursued his life if he hadn't been born with a fortune, he said, "I would think of making one"—something Junior could not have said, could not have believed, and in all likelihood could never have accomplished. But it was an attitude that Junior could definitely admire. Just as Junior worshipped Abby for all of those qualities that he himself lacked, he found in Nelson the person he could never be yet someone whom he could nonetheless see as a surrogate. Abby brought taste, sociability, and adventurous spirit into Junior's life; Nelson brought confidence, daring, and ambition. No wonder Junior did not blame Nelson for the Rivera affair, even if it clouded the family name more than any single event since Ludlow. (Admittedly, it also won the family some friends, but among their number were some right-wing editorialists whose other views would have made Junior blanch.) In fact, if the whole ugly business was responsible for the letter Nelson sent his father on July 3, 1933, less than two months after the tarpaper went up on the wall of the RCA lobby, Junior would have owed Diego Rivera the greatest of debts. "I simply want you to know by this letter than I am back in the fold again," Nelson told his father, ". . . and that from now on my one desire will be to be as much of a help to you as I possibly can with my limited experience. I assure you that I will spare nothing toward this end."

By the winter of 1933–34, at roughly the same time the Heckscher suit was filed and the Rivera mural was destroyed, not long after word of the ill-conceived plans to develop a German building had begun to leak into print, and only a year after the catastrophic opening of Radio City Music Hall; as the brief economic recovery occasioned by the first days of Roosevelt's New Deal evaporated into the chill air; as Junior spent more and more time away at various spas seeking to preserve not only his own precarious health but his wife's as well (during times of stress, he said, Abby was "depressed and discouraged and lacking strength"); and as John R. Todd was about to confront the fact that he wasn't the boss's son—amid all this turmoil, discomfort, and doubt, something new and different began to occur around Rockefeller Center. People began to admit that they liked it.

The first public renunciation of previous criticism couldn't have been more forthright. "After all the carping we have done about Rockefeller Center, it pleases us to eat dirt," read a "Notes and Comment" item in the December 9, 1933, edition of *The New Yorker.* Mumford's signed pieces notwithstanding, the magazine's editorial "we" atoned for the snarky sarcasm and indignant harrumphs that had characterized its earlier commentary. "We are prepared to admit that the Center is beautiful," E. B. White wrote in the magazine's behalf. "If Mr. Rockefeller will send us over a level teaspoonful of strained dirt, we will eat it publicly, in the sunken garden below his monument." White himself elsewhere described how much he enjoyed walking a few blocks uptown from his office to take an elevator to the RCA's open-air observation deck and relax in one of the handsome Adirondack chairs provided for the crowds he so contentedly joined.

The *Times,* in its *Times*ian fashion, incrementally moderated its editorial page doubts about the enterprise, but its editor, John H. Finley, was privately direct. "I wish that you could have seen your high tower as I saw it from a *Times* window in the late afternoon light on Thanksgiving Day," Finley wrote Junior. He invoked a description of the desert city of Petra ("a rose red city half as old as time") and admitted that "I am now quite reconciled and grateful." At the Music Box Theatre, where sold-out audiences had been laughing as Senior rejected his son's "gift" of unrented and unrentable buildings, the producers of *As Thousands Cheer* recanted quietly but convincingly. All along they had kept in reserve an alternate piece they could drop into the show upon Senior's death. But Senior lasted longer than the Center's reputation as a loser, and in the summer of 1934 the skit was dropped from the show, a victim of its irrelevance.

In the following year Rockefeller Center received the endorsement that signaled its elevation from scorned commercial exploit to revered architectural masterpiece. The man who could offer this priceless gift arrived in New York in the fall of 1935. As he prepared to disembark from his ship, his first comment was a question directed at his translator. "Jacobs," he asked, "where are the photographers?" Charles-Edouard Jeanneret certainly looked odd enough to attract a camera or two: pale and thin, on his dome-like head a bowler hat, on his beakish nose a pair of glasses—goggles, almost—consisting of round lenses encircled and supported by black frames as thick as a finger. But Jeanneret, aka Le Corbusier—architect, theorist, agitator, egomaniac—believed he deserved the attention of the press on merit. Jacobs dug up a compliant photographer who had expended all his film on the *Normandie*'s more obvious celebrities but nonetheless agreed to snap away at Le Corbusier with his empty camera. His subject seemed pleased.

You could reasonably think that Corbu, as several generations of acolytes would call him, was invented by Merle Crowell, given the role he would soon play on his first trip to America. Corbu, however, was his own creation. Geoffrey Hellman, in *The New Yorker,* said, "Except, perhaps, for Frank Lloyd Wright, no living architect has been more widely discussed, by others or by himself."* His visionary declarations about architecture and cities had provided philosophical justification for the proponents of the International Style, and one of his books, *Toward a New Architecture,* which declared itself for the rational over the emotional, the functional over the decorative, the planned over the organic, had even provided inspiration for the dogmaphobic Raymond Hood. His detractors believed he "showed everybody how to become a famous architect without designing any buildings." Even his supporters believed "his opinion was of equal value to his architectural achievements." For years he had been lobbing ideological grenades into design studios and drafting rooms, the shrapnel invariably gouging the "pathetic paradox" that was skyscraper Manhattan. He characterized New York's towers as "tumult" and "hairgrowth" that had "petrified the city," turning pedestrians into lice.

But now, in the fall of 1935, sailing into Manhattan on Rockefeller-sponsored breezes, he began a twenty-city tour of America initiated by the Museum of Modern Art, supported by the Rockefeller Foundation, and launched out of the RCA Building. Two hours after posing for the filmless photographer, Corbu was speaking to reporters at MOMA. Three days later, wearing his inevitable tight-fitting suit and bowtie, his owlish glasses glinting in the lights, he delivered a speech in the Rainbow Room on the RCA's sixty-fifth floor, and shortly afterward took the elevator down to the NBC studios to address a fifty-station nationwide radio hookup. His message was that Manhattan was an abomination, save for one redeeming exception. Rockefeller Center, he believed, was "rational, logically conceived, biologically normal, harmonious." Unlike the rest of petrified Manhattan, Corbu declared, Rockefeller Center embodied "architectural life."

The heroics of generals are memorialized by poets; the brilliance of architects is declared by polemicists. Corbu had blessed the men who designed Rockefeller Center with that most precious of gifts for ambitious architects: a theory.

The one member of the Associated Architects who would have been more amused than impressed by Corbu's endorsement did not live long enough

---

*Corbu threatened to sue Hellman for mentioning the fact that he was Swiss—a libel, he said, because the Swiss are a nation of hotelkeepers.

to learn of it. Roughly two years before Corbu's visit, Raymond Hood became seriously ill. The pace in the Associated Architects' office had slowed substantially with the completion of the British and French buildings, and though many members of the design staff had been laid off Hood himself continued to stay up too late, drink too much, and work too hard. By November 1933 he was in the hospital. The official diagnosis was rheumatoid arthritis. Hood's was this: "The monkey business is that I have too many Streptococi [*sic*] inside my carcass and possibly too many doctors on the outside," he wrote his friend, the designer Norman Bel Geddes. "At any rate I am being manhandled like an architect manhandles clients."

He was in and out of various hospitals throughout his last year, living under rules, he said, that mandated "no smokee—no drinkee— . . . a beautiful diet of Brussels Sprouts, spinach, cauliflower, carrots, peas," and, if she could swing it, booze smuggled in by his wife. In between confinements he continued to display the equanimity and generosity of spirit that had made him so widely loved even in the fractious and faction-ridden world of big-time architects, where the battle for Most Ubiquitous Emotion was a neck-and-neck race between envy and schadenfreude. For years Frank Lloyd Wright had taken potshots at "Hood and his tribe. " He had refused to participate in Philip Johnson's International Style show at the Museum of Modern Art because Hood's work was included. Yet when Wright was in New York he likely as not dined with the same companionable man ("good old Ray Hood," he called him) he castigated from every available platform. On one of his hospital furloughs, Hood and his wife even spent several weeks in Bermuda as guests of Ralph Adams Cram, the arch-Gothicist who had written the most blistering of all the attacks on Rockefeller Center, calling it (among many other juicy things) "the apotheosis of megalomania." Hood held neither ideologies nor grudges.

He continued going to the office whenever he could, right up until three weeks before his death in August 1934. His obituaries made surprisingly little mention of his role in Rockefeller Center, presumably because, at the time, the specific contributions of the various architects were not clear. Hood never once attempted to claim credit due him for the design triumph that was Rockefeller Center, and once even said, "I am not sure that what has come out of [the group design process] isn't . . . better than any scheme any one of us would have worked out if he'd had everything his own way."

His fellow architects, however, knew exactly the measure of Hood's greatness. Forget for a moment the way Frank Lloyd Wright revealed the deficits of his own personality while he paid tribute to Hood: "Ray Hood was a good egg," Wright told a friend. "Architecture needs about ten first class funerals of the higher-ups more than it needs his." Two other colleagues got it much better. Summarizing the twelve brief years of success Hood enjoyed, Harvey Corbett said, "He understood the economic necessity of rational building but ever kept his imagination free." And, decades later, expressing the loss a culture endures when so talented a man dies at fifty-three, architect Donald M. Douglass wondered, "What if he had had ten more years, or thirty as Wright had?"

Of Rockefeller Center's three senior architects, Ray Hood had the least use for the theoretical. Corbett had made his reputation more with his "paper architecture," in Mumford's derisive term, than with his buildings, and Harrison was young enough, modern enough, and international enough to have become swept up in the Bauhaus doctrines that had begun to dominate architectural thinking. Late in life Harrison insisted that Le Corbusier "had absolutely no influence" on Rockefeller Center, but this judgment likely arose from the quarrels the two men engaged in during their collaboration on the United Nations headquarters in the late 1940s. In fact, as Brendan Gill put it, Harrison was "Corbu's chief sponsor in this country."

Corbu's trip took place in October 1935, fourteen months after Hood died. In the gap between the two events, architectural responsibilities at Rockefeller Center were necessarily reconfigured. John R. Todd had earlier taken care to acknowledge Hood's role even as his condition worsened ("We will treat him like a brother," Todd assured Junior.) But after Hood died, Todd's concern about the future was evident. "I have just heard that the doctor has ordered you to take a real rest," Todd wrote Harrison. "I hope you will have sense enough to stay away until you get in good shape."

Todd was anxious because he knew Harrison would have to carry the effort forward. Andy Reinhard (who got his own please-stay-well note from John R. just after Hood died) would play a large role dealing with tenants, and Reinhard's partner Henry Hofmeister would continue to manipulate the positioning of the trusses, beams, utility conduits, and other viscera in any new buildings, abetted by André Fouilhoux, the courtly French-born engineer who had been Hood's business partner. Corbett drifted away from Rockefeller Center to pursue projects of his own, notoriously the brooding Men's House of Detention (aka the Tombs) in Lower Manhattan. Though he continued to collect a nominal consulting fee for a few years, Corbett ceased playing his accustomed role as resident publicist and polemicist.

Those jobs, as well as the critical one of chief designer, would have to be taken by Harrison. He had the interest, he had the talent, and he had a daily breakfast partner whose rise in the organization made Harrison's parallel progress inevitable. Harrison's biographer Victoria Newhouse wrote that his relationship with Junior's second son "was not a conventional friendship of equals, but rather an amiable relationship between artist and patron." This was all either of them could ask for, and for nearly four decades it served them both very well indeed.

When Nelson Rockefeller joined the family office in May of 1931, the only thing he brought to work was his name. The honorific created for his father thirty-four years earlier—"Mr. Junior"—had arisen out of necessity in an office already dominated by a Mr. Rockefeller. The next generation bearing the family name required additional classification, and once the eldest of Junior's boys became "Mr. John," the second son was a foreordained "Mr. Nelson." It was a tradition that would continue for decades, even extending to each brother's personal staff. At office Christmas parties in the 1970s, name tags displayed an elaborated taxonomy: "Mr. Jones—Mr. David's staff" or "Mr. Persico—Mr. Nelson's staff." At least one brother took the nomenclature home. "Mrs. John and I enjoyed so much your letter," began a note from Mr. John to one of his associates.

So formal an identifer suited John; on Nelson it seemed out of place. From the beginning he mixed comfortably with his father's senior advisers, with the socialites he was getting to know on the Junior Committee of the Museum of Modern Art, with the artists (like Diego Rivera) whose work he collected, with the elevator men and the lunch counter waitresses and anyone else he met. The formal etiquette of the day, wrote David Gelernter, "was as likely to equalize classes as to separate them. . . . If the ranking bureaucrat had any manners, he removed his hat when addressing the unemployed laborer." But with Nelson it was not a matter of formality; his skin fit him so well he could wear it anywhere.

Like his older brother, or his father long before that, he had no specific responsibilities assigned to him when he started work. Unlike either man, though, he didn't wait for anyone to formalize an assignment. If there was work to be done, he did it; if there wasn't, he created some. He got involved in the Rockefeller Center rental operation. He put in some time at the Chase, learning the banking business from Uncle Winthrop Aldrich. He peppered the Todds, Roxy, Joe Brown, and various others with requests that

they consider hiring a particular friend or contracting with a particular supplier ("It would be well to humor him wherever it is possible," Brown wrote
to Web Todd). He served as intermediary with family friends and acquaintances who had proposals for Rockefeller Center (Mrs. Samuel Seabury,
wife of the distinguished jurist, insisted on discussing her idea for the New
York Horticultural Society and Garden Club with Nelson "personally").
Pretty frequently Nelson poked his nose into random aspects of the Center's development, from the roof gardens to the allocation of tickets for
opening nights at Radio City Music Hall.

The one area from which he removed himself was the one closest to his
own interest—art. After the Night of the Murdered Fresco, he by and large
stepped away from the selection process. This could not have been easy.
Nelson was now a trustee of the Metropolitan Museum as well as the Museum of Modern Art, and a collector whose ample resources served a taste
so thoroughly cultivated that MOMA director Alfred Barr was led to say,
"Nelson needs art more than any man I know." After the Rivera affair, no
doubt wishing to avoid the trouble that art could bring to his professional
life, he satisfied his aesthetic impulses at home. Henri Matisse may have
chosen not to execute a mural for the RCA Building, but he was happy to
create one for the fireplace wall in the living room of Nelson's apartment at
Fifth Avenue and 63rd Street. Fernand Léger, having lost the commission
for the "moving mural" in the lobby of the International Building, didn't go
away empty-handed; Nelson hired him to create murals for other walls in
the living room at 810 Fifth, and was so pleased with the results that he
asked Léger to keep on painting, down the hallways and up the apartment's
marble staircase—as Nelson's biographer Cary Reich wrote, "much as a
lesser mortal might ask a housepainter to touch up a closet while he was at
it." Nelson's extravagant walls were of a piece with the fireplace andirons
forged by Alberto Giacometti, the rugs crafted by Christian Bérard, and the
impressive suite of sculptures by Gaston Lachaise.

Of all the artists whose work actually reached the walls of Rockefeller
Center, the only one with whom Nelson remained involved was the im-
measurably gifted but personally erratic Lachaise. The sculptor's bizarre behavior had offended a number of his patrons, eventually plunging him into
desperate straits. By the spring of 1935, just months after MOMA had
mounted a successful retrospective of his work, Lachaise was looking for
work as a day laborer and eating just two meals every other day. On hearing
from Lincoln Kirstein how desperate Lachaise had become, Nelson began a
program to help him out. With Kirstein acting as a go-between, he purchased

a series of Lachaise pieces "as a way of helping to support" the sculptor and his wife. Nelson bought the pieces anonymously, presumably to spare Lachaise the sting of feeling like a charity case, but there was a side benefit that Nelson well realized. "I stressed [to Lachaise] the fact that the [unnamed buyer] is in moderate circumstances," Kirstein wrote to Nelson, ". . . so he [quoted] a price which in a way rather embarrasses me, inasmuch as it is extremely low." In reply, Nelson congratulated the guilt-stricken Kirstein for his "most satisfactory deal."

Even if Junior could not have understood his son's interest in Lachaise's work, he would have appreciated both the charitable aspect of Nelson's buying program and its penny-wise meanness. It seemed an inbred Rockefeller trait, this need to demonstrate financial responsibility on a small scale while engaging in jumbo-sized indulgences. Junior could run up a five-million-dollar tab acquiring Chinese bronzes and other pieces, and though he was forty-one years old still feel compelled to explain it to his father with a peeved defensiveness: "I have never squandered money on horses, yachts, automobiles or other foolish extravagances. . . . This hobby, while a costly one, is quiet and unostentatious and not sensational." But when his own passions were in their customarily quiescent state, Junior appreciated a bargain and valued thrift. Even more, he valued those people around him who watched his money as if it were their own—people like Robert Gumbel, the self-described "office boy" and general factotum who in 1934 complained to one of the building managers that "Mr. Rockefeller should not be asked to bear the expense, amounting to sixty-five cents, for repairing the glass" on a clock broken by the cleaning staff. Nelson fit right in: that same year he sent Junior a memo urging him to press John R. Todd to speed up a minor build-out on the eleventh floor of the RCA Building. "We will get a very high rate per square foot," Nelson wrote, "and I hate to see this potential money slipping through our fingers."

Well he might: one-sixth of it would someday be his. In the spring of 1933 Nelson enlisted his siblings in an effort to get Junior to begin passing along some of his great wealth to them. Until that point Babs and the boys had fundamentally been living on allowances controlled by Junior, allowances large enough to sustain a small country, perhaps, but allowances nonetheless. "As a result of our various talks together we have begun to realize how much you and Mother have done for us and the importance of your influence in our lives," they said, near the beginning of a four-page, single-spaced letter. Near the end, in language equally decorous but far less direct, the six members of the third Rockefeller generation essentially said: Give us the money.

Over the course of the next year Junior complied. First came direct grants of 200,000 shares of Socony-Vacuum stock, worth $3.2 million each, for the three oldest children (the younger ones, still in school, would have to wait). Then, as the Depression-stoked clamor for the redistribution of private wealth grew louder, Junior moved to shelter the family fortune by creating the so-called 1934 Trusts, the vehicles through which, over the years, he would transfer his wealth to his children.

Eventually, the single most valuable holding in Junior's portfolio would be Rockefeller Center, and if Nelson couldn't exactly be sure of that in 1933 and 1934, he nonetheless wasn't going to take chances. From the moment he sent his post-Rivera note of fealty to Junior ("my one desire will be to be as much of a help to you as I possibly can") until he embarked on his political career in 1940, then for two more periods in the years before he became governor of New York in 1958, Rockefeller Center was the core of Nelson's professional life.

By the summer of 1934, just turned twenty-six and with only a year of full-time work at the Center behind him, he had begun to solidify his position as Junior's primary adviser. Ivy Lee had started to fade from view with the rise of Merle Crowell, and by the time Lee's dealings with the Nazis became known he had been relegated to the periphery of Junior's vision.* Illness forced Arthur Woods to step down as president of Rockefeller Center, Incorporated. Thomas Debevoise continued to whisper in Junior's ear, but even he recognized that Nelson's rise would require him to adjust his posture; as Peter Johnson and John Ensor Harr wrote in an authoritative book funded by the Rockefeller family, "like a good prime minister [Debevoise] realized that the wave of the future lay with the monarch's sons." Little good it did him; in time the sons, led of course by Nelson, would push Junior's aging counselor out the door.

Nelson in some respects was suited to the advisory role. Like Debevoise among Junior's associates, he presumed an intimacy with his father that his brothers didn't dare: their letters to Junior were usually (in Johnny's case always) addressed "Dear Father" and signed with a comparably formal valedictory, while Nelson was likely as not to begin with a breezy "Dear Pa" and

---

*After Lee died of a brain tumor in November 1934, Junior did send his widow a condolence note—but he took nearly ten months to do it.

sign off "With loads of love." Neither did he shrink from addressing sensitive issues with his father, as his brothers often did. Yet Nelson was never cavalier about the advice he gave Junior, and prepared carefully before raising important matters with him, just as any responsible consigliere would.

On the other hand, Nelson's very Nelsonness was at odds with the discreet whispers and eyes-only memoranda of the confidant. Junior recognized this early on when he told Senior that "Nelson's temperament is such that he is happier when he is creating something himself and directly responsible for its success." Nelson's own spin on it, delivered decades later, was more concise: "I never wanted to be vice-president of anything."

From the diaries of John D. Rockefeller 3rd:

January 2, 1935: *"Had lunch with Nelson. . . . Discussed mainly our relationship to Rockefeller Center and a general division of the family's responsibilities. . . . [I told him] that, frankly, Rockefeller Center had the more appeal to me at the moment."*

March 25, 1935: Lunch with Nelson, *"at my suggestion . . . Spoke particularly of characteristics which we each had which might be annoying to the other."*

February 13, 1936: *"Had lunch with Nel. . . . Discussed with him means whereby he and I could better keep in touch and work more closely together. . . . Nelson was quite sympathetic to everything I said as to the importance of our pulling together."*

December 18, 1936: *". . . had a long talk with Nel. . . . Stated that I felt the handling [of a recent negotiation] had been most unfortunate, particularly as between him and myself. . . . [I said] it would be essential that we agree and have a basis of working together harmoniously. . . . He admitted the desirability of working together more closely . . . but seemed to feel less strongly about it."*

It's almost excruciating to read John's diaries from the years when he believed he was sharing responsibility with his younger brother or even, on occasion, jousting with him for position. It didn't matter if Junior told his sons that responsibility for planning the move from 26 Broadway to the RCA Building was "to be assumed by John entirely and not partly by Nelson"; not three months later Nelson told his father that "I talked with John . . . and he said that he would approve my going ahead and making all the arrangements." After John stated that "the position of chief executive officer of Rockefeller Center would have very real appeal to me," Nelson declared his interest in the job and John immediately surrendered. Even in the post John was eventually handed—office manager of the staff in Room 5600—he was frequently overruled by Junior, who did not refrain from adding to his veto of one of John's painstakingly drafted plans these un-comforting words: "I have discussed the matter with Nelson and he is in-clined to feel that my suggestions are perhaps the best way of dealing with the situation." John's sympathetic biographers described Nelson, during the years he and John worked together in the family office, "chafing at being preempted from most of the opportunities there by his older brother." If this was chafing, then World War I was a game of jacks.

John, of course, was in no way a formidable opponent. Even when he tried in his stumbling fashion to assert himself, he would back off as soon as people began paying attention. Through much of 1934 he campaigned against Webster Todd's continued supervision of the Center's theater oper-ations. When after seven months of this John learned that Todd's father and Robertson had finally concluded he was right, he reacted like a startled bunny, telling Robertson "that I hoped very much that they had not come to this conclusion because of anything which I have said or done."

Motivated by either arrogance or sympathy, Nelson once took pains, as John described it, "to outline to me his philosophy of life." The older brother did not record anything the younger brother said that day (needless to say, John wrote only that he found it "very interesting"), but one suspects that an obvious element of that philosophy—"using my weakling brother as a shield," perhaps?—wasn't part of it. John's repeated acquiescence to Nelson's plans, even when he disagreed with them, enabled Nelson to pre-sent these schemes to their father as if they expressed a shared vision for Rockefeller Center when in fact they were part of Nelson's campaign for his own ascendancy. In the summer of 1934, Nelson persuaded John to sign on to a proposal he sent off to Junior in Seal Harbor: the creation of a new ex-ecutive committee to supervise the work of Todd and Robertson, its mem-bership consisting of Nelson, John, and Barton Turnbull, a financial adviser who'd joined the family staff just months earlier and whose head had al-ready been turned by Nelson. It was not difficult to figure out who would control such a committee.

That fall, on Debevoise's strong recommendation, Junior rejected the plan that "the boys" (as Junior would always call them) had presented. "Within a month," wrote Peter Johnson and John Ensor Harr, "Nelson's reorganization was reorganized." Both brothers signed a letter to Junior apologizing for overreaching in the reorganization plan. But minutes of a reconstituted executive committee reveal that only one of the brothers was named vice chairman; that the same brother was designated the executive committee's official liaison with Todd and Robertson; and that this brother presided at the committee's meetings, even when C. O. Heydt, the nominal chairman, was present.

The other brother, frustrated at every turn, rendered a supernumerary, his most ardently held positions all but disregarded by the Todd organization and by his father and brother, simply tiptoed away. In a 337-page reminiscence recorded and transcribed in 1962, John devoted exactly three sentences to Rockefeller Center.

He may have taken on Johnny one-on-one, but Nelson generally did not work alone. In the middle thirties, before he consolidated his power at Rockefeller Center, Nelson began to create a storehouse—not of material resources, which he did not need, but of people. Nelson knew that talent was both rare and costly. In his later years he gathered capable associates by spending top dollar to acquire their services and their loyalty.* But when Nelson was young, association with the Rockefeller family was lure enough. Wallace Harrison said that working for Nelson "was like being handed a meringue glacee; it was almost too easy."

At Rockefeller Center, Harrison was Nelson's closest professional associate. While Johnny was still around he was his younger brother's declared ally, but it was an alliance similar to one that an occupied country would enter into with its conqueror. Laurance—Bill—moved into Room 5600 after dropping out of Harvard Law School in 1935 (he had flunked out the year before, then given it one last, futile stab), but he had little to do with Rockefeller Center early in his working life, instead pursuing a separate career as a venture capitalist. Most of the associates on the staff of Room 5600 were helpful to Nelson, but they were nonetheless Junior's men. Besides, it was Nelson's nature to look outward—to look, as Cary Reich suggested in the subtitle of his superb biography of Nelson, for "Worlds to Conquer," and for the allies who would cover his flanks, provide reinforcements, manage the supply lines, and do whatever else was necessary to make his con-

---

*He purchased quantity as well as quality: his 1970 gubernatorial campaign had 476 paid employees; his opponent, Arthur Goldberg, had only 35.

quests possible. Wally Harrison was an obvious choice for Best Pal: a compatible figure, an enthusiast of modern art, a member of Nelson's social set, and professionally up to his ears in Rockefeller Center. Harrison also possessed the one characterological trait that was essential for those who worked in Nelson's orbit. His success with Nelson, as Victoria Newhouse phrased it, arose from "his easy acceptance of the existing power structure." Harrison himself put it this way: "The things Nelson ran, he ran."

If you could buy into the prerogatives of the padrone, and if you had talent, brains, and the skills Nelson needed, you had an admission pass into an enduring confederation of friends and advisers whom Nelson called "the Group." These were men who worked for him at Rockefeller Center, at the State Department when he was coordinator of the Office of Inter-American Affairs during World War II, in Albany during his fifteen-year governorship. Their roles were defined not necessarily by their professional specialties but by a highly personal one: they were willing to specialize in Nelson. (Harrison himself spent the war years directing the cultural program of Nelson's Inter-American Affairs operation.) In 1952 a grateful Nelson even provided the Group with a clubhouse. The limestone mansion that had been Junior and Abby's first home in New York became the 13 West 54th Street Club, its membership consisting of Nelson and just eleven others: his four brothers; five members of the Group, including Harrison; Thomas Debevoise; and a surprising wild card, physicist J. Robert Oppenheimer (whom the seventy-eight-year-old Debevoise said he could not hear from his end of the lunch table). When Junior gave Nelson the house in 1946, son thanked father for its "usefulness," an attribute it maintained for thirty-three years, until the night Nelson died in one of its upstairs rooms.

The membership committee of the 13 West 54th Street Club consisted solely of Nelson and Harrison, a measure of the closeness of a relationship cemented years before at Rockefeller Center. Beginning in the mid-1930s, the two men met roughly once a week at the Union News Company's Gateway Restaurant in the underground concourse just behind Manship's Prometheus statue, whenever Nelson called Harrison to ask, "Do you want to have a cup of coffee?" That was the pretext for a meal that Nelson had invented—toasted rolls held together by a mortar of butter, bacon, and orange marmalade—and a discussion of any new ideas that Nelson had hatched. Around them in the enormous restaurant (according to Merle Crowell, its oyster bar was—surprise!—"said to be the largest in the world") photomurals depicted "the architectural development of New York City," a suitable inspiration for their plans.

It was in the Gateway that Harrison and Nelson cooked up a scheme to design and develop an International Style apartment complex on Rockefeller property running mid-block from 54th to 55th Streets, west of Fifth. It would turn out to be Harrison's finest work, two eleven-story structures in blond brick, joined by a single garden courtyard, their elegant facades distinguished by cantilevered, semicircular dining bays that seemed to billow out of every apartment. Rooftop terraces, "all-metal kitchen equipment," streetside air filters, "intercepted call" telephone service ("useful and convenient for tenants who do not have their own servants")—it was all modern, and all Nelson. He even wanted to patent the dining alcove arrangement.

Johnny opposed the idea. So did Junior's chief tax adviser, Philip Keebler. Even Laurance, uncharacteristically disloyal to Nelson, said he "could not see any reason [to develop the property] excepting that Father might enjoy it as a hobby." The *Herald Tribune* reminded its readers that Junior had originally bought up all that property in the West 50s to *prevent* the construction of apartment houses in his neighborhood. But Nelson presented his father with three muscular arguments. First, there was a clear market—as Junior told his own father, "There has been practically no building of apartment houses since the depression began." Second, the rise of Rockefeller Center had vastly increased the value of all the property Junior controlled in the blocks to the north, and putting some of it on a paying basis appealed mightily. And third, Rockefeller Center itself could be used as a marketing device. Nelson named the building the "Rockefeller Apartments." He commissioned a real estate firm to seek tenants by canvassing every single firm that had offices in Rockefeller Center. He ordered Merle Crowell to beat the publicity drums. He installed "a full-size replica of a typical suite" on one of the RCA Building's setbacks, and even charged admission to those who wished to tour it. By the time the Rockefeller Apartments opened on October 1, 1936, Nelson told his father, every one of its 138 units had been rented.

Replied Junior, "I am proud to be your silent partner."

It was a story John R. Todd loved to tell. Early in 1936 the men in the Rockefeller Center rental office had come to him with a problem. In another year, they said, the first group of buildings would be "substantially" filled up "and the best Renting Department in this little world will be out of business. You must get us a new building at once." It couldn't have been true; though renting had picked up substantially, the overall occupancy rate was hovering somewhere around 80 percent, which sounded decent enough but rang a little tinny when perceived from the opposite direction: you could lose a lot of money in the skyscraper racket with a 20 percent vacancy rate. Even the tiny British Empire Building and La Maison Française, which had everything going for them—Fifth Avenue frontage, the duty-free warehouse, only two hundred thousand square feet of carpet space between them—weren't full after more than four and a half years on the market.

Even one-fifth empty, though, the existing buildings made for an impressive suite. The RCA, the RKO, the Music Hall, the Center Theater, the British and French buildings, the International Building and its two Fifth Avenue adjuncts—this first phase of the Center's construction had yielded more than $100 million worth of limestone, imagination, and faith. To date, Junior had spent roughly $60 million of his own money and another $44.6 million of Metropolitan Life's. (In 2003 these sums would translate to approximately $805 million and $599 million.) But by Hugh Robertson's computation, "it would never be possible for the development as a whole to meet its expenses" without building on the three parcels of land that remained undeveloped in 1936: on the north block between the Music Hall and the western entrance to the International Building; on the south block running eastward from the rear of the Center Theater; and, also on the south block, the Sixth Avenue properties once owned by William Fox, occupying the block's southwest corner, and an adjacent row of empty lots running along the north side of 48th Street.

The northern parcel was in fact only superficially undeveloped. That is, although no building occupied the land just east of the Music Hall, what existed just below street level was absolutely essential to Rockefeller Center's success. On the north side of 50th Street stood the entrance to a steel-framed ramp that spiraled 34 feet below grade, a 450-foot roadway that flowed into a pair of enormous shipping rooms. There, by the end of the 1930s, a buzzing complex of loading platforms, truck turntables, and electric cargo-handling equipment each day disgorged the contents of 800 delivery trucks into the freight elevators of the Center's various buildings. Lined in glazed brick, absolutely windowless, its air cleansed and replaced every ninety seconds by powerful ventilators, the truck terminal was the outgrowth of an idea Harvey Corbett had proposed in 1927 as part of his "basket weaving" scheme to relieve urban traffic. Three quarters of a century later, it differentiates 49th and 50th Streets between Fifth and Sixth

Avenues from virtually every other block in midtown Manhattan: absent any trucks idling along the curb or double-parked in the center of the roadway, the two streets remain unclogged arteries in a body otherwise desperate for a multiple bypass.

The undeveloped land on the south block in 1936 was not nearly so well utilized. The sagging old Fox properties on Sixth Avenue limped through the last years before their demolition, grimy remnants of the world beneath the el tracks that would soon disappear; in the meantime, they yielded a little rent money. The 90,000-square-foot parcel stretching east from the back wall of the Center Theater produced a few dollars more, from the hundreds of cars parked there each day at fifty cents per. It could have handled even more had the demolition crews taken their wrecking balls to the three row houses along 49th Street that abutted the lot. From a window high in the RCA Building these buildings resembled the last teeth in a battered mouth. Two of them were empty of human habitation altogether, and the middle one was occupied only on those fairly rare moments when William Nelson Cromwell was in town.

Puttering about his four-story limestone home at 12 West 49th, the two neighboring buildings doing little more than buffering number 12 from the twentieth-century city rising around them, Cromwell had become an expensive burden to Columbia University. His valuable collection of bronzes and other artifacts, the statuary resting on pedestals, the resplendent chandeliers poised over polished tables gave the place the look of a slightly musty museum. But Columbia had no interest in subsidizing the collection, the building that housed it, the neighboring properties, or the wealthy eighty-two-year-old man who not only acted as if he had life rights to the three buildings, but who showed no inclination to die anytime soon.

Cromwell's refusal to give up his houses and the land beneath them, even though his ground leases had expired in 1927, was by 1936 costing his alma mater $41,250 a year in rent payments withheld by Rockefeller Center. If he held out so long that any new building would have to be built on a smaller footprint than otherwise possible, a portion of that rent would be lost forever. Climbing nimbly through a loophole in his original lease, Cromwell had even suspended his own rent payments on the land beneath number 14 nearly nine years earlier, at the outset of his stare-down with Columbia. As Columbia treasurer Frederick Goetze noted, Cromwell "expresse[s] his great love for Columbia," but at the same time "our minimum loss in income on account of [his] obstructive attitude" had reached $575,000. The old lawyer's implicit threat to cut Columbia out of his will if he were pushed too hard could cost the university hundreds of thousands more, as would a battle against the waves of lawyers he threatened to set in motion if Columbia really wanted to fight.

Ready to begin the next step of the second phase of the construction process, the Rockefeller Center executive committee considered suing Columbia for damages caused by the university's failure to deliver the Cromwell-occupied land. This compelled Goetze to call to action "the only man," he believed, who had a chance of persuading this plutocratic squatter to cooperate. Thereupon Nicholas Murray Butler and William Nelson Cromwell played a duet of such operatic grandiosity it deserved to be on-stage at the Met. "The questions at issue [concerning your houses] are of such importance to the City of New York and its development that I hope we can all cooperate to solve them," sang Butler. Intoned Cromwell, "I realize the consummation of this improvement"—the construction of a new Rockefeller Center building—"will result in creating for the City of New York an enormous increase in its tax roll; furnish relief in congestion of traffic; aid the unemployed; turn the wheels of manufacture and will constitute a great public benefaction." He was not being ironic; this is the way these men spoke.*

At the conclusion of their negotiation Cromwell agreed to give up the westernmost of his houses, number 14, in exchange for a ten-year lease extension on the land beneath number 12 (which in turn mooted Rockefeller use of the land beneath number 10), plus Rockefeller Center's agreement to connect number 12 to the city's steam tunnels. With a flourish of generosity, he agreed as well to pay his ten years' rent for number 12 in advance; that sum roughly equaled the nine years' rent he had *not* paid on number 14. With a greater flourish of pomposity, he insisted on signing the agreement and personally handing over his check to Butler at the President's House on Morningside Drive. Butler was satisfied, but his treasurer demurred: "Mr. Cromwell still owes us nearly four hundred thousand dollars for loss of Rockefeller rent," said Frederic Goetze. "I hope he will remember us to at least that extent in his will."

---

*The outstanding example of Cromwellese appeared in a letter he wrote Butler six years later, on the occasion of the Columbia president's eightieth birthday: "The effulgence of your glorious career obliterates time which gave to the world the miracle of your existence. If my heart had voice, it would become speechless in the endeavor adequately to convey to you my devotion, admiration and gratitude for the marvel of such a unique and unparalleled life as you have exemplified to all mankind."

Four buildings went up on Rockefeller Center's undeveloped land in the second phase of construction, which began in 1936: the first Time & Life Building, the Eastern Airlines Building, the Associated Press Building, and the U.S. Rubber Building. They were half siblings to their predecessors. Dressed in the same shot-sawn Indiana limestone, united by their proximity to one another, the family resemblance was unmistakable. But the death of Hood and the consequent ascent of Harrison altered a portion of the genetic code. The Time & Life, on the easternmost portion of the Cromwell/ parking lot site, featured a sheer facade with no setbacks, exactly what Harrison had vainly lobbied for when Hood was molding the RCA Building. Just to its west, the Eastern Airlines Building was yet more Harrisonian, its sixteen-story slab rising from a horizontal pedestal, a sort of precognition of the similarly arrayed United Nations Building still a decade in Harrison's future.

On the Eastern building, Harrison further announced his allegiance to the International Style by dispensing with Hood's aluminum spandrels, the element that gave the other towers their verticalizing stripes. To Harrison, the spandrels were evidence of the superfluous ornamentation he and the other Internationalists eschewed. Even more so were the sculpture groups, the mosaics, the painted bas-reliefs, the stone cartouches, the Pyrex screens, and all the other romantic thumbprints that adorned every entrance to every one of the earlier buildings. Not only did the Eastern Airlines Building have nothing over its doorways, but the entrances themselves were virtually transparent, part of an unprecedented two-hundred-foot expanse of glass, two stories high, that enwrapped much of the building's pedestal. This was an architecture not of solidity but of sleekness.

An evolving change in management policy also affected the look of the new buildings. Although John R. Todd jollied himself with his endless teasing of architects and his profit-celebrating aphorisms, he never refrained from using his throw weight to dissuade Junior from acting on his duller aesthetic impulses, such as those concerning the RCA roofline or the Friedlander sculptures. Now, however, prospective tenants were beginning to drive the architectural decisions and Hugh Robertson was driving the architects.

The Associated Press Building, straddling the entrance to the trucking ramp in the north block, was the first structure in Rockefeller Center to be built out to the limits of the lot line, and the first to deviate from the stricture that no interior space could be more than twenty-seven feet from a window. With a potential lead tenant requesting huge, open space for its newsrooms, Robertson ordered the stolid Henry Hofmeister, who had virtually no design experience, to "Go over in a corner, speak to no one and get this building done." There's nothing wrong with satisfying a tenant, but as Carol Herselle Krinsky has pointed out, the squat and relatively frumpy AP Building was truncated at an unimposing fifteen floors partly because there weren't enough other tenants interested in the place.*

Robertson's ascension was nothing that Todd rejected or resisted; as John R. grew older and Rockefeller Center grew more successful, he found the glow of his own glory more satisfying than another day in the office. Back in 1933 he could not only comfortably disagree with a unified opposition of his son, his brother, Robertson, and Joe Brown, but he had the power, and the will, to outvote them 1–4. By 1936 he no longer bothered with any but the major issues, often as not ceding his decision-making authority to Robertson, and gave more time to being profiled by *The New Yorker* than to the day-to-day running of Rockefeller Center.

During all the years that Todd had been focusing his attention on Junior, Robertson had been building relationships with Junior's boys over lunches in Rockefeller Center, dinners at the River Club, and, on at least two occasions, shooting weekends at his South Carolina plantation, near Charleston. Robertson had no trouble cleaning up Nelson's messes, as in the Rivera affair, and also appeared better able than Todd to handle the flow of ideas, questions, hiring recommendations, and the like that poured out of Nelson. Todd disliked some of Nelson's notions, had already thought of many of the others, and wasn't very politic in the way he dismissed them. According to Francis Christy, who had a front row seat, open clashes between Todd and Nelson became frequent and serious. Nelson and those close to him, Christy wrote, "had gradually become disenchanted with John R.'s occasional attitude of imperiousness."

The only surprising word in the preceding sentence is "gradually." (Make that two: regarding Nelson, "gradually"; regarding Todd, "occasional.") Nelson's rise in the affairs of Rockefeller Center was as gradual as

---

*The AP Building's dull earnestness was lightened only by the marvelous nine-ton stainless steel sculptural frieze, called *News*, placed above the main doorway. This was the work of the thirty-four-year-old Isamu Noguchi, who was already well known in art circles when he won the commission in a competition but had not yet become famous, as architectural historian Francis Morrone phrased it, "for putting a rock in every plaza in America."

a geyser. His personality required it, and the confidence of his father, sealed with the success of the Rockefeller Apartments, guaranteed it. "Hardly ever did his father ask Nelson to do something. Nelson would walk in and see something to be done," Wally Harrison remembered in 1978. "That was the way they transferred responsibilities. Nelson just sort of took them until he—well, until he became president of Rockefeller Center."

CHAPTER 20

The S. L. Rothafel who awoke on the last Wednesday of 1932 (this presumes, of course, that he had gone to bed on that horrible last Tuesday) must have been

very different from the man he had been just twenty-four hours before. For three weeks Roxy had been ill, but Radio City Music Hall's catastrophic opening night was a blow beyond reckoning. Junior's congratulatory telegram probably didn't allay his woe. If you wanted to be really frank about it, Junior's carefully chosen words, though admiring on the surface, were tinted by an ambiguity even Roxy might have noticed: "You have achieved the impossible," the wire read in part, and there was no denying it.

The prostatitis that had plagued him during the frantic preparation for the opening had drained Roxy of the inner resources he might have called upon to deflect the hoots and howls resounding around him. He was also taking hits for what he had put his people through ("After the show opened," recalled dancer Margaret Dunne, "the girls started collapsing—about, oh, at least seven every day. The curtain would go down, and you'd just see them drop"). He dragged himself to the opening of the RKO Roxy, and this time he even had a role onstage, introducing the formal dedication ceremonies. His speech brief and his voice hoarse—"almost inaudible," according to the *Herald Tribune*—he nonetheless managed to get off a quintessential Roxyism. The new Roxy, he croaked, was designed to "seat 3,700 patrons in drawing room intimacy." It was the first time he had presided over the creation of a theater that wasn't larger than the one that had preceded it, but that didn't keep him from quivering with quantification (and exaggeration—its capacity was a few seats shy of 3,600).

The next day Roxy was hospitalized. The day after that, New Year's Eve, he underwent abdominal surgery, and two days later the newspapers announced that he would be taking a six-week leave. His last act before beginning his convalescence was firing the Martha Graham company. Under instructions from her lawyer, Graham and her troupe continued to report to the Music Hall each day before show time, knowing they would not go on but conforming to the verbal contract she insisted was still in force. Eventually she was paid, and Martha Graham and her dancers, perfect symbols of Roxy's folly, went away.

In the normal course of events John R. Todd and Junior would speak frequently, particularly in the Center's early days. Only occasionally did memos pass between them, and Junior requested a formal presentation very rarely. But in September 1933, after the RCA Building, the RKO Building, both theaters, and the first two foreign buildings had been open several months, Junior asked Todd to give him a detailed report "with a view of seeing what changes should be made as we enter upon the next stage of the work."

It took John R. two months (and a little peckish nagging from Junior) to respond, but when he did he produced a remarkable twenty-nine-page letter, a building-by-building, program-by-program, problem-by-problem elucidation of every issue facing Rockefeller Center. Todd addressed the budgeting system, the schedule for the development of the remaining empty land, the complications surrounding the Metropolitan Life mortgage. He described an effort to get the federal government to pay for the extension of New Jersey rail lines under the Hudson to Manhattan (it failed), and an even nervier effort to get Columbia to allow postponement of $500,000 in rent each year without interest (it succeeded). But the largest issue, he suggested, was the need "to get people in very large numbers, from this country and from abroad, to Rockefeller Center." He explained that the "office rentals we are getting are not as high as we originally figured and do not . . . permit us to look forward to as favorable a balance sheet as we hoped." Shoppers and theatergoers, he said, could turn that around.

Because of the bankruptcy of RKO in January 1933, Rockefeller Center itself now owned a big piece of the theaters and had taken essential responsibility for operating them. (It would take over full control in 1934.) If those ten thousand seats could be filled a few times a day, and if the theatergoers spent a little money in the Center's restaurants and stores, success was guaranteed. "If we can bring people in sufficient numbers to Rocke-feller Center," wrote Todd, the return from the stores and restaurants would accomplish what he described—both capitalized and underscored—as his foremost objective: "PUTTING THE ENTIRE DEVELOPMENT IN SUBSTANTIAL BLACK."

"Our first step in that direction," he added in proud summary, "was the completion of the Radio City Music Hall. The fame of it has gone around the world. The adverse criticism is negligible but the praise and admiration for it are all that we could expect." Eleven months had not yet passed since "The Fall of the House of Ushers," as Heywood Broun had called the disastrous opening night, and already the Music Hall had moved from the column reserved for major problems into the one designated for unqualified successes.

This had happened despite Roxy. Shoved out of the picture at least for a time by the double whammy of failure and illness, he had barely emerged from anesthesia when Merlin Aylesworth, president of NBC and point man in the shared Rockefeller-RCA management of the Music Hall, announced two weeks after opening night that the theater that would never show motion pictures, as Roxy had once proclaimed, was now a motion picture theater. When Roxy returned from what turned out to be nearly twelve weeks of semienforced leave, he found his programming ideas discarded, his personal assistant and his business manager fired, and the nude statues he had banished from the Grand Foyer back in place. Helen Keller, touring the Music Hall around this time, ran her hands over Robert Laurent's *Goose Girl* and pronounced it "very saucy."*

Roxy had no leverage at all. Before the first movie to play the Music Hall opened on January 10, 1933—*The Bitter Tea of General Yen,* starring Barbara Stanwyck and Nils Asther—the contagion of empty seats spreading through the enormous auditorium had sent losses past $100,000 a week. Aylesworth's formula of first-run movies introduced by a fifty-minute live show, repeated four times a day, turned things around. By midsummer the Music Hall was showing an operating profit. Roxy still produced the now-abbreviated stage shows, but he was no longer involved in policy decisions. He did not like this, and behaved just as one might expect, throwing tantrums and loudly proclaiming his indispensability. He brutalized his creative team, belittled their work, and repeatedly threatened to quit.

*Keller returned a year later and this time praised the "impressively and poetically" portrayed message of Ezra Winter's mural, thereupon establishing that Junior's high opinion of the painting was shared by at least one other person, even if a blind one.

"Living in a self-centered world bedecked with iridescent dream-colors," wrote Terry Ramsaye, Roxy couldn't believe it when he was fired, in early 1934. "With cheeks trembling and eyes filled many times with moisture," read an article in the *Sun,* he insisted "he would be called back to head the great enterprise that had meant so much to him." When he failed to stimulate a press campaign for his return, he turned directly to Nelson Rockefeller, whom he nearly suffocated with unctuous entreaties: "COMMAND ME IF YOU THINK IT ADVISABLE I AM AT YOUR SERVICE," read one telegram. Nelson didn't think it advisable. Instead Roxy tried his hand at Roxyizing a large theater in Philadelphia, and he ventured a brief return to the road with a few members of his old "Gang." Nothing worked. In 1936, still dreaming of a comeback, he died of a heart attack, at fifty-three. "Death is just a big show in itself," he had said the year before, and he was right, in a way: more than two thousand people attended his funeral at the Central Synagogue, and there were elements of the event that were pretty impressive—a Marine Corps escort for the flag-draped coffin, the kaddish chanted by Jan Peerce. But beyond some back pay from RKO that his estate could collect only through lawsuit, he left little beyond some worthless holdings in a variety of failed theatrical enterprises and a name that over the next several decades would be attached to hundreds of ventures all over the world, not one of which had anything to do with him.

The new man at the Music Hall couldn't have been more dissimilar from Roxy. W. G. Van Schmus was an avuncular, slow-talking former advertising man, a New Jersey neighbor of John R. Todd. Portly and courtly, prone to an amiable long-windedness that disguised his sharp analytical skills, "Mr. Van" claimed to have seen only three movies in his life before his appointment as head of the world's largest movie theater. His greatest accomplishment up to that point may have been his role, as a consultant to Macy's, in the promotion and popularization of twin beds. But the substance of his experience was less important than the aura created by his manner. Van Schmus allowed people to do good work away from the shadow of supervision, free from the egomaniacal credit-mongering of the Roxy-style impresario. The enormous success the Music Hall would soon (and long) enjoy was consequently an unlikely hybrid, the crossing of "the vision of a demented prophet"—Brooks Atkinson's description of Roxy—with the calm and rational leadership of the dignified Van Schmus.

You could tell that the troops were ready for a change: when RCA and the Rockefellers grabbed Roxy's final melodramatic "resignation" as if it were the key to El Dorado, among all Roxy's ranking colleagues only the house manager, Charles Griswold, walked out with him. Almost everyone else—associate producer Leon Leonidoff, Roxyettes director Russell Markert, conductor Erno Rapee, art director Vincente Minnelli, ballet mistress Florence Rogge—marked Roxy's departure by ignoring it. Even Roxy's nurse, Anna Beckerle, stayed with the Music Hall. According to Minnelli, whom Roxy had alternately lacerated with sarcasm and soothed with oleaginous flattery, "there were no drawn out tearful goodbyes."

But Minnelli also acknowledged that Roxy had "pushed me to creative heights that even I didn't know were in me," and any of the others would have had to acknowledge the same. Only someone with Roxy's unembarrassed passion for excess could have trained them in the art of spectacle that they would jointly master. Leonidoff, who assumed Roxy's role as lead producer, was as subtle as a shriek. Friendly entertainment writers might refer to him as a "dynamic, diminutive Russian," but he showed up in other sections of the newspapers for screaming at cabdrivers (once with such vein-popping rage he was arrested), being sued by prominent businessmen for alienation of affections, or remarrying (and then redivorcing) the woman who had publicly accused him of having an affair with the Chicago gold digger Peaches Browning. To colleagues he was a terrorist. Adventure novelist Ernest K. Gann, who as a young man out of the Yale Drama School worked as his assistant, maintained that the staff labored for Leonidoff out of "masochistic loyalty." At least some, however, managed to suppress both their masochism and their loyalty: one colleague threw a telephone at him, another knocked him down with a punch, and at one point in the 1950s he so enraged Raymond Paige, the Hall's music director at the time, that Paige was led to "grab Leonidoff around the neck from in back and pull him over the rail into the orchestra pit."

Erno Rapee, the Hall's first music director, was a match for Leonidoff. For one thing, he was incontrovertibly the best in the business, albeit the rather peculiar business of leading a seventy-piece symphony orchestra, two soloists, a thirty-voice chorus, and an entire ballet company through, say, a twenty-minute condensation of *Carmen.* For another, Rapee, who looked like a small, predatory bird and moved just as fast, did not trouble himself over the finer sensibilities of his musicians. He could not possibly have committed all the deeds attributed to him in a *New Yorker* profile in 1944, but the citation of a few may define the edges of his personality. According to Barbara Anne Heggie and Robert Lewis Taylor, Rapee liked to order the members of a particular section to bring their instruments to his office for pop quizzes on the orchestra's vast repertoire. "Number fourteen, tenth bar!" he would shout in his flavorful Hungarian accent. "Ready? One, two, three, four, *toot!*" He thought nothing of asking a staff composer to, say, "Turn me out a gloomy ballet by noon—something like 'Swan Lake,' but only better." During one show in the mid-1930s, a horn player collapsed with a heart attack in midoverture; as a couple of colleagues rose to assist him, Rapee hissed, "Sit down you sons of bitches and play!" Still flailing away with the baton in his right hand, with his left he punched the button to lower the bandstand elevator. "Once out of sight of the audience," wrote Heggie and Taylor, "he signaled two stagehands to carry the stricken man off the platform; then he brought up his musicians, still playing at full tilt, and finished the overture." Rapee "was much concerned over the horn-player's collapse. 'The poor fellow . . . he was in bad shape. We didn't lose a bar.'"

Leonidoff and Rapee shaped and perfected the Music Hall style, along with Minnelli (who stayed for just three years) and Markert (whose Roxy-ettes segued into their new name, the Rockettes,* when Roxy segued out the door). The vastness of the stage and its distance from many of the seats demanded an outsized mode of entertainment. Minnelli's successor, the great theatrical designer Boris Aronson, soon realized how ill suited he was to the Music Hall's singularity: "My basic inclination was to make things smaller so that the set would be related to people and happenings," he said, by way of explaining the brevity of his tenure. "The tendency of the Music Hall [was] to enlarge, to make things big, and bigger than anything anybody else has to show." Leonidoff said he brought in "a certain type of act—acrobats, knock-about comics, circus-style acts—because our stage is so big you can't fill it with talk." Instead he filled it with an imaginative extravagance that approached surrealism. If "the Music Hall style" conjures up visions of dancers tricked up as "West Point Cadets, Israeli Paratroop Women, Can-Can Girls, Canadian Mounted Police, squirrels, typewriters, birds, zebras, dollies, soldiers, waitresses, cowgirls, femmes fatales," as ex-Rockette Judith Anne Love described her various roles in her three-plus years in the company; if the costume designers specified that the mermaids in an "undersea

*Markert never quite caught on; nearly four decades later he still pronounced the word "rockets."

ballet" should have their hair dyed "fluorescent pistachio"; if the menageries brought in for assorted nativity scenes, cowboy scenes, dairy-maid scenes, and other exercises in theatrical husbandry led one ballerina to consider writing a memoir called *Manure on My Mark*—if all this was true, then so, inescapably, was this: Leonidoff, Rapee, and the rest of them did it in pursuit of something that for all the immoderation still aspired to art.

Consider: the corps de ballet headed by Florence Rogge at various times featured some of the twentieth century's finest dancers, including Patricia Bowman, Paul Haakon, Melissa Hayden, and Nora Kaye. The thirty-voice Glee Club was the incubator for the operatic careers of Leonard Warren, Robert Weede, and, most prominently, the Music Hall's lead tenor for six years, Jan Peerce. Baritone Robert Merrill, whose own distinguished career was launched out of a soloist's gig at the Music Hall, said Rapee led "a first class symphony." And Markert's Rockettes were, in a word, the Rockettes.

John D. Rockefeller Jr.—donor of the Cloisters, restorer of Williamsburg, patron of the Grand Tetons, and source of the funds that launched the Museum of Modern Art—must have been at least bemused by the fact that his single greatest contribution to American culture turned out to be thirty-six pairs of long, long legs. He loved to watch the Rockettes, found their act "exquisite and thrilling," and admired their offstage poise as well: once when they were all turned out for a tea with Rockefeller Center's management, each of the girls dressed to Markert's demure specifications, Junior exclaimed, "My, they look like the young ladies at Southampton!" An adventure that had begun with an effort to provide a home for the Metropolitan Opera may have culminated in something a little less exalted, but Junior found a redemptive moral in the daily disposition of those long and shapely legs. He said he "learned a lesson from the dancers—that of working together as a group and not striving for personal aggrandizement."

The unbroken, unchanging, utterly uniform line was everything to Markert. "As long as a Rockette is in the line," Markert declared, "she has no chance for individual success." He didn't like foreign-born dancers because they were generally too individualistic to become "part of a regiment." In the early days every Rockette was between five feet four and five seven (by 2002 the range had modulated to five five and a half to five nine), the taller ones in the middle of the line, shorter ones at the ends, the differences evened out by visual perspective. Black Rockettes were out of the question: Markert made such a fetish out of sameness that dancers who got suntans were either made to use liquid whitening makeup or they were laid off until their natural pallor returned. Girls who gained weight—who strayed into what Markert called "the Malted Milk Department"—were first given copies of diet books, then were publicly excoriated ("I've lost nine pounds," said one; replied Markert, "Never mind the pounds off your face, take them from your fat rear!"); and if they still didn't respond, they were fired. Challenged to justify his mania for sameness, Markert shrugged. "The girls still have their faces and their individual personalities," he said.

But that was wishful. It's hard to perceive individual personalities when a seventy-two-legged dancing machine is slicing the air with its ritualized closing sequence of eye-level kicks (the applause usually began around the tenth one). Besides, the schedule was so killing dancers were hard-pressed to stay awake long enough to express their personalities. Each Rockette did four or five shows a day (depending on the time of year), seven days a week, for three weeks. After a week off, the cycle started again. For the orchestra, the ballet, and the glee club; for the forty full-time seamstresses in the costume shop and the platoons of carpenters, painters, and electricians in the set department; for the crowds of howdah builders, pom-pom acquirers, and lasso knotters in the property department; for the stage manager and his staff, running through the hundred different trims in which the enormous curtain could be arrayed—for the entire company, which at times numbered more than five hundred members, the schedule became especially brutal whenever a new show was about to be introduced, which happened every time the movie changed. Judith Anne Love remembered the preparation as "a merciless round of rehearsals, wardrobe fittings, criticisms, turmoil, and tension that began at 7:00 A.M. on a Monday and that, in addition to the regular four shows a day, never let up until noontime Thursday" when the new show opened. One of Florence Rogge's successors described it like this: "In the old days, before the girls were protected by the union, they rehearsed day and night until they died like flies." When Van Schmus picked three popular films in a row in 1938—*Bringing Up Baby, Jezebel,* and *Algiers*—it almost seemed like a vacation. When he picked the rare loser that had to be pulled (with its accompanying stage show) after only one week, it seemed like hell.

Come with me
And you won't believe a thing you see.
Where an usher puts his heart in what he ushes,
Where a fountain changes color when it gushes . . .
Where the stage goes up and down when they begin it.
Where they change the lights a hundred times a minute.
It's a wonder Mrs. Roosevelt isn't in it,
At the Roxy Music Hall . . .

It wasn't one of Lorenz Hart's greatest lyrics (and it definitely wasn't one of Richard Rodgers's best tunes), but when Audrey Christie introduced "At the Roxy Music Hall" in *I Married an Angel* in 1938, the audience reaction paralleled the one that had greeted the Rockefeller Center skit from *As Thousands Cheer* in 1933: everyone got it. Anyone puzzled by the use of "Roxy Music Hall" instead of "Radio City Music Hall" could have written it off either to the metric requirements of Rodgers's melody or to the fact that long after he was gone, the place was still Roxy's creation.

To the crowds entering the theater at 11:00 A.M. for the first show of the day, his influence was apparent from the very first moment, when one of the imposing doormen—they were all over six feet tall—opened the Music Hall. At precisely the same instant, a bugle would signal the hour, and the ushers and pages would snap to attention at their positions. By then they had already completed their daily half-hour drill (held during the winter in one of the rehearsal halls, in the summer on the cork surface of the Music Hall roof); their required showers; and the inspection of everything from their uniforms (military style in the daytime, black tie at night) to their fingernails (even though all the ushers wore gloves) to their socks (garters required). From then until the end of their shift, when they'd march in tight formation down the grand staircase and through the lobby, the ushers were like a military parade unit—only better dressed, and with more responsibility.

Up in the first mezzanine, the ranking ushers took positions in the theater's sole reserved seat section, where wall brackets held cards displaying the name of the usher in charge of each aisle. Downstairs in the loge, ushers assigned duty near the front row prepared to scout for—and politely eject—the notorious miscreants the Rockettes called "crotch-watchers." Throughout the house, the ushers, all wearing sleeve stripes conveying their rank, communicated with one another with an elaborate series of hand signals, their white gloves flashing a code covering everything from "patron wants better seat, do you have any available?" to "executive is being bothered by a bore; tell him he has a phone call." Accepting tips was forbidden. So was watching the movie.

As the house lights came down, primary responsibility for the evening passed from the head usher to the stage manager. The first man to hold this position, William Stern, always wore a tuxedo even though no one in the audience ever saw him.* On Stern's signal, the curtain began to assume one of its myriad dispositions as organist Richard Liebert reached a crescendo on the mightiest of all Wurlitzers (two consoles, fifty-eight sets of pipes). The show was about to begin, but Music Hall audiences, dazzled by the splendor of the furnishings, the plushness of the lounges, and the gilded ceiling with the sunset motif, didn't trouble themselves overmuch with the details of what occurred on stage. Though this was frequently a relief to those collapsing under the relentless performance schedule, it was an irritant, too. Jan Peerce said he spent his career at the Music Hall "singing over crackling candy wrappers and missed cues." A member of the glee club said, "We do all this work, sweating and straining, and all they say is, 'What beautiful toilets.'"

Except at Christmas and Easter once those seasonal shows acquired independent reputations, for the forty-five years the Music Hall maintained its show-and-a-film policy it was the appeal of the movie that determined the size of the crowd. But the Rockettes and the ballerinas, the orchestra and the glee club, the colossal sets that strained to fill the enormous proscenium and the immaculate ushers who patrolled the endless aisles—none of this was incidental. As a writer for *Film Daily* pointed out, instead of saying "I went to [film's title] yesterday," millions of Americans told their friends, "I went to Radio City Music Hall yesterday."

And that was precisely what Todd had in mind when he stressed to Junior the importance of promoting the entertainment and the shopping: the *experience* of Rockefeller Center had developed a palpable value. According to a survey, three out of four visitors to the Music Hall patronized some other Rockefeller Center facility—a store, a restaurant, maybe the Museum of Science and Industry downstairs in the RCA Building, or the "Gardens in the Sky" up on the setback roofs. Exhibits temporary and permanent, as

---

*It was a mythicizing touch appropriate to his latest career as host of the popular radio show *Bill Stern's Sports Newsreel,* in which organ music, sound effects, and other Roxyian influences augmented Stern's grossly exaggerated tales of the day's athletic heroes.

well as events ephemeral as air, opened throughout the Center with such frequency a tenant could feel he was living inside a promoter's daydream. A man named Jules Charbneau displayed his collection of "tiny things" in the Grand Lounge of the Music Hall—ivory animals (including a camel) small enough to pass through the eye of a needle, three thousand gold spoons stored inside the shell of a single hazelnut, an eighty-eight-key, fully functioning grand piano "you can hold in the palm of your hand; it's made to give good music, but you have to hit the keys with a toothpick." An "auto-gyro parade" over midtown Manhattan, best viewed from the sunken plaza, marked the topping-off of one of the buildings. Twenty-two trained canaries put on a musical performance every day at 4:00 P.M. in an exhibit space on the eleventh floor of the RCA Building. If something had the potential to attract a crowd, it had a place at Rockefeller Center. Unless, of course, it offended Rockefellerian sensibilities: the publicity department turned away a garment manufacturer who wanted to photograph models wading into the Prometheus fountain in their underwear.

"Mr. Rockefeller gives visitors dimes; visitors give him dollars," said the *Portland (Maine) Press Herald,* and although the paper conflated two generations of Rockefellers—it was Senior who handed out the iconic dimes—it got the essential fact exactly right. The crowds who began showing up in large numbers in the mid-1930s brought dollars straining to leap from their wallets. Rockefeller Center encouraged these acrobatics with the opposite of a hard sell. "Say what you want about Radio City," read a "Talk of the Town" piece in *The New Yorker,* "it is the metropolis of good manners." The front lines of politesse were manned by the Center's official tour guides and their associates, the "Ask Me" guides. The latter were twelve young men scattered about the outdoor spaces, identifiable by the sort of uniform that could make a matron from Mineola swoon: silk ascot, double-breasted jacket, an embroidered "RC" crest on the chest. The tour guides were well-spoken young men on their way to better things. Thus did one Californian quickly make his way from the Music Hall usher corps to a guide's position to a career in Hollywood, despite the unfortunate screen test administered by the New York office of Selznick International Pictures, in the International Building. David Selznick's New York story editor, Kay Brown, liked Gregory Peck a great deal, but Selznick thought the ambitious tour guide would be "hard to cast—bad ears."

The busiest guides were stationed on the Observation Roof, atop the RCA Building. Under the direction of John Roy, a former English teacher at the Hotchkiss School, the Observation Roof acquired a Rockefeller-suited dignity. Large pots held handsome evergreens, and two lines of Adirondack chairs ran the 190-foot length of the open promenade to a group of "air conditioning stacks and other funnels . . . painted in bright colors to give the appearance of a ship's deck." The guides stationed there sometimes had to handle as many as three hundred questions a day, which required them to "be versed in architecture, history, geology, astronomy, art, human nature, night club couvert charges, ship sailings, places of interest in Manhattan, United States highways, Broadway shows, and the time." To Tom Merton, a Columbia undergraduate who liked the $27.50 a week but hated the customer contact, this was not appealing. He didn't like having "to stand there and talk to the people pouring out of the elevator with all their questions," he recalled several years after he had taken the vows of a Trappist monk.

Despite the presence of guides as literate as Thomas Merton and a manager as high-toned as John Roy, who looked and behaved more like a banker than an impresario, the Roof was unquestionably a business enterprise. Accountants calculated that it cost a nickel to get each customer up there by elevator and a nickel more to get each one down, and there wasn't a chance that this investment would not be recouped. In addition to the admission charge to the deck, there were refreshments to be consumed (tongue sandwich, twenty cents; limeade, fifteen cents; buttermilk or sarsaparilla, ten cents) and souvenirs to be carried home: ashtrays, lighters, compacts, perfume bottles, tiepins, bracelets, tableware, lamp shades, even crucifixes bearing a Rockefeller Center medallion just below the body of Christ. If the words "Rockefeller Center" could fit on it, the souvenir stand sold it.

On his days off, Pete McGuire was a frequent visitor to the RCA roof. He always had a question for the guides, always the same question, and he made sure to ask it when there were plenty of other visitors within hearing range. Could the guide point out the Statue of Liberty? McGuire would inquire. The guide had no choice but to acknowledge that it couldn't be seen, that the Empire State Building was in the way. The same guide might have wanted to add a less polite comment but was obliged by the presence of paying customers not to point out that the amiable McGuire was head guard at the Empire State's observatory, an operation so successful (atop a building so otherwise unsuccessful) that in its first year it brought in almost exactly $1 million when the building's entire rent roll amounted to only $1.015 million. The RCA deck was never quite that important to Rockefeller Center's financial health, but a feature that could average thirteen hundred paying customers a day, as the Roof did by the time it was two years old, occupied a comfortable position in the scheme to make the Center a tourist attraction.

The Center's other roofs, however, were much less productive. This was especially disappointing for those whose tastes ran more to marigolds than to murals. Todd, breeder of camellias, couldn't expose that southern strain to the New York climate, but he successfully held out for dogwood "against a powerful forsythia bloc," and hired on as consultants the Georgia nursery firm that had planted the Augusta National Golf Club. Andy Reinhard got involved in creating a bird sanctuary on one of the setbacks, where at times he could be found wandering around in a double-breasted blazer and straw boater, enjoying his afternoon cigar. Nelson engaged himself in earnest consultation with "Uncle Winthrop's lawn expert." Even Abby stepped forward to make the case for grass walkways instead of gravel.

But no one cared as much as Junior, who believed that gardens would attract sightseers as well as tenants. Although Ray Hood's initial, more lavish plans were never realized—early renderings show glassed-in conservatories on the low roofs, flower-covered bridges spanning 49th and 50th Streets, fountains, colonnades, even a marionette theater and a music conservatory—Junior seemed willing to bear quite a lot of expense to get the gardens right. He urged Todd to consult with the plantsmen responsible for his own New York gardens, with a swank Boston landscape architect who fancied metal trees and spelled roofs "rooves," and with the man who "designed Miss Choate's garden." For his own counsel Junior sought out the expatriate American architect Welles Bosworth, who had played a large role in the restorations of Versailles and the Rheims cathedral. Bosworth suggested to his old client that the garden atop the French building should be modeled on "Courances, near Fontainebleau, where you lunched with the Marquis de Ganay."

The roofs of the four low buildings on Fifth were done up in styles appropriate to the buildings' themes—cobblestones from the streets of Italian towns and two stone plaques from the Roman Forum framed the plantings on the Palazzo d'Italia, for instance, and the British Empire Building's umbrella-topped garden tables, where tenants could take tea in clement weather, were surrounded by well-trimmed yews and other hedge plants. But the gardens meandering around the eleventh-floor setback on the RCA building, 140 feet above street level, were so lavish they made the tops of the low buildings look like suburban backyards. The man who designed them, a fellow of the Royal Horticultural Society named Ralph Hancock, called his conception for the RCA setbacks the "Gardens of the Nations." The twelve distinct gardens he installed were linked by manicured pathways and a meandering, 125-foot stream, and were united by the internationalist theme so close to Junior's heart. In the Spanish garden, for example, a stucco cloister with orange roof tiles enclosed a stone patio, where a hundred-year-old wrought-iron Spanish wellhead was surrounded by yucca, agave, hibiscus, and other Iberian plants. The English garden, set amid rocks imported from the Lake District, was described by the *Times* with a sigh of longing: "Here the buds of pink dogwood are swelling, the bluebells nod and the narcissus looks out starry-eyed, while the yellow primrose bloom upon the bank where grow the weeping birch with the spruce and the hemlock." Even Merle Crowell couldn't have written that, but he might have been behind this piece from the *Racine (Wisconsin) Journal News:* "The scheme . . . will be a novelty in New York, thousands of whose citizens have never seen a flower or a plant."

Non–New Yorkers, on the other hand, apparently had seen enough at home not to bother much with gardens when they came to New York. The Gardens in the Sky were more popular with the press than with tourists, and press got in for free. "The gardens are an attraction," one Rockefeller Center manager wrote in 1936, "almost entirely because they are 140 feet up in the air." By the next year, burdened with a full-time staff of seven gardeners plus a complement of guides, ticket takers, and other functionaries, the gardens were operating at an annual loss of $45,000. That didn't include a penny allocated to amortization of the enormous cost of the gardens' creation. Hoisting two thousand species of plants, a grove of thirty-foot trees, and three thousand tons of soil* up to the eleventh floor of a midtown building was an expensive proposition. So was the installation of the pipes, pumps, and other paraphernalia required for the ninety-six thousand gallons of water circulating through the gardens' streams and fountains. The only real break Junior got came from the cost-free importation of a herd of chipmunks rounded up in the Pocantico woods and set loose in the Gardens of the Nations "to eat excess roots of plants, hard-shelled beetles, and, in the fall, acorns from the stripling oaks."

In the beginning, things weren't much better belowground, either. The extensive (and unprecedented) concourse connecting all the Center's build-

---

*By 1986, when a portion of the gardens was refurbished, an additional 225 cubic yards of soil had accumulated simply from the decay of plant material, the deposits of winds, and the various other natural processes that even midtown Manhattan was able to support.

ings one floor below street level was an impressive feat of planning, engineering, and politicking (the city had to cede its right to claim ownership of anything built directly above or below its streets), but for a long time it was a commercial dud. Hungry to build traffic to support the shops, whose rents were a function of their gross volume, management did what it could to make the concourse a destination. A lengthy lease was granted to Charles DeZemler, barber to Teddy Roosevelt, Lord Kitchener, William K. Vanderbilt, and more recently "half the males in the Social Register." DeZemler installed in his three concourse shops larchwood paneling, chromium-plated fittings, telephone-equipped chairs, and the thirty-two hundred pieces in his "DeZemler Museum of Tonsorial Art"—as well as thirty-eight barbers well drilled in the celebrated DeZemler methods (always start on the right side, always daub the nostrils with peroxide, no talking during the DeZemler Special Facial Massage). The U.S. Post Office was considered such a magnet that Todd and Robertson treated it as their own: Rockefeller Center paid for its build-out, picked up much of its nonpersonnel operating expense (electricity, private elevator maintenance, and the like) and even saw to the regular replacement of its inkwells. Banks of pay phones placed throughout the concourse drew nearly seven hundred people a day. Joe Brown resisted the installation of public bathrooms "because they become nuisances," but generations of shoppers and commuters have been grateful that he was overruled.

Still, the concourse could not overcome a built-in problem: it was a passageway that went from nowhere to nowhere. On its western end, excavation for the promised Sixth Avenue subway did not even begin until 1936. On the east, a connection to the capillary system of pedestrian tunnels emanating from Grand Central Terminal was vetoed by the owners of the intervening Saks Fifth Avenue. At the precise center of the Center—the sunken plaza in front of the RCA Building—where doors on either side of the Prometheus statue led directly into the concourse, the architects had made their most serious misjudgment. The descending Channel Gardens may have drawn people from Fifth Avenue, but the stairs leading into the plaza and the shops that ringed it seemed to be regarded as the entrance to a mild form of hell. "People look down into the Plaza," John R. Todd told Junior, "but they do not go down into it."

This was doubly unfortunate because in other ways the plaza, at least as a piece of urban design, was a huge success. For Rockefeller Center, a version of the plaza was like a tree from the Garden of Eden—it dated back to Ben Morris's initial plans, the very first architectural element imagined for land that was supposed to accommodate an opera house and a great cere-monial square in front of it. For the Associated Architects, keeping it open increased the size of the RCA Building's zoning envelope and thus enhanced the building's financial success. The plaza area also brought light into the en-tire development, an effect enhanced by one of Ray Hood's last suggestions: by setting the Time & Life Building on a north-south axis, rather than an east-west axis parallel to the International Building across the plaza, Hood created what architectural historian Carol Herselle Krinsky called a "pin-wheeling motion"—not an inert, symmetrical, Beaux-Arts composition, but one with a rhythmic action to it. The Channel Gardens and the walkways surrounding the sunken plaza in warm weather became the arena for a con-stantly changing flower show, beginning each year with crocuses, passing through tulips and summer annuals, and concluding each fall in a tumult of asters and mums (but few white blossoms of any variety: spring's Easter lilies inevitably acquired a coat of soot and had to be washed by hand).

Best of all, the plaza was open space in the heart of the city's concrete ravines, its accessibility—and, consequently, its integration into the life of midtown—enhanced by the disposition of the lobbies in most of the Cen-ter's buildings: these were true "lines of communication, not private cul-de-sacs." As James Marston Fitch and Diana S. Waite have pointed out, in American office buildings this was a feature "unheard of then and uncom-mon even now." Walk into a Rockefeller Center building at one end, and in most cases you can walk out the other. It is a system of circulation so ef-fortless and comfortable that when Wallace Harrison designed the Eastern Airlines Building in 1938 and 1939, he intentionally disrupted it: in order to attract people to the concourse, he made the most prominent feature in the Eastern Building's lobby a staircase leading one flight down.

Harrison understood the problem: in 1935, 63,000 people entered the RCA Building's lobby corridors each day, while only one-tenth as many used the concourse just below. The stores there, consigned to what quickly became known in the Manhattan commercial real estate business as "the catacombs," were suffering. The shops opening directly onto the sunken plaza—silversmiths, antiques purveyors, high-end milliners—were near death. The plaza itself, where Prometheus lolled distractedly on his side, was usually empty, its failure as insistent as a toothache.

Omero C. Catan entered the history of Rockefeller Center on Christmas morning, 1936. The night before, Mr. and Mrs. Santa Claus handed out gifts to five hundred poor children, a chorus sang carols, and four thousand decorative lights flashed on. The modest balsam under whose branches excavation workers had collected their paychecks in 1931 had been followed by a series of stately (and increasingly large) evergreens installed in the plaza. This was Merle Crowell's idea, as was the accompanying show of glee clubs, girl scouts, "the best Catholic choir in the city," organ music piped in over a PA system from the Music Hall, and the Gloria Trumpeters—three women, Crowell told Nelson Rockefeller and Arthur Woods, who were internationally known for their "wizardry with trumpet music."

Over the following decades the annual arrival of the Christmas tree would provide the downbeat for a ritualized minuet born of botany, shipping, publicity, and the irresistible tug of seasonal emotion. These were trees trucked in from New Jersey, trees floated down the Hudson, trees hauled slowly through the predawn streets of Manhattan, much like the marble columns for St. John the Divine that decades before had been dragged through those streets by steam winches. At times the installed tree was enhanced by reindeer in adjacent pens, more often by the 190 men and women from ninety tenant firms who comprised the Rockefeller Center Choristers. In one unfortunate season the tree's luster was tainted by the long aluminum icicles hanging from its branches that, loosened by the wind, "flew around the area like spears." Upsetting as this was, it did not diminish the mountain of newspaper articles and broadcast reports— Crowell made sure that even the first ceremony in 1933 was broadcast nationally by NBC—that annually arose from what must be the single most productive publicity event ever conceived in the city of New York.

But in 1936, no tree could upstage the phenomenon that had lured Omero C. Catan to Rockefeller Center. Catan was the somewhat less than celebrated author of *Secrets of Shuffleboard Strategy,* but was widely known in metropolitan New York for his other life as "Mr. First." For more than twenty years, stretching from the early 1930s well into the 1950s, Catan would have been happy to attend the opening of a can of peaches if he could be sure he'd get the first bite. He was the first man to buy a token when the Eighth Avenue subway opened for business. He was the first man to pay a toll in the center tube of the Lincoln Tunnel (later, when the north tube opened, Catan was in a military hospital in England and his brother, "Mr. Second," had to stand in for him). He would be the first passenger to land at Idlewild Airport, the first to put a coin in one of the city's new parking meters, the first to drive across the Tappan Zee Bridge.

On December 25, 1936, "Mr. First" strapped on his skates and inaugurated the Rockefeller Center Skating Rink. For a fee of $2,000, a Cleveland engineer named M. R. Carpenter had designed the system of tubes and pipes and compressors that enabled this anomalous addition to a business development. Meant to be temporary, another promotional exhibit that might yield some newspaper coverage, it proved so brilliant a success that it would be hailed by one commentator as "a great decision, a surrealistic decision, a fairy-tale decision." Of course, it wasn't a decision at all, but the ricochet from an earlier fumble. In 1949 the *Saturday Evening Post* confided that "the management [of Rockefeller Center] still speaks in hushed tones of the hundreds of skaters a day who happily contribute a yearly total of $80,000 for the privilege of putting on a free show." While they were at it, the writer added, those accidental skaters also managed to "salvag[e] the Center's biggest architectural mishap."

Contrarily, one of Rockefeller's Center's greatest architectural successes turned out to be a commercial disaster. Where the gloomy old brownstones at the western end of the southern block had languished for decades, a gorgeous theater rose in 1932, shone briefly, and then disappeared. Until it was torn down in 1954, what *The New Yorker* called the "poor, never-not-doomed" Center Theater had everything going for it, including a handsome design, gorgeous interior decoration, and a manageable size—everything, that is, except for a reason for existing.

After the Music Hall was hurriedly transformed from vaudeville palace to movie house following its disastrous opening, the RKO Roxy (as it was still called at the time) was treated like a stepchild forced to give up her room to a favored sibling. Two first-run motion picture theaters was one too many, and after all the first-run films had been hijacked by the Music Hall the RKO Roxy was converted into a vaudeville house. In 1933 this was akin to trading in your new Chrysler for a goat.

What a shame it was. In some ways Eugene Schoen outdid Donald Deskey, not least because the German-born Schoen, who taught interior design at NYU, knew the value of restraint. For all of Deskey's innovation at the Music Hall, his catalog of novel materials and his lengthy roster of contributing artists were a little overwhelming. Schoen seemed more interested in burnishing his hall than in gilding his reputation. He used the same sort of modern furniture in the lounge areas that Deskey brought to the Music Hall, but the decorative elements were both more modern and more subdued. The two outstanding works he commissioned were a striking, sixteen-foot long etched-glass screen by Maurice Heaton, depicting Amelia Earhart's 1932 Atlantic crossing, for the ladies' lounge, and an enormous "photo mural" by Edward Steichen, also on aviation themes, for the men's lounge. Steichen had devised a new art form—six-foot-high enlargements of original black-and-white photographs shot expressly for this purpose, arrayed in a continuous line around the entire room. It was an efficient art, too: he could produce 150 feet of murals in three weeks. Steichen was at the height of his celebrity in 1932, chief photographer for both *Vanity Fair* and *Vogue,* and exactly the sort of artist—widely admired, aesthetically innovative—that Rockefeller Center's managers favored B.R.: Before Rivera. Nor were leftist politics yet a disqualifier. Schoen commissioned a piece from Hugo Gellert, whose *Us Fellas Gotta Stick Together* for the Museum of Modern Art's mural show had provoked Nelson Rockefeller's apology to J. P. Morgan.

Schoen's real triumph, though, was the Center's auditorium. It may have been the most beautiful theater New York has ever known, an expression of contemporary sensibility that would still have looked fresh half a century later. It was the first modern theater paneled entirely in wood, its warm, unornamented veneer of bubinga mahogany reaching from the baseboards to the ceiling sixty feet overhead, "free from the French-pastry and animal-cracker magnificence of the movie-palace tradition." "It is an extraordinarily beautiful theater," Mordaunt Hall wrote in the *Times;* the *Sun's* Henry McBride, dean of the city's art critics, deemed it "overpoweringly chic" and declared its acoustics extraordinary.

But "the little house," as Rockefeller Center officials called it, had nearly 3,600 seats, and when vaudeville failed to fill them management tried everything but turning the place into a midtown haven for the unemployed. Even that was considered, after a fashion, when shortly after its conversion Roxy suggested enlisting the city's 12,000 jobless musicians to rotate through two concerts a day, seven days a week. That wasn't much worse an idea than many of those put into practice. The Center became, serially, home to elephantine operettas (one required 94 stagehands, 56 musicians, 136 actors and 500 costumes), elaborate ice shows ("America's only ice theatre," read the press release), full-length operas staged on a platform just above the ice (the cast "has been a bit chilly these spring nights," noted one official). For a while it was an outsized home for Ballet Theatre, the great dance company promoted by Sol Hurok out of his office on the fifth floor of the RCA Building. One producer wanted to stage Cole Porter's *Nymph Errant,* starring Gertrude Lawrence, but was rejected because management found it "an extremely risqué type of play which has no place in The Center Theatre." Other suggestions included "Hippodrome Spectacles"; an "American Indian Romantic Music[al]" called *Minnehaha;* and *King Solomon,* "a gorgeous and impressive spectacle . . . supposed to be of particular interest to Masons and people of the Jewish faith." Leon Leonidoff contacted ten members of the New York Rangers to see if they would be willing to play a ten-minute hockey game every night, but Leonidoff's collaborator in this venture, designer Norman Bel Geddes, demurred because he thought audience members who weren't hockey fans wouldn't be interested, and those who were would miss the fighting and the betting. Eva Le Gallienne wanted to bring in her Civic Repertory Theater, but she expected the landlord to put up the producing cash.

Amazingly, Rockefeller Center did eventually decide to get into the producing business; inevitably, the committee charged with this responsibility picked a series of losers. The last effort in this line of failures had an outstanding pedigree: written by George S. Kaufman and Moss Hart, produced by Sam Harris, and starring Frederic March. But *The American Way* was a bloated, tendentious, and earnestly patriotic turkey, an expensive disaster for everyone involved. It called for an army of performers and backstage personnel, seven full-time stage managers, and, even though it wasn't a musical, a full orchestra that was for some reason ensconced in an upstairs studio, where conductor Oscar Levant was alerted to the progress of the stage action by a series of flashing lights. Margaret Case Harriman, exaggerating a little in the first half of her appraisal but not at all in the second, said the show had been staged in a theater "holding four thousand persons, most of whom stayed away."

Apart from the post–Roxy Music Hall, nothing drew larger crowds to 49th and 50th Streets than the institution that had made an economically sound Rockefeller Center possible, and that had also guaranteed that Roxy-style entertainment could no longer survive in theaters. By virtue of its thirty-five studios stacked up in the western portion of the RCA Building, the National Broadcasting Company was from the beginning the Center's largest tenant. By virtue of the 60 million American households that could now find their entertainment in the box with the glowing dial, a generation of singers and comics and musicians and elocutionists looked out from the stages of the nation's music halls and palaces and saw rows of empty seats.

In the early 1930s the primary responsibility of RCA's chief engineer,

O. B. Hanson, was figuring out how to place thirty-five broadcast studios inside a giant office building. His initial determination, acknowledged by the architects, was that a series of large, columnless rooms could not support fifty-plus stories of limestone and steel. Thus, the western portion of the RCA Building, housing the broadcast facilities, was terminated at sixteen floors. For sound insulation, the studios were suspended from the building's structural elements, virtually rooms within rooms, their floors floating on enormous, felt-covered steel springs. None had windows. Beneath the studio floors more than fifteen hundred miles of wires and cables assured a technological overcapacity engineered by the farseeing Hanson, who "expected the industry to catch up with his engineers." Two stories of studios remained unused in the early days: they were designed for the coming era of television. Hanson even wired most of the structure for direct current, for he knew that "the flicker of an alternating current would play havoc with the [television] scenes and images" that would someday emanate from Rockefeller Center.

But Hanson also had to provide for something decidedly nontechnical—studio audiences. Vaudeville hadn't died with the coming of radio; like the audience, it just moved. Vaudeville headliners, weaned on the elixirs of laughter and applause, at first found themselves at sea when asked to perform in a room occupied only by sound equipment and bored technicians. By the time Hanson had begun to lay out plans for the NBC facilities, complaints from Eddie Cantor, Ed Wynn, and other performers had made the studio audience a broadcast necessity. Consequently, five stories of the studio complex contained audience galleries and reception rooms. Studio 8H, the world's largest, could seat fourteen hundred.* With two shows on the air at all times (one on NBC's Red Network, one on the Blue), and another eight or ten in rehearsal at any given moment, tourists wanting to join a studio audience were easily accommodated. NBC went on the air from its new Rockefeller Center headquarters in November of 1933; in its first year, more than three-quarters of a million people witnessed a live broadcast.

Studio 8H was the broadcast equivalent of Yankee Stadium. It belonged to Cantor on Sunday nights, Wynn on Tuesdays, and on Wednesdays beginning in January 1934, to the most popular man on radio. Fred Allen did two broadcasts each week, the first at 9:30 and the second three hours later for the West Coast audience. As the *Times* explained it, the people who'd

---

*Publicity materials said the stage in 8H could accommodate a four-hundred-piece orchestra, but cited no reason why anyone would ever want to assemble a four-hundred-piece orchestra.

been lining up for hours for the chance to see their favorite performer "may enter the studio expecting to see a hilarious Fred Allen, sparkling with facial expressions and cavorting around the microphone in funny regalia and with comic gestures. But no; the studio audience beholds the comedian as a calm figure standing at the microphone in a double-breasted suit, with collar open and tie loosened," perhaps keeping his eye on the network censor in the control booth—the man Allen called the "vice president in charge of waving fingers at comedians."

More imposing was 8H's other star occupant, Arturo Toscanini. Brought in by Sarnoff in 1937 to lead the NBC Symphony, the great conductor was such a draw that more than thirty thousand people requested tickets to his first broadcast; those fortunate enough to attend were presented with programs printed on satin, lest the turning of pages intrude on the sonic quality of the broadcast (for subsequent performances, cork or cardboard were the preferred materials). At home, audiences in the millions acquired their knowledge of music through Toscanini's immensely popular broadcasts; in 1939, *Life* asserted that the conductor was as well known to the American public as Joe DiMaggio. In the studio, those fortunate enough to hold tickets (although they were free, a black market quickly developed) could watch the great man make history every Saturday night: as music historian George Marek has noted, whatever piece Toscanini and the NBC Symphony played was heard at that instant by more people than had ever heard it before, in all its thousands of live performances, since the day of its composition.

Even though he'd change clothes at intermission, Toscanini concluded his broadcasts soaking wet from his exertions; he'd sit in a chair in his eighth-floor dressing room while one NBC staff member wiped his brow and untied his tie, and another brought him a glass of champagne sent down from the Rainbow Room. For his part, after completing a broadcast at 1:00 a.m., Fred Allen and his crew* would retire to a Sixth Avenue deli to work on the next week's show. Others among their NBC colleagues unwound at Hurley Bros. & Daly, the saloon on the northeast corner of Sixth and 50th that had survived the demolition of most of the Upper Estate and in time became so popular a drinking place for NBC talent that forever after insiders knew it as Studio 1H.

---

*His chief writer was a twenty-one-year-old aspiring novelist named Herman Wouk, his producer twenty-five-year-old Sylvester "Pat" Weaver, a Dartmouth classmate of Nelson's who would later create both the *Today* and *Tonight* shows, and become chairman of NBC.

—————

Seeing a show was only part of the radio experience that brought visitors in the millions to the RCA Building. At the daily 9:00 A.M. opening of the Guest Relations center on the building's mezzanine, the hordes of pilgrims from all over the country who had procured guest cards from their local NBC affiliates entered a room that on its own was a dazzler. The entrance rotunda was decorated with a stunning photomural created by Margaret Bourke-White. The 160-foot-long piece, nearly eleven feet high, circled the room, a collage of microphones, transmission tubes, condenser coils, antenna towers—"everything that makes radio possible," Bourke-White explained. You couldn't help but be overwhelmed by the size and power of the photographer's work (in notes for her memoirs Bourke-White wrote of the NBC mural, "this wd be the biggest m in the w & nobody was going to stop me"). Her publicity materials said the mural was "the first of its kind in the world," which ignored Steichen's piece a block away in the Center Theater, but as the twenty-nine-year-old Bourke-White said, "I am not interested in anything or anybody except as my work may be helped or affected."

The studio tour itself was like a trip through a fun house. Those actors walking the corridors in green makeup and purple lipstick? They're on the way to 3H, where NBC is testing television technology; the ghoulish look neutralizes the effects of the lighting. Yes, that's Fred Astaire you see through the triple-paned glass in 5B; he's in town to appear on the Lucky Strike Hit Parade on Saturday, and that big platform he's dancing on has been miked so your friends will be able to hear his taps all the way to San Diego. Now— in a conspiratorial whisper—do you see that fellow coming out of the men's room? That's John B. Kennedy, the announcer from Radio City Dance Party!

Of course, although they may have known the sonorities of his voice, few if any of the customers knew what John B. Kennedy looked like. But there was a chance the guide was telling the truth, and when you've traveled to New York City to revel in the fabulous fantasy world that was Rockefeller Center, where Lorenz Hart said, "You won't believe a thing you see"—well, wasn't that more than enough?

In the fall of 1934 the Rainbow Room—the most glamorous of Rockefeller Center's entertainment venues and, after the Music Hall, its most celebrated one—was about to open, and Francis Christy was assigned an unlikely responsibility. The Harvard-trained lawyer and legal scholar (his authoritative *The Transfer of Stock* would remain in print more than half a century) had recently given up his partnership at Milbank, Tweed, Hope and Webb to take a full-time executive position at Rockefeller Center. Neither his training nor his job description, however, could have prepared him for this particular task. Since New York law required nightclub operators to be fingerprinted, and since the actual owner of the nightclub in question was less than eager to make the trip to the local precinct house, Christy volunteered to press hand to ink to paper and thus enter the permanent files of the New York Police Department. The nominal president of Center Restaurants, Incorporated, Francis Christy thereby made legal the upcoming opening of "Jack Rockefeller's saloon and dance hall."

That was Westbrook Pegler's phrase for a venture that became candy for columnists. How could they resist the easy material Junior provided when he agreed to crown his real estate development with a glittering tiara where society would frolic, celebrities would parade, and great quantities of liquor would flow night after glamorous night? This was about as likely as famous communists being commissioned to paint Rockefeller walls. "Throughout his life," wrote a *Daily News* entertainment reporter, "whenever he has been asked 'Wot'll it be?,' the junior John D. has always replied, 'milk.'" In the *Mirror,* Mark Hellinger wrote a "Dear Johnny" letter to Junior that began, "If you hadn't gone into the café racket . . ." The Rainbow Room, wrote a visiting Englishwoman, was a place where one was meant "to dress high and snap the rubber-band off the bank-roll," and any journalist who could attach that concept to an image of Junior in evening clothes would have been well advised to give up newspapering for science fiction.

Junior himself knew how improbable, perhaps even hypocritical, this all was. Having favored Repeal, he told Arthur Woods, he did not feel he could deny Rockefeller Center restaurants run by others the right to serve liquor, "much as I might like, for personal reasons and because of personal convictions, to do so." Stuck with running one himself—more precisely, a corporation he owned and controlled stuck with running it—those reasons and convictions largely went into hiding. There had always been plans for a dining facility on the sixty-fifth floor of the RCA Building; the conventions of the time all but required a luncheon club for tenants, and it would take forever to amortize the cost if you didn't make use of the place at night. But when no outside operator would assume the risk, Junior had to take it on himself. "Not being sufficiently familiar with the usual method of dispensing alcoholic beverages in the average high grade club," he told Woods with polite understatement, Junior effectively ducked behind a pillar and hoped for the best.

From the beginning, it *was* the best. Fred Allen told the NBC guides in 1935, "If you behave and do your jobs right . . . when you die you'll go way up to the Rainbow Room." All those tourists on the observation deck just above the Rainbow Room as well as those circulating through the stores, plazas, theaters, and exhibits way below were good for business, but their mission was to enjoy the aura of Rockefeller Center, not to add to it. That was what the Rainbow Room was meant to do. The morning after its October 1934 debut, the *New York Journal* ran an eight-column headline across the first page of its second section: "SWANK CROWD SEES RAINBOW ROOM OPENING." The *Times* listed the attendees, a dazzle of surnames that ran from Astors and Auchinclosses to Warburgs and Whitneys, salted with a few delegates from the business aristocracy that had risen in recent years—lawyers Paul Cravath and Jeremiah Milbank, press eminences Arthur Brisbane and Herbert Bayard Swope, merchant Marshall Field. Of course, once you'd let in lawyers, editors, and merchants, the old crowd wasn't what it used to be; the British journalist Molly Castle wrote that the roll that night included "five or six hundred of New York's Four Hundred."

Junior, host to a party of sixteen, may have been unsettled more by the talent than by the 1921 Moët et Chandon Imperial Crown being poured all around him that night. He might well have liked some of the viscous dance music supplied by Jolly Coburn and His Orchestra, and the Music Hall's organist, Richard Liebert, was on the program, too. But the headliner was a French *diseuse* named Lucienne Boyer, who arrived in New York a few days before the opening with "a manager, a pianist, a violinist, three maids, 23 trunks, 50 pieces of hand luggage," and a flair for publicity. "I am the slave of my pleasure and the slave of the pleasure of those who like me," Boyer told the *Post,* whose reporter apparently did not ask if John D. Rockefeller Jr. was among those who liked her. One journalist said Boyer sang "slightly purple songs in French and broken English—so broken that the pieces rattled." Her big number was "Parlez-moi d'Amour," but it's safe to say that Junior, who had both an excellent table and perfect French, did not oblige her.

In fact, after that first night he pretty much stayed away from the Rainbow Room. He neither bathed the men responsible for it in congratulatory telegrams nor bruised them with his characteristically gentle criticism. Occasionally he would accompany his sons to the room to see a particular act (like, for instance, the blind pianist Alec Templeton, of whom John D. 3rd said, "He seems like a terribly nice boy"). But the Rainbow Room and its components—liquor, indulgence, worldly entertainment—seemed to be something best left to others.

Skyscraper entertainment was very stylish in the mid-1930s—Vincent Astor owned the popular St. Regis Roof, and the Starlight Roof at the new Waldorf-Astoria had its fans—but the Rainbow Room was higher, larger, shinier, and more audacious than any competitor. Hood and the other architects had situated the room eight hundred feet above sea level and had surrounded it with twenty-four windows, each two stories high, that from within made the place seem to float in the Manhattan sky. The decor was the work of Elena Bachman Schmidt, a protégé of Elsie De Wolfe, the great decorator who introduced a light, French style into American homes previously entombed in Victorian gloom and who "made it fashionable for older women to tint their hair blue."

Assisted by a capable consultant—Vincente Minnelli, on loan from the Music Hall to help pick wall colors—Schmidt created a room built of classical elements that created the illusion of modernity. On their own, the green leather chairs, the aubergine satin drapes, the crystal and the brass and the rest were straight from the De Wolfe tool kit; put together and then suspended among all those fabulous two-story windows, the place seemed to have been designed "not as a room, but as a background for people." In the Astaire-Rogers film *Swing Time,* the Rainbow Room was apotheosized as the "Silver Sandal"; for the 1937 George Murphy vehicle *Top of the Town,* it was the model for the "Moonbeam Room" (a Universal Pictures press release said the $100,000 Moonbeam set was "the greatest and most pretentious ever built in Hollywood"); in the popular imagination for nearly three-quarters of a century, it has been the embodiment of Art Deco chic. But it wasn't the room that was Deco, it was the people in it.

The crowd that frequented the Rainbow Room in the 1930s was composed of the sorts you see at the tables watching Fred and Ginger in most of their movies—as elegant as caviar, as rich as butter, and most of all *not common.* The masses were kept out not by the airs of headwaiters (those accepting a tip in exchange for a good table were immediately fired) but by a price structure that required a trust fund and a dress code that required white tie. ("As the quality of the audience deteriorated," wrote Francis Christy, the code was relaxed to admit men merely wearing tuxedos; still, one of the direct elevators from the lobby floor was reserved for those in full white tie.) *Fortune* said that Rainbow Room management catered to "the nonflashy strata of the upper crust," suggesting that the highly visible nightclubbers at places like El Morocco and the Stork Club were not only flashy but not quite so upper. An internal memo noted that without the Rainbow Room, "the very impressive and dignified society people" would have nowhere else to go in nighttime New York.

At the same time, the celebrity culture that had begun to take shape during the dark Prohibition years, when rascality was a virtue and renown became a reward, now flowered extravagantly at the Rainbow Room. Press releases sedately noting, say, the small party last night given in honor of Mr. and Mrs. Wyckoff Vanderhoef quickly went on to announce that Miriam Hopkins, Norma Talmadge, and Jean Harlow (so much for "nonflashy") happened by as well. One release enumerated a range of celebrities that included Mr. and Mrs. Peter Arno, Mr. and Mrs. Gene Tunney, Walter Pidgeon, and Nita Naldi (not to mention one "Captain Jefferson Davis Cohen," whose fame proved temporary). Douglas Fairbanks Jr. recalled how he'd "go up to the Rainbow Room, go to the bar, and wait and see who showed up"; his Rainbow cronies included Laurence Olivier, David Niven, and Marlene Dietrich, who would demand an enlivening tango if the band persisted in too many waltzes and fox-trots. On "NBC Radio Star Nights" the network would provide two tables' worth of radio celebrities, who were promised they would not be asked to perform so long as they agreed to take a bow when introduced from the bandstand.

Still, the room needed to retain its social cachet if its celebrities were to be protected from a déclassé element that "might create the impression that the Rainbow Room was *sans chic*" (as a later operator of the room put it, "Dacron not Dunhill"). That required coverage on the society pages, and apart from great events like the room's opening night, the editors were more interested in the new generation of bright young things than in the grande dames left over from the Mauve Decade. When typewriter heiress Burnice Smith eloped with the Venezuela-born "tango-rhumba maestro" Eddie LeBaron, one of the Rainbow Room's regular bandleaders (he "goes with the lease—and should," wrote Abel Green in *Variety*), everybody was well served: the newspapers, for the scandal value; the Rainbow Room, for the publicity (performers so glamorous they can marry millionaires!); even Burnice's grandmother, the society doyenne Mrs. George Washington Kavanagh (who was immortalized in a different context as the begowned, bejeweled, and benighted older woman being scrutinized by a bag lady in Weegee's famous photograph "The Critic"). Mrs. Kavanagh was more than happy to welcome a *Daily News* reporter into her house on East 62nd Street after her granddaughter's elopement and announce that she felt no ill will. "Of course," she added, "our family is an old American one and I always like to see girls marry American men."

But when you can't count on regular elopements, you find other ways to get your establishment's name into the newspapers. One of the most effective gambits was the hiring of a Yale graduate named Jerome Zerbe, who was paid $75 weekly (plus all he could eat) to bring his stylish young friends to the Rainbow Room for dinner three times a week. The payoff came when the elegant Zerbe—"the boy with the patent-leather hair," Helen Worden called him—took flattering pictures of his dinner mates and sent them off to grateful society editors, thus launching his four-decade career as court photographer to the rich, the beautiful, and the idle. Zerbe professed amazement that anyone would want to look at his pictures when the front pages were still chronicling unemployment, bread lines, and generalized economic woe. "My friends and I were all more or less Marie Antoinettes in our attitudes," he said many years later, "but instead of having our heads chopped off we were applauded. Very strange."

A new generation of heedless sybarites was prepped for graduation into the Rainbow Room once the less formal Rainbow Grill opened up down the hall, in 1935 (black tie in season, white linen acceptable in the summer). No Royal Squab en Cocotte Richelieu here; this was a room for fun. In the Grill, a staff member confided in a memo, the "college boys [who] are not noted for their good behavior when drinking" would be able to "frolic and make merry with no disadvantage." Advertisements in Ivy League newspapers solicited the potential frolickers to come to the "Manhattan Mecca for College Men and Women Who Do the Right Thing." In keeping with Merle Crowell's philosophy of getting something for almost nothing, the ads were virtually free: the papers in which they ran were compensated in waived cover charges for their student editors. It was among the "college men and women" in the Grill that New York encountered the "freak dance craze" that would help endow the city with its enduring nickname. "The Big Apple" was an after-hours joint on the outskirts of Columbia, South Carolina, that gave birth to what the *Daily News* called a "combination of Truckin' the Susi-Q, the Charleston and the Shag, with a touch of St. Vitus' Dance thrown in." It traveled rapidly, and when it hit the Grill (and consequently the newspapers), the dance was established.

Not, however, down the corridor in the Rainbow Room. "I LOATHE THE BIG APPLE," read the headline on a Saks Fifth Avenue newspaper ad. "Are you against the Big Apple, too?" the copy continued. "Ruby Newman, at the Rainbow Room, definitely is." If you want to waltz, the ad suggested, go heed Newman and his orchestra at the Rainbow Room on Monday nights; and if you want to be dressed right for a waltz in the Rainbow Room, come visit Saks' Debutante Shop. But if the Rainbow Room did not accommodate the Big Apple, there must have been something among its component twists and gyrations and grinds stranger even than St. Vitus' Dance. For virtually nothing else—except, it's horrifying to note, black performers—was automatically disqualified from an entertainment lineup that not even the most deranged impresario could have conceived.*

One might speculate that the Rainbow Room's peculiar entertainment policy arose from a sort of whistling-past-the-graveyard determination to ignore the ravages of the Depression. But it's probably safest to say that the room's bizarre collection of high- and low-end entertainers, animal acts, athletes, dancers, and uncategorizables was assembled out of a need to amuse its jaded clientele. Not that it began badly. Lucienne Boyer may not be remembered, but she was top-billed talent wherever she went in 1934. And Boyer was followed by Beatrice Lillie, whose opening night audience included Cole Porter, Elsa Maxwell, and Noël Coward, the last of whom joined her onstage for a duet. But Boyer's fee was $3,000 a week, Lillie's was $2,375, and the Rockefeller tropism toward economies commanded a still steeper decline in talent expenditures. Besides, every evening also featured a dance band, an opening act, a magician who wandered from table to table trailed by a palm reader and maybe a numerologist, and whatever else it took to get the crowd not to depart for "21," where all they had to do was drink.

Soon the headliners in "this sky-high temple to Bacchus and Terpsichore" were monologists, impressionists, or maybe the "Viennese *conferenciere*" Marcelle Luzzato. Opening acts ran from the Three Pitchmen (offering "capers with kazoos") to Beth Pitt, billed as "the Lighted Balloon Girl" (she promised that "the climax to her career will be the act she hopes to put on at the Triboro Bridge opening") to Zingo the London Hippodrome Horse. Ping-Pong champion Ruth Aarons took on all comers (beat

---

*"You know the group which comes to the Rainbow Room," said John Roy when Nelson inquired about the possibility of integrating the roster of performers. "Many would leave were we to offer colored entertainment. Our group is not the one which patronizes Cafe Society Uptown, nor one expecting to find Harlem entertainment here. Also, we would have an additional problem concerning admission of negroes as guests in the Room and the Grill were we to use colored entertainment."

her and you won a bottle of champagne), and she was such a success that a badminton team soon followed. Every show had to include a pair of "adagio dancers," and if you strung together a couple of seasons' worth of them, you'd end up with something sounding like roll call in a Mediterranean fishing port: Maurice and Cordoba, Gomez and Winona, Lydia and Joresco, Enrica and Novello, Medrano and Donna, Ramon and Rosita. Ramon and Rosita caused a problem: after the couple divorced, Ramon hired someone named Amy to serve as his new Rosita, and the original Rosita brought an infringement suit against Rockefeller Center—even though her own real name was Maria Louise.

Not all the talent was gimmicky, suspect, or litigious. A comic act called the Revuers arrived in the Rainbow Room fresh from a big success downtown at the Village Vanguard; its members included the very young Betty Comden, Adolph Green, and Judy Holliday, and although they flopped, said George Ross in the *World-Telegram,* it was nonetheless "a nice gesture on the Rockefellers' part" to book them. Agnes de Mille performed a balletic duet with a dancer named Hugh Laing. Sometimes a rising star would get a showcase, as when the twenty-two-year-old Mary Martin accepted two hundred dollars a week to sing four numbers each evening right after concluding her work on Broadway in *Leave It to Me.* But Martin had to share the bill with a trained crow.

As irritating as that might have been for Martin, it would have been worse to headline a bill whose opening act was so successful that the headliner faded into oblivion. That was what happened to the singer Milly Monti on November 11, 1936, the night an unknown young ventriloquist named Edgar Bergen appeared in the Rainbow Room on the recommendation of Noël Coward. (The audience included Bette Davis, whose blue damask gown, wrote the columnist Cholly Knickerbocker, was "very becoming to her blonde pulchritude.") Within a month Bergen was appearing on Rudy Vallee's radio show; a few months later he was a national celebrity; a few months after that, his *Chase & Sanborn Hour* with Charlie McCarthy and Mortimer Snerd was the top-rated show on Sunday nights.

Think about it: a ventriloquist becomes a huge star—*on the radio!* How good an act must that have been when it played for the swells way up there in the Rainbow Room?

CHAPTER 21

Nelson may have needed art, but he also relished the high life. He never went nearly so far as his little brother Winthrop, whose postgraduate club hopping culminated in his marriage to a former beauty queen (well, sort of; before she be-

*You have caught **the snake** in the process of **changing its skin.***

—NELSON A. ROCKEFELLER,
DECEMBER 1936

came Bobo Sears Rockefeller, Jievute Paulekiute was Chicago's Miss Lithuania in 1933). Nelson's social life had a shinier gloss—visits at George Gershwin's penthouse on Riverside Drive during the cocktail hour (Nelson favored a mix of orange juice and sherry), dinners with Roxy, evenings out with Queen Mary's brother Lord Athlone and his wife, Princess Alice ("Enclosed please find the $100 which you so kindly loaned me" last night, Nelson wrote to an associate after that particular date. "Fortunately, the royal party decided not to go to a night club").

Nelson called the Rainbow Room, whose operations he supervised in his role as chairman of the Center's Roofs and Restaurants Committee, "our restaurant," and the possessive suggested a fondness that he didn't expend on, say, the gardens. His enthusiasms, which no one around him would ever try to contain, reached every part of the operation. He urged the hiring of particular entertainers (he was especially keen on having "Dudley & Cole attempt their 'Two Cigarettes in the Dark' dance on the balcony . . . and [their] 'Bolero' on the floor"). He came up with ideas, like Saturday afternoon tea dances, that he knew would make no profit but might, as a colleague said, draw "the right kind of people" to the room. Fond of the baked beans in small earthenware crocks that the Pennsylvania Railroad served in its dining cars, he seemed to think the dish would make a nice addition to the menu (but dropped the matter when he learned that the Pennsy's chefs simply emptied large cans of Heinz Baked Beans into the handsome little jars). One of Nelson's enthusiasms that didn't pan out involved a former Olympic diver named Jane Fauntz, who sent him a series of notes on elegant stationery, ostensibly pitching for a job as an "art diver" in the Rainbow Room ("I am very feminine," she assured him). This correspondence led to at least two meetings, one of which Fauntz commemorated with a broad wink: "As for old 'Promiscuous,' the golden gent in the fountain—perhaps he'd like someone to talk to for company—he looks rather lonesome.'"

None of this meant that Nelson didn't regard the Rainbow Room as a business, but it did require a certain deftness insofar as that business intersected with his social life. The bandleader Meyer Davis, who had played at his wedding, wheedled Nelson to "personally favor my orchestra for the Night Club" (in vain, as it turned out). Mrs. Kermit Roosevelt agreed to hold a benefit in the room after exposure to Nelson's effortless charm, but in the next breath he had to explain why the price she had initially been quoted would have to be raised. When one or another business titan or socialite sustained a bruised ego or an offended sensibility because of something that happened in the room, Nelson was instantly alerted and, if necessary, called in to apply his mollifying balm. But the delights of the Rainbow Room compensated for such complications. One evening, arriving late on the sixty-fifth floor with a group of friends, he discovered that Ray Noble and his orchestra had already left the bandstand for the night. What good was owning a club if you couldn't ask the talent to put on a command performance? Nelson asked, and Noble complied.

As much as he enjoyed the privileges afforded him throughout the Center, Nelson was as polite as the Rockefellers who preceded him and as politic as the Rockefeller he was on his way to becoming. He wrote in gratitude to the bartender who concocted a "Rainbow" cocktail that had become very popular and, priced at a ten-cent premium above the standard cocktail, was also pretty swell "from a financial point of view": it brought in an unanticipated profit of $309.80 over four months. In the Music Hall he held eight seats, first row center mezzanine, for every opening night. When he entered the building the ushers instantly began flashing their signals to one another. One hand in front of the chest in a pistol shape meant a "big shot" was in the house, two hands doing the same thing meant "bigger shot," and Nelson was as big a shot as the place might see. Still, he never missed a chance to present awards to outstanding workers, speak at employee ceremonies, or announce scholarships for employee children. One year he gave the Music Hall's service staff a radio for their clubroom so they could listen to the World Series on their breaks.

But those were gestures suited for good times; when the going got tough, that Nelson disappeared. In 1935, Henri Charpentier, the great chef who had brought crepes suzette to his elegant restaurant in the Maison Française, found himself tumbling over the brink of failure, unable to meet his rent payments. Nelson, who dined often at Charpentier's, wrote him on April 2 to thank him for the *poisson d'Avril* he had enjoyed the previous evening. Just nine days later, at four in the afternoon, a constable and six deputies sent the customers home, dismissed the waiters, then "loaded foodstuffs and liquors into baskets and boxes, turned out the lights, locked the doors and drove away." Abandoning "the sheer oppressive voice of his good cheer" (as the *Times* once characterized the chef's usual form of address), Charpentier fired off a melodramatic telegram to Nelson. "Naturally," Nelson told Hugh Robertson, "I have sent no reply."

Naturally: as he had done at the time of Diego Rivera's firing, Nelson turned over the ugly part of the affair to someone else. His disengagement from his friend Charpentier also reflected his ability to separate his nominal pleasures from the steely realities of business. This wasn't ruthlessness; Charpentier was a horrible businessman, and unpaid rent is unpaid rent. At the time Charpentier signed his lease in 1933, he and the other restaurant operators were to some degree subsidized by Rockefeller Center, for you couldn't attract office tenants if you didn't have places for them to eat, and you couldn't expect a restaurant in an office center to make a profit if there weren't yet enough tenants. But by the time the deputies "brutally destroyed the fruit of my work," as Charpentier had exclaimed in his flavorful telegram,* both Nelson Rockefeller and Rockefeller Center were sailing toward success.

A memo Nelson wrote to key associates in early 1936 indicated the position of strength both he and the business had attained. Complimenting them for overcoming "insurmountable difficulties," he went on to marvel at how "organizations have been brought out of chaos [and] a center of great beauty has been created." He praised the design process, the publicity efforts, the purchasing process. The results of the "whirlwind renting campaign," he continued, "have absolutely staggered the whole city." Then he

---

*The chef was even rougher on Junior: a five-year campaign of letters and telegrams culminated in 1941 with the ultimate insult. "You might talk plenty about charity," Charpentier wrote, "but your kindness is Godless."

concluded the memo with a 180: perhaps it was time to revisit the contract with the professional managers who had brought the development so far.

Later that year, in an extravagant eleven-page takeout on Rockefeller Center's "changing reputation," *Fortune* said the development "is now passing from the promotional to the operating phase of its ordained life cycle." Then the magazine quoted Nelson directly: "You have caught the snake in the process of changing its skin."

In the first seven years of the Center's evolution, Junior's mood migrated from defiant (he wasn't going to let the opera group push him around) to engaged (crawling around on the blueprints with his collapsible yardstick in hand) to distraught *(where will all the money come from?)*. By the time planning for the second phase of construction was under way in 1935, he had landed on the shore of something close to contentment. For one thing, he was sleeping better. He also reported that his indigestion was improving, and that he had even managed to go four straight days without a headache—"something that has not happened to me for years."

A stroll through the International Building shortly after it opened led Junior to tell Joe Brown, "I really do get more thrills from the Development as new units are opened or new projects are launched." (Catching himself, he did ask Brown to "please excuse this burst of enthusiasm.") The maquette for Lee Lawrie's powerful *Atlas* for the International's forecourt so pleased him that he authorized the additional expense required to cast it in seven tons of bronze rather than the cheaper aluminum. Several weeks later he demonstrated his new sense of calm when he announced that his associates no longer had to advise him about cash needs on a quarterly basis; he would "assume things are running within the year's appropriation unless you call [it to] my attention." At this point Junior's outlay had already passed $50 million, but the income stream was freshening rapidly. He barely blinked when he was asked for the go-ahead to proceed with construction on the last four buildings. After the first of these was built, he no longer even felt the need to tap into the Met Life mortgage, from which he had drawn down only $44 million of the authorized $65 million. He covered the new buildings' costs with cash.

Nelson and Junior were moving in opposite directions. As one took on responsibility and authority the other began to shed them. This may not have been intentional on Junior's part but it was irresistible. Nelson was capable, and Junior was comfortable. The time was right for transition in many aspects of his life. He had finally completed his reconstruction of the cathedral in Rheims (when his grateful French associates toasted him with three different vintages of champagne, he returned the salute with Perrier). Fort Tryon Park opened to the public in 1935, and Junior often found himself stopping there with Abby on the way to Pocantico for a walk "overlooking the river, up and down the smooth, well graded paths, among the trees, the shrubs and the beautiful rocks." The youngest of their children gone from home, Junior and Abby made plans to leave 10 West 54th Street. The empty nest to which they moved evolved into a forty-room triplex at 740 Park Avenue, partly a residence (including a dining room that seated forty-eight) and partly a private museum for Junior's collection of Asian art and artifacts. The old place was razed, and the land it stood on became the sculpture garden for the Museum of Modern Art.

Junior's last apparent contribution to Rockefeller Center fit perfectly with the image of a contented man moving toward retirement. It was also so affecting that it triggered what one would least expect John D. Rockefeller Jr. to inspire: a nationwide craze. As history would record it, Junior paused one day on a truck ramp to watch some of the men and machines building the Eastern Airlines Building in the southern block. A guard clapped his hand on his shoulder and said, "Keep moving, buddy. You can't stand here all day." Junior being Junior, he kept moving and didn't stand there all day. Merle Crowell being Merle Crowell, within weeks an eighty-foot-long viewing platform went up on the east side of the site, dedicated to "the gentle art of gaping at construction activities" and christened the Sidewalk Superintendents' Club. George Atwell was named the club's "honorary president," qualifying for the position partly because he owned the excavation company that had done most of the digging for Rockefeller Center but mostly, one suspects, because he looked like Lionel Barrymore. Membership cards were handed out to twenty thousand people in the first week, to three-quarters of a million in the first three months. Early visitors included architects William Lescaze and Albert Kahn, and designer Raymond Loewy. Atwell/Barrymore's grandfatherly face showed up in newspapers across the nation. "Chapters" of the club opened in cities stretching from Cambridge, Massachusetts, to Fort Worth to Los Angeles, and Crowell brought some of their members to New York for a photogenic convention.

Press coverage was extensive and ecstatic. The *Lincoln (Nebraska) Evening-Journal,* for example, said the Rockefeller family may "have given millions to charitable enterprises" but "no greater benefaction to mankind has been made than that by John D. Rockefeller Jr., when, at comparatively small cost, he provided a gallery for the steam shovel watchers at the site of new construction work in Rockefeller Center." Yet to his credit, Merle Crowell admitted elsewhere that the idea had nothing to do with Junior and a rude watchman, but came from "a platform for kibitzers in Des Moines." Someone had sent a clipping about it to Nelson. When an awe-struck C. D. Jackson, publisher of *Life*, offered "three loud cheers . . . to the person who had the marvelous public relations instinct" to capitalize on the notion, Hugh Robertson replied, "This was an idea of Nelson Rocke-feller's which has gone over in grand shape." The *Chicago Daily News* was more precise: "It's a better idea even than giving away dimes."*

"By 1937," wrote the anonymous author of a commemorative volume pub-lished after Junior's death in 1960, "Mr. Rockefeller saw Nelson work his way through the Center to the position of Executive Vice President and be-gin to take command of some of the major problems facing the Center." Nelson "worked his way" to his eventual command the way a tsunami works its way through a tidal stream.

As he began to consolidate his authority, he relied less and less on the ad-vice or involvement of John R. Todd. He had fought with Todd quite a bit, and chafed at John R.'s tendency to kill his ideas by simply failing to act on them. Nelson's frustration was aggravated by his exclusion from discussions concerning the periodic extensions of the managers' contract, which con-tinued to be negotiated by Junior and Debevoise despite Nelson's rise within the organization. This was no small issue: Debevoise, who had brought his neighbor Todd into the project, remained his champion. At one especially tense time in the Rockefeller Center offices in late 1934, when a confidential memo warned of the "jealousies, friction and politics" that had gripped the apparatus, Debevoise dictated a four-page defense of Todd and his partners. "They have done a stupendous job," Debevoise said, "spent a stupendous amount of Mr. Rockefeller's money, have created an

---

*The idea reached its apotheosis in 1957, by which time the Sidewalk Superintendents' Club had become a Rockefeller Center fixture. The clubhouse that opened that year when construc-tion began on the new Time & Life Building was covered with a striped canopy, decorated with flower boxes and colorful pennants, fronted by ten large Plexiglas windows, and outfitted with toy cranes and bulldozers so members could "pit their construction skills against one another." And it was dedicated by someone very different from George Atwell, but likelier to attract a few more cameras: Marilyn Monroe.

excellent public attitude toward the project, and have not only kept us out of trouble but done the best kind of work for us in all our relationships." He concluded with this: "It is time that we made the Managing Agents realize that we are with them, that our only object is to do what we can to help them, and that from now on cooperation is to be our first name."

Unless your first name was Nelson. Through 1935 the communication between the chief manager and the chief son was almost entirely disputatious. Nelson wanted to spend more money on the *Rockefeller Center Weekly;* Todd did not. Nelson had specific ideas for the Wailing Wall in the RCA lobby; when Todd demonstrated their impracticality to Junior, Nelson became petulant and complained that Todd was being unfair. Not only was Nelson's first name not "cooperation," his last name was indubitably Rockefeller, just like the man who paid Thomas Debevoise's salary. Thus, just six months after offering his gaudy praise for Todd and his partners, the lawyer threw in with the boss's son. And six months after that, Debevoise directed an eyes-only memo to Nelson. "Only three copies were made of it," Debevoise began, "one for you, one for your father and one for me." At its heart was a question that, through the very asking, changed everything: What would be the effect on the "public and official mind," asked Debevoise, if John R. Todd were fired?

Throughout Nelson's long, trench-by-trench battle with Todd he remained on good terms with Hugh Robertson, and turned to him from time to time not only to clean up after him (viz. Rivera and Charpentier) but for counsel as well. They didn't have quite the mentor-student relationship that Robertson offered John D. 3rd, but Nelson wasn't as needy as his older brother. Besides, he had his pal Harrison, ready to emerge from the collaborative huddle of the Associated Architects just as Nelson prepared to act on his own.

Unquestionably, the immediate success of the Rockefeller Apartments energized both men. It wasn't really a Rockefeller Center project, so they had not had to suffer Todd's supervision. It also led directly to a much grander idea, born over one of their marmalade-and-bacon breakfasts in the Gateway Restaurant, that was potentially as imposing as Rockefeller Center itself: Nelson wanted to extend Rockefeller Plaza, the midblock street that ran between the skating rink and the RCA Building, up to 53rd Street, to serve as the fulcrum of an arts center modeled after the business center two blocks to the south. Nelson's vision, said Harrison, would have turned the extended street into "a walking plaza, more like a Venetian plaza without traffic": San Marco in Manhattan. On either side of this northern extension of the plaza would stand new homes for the Metropolitan Opera, the Museum of Non-Objective Painting (precursor of the Guggenheim Museum), and, as a commercial (but slightly artsy) anchor, the Columbia Broadcasting System. At its northern terminus the plaza would lead directly to the front door of "Mother's Museum"—the Museum of Modern Art, ready to rise on land owned by Junior, under the auspices of the chairman of its finance committee and its building committee, Nelson Rockefeller.

It was a scheme that had much to recommend it. The Metropolitan Opera would finally get its new house. Solomon R. Guggenheim, heir (along with his sister Peggy) to an enormous mining fortune, had announced his intention to open a museum for his vast collection of abstract art, and here was a perfect site. It was good business, too. As Nicholas Murray Butler had perceived more than a decade earlier, the creation of new corner lots—there would be four in each block—would greatly enhance the value of the real estate on either side of the street. And to the north of Rockefeller Center, much of that real estate already belonged to the Rockefeller family. Including the land reserved for the Modern Art museum, Junior and entities he controlled owned fifty lots in all.

But there was one critical piece of land that Nelson needed to acquire if he wished to complete his scheme, and it was far better defended than even William Nelson Cromwell's fortress on 49th. Right smack in the path of Nelson's grand promenade, on the north side of 52nd Street, in a block teeming with so many bars, nightclubs, and jazz joints that *Variety* called it "the illegitimate offspring of Rockefeller Center," stood the "21" Club. When on New Year's Eve 1929 the owners trundled all their possessions, and many of their drunken habitués, up from their condemned building on 49th Street, they had vowed they'd never move again. Why would they, when they had created the most successful drinking spot in New York? Where, John D. Rockefeller 3rd was surprised to learn when he was taken there by his brother Winthrop, you could on any given night find people like Grover Whalen, Jock Whitney, or Eddie Warburg having the time of their lives. (Poor, clueless Johnny: On his first visit to "21," in 1940, he informed his diary that "It seems that it used to be a speakeasy but now is run as an expensive restaurant.") Even more impressive than the crowds who filled the place nightly were the prices those crowds were willing to pay. Damon Runyon insisted that the Kriendler and Berns families, who owned the place, maintained a secret "Laughing Room, well-insulated for sound, where [they] got together to plan the day's price list."

There were only two ways Nelson could hope to remove "21" from its position blocking his incipient Venetian-style plaza. First, he could buy it and evict the tenants. Except the Bernses and the Kriendlers weren't tenants, and the place wasn't for sale. When they moved in they had bought the building and also the land beneath it; part of the down payment came from the eleven thousand dollars of Junior's money they had been paid to abandon their old place on 49th. Nelson's other option was political. He could try to get the city to condemn the property. But it appears that the only people in New York who had as much political juice as the Rockefeller family were the Bernses and the Kriendlers, thanks to the support of the Whalens, the Whitneys, the Warburgs, and all the other heavy hitters who called the place their own. Nelson lost.

Within a year Junior began unloading all his property in the West 50s. A large portion of the south side of 53rd Street he gave for a new branch of the New York Public Library (here was family revenge—construction of the library basement set off an unintended chorus of popping corks among the jereboams of champagne in "21"'s abutting wine cellar). The north side, of course, went to the Museum of Modern Art. The museum's director, Alfred Barr, wanted to hire Ludwig Mies van der Rohe to design the new building, but the two-man MOMA building committee—half of whose members were named Nelson Rockefeller—picked architects Philip Goodwin (himself a MOMA trustee) and Edward Durell Stone, who had worked his way back into Rockefeller graces since his dismissal on Christmas Eve in 1932.

When they got the commission, Goodwin and Stone didn't know whether "21" would yield to Nelson, so they designed the museum, Goodwin asserted, to be "equally adapted to face either a comparatively narrow street or an open plaza." But that's unconvincing: the visual evidence and simple logic indicate that the architects thought Nelson was going to get his way. The sleek facade of the most declaratively International Style building erected in prewar New York was clearly designed to be a glistening tableau at the head of Nelson's stately plaza. No architect, not even Ed Stone, wants to put an ambitious building in the middle of the block on a narrow street, where it can be viewed in its entirety only from the sides. Actually, Stone must have been conflicted in any case—while spending his days designing for Nelson, he was spending most of his nights getting plastered at the bar of "21."

The truncated version of Rockefeller Plaza was dedicated on April 1, 1937, coinciding with the opening of the Time & Life Building on the east side of its southern end. The 720-foot street may have been situated right in the heart of the heart of the world, but it led from nowhere to nowhere—the dreary brownstones at its southern end were well matched by an equally mundane vista at the northern end. At the dedication ceremony it's unlikely that Nelson dwelt on his plan's failure. (It was probably much tougher on Harrison, whose many drawings for the project included a version he sketched out in 1977, when he was past eighty.) To Nelson, failure was something you escaped by moving rapidly to the next task. Wrote Cary Reich, "Finally, in April 1937, Nelson made his conclusive bid for power."

He now had the full support of Thomas Debevoise, and the man he had to defeat had been grievously wounded, a victim of his own vanity. Todd said that he never wanted *The New Yorker* to publish a profile of him. He consistently maintained that the twenty-nine-year-old author of the piece, Geoffrey Hellman, was a friend of his daughter's but otherwise had no connection to him. "I did not want [the article] at all," he told Debevoise. Certainly that was the case once Hellman showed him a draft of the piece. It was, Todd said, "very bad. Not alone from my standpoint . . . but from the standpoint of Rockefeller Center, from [Junior's] standpoint, and from the standpoint of my relationship with him." He knew that even the appearance of self-promotion was enough to convict him.

But in the spring of 1936, when Todd agreed to cooperate with Hellman (it is unclear whether this was his decision alone or the result of a recommendation from T. J. Ross, a public relations man who had been Ivy Lee's partner), he had not been able to restrain himself. Under the guise of offering to verify the facts in the piece, he began an elaborate dance dedicated to his own glory. A memorandum of "miscellaneous notes" on the piece, while written in the third person, was unmistakably his. He boasted of his four houses and his "collection of early English and early American furniture that is pretty important." He said that his "work on the book 'Prince William's Parish and Plantations,' with its beautiful photographs and format is worthy of note." He extolled his business skills, bragged that his firm's payroll had been "running for years [at] about $1,000,000 a month," and took pains to add that "the family relations of Mr. Todd and his children have been just about ideal." And in case Hellman felt that he had addressed every aspect of his subject's personality, Todd enlightened him. "Mr. Todd's ideas on religion are worth exploring. If you think he knows nothing about music, try him."

It got worse. Just a few days later, Hellman received twelve more pages of corrections and comments from T. J. Ross, if not dictated by Todd then certainly ordered up by him. This time he assumed the role of editor: while Hellman's version of one event in Todd's life was "substantially correct," the memo suggested that it "should be omitted or told in a more dramatic manner, as it is not interesting." This was like a patient telling a surgeon where to cut. Motivated by his survival instinct, Todd also indicated that he "would like for the article to include a reference to the fact that his acquaintanceship has produced for him the greatest esteem for Mr. Rockefeller Jr." By the end of September he had actually taken a galley proof of Hellman's piece and rewritten it, top to bottom.

It was around this time that Nelson first learned of the piece. Had he been informed before, he claimed, he would have been able to block its publication, presumably by the application of a little flattery and a little pleading with *The New Yorker*'s editor, Harold Ross; just that summer Nelson had persuaded Vincent Astor, publisher of *Today*, to kill a piece about him. At this point, however, the Hellman article was an inevitability. Although he would spend much of his career writing about the rich and powerful, Hellman in this instance heeded Harold Ross's admonition "A journalist can have no friends." On October 31, the writer informed T. J. Ross that he had made "some modifications," but if anyone wanted "to see how the latest commas have been changed they had better get in touch with the New Yorker direct. To be frank," he continued, "if I had known how much badgering there was going to be about this piece I would never have agreed to show you the proofs in the first place. . . . I think in future I will confine my New Yorker profiles to parachute jumpers, artists, and other reliable people." Todd made a last stab at getting the piece killed, but Nelson did not support him. In fact, Nelson said he "more or less agreed with the sentiment expressed by Mr. Hellman in his letter."

As published—in two parts—Hellman's article, called "The Man Behind Prometheus," portrayed Todd as a brilliant, imaginative, competent, vain, and self-important man without whom the wonder of Rockefeller Center could not have been realized. In other words, it got him exactly right. But he was finished. Nelson had already begun to make provisions for a managerial succession, and had suggested to Debevoise that it might be wise to jettison both Todd and his son, yet keep Robertson and Joe Brown on board. Debevoise almost choked on the notion: if the two men were willing to stay, he wrote, "would that not be an act of disloyalty which would show that they are not the type of men whom Rockefeller Center would want as important associates?" Apparently not. While Todd was looking in another direction during the Hellman commotion, Robertson had become Nelson's co-conspirator: he suggested that Webster Todd be detached from Rockefeller Center and shunted into some sort of role representing the Rockefeller interests at RKO. This way, Robertson argued, the question of renewing the managers' contract would go more smoothly, as John R. would "not have his son's interests to consider."

The negotiations were arduous, occasionally contentious, and not irrevocably concluded until the spring of 1938, but they were conducted entirely by Nelson and landed at the spot he had long been aiming for. Effective April 30, 1938, John R. Todd and Webster Todd retired as managers; so did Joe Brown, who decided to continue in business with Web. (Doc Todd had retired the previous year.) Each was granted the equivalent of a year's pay. Three weeks later Nelson was elected president of Rockefeller Center, Incorporated, Hugh Robertson was appointed executive manager, and both Robertson and Wallace Harrison were elected to the RCI board.

John R. Todd's valedictory was brief. "My dear Mr. Rockefeller," began his letter to Junior. "Now that a new relationship has been established, may I say,—the task of making Rockefeller Center the full success we all want it to be is not yet completed. If and when I can help you may depend on my best effort. Sincerely yours, John R. Todd." That was it. Junior, traveling abroad, did not reply until a full month after his return. Then, just before sending Todd a letter of thanks that was both gracious and formal, he passed it by Debevoise for comment. Debevoise told Junior, "In spite of all Mr. Todd's omissions and commissions, his vanity and his love for publicity, I think he deserves what you say and I know it will please him immensely."

Undoubtedly. But John R. probably would have liked—and he definitely deserved—Francis Christy's notion even more. "There is no plaque in Rockefeller Center commemorating the part the managing agents played in producing this masterpiece," the lawyer wrote near the end of his life, "and no statue of John R. Todd. But there should be."

Dead End, the movie was called, and the title doubled as a description of a place and the condition of the lives lived there. This dead end sat at the edge of the East River, in the vicinity of 53rd or 54th Street, a slum as rotten as the old pilings just offshore that looked like the stubble on an old man's face. Humphrey Bogart, now a big-time mobster, comes home in a swagger of arrogance, tormenting his long-suffering mother (Marjorie Main, of course), thrilling the incipient thugs hoping to follow his path (Leo Gorcey and Huntz Hall before they became comic), and getting into a bad guy–good guy showdown with Joel McCrea. McCrea's character has the perfect career for a man meant to represent the high aspirations and low prospects of an ambitious and righteous young man in Depression-era New York: he's an unemployed architect.

The first thing you see in the movie is the RCA Building in the distance, looming over Manhattan like the Emerald City. Then the camera pans down to the near foreground, where the rest of the movie will reside: the squalor of the dead end neighborhood. Playwright Sidney Kingsley described the effect in his script for the original Broadway production on which the movie was based: "Up the street, blocking the view, is a Caterpillar steam shovel. Beyond it, way over to the west, are the skyscraping parallelepipeds of Radio City." The play and the subsequent movie, Kingsley wrote, were inspired by a quotation from Tom Paine: "The contrast of affluence and wretchedness is like dead and living bodies chained together."

This was New York in the latter half of the 1930s, when the living body of Rockefeller Center had affirmed its role as the dominant symbol of affluence,* in turn dominated by the family whose name it bore. "The great masters of economic destiny are up there," Le Corbusier wrote after visiting the fifty-sixth floor of the RCA Building in 1935, "like eagles in the silence of their eminences." The office that Junior, his two eldest sons, and fifty-three family employees first occupied in October of 1933 covered two-thirds of the floor's usable space. Visitors stepping off the elevator entered a room done up in red satin, green leather, and six coats of eggshell enamel, there to be greeted by Charles Garland, a receptionist/messenger who spent nearly four decades working for the family. Just before the office opened, *The New Yorker* informed its readers that due to the rotation of the Earth, "the building, rushing giddily to the eastward, has a higher velocity at its top than at the bottom." As a result, the magazine said, the occupants of Room 5600 would travel "more than a mile farther each day than the man in the street."

---

*The movies loved Rockefeller Center; every time Rosalind Russell played a business executive, she said, "the opening shot was always an air shot over New York. Then it would bleed into my suite of offices on the fortieth floor of Radio City." *The Man in the Gray Flannel Suit, The Solid-Gold Cadillac, Marjorie Morningstar, Sleepless in Seattle,* and numerous other films had scenes set in Rockefeller Center, every one of them thus signaling three key concepts to the audience: New York, success, and glamour. Producers of *The Naked City* and *The Hucksters* also wanted to shoot in the Center, but were turned down by management because the films "suggested an unpleasant association."

In the southwest corner of the floor, looking out over the low-rise buildings and the Hudson River in one direction and toward New York Bay and the Statue of Liberty in the other, Junior spun eastward while seated in the same room he had occupied at 26 Broadway. The heavy dark furniture, the antique fireplace with its hidden flue venting into the Manhattan sky, the sixteenth-century paneling on the walls had rematerialized intact, installed by the same decorator who had designed the room in its downtown incarnation.* A fifty-two-lamp annunciator enabled Junior to summon anyone from any fifty-sixth-floor office by flipping a switch. He addressed less urgent matters by inserting a note or a memo into the bank of pigeonholes arrayed nearby, one for each member of the office staff.

The family payroll extended far beyond the boundaries of the fifty-sixth floor. In May 1937 some 392 accountants, lawyers, real estate specialists, stenographers, golf instructors, chauffeurs, scullery maids, stablemen, security guards, housekeepers, and other functionaries attended to the needs of the four generations of Rockefellers. (By the time of Senior's death that same month at ninety-seven, the third generation had produced seven great-grandchildren for the ancient patriarch.) After World War II, the office staff alone expanded to such a degree that "Room 5600" included not just the entire fifty-sixth floor but the two floors immediately below it.

The staff of Room 5600 concerned itself with matters ranging from the august affairs of business, social policy, and philanthropy to such clerical effluvia as, say, maintaining records pertaining to the family's gun permits (Junior, John, Nelson, Laurance, and Winthrop all owned pistols; John, in 1941, said he wanted "a quick-draw holster" for his). Robert Gumbel, a small, thin man in starched collar and wire-rimmed glasses who would work for the family for nearly sixty years, was Junior's executive assistant and also chief petty officer in charge of the entire operation. From his windowless office he supervised the clerical staff, monitored Junior's in-box, and deflected pestiferous favor-, job-, or money-seekers with a ritualized courtesy. Even the most arrant beggars were rejected with a signed reply; a Mme. Maud de Wagstaffe, who first wrote Junior with her ideas for Radio City Music Hall in 1933, and who asked for a job as a typist in 1943, was still getting polite answers in Laurance's behalf in 1961. Gumbel saw to 5600's material needs as well. More than a dozen years after the office

---

*The designer wanted $4,500 to execute the transplantation, but Junior asked Robert Gumbel to instruct him that "[if] you find the work has actually cost you less and you can bill it for say $3500 or $4000 and make a reasonable profit, you will do so."

opened, realizing that it would be nice to be able to store milk for coffee, he told a co-worker, "The chances are we could get a refrigerator from one of the houses and bring it around here."

Nelson's office was opposite Junior's on the northwest side of the building. His view took in the Hudson up beyond the Rockefeller-preserved Palisades, all of Central Park, and the northern half of Manhattan. His instinct for control was never dormant. "He will get up from a conference table to adjust a picture that is a quarter inch awry on the wall of his office—or, for that matter, in any office he happens to be in," wrote one journalist. Not quite ready to declare aesthetic independence in a business setting, like his father he decorated in antiques, but favored the flowing lines of Chippendale and other eighteenth-century styles over the lugubrious Jacobean to which Junior was partial.

The world Nelson surveyed from this aerie was filled with opportunities that extended far beyond his command of a real estate operation. He took over as president of the Museum of Modern Art in 1939, and brought a Roosevelt adviser named Anna Rosenberg onto his staff to help him find his way in the political world. With David Sarnoff he recruited a new head of production for RKO Pictures. He joined the board of a Jersey Company subsidiary that controlled most of the oil fields of Venezuela, studied Spanish, and forthwith developed an interest in Latin America characterized, wrote Cary Reich, by "an ardor startling even to those who were well accustomed to his enthusiasms." He made few distinctions among his professional interests, or between his professional interests and his family interests, seeming to see all Rockefellerdom as a continuous landscape, the people employed within it or connected to it available to be called upon as needed. He was that way his entire life: at twenty-four he had no problem asking the president of NBC to send someone over to 10 West 54th Street to fix his mother's "radio set"; at fifty-nine, he dispatched the director of stage operations at the Music Hall to Pocantico, to set up the lighting and decorations for his wife's birthday party.

Nelson's wider engagements made Hugh Robertson's role as "executive manager" that much more important. It could also be said that Robertson's matchless competence made those wider engagements possible. Operating out of the Rockefeller Center, Incorporated, offices in the Associated Press Building, serving as chief of staff to a distracted head of state, Robertson directed a huge organization that was now humming along with maximum efficiency. The renting department no longer needed its a-deal-at-any-price policy. Digging for the Sixth Avenue subway had begun in 1936, and now

Charles Heydt, who had taken responsibility for lobbying the city government to speed the new line into existence, could report that the hateful el was at last coming down; its dismantling began in December of 1938, and five months later the Music Hall's fabulous marquee could finally be seen from across Sixth Avenue.

Close ties with Fiorello La Guardia's City Hall had been cemented so thoroughly that when the youngest of the Rockefeller brothers, David, completed work for his Ph.D. at the University of Chicago, he joined the mayor's staff (and, according to journalists Peter Collier and David Horowitz, developed the habit of answering the phone, "City Hall, Rockefeller speaking!"). Warm relations between the Rockefellers and their fellow Republican had not been easily established. In 1932, Thomas Debevoise had chased away La Guardia backers who had come to Junior for campaign funds because of "La Guardia's attitude . . . in regard to Rockefeller assessments." Once in office the new mayor came close to appointing a tax commissioner whose candidacy for the job terrified Charles Heydt. Pleading to lawyer Raymond Fosdick, Heydt said, "You know the animus which he has for my principal. Is there nothing to be done to prevent this calamity?"

There was. Heydt and Fosdick weren't the only men interested in blocking the appointment of William H. Allen; few in the real estate community liked Allen, a good-government reformer who was both well intentioned and highly outspoken. Consequently, Allen had to launch his attacks on Junior from outside city government. He used cannons. Allen called Junior the city's "Chief Tax Dolee," and noted how the assessments for the Center's Fifth Avenue lots had *decreased* after the land was developed. An Allen computation indicated that ridiculously low assessments enabled Junior to escape something between one and two million dollars a year in tax obligations. The land the Music Hall stood upon, he pointed out, was assessed at a lower rate than the land beneath a theater in Jamaica, Queens. In an oral history he prepared in 1950, a still apoplectic Allen explained how this had all happened: "Go to almost any group or person in this town," he told his interviewer. "A reference to Rockefeller tax favors will bring this: 'Maybe, but look at that skating rink, look at the tallest Christmas tree, look at the tulips!'"

The political sophistication of Junior's associates didn't hurt, either. They worked the Democratic side of the street as well as the Republican. Political fixer Lester Abberley, whose association with Robertson went back to the early days of Todd, Robertson & Todd, would represent Rockefeller Center in venues as varied as the Manhattan borough president's office and the U.S. Capitol for half his sixty-year legal career. Abberley had direct ties to John F. Curry, the Tammany Hall boss, and persuaded him to engineer the deal that had New York City concede its rights to the concourse, the truck ramp, the bonded warehouse, and everything else that passed beneath the city-owned streets, all in exchange for less than $10,000 a year. Peter Grimm of William A. White & Sons received a $7,500 bonus for helping win reduced assessments in the years the Democrats controlled City Hall, and on at least one occasion represented Rockefeller Center in Washington once he had returned to private life after two useful years in Franklin Roosevelt's Treasury Department.

No one, least of all Hugh Robertson, underestimated the value of all this political influence. An entry in the draft minutes for one executive committee meeting said that the Center's tax assessment had come in at 79 percent of costs instead of "the customary 90%." The committee therefore decided, on Robertson's recommendation, to accept the assessment "without protest." It also decided to omit the entry and its revealing numbers from the official minutes.

Over time the political influence that accumulated in Room 5600 and across the street in Robertson's office was like energy stored in a powerful battery, ready to be tapped as needed. In 1935 a used-jewelry dealer named Isidore Mitchell rented some space in the RKO Building and immediately tried to assign his lease to the "Rockefeller Purchasing Corporation," a company he had just created. When the legal department blocked the assignment, noting that Mitchell had no claim on the use of the name, the jeweler went to court and announced his intention to appoint Dan Rockefeller, a Rochester short-order cook, an officer of the firm. Francis Christy directed the court response but also drafted a legislative act that Abberley forwarded to Charles Poletti, counselor to Governor Herbert Lehman and chairman of the New York State constitutional convention. Christy's proposed law was an addition to the penal code making it a crime to use a name "with intent to deceive or mislead the public." It was Christy's belief, said Abberley, that "a provision in the penal law would make a person think twice before doing what our friend Mitchell and others have done."

It's no surprise that the bill was enacted by the legislature and signed into law by Governor Lehman; it was certainly reasonable public policy, even if levying a criminal penalty for unfair competition was a little unusual. But Christy's next legislative triumph was an eyebrow raiser. In 1938, Rockefeller Center managed to bring about a change in Section 161 of the New York State Labor Law. The newly amended law provided that all theater employees were entitled to one day off each week—except employees who worked in a theater that produced stage presentations in combination with motion pictures. Christy's amendment, which crept into the Labor Law under dark of night, wasn't called the Radio City Music Hall Indentured Servitude Act, but it may as well have been. The performers in the Music Hall, years away from winning union representation, were working under conditions that tended to mitigate the romance of a life in the arts. Said one member of the ballet corps about their four-a-days on that enormous stage, "I did piqué turns from 50th Street to 51st Street, then relevés and arabesques from 51st back to 50th, then it ended with God knows how many fouettés, four times a day, seven days a week"—a schedule officially sanctioned by the legislature of New York State.

Unions may have been slow in coming to the stage of the Music Hall, but they were a fact of life in virtually every other aspect of Rockefeller Center, from the construction crews to the elevator men to the waiters in the Rainbow Room. In reality, they were more than a fact of life: these working people were, to some degree, the lineal descendants of the men, women, and children who had died at Ludlow in 1914. That horrible event not only reoriented the direction of Junior's life but his self-definition as well: John D. Rockefeller Jr., friend of the workingman.

Relatively speaking, he was. Junior devised an approach to labor issues that could be summarized in one of his favorite homilies: "Neither scorn nor fear the common man." This formulation conveyed his wish to treat working people as equals yet implicitly acknowledged that "the common man" was, to one of Junior's wealth and background, a breed apart. He once said of some new social acquaintances, "They have very little money but are delightful." The "but" on which the sentence balanced indicated how thoroughly his wealth had isolated him.

As Hugh Robertson was about to assume responsibility for the operations of Rockefeller Center, Junior sent him a letter that could have been an excerpt from a speech: "I believe that employers and employees are partners, not enemies. That their interests are essentially common interests, not antagonistic. That the highest well-being of both can best be obtained by cooperation, not by warfare." It sounded good, and he no doubt meant it (even though it did not extend to the staff at Pocantico, whose unionization he adamantly resisted on the grounds that the 3,300-acre estate was not a commercial venture). In practice Junior's recognition of the interests of workers was something like his feelings about serving alcohol in the Rainbow Room. He knew it was right, but he really had little idea how it was done.

The Rockefeller mythmaking machine stressed that Junior believed in unions, and official histories (not to mention other works that rely too much on official histories) note that Rockefeller Center never lost a day to a strike. In fact an elevator operators' strike in 1932 delayed the start of the British Empire Building, a sheet-metal workers' strike a few months after that came close to shutting down a great deal of construction activity, and in 1938 electrical workers walked out and threw up a picket line that was honored by other unions. The union that won Junior's approval was the Independent Association of Rockefeller Center Employees, a teddy bear of a company union unconnected to the larger labor movement. If a pro-union (as opposed to pro-worker) feeling was meant to emanate from Room 5600, it never reached John Roy, the former English teacher who ran the Rainbow Room and the Observation Roof. Roy consulted with the notorious P. L. Bergoff, "King of the Strikebreakers," and thoughtfully forwarded a report on Bergoff's services to N. A. Kenworthy, who ran all on-site operations for Todd & Brown. A couple of months later Kenworthy could have gotten a full description of Bergoff's operation in the pages of *Fortune,* where it was called "the oldest, toughest, hard-boiledest practitioner in the field of professional strikebreaking," especially adept at recruiting platoons of goons, thugs, armed guards, and replacement workers.

It would be unfair to tar Junior with a direct connection to the unsavory Bergoff. But his benign paternalism toward the labor force, along with John Roy's and Joe Brown's open antagonism, was discarded as ineffectual and wrongheaded just weeks after Nelson and Robertson took control of Rockefeller Center. The change in labor policy was a perfect illustration of the practicality that motivated them and the symbiosis that would enable them to work together so effectively. After consulting with the "tough as a teamster" Anna Rosenberg, Nelson determined that labor peace could be secured by working directly with the New York Building and Construction Trades Council of the American Federation of Labor. This would entail recognizing its component unions; ceding the council authority to handle all intra-union jurisdictional disputes; and paying the workers slightly more than their counterparts received from other employers. The unions agreed to a no-strike clause, Robertson to a no-lockout clause, and both sides to

compulsory arbitration of disputes. Robertson also soon fired his labor relations chief, the anti-union C. A. Hodgins, and replaced him with Nelson's
old Dartmouth buddy Victor Borella, an orphaned scholarship boy whose
working-class background enabled him to speak both Introductory Blue-
Collar and Advanced Nelson. He was fluent in Junior, too: by late 1939,
Borella and Robertson had persuaded Junior to allow Rockefeller Center to
become a closed shop—if you wanted to work there, you had to join the
union.

The AFL contract was a stunning achievement. As a model for other labor disputes, said the *Detroit News,* the Rockefeller Center solution might
bring peace to American industry's "long and bitter civil war." After the
contract had been in place for two years (and already extended for an additional four), the *Journal-American* commemorated it with the headline
"LABOR UTOPIA IN RADIO CITY." AFL leaders announced their desire to
replicate the Rockefeller Center contract elsewhere.

So different from anything Junior would have promoted, the labor contract made it clear that Nelson's authority at Rockefeller Center was as firm
as the limestone of which it was built. He may have been arrogant, ruthless,
occasionally cowardly, but Nelson's greatest single gift was the propulsive
self-confidence that enabled him to forget about conventional processes or
precedental niceties and simply get things *done.* More than thirty years
later, George Meany, the heavily barnacled president of the AFL-CIO, explained this self-confidence in economic terms. Meany had been president
of the New York State AFL back when Nelson was running Rockefeller
Center, so had formed his opinion about him over the negotiating table.
Said Meany, "Nelson is satisfied with his own share, and he don't try to keep
the other feller from getting his."

CHAPTER 22

The driving of the last rivet into the steelwork of the U.S. Rubber Building didn't complete Rockefeller Center. It didn't even complete the U.S. Rubber Building, which would not be ready for occupancy for another five months.

*Looking out my window, I knew that I had been brought to the top of the mountain and shown **the kingdom of the world.***

—ALFRED KAZIN

But there was sufficient symbolism in the rivet driving to justify the ceremony held in the building's unfinished lobby on November 1, 1939. There was also an abundance of promotional benefit to be had: with Junior himself wielding the forty-pound rivet gun, it was a page one feature across the country. Editorialists added triumphant harmonies to the news stories: "In all the building history of the world . . . ," intoned the *Washington Star,* "it is probable that nothing has been so daring and dashing and so meaningful in its conception as Rockefeller Center." NBC broadcast the entire event nationwide.

Although the publicity may have focused on Junior, it was really Nelson's day. Not only was this, the Center's twelfth building, the first one planned, designed, and erected entirely under his leadership, but as he had told his father the previous February, when construction was about to begin, the Rubber Building promised "a maximum of return at a minimum of investment." For its coming-out party Nelson had chosen the speakers, approved the order of business, and now presided as master of ceremonies. In the Rubber Building's drafty lobby, its unfinished concrete walls brightened with an array of patriotic bunting, guests guided to their seats by a battalion of Music Hall ushers kept on their coats and hats. With the sole exception of Nelson, who was his own source of heat, so did the other speakers lined up with him on the platform: David Sarnoff, Nicholas Murray Butler,

Fiorello H. La Guardia, Thomas Murray of the AFL, and Junior. The other man on the dais, silent through the proceedings but hailed by Nelson near the conclusion for his "imagination and brilliant leadership," was Hugh Robertson. John R. Todd was present, seated next to John D. 3rd. Neither was on the platform or mentioned in any of the speeches.

The guests had filed in to the strains, for some reason, of "Auld Lang Syne," played by the Seventh Regiment Marching Band. The invitation list included the Center's architects, engineers, and department heads, many of the artists who had created its murals and sculptures, and nearly all the major tenants. It also glittered with names that defined the boundaries of New York's public life: Vincent Astor; August Belmont; the old governor, Al Smith; the new Cardinal, Francis Spellman; Adam Gimbel of Saks Fifth Avenue; Walter Hoving of Tiffany; the presidents of the University, Metropolitan, Yale, and various other clubs. Understandably, if not eagerly, someone had put William Nelson Cromwell on the guest list. Surprisingly—this was probably Junior's doing, as no one else would have had the nerve—Ida Tarbell, the muckraker who had been the family's most prominent scourge more than three decades before, was present as well.

Let them all sit for a while; look, for a moment, at what they had come to celebrate.

Rockefeller Center, an autumn weekday, 1939:

In his office in the International Building, Jock Whitney sits at the desk that had belonged to his grandfather John Hay, Theodore Roosevelt's secretary of state. The painting on the wall behind him had been Whitney's own acquisition: Georges Seurat's *L'île de la Grande Jatte*. Whitney's primary concern at the moment is the film that he and David Selznick, his best friend and business partner, are about to release. Both men need to "go to work on the struggle on 'Frankly, my dear, I don't give a damn'"—in other words, to persuade the Hays office to allow Clark Gable to utter that final, frightening word at the climax of *Gone with the Wind*.

Across the way in the Time & Life Building, *Time* senior editor Whittaker Chambers can see the skating rink from his twenty-ninth-floor window, just down the hall from his colleague John Hersey, just upstairs from James Agee. To the very young Alfred Kazin, who had made the voyage from an immigrant household in Brooklyn to this auspicious spot, the view from the *Time* office has a quality that goes beyond the merely visual:

"Looking out my window," Kazin wrote years later, "I knew that I had been brought to the top of the mountain and shown the kingdom of the world."

On three loftlike floors in its own building on the other side of the skating rink, the Associated Press sends its daily fare of one million words zipping around the globe; its subtenants—a range of foreign news providers including Reuters and the Soviet agency Tass—hitchhike on the four million feet of wire the AP has embedded in conduits on the fourth floor, connecting to all five of New York City's main power lines. Upstairs on the eighth floor, Norman Bel Geddes applies his imagination, his nerve, and his growing staff—his firm will soon occupy twenty-two rooms in the AP Building—to the design of locomotive engines, office furniture, seltzer bottles, airplane interiors, the Ringling Bros. circus, and the Hydrox Cookies box. Eleven miles to the east, almost 30,000 people are standing in line to see Geddes's most recent triumph, the "Futurama" exhibit he created for the 1939 world's fair. This painstakingly detailed (500,000 model buildings, 50,000 tiny cars) and frightfully expensive ($7 million) representation of the world of tomorrow looks remarkably like the suburbs of a large American city circa 1975. The space it occupies, twice as large as Radio City Music Hall, is enclosed by the globelike Perisphere poised next to the conical Trylon—the fair's indelible symbols, designed by Wally Harrison in his Rockefeller Center office.

On the thirtieth floor of the International Building, producer-director George Abbott picks his way around the huge piles of scripts that pour in for his consideration. Plays on war and fascism, he had told an interviewer, "come in at a rate of a gross a month," but he was still seeing plenty of that staple, the Noël Coward–type play "in which everyone is very tan, very amorous, and lives on the Riviera." Ten floors below, Gloria Swanson, long retired from the movies (and long disentangled from Joe Kennedy, who keeps a New York office on the forty-sixth floor of the RCA Building), presides over Multiprises, Incorporated, a firm she created to underwrite the efforts of some refugee European scientists to develop, among other things, luminescent paint. "I could sell carloads of it in Los Angeles alone," Swanson said. When she lived there, she recalled, "Hollywood dinner invitations routinely included road maps, but still guests often ended up sitting in a car on a dark street while the chauffeur ran up and down with a flashlight looking for a number on a mailbox or a curbstone."

In their twenty-ninth-floor boardroom in the RCA Building, the five members of the executive committee of Standard Oil of New Jersey arrive for their daily 11:00 A.M. meeting. Along one wall stand a piece of teak railing and the ship's bell from the SS *Mauretania;* on the sturdy oval table in the center of the room, a clipboard, a notepad, and a brass ashtray sit at each man's place. For two hours the committee members will discuss the affairs of some of the 240 subsidiaries that comprise the Jersey Company before adjourning to a shared lunch among the potted palms of their private dining room on the sixty-fourth floor. When that opened back in 1934, Junior wrote his father to let him know that the company's executives were "delighted with the lunchroom and the lunch, which was served to them at a dollar a plate."

On the northwest corner of the RCA Building's fifty-third floor, fluted Corinthian columns carved from limed oak anchor the corners of David Sarnoff's office, where he rules the vast company whose commitment to Junior, made nearly ten years before, had launched Rockefeller Center. Next to one of those columns, a secret panel opens onto a white-tiled room furnished with a wardrobe, a shower, a toilet, and a telephone-equipped barber chair. In the afternoon Sarnoff luxuriates in a shave administered by Charles DeZemler himself, taking daily leave of his domain in the concourse.

The grandeur of Sarnoff's suite is the apotheosis of the imperial style affected by the moguls of the day, and nothing mars its calculated air of ordered perfection. Even his desk is immaculate, as nothing more than a single sheet of paper is ever allowed to occupy its polished leather surface. Memoranda that make it that far do not get the chance to linger; each one is immediately labeled with one of Sarnoff's all-purpose responses, "Yes," "No," or "PSM" ("Please see me"), then expressed back to its writer. When he's alone Sarnoff presses a button that reveals an amenity less prepossessing than his private spa but just as essential to his self-image. A panel slides open and out rolls a small shelf bearing a two-dollar telegraph key. When he isn't running the Radio Corporation of America, the former telegraph operator likes to tap out messages to his old friend George Winterbottom in the RCA Communications office downtown on Broad Street.

This was also Rockefeller Center, autumn 1939:

Begin on the east, with the trees. "Trees should have no place on Fifth Avenue," the president of Best and Company had once said, and until late 1938 there wasn't a twig on the avenue from Madison Square all the way up to Central Park. The Fifth Avenue Association had been especially antiarboreous, determined to make sure that no foliage would block the view of shop windows from passing buses. But Nelson encouraged the tree-planting efforts, ignoring the opposition of some FAA members who had not yet reconciled themselves to the giant in their midst.* Now even the double-decker buses traveling up and down Fifth afford unimpeded views—the eight mighty elms imported from Westchester County tower forty feet above the pavement, not a hedge but a canopy.

If you get off one of those buses midway between 49th and 50th Streets, the Channel Gardens draw you westward. The Channel's downward slope supplies gravitational pull, the retail shops along its sides contribute contextual interest, and gilded Prometheus lolling at the base of the RCA Building's dramatic upthrust forms a visual goal. You can buy a cigar at the Dunhill shop in the British Empire Building (if you are a particularly fortunate Dunhill customer, you can dip into your private stash in your own wooden humidor), or pick up the latest Colette across the way at the Librairie de France. The Channel would be a nice place to enjoy your cigar or your book on your lunch hour, if only you were allowed to sit down. By design there are no benches, and when salesgirls from across the street at Saks Fifth Avenue began to perch on the granite coping around the Channel's six pools "for a smoke and a box lunch," ivy plantings were put in place to discourage them. The sitters, one of his associates told Nelson, were "interfering with business." In the Channel, the idea is to pull people past (and, it is hoped, into) the stores, then down to the sunken plaza.

The plaza is a fine place for lunch, in the café that now occupies this once barren expanse. Frederick Lewis Allen's description of the plaza on a sunny day is irresistible: "Looking out on the people strolling by," Allen wrote, "the bright yellow-green and blue-green umbrellas, the silver water coming down over the fountain steps below Prometheus, and beyond, the shadowed rear wall of the Time and Life Building[,] I tried to think what the scene reminded me of, and realized that it was a shipboard scene, full of animation and sunlight and the sense of holiday." Clement evenings find the plaza filled with diners, dancers, and live music. Soft and stately waltzes once bubbled forth from a string orchestra, until Nelson ordered up a swing band. Now, said the *World-Telegram,* a passerby can hear "the lively sounds of a hot trumpet or restless clarinet waft from below."

In the winter ninety-nine cents gets you onto the rink; if you want the

---

*The irritating Captain Pedrick had grown much more accommodating of Rockefeller Center after moving his office into the International Building.

whole place for an evening party, it's yours for fifty dollars an hour. Day or night you can stumble on your skates to the bar in the adjacent English Grill and enjoy a drink while surrounded by murals rather less portentous than those in the RCA lobby: cartoonist William Steig had been commissioned to paint several dozen of his "Small Fry" in skating poses on three of the grill's walls. Through the floor-to-ceiling window you can watch other skaters, and beyond them, on the opposite side of the rink, you just might be able to make out the James Thurber chalk drawings that adorn the rear wall of the Café Francais. It took Thurber two hours to complete the entire ninety-foot composition, a characteristic menagerie of Thurber women barking at Thurber men—except everyone is on skates, skis, or sleds. The Steig and Thurber murals suggest that the Union News Company, which operates both restaurants, isn't entirely philistine. But neither is the company sentimental: a few years later both murals will be painted over, disappearing forever.

Since July of 1939, the tenant who arrives at work by car no longer has to pay fifty cents for a space in the large midblock lot between 48th and 49th Streets. William Nelson Cromwell's town house still huddles against the eastern side of the thirty-four-story Time & Life Building, but to the west, on the site of the old parking lot, stands what is known for now as Holland House, but will soon be named the Eastern Airlines Building. Wallace Harrison designed a twelve-story tower to rest atop a large, four-story base; at sixteen stories in all, the building required only one elevator bank, which enabled him to configure the tower portion as a pure slab and still position every inch of office space within the optimum twenty-seven feet of a window.* Excess interior space embedded deep within the lower floors has been put to profitable and convenient use: the core of the first three floors, plus another three floors below street level, are a parking garage.

It is the first garage ever contained within the walls of a New York City office building, and as such has nearly become a tourist attraction itself. To the tenants who use it, the garage is a daily luxury. Attendants in quasimilitary uniforms slide down brass firemen's poles to return to the lobby from the floors above, or to retrieve cars from the floors below. Bright red interior pillars give the place an air of unexpected gaiety, and their coloring

---

*The building's access to sunlight was enhanced by a clause in Time Inc.'s lease for its own building just across Rockefeller Plaza—nothing could be built within two hundred feet of the upper floors of the Time & Life Building.

has a practical purpose—a patron complaining of a scraped fender can prove his case by the presence of telltale red on the bruised vehicle. The handsome furnishings of the ladies' lounge—sofas, upholstered chairs, makeup tables and mirrors—make the room seem as if it belongs in the Music Hall or the Center Theater, and make the lounging ladies just as comfortable.

In unpleasant weather the walk from the garage to one's office in any of the Center's buildings through the underground concourse is dry, warm, and convenient. On fair days, though, to walk across the side streets or around the plaza is to experience what Frederick Lewis Allen identified as "the tingle of metropolitan success," even if the reasons for this impression are not fully comprehended. Yes, there are the lovely gardens, the handsome buildings, the artful way those buildings are arranged so that sunlight is abundant. But subtler things distinguish this piece of ground from any other in midtown Manhattan. Because of the underground trucking ramp, 49th and 50th Streets are generally free of the traffic that clots every other crosstown block in midtown. Because of the ministrations of the Center's maintenance staff, the streets are bare of litter and the sidewalks have their own coloration: flattened and blackened blobs of discarded chewing gum are regularly steamed into oblivion, so that the Rockefeller Center pavement is free of the acne that scars the rest of the city's sidewalks.

At all the larger buildings "Special Officer Doormen" in brown uniforms greet visitors and tenants with the mandated touch of the cap. Never, though, do they greet "important people" by their names or reveal to others "the name of anyone going in or going out of the building, or whether or not any particular person is in the building or in his office"; violation of either rule is cause for immediate dismissal. The opening of the garage has cleared the private street between the plaza and the RCA Building of the chauffeured cars that, to Junior's dismay, had previously "interfere[d] with the general vista and architectural effect." It has also cleared the lobby of the crowd of chauffeurs who used to loiter on cold days just inside the doors: the chauffeurs' room in the garage is warm, dry, and equipped with Ping-Pong tables.

A common expression held that you could do anything you wanted in Rockefeller Center except sleep (no hotels), pray (no churches), or not pay rent to Junior. Some people incorporated the place so deeply into their lives it became a virtual fetish. Mrs. Equinn W. Munnell of 1 Lexington Avenue first skated on the Rockefeller Center ice the day the rink opened in 1936, then came back twice a week, every winter week, for the next three decades. Henry W. Clark, who worked for the Union Pacific Railroad at 120 Broadway, was so conscientious in his attendance at Radio City Music Hall that he made a point of reporting complete details of his annual patronage to the Hall's box office treasurer, Arthur Clary, "showing also the comparison with the two preceding years." But no one displayed his loyalty to Rockefeller Center as avidly as George Street, manager of the RCA Communications office in the concourse. Street proudly ate his meals at the Gateway Restaurant, got his daily shave at DeZemler's barber shop, and bought his clothing from two Center haberdashers, Berry-Ryder and Doyle and Black's. He parked in the Rockefeller Center Garage, saw every movie that played the Music Hall, and entertained visitors in the cocktail lounge adjacent to the Rainbow Room. He bought his flowers from J. Trepel's and his toothpaste from the Kaufman-Bedrick pharmacy, both in the RCA lobby. If he needed a new hat, Street said, he'd get it from Chapeaux Tardy, in the Maison Française—"but he says there's no use him getting a hat," the *Rockefeller Center Weekly* reported, for "he doesn't leave Rockefeller Center long enough to need a new one."

The *Weekly*'s effort to make Street a poster boy for the wonders of the Center didn't even hint at how much of one's life could be lived within these three blocks. If Street had concerns about his health, he could entrust his welfare to one of the doctors ensconced on the twenty-second floor of the Time & Life Building, one of the thirty dentists on the eighteenth floor of the International Building (which had been piped for gas, compressed air, and other dental necessities), or to the comforts of a "scientific massage" and other therapeutic services offered by Harold Reilly's Health Service on the eighth floor of the RCA Building ("as new as Rockefeller Center," Reilly boasted in his ads, "is our method of generating indoor sunshine in both the Gymnasium and the Hand Ball Court"). He could conduct his banking at any of three Chase branches in the Center, and if his account was healthy, he might even fantasize about buying one of the gems that had been cut from the fabulous 726-carat Jonker diamond in jeweler Harry Winston's well-guarded suite in the British Empire Building. If Street didn't keep up on the news of the world by reading any of the fifty-nine magazines published in Rockefeller Center, he could find both information (an hour of filmed news every hour on the hour) and comfort ("seats so capacious that the fat man [would] not run over the edges") at the Newsreel Theatre, tucked into the curve of the trucking ramp beneath the Associated Press Building. If he needed a reliable interpretation of a federal regulation pertaining to his business, he could turn to the U.S. Government Information Service in the concourse, where Edythe Roberts and four associates stood ready to answer questions ranging from "Can I import a penguin?" to "Is there a bounty on twins?"

For distraction, Street could have turned to the Leisure League of America on the twelfth floor of the RCA Building, where a gas station operator named James S. Stanley had opened "a national clearing house for leisure ideas" dedicated to "helping thousands of Americans to develop new hobbies and to get greater satisfaction out of the ones they already have." Or he might have tried writing a sonnet or two and submitting them to the National Poetry Center on the forty-fourth floor; if director Anita Browne found them worthy, said *The New Yorker,* they could be "mounted tenderly on colored cardboard and hung along the walls of the room, where editors can come and look at them." And if he just longed for a night on the town, he could patronize Frank C. Kay's valet service on the ground floor of the RCA Building. Kay offered tenants dressing booths, plus storage space for "formal or evening clothes" and "competent valets" to care for them.

The emphasis on service extended to a trio of beverage purveyors based in the concourse. If a tenant was thirsty, the Coca-Cola "refreshment headquarters" could instantly dispatch "one of our uniformed attendants" to deliver a cold Coke to any office in the Center. Borden's "corps of trained men" working out of "special storage facilities right here in Rockefeller Center" fought over the straight-to-your-desk milk delivery market with the men from the Dairylea Office Service—Borden offering all milk products, Dairylea specializing in chilled half-pint bottles.

Food was a bit of a problem. Not that there wasn't enough of it; the Center's restaurants, all except the Rainbow Room run by the Union News Company, served meals by the trainload.* But Union News was not exactly a culinary pacesetter. Its high-end Restaurant Mayan in the International Building, wrote Justin Kaplan, was physically an evocation of "Chichen Itza minus human sacrifice," but it offered a menu about as Mayan as macaroni, with far greater pretensions: escargots Bourguignonne, curried chicken à

---

*After World War II, when Union News's exclusivity expired, Schrafft's opened a restaurant that unashamedly declared itself the world's largest, capable of seating 1,283 people and serving 7,500 meals a day.

l'Indian, veal Viennoise, and that exotic import from the east, chow mein. Most of the other restaurants were no more imaginative than dry toast— they existed to feed the daily crowds. This was all a far cry from Henri Charpentier and the glories of his doomed restaurant in the Maison Française. Lunchtime dining for tenants unaccustomed to the press of the common crowds was a largely private affair conducted in the corporate dining rooms on the sixty-fourth floor of the RCA Building and in the Rockefeller Center Luncheon Club on the sixty-fifth. Junior had a permanent reservation in the Rockefeller Foundation lounge on the sixty-fourth floor but rarely took advantage of it (nor did he much use the foundation's Ping-Pong table). According to Edwin Cox's syndicated newspaper feature, "Private Lives," Junior always dined alone, in the Rainbow Room, reading the newspaper and cooling himself with a small ivory fan. When his friend James Farley, the U.S. postmaster general, forwarded him a copy of Cox's item, Junior was quick with a reply: "Aside from the fact that I never read the newspaper at lunch, never lunch alone in the Rainbow Room and never use a little ivory fan," he told Farley, "the statements are accurate."

As surprising as was this playful irony from this most unironic of men, Junior's comment was nonetheless characteristically literal. No, he didn't eat in the Rainbow Room, but only by inches. His favored midday dining venue was the extensive complex of suites and salons adjacent to it. As the sun rose each weekday, the sixty-fifth floor shed its white tie and tails and reached for a J. Press suit. Head chef Bernard Richter turned his staff's attention away from last night's "roasted English pheasant mounted with its natural feathers prepared on a silver spike" to today's club sandwich, fruit Jell-O, and other staples on the menu of the Luncheon Club (not "Lunch Club," the board determined, having "ascertained that . . . 'lunch' is a verb"). At midday the sixty-fifth floor became the mess hall for Junior, his sons, several key associates, and roughly six hundred of the Center's most distinguished tenants. Women were barred from membership because, as Thomas Debevoise told Nelson, "men do not like to have their women friends around during business hours." A quota capped Jewish membership at 3½ percent—a reasonable number, felt the club's president, General James C. Harbord, because it was exactly the proportion of Jews in the American population. Harbord seemed not to recognize that this was New York, where some 30 percent of the population was Jewish, or that Rockefeller Center had already become the cynosure of the entertainment industry, which was so heavily Jewish. This was especially odd considering that Harbord was chairman of the board of RCA and David Sarnoff's boss.*

Some statistics, courtesy of Merle Crowell and his loyal chorus of publicists, journalists, and numerologists: in the fall of 1939 more than 26,000 tenants occupied Rockefeller Center's 5,107,910 square feet of office space. Another 125,000 people visited each day, a number equivalent to the population of America's fifty-first largest city. Together, visitors and tenants consumed 117,000 kilowatt hours of electricity daily, enough to "light and give service to every home in Omaha." The Post Office each day dedicated thirty-two mailmen to the task of delivering a hundred thousand letters and twelve thousand packages to the sixteen hundred tenant firms. Over the course of the year seven million people attended performances at the Center's theaters; six million passed through the doors of its two hundred shops and service establishments; more than 1.3 million took the guided tour or visited the Observation Roof.

Few cleaned up after themselves. That fell to a maintenance staff that was by far the largest component of the Rockefeller Center workforce and arguably its most important one. John R. Todd said it was their job to "bring the operation as near perfection as possible, because that gives the buildings their atmosphere." Nelson handed out certificates, ribbons, and trophies to outstanding maintenance workers as if he were the swimming coach at a children's day camp. A sure winner for the picture newspapers was a photo of the cleaning staff lined up like the Marine Band in full parade dress; for cityside columnists, an interview with a charwoman who recovered a lost diamond earring from the nightly trash couldn't miss.

The antique desk, the Seurat on the wall behind it, the Dufys and Ma-

---

*Odder still, at least from the perspective of the first decade of the twenty-first century, was the way the Rockefellers, especially Nelson, accepted the quota. "As you probably know," Nelson wrote to the board of governors in 1935, "Mr. Ellinger"—the father of one of Nelson's friends— "is Jewish. However, he is of very high type and has none of the characteristics which are so often associated with his race." The statement is shocking for two reasons: first, because in Nelson's social world, his cultural world, and his incipient political world (Anna Rosenberg had become his closest adviser), he showed not the slightest prejudice; but more so, perhaps, because Nelson undoubtedly could have broken the quota by fiat. The club's independence was a sham: the dues it collected from members were handed directly to Rockefeller Center, Incorporated. It took Nelson three years to get Edgar Ellinger into the club, a slot opening up only when an increasing overall membership, Nelson was informed, made "room for a few more" Jews.

tisses and Braques hanging here and there—one might imagine that the *Rockefeller Center Weekly* had Jock Whitney's office in mind when the magazine apotheosized the typical Rockefeller Center charwoman. She "intimately lives and has her being among the luxurious objects which daily surround the potentate she has never seen," wrote Mary E. Learned. "The shining desk is as familiar to her as it is to him. Nightly, her capable hands maintain its satin perfection. . . . She treads his thick rug, dusts his chair and pictures, plumps the pillows on his luxurious sofa. From observation of his vacant office she has built the mosaic of his personality. Unknown, she has been with him months and years."

It almost begs for Cary Grant as Whitney, returning to his office late one night to retrieve something he'd forgotten after a white-tie frolic in the Rainbow Room, only to discover his desk being lovingly massaged by, oh, Hedy Lamarr, an immigrant working girl who is really a down-on-her-luck Ruritanian princess. Except Hedy would have been monitored by a crew boss, and Cary would have had to go off to late drinks at "21" on his own. The Rockefeller Center cleaning staff was managed with a precision that rivaled the rituals of the Music Hall usher corps. At times, this formality was enforced with an unbecoming ferocity. In 1943 a forewoman the union called "a female Simon Legree" and "a petticoated despot" provoked a wildcat strike. But rebellion was neither in the nature of this workforce nor in its interests. The three hundred men and women who cleaned the Center's floors, windows, cuspidors, toilets, corridors, and ashtrays were mostly foreign born, supporting families, reasonably well paid considering the unskilled nature of their work, and most of them needed their jobs desperately.

The workday began each evening in a subbasement, where the employee locker rooms adjoined a sort of mechanics' row—the Center's plumbing shop, the tinsmith shop, the rooms reserved for the large staff of carpenters and locksmiths and electrical workers and metalworkers. The women, known as "low-dusters," lined up single file, each holding a mop in her right hand, handle up. After collecting the rest of their supplies from a quartermaster, they mounted their nightly assault on a total square footage comparable to more than three thousand six-room houses. As the women finished their work, "high-dusters"—all men—would come in with ladders and elongated vacuum hoses to clean the upper walls, light fixtures, cabinet tops, Venetian blinds, and other spots the women couldn't reach. Midway through the shift, elevators operating on a precise schedule brought couriers from the subbasement cafeteria to hand out lunches to designated dusters on each floor, all in the time it took for the doors to open and close.

This army had its specialists as well. Five full-time chewing-gum removers. Three "butt pickers," charged with cleaning up the remnants of hundreds of thousands of cigarettes. Three more men who did nothing but clean elevators. There was a crew dedicated to hosing down the sidewalks, another to polishing every last piece of brass trim, and another that did nothing but clean, varnish, or replace the threshold "saddles" at the entrance to each office suite. Every night the cleaning crews collected two tons of refuse from the offices' wastebaskets and turned it over to a paper recycler who was contractually obligated to keep it for two days in the numbered bags in which it had been collected. That way, the tenant who had mistakenly discarded a legal document, a hundred-dollar bill, or a chip off the Jonker diamond could order a search, and the "potentate she had never seen" might offer his gratitude to the charwoman who polished his desk, plumped his pillows, and carefully labeled his trash.

Back, then, to the unfinished lobby of the U.S. Rubber Building, November 1, 1939. At some point while the crowd settled in, the band modulated from "Auld Lang Syne" to a chorus of "Roar, Lion, Roar," the Columbia fight song. Nicholas Murray Butler was seventy-seven years old, in his thirty-eighth year as the university's president. If you made a list of Butler's every request, recommendation, suggestion, or tantrum concerning Rockefeller Center over the past decade, you would quickly discover that his wishes had been all but entirely ignored. His one victory was the installation of a plaque in the Channel Gardens saluting David Hosack (actually, there was a second victory: the inscription on the plaque incorporated Butler's correction of Merle Crowell's punctuation). Butler had otherwise found solace in Junior's monthly rent check, which covered 29 percent of Columbia's operating expenses.

For the rest of the men on the platform, their pride and sense of satisfaction was unmitigated. A jocular La Guardia asked Junior to "see if you can put a few more Centers around the city." Murray reminded the audience, which included a number of people substantially less labor-friendly than Nelson, that all of the buildings had been constructed by unionized tradesmen, at union wages, under union conditions. Sarnoff saluted the power of radio and promised the imminent advent of television. The Rockefeller Center Choristers provided the kind of entertainment the management liked best—the unpaid kind. Bizarrely, they were not on the scene, their voices piped in from a studio in the RCA Building. Even more bizarrely, the selection they had been asked to sing was Strauss's "Tales from the Vienna Woods."

Junior's speech invoked freedom, democracy, economic well-being, social service, world peace, and God. He did not express a syllable of the peevishness he had displayed just a month earlier at dedication ceremonies for the employee gymnasium in the Eastern Airlines building, when he took a shot at the Metropolitan Opera nabobs who had left him holding an eleven-acre bag in 1929. His only remotely cranky statement was an admonition to those who placed blame for war "at the door of business. On its very face such an imputation is as absurd as it is false. Any intelligent business man knows that, while war may temporarily stimulate certain kinds of business, in the long run it is far more destructive of property and other values."

It was a timely cautionary: Congress was at that moment debating an act that would make it legal for American firms to sell war materiel to the British and the French. But Junior's speech this day was less noted by the mob of newspapermen than was his deed. The main event began when he removed his overcoat, put on a pair of oversized White Chief work gloves, and hefted the rivet gun. His suit jacket remained buttoned, his silvery hair faultlessly combed. According to his appointment diary, Junior had attended "Rivet practice" earlier in the day, and judging by his afternoon performance he'd been a good student. A look of genuine pleasure brightened his face as he leaned into the task. A steel foreman helped him steady the gun, and a union "clincher" held the two-pound silver-alloy rivet in place. "He's pretty good," an experienced riveter told the *New York Sun,* "but his stance could bear correcting and a good pro would make him put his right hand over a little more." Hardly a newspaper in the country failed to grab this quotation off the wire and slap it into the picture caption. When Junior was done with the various repeats requested by the photographers and newsreel cameramen, his son—his "devoted son," Junior had called him in his speech—patted him on the back. Then Nelson returned to the platform and announced to the crowd, "And so the story ends."

But it hadn't, not quite yet. What no one had said at the ceremony, and what no one not in the management of Rockefeller Center could have known, was that there were still a few plot twists left in this tale. For as nice as it was to behold these eleven acres embroidered in flowers and trees, restaurants and a skating rink, strolling shoppers and hurrying office workers, the new buildings had pushed Rockefeller Center's vacancy rate to 15 percent, and that was nowhere near a happy ending.

CHAPTER 23

Sunday was a work day for Robert Eisenbach, an editor in the news department of the National Broadcasting Company. The rumblings of the European war had already reached across the Atlantic and into Rockefeller Center, but the threat of war was no match for that crisp late autumn air that could sharpen the senses and make New York seem like an idealized version of itself. The post-Thanksgiving crowds lining up at the Music Hall to see Cary Grant terrorize Joan Fontaine in Alfred Hitchcock's *Suspicion* had led management to hold the movie over for its third week. In the Channel Gardens, fall's hardy chrysanthemums had given way to the seasonal plantings that led one's eye to the gorgeous eighty-three-foot spruce astride the sidewalk above Prometheus. This year two pens on either side of the tree were set up to provide a holiday home for four reindeer whose names were, in a way, rooted in Rockefeller Center's history. A century and a quarter had passed since the man who dreamed up Dasher, Dancer, Cupid, and Vixen had lived here, when he was managing David Hosack's old gardens in behalf of the Columbia trustees.

In the newsroom Eisenbach occupied on the fourth floor of the RCA Building's western extension, at 2:27 that Sunday afternoon, the Associated Press machine stopped chattering away in its usual fashion and suddenly began to gong. Eisenbach followed the words as they formed on the paper: "The White House has just announced that the Japanese have attacked Pearl Harbor, Hawaii." Immediately he grabbed the emergency phone connecting him

The demand for additional space in Rockefeller Center from present tenants, large and small, is almost unbelievable, not to speak of the long and ever-growing waiting list of new applicants.

—JOHN D. ROCKEFELLER JR.,
FEBRUARY 11, 1946

to the master control room. "Send it down," he said—cut off all programs. On the NBC Red Network, the glutinous strains of *Sammy Kaye's Sunday Serenade* halted in midmeasure. On the Blue Network, a *Great Plays* broadcast of Gogol's *The Inspector General* went silent. In moments all 246 stations on both networks had been seized by the network engineers and connected to the emergency microphone in the newsroom. Eisenbach had never been on the air before; now, in his debut, he told America that it was at war. At the next station break, two minutes later, the three familiar chimes that identified NBC were followed by a fourth note. This was the emergency alert to all NBC personnel, signaling them to call in immediately for instructions.

Just outside the RCA Building, the news arrived on less technological wings. Holiday crowds in the Channel and around the tree, skaters carving the ice, moviegoers waiting on line at the Music Hall could see paper airplanes drifting down from the offices of *Time* and *Life*. Editors and writers leaning out the windows had inscribed each with a brief message: "We are at war with Japan." As the first one hit the ground, Rockefeller Center's role in the worldwide conflict could have been said to have officially begun. So, too, could this have been said: with the onset of war, Rockefeller Center's ultimate success was at last assured. Two years earlier, when Junior told the chilly audience in the U.S. Rubber Building that war was bad for business, he had been motivated by all the right instincts. But in the instance of Rockefeller Center, he turned out to be wrong on the facts.

In a sense World War II had come to Rockefeller Center long before America's entry into it, with Hitler's May 10, 1940, invasion of the Low Countries. Not two months had passed since the opening of Holland House, which had been developed on the same promotional model perfected in the marketing of the French, British, and Italian buildings. Suddenly the elaborate Dutch garden on the setback roof, the club for Dutch businessmen on the second floor, the displays of tulips and delft tiles in its lobby showroom were of small interest to the Dutch and Dutch-American concerns that had spoken for one-fifth of the space in the twenty-story building. The elevator attendant who greeted Dutch tenants with a courtly "Goeden Morgen, mynheer" forthwith had far fewer people to say it to. The Netherlands Consulate no longer had a government to represent; the Royal Dutch Airlines office no longer had travelers to sell its tickets to; Rockefeller Center, Incorporated, no longer had a plausible theme or an anchor tenant for its newest building.

The local beneficiary of the blitzkrieg was Eddie Rickenbacker, war hero, race-car driver, and latterly one of the most successful men in the airline industry. Rickenbacker had been installed as general manager of the limping Eastern Airlines in 1933 by General Motors, its controlling shareholder; almost immediately he turned it around, making it, he claimed, the first airline to operate profitably without government subsidy. Under Rickenbacker, Eastern had none of the pretensions to glamour of, say, Pan Am, which had commissioned Norman Bel Geddes to design the Pullman bunks and the white-gloved waiters' costumes for its stylish Clippers. Rickenbacker paid the lowest salaries in the business, shrank from hiring female flight attendants (they were always "marrying the customers," he complained), and believed, wrote Finis Farr, that "a plane ride was, in fact, a bus ride with the miracles of takeoff and landing at the start and finish."

So closely was its leader associated with the business that Eastern soon became known as "the Rickenbacker line." Had he chosen, he could have made the name official: in 1938, Rickenbacker bought the business from General Motors for $3.5 million, with the backing of the investment bank Kuhn Loeb and the budding twenty-eight-year-old venture capitalist Laurance Rockefeller (who brought in a few colleagues, among them Rockefeller Center rental manager Lawrence Kirkland). Apart from a shared business interest and the parallel rhythms of the two names, Rickenbacker was no Rockefeller. His speech was a garble of embroidered-sampler clichés and the odd "Columbus Dutch" of his central Ohio upbringing ("I tolded you" was one favored locution). He called black people "darkies." He was devoted to right-wing radio commentators, and his cultural interests didn't extend much beyond his loyal attachment to *The Lone Ranger.* But as a Rockefeller business partner at a time when the Rockefellers had a brand-new and suddenly imperiled building on their hands, Rickenbacker grabbed the opportunity. Less than a month after the fall of the Netherlands, the *Herald Tribune* reported that "Airline history was made 10,000 feet in the air yesterday when Capt. Eddie Rickenbacker . . . signed a lease that will give the name of Eastern Air Lines to the sixteen-story building at 10 Rockefeller Plaza." A photograph that the wire services zipped to newspapers across the country showed Rickenbacker, Laurance, and Kirkland signing the lease aboard an Eastern Silverliner, somewhere over Philadelphia—great publicity for Eastern, great publicity for Rockefeller Center, and thus doubly pleasing to all involved.

Soon other tenants besides the Dutch had to be replaced. Seven of the eight travel bureaus in the Center were all but wiped out by the dislocations caused by the European conflict. A similarly beset foreign-coin dealer in the International Building asked to be allowed to continue to rent his space in exchange for 50 percent of his net profits, but the likelihood of profits was now so slim the rental committee rejected his request. The Italian consul general turned over the keys to his space in the Palazzo d'Italia and sailed home. In February of 1941, William Rhodes Davis, an American oilman with well-known ties to the Axis powers—he had shipped 12 million barrels to Germany and 8 million to Italy before a British blockade put an end to the traffic—was denied a lease renewal. His was an extreme case; Davis had promoted a putative "peace plan" devised by Hermann Goering, and the *Herald Tribune* said he was "liberally blamed for supplying the oil with which Germany was carrying on her blitzkrieg." Less arrant traders with the Nazis did not suffer eviction: ten days before Davis's renewal was rejected, John D. Rockefeller 3rd called on David Sarnoff to solicit his involvement in the British War Relief Society. Sarnoff declined on the grounds that his company had extensive contracts with Germany, and signing on to the British aid effort might be considered "an un-neutral act."

The lead-up to America's entry into the war was not entirely grim. Landlord and tenants alike embraced the remaining manifestations of peace. The cheery caption on a publicity photograph of an attractive young woman lounging in one of the roof gardens read, "Miss Bernice Thimm ponders in amazement the first crocus to brave the March winds." The gardens had been closed to everyone but tenants and, apparently, Merle Crowell, who knew that any amazed pondering by newspaper readers would be directed not at the brave little crocus but at Miss Thimm's exceptionally photogenic legs. For another Crowell stunt, meant to illustrate how easy it was to get to Rockefeller Center via the new Sixth Avenue subway, six homing pigeons borrowed from the Army Signal Corps were taken to the line's distant termini and released; their arrival back at Rockefeller Plaza merited cheering crowds and a national radio broadcast.

Speaking at the February 1941 dedication of Carl Milles's striking wooden sculptures in the lobby of the Time & Life Building, Henry Luce evoked the threat of war and the wonders of peace. "These winter evenings . . . ," he told his audience, "I walk out the door of the Time & Life Building and look down at the figures of the skaters on the rink below and up to the blazing windows of the sky-reaching summits of the Center. They are the windows of the only world city which today still shows light." But the audience could abide only so much dramatic drumroll, so the ceremony reached its climax on a less solemn note, when a mechanical bird perched above the head of the woodsman in the central piece of Milles's triptych trilled a gay little song. The effort that had been put into this performance demonstrated that the struggle between war and peace was not the only thing on the minds of Luce, his key associates, the RCA engineering department, and Crowell's publicity staff. The chirping was the recorded song of a clarino, or Mexican thrush, that belonged to Fairfield Osborn, president of the New York Zoological Association. At his townhouse on East 61st Street, Osborn had auditioned several birds for the NBC engineers who had been dispatched on this critical mission. Osborn's Persian leaf bird failed the test, as did a bulbul. But at the other end of a remote hookup in the RCA Building, the clarino's song was finally committed to acetate. A week later, on the eve of the formal dedication ceremony, a relieved Time Inc. bureaucrat filed a report to Roy Larsen, the company's president. "Mr. Bailey and Mr. Johnson of this office were present at the test of the singing bird last night," the memo read, "and they advise me that the song is not unpleasant."

The war itself changed everything. Within days of Robert Eisenbach's announcement to the nation and the fluttering paper airplanes launched from the windows of the Time & Life Building, the federal government seized the offices of the Center's remaining German, Italian, and Japanese tenants. The royal Italian coat of arms over the entrance to the Palazzo d'Italia, as well as Attilio Piccirilli's crypto-fascist laborer, were covered with planks. The French consulate closed, and though it would be a few years before the Free French opened it back up, downstairs on the Channel bookseller Isaac Mohlo soon turned his Librairie de France into a meeting place for exiled French intellectuals. Sir William Stephenson—the celebrated "Man Called Intrepid"—ran worldwide British intelligence from several nondescript office suites in the International Building; one, Room 3663, was the base of operations for the future head of the Central Intelligence Agency, Allen Dulles.* The "exotic Nipponese blooms" in the Japanese garden on the eleventh-floor setback of the RCA Building were ripped up and replaced by

---

*Another of Stephenson's colleagues was the British naval intelligence officer known as Agent 17F, later to become famous as the novelist Ian Fleming. In the first James Bond novel, *Casino Royale,* Fleming has James Bond earn his "license to kill" with the rifle assassination of a Japanese cipher expert operating out of the RCA Building. "They have tough windows at the Rockefeller Center to keep the noise out," Bond explains. "It worked out well [when] I got the Jap in the mouth as he turned to gape."

a Chinese Garden named for Madame Chiang Kai-shek. This action was not provoked by the *Life* magazine article that addressed the U.S. citizenry's "distressing ignorance on the delicate question of how to tell a Chinese from a Jap," but the instinct behind it was identical.

People working in the Center saw their routines disrupted by the petty irritations of wartime. Meatless Tuesdays came to the Rockefeller Center Lunch Club ("PLEASE COOPERATE AND DO NOT ASK FOR MEAT ITEMS," the menu instructed). At the Music Hall, Russell Markert, having trouble finding blond Rockettes, grumbled that "all the good dyes must have gone to war." The loss of many of the Center's elevator operators to the draft compelled the hiring of older, married men; as a result, Victor Borella warned Hugh Robertson, "We may have to lose something in snappiness and appearance." By 1943 the male shortage was so severe that the corps of tour guides became entirely female. "As the boys step out the girls are stepping in," a press release said, and when Charles de Gaulle made a well-publicized visit to the Observation Roof shortly after D day, it was a bilingual "Centerette" who answered the one question burning in the great man's mind: "*Où est* Coney Island?"

Other changes were more serious. The Rockefeller Center security department distributed nine thousand sandbags throughout the Center so that tenants could use them to put out fires started by incendiary bombs. The lamps Hugh Robertson had had installed on top of the AP and Time & Life buildings, their powerful beacons washing dramatically over the RCA facade each night, were extinguished. What-to-do-in-a-blackout posters appeared on corridor walls throughout the Center, and emergency instructions were placed among the china and napery on every table in the Rainbow Room. (These instructions failed to include one of the admonitions addressed to the Center's tenants in a separate handout: do not remain in the top four floors of a building during an air raid.) When Mayor La Guardia announced a dim-out policy in the spring of 1942, Robertson sent a memorandum to all tenants ordering them to install blackout shades; those slow to conform, he said, would be denied night cleaning services.

The war had not caused Robertson to cede a single degree of his icy calm or acquire an ounce of sentiment. After W. G. Van Schmus reported to Robertson that Roxy's widow had requested a pass to the Music Hall, Van Schmus dictated a memo for his own files: "Mr. H.S.R. did not see any reason why this should be done." (Others did: friendly ushers were still smuggling an elderly Mrs. Roxy through unmarked doors nearly two decades later.) But Robertson did begin to slow down a bit. Beset by a case of shingles that kept him away from work for six months, and passing his sixtieth birthday during his convalescence, he agreed to a pay cut that knocked him down from $80,000 a year to $60,000. Still, he bore ultimate responsibility for all the key issues: labor agreements, major lease negotiations, political relations with the city, and—there's no other way to describe it—using the war as an excuse to save a buck.

It wasn't like, say, the Orson Welles character in *The Third Man,* making a killing in postwar Vienna by compromising the medicine intended for seriously ill children, but given that Rockefeller Center was approaching real profitability in 1942, and even more so given Junior's hard-won and zealously defended reputation for probity, Robertson's maneuvers with the union representing the Rainbow Room waiters were pretty distasteful. In the summer of 1941 the nightclub had recorded the greatest profit in its seven-year history. That fall, the *Sun* described one Saturday as "almost like New Year's Eve," the 350-seat room serving 575 meals in the course of the evening, not including another 312 down the hall in the Grill. Though Robertson acknowledged in negotiations with the union several months later that gross receipts had increased, profits were rapidly plunging. In September 1942 his strategy was outlined for Junior by a rising member of the office staff, Barton Turnbull: if the union leaders held firm to their wage demands, Robertson would tell them "the operation of these rooms at night will be discontinued." Further, Turnbull added, any closing would be accompanied by a public statement "that the step had been taken in line with reducing activities not connected with war work." Such a statement, the memo concluded, was likely to "be well received."

It played out exactly that way, even though the waiters' union asked for only a pipsqueak of a raise: two dollars a week. On December 19, Robertson announced that both the Rainbow Room and the Rainbow Grill would be closed at the end of the month because of the "increasing shortage of manpower due to the demands of the armed forces and the war production industries." Union officers, fearful for their reputations, played along shamelessly, the local's president privately thanking Robertson for not blaming the shutdown on the waiters. Robertson acknowledged the "many deep expressions of regret," but told a *Variety* reporter that continued operations were "non-essential to the war-effort."

The Luncheon Club must have been deemed essential. It reopened on February 15, 1943, with a credit for the six dark weeks extended to all members and an outside caterer brought in to provide their lunches. The evening lights didn't go back on in the Rainbow Room until 1950.

In the spring of 1942, when Robertson ordered all the Center's tenants to install blackout shades, about 10 percent of them objected—not about the shades, but about the price. Barton Turnbull sent a letter to Nelson reporting that the complainants felt Rockefeller Center should cover the nine-dollar cost of each shade. A lot of these tenants, Turnbull assured him, "need to be brought into line." Turnbull was communicating to Nelson through the mails because the president of Rockefeller Center was no longer in New York. In the summer of 1940, less than four months after tenants began moving into the U.S. Rubber Building, Franklin D. Roosevelt had appointed Nelson coordinator of Inter-American Affairs, a new sub-cabinet-level position created to supervise U.S. policy in Latin America. Turnbull stepped into the position of "acting president," and for the next five years, including one last year in which Nelson served as an assistant secretary of state, he sent his boss regular reports describing affairs at Rockefeller Center.

Sometimes Turnbull's letters addressed substantive issues, particularly labor matters, that required Nelson's involvement. Usually, though, they read like the sort of chatty reports a camper might send home to his parents. A Victory Garden had been installed in the Channel, Turnbull reported in June of 1942; Junior, he added, was "skeptical that we can keep the tomatoes on the bushes after they have ripened," but "[Bertram] Cutler thinks that 'most people in New York don't even know that they are tomatoes!'" At the Center Theater, Turnbull wrote, "the barrel jumper [in the ice show] had to be replaced because he wanted too much money." The Music Hall, showing *The Philadelphia Story,* just had "the second largest week in its history." When the subject was *really* trivial, Robert Gumbel took the initiative and wrote in Turnbull's stead: Did Nelson want to contribute five dollars to the 1943 employee Christmas fund? (He did.)*

What the Turnbull letters revealed more than anything else was the sort of thing written between the lines of letters from all happy campers: everything was just fine. The investment that Junior had made at the onset of

---

*Nowhere in all this correspondence is there any acknowledgment of another wartime phenomenon: certain of the Center's bathrooms, especially one on the eighth floor of the RCA Building, had become secret trysting places for gay men. The situation of such a "tea room" (derived from "t-room," in turn derived from "toilet room") at the end of a lengthy corridor enabled sentries to signal the approach of an unknowing visitor.

one national earthquake was now redeemed by the country's sustained response to another one. The completion in 1940 of the Depression-spanning construction program had turned out to be the perfect preface to the quickening war economy. By late that year the vacancy rate had dropped to 10 percent, and Turnbull initiated a series of rent increases. Just before Pearl Harbor, vacancies were down to 6 percent, and John D. 3rd noted that "The Center is now more than breaking even" on an operating basis. In 1941 federal and state governments occupied 3.75 percent of the commercial office space in the United States; by 1945 the prosecution of the war and the attendant expansion of government programs had increased that figure to more than 10 percent, and along the way Rockefeller Center absorbed its share of the growth. Positive cash flow could now be used to pay down the Metropolitan Life mortgage. The renting department stopped granting options on available space. In a 1942 letter to Junior, who was vacationing at his eighteenth-century house in Williamsburg, Hugh Robertson wrote, "Our October statement shows the best net return of any statement we have ever had, and I think we have definitely 'turned the corner.'" Replied Junior, "How pleased I am with the news contained in the last paragraph of your letter, you can well imagine."

By the time Lily Pons sang the "Marseillaise" to a crowd of thirty thousand people jamming the plaza, filling the adjacent streets, and leaning out their office windows to celebrate the liberation of Paris in the summer of 1944, Rockefeller Center had reached what an awed *New York Times* called "the saturation point": of its 5,290,000 square feet of rentable space, 99.7 percent—all but 15,000 square feet—was occupied. Turnbull had already "notified all of our own government agencies . . . that in their future plans for expansion they must look elsewhere for space." Robertson wrote to Nelson to tell him that he was holding applications from present tenants for a million additional square feet of office space, and requests for 500,000 more from people pounding on the walls to get in.

The war was not even over yet; the soldiers had not yet come home; the postwar economic engine had not yet begun to roar. That would all begin in 1945, just as three figures who went back to Rockefeller Center's origins passed from the scene. Charles O. Heydt had retired four years earlier but had continued to use an office in Room 5600; now, Heydt's forty-eight-year tenure in the family office would have to conclude: "Already, and quite naturally," Junior wrote to his old friend, "the boys"—Nelson and his brothers—"are inquiring about permanent and larger quarters."* Nicholas Murray Butler turned eighty-three in 1945. He had spent almost exactly half his life as Columbia's president, and though he remained whole of mind, blindness, deafness, and the other debilities of age had overtaken him. No longer even able to sign his name to his letters, Butler was compelled to accept retirement. (A year before his death in 1947, he gave up his presidency of the Carnegie Endowment for International Peace as well, ceding the position to a youthful diplomat named Alger Hiss.) John R. Todd, five years younger than Butler, died while on vacation in Florida, on May 12, 1945; in his posthumously published memoirs, he devoted seventy-nine pages to his half-century in business—sixty-six of them to his nine years at Rockefeller Center.

Five days before Todd's death the final triumph of Rockefeller Center was heralded by a storm of paper tumbling from its windows into the streets and gardens below, an exultant celebration of the end of the war in Europe. This spasm of joy and relief and brightest hope had been provoked by a false report; the next day, the official day, the blizzard began anew. For four years newsreel cameras documenting war-bond rallies, WAC induction ceremonies, propaganda displays, and other manifestations of wartime spirit had made this piece of land nearly as familiar a national monument as the temples and obelisks of Washington. Now the cameramen came to document the wild celebrations and solemn ceremonies of peace. V-J Day was a variation on V-E Day, even inside the buildings: Arturo Toscanini marked the end of the European war by conducting Beethoven's Fifth Symphony and the end of the Pacific war with the Third. In October the return of the fleet brought a record eight thousand people to the RCA Building's Observation Roof during the course of the day to salute the forty-seven ships steaming into the Hudson and the hundreds of planes humming overhead.

The flags of the United Nations, first lofted on poles circling the skating rink for a special event in 1942, now became a permanent fixture. The colony of bees originally imported to pollinate a Victory Garden on the terrace of the Associated Press Building soon numbered one hundred thou-

---

*Nelson, with Laurance, laid claim to the eastern end of Room 5600, and commissioned Wally Harrison to redecorate it to accommodate his modern tastes. When he gave his father a tour of this veritable showroom of the International Style—blond wood walls, flush-set doors, Scandinavian furniture—Nelson couldn't contain his pride. "Gee, Pa, isn't this impressive?" he asked. "Nelson," Junior replied, "whom are we trying to impress?"

sand, and was well on its way to producing two hundred pounds of honey each year. Tenants who three or four years earlier had left their cars in "protective storage" in the Eastern Airlines Building garage came home from the war to find them jacked up off the floor, covered with cloth blankets, and, thanks to twice-monthly engine revvings, ready to roll. The revival of tourism brought ten thousand people to the NBC studio tour during just one week in December; that same week the lines for the five daily shows at the Music Hall ran from Sixth Avenue all the way to Fifth, turned the corner, and extended two more blocks to 52nd Street.

In 1940 the gross national product stood at $101.4 billion; five years later—three of them braked by the drag of wage and price controls—it reached $215.2 billion. Cash from redeemed war bonds, added to the smoldering fire of four years of pent-up consumer demand, accelerated a boom like none the country had ever known. In the heart of the commercial capital of the richest and most powerful nation on earth stood the only first-class office space—virtually the only private office space of any grade, really—built in New York since the opening of the Empire State Building in 1931. Over those same fourteen years a transportation infrastructure just waiting to move the cars, trains, and planes of a revived economy had been put in place: the George Washington, Triborough, and Henry Hudson Bridges; hundreds of miles of highways and parkways; the Lincoln and Queens-Midtown Tunnels; La Guardia Airport; the Sixth Avenue subway. The private development and the public development made a fertile coupling.

By April of 1946, four hundred firms were on the renting department's waiting list; by July the negative inventory—the space they could rent to new tenants if only it existed—reached a million square feet. Time Inc. wanted so much more space that the company, which contemplated a move to the suburbs until an internal report noted that the staff would "rather live on pate de foie gras in New York than roast beef in Pelham, Riverdale or Chappaqua," took an option on the land beneath the Hotel Marguery on Park between 47th and 48th. This was not a meaningful threat to Rockefeller Center's sold-out glory: NBC, gearing up for television, immediately raised its hand for any space Time might be abandoning.

Even while he was still in Washington, Nelson's in-box had been swamped by entreaties from friends, acquaintances, tenants, and foreign governments desperately hoping he could intervene and find them a few more rooms in Rockefeller Center; the Brazilian consul general, wrote Nelson to Robertson, came to him "with tears in his eyes," so desperate was his government to acquire additional space adjacent to its offices in the Eastern

Airlines Building. War's end brought the requests to flood tide. The Ecuadorian consul asked Nelson to put his country on a list "with some special mark of yours, so that we may thus have a chance"; the Costa Ricans pleaded for just enough space to house their files. "Dear Nelson," said Norman Bel Geddes; "Dear Nelson," said playwright Robert Sherwood, who said he felt justified "asking for special favors"; "Dear Nelson," said, it seemed, half the movers, shakers, operators, players, and creators in New York. When Sol Rosenblatt, counsel for the Democratic National Committee and one of the very first tenants in the International Building, came asking for more space, Nelson sent a memo to the renting department: "In view of the fact that he came to us when we were a small voice crying in the wilderness . . . ," he wrote, "we should give his case every possible consideration." The renting department couldn't help. The International Building didn't have room for a mouse.

Junior reacted to this "almost unbelievable" demand for space with prudence. He sent a letter to his sons urging them to refer "all applicants without exception to the Managing Director's office," lest the family's fairness be called into question. Noting the black ink flowing in an unbroken current, he asked Debevoise and others to begin the process of squaring his estate, much of which was tied up in Rockefeller Center. Changing its corporate ownership required the landlord's permission, and negotiations with Columbia began, stopped, began again. Finally, the university assented. In the summer of 1948, in a letter formalizing what was about to occur, Nelson wrote to his father: "Because this center has become so closely identified in the public mind with you and your dynamic belief in a free society, my brothers and I would like to keep it in the family as a living symbol of the great tradition which you and grandfather before you have built."

And soon it was done. Ownership of Rockefeller Center passed to Junior's sons. He had not always treated his children equally; during the war his distribution of $55 million provided a vivid expression of their standing with him—Nelson received $12.6 million, the other favored brothers comparable amounts, and the rebellious Babs and the occasionally dissolute Winthrop (the only brother, it might be noted, to see combat duty) just half a million each. Now, though, Junior could understandably regard this collection of buildings as central to the very definition of the word "Rockefeller." He presented it, in equal shares, to the sons who would bear the name forward.

Years later, Junior's brother-in-law Winthrop Aldrich offered a bankerly appraisal of Rockefeller Center when he said that the decision to build it "was probably the greatest thing that ever happened for the family." But if Junior ever saw Rockefeller Center as his own personal triumph, he never said so. How could he have? His natural diffidence would not have allowed him to brag. His self-image would have made him reluctant to exalt the success of an endeavor that may have begun with a socially beneficent objective but, through two decades of great fortune, had concluded in a thoroughly commercial success. How could Rockefeller Center be a reflection of who he was, when even after its completion Junior had acknowledged that "I really belong in Williamsburg"? How could Junior understand that he, a child of the nineteenth century who longed for the eighteenth, had in two decades of the twentieth created a beacon that would shine into the twenty-first?

EPILOGUE

1948–2003

In April of 1948, at roughly the same time that he was arranging the transfer of Rockefeller Center to his sons, Junior suffered a grievous loss. Abby died of a heart attack, at seventy-three. He was so shaken he commanded that her body be cremated at once—"take this blow away," he pleaded. Johnny and Nelson spent the night with him, and in the months to follow their wives took turns looking after him at Bassett Hall, his home in Williamsburg.

With the tools granted someone whose faith is devout and whose belief in what he called "the purifying fire of sacrifice" is absolute, Junior eventually managed to reassemble his life. "We know little of the sources of strength, physical as well as spiritual, that await our great need . . . ," he told an associate. "But there they are. . . . I have found them." In 1951 he wed Martha Baird Allen, the widow of a friend from his college years at Brown. They were married in her home in Providence before only six guests, including Junior's longtime secretary, Robert Gumbel. On the application for his marriage license, Junior entered his occupation as "real estate developer."

Some four decades after Junior's death, David Rockefeller wrote that "It might surprise people to know that . . . Father received no income from [his] massive investment [in Rockefeller Center] and recouped less than half of the capital he had invested." This would surprise only those who believe that money or property passed on to one's heirs doesn't count. A deftly executed tax dodge enabled Junior to transfer the $57.5 million he was still owed by Rockefeller Center, Incorporated—his total cash investment, which had been made in the form of a loan, had peaked at $75 million—to his sons' charitable foundation, the Rockefeller Brothers Fund. His un-recouped capital would eventually be returned to the five boys as a $10.6 million tax loss for each of them. In time the Center became, in the words of family associates John Ensor Harr and Peter Johnson, "by far the largest single repository of [Rockefeller family] wealth." Elsewhere Harr and Johnson called the Center "the salvation of the Rockefeller family fortune." Laurance Rockefeller, the son with the best business head, told an interviewer, "Father did a lot better for us than he'd ever intended. . . . I don't think he had any idea at all Rockefeller Center would be as big as it was."

Junior spent the last years of his life largely in a seasonal cycle of rest—springtime in Williamsburg, summer in Seal Harbor, fall in Pocantico Hills, winter at the Arizona Inn in Tucson. Save for the occasional visit with one of his sons at the Rockefeller Center Luncheon Club, he all but stopped going to the office in 1956. Asked by a colleague around this time whether he considered his decision in 1929 to proceed with the development of the Upper Estate a courageous act, he replied, "Often a man gets into a situation where there is just one thing to do. There is no alternative. He wants to run, but there is no place to run to. So he goes ahead on the only course that's open, and people call it courage." Not even remotely concerned with the sturdiness of his reputation, in 1958 he issued a new public relations policy: "No further efforts will be made to correct inaccuracies in published articles." Weakened by prostate surgery, he died in 1960 at eighty-six. He had spent his last days sitting alone in a chair by a window, a blanket pulled around him.

In the 1950s, Junior's five sons gathered regularly, usually at Pocantico Hills. The brothers' meetings addressed their philanthropic efforts, their business ventures, the staff in Room 5600. After the war they had effectively divided up the Rockefellerian world: John presided over the Rockefeller Brothers Fund; Laurance directed their joint investment partnership; David went to work at the Chase Bank; Winthrop entered the oil business; and Nelson chose politics. Rockefeller Center, of course, was also his.

Nelson's spheres of interest became balls for him to juggle. In 1953, appointed undersecretary of health, education, and welfare by Dwight Eisenhower, he returned to Washington, tossing the keys to the Center to Laurance as he left. Shrewd and unsentimental, Laurance made the decision to take the loss and tear down the Center Theater. He also planned the westward leap across Sixth Avenue that would expand the family's midtown holdings to twenty-five acres and its rentable office space to nearly fifteen million square feet. Commuting from Pocantico Hills down the Hudson to midtown on his own PT boat, assembling the string of "Rockresorts" that became vacation hideaways for the American wealthy, Laurance was comfortable in the cloak of privilege. He was also so confident in his sense of self that he did not object when Nelson returned from Washington in 1956 and took his old job back. It was harder for Johnny, who had run the Rockefeller Brothers Fund since its inception. Johnny at first objected when Nelson announced his wish to take over that as well, but it was like trying to resist a bulldozer. He ceded the fund to Nelson and thereafter focused much of his attention on an old family interest: as chairman of Lincoln Center, he finally freed the Metropolitan Opera from its yellow-brick slum on 39th Street and installed it on the Upper West Side in a new home made of glass, travertine, and aesthetic sentimentality—Wallace K. Harrison, designer.

Elected governor of New York in 1958, Nelson conducted a fifteen-year object lesson in the exuberance of activist government, the extremes of presidential ambition, and the excesses of grandiose building projects (as governor, said Nelson's speechwriter Joseph Persico, "Concrete excited him most"). But he did not leave Rockefeller Center far behind. He received the same sort of regular updates Barton Turnbull had sent him during the war, messages like the one in 1961 informing him that a fully equipped fallout shelter accommodating 30,500 people would cost nearly $3 million (it was never built, but Nelson did have a shelter installed in his basement at 810 Fifth Avenue). The Rockefeller Center medical staff was for years responsible for emergency medical service at the governor's Manhattan office on 55th Street. When Nelson needed to hold a truly important, and private, political meeting, he used the glossy Roxy Suite upstairs in the Music Hall.

After his governorship and his subsequent brief tenure as Gerald Ford's vice president, Nelson returned to New York to stay in 1977. Once again he attempted to assert his familial dominance, but finally his older brother resisted. Johnny's five decades of frustration, abasement, and deference gave way to a spasm of surprising vehemence. "You have always indicated to me that there were two things you wanted to accomplish in your lifetime," Johnny wrote in a letter he hand-delivered from his corner of Room 5600 to Nelson's on the opposite end of the floor. "The first was to become President of the United States, and the second was to become the leader of the family and be sure it lived up to the great traditions bequeathed to us by Father and Grandfather. Obviously, you have failed in the first of these objectives, and you are in danger of failing in the second, unless you modify your behavior." Nelson did not. A quarrel ensued, and the brothers never spoke again. Johnny died in 1978, Nelson the following year.

On June 30, 1950, Rudolph Travers concluded nineteen years of monthly visits to the offices of the Metropolitan Life Insurance Company when he handed over a check for $533,000—the last payment on the record-setting mortgage. By 1953, Rockefeller Center was throwing off $5 million annually in net profit, irrespective of the enormous tax advantages accruing to its owners. Space that had been set aside for amenities was given over to more productive crops: the employee gymnasium made way for offices, the post office moved to less valuable space. The Jersey Company, needing room, had commissioned the Center's first postwar structure, the midblock Esso Building on 51st Street, on a piece of land acquired when Nelson was trying to build the triumphal avenue leading to the door of the Museum of Modern Art. Portions of the RCA Building's lower floors occupied by the Museum of Science and Industry at a $90,000 annual rental became retail and office space bringing in more than double that. Toscanini and the NBC Symphony were booted off-premises when 8H was converted to a television studio, and a prime chunk of street-level space was turned over to Nelson's old classmate Pat Weaver for his new invention, the *Today* show—within a year, according to *Billboard,* "probably the largest-grossing venture in the history of show business."

The Center Theater wheezed its last in 1954 and became an organ donor to more fortunate buildings. The brass handrail in the lobby and the dressing room furnishings were sold to the Cherry Lane Theatre in Greenwich Village; many of the chandeliers went to the Hammond Street Pier in Atlantic City; the auditorium seats were shipped off to Bowdoin College, Grand Teton National Park, and a synagogue in Lakewood, New Jersey. The revolving stage and its grand curtain were relocated intact, to South Carolina, where they formed the centerpiece of a new theater at Bob Jones University. The Steichen photomurals and almost all of the Center Theater's other artwork disappeared.

This should not suggest that art was no longer valued at Rockefeller Center. After Italian democracy was restored, a new bronze piece by Giacomo Manzu replaced Piccirilli's laborer and the Savoy coat of arms on the Palazzo d'Italia.* And on the site of the Center Theater, the lobby of a

---

*Along with the insignia of Italy's earlier eras, the fascist emblem carved into the stone at the top of the building's facade remained in place, but the letter and numerals denoting the date of Mussolini's ascension were chiseled away. The disassembled glass bricks of Piccirilli's piece were placed in storage and later discarded.

nineteen-story addition to the U.S. Rubber Building featured an abstract bas-relief of aluminum, plastic, and phosphor-bronze by the constructivist sculptor Naum Gabo. Lessons had been learned: Gabo's piece told no story, made no statement, expressed no ideology. Said the artist, "It represents the image of itself."

Hugh Robertson stepped down from his staff position at Rockefeller Center in 1948 but retained a seat on the board and an annual twelve-thousand-dollar pension. His passage into retirement was storm tossed. Early in 1949 he received a letter from Frederic Goetze, who had just concluded thirty-two years as Columbia's treasurer. "I was shocked and astonished," Goetze wrote, to hear "that a member of the Rockefeller family had stated that the personal relations between Columbia and the Rockefeller Center could not be worse." It was as if Robertson had been waiting to be challenged to this particular duel; he responded with a fusillade of reproach that made it seem that the Rockefellers had for two decades been gouged, robbed, and kneed in the groin by Columbia. The ground rent was "extremely excessive." The Cromwell settlement, he said, was overly generous to the university. Columbia's $2.5 million rent postponement in the mid-1930s was inadequate acknowledgment of Depression reality. He concluded that although he had no knowledge of the complaint that had "shocked and astonished" Goetze, "if such a complaint was made I think these and other reasons are sufficient to back it up."

Robertson was a sore winner. He was also a slightly greedy one. Not two months after sending his bill of complaint to Goetze, he asked Nelson for permission to consult with the Massachusetts Mutual Life Insurance Company, which was preparing to develop the plot at the northwest corner of 48th and Fifth that had been occupied by the Dutch Reformed Church. It was an obvious conflict of interest. Mass Mutual wanted to extend its building west to the Time & Life Building, then make an L-turn north to 49th Street, which required access to the Rockefeller-controlled Cromwell properties. Nelson told Robertson he considered it "quite improper" for him to pursue the Mass Mutual relationship; Robertson harrumphed a defense ("You should, I think, know me well enough to realize . . ."). Robertson turned down the job and stayed on Nelson's board. When he died, in 1951, Rockefeller Center made a two-hundred-dollar contribution in his name to a hospital near his South Carolina plantation.

Thomas Debevoise continued to come to the office after Nelson eased him out of his position as lord chamberlain of Room 5600, but the tasks he took on were increasingly peripheral and his drinking was increasingly nettlesome to those who worked with him. By 1957 he could tell Junior he didn't want to be paid for doing nothing, but clearly he meant that he wanted the work more than the pay. Junior hinted that it was time to go: "We must not forget, you and I, Tom, that we are over eighty and we must both of us readjust our way of living and working with that in mind." A year later Junior was more direct. He asked Debevoise to give up his remaining committee memberships in the Rockefeller organization, his trusteeships, everything. "I urge you my good friend from college days [to] heed and take this counsel," wrote Junior. The *Times* obituary reporting Debevoise's death three months later marked only the fifth time in his long career that his name had appeared in the paper. The depth of his relationship with Junior was marked by the condolence letters Junior received— condolence letters not to a family member but to a client.

You could tell who designed the addition to the U.S. Rubber Building at a glance: the plain slab had to be the work of Wallace Harrison. The two other buildings that had been added in the years after the war—the Esso Building and the Mass Mutual project, which opened as the Sinclair Building in 1952—had been designed by Robert Carson and Earl Lundin, veterans of the Associated Architects' buzzing hive in the Graybar Building. The Sinclair wasn't formally part of Rockefeller Center until it was purchased from its developers in 1963, but from the day it opened it was a kissing cousin. In exchange for ground leases on the last two Cromwell lots, as well as pedestrian and freight connections to the rest of the Center's buildings, Mass Mutual allowed Rockefeller Center to dictate its design.

Carson and Lundin reigned only briefly. When Harrison completed his postwar work on the United Nations headquarters (land donated by Junior, renderings executed by Hugh Ferriss, models fashioned by René Chambellan, and public perceptions dominated by Le Corbusier), he resumed control of the Rockefeller Center design program, beginning with the U.S. Rubber addition. He also continued to nourish the gross misapprehension that he had been the Center's chief architect. At least three times between 1947 and 1953, Andrew Reinhard was moved to complain—twice publicly, in architecture trade magazines—about what he called "Harrison's publicity campaign." Though Harrison repeatedly apologized, he apparently did not disabuse the chorus that helped him create the myth. He was

"Wally Harrison, who built Radio City," as Walter Winchell called him, and two decades after his death newspapers were still giving Harrison credit not due him.

What he did deserve credit for was what Vincent Scully called the "incoherent splatter of skyscrapers" marching down the west side of Sixth Avenue. This western expansion of Rockefeller Center began with Harrison's new Time & Life Building in 1959 and degenerated from there, a row of marble megaliths that seemed informed less by the doctrines of the International Style (although they were clearly inspired by them) than by some form of totalitarian nightmare. A publicity release read, "The new buildings, with their broad plazas, generous promenades, and underground concourse system . . . are an exciting integral extension of Rockefeller Center in design, concept and philosophy." But this was like saying that nuclear war is an integral extension of Quakerism; if Harrison had learned anything from Hood or Corbett, it had long been forgotten. Cyril Connolly's unfair description of the original Rockefeller Center buildings would have been spot-on for the Sixth Avenue slabs: "the sinister Stonehenge of economic man."*

The harsh reaction to the Sixth Avenue buildings lost Harrison the sponsorship of his patron. Nelson, who had once given Harrison, outright, an apartment in a glamorous Fifth Avenue building along with a budget for furnishings and renovations, now turned against him. "After a lifetime devoted to building for the Rockefeller family," wrote Victoria Newhouse, "Harrison was faced with the kind of dismissal an unsatisfactory tradesman might expect." He quickly sank into depression and became a barely recognizable facsimile of the companionable fellow whose openhearted collegiality and shambling charm had carried him so far. Excoriated by critics—"I'm sure all the critics say I'm no good," he acknowledged—he turned against the modernists with whom he had long identified but who had since dismissed him as a "compliant servant of the rich." His late life, he claimed, was "ruined . . . by the German Bauhaus and its groups of friends who have

---

*The one aspect of the westward leap that was both integral and salutary took place underground, when Rockefeller Center leased the north mezzanine of the Sixth Avenue subway station. Rockefeller assumption of responsibility for its upkeep, its layout, and the shops and services tenanted there instantly made it the best-maintained and most congenial subway station in the entire city. It was the first privatization of a station since the period when the lines themselves were still private, but with a rather different attitude toward maintenance than the one expressed by Frank Hedley, president of the IRT line, in 1927: "I saw a car with clean windows today," Hedley said, "and when I got back to the office I raised hell to find out who cleaned those windows and spent all that money."

had a disastrous effect on American architecture." Elsewhere he characterized the proponents of the International Style as "homos who found it a good public relations [*sic*] to hang their hats on." He died in 1981, described by a eulogist as "puzzled and . . . left out," an old man consumed by a spirit-shriveling bitterness.

Just as Rockefeller Center's fortunes had soared with the postwar boom, they suffered whenever New York's economy began to drag. In the worst of times—during, for instance, the city's real estate slump in the early 1970s—vacancy rates reached as high as 12 percent. This was not entirely bad news for the managers of Rockefeller Center, who exploited each downturn by pressing negotiations with Columbia for either a lease extension or an outright purchase of the land. However deep the shadows that periodic recessions cast over 50th Street, they were as nothing compared to the total darkness that repeatedly threatened Morningside Heights; in 1972 the university had to dip into endowment capital to meet current expenses. Well-timed pressure consequently enabled the Rockefeller interests to strike a series of renewals that left Columbia's annual income from the most valuable eleven acres of Manhattan at just $11 million in 1984. Factoring in the value of the Underel properties along the east side of Sixth, which the university had bought in 1953 and leased back to the Rockefellers, the rent had increased at a compound rate of less than 2 percent over the previous forty-five years. Inflation alone, irrespective of the inherent increase in the land's value, would have brought the 1984 rent to nearly $25 million.

Rockefeller desire eventually aligned itself with Columbia need in 1985, when the university sold its 11.7 acres to Rockefeller Center for $411 million (the ghost of Butler must have been hovering in the Columbia press office: the announced figure was an even $400 million). The sale immediately increased the size of Columbia's endowment by 48 percent and, assuming a 5 percent yield, its annual revenues from the land by 85 percent.

This was a much better return than the one Columbia realized from the earlier conclusion of a complex lease situation. In 1948, when William Nelson Cromwell finally expired at ninety-four, his will stipulated a $600,000 bequest to the university—almost precisely the amount Frederic Goetze had figured, back in 1936, that the old lawyer's delays and manipulations had cost his beloved alma mater.

For years, the one part of the Center that seemed immune to local or national economic woes was Radio City Music Hall. Throughout the 1950s and 1960s, defying every known trend in the entertainment industry and in the business cycle, the crowds continued to line up for the Music Hall's increasingly anachronistic shows. From the moment the show-and-a-movie policy was instituted in 1933 until 1968, not once did annual attendance drop below five million. In 1965 maintenance workers were still scraping twenty pounds of chewing gum off the undersides of the auditorium's seats *each day.* That same year the place was given a top-to-bottom facelift; it closed for five days so more than three decades of accumulated grime could be scoured off the walls and ceilings, enabling management to turn up lights that had been dimmed a few years before, the *Times* reported, "to make the dirt less noticeable."

But then the earth shifted. In 1961 Gus Eyssell, who had succeeded Hugh Robertson as executive manager, had boasted that the Music Hall was "the one place where you can go and never be offended." Ten years later that had become a dubious virtue. Eyssell attributed the rapid decline in attendance to "those French and Italian [movies] with those subtitles at the bottom." Yet the most highly publicized Hollywood pictures were not deemed suitable for the Music Hall either, and, Eyssell said in an internal memo, "there is no assurance that the industry will make quality type attractions in the future." In one typical year the Music Hall booked *The Black Windmill, Superdad,* and *Herbie Rides Again,* turning away *Chinatown, Blazing Saddles,* and *The Godfather Part II. Variety* said that "the Music Hall has been hit hard both by the radicalization of entertainment styles and the deterioration of the midtown area." The latter was beyond management's control, the former beyond its imagination. The stage shows, still produced by Leonidoff and Markert, men whose sense of popular entertainment had been forged in the 1920s, embarrassed even the performers. One dancer said, "Some of the things we have to do are so old-fashioned that we can hear the audience laughing at us." That might have had something to do with the new acoustics: when there were only six hundred people sitting in the cavernous theater, as there were on one grim Wednesday in the fall of 1972, you could almost hear them breathing.

Management responded with cuts. The glee club had been discontinued in the 1950s, but now the ballet company was disbanded as well. Leonidoff was let go. The performers' unions, who believed that Rockefeller Center would never take a strike because the Music Hall was the draw that brought people to the Center's shops and restaurants, suffered defeat after defeat. Even the Rockettes line was cut back from thirty-six to thirty. The Stuart Davis painting in the men's lounge, presumably more valuable as a tax deduction than as a piece of décor, was donated to the Museum of Modern Art. By 1977 attendance had bottomed at 1.5 million. Considering the movies offered to audiences that year—*Mr. Billion, The Littlest Horse Thieves, Pete's Dragon*—it's a wonder that many showed up. Reviewing a family-oriented turkey called *Crossed Swords* in *Time,* Frank Rich said, "By making a fetish of booking such movies, Radio City Music Hall has in effect willed its own death."

It almost happened. For much of 1977 and 1978 the Music Hall lay in a coma, its struggle for survival a front-page story in the New York papers. Alton Marshall, the Center's president, threatened. Editorialists yelped, politicians pounded tables, Rockettes picketed. It was going to close. A garage would go up on the site. It was going to be torn down. It was designated a landmark so that it could not be torn down. It was dragged toward court so its landmark designation could be rendered invalid. In fact, internal documents reveal that as early as 1969, management had been considering replacing it with an office building. By 1978 alternative uses under consideration included a shopping mall, a theme park, a hotel, a new home for the American Stock Exchange, and an aquatic environment developed with the Cousteau Society.

The near panic led the state to offer urban development funds to cover operating losses, but in the end the episode had accomplished two things: all the publicity had improved business so much that the state never had to write a check, and the entire desperate exercise allowed management the cover under which it could discard the hallowed stage-show-and-a-movie format. "It was like the Catholic Church going from Latin to English," said Alton Marshall years later. Big-name entertainers replaced the movies, and the Music Hall–produced live shows were radically deflated and reserved for the holiday season. In 1987, sixteen years after Russell Markert's retirement and five years after the five thousandth Rockette high-kicked her way into the line, the first black dancer finally joined the troupe. In time the re-vivified Music Hall became the number-one performance venue in the nation, and its new operators could confidently spend $70 million on a complete renovation that could almost make you think Roxy had never left.*

---

*The Stuart Davis mural was even returned to its original spot in the men's lounge, loaned to the Music Hall by the institution to which it had been donated, the Museum of Modern Art.

Ray Hood believed that the proper life for a skyscraper was roughly twenty years, which gave architects the chance to experiment. After the Music Hall had survived for forty-five only to require life support, Wally Harrison said, "It's dead. That's that. Why worry about it?" But the campaign to save the Music Hall, and the Rockefellers' subsequent purchase of the Columbia land, guaranteed the future of Rockefeller Center. While fearing for its mortality the public had become aware of the Center's glory; by assuring its ownership the Rockefellers had acquired a reason to reinvest.

And, as it turned out, to sell. After consolidating their ownership of the land and the buildings, they initiated a $200 million capital improvement program, including $20 million just for a "Williamsburg-level" restoration of the Rainbow Room (the new managers may have fretted about "mix[ing] the Dacron crowd with the Dunhills" but they largely solved the problem with an extremely anti-Dacron pricing policy). Soon the Rockefeller family commenced an ornate series of financial maneuvers involving an array of corporate entities, family trusts, private investment partnerships, publicly held real estate investment trusts, and mortgage holders (along the way, David Rockefeller, the last brother to retain a personal ownership interest, alone realized a $170.9 million profit on one sale maneuver). Those who shuttled in and out of the bewildering Rockefeller Center equity structure included Goldman Sachs, the Whitehall Group, Tishman Speyer, NBC (which bought its 1.6 million square feet of space outright, for $440 million), the Crown family of Chicago, the Italian Agnelli family, the Greek Niarchos family, and the Japanese Mitsubishi Estate Company. News of the sale of a controlling interest to the last of these was received as evidence of the moral exhaustion of American capitalism. An overextended Mitsubishi's subsequent bankruptcy and abandonment of its interest in "the Hope diamond of world real estate" was received as evidence that maybe something was wrong with Mitsubishi.

In 2000, Tishman Speyer and the Crown family bought out everyone else and for $1.85 billion assumed total ownership of everything but the NBC space. Jerry Speyer, chief executive of Tishman Speyer Properties, called his acquisition a "singular real estate asset that has transcended time."

In May of 2003, exactly seventy-five years after Benjamin Morris unveiled his pasteboard model of a new opera house before the gentlemen of means gathered in the Metropolitan Club, a visitor to Rockefeller Center looking for words to describe the place could not have improved on a few that had appeared in the introduction to a book published to promote it. "Rockefeller Center amounts to an extended family of buildings," wrote Brendan Gill, "none of which, though they grow older, appears to grow old."

This did not mean they were changeless; modifications had been constant, even after the Center earned landmark designation in 1985. The concourse was redone in 1999 so that it more closely resembled a contemporary Los Angeles mall than the lower decks of a 1930s luxury liner. The visitor in 2003 could no longer find the Great Hall of the International Building, which had been gobbled up for a health club, or the Newsreel Theatre, which had become the Guild Theatre and then, finally, turned into shops. The playground on top of the Music Hall had long been closed due to leakage into the auditorium, and access to the Observation Roof of the RCA Building was discontinued around the time of the Rainbow Room renovation. Most of the consulates had skipped across town to the vicinity of the UN years ago; the Passport Office moved out of the International Building in 1997. Eastern Airlines no longer existed, and the Jersey Company, after moving across Sixth and changing its name to Exxon, had been propelled by the centrifugal force of a changing economy to take up residence in a Dallas suburb. There was no RCA Building any longer, at least by that name: in a nifty exercise in historical synchronicity, the RCA Corporation, nearly destroyed by David Sarnoff's son Robert, had been acquired by General Electric, the company—Owen Young's company—from whose loins it had sprung and whose gigantic neon logo now hung from the top of the building. The Associated Press had recently announced it was abandoning the high-rent environs of its building, where only twelve years earlier it had welcomed back correspondent Terry Anderson, held hostage in Lebanon for seven years, with a shower of yellow rose petals.

Some things hadn't changed at all. The Librairie de France, though shrunken in size (part of its former space had been taken over by a chain operation called the Sunglass Hut), remained in La Maison Française; the Center's oldest continuous retail tenant, it was still owned by the family that had founded it. Dentists were still tapping into the gas lines on the eighteenth floor of the International Building, business people (quota free) were still dining daily in the Rockefeller Center Luncheon Club, Rockettes (now unionized) were still working on their fan kicks in the rehearsal rooms upstairs in the Music Hall. In Room 5600, the needs and interests of a growing cadre of Rockefellers, reaching into the sixth generation of Senior's descendants, were still looked after by a private army of associates.

On the street, a time traveler walking east from the other side of Sixth Avenue or west from the other side of Fifth could enter Rockefeller Center and immediately see that in the essential respects, everything was the same as it had always been. But why had no one been able to successfully duplicate it? Why had none of the scores of office or cultural complexes all over the country, every one of them inspired by Rockefeller Center, even approached the original's aesthetic, commercial, and—there's no other word for it—emotional success? "An infinite number of superimposed and unpredictable activities on a single site," as Rem Koolhaas phrased it, guaranteed a life that a dedicated cultural center or shopping center or business center never could, a point vividly illustrated barely a mile uptown, amid the desolate daytime expanses of Lincoln Center. It was also evident that Rockefeller Center's placement right in the heart of Manhattan, part of the city's grid, made it real in the way that, say, a waterfront development never could be. Pedestrians didn't just go *to* Rockefeller Center, they went *through* it.

It wasn't a destination in the city; it was, organically, the city itself—a city where the privately maintained sidewalks were spotless, where the ramp-relieved cross streets were free of delivery trucks. Where the flowers and the flags and the sun slicing down between the buildings and into this surprisingly small open space conveyed exactly the same thing it had suggested to a *Fortune* writer in 1936: "Rockefeller Center begets a sauntering mood," he said—and by the evidence, it always would.

NOTES

Documentation exists for every fact in this book, but if I were to include here a reference for each one, there would be more notes than narrative and a book about the size of the British Empire Building. I have consequently confined the published notes to direct quotations; to assertions of fact that may be in dispute; and to certain published sources heavily leaned upon. However, readers wishing citations for material not referenced here may write to me in care of my publisher (Viking Penguin, 375 Hudson Street, New York, NY 10014) or directly to me by e-mail (dan@okrent.com). The citation "author interview" indicates interviews conducted either by me or by my research assistant, Randy Hartwell.

ABBREVIATIONS USED IN NOTES

Archives

AAA: Archives of American Art, Washington, DC.

AL: Avery Library, Columbia University.

CA: Columbia University Archives, Columbiana Collection, Columbia University.

CentA: Century Association Archives, New York, NY.

CBF-I: Transcripts of interviews conducted by Charles B. Fowler for his unpublished history of Radio City Music Hall, Radio City Music Hall Archives, New York, NY.

CHK-I: Transcripts of interviews conducted by Carol Herselle Krinsky for her *Rockefeller Center*, published 1978.

CHRIS-1: Unpublished internal history of Rockefeller Center by Francis Christy, located in the Rockefeller Family Archives, 2C, Box 82, Folder 619, 8/9/49.

CHRIS-2: Unpublished personal memoir by Francis Christy, in possession of his son, Arthur Christy.

COHP: Columbia Oral History Project, Columbia University. Specific interviews are identified with the name of the subject, e.g., "COHP, Wallace Harrison."

DDP: Donald Deskey Papers, Cooper-Hewitt National Design Museum, New York, NY.

HRC: Humanities Research Center, University of Texas, Austin.

JB/RR: Joseph Baum Rainbow Room files, New York, NY.

MOA: Metropolitan Opera Archives.

MOMA: Museum of Modern Art Archives, New York, NY.

NYA: New Yorker Archives, New York Public Library.

OHK: Otto H. Kahn Papers, Firestone Library, Princeton University.

RCAC: Rockefeller Center Archive Center, New York, NY. Citations that include a number (e.g., "RCAC, #152") reference press releases from the Rockefeller Center publicity department, which were numbered consecutively and are stored at the archive in chronological order. Citations that include the signifier "cap" come from captions and photographs stored at the RCAC, with volume name and/or number as appropriate. Letters, inter-office memoranda, and other RCAC material cited here have been stored for reference at the archive in a separate file entitled "Okrent, Great Fortune."

RCMHA: Radio City Music Hall Archives, New York, NY.
RFA: Rockefeller Family Archives, Rockefeller Archive Center, Sleepy Hollow, NY.
TIA: Time Inc. Archives, New York, NY.
TIEF: Time Inc. Editorial Files, New York, NY. This subset of the Time Inc. archives consists of original reports from correspondents and other research files for articles published in the company's various magazines.

Publications
AF: *Architectural Forum*
AmArch: *American Architect*
CB##: *Current Biography* (where ## = year)
JSAH: *Journal of the Society of Architectural Historians*
NYDN: *New York Daily News*
NYHT: *New York Herald Tribune*
NYP: *New York Post*
NYT: *New York Times*
NYW: *New York World*
NYWT: *New York World-Telegram*
RCW: *Rockefeller Center Weekly*
RCM: *Rockefeller Center Magazine*
RERBG: *Real Estate Record and Builders' Guide*
TNY: *The New Yorker*
WSJ: *Wall Street Journal*

Other periodicals are identified by their full name. Periodical citations that contain no page numbers reference incomplete clippings in various files and scrapbooks.

Reference Works
DAB: *Dictionary of American Biography*
ANB: *American National Biography*

PROLOGUE

2   **a simple:** RFA 2Z, B2 F25, Junior to Senior, 5/23/28.

2   **The Opera Company itself:** RFA 2C, B81 F607, Lee to Junior, 5/25/28.

3   **gave the meeting:** RFA 2C, B100 F761, W. G. Van Schmus to Nelson, 10/2/39.

3   **I was asked to join:** Fosdick, 264.

CHAPTER 1: *The Heart of This Great City*

5   **most erudite:** *Life,* 11/24/45.

5   **bootlicker:** Marrin, 14–15.

5   **aggressive and violent:** ibid.

6   **harvesting machine:** Alva Johnston, "Cosmos," *TNY,* 11/8/30, 29.

6   **belt of forest trees:** CA, public relations department memo, 6/10/53.

6   **a man of profuse:** ibid.

8 **the most courageous act:** Koolhaas, 18–19.

9 **at what point:** Christopher Trump, "Columbia's Million Dollar Deal," *Change,* 3/73, 15–19.

9 **chocolate-coloured:** quoted in Conrad, 33.

10 **Hughes believed:** William J. Stern, "Urbanities: How Dagger John Saved New York's Irish," *City Journal,* Spring 1977, 103.

10 **there is no noise:** quoted in L. Morris, 113.

11 **I can still hear:** quoted in Chernow, 219.

11 **a visual summary:** quoted in Hawes, 79–80.

11 **If they want:** T. Wolfe, 4.

11 **narrow houses:** quoted in Simon, 126.

11 **unofficial Mrs. Huntington:** ibid.

12 **gaslit carnival of vice:** Daley, 88.

13 **The attention of the trustees:** Butler, vol. 1, 135.

14 **I am told:** CA, Butler to Goetze, 1/20/28.

14 **We have only to look at:** CA, Goetze to Butler, 1/21/28.

15 **slapped down:** Eaton, 241–43.

15 **insulted, abused:** Matz, 4–5.

15 **the Astors, the three Vanderbilts:** Kolodin, *Metropolitan Opera,* 4.

15 **a more amazing example; enormous malt-house:** *NYW,* 10/28/1883, cited in Stern, *1930,* 818.

15 **sidesaddle:** Kolodin, *Story,* 24–25.

16 **in which ladies:** unattributed, quoted in Matz, 101–2.

16 **exceptional sightlines:** Harry Jameson, "The Ordeal of the Opera," *TNY,* 8/27/27, 28.

16 **the flyleaf between:** Wecter, 155.

17 **in two or three years:** Matz, 61–62.

17 **feudal barons:** ibid., 99.

17 **one historian suggests:** Stern, "Urbanities."

18 **a town frequently:** unattributed, quoted in Matz, 4–5.

20 **The accommodations for those patrons:** RFA 2C, B81 F607, Kahn to Cutting, 1/26/26.

20 **If the music lovers:** quoted in Kolodin, *Story,* 21.

21 **be in a position themselves:** quoted in Mayer, 159.

21 **cultured rail-splitter:** "Opera Houser," *TNY,* 4/9/27, 19.

22 **very well heartily approve:** OHK, B395, Cutting to Kahn, 2/23/27.

23 **conferences with statesmen:** *NYT,* 6/2/27, 28.

23 **As well commission Brangwyn:** Jameson, *TNY,* 8/27/27, 28.

24 **a democratic house:** quoted in Matz, 101–2.

24 **And where is Broadway:** CHK-I, Robert O'Connor.

24 **not congested:** *NYT,* 2/4/28, 2.

25 **Why not put it:** quoted in Collins, 6.

25 **succumb[ed] to a stress:** OHK, B333, Morris's meeting notes, 10/28/27.

25 **woke up one morning:** *NYHT,* 5/25/49, 18.

26 **twelve new corners:** CA, Butler remarks to trustees, 5/3/26.

27 **The Heart of This Great City:** quoted in Page, 32.

27 **It was I who conceived:** MOA, Tonnelé to George Sloan, 12/22/43.

27 **but it fathered my thought:** Winston Weisman, "Who Designed Rockefeller Center?," *JSAH,* 3/51, 12.

28 **richest, most exclusive:** Strouse, 362.

28 **the property contiguous:** CA, Goetze to Butler, 1/20/28.

28 **show a way out:** Morris to Cutting, 2/17/28, quoted in Weisman, 14.

29 **permanency of income:** OHK, B372, Morris file memo, 3/10/28.

29 **Mr. R. Fulton Cutting called up:** C. A. Cochran to Morris, 4/24/28, quoted in Weisman, 144–45.

29 **Pulling teeth is a delectable:** MOA, B394 F2, Kahn to Cravath, 4/10/28.

29 **family physician to big business:** *WSJ,* 11/10/34.

30   enlightened self-interest: Hiebert,59.
30   This is the first advice: quoted in Hiebert, 100.
31   Poison Ivy: ibid., 297.
31   Paid Liar: *New York Call,* 3/7/15, 2.
31   has devoted his energies: quoted in Hiebert, 297–99.
31   I cannot come to any other: OHK, B354, Lee to Kahn, 5/5/28.
32   The whole thing stands or falls: quoted in Weisman, 15–16.
32   The key to the whole situation: RFA 2C, B81 F607, Lee to Junior, 5/25/28.

General sources for Chapter 1: **Butler:** Dorothy Bromley, "Nicholas Murray Butler: Portrait of a Reactionary," in *American Mercury,* 3/35; Johnston, in *TNY;* author interview, Michael Rosenthal, 12/17/02. **Hosack and the Upper Estate:** Bender; Robbins; David Garrard Lowe, "The Triumph of Rockefeller Center," *City Journal,* Summer 1995; Trump, in *Change.* **Development of Fifth Avenue:** Hawes; Simon; Lowe, "The Triumph." **Sixth Avenue El:** Daley. **Kahn and the opera:** Collins; Eaton; Kolodin; Matz; Mayer. **Hearst and 57th Street corridor:** Nasaw; Swanberg, *Citizen Hearst;* Stern, *1930.* **Lee:** Hiebert. **Metropolitan Club:** Porzelt; Strouse.

CHAPTER 2: *A Commonplace Person*

34   You know, I didn't: "The House of John D.," *Fortune,* 12/31, 54.
34   You can never forget: RFA 2Z, B20, Laura S. Rockefeller to Junior, 7/23/99.
34   it was his mother who: quoted in Stasz, 106.
34   there, like air or food: quoted in Chernow, 187–88.
34   I am glad my son has told me: quoted ibid., 198.
35   nervous collapse: Stasz, 98–99.
35   shy [and] ill-adjusted: quoted ibid.

35   I do not make friends: quoted in Chernow, 347.
35   Only at Brown did I enjoy: *NYDN,* 11/26/61, 98.
36   He could spend a half-hour: Stasz, 131.
36   a plain, simple, earnest: quoted in Chernow, 357.
36   eager, impetuous, insistent: quoted in Schenkel, 37.
36   a postgraduate degree: quoted ibid., 38.
36   sickened him: quoted in Chernow, 550.
36   Of my ability: quoted in Collier and Horowitz, 99.
37   Your fortune is rolling: quoted in Chernow, 563.
37   she was so gay and young: quoted in Kert, 3.
37   I don't think too much church: quoted in Manchester, 32.
37   a zest for everything: Kert, 41.
38   miss you so sadly: quoted ibid., 204.
39   the charred bodies: Hiebert, 99.
39   one of the most important: Collier and Horowitz, 131.
39   marvelous, vigorous, courageous: Fosdick, 148.
39   adopted any spirit of conciliation: Schenkel, 48.
39   he has never said anything: Chernow, 621.
41   the world's most famous business address: ibid., 222.
41   It was rather expected of me: quoted ibid., 509.
41   defending himself: L. J. Horowitz, 73.
42   a potential power: "The House of John D.," *Fortune,* 12/31.

General sources for Chapter 2: **Junior:** Chernow; Fosdick; Reich; Schenkel; Stasz; Harr and Johnson, *Century;* D. Rockefeller, *Memoirs;* author interview, David Rockefeller, 4/02. **Abby:** Kert; Stasz; D. Rockefeller, *Memoirs.*

CHAPTER 3: *These Properties Will Be Greatly Increased in Value*

43 auto-intoxication: Reich, 9.
44 I am happy to enclose: RFA 2Z, B2 F26, Junior to Senior, 7/5/29.
44 when the sunset; cream soups: RFA 2Z, B2 F160, Junior diaries.
44 Advice, etc.: RFA 2Z, B32, Junior reference files.
44 cabinet: "The House of John D.," *Fortune*, 12/31.
45 the man who votes: *NYT*, 2/15/52.
45 rotogravurish: "A Phenomenon of Exploitation," *AF*, 10/34, 292–98.
45 Your barrel is full: quoted in Fosdick, 411.
45 would have office papers with me: RFA 2H, B123 F913, Heydt to Debevoise, 5/8/29.
46 adopted son: RFA 2H, B124 F920, Junior and sons to Heydt, 11/6/41.
46 a service department from which: *NYT*, 5/24/25.
46 Chauncey Depew was at Number 17: quoted in Fosdick, 22.
47 only a Rockefeller can afford: COHP, Peter Grimm.
48 that large majority of business men: RFA 2Z, B2 F25, Kahn to Jr., 2/14/28.
48 ten minutes of your time: RFA 2C, B81 F607, Kahn to Junior, 5/25/28.
48 would be very noticeable; in view of the possible: Krinsky, 202.
50 not a single dissenting voice: RFA 2Z, B57 F499, Heydt to Junior, 9/6/28.
50 whether the opera: RFA 2 C, B77 F572, Albert B. Ashforth to Heydt, 9/5/28.
50 rather unfriendly: RFA 2Z, B57 F499, Junior to Heydt, 9/6/28.
51 I feel sure: RFA 2Z, B57 F499, Heydt to Junior, 9/8/28.
51 Some time when occasion; I had hoped; I found that the lowest: RFA 2C, B71, Butler to Junior, 9/27/28.
51 the principal from the other side: CA, Butler to Goetze, 12/20/28.

52 it encourages several: CA, Butler to Goetze, 9/17/28.
52 detailed as they are: CA, Butler to Goetze, 9/29/28.
52 whenever Butler pronounced: COHP, James T. Shotwell.
52 I know perfectly well: CA, Butler to M. Hartley Dodge, 12/17/28.
52 Were he to die: CA, Butler to Hall, 12/12/28.
53 Is it ready; Mr. Aldrich drew: Harrison Dimmitt, "That Was New York," *TNY*, 8/18/34, 46–48.
53 severely censured: CHRIS-2.
53 Columbia . . . has nothing to do: *NYHT*, 1/29; date on clipping missing.
53 to the mutual advantage: CA, trustee minutes, 12/3/28, 261.
54 No, we're not going to sell: author interview, Alton Marshall, 5/5/00.
54 expedition to Africa; president's oil can: CA, Butler memo to trustee committee, 2/21/29.
54 the persistent belief: CA, Butler to Jackson Reynolds, 2/18/29.
55 the most important real estate transaction: *NYW*, 1/24/29.
55 commercial paradise: *NYHT*, 1/29 (exact date unclear from clipping).
55 huge: *NYT*, 1/23/29.
55 the pressure of population: *NYT*, 5/24/25.
55 the requirements of existence: Angly, 5.
55 Select your real estate: *NYA*, 1/24/29.

General sources for Chapter 3: **Junior:** see Chapter 2 sources. **Heydt:** Kert. **Real estate in West 50s:** Allen, *Rockefeller;* Weisman.

CHAPTER 4: *I Chose the Latter Course*

57 neo-frumpy: White and Willensky, *AIA Guide,* 872.
58 rental architects: Newhouse, 36.
58 good, prompt: CHK-I, Webster Todd.

58   a combination of many of the best: RFA 2C, B77 F572, Albert Ashforth to Heydt, 9/5/28.

58    $5 million: RFA 2Z, B57 F499, Heydt to Junior, 9/6/28.

59   Hofmeister: Krinsky, 34–35.

59   in a big operation like this: *RCW,* 3/14/55.

59   Romance is the greatest: Geoffrey Hellman, "The Man Behind Prometheus, I" *TNY,* 11/14/36, 32.

59   We had heard of Princeton: Hellman, "The Man Behind Prometheus, II," *TNY,* 11/21/36, 24.

59   selling, romance, dog fights: Hellman, *TNY,* I, 32.

59   Life . . . is made up of music: Todd, *Living,* 160.

59   For an architect: Hellman, *TNY,* I, 34.

59   He was a master: William P. Vogel Jr., in Todd, *Living,* xix.

60   Changing from: *The Boulevard,* 11/31, 25.

60   the obstruction department: "A Phenomenon of Exploitation," *AF,* 10/34, 292–98.

60   the largest tourist business: *Life,* 1/12/42.

61   benevolent acerbity: Vogel, in Todd, *Living,* xix.

61   it was simply one building: Todd, *Living,* xiii.

62   If the Graybar Building: Kilham, 116.

63   I am now plaettbar: OHK, B409, 5/9/29.

63   I wish you'd figure out: COHP, Peter Grimm.

63   What is causing delay: RFA 2C, B107 F799, Junior to Heydt, 8/17/29.

63   It does not seem that: RFA 2C, B107 F799, Heydt to Junior, 8/15/29.

65   caressing, almost hypnotic: Hellman, *TNY,* II, 25.

65   Mr. Todd has never made a failure: RFA 2C, B107 F799, Heydt to Junior, 8/15/29.

65   All of my time: Todd, *Living,* 9.

66   a great disappointment: RFA 2C, B107 F797, Junior to Debevoise, 8/31/29.

66   Harvard, of course: RFA 2C, B107, Words to Debevoise, 8/21/29.

66   in-house executive organization; borders on absurdity: RFA 2C, B78 F581, Aldrich to Debevoise, 9/24/29.

66   Defend high salaries: Hellman, *TNY,* II, 26.

66   largely dissipated; frank to say: RFA 2C, B78 F581, Aldrich to Debevoise, 9/16/29.

67   closed mind and an open fly: Reich, 249.

67   I never smile south: quoted in *Century Association Yearbook, 1975,* 183.

67   contemplated that the Opera; so tender and considerate: RFA 2C, B107 F799, Heydt to Junior, 8/19/29.

68   way beyond his powers: RFA 2C, B107 F799, Woods to Debevoise, 8/21/29.

68   The Opera House would be a dead spot: RFA 2C, B81 F607, Todd to Aldrich, 12/4/29.

68   can't be used for anything else: Todd, *Living,* 91.

68   if I could only stick the Opera House: Hellman, *TNY,* I, 33.

68   genteel blackmail: Harr and Johnson, *Century,* 323.

68   John, I've just come from a meeting; Winthrop, go back: quoted in Johnson, 59.

69   the primary cause, he believed: Kolodin, *Story,* 299.

69   no longer found much dignity: Collins, 262.

69   board of directors . . . was very dumb: COHP, Peter Grimm.

69   Now that we don't dare: Vanderbilt, 227–29.

69   pressed the least shiny: CHRIS-2.

70   unthinkable: ibid.

70   Mr. Rockefeller lost no time: ibid.

70   it came about; only two courses; the latter course: Fosdick, 264.

General sources for Chapter 4: **Reinhard and Hofmeister:** Krinsky; Newhouse; Weisman. **Todd:** Hellman in *TNY;* Kilham; Todd, *Living.* **Seal Harbor and Mount Desert:** Harr and Johnson, *Century;* Todd, *Living;* www. wam.umd.edu/~sepsmith. **Junior and opera:** Christy memoir.

CHAPTER 5: *Architecture Never Lies*

71   **catalytic:** Huxtable, 291.
71   **influenced my generation:** CentA, Edward Steese, in memorial letter, Hugh Ferriss file.
72   **closely juxtaposed:** Ferriss, 15.
72   **Is God in:** unattrib., quoted in Burns and Sanders, 232.
72   **the enterprise of business:** quoted in Stern, *1900,* 145.
73   **ambassador of the arts:** Hawes, 15.
73   **palatial urbanism:** N. White, *Architecture Book,* 31.
73   **dominate the field:** Kilham, 64–65.
74   **some mighty force:** quoted in Burns, 231.
74   **a machine:** quoted in Willis, *Form,* 19.
74   **giant signboard:** Heilbrun, 285n.
75   **finger of God:** www.newcolonist.com/ aynrand.html.
75   **hopelessly degraded:** quoted in Giedion, 570.
75   **monster office:** L. Horowitz, 152.
76   **beauty by mistake; final phase:** Kundera, 101.
76   **If the present tendency:** quoted in Wist, 38.
77   **crude clay:** quoted in Tauranac, 58.
77   **remarkable drawings:** *NYW,* 2/5/22.
78   **lilliputian; uncouth; yesterday's critics:** Ferriss, 30.
78   **compulsory cubism:** Conrad, 127.
78   **Architecture never lies:** Ferriss, 16.
79   **parallel effort:** Hanks, 9.
79   **Trivial reminiscences:** Bletter and Robinson, 14.
80   **jaw load:** quoted in Pritchett, 81.
80   **as a whole:** Ferriss, 50.

80   **American cities [are] in danger:** *NYHT,* 11/1/39, 19.
80   **hedonistic Urbanism:** Koolhaas, 204.
81   **disease of growth:** D. L. Miller, 79.
81   **mechanized romanticism; motives; popularized:** AL, Hugh Ferriss Papers, Box 7, Mumford to Jean Ferriss Leich, 7/19/76.
81   **reckless, romantic:** Mumford, "Notes on Modern Architecture," *The New Republic,* 3/18/31, 119–22.
81   **people swarm:** quoted in Kilham, 188.
81   **Congestion is good:** quoted in "In Praise of Congestion," *Time,* 12/14/31, 16.
81   **to assure an appropriate:** RFA 2C, B106 F794, "Board of Consulting Architects Report," 2/20/29.
81   **greatest skyscraper architect:** quoted in Stern, *Raymond Hood,* 25.

General sources for Chapter 5: **New York architecture:** Stern, *1900;* Stern, *1930;* Page; Hawes. **Skyscrapers:** Bletter and Robinson; Goldberger, *Skyscraper;* Willis, *Form.* **Congestion:** Koolhaas.

CHAPTER 6: *Tears of Joy to a Small Business Man*

82   **the most diligent:** *Vanity Fair,* 2/33, 12–13.
83   **great prominence; moral rectitude; beautician:** CHRIS-2.
83   **from and after the date:** CA, Goetze to tenants, 1/15/29.
83   **If there is one thing:** F. L. Allen, "Radio City: Cultural Center?," *Harper's,* 4/32, 537.
84   **a sort of Montmartre:** RFA 2C, B78, translation of article by Pierre Lamure, in *Le Jour,* 8/19/34.
84   **sold Rockefeller:** Claire Klein, "The Rockefeller Center Property," *Columbia University Quarterly,* 2/41, 59–60.
84   **pool rooms; bare-faced use:** Fifth Avenue Association, 37.

85 considerable uneasiness; press statements: RFA 2C, B78 F581, Pedrick to Junior, 4/14/30.

85 All you need: Kobler, *Ardent,* 224.

85 a highly respectable: CHRIS-I, 27.

85 in order to avoid: Kobler, *Ardent,* 228–30.

86 Graham and Reilley: CHRIS-2, "Rider."

86 a character straight out of: CHRIS-1, 30.

86 instrumental in inducing: ibid.

87 a boom trading: "Rockefeller City," *TNY,* 2/16/29, 11.

87 unscrupulous speculators; extortion: RFA 2C, B106 F796, Hall to Heydt, 8/5/29.

87 if, by any chance; create conditions: RFA 2C, B106 F796, Heydt to Junior, 7/19/29.

87 He was crazy: "Nostalgic Twins," *TNY,* 3/2/63, 24.

89 you are . . . the one man: CA, Goetze to Butler, 7/31/30.

90 the Wendels never: Louis Reynolds, quoted in Page, 46–47.

90 Tenant shall make: Rosenman, 18.

91 From abroad we have claims: quoted ibid., 46.

93 The . . . southeast corner: RFA I2C, B77 F573, Heydt to Junior, 6/4/31.

93 a Scotsman: CHRIS-1.

93 furnished rooms: "Bad Boys," *TNY,* 10/31/31.

94 he was motivated: RCAC, #103, 12/9/32.

95 my fair Portia: Dean, 117.

96 devote the entire: CHRIS-1.

96 university's want of honor: CA, Saxe to Trustees' Committee on Legal Affairs, Cromwell subcommittee, 12/17/30.

96 take [my] pants off: ibid.

97 interest and friendship: CA, Butler to Goetze, 8/2/30.

97 a loss of income; impairment of the aesthetic: RFA 2C, B72 F555, Christy to Heydt, 1/24/30.

97 steadfastly refusing: CA, Saxe to Trustees' Committee, 12/17/30.

97 something fine in exchange: quoted in CA, Saxe to Butler, 11/19/30.

97 our good friend: CA, Butler to Goetze, 8/2/30.

97 Lawyer Cromwell's: "Faces of the Month," *Fortune,* 2/32, 129.

98 I should have cancelled; very much averse: RFA 2C, B77 F578, Heydt to Debevoise, 3/9/32.

General sources for Chapter 6: **Upper Estate residents:** Dau. **Speakeasy culture:** Kaytor; Kobler; Morand. **Lease purchases:** CHRIS-2. **Wendels:** Rosenman; *NYT* coverage of Ella's death and will. **Maxwell and Hurley's:** Alpern and Durst. **Cromwell:** Dean; Loth.

CHAPTER 7: *I Like Having a Lot of People Against Me*

99 The contemporary designer: quoted in Bletter and Robinson, 35.

100 strange, irresponsible objects: quoted in Kert, 283.

101 gentlemen—not kikes: quoted in Irish, 97.

101 The blue book: Allene Talmey, "Man Against the Sky," *TNY,* 4/11/31, 24–27.

101 fighting spooks: quoted in Francis S. Swales, "Draftsmanship and Architecture as Exemplified by the Work of Raymond M. Hood," *Pencil Points,* 5/28, 259.

102 has had to do with: RFA 2C, B106 F794, Pope to Junior, 10/19/28.

102 a possible treatment: AL, Corbett Papers, B6, F1, 2/20/29.

102 in no sense a competition: ibid.

102 former architect and decorator: RFA 2C, B107 F799, Melzer to Junior, 5/21/29.

103 focal tall building: J. Adams et al., 15.

103 Sixth Avenue subway: ibid.

103 a conservative type of architecture: RFA 2C, B107 F862, 7/9/29.

103 great architectural interest: quoted ibid.

104 final plans will not differ: Kilham, 150.

104 tall, spare; So you're the writer: Todd, *Living*, vii; Vogel's introduction.

104 slow to hire: NYA, unsigned correction memo to Hellman, 4/23/36.

105 Morris partisans: CHK-I, Robert O'Connor.

105 comfort and satisfaction: OHK, B333, F1, 7/15/27.

105 word from Todd: RFA, B107, F799, 10/1/29.

105 violent disagreements: MOA, Edward Ziegler to George A. Sloan, 5/10/44.

105 the largest single opportunity: "The House of John D.," *Fortune*, 12/31, 54.

106 a happy combination: *NYW*, 8/16/34.

106 undoubtedly provoked: Ferriss, 28.

107 Hire another man: AL, Hood Papers, F1, Donald M. Douglass to Walter Kilham Jr., 3/12/70.

107 working all day; a scheme for: quoted in Kilham, 113.

107 architectural style and grouping: quoted in Newhouse, 38.

108 Because he had *ideas*: CHK-I, Webster Todd.

108 I like having a lot of people: Todd, *Living*, 68.

109 this time he wasn't an architect: Kilham, 115.

109 subject at all times; Todd & Brown: RFA 2C, B75 F564, agreement between Metropolitan Square and architects, 7/1/30.

109 Still, the only architects: *see* Canato, 114.

109 architects were unemployed: Newhouse, 58.

109 sound of the riveting machines: Koolhaas, 117.

109 redesigning of the very heart: *Fortune*, 12/31.

110 For the client; There remains: quoted in Kilham, 185.

General sources for Chapter 7: **New York architects in the twenties**: Bletter and Robinson. **J. R. Pope**: Stern, *1900*. **Todd**: Hellman in *TNY*. **Hood**: Kilham; Talmey in *TNY*.

CHAPTER 8: *A Genius*

111 a joy ride: T. E. Tallmadge, quoted in Kilham, 185.

111 Intersections are where: quoted ibid., 151.

111 designing arm: quoted in "The Editor's Diary," *Architecture*, 11/29, 309.

111 Little Ray Riding Hood: Francis S. Swales, "Draftsmanship and Architecture as Exemplified by the Work of Raymond M. Hood," *Pencil Points*, 5/28, 259–69.

111 Never decide: quoted in J. B. Griswold, "Nine Years Ago Raymond M. Hood Was Behind in His Rent," *American Magazine*, 10/31, 52.

111 patron saint: Rayne Adams, *Architecture*, 3/31, 129.

112 custodian of nineteenth: Balfour, 213.

112 The instruction of the Ecole: Le Corbusier, 118.

112 Beaux-Arts aroma: Kilham, 38.

112 Downtown, where you pass: AAA, Hood Papers, R795, 10/28/06.

113 in some dirty but: AAA, Hood Papers, R795, 9/6/06.

113 the greatest architect: Kilham, 50.

114 anyone who could eat so much: quoted in *NYHT*, 8/15/34.

114 A Vocabulary: *Pencil Points*, 6/22 and 7/22.

114 left raw; four visible faces: *NYT*, 8/23/31.

116 clarity and logic: quoted in Kilham, 60.

116 It is not a tower: *International Competition*, 37.

116 illogical: Solomonson, 146.

116 put the sky within: Kamin, 14.

116 his finest spree: Talmey, "Man Against the Sky," *TNY*, 4/11/31, 24–27.

117 must absolutely be stopped: *Chicago Tribune*, 12/17/22.

117   the *Tribune* [had] cast itself: Solomonson, 39.

117   literally camped: Frederick W. Revels, Syracuse University, quoted ibid., 95.

118   a flea: Walker, 25.

118   smote [the jury]: *Chicago Tribune,* 11/30/22.

118   a priceless pearl; a mind unaccustomed: quoted in Solomonson, 171.

118   embroidery was in vogue: Kilham, 60.

118   gathered such praise: N. White, *Architecture Book,* 266.

119   the unpleasant effect; black holes: *NYT,* 8/15/34, editorial page.

119   a negro prizefighter: quoted in Koppe, 11.

119   the first- and second-prize: Goldberger, *Skyscraper,* 61.

119   My tablecloths are all covered: quoted in *NYT,* 8/15/34.

120   honest architecture: Raymond M. Hood, "The Spirit of Modern Art," *AF,* 11/29, 445–48.

120   Utility produced beauty: quoted in Canato, 7.

120   The Tribune and Radiator buildings are both: quoted in Witold Rybczynski, "The Lure of the New," *Preservation,* 5/91 and 6/91.

121   sane enthusiasts: Stern, *Raymond Hood,* 8.

121   Make it look as if: Solomonson, 16.

122   beauty stuff: quoted in "Hood," *AF,* 2/35.

122   After waiting till: Kilham, 19–20.

122   things which [the client]: Walter H. Kilham Jr., "The Way of an Architect with a Client," *AIA Journal,* 9/72.

122   do[ing] a little zoning: quoted in Kilham, 23.

122   the first and almost dominant: Raymond M. Hood, "The New Building," *AF,* 11/30.

122   plans, exteriors: ibid.

123   unrolled newsprint: Kenneth M. Murchison, "As I See the News Building: Critical Comment," *AF,* 11/30.

123   a pair of red: ibid.

123   If a man asks: Hood, "The Spirit of Modern Art," *AF,* 11/29.

123   a factory at a factory price: Talmey, *TNY,* 4/11/31.

123   as though a shining new world: Jordy, 59.

123   Why not try nothing: Hood, "The News Building," *AF,* 11/30.

123   That's not architecture; So much: quoted in *New York Sun,* 8/14/34.

General sources for Chapter 8: **Hood's life:** Kilham; Stern, *Raymond Hood;* Talmey in *TNY.* **Tribune competition:** Solomonson; Kamin.

CHAPTER 9: *A Hundred Lawsuits*

124   the whole economy: quoted in Swanberg, *Luce,* 82.

124   to relieve the suffering: RFA 2C, B68, Christy to Debevoise, 10/31/30.

124   no housing shortage; borrowing trouble: RFA 2C, B68, Debevoise to Christy, 11/3/30.

124   who else had any money: quoted in Shachtman, 140.

125   Just to work my way up: Persico, 30–31.

125   wealthiest young woman: *NYT,* 10/1/30.

125   ABBY ROCKEFELLER WEDS: *NYT,* 2/26/25.

125   According to a family member: Laura Rockefeller Chasin, quoted in Harr and Johnson, *Century,* 101–2.

126   uncomfortable with himself: author interview, David Rockefeller, 4/02.

126   had not done much of anything: unattributed, quoted in Geoffrey Hellman, "Out of the Cocoon on the Fifty-sixth Floor," *TNY,* 11/4/72, 66.

126   associated with father: *Time,* 11/21/32.

126   He suffered from being outstripped: quoted ibid. 63.

126   Art is one of the great resources; enriches the spiritual: Chase, *Abby,* 130.

126   granite indifference: quoted in Kert, 283.

127   $25,0000 in purchases; Affectionately, John: Collier and Horowitz, 99.

127   I showed Papa the pictures: quoted in Reich, 101–2.

127   a wonderful trip to Boston: quoted in J. A. Morris, *Nelson Rockefeller,* 72.

128   a grand state visit: Reich, 81.

129   showed no interest in me: quoted ibid., 82.

129   HE MUST DO WHAT HE THINKS: RFA 2H, B122 F909, Junior to [unknown], 10/20/30.

129   No one would have believed: *Chicago Tribune,* 1/16/29.

130   very much of a gent: quoted in Newhouse, 38.

130   will not differ radically: Kilham, 150.

130   the first architect: Ivy Lee Papers, Seeley Mudd Library, Princeton University, Box 83, F5: Todd, Robertson, and Todd press release, 10/28/29.

131   a conservative type of architecture; buildings to build; sound financially: RFA 2C, B107 F802, Morris to Woods, 12/21/29.

131   Should Mr. Rockefeller feel: ibid.

131   rather have a hundred lawsuits: RFA 2C, B69 F515, quoted in Raymond Fosdick to Debevoise, 8/27/30.

131   I suggest no charge: RFA 2C, B107 F802, Morris to Junior, 7/13/29; quoted in RFA 2C, B69 F515, Heydt to Junior, 12/23/29.

132   $2,250, for the few sketches: RFA 2C, B69 F515, quoted in Heydt to Junior, 12/23/29.

132   similarity to the present scheme: Raymond M. Hood, "The Design of Rockefeller City," *AF,* 1/32, 1–12.

132   Morris put away: *NYA,* unsigned correction memo to Hellman, 4/27/36.

132   Ben Morris declined; stayed loyal: Todd, *Living,* 90.

132   Metropolitan Sq. Site: AL, B. W. Morris Papers, flat file.

General sources for Chapter 9: Depression: F. L. Allen, *Since.* Junior's finances: Chernow. Babs: Stasz. Abby: Chase, Abby; Kert. Johnny: Harr and Johnson, *Century;* Harr and Johnson, *Conscience.* Nelson: Reich; Persico.

CHAPTER 10: *Let Owen Young Do It*

133   He did not have intimate: author interview, David Rockefeller, 4/02.

135   making this new site; worth looking into: RFA 2C, B87, Junior to Todd, 12/27/29.

135   As you know, . . . one can fly: RFA 2C, B87, Harden to Junior, 1/27/30.

135   the most marvelous thing: quoted in Newhouse, 39.

135   This man Owen D. Young: William Soskin, *NYP,* quoted in Case and Case, 581.

135   miracle man: "Life of Owen D. Young, Part III," *Fortune,* 3/31, 90.

136   Instead of saying: *Forbes,* 10/32.

136   makes Governor Roosevelt: quoted in Case and Case, 567–71.

137   lien on science: "Blue Chip," *Fortune,* 9/32, 45.

138   radio's educational possibilities: quoted in Case and Case, 488.

138   adamantly opposed: D. Rockefeller, 55n.

138   no longer considered apart: RFA 2C, B87, file memorandum, 1/17/30.

138   Excluding Jews: Collins, 46.

138   hope to divert immigrant students: Bender, 288–89.

139   I want to make an appeal: quoted in Kert, 208.

139   slippery Jew speculator: RFA 2C, B69 F517, Junior to Debevoise, 8/25/31.

139   a good mixture of prominent men: RFA RG5, B195 F878, Debevoise to John D. Rockefeller 3rd, 7/22/36.

139   extremely competent; no more strange brothers: RCAC, John Roy to Joseph Brown, 10/31/34.

139   people of the chosen; serious mistake; sorts applications: RCAC, Brown to John Roy, 11/1/34.

139   preferred dealing with [Young]: Bilby, 89.

140   No. 1 Boy Wonder: "Toscanini on the Air," *Fortune,* 1/38, 62.

140   a communist's idea: Marek, 220.

140   simple Radio Music Box; thought well of the idea: quoted in Lewis, 115–16.

141   merchandised one miracle: *Fortune,* 9/32, 45.

142   Thinking out loud: Todd, *Living,* 140.

143   Rockefeller Plans Huge: *NYT,* 6/14/30.

General sources for Chapter 10: **Young:** J. and E. N. Case, Lewis. **RCA:** Lewis; Barnouw, *Tower.* **Sarnoff:** Barnouw (both); Bilby; Lewis; Sobel.

CHAPTER 11: *Who Designed Rockefeller Center?*

145   The architects cooperated: AL, Harrison Papers, B3 F2, 11/10/37.

146   From now on . . . this square: RCAC, Todd memo, 12/6/29.

146   six-year charrette: *Century Association Yearbook, 1999,* 322.

146   almost a factory like: TIA, Webb & Knapp Report, 7/19/37.

147   order and the efficiency: Kilham, 13.

147   gang planning: quoted in Josh Greenfeld, "Curtain Going Up for Wallace Harrison," *NYT Magazine,* 8/21/66, 36.

147   unusual interest: *AF,* 1/32, 1.

147   You are hereby authorized: RCAC, overtime approval form, 12/2/31.

148   If the drawing you wanted: Kilham, 136.

000   ask for a little indulgence: *AmArch,* 11/19/24, cited in Bletter and Robinson, 10.

149   We have vertical: quoted in W. Taylor, *In Pursuit,* 36.

149   basket weaving: Corbett, "The Problem of Traffic Congestion, and a Solution," *AF,* 3/27, 201–8.

149   Venice: AL, Corbett Papers, "An Architect's Vision of the Titan City—1975," B4.

150   Seven or eight years; Once a shining: John Cushman Fistere, "Poets in Steel," *Vanity Fair,* 12/31, 58.

150   man who got the work out: quoted, unattributed, in J. Adams et al., 20.

150   Can I be of any help: AL, Harrison Papers, B2 F9, book proposal for biography of Nelson, 3/76.

150   You and the building: CHK-I, Harrison.

150   equable, accommodating: Gill, 155.

151   America . . . is the only: AL, Harrison Papers, B6 F1, notes on WNET questionnaire, 1978.

151   like a column: Ellen M. Harrison, quoted in Newhouse, 28.

151   born somewhere else: E. B. White, *Here Is,* 20.

151   clear glass bowl: quoted in Newhouse, 12.

152   architectural washing: Herbert Warren Wind, "You're Lucky If You Can Come Close," *TNY,* 11/20/54, 51.

152   half related: CHK-I, Webster Todd.

152   compliant servant: Gill, 156.

152   When all is said: quoted in Wind, *TNY,* 11/20/54.

152   It is needless to say; approach to the problem; cobwebs of whimsy: Hood, "The Design of Rockefeller Center," *AF,* 1/32, 1–12.

153   jobs: quoted in H. J. Woolf, "An Architect Hails the Rule of Reason," *NYT Magazine,* 11/1/31, 6.

153   If you men; Don't shoot us: quoted in Todd, *Living,* 97.

153   spokesman for my associates: *NYT,* 8/23/31, V-1.

153   too timid: CHK-I, Kilham.

154   How could [Junior] look: CHRIS-2, 10.

154   loved projects: author interview, David Rockefeller, 4/02.

155 **artistic handyman:** J. Adams et al., 253.

155 **ideal client:** quoted in Gill, 156–57.

155 **Egyptian style:** *NYT,* 3/36/31, 1.

155 **guild of master:** Reinhard, "Organization for Cooperation," *AF,* 2/32.

156 **jumping into a bull ring:** CHRIS-2, 8–9.

156 **whims are reasonable:** quoted in Stern, *Raymond Hood,* 24.

157 **Form follows finance:** Willis, *Form.*

157 **The view from the tower; landscape those roofs:** *NYT,* 8/23/31, V-1.

157 **very charming and serious:** MOA, Edward Ziegler to George A. Sloan, 5/10/44.

157 **Benign Compromiser:** N. White, *Architecture Book,* 141.

158 **Goddamn it:** AL, Harrison Papers, B2 F9, book proposal, 3/76.

158 **alarmed; had produced so great a number:** Gill, 154.

158 **just tried to get things:** August Heckscher, *Century Association Yearbook, 1982,* 237.

158 **looked in the direction:** Suzannah Lessard, "The Towers of Light," *TNY,* 7/10/78, 32.

159 **I was told; I wish we could all work:** "Symposium, International Style, Exhibition of Modern Architecture, MOMA," *Shelter,* 4/32.

160 **People are always asking:** AL, Harrison Papers, B3 F2, speech to New York City Building Congress, 11/10/37.

160 **fling of imagination:** Weisman, 41–42.

161 **draw[ing] the public interest:** AL, Corbett Papers, B6 F1, "Report from One of Board of Consulting Architects . . .".

161 **plain, beautiful slab:** COHP, Wallace Harrison.

161 **slat:** *NYT,* 8/23/31, V-1.

161 **I have never collected:** quoted in Winston Weisman, "Slab Buildings," *Architectural Review,* 2/52, 119–23.

161 **bad space:** quoted in Jordy, 46.

161 **from the outside in:** Todd, *Living,* 88–89.

161 **our chief architects:** ibid.

161 **expand his ego; man as ant:** Lessard, *TNY,* 7/10/78, 43.

162 **As each elevator:** quoted in Giedion, 573.

162 **an abrupt climax:** quoted in Canato, 27.

162 **largest frozen fountain:** Thomas van Leeuwen, quoted ibid, 29.

162 **It is not the way:** Stein, 202.

162 **tapestry effect:** quoted in Newhouse, 45.

162 **mere lineations:** Giedion, 573.

163 **wondering what sort:** quoted in Kilham, 88.

163 **a camel should have been:** author interview, Paul Goldberger, 2/00.

163 **The view of Rockefeller Center:** *RCW,* 2/14/35.

General sources for Chapter 11: **Harrison:** Gill; Newhouse; Wind, *TNY.* **Graybar offices:** Kilham; *AF,* 1/32–10/32. **International Style:** Hitchcock and Johnson; Stern, *1930;* T. Wolfe.

CHAPTER 12: *Wondering Where I'm Going to Get the Money*

165 **We considered several:** quoted in Kobler, *Ardent,* 228–30.

165 **you can *see* the noise:** quoted in Douglas, 17.

165 **No experience:** quoted in C. Hood, 54.

165 **a dissonance comprised:** quoted in Douglas, 17.

165 **I feel deeply:** *Life,* 11/17/41, 49.

166 **the number of Negroes:** "The Union: Mother of Clubs," *Fortune,* 12/32, 47.

166 **Stretching . . . from old St. Pat's:** "Hymn to the Citadel of Static," *TNY,* 12/31/32, 12–13.

166 MUST VACATE; TAKE ADVANTAGE: AL, Corbett Papers, B6 F2, photograph.

166 **fight this destroyer:** *The Boulevard,* 11/31, 10.

166 **of Turkish design:** RCAC, chronology.

167 synonym for luxury: *NYHT*, 5/5/49, 18.

167 Committee of Five Hundred: RFA 2C, B112 F10, Jenkins to Junior, 11/19/29.

167 You are going to benefit: RFA 2C, B70 F538, Jenkins to Junior, 2/19/30.

168 a gigantic theatrical; alarming rumors: RFA 2C, B78 F581, Pedrick to Junior, 4/14/30.

168 repulse the invasion; charitable and philanthropic: RFA 2C, B78 F581, Pedrick to Junior, 1/27/30.

168 altogether too officious: RFA 2C, B107 F797, Junior to Lester Abberley, 10/11/30.

168 perfect harmony: *NYW*, 10/16/30.

168 a slippery Jew: RFA 2C, B69 F517, Junior to Debevoise, 28/25/31.

169 take the Columbia Tract; not in good faith: RFA 2C, B71 F540, Debevoise to Woods, 7/16/30.

169 it would only bother him: RFA 2C, B69 F517, Todd to "Miss Adams," secretary to Junior, 8/24/31.

169 Stotesbury . . . telephoned me: RFA 2C, B69 F517, Junior to Debevoise, 8/25/31.

170 Greenfield: CA, Hugh Robertson to Goetze, 1/25/49.

170 I feel all right: quoted in Manchester, 118.

170 A large body: Dwight Macdonald, quoted in Manchester, 67.

171 There has been no financial; Is it worthwhile: RFA 2Z1, B7 F73, Junior to Senior, 10/2/31.

171 equitable adjustment: cited in RFA 2H, B57 F421, Junior to Debevoise, 5/12/32.

171 For my own self-respect; I have never sought: ibid.

172 I did not seek: ibid.

172 immense capital outlays: quoted in Fosdick, 263–64.

172 rock bottom: Todd, *Living*, 109.

173 the production of income: Richmond Shreve, quoted in Abramson, 44.

174 prototypical white shoe: Jackson, 761.

174 very satisfactory: F. W. Ecker, testimony, Temporary National Economic Committee, 2/27/40.

175 the only thing that kept: CHRIS-2, "Rider," 13.

175 Cocktail Caddie: RFA 2C, B78, Travers to Nelson, 8/10/34.

General sources for Chapter 12: "21": Kaytor. Junior's finances: Chernow. Empire State Building: James; Shultz and Simmons; Willis, *Building*. Metropolitan Life and mortgage: CHRIS-1; CHRIS-2; Harr and Johnson, *Century*; James; Todd, *Living*.

CHAPTER 13: *Our Architects Deserve to Remain in Chains*

176 delight and deep satisfaction: RFA 2C, B71 F541, Butler to Junior, 2/9/31.

176 details of the Rockefeller: *RERBG*, 7/5/30, 3.

176 temporarily withheld: *RERBG*, 7/12/30, 3.

177 a marked absence: Hood, *AF*, 1/32, 1–12.

177 You'd never have drawn: COHP, Wallace Harrison.

178 No old stuff: quoted in Stern, *1930*, 606.

179 will be disclosed tonight: *NYT*, 3/5/31, 1.

179 lofty exteriors: *NYT*, 3/6/31, 3.

179 glisten[ing] like a mirage: ibid.

179 the new acropolis: *NYHT*, 3/6/31, 1.

179 a jewel box: ibid.

179 jeweled powder box: *NYT*, 3/6/31, 3.

180 severe simplicity: ibid.

180 addressed himself: Kazin, *Starting Out*, 36.

181 inane romanticism: Mumford, "Notes on Modern Architecture," *The New Republic*, 3/18/31, 119–21.

181 The weakly conceived; failure; wantonly; If Radio City: ibid.

181 affair of bald cubes: *NYHT*, 3/31/31, editorial page.

181 the last atrocity: quoted in Kilham, 155.

181 By all means: ibid.

181 aroused the public: *Pencil Points,* 5/31, 387.

181 ugliest conglomeration: *NYT,* 3/12/31, editorial page.

181 hopeless hodgepodge: *NYT,* 3/9/31.

181 disgraceful symbol: quoted in "The Layman Rebels," *The Nation,* 4/13/31.

181 lacking in imagination: *NYT,* 3/24/31.

182 adventures among buildings: *NYHT,* 4/4/31.

182 intervene before: *NYHT,* 3/31/31.

182 high-power commercial: *NYT,* 4/15/31, IX-4.

182 I should avoid: COHP, Wallace Harrison, 94–95.

182 smiling countenance: "The Radio City of New York," *Shelter,* 5/31, 32.

182 but . . . with a wee bit: quoted ibid.

182 It may be my building: quoted in *NYW,* 8/16/34.

182 fact find: RFA RG 2H, F568 B74, Ivy Lee to Junior, 5/29/31.

183 We're all for Hood: quoted in Kilham, 155.

183 a certain magic: *NYT,* 8/23/31, V-1.

183 figure from classical Athens: quoted in Canato, 115.

183 famous California philosopher: ibid., 158.

184 rejuvenated provincialism; present chaos: Rather, 146–49.

184 Not the victory: www.huskernews.com.

184 expressed considerable interest: RFA 2C, B107 F803, Todd to Woods, 3/1/32.

184 All excerpts from Alexander: RFA 2C, B93 F704, "Thematic Synopsis—Rockefeller City."

185 He practically threw me: quoted in Kilham, 126.

185 People willfully: Mumford, "Frozen Music or Solidified Static? Reflections on Radio City," *TNY,* 6/20/31, 28.

185 this frightened magazine: *TNY,* 7/4/31, 9.

186 I cannot find a word: Mumford, "Mr. Rockefeller's Center," *TNY,* 12/23/33, 29.

186 little scratchy tooth; juvenile badness; inverted mustaches; bad guesses: ibid.

186 not architectural features: Mumford, *TNY,* 10/12/35, 63.

186 This group: Mumford, "The Skyline," *TNY,* 3/11/39, 37.

186 the most exciting mass: Mumford, "Rockefeller Center Revisited," *TNY,* 5/4/40, 73–74.

General sources for Chapter 13: **Mumford:** Jacobs; D. L. Miller. **Alexander:** Canato; Kilham; Masters.

CHAPTER 14: *Desperate for Business*

187 gobble up mouthfuls: F. L. Allen, "Radio City—Cultural Center?," *Harper's,* 4/32, 534.

188 We are having an awful: RCAC, S. W. Straus to Todd, 9/25/31.

188 Let the men: RCAC, Todd to Todd & Brown, 9/25/31.

189 160,000 of them: Hoopes, 153.

189 We wonder if there will ever: quoted in Elson, *World, 1923–1941,* 186–87.

189 civic improvement; participate: quoted in Fosdick, 263–64.

189 Unto he: quoted by Laurance Rockefeller, in PBS series *The American Experience,* "The Rockefellers."

190 Liquidate labor: quoted in Kessner, 169.

190 The practical answer: quoted in L. H. Robbins, "Our 'City Within a City' Lifts Its Final Towers," *NYT Magazine,* 2/13/38, 6.

190 Idle capital: RCAC, press release, 1/18/38.

190 worked elsewhere preparing: Fosdick, 266.

190 army of supply; miners; lumberjacks: RCAC, #2, 7/30/31.

190 most of the business done: RCAC,
N. A. Kenworthy to Todd & Brown,
3/13/33.

191 could never forget: RFA 2C, B68,
Victor Borella to Junior, 10/28/55.

191 In behalf of Humanity: RFA 2C, B78
F580, Welfare Committee of Local 28
of the Sheet Metal Workers International Association to Junior, 7/27/32.

191 the magnanimous spirit: ibid.

192 what with the Depression; you
couldn't blame: quoted in Desmond,
49–50.

193 a time of relaxation: Todd, *Living,* 79.

193 It does give one: quoted in Beard,
Growing Up Republican as cited by
Alan Ryan, the *New York Review of
Books,* 6/26/97.

194 absolutely disgraceful: RCAC, Brown
to E. L. Smith, 9/25/36.

194 convinced that there is nothing: ibid.

194 what we have is good: RCAC, various.

194 Whether the scheme: Kilham, 133–
34.

194 I think brown: RCAC, Brown to
E. L. Smith, 5/22/33.

194 This is what; joe brown: Kilham,
133–34.

195 I doubt if anyone: Webster Todd,
"Testing Men and Materials for Rockefeller City," *AF,* 2/32, 199.

196 gracious; necessary for political:
ibid.

196 provided [they] make satisfactory:
RCAC, Junior, cited in Webster Todd
to E. L. Smith, 2/26/32.

196 if the price of cement: RCAC, Brown
to C. O. Heydt, 3/10/32.

197 You can't even begin to realize:
CHRIS-2, 159.

197 expression of faith in the future: Edwin C. Hill, CBS radio, 12/27/32,
quoted in Fosdick, 271.

198 the tremendous load: Todd, *Living,*
131.

198 the accepted badge: quoted in Abramson, 71.

199 only 50,000 man-hours: RCAC, #792,
3/35.

200 will not bar a colored person:
RCAC, Brown to W. S. Richardson,
5/7/31.

200 agile as goats: Mitchell, 267–79.

200 aristocrats of the site: Abramson,
80–81.

General sources for Chapter 14: **Depression
New York:** F. L. Allen, *Since;* Caro; Gelernter;
Kessner. **Construction during Depression:**
Abramson; Grant. **Rockefeller Center site:**
*Skyscraper Building: The Story of Rockefeller
Center,* film by Walter H. Kilham Jr. **Mo-
hawks:** Mitchell.

CHAPTER 15: *Give 'Em Something
Better*

203 the greatest genius: *NYT,* 4/3/27,
VII-7.

204 high-toned little theater: Hall, 26.

205 only a young man; a national reputation: *Minneapolis Journal,* 10/1/11, 9.

205 Revue de Luxe: *Chicago Tribune,*
6/6/12.

205 It matters not how humble: quoted
in Gabler, *Empire,* 94–105.

205 my ancestors were peasants: *New
York Tribune,* 2/17/18, quoted ibid.

205 an environment so pleasing: *Motion
Picture News,* 12/6/13, quoted ibid., 32.

206 Nothing he ever said or did: quoted
ibid., 34.

206 largest life insurance policy: *NYT,*
6/11/15, 15.

206 Forest City-style: Francisco, 5.

207 Newest, Latest: ibid., 6.

207 Presentations by S. L.: Hall, 66–67.

207 a cultural orgy: Atkinson, 182.

207 somewhere in 1808: Hall, 51.

208 My friends call me: *New York Sun,*
1/13/36.

208 Hello, everybody: *Time,* 2/9/31.

208 Roxy's benediction: Hall, 72.

209 greatest little girl: *Time,* 2/9/31.

209 difficult to conceive: *NYP,* 1/14/36.

209 When science shot lilting: quoted in
Hall, 71–72.

210 Why do you do this: CBF-I, James Stewart Morcom.

210 When Roxy thanks a friend: Talmey, 173–81.

210 I'm just Mrs. Roxy: *NYWT,* 4/21/31.

210 I fell desperately: John Gruen, interview with Bowman, *Dance Magazine,* 10/76, 49–58.

210 It's the Roxy and I'm Roxy: Hall, 10.

211 A shipwrecked man: quoted in Manchester, 150.

211 It was bigger: *Motion Picture Herald,* 1/18/36, 13–16.

211 Dear Roxy—I Love You: Hall, 132.

212 Be careful: quoted in Talmey, 173–81.

212 the largest similar: quoted in F. L. Allen, "Radio City—Cultural Center?," *Harper's,* 4/32, 542.

212 playing an intricate: Hall, 131.

212 world figure: *NYT,* 3/26/27, 1.

212 Let us tell you, Roxy: CBF-I, Sydney Goldman.

212 general plan of development: RFA 2C, B71 F540, referenced in Woods to Columbia Trustees.

213 tend to give our property: RFA 2C, B71 F540, Goetze to Metro Sq., 8/4/30.

213 I'll make a bet: *NYT,* 2/27/27, VII-7.

213 Mayor of Radio City: *NYT,* 3/6/31, 3.

213 elevated esplanade; audience is . . . as much: *NYT,* 4/15/31, IX-4.

214 tenant appeal: "A Phenomenon of Exploitation,"*AF,* 10/34, 292–98.

214 not at any time . . . remove: RCMHA, *Radio City Music Hall Bulletin,* 6/10/36.

214 colossal anonymities: Clark obituary, *NYWT,* 8/34, exact date illegible.

215 theater notables: *NYT,* 10/1/31.

215 You might be: COHP, Wallace Harrison, 106–7.

215 Hello, everybody!: Associated Press, 10/6/31.

216 Ed Stone . . . could draw: *Time,* 3/31/58, 56–64.

216 soul of the school: quoted ibid.

216 architects who hoped to work: quoted in *TNY,* 1/3/59.

217 pretty heavily laced: Stone, 80.

217 Nobody's going to be: quoted in COHP, Wallace Harrison, 107–8.

217 laugh and cry together: quoted in Kilham, 131.

217 The picture of thousands: Jordy, 84.

217 He didn't know of one: Kilham, 132.

218 calls for Packards: Jordy, 79.

218 Words fail me: RFA, Junior to Todd, 11/10/32.

218 Only by reading Alexander: Balfour, 140–41.

218 great wormy intestine: Manuel Komroff, "Putting Modern Art in Its Place," *Creative Art,* 1/33, 37–44.

218 "God-awful": DDP, Deskey interview by J. Stewart Johnson, 9/6/75.

219 from a pen to a city: quoted in Ada Louise Huxtable, "Design Notebook,"*NYT,* 5/24/79, C10.

219 an artist . . . with a good sense: Hanks, 1–3.

219 only designed an ashtray: DDP, Deskey interview by Johnson, 9/6/75.

220 On Monday I got: RFA 2Z, B1 F10, Abby to Junior, 4/3/31.

220 a prototype of the cosmopolitan: DDP, Marco Polo Room files, "Biography of Donald Deskey," typescript.

220 had never had a piece: DDP, Deskey interview by Johnson, 9/6/75.

221 you're the famous Brazil nut: ibid.

221 Portuguese rococo: Roberta Brandes Gratz, "Is Rockefeller Center Losing Its Heart?," *Soho Weekly News,* 1/12/78, 10–11.

221 modern rococo: Hanks, 100–108.

221 The introduction of sound: quoted in Hall, iii.

222 116 petty offenders: *NYT,* 6/28/32, 18.

222 I would rather be: J. Morris, *Manhattan,* 58.

223 gilt-ridden: DDP, RC press release #89, 6/27/32.

223 noted modernist: *NYT,* 6/27/32.

223 sane modern design: quoted ibid.

223   bas-reliefs in cork: DDP, RC press release #65, 6/27/32.

223   Ezra Winter's mural: DDP, RC press release #88, n.d., 1932.

223   American Art has been used: Komroff, "Putting . . . ," *Creative Art*, 1/33, 37–44.

224   It was an opportunity: quoted in "Music Hall Mural Going to Museum," *NYT*, 4/3/75.

224   everything from zoology lessons: Hills, 105–6.

224   made urgent by the problem: quoted in *Art Digest*, 4/32.

224   grotesque little man: quoted in Ciment, 33–35.

225   sheer, dismal ineptitude: quoted in Reich, 104.

225   unpleasant situation: RFA 2E, B21 F211, Nelson to Conger Goodyear, 4/26/32.

225   come the Revolution: quoted in Collier and Horowitz, 668.

225   first aid: Henry McBride, "The Palette Knife," *Creative Art*, 5/32, 424–25.

225   outstanding individual patron: *Time*, 1/27/36, 28–29.

226   potential art-loving: DDP, RC press release #89, 6/27/32.

226   We have long since overcome: ibid.

226   One of the artists recently: Komroff, "Putting . . . ," *Creative Art*, 1/33, 37–44.

226   Donald's chest expansion; the whole outfit: AAA, R2065, Edith Halpert to Robert Laurent, 7/15/32.

226   address him as "John": ibid., Halpert to Laurent, 9/9/32.

226   Deskey is more slippery: ibid., Halpert to Laurent, "Wednesday," n.d.

227   very bad; the last time I saw my mural: AAA, R688, Bouché's autobiographical notes.

227   I have such a desire: quoted in R. Robinson, *Georgia*, 371.

228   devoted the past sixteen years: Lisle, 204–6.

228   the Mexican disease: quoted ibid.

228   a child not responsible: quoted ibid.

228   came back a few; Except she won't: DDP, Deskey interview by Johnson, 9/6/75.

228   No one in my world: quoted in Eisler, 431–36.

228   I'll get Hell: ibid.

228   charged with some high explosive: quoted in Lisle, 204–6.

229   I can't paint: quoted in Cowart et al., 207.

229   put the canvas up: DDP, Deskey interview by Johnson, 9/6/75.

229   half the human race is barred: Lewis Mumford, "The Skyline," *TNY*, 1/14/33, 55.

230   Proto-WPA: J. Adams, 21–22.

230   some giant [who] had spat: M. R. Werner, "Radio City: From Real Estate to Art," *Atlantic Monthly*, 5/33, 471.

230   I'm smothering: quoted in "Off the Record," *Fortune*, 2/33.

230   Carpet so thick: *Richmond News-Leader*, 6/2/33.

231   nap or spend the night: CHRIS-2, 228.

231   I didn't conceive: quoted in Werner, *Atlantic Monthly*, 5/33, 473.

231   experience gained: *NYT*, 2/20/32.

231   Roxy's electrons: Walter Gutman, "News and Gossip," *Creative Art*, 12/32, 319–20.

231   gasoline stations: *NYT*, 6/26/64.

231   feminine makeup: RCMHA, B54, S. R. McCandless to "Mr. Lewis" of RKO, 10/18/32.

232   young, very busy man: *Chicago Tribune*, 8/21/32.

232   Modern clothes: quoted ibid.

232   most important single step: Louise Cross, "The Sculpture for Rockefeller Center," *Parnassus*, 10/32, 1–3.

232   solved the problem of acoustics: quoted in *New York Sun*, 12/17/32.

232   It is not difficult to believe: Frank Settele, "The Best for the Biggest; Plastics in Radio City," *Plastic and Molded Products*, 1/33.

233 No one ever turned his back: Dolores Pallet, quoted in RCMHA, BB.

233 carrying [Roxy's] lap robe: AAA, R688, Bouche's autobiographical notes.

234 Shake it up: quoted in Francisco, 54.

234 with longer legs: quoted in *Christian Science Monitor*, 5/26/71, 13.

235 Hide your daughters: Robert Roman, "Hide Your Daughters, Here Comes Russ Markert," *Dance Magazine*, 9/69, 46.

236 full admirals: quoted in Hugh Blake, The New Roxy," *TNY*, 12/17/32, 36.

236 epaulette, gold-braid and frogging: ibid.

236 surrounded by confusion: "Rothafeller Center," *Time*, 1/2/33, 29.

236 Take those tables; Get the house manager; Of course she'll laugh: quoted in *NYHT*, 12/19/32.

237 That's ordinary!: TIA, Montrose J. Moses, "Mayor of Radio City," unidentified clipping.

237 somewhat in advance of popular: quoted in *New York American*, 12/14/32.

237 I found myself unable: quoted ibid.

237 175,000 office workers: RCMHA, photo caption, summer or fall 1932.

237 no moral objection; maybe that's because: quoted in *New York Evening Journal*, 12/32, exact date illegible.

238 I've had six wives: *Time*, 1/2/33, 29.

238 the first completed unit: *NYT*, 12/18/32.

238 The last six days: author interview, Margaret Dunne, 6/18/99.

238 Will take care of the seats: RFA 2C, B88 F664, Roxy to Nelson, 11/14/32.

238 almost abject humility: quoted in *NYT*, 11/22/32.

238 Graham Crackers: McDonagh, 90–92.

238 [we] were Greek: Graham, 144–45.

238 This thing will make: *NYHT*, 12/18/32.

239 a Lilliputian: Gutman, *Creative Art*, 12/32, 319–20.

239 Then . . . our Depression began: TIA, file interview with Orlean Stone.

240 Maxfield Parrish sky: RCMHA, B1, RKO press release, 5/26/3.

240 Never . . . were so many top hats: *NYHT*, 12/28/32, 1.

240 that great genius: Kilham film, *Skyscraper Building: The Story of Rockefeller Center*.

240 Sure, it's my brown: *New York Sun*, 12/28/32.

240 Six thousand famous: quoted in *NYT*, 1/29/33, IX-7.

241 Roxy, the theater is ready: quoted in *NYP*, 12/28/32.

241 finest entertainment: RCMHA, *The Radio City Theatres: The Radio City Music Hall, The RKO Roxy Theatre, Under Personal Direction of Roxy*, n.d.

241 and thus it rose: quoted in *New York Journal*, 12/28/32, 11.

241 seemed to get lost: ibid.

241 I want more light: *NYWT*, 12/30/32.

242 children; I'm proud of you all: ibid.

242 The mountain labored: *NYHT*, 12/28/32.

242 If the seating capacity: Terry Ramsaye, "Static in Radio City," *Motion Picture Herald*, 1/14/33.

242 notion of perfect entertainment: "All Men Dream," *TNY*, 1/7/33.

242 only when forty-five: Werner, *Atlantic Monthly*, 5/33, 474.

242 mistook, in the great distance: quoted in *Chicago Daily News*, 3/25/33.

242 I shall let the place: *New York Evening Journal*, 12/28/33, 11.

243 banged his fist: quoted in *CB42*, 655–56.

243 They were terrible: AAA, R688, Bouché's autobiographical notes.

243 mouth of a cannon: "All Men Dream," *TNY*, 1/7/33.

243 They went around; looked like a mouse: CBF-I, James Stewart Morcom.

243 found themselves satiated: *NYHT*, 1/8/33.

243 It's the greatest moment: *NYWT*, 12/30/32.

244   **broken-hearted:** CBF-I, Sydney Goldman.

244   **disappointed with himself:** Francisco, 92.

244   **unmistakable stamp:** *NYP,* 12/28/32.

244   **a negative triumph:** Ramsaye, "Static," *Motion Picture Herald,* 1/14/33.

244   **less effective than the . . . mirrors:** *NYT,* 1/33, date left off clipping; AAA, R2067.

244   **theater which is so long:** *NYHT,* 12/30/32.

244   **I never saw anything like it:** *New York Sun,* 1/n.d./33, date unclear; AAA, R971.

General sources for Chapter 15: **Roxy:** Hall; Francisco; Talmey; CBF-I files and clippings. **Movie theaters:** Hall. **Stone:** Kilham; Stone; *Time,* 3/31/58; *The New Yorker,* 1/3/59. **Deskey:** Hanks; *The London Studio,* 1933, vol. 5. **O'Keeffe and Stieglitz:** Cowart et al.; Eisler; Lisle; R. Robinson.

CHAPTER 16: *Ruthlessness Was Just Another Word for Good Business*

246   **leaders in various walks; prohibition experiment:** quoted in Fosdick, 255–57.

246   **two-martini man:** John Lockwood, quoted in Reich, 388.

246   **honestly convinced:** Dorothy Bromley, "Portrait of a Reactionary," *American Mercury,* 3/35, 286.

247   **made the wet cause; a little obnoxious:** Alva Johnston, "Cosmes," *TNY,* 11/8/30, 30.

247   **My position may:** quoted in Fosdick, 256–57.

247   **If any single:** Behr, 233–34.

247   **broke the deadlock:** Johnston, "Who Won the Repeal?," *TNY,* 9/9/33, 36.

247   **Young Rockefeller:** *New York Evening Journal,* 6/8/32.

247   **has done the country an inestimable:** *New York American,* 6/8/32.

247   **Now that you and Tom:** Winthrop W. Aldrich Papers, Baker Library, Harvard Business School, B156, Junior to Aldrich, 6/17/32.

248   **America's most useful:** Will Hays, quoted in *NYT,* 12/30/32.

248   **You are a fine looking group:** RFA 4L, B219 F2224, quoted in Robertson to Junior, 12/17/48.

248   **Experienced men:** F. L. Allen, "Look at Rockefeller Center," *Harper's,* 10/38, 508–9.

248   **It is true that Todd:** RFA 2C, B107 F799, Debevoise to Junior, 8/21/29.

248   **as far away as trains:** Todd, *Living,* 9.

248   **furniture-buying binges:** Hellman, *TNY,* 11/21/36, 23.

249   **I'm glad to take responsibility:** RCAC, Todd to Reinhard and Harrison, 8/7/34.

250   **Business is not discussed:** NYA, T. J. Ross to Geoffrey Hellman, 4/27/36.

250   **crushing vacancy rates:** Grant, 96.

252   **to look at that damn thing:** quoted in Reich, 100–101.

252   **we would trade the whole:** *TNY,* 7/4/31, 9.

252   **Citadel of Static:** *TNY,* 12/31/32, 12–13.

252   **What I should like:** Leslie Nelson Jennings, "Open Letter to Mr. Rockefeller," *TNY,* 12/3/32, 83.

253   **symbols in stone and steel; No other single:** quoted in Rockefeller Center, *John D. Rockefeller Jr.,* Junior to Lord Southborough, 21.

253   **uncanny ability to overcome:** CHRIS-2.

253   **figure balance of space as follows:** RCAC, unsigned, undated.

253   **The battle of the leases:** Todd, *Living,* 100.

253   **zeal . . . became proverbial:** *Time,* 1/22/34, 43.

255   **is not Greek:** Rockefeller Center, *Rockefeller Center,* 38.

255   **Where there is a possibility:** RCAC, Brown to Heydt, 3/11/32.

256 give preference to their products: RCAC, quoted in E. L. Smith staff memorandum, 1/29/35.

256 accommodating 20,000: Léger, 88.

256 the greatest price of height: Willis, *Form,* 45–46.

257 We told him that we needed: Todd, *Living,* 121.

257 OK, you want to sell: CHK-I, Webster Todd.

257 you will feel at home: RCAC, speech by I. W. Baldwin, 4/13/33.

257 plastered on a real estate: quoted in Fosdick, 269.

258 substitute a phrase; At least half: CA, Butler to Corbett, 4/8/31.

258 The newspapers will do almost: CA, Butler to Goetze, 8/19/31.

258 It's your money: quoted in Fosdick, 269.

258 flamboyant and distasteful: ibid.

260 tenant usually pays between: RCAC, "Dunning Notice—Form 155," 11/6/39.

260 A large number of small: Shultz and Simmons, 33–34.

261 largest collection of aeronautical: RCAC, #561, 8/10/34.

262 we should use every influence: RFA 2C, B91 F683, Heydt to Debevoise, 5/27/32.

262 Yardley & Co. Ltd.: RCAC, #138, 4/18/33.

262 The Leisure League: RCAC, #451, 4/17/34.

262 Things at Rockefeller: RFA 2Z, B3 F30, Junior to Senior, 6/1/34.

262 desolate acres of unrented: "Radio Gala," *Time,* 11/20/33, 37.

263 very close to exhausting; The progress: RFA, B91 F683, Kirkland to Todd and Robertson, 3/17/33.

263 find[ing] the proper: quoted in "A Phenomenon of Exploitation," *AF,* 10/34, 292–98.

263 Tenants . . . will object to having: RCAC, Per-Lee to R. Pollak, 8/11/33.

263 Conditions over which: RFA 2C, B91 F683, Junior to Debevoise, 3/21/33.

263 investments . . . in tenant enterprises: ibid.

264 coercion; unfair; monopoly: *NYT,* 1/11/34, 1.

264 In real estate circles: Todd, *Living,* 102.

264 uncordial: "A Phenomenon of Exploitation," *AF,* 10/34, 292–98.

264 The high powered methods: RFA 2C, B79 F589, unsigned memorandum, 2/21/33.

264 without outside brokers; good: RFA 2C, B108 F804, Todd to Junior, 11/18/33.

264 ROCKEFELLER GROUP SUED: *NYT,* 1/11/34, 1.

265 The 100 Men: RFA 2C, B74 F569, brochure, undated.

265 pleading: Kessner, 371.

265 consisted largely of thumping: *NYT,* 4/27/41, 1.

266 this modern Frankenstein: quoted in *NYT,* 1/11/34, 1.

266 Where will [the Center's] tenants: F. L. Allen, "Radio City—Cultural Center?," *Harper's,* 4/32, 540–41.

267 common practices; inducements; absolutely clean: quoted in *Chicago Tribune,* 2/2/41.

267 If no new and improved: Ivy Lee Papers, Seeley Mudd Library, Princeton University, written answers provided to interviewer Roy Howard, 2/27/34.

267 details of all leases: RCAC, board meeting minutes, 1/19/34.

267 philanthropist, real estate and steel: *NYT,* 4/27/41, 1.

267 individuality and personal charm: *NYT,* 4/30/41, 14.

267 canny Scotchman: *Chicago Tribune,* 2/2/41.

268 absolutely and unqualifiedly: RFA 2C, B92 F690, Junior's handwritten comment on Debevoise to Junior, 7/2/35.

268   buy or take over: RFA 2C, B92 F690, Debevoise to Junior, 7/2/35.

268   **$250,000 when they move:** RFA 2C, B93 F702, Heydt to Debevoise, 12/1/39.

General sources for Chapter 16: **Junior and prohibition:** Fosdick. **Butler and prohibition:** Johnston, *TNY,* 9/9/33. **Manhattan real estate glut:** Abramson, Grant. **Robertson:** Weisman; *The Boulevard,* 11/31; *AF,* 10/34; CHRIS-2. **Wenrich:** author interview, John A. Wenrich, 9/02. **Vizetelly:** *ANB.* **Heckscher:** Caro.

CHAPTER 17: *All the Finns in Helsingfors*

269   **excavation work; largest building project; $1,000,000,000:** RCAC, #1, 7/25/31.

270   **If it is a question:** quoted in Hiebert, 297–99

270   **largest; mammoth:** RCAC, #1, 7/25/31.

270   **All the Finns:** quoted in *NYHT,* 7/23/33.

271   **If the 1,000,000:** RCAC, #2, 7/30/31.

271   **If all 14 buildings:** RFA 2C, B81 F609, "Rockefeller Center," 4/1/45.

271   **If one man were:** RCAC, chronology, 9/11/31.

271   **for publicity purposes:** RCAC, Crowell office memorandum, 10/1/35.

271   **2,100 miles:** RFA 2C, B81 F608, press release, 1/29/32.

271   **after reading about:** "Rockefeller Center," *Fortune,* 12/36, 139.

271   **most rampant boasting:** RFA 2C, B81 F612, Debevoise to Lee, 1/21/33.

271   **Now that the Rockefeller Centre:** RFA 2H, B77 F584, Junior to Lee, 4/21/32.

271   **appeared in newspapers:** RFA 2C, B78 F580, Todd to Junior, 11/18/33.

272   **another mid-city:** RCAC, caption, Construction IV, 12/7/32.

273   **appreciate mention in the caption:** RCAC, #2180, 9/8/38.

273   **Oscar:** RCAC, #1201, 2/36.

273   **Every informed man:** RFA 4L, B214 F2160, "Rhododendrons and Public Relations," draft ms. by Ken Clark, circa 1939.

273   **All these people are smiling:** *NYT,* 2/9/97, 39.

273   **Mr. Chairman; better understanding:** quoted in *NYT,* 7/13/33, 9.

274   **easygoing charm:** Hellman, *TNY,* 4/18/42, 26.

274   **permanent Secretary of State:** RCAC, #190, 7/10/33.

275   **tenants which we:** RFA 2C, B92 F697, Junior to Debevoise, 8/5/31.

275   **Palais de la République:** RFA 2C, B78, Butler to Junior, 12/2/33.

275   **were much interested:** RFA 2C, B92 F696, Southborough to Junior, 1/26/32.

275   **foremost peers:** CHRIS-2, 141.

276   **entry under bond:** Public Law No. 296, 72d Congress, S. 4747.

276   **carry on the practice:** quoted in *NYT,* 1/11/34, 1.

277   **at all times be maintained:** RFA 2C, B92 F696, Abberley memorandum, 3/9/34.

277   **200 foot long steeply:** Adams, 159.

277   **To have landed Crepes:** "Notes and Comment," *TNY,* 11/25/33, 13.

277   **has been criticized time and again:** CA, Butler to Todd, 11/15/34.

277   **constant scoffing:** RCAC, Butler to Todd, 4/13/36.

278   **therefore it will be necessary to go ahead:** RCAC, Schley notes on architects' meeting, 3/1/34.

278   **saving . . . under these:** RFA 2H, B124 F920, Heydt to Senior, 6/7/34.

279   **This lease is of the utmost:** RCAC, "Information Bulletin: Confidential," 8/10/34.

279   **most of the major steamship:** Ruth B. Shipley, quoted in RCAC, #1105, 11/21/35.

279   **Your Excellency:** RFA 2C, B92 F695, Junior to Mussolini, 3/10/32.

280   **attempted to cartelize:** Sheldon Rich-

man, "The Concise Encyclopedia of Economics," www.econlib.org.

280 **democracy is dead:** "The State—Fascist and Total," *Fortune,* 7/34, 47.

280 **must recognize:** "An Introductory Guide," ibid., 45.

281 **more powerful than any monarch:** RCAC, Italian Minister of State Vittorio Scialoia, presentation in behalf of Palazzo d'Italia, in Rome, 2/20/33.

281 **ROCKEFELLER 3RD GOES TO WORK:** *NYT,* 12/3/29.

281 **I am not going to urge:** RFA, unidentified clip in Junior's scrapbook, 1929.

281 **smothered by the number:** author interview, David Rockefeller, 4/02.

281 **very interesting:** see RFA 5.1.1, B4-6, JDR3 daily diaries.

281 **was like a sun:** quoted in Reich, 388.

282 **Several post office:** RFA 5.1.1, B5 F46, JDR3 diary, 1/22/34.

282 **Twin Buildings:** *NYT,* 6/1/32, 25.

282 **mostly men of very high grade:** RCAC, Douglas S. Gibbs to Robertson, 7/21/32.

283 **the belief prevalent:** RFA 2C, B92 F697, Ellery G. Huntington to board of directors, 3/10/33.

283 **express publicly his approval:** RCAC, unsigned "Memo re Foreign Buildings in Rockefeller Center," 12/21/33.

283 **his aid in smoothing:** *WSJ,* 7/12/34.

284 **Jewish agitation:** RFA RG 5.1.1, B4 F45, JDR3 diary, 10/3/33.

284 **[Lee] has complete confidence:** Ivy Lee Papers, Seeley Mudd Library, Princeton University, B3 F33, JDR3 file memo, 9/8/33.

284 **several . . . Jews about the possibility:** RFA RG 5.1.1, B4 F45, JDR3 diary, 8/30/33.

284 **prominent Jews:** RFA 2C, B92 F692, JDR3 to Junior, 9/7/33.

284 **misgivings about:** quoted in RFA RG5.1.1, B4 F45, JDR3 diary, 9/5/33.

285 **mak[ing] no statements:** RFA 2C, B92 F692, JDR3 to Junior, 9/14/33.

285 **one of the main purposes:** RFA 5.1.1, B5 F46, JDR3 diary, 2/21/34.

285 **unnamed building:** RCAC, minutes of executive committee meeting, 10/25/34.

285 **various people, recently consulted:** RCAC, draft minutes of executive committee meeting, 10/25/34.

285 **and we were decidedly:** quoted in Balfour, 44.

286 **I never heard:** AL, Harrison Papers, B16 F5, interview, 2/9/76.

General sources for Chapter 17: **Crowell:** Bernays and Kaplan; *Fortune,* 12/36. **John 3rd:** His diaries, in RFA 5.1.1; author interview, - David Rockefeller, 4/02; Harr and Johnson (both).

CHAPTER 18: *What Do You Paint, When You Paint on a Wall?*

287 **What do you paint:** E. B. White, "I Paint What I See," *TNY,* 5/20/33. The complete poem:

"What do you paint, when you paint on a wall?"
    Said John D.'s grandson Nelson.
"Do you paint just anything there at all?
"Will there be any doves, or a tree in fall?
"Or a hunting scene, like an English hall?"

    "I paint what I see," said Rivera.

"What are the colors you use when you paint?"
    Said John D.'s grandson Nelson.
"Do you use any red in the beard of a saint?
"If you do, is it terribly red, or faint?
"Do you use any blue? Is it Prussian?"

    "I paint what I paint," said Rivera.

"Whose is that head that I see on my wall?"
    Said John D.'s grandson Nelson.
"Is it anyone's head whom we know, at all?
"A Rensselaer, or a Saltonstall?
"Is it Franklin D.? Is it Mordaunt Hall?
"Or is it the head of a Russian?"

"I paint what I think," said Rivera.

"I paint what I paint, I paint what I see,
   "I paint what I think," said Rivera,
"And the thing that is dearest in life to me
"In a bourgeois hall is Integrity;
   "However . . .

"I'll take out a couple of people drinkin'
"And put in a picture of Abraham Lincoln;
"I could even give you McCormick's reaper
"And still not make my art much cheaper.
"But the head of Lenin has got to stay
"Or my friends will give me the bird today,
   "The bird, the bird, forever."

"It's not good taste in a man like me,"
   Said John D.'s grandson Nelson,
"To question an artist's integrity
"Or mention a practical thing like a fee,
"But I know what I like to a large degree,
   "Though art I hate to hamper;
"For twenty-one thousand conservative bucks
"You painted a radical. I say shucks,
   "I never could rent the offices—
   "The capitalistic offices.
"For this, as you know, is a public hall
"And people want doves, or a tree in fall,
"And though your art I dislike to hamper,
"I owe a *little* to God and Gramper,
   "And after all,
   "It's *my* wall . . ."

"We'll see if it is," said Rivera.

Reprinted by permission; © E. B. White. Originally published in *The New Yorker*. All rights reserved.

287   **lack[s] symmetry; colonnade; symmetrically designed:** RFA 2C, B78 F582, Junior to Todd, 3/31/33.

287   **frank expression:** quoted ibid.

287   **Rockefeller Equinox:** *TNY,* 4/4/36, 15.

288   **I sat in the front seat:** Rockefeller Center, *John D. Rockefeller Jr.,* Todd to Junior, 4/13/33, 27.

288   **from Mrs. Carnegie's:** RFA 2C, B78 F581, Junior to Todd, 4/11/33.

288   **gross and unbeautiful:** RFA 2C, B78 F581, Junior to Todd, 9/19/33.

288   **Although I do not personally:** RFA 2C, B93 F704, Junior to Hood, 10/12/32.

289   **It has been decided:** RCAC, Webster Todd to Smith, 2/16/32.

289   **a list of artists:** RCAC, Brown to Smith, 10/3/32.

289   **cheaper than plaster:** quoted in Kilham, 124.

289   **constant study of finance:** Andrew L. Reinhard, "Gardens of the Roofs of Radio City," *AmArch,* 11/31, 75.

290   **the futility into which:** RFA 2C, B107 F803, Vincent to Woods, 3/23/32.

290   **one of the most carefully:** RFA 2C, B107 F803, Junior to Woods, 5/5/32.

290   **The New World:** RFA 2C, B107 F803, undated, unsigned memorandum.

290   **moving mural:** COHP, Wallace Harrison, 153.

291   **Let us be ever watchful:** *NYT,* 2/19/65.

291   **twisted temperament:** COHP, Holger Cahill.

292   **Father feels so strongly:** RFA 2H, B140 F1041, Junior to Welles Bosworth, 1/31/21.

292   **the finest work:** RFA 2H, B140 F1041, Bosworth to Junior, 3/16/20.

292   **If I were contemplating; delightful man:** RFA 2H, B140 F1041, Junior to Elbert Gary, 4/16/27.

292   **Pardon me:** cited in "Rockefeller Center," *Fortune,* 12/36, 139.

292   **Let's tie up:** *RCW,* 10/25/34, 6.

292   **look[s] like he [has] just sprung:** cited by Andrew Dolkart, on the *Today* show, 3/2/98.

292   **much wider:** *RCW,* 1/17/35, 5.

293   **young man escaping:** *Fortune,* 12/36, 139.

293   **I don't like it:** AAA, Manship interview with J. D. Morse, 2/18/59.

293   **strikes a new note:** RCAC, caption, Art XI.

293   **I have been trying to decide:** *NYT,* 12/24/33.

294 representative of the Renaissance: "The Sculpture of Lee Lawrie," *AF,* 5/31, 587–600.

294 no more exciting: AL, George De Ris Papers, B1, F2, quoted in unidentified clipping.

294 up on the walls: *Century Association Yearbook, 1964,* 186.

294 Guided by Light: Balfour, 144.

294 Day unto Day: RCAC, notes on architects' meeting, 12/11/33.

294 would prefer to have: RCAC, quoted in notes on architects' meeting, undated, 1933; Balfour, 144.

295 I shall not be able: quoted in Balfour, 144.

295 convergence: Koolhaas, 125.

295 Lenin of Mexico: quoted in Marnham, 182.

295 We had an amusing: quoted in Kert, 352.

295 I have never known: quoted in Marnham, ix.

296 a monster: B. Wolfe, *A Life,* 578.

296 created a vision; a liar: Hamill, 9.

296 attractive ugliness: B. Wolfe, *A Life,* 244.

296 great fun, charming: author interview, David Rockefeller, 4/02.

297 a monkey who: quoted ibid.

297 I can not forget: RFA 2C, B94 F706, Kahlo to Abby, 1/24/33.

297 [Diego] misses: RFA 2C, B94 F706, Kahlo to Abby, 1/27/33.

297 Pierre Picasso: RCAC, W. Todd to office, undated telegram, 1932.

297 society artist; geared: Gold and Fizdale, 271.

298 give preference: *NYT,* 3/7/32.

298 unfounded rumor; most important work: Merle Crowell, "The Story of Rockefeller Center: VII: A Question Answered," *AF,* 5/32, 424–30.

298 so as to suit everybody: *NYT,* 11/20/32.

299 art should be pretty: COHP, Holger Cahill, 297.

299 If that's a bird: Heckscher, *When,* 117.

299 Uncle Peach: C. Gray, "Six Brothers," *NYT,* real estate section, 10/17/99.

299 architectural sculpture is essentially: Zorach, 93.

300 ancient war galley: RCAC, Lawrie to architects, 10/19/35.

300 All his paintings are: quoted in Marnham, 188.

301 tireless giant: B. Wolfe, *A Life,* 578.

301 undigested mixture: ibid., 577.

301 trading with the enemy: Frances Flynn Paine, in Museum of Modern Art, *Murals,* 32.

301 I continued to regard: Rivera, *My Art,* 98–100.

302 painted the fruits; productive labor; no mortgage-holding: Rivera, *Portrait,* 15.

302 best and most fruitful: ibid., 18.

302 May I take: RFA 2C, B94 F706, Nelson to Rivera, 10/13/32.

303 You signed my sketch: quoted in Lucienne Bloch, "On Location with Diego Rivera," *Art in America,* 2/86, 108.

303 two members: Rivera, *Portrait,* 22.

303 Avec mes hommages: original in Museum of Modern Art, Department of Drawings.

303 I assure you that . . . I shall: RFA 2C, B94 F706, office translation of Rivera to Abby, 11/5/32.

303 if a whole population: RFA 2C, B107 F803, file memo on "Thematic Synopsis," 12/28/31.

304 My panel will show: quoted in B. Wolfe, *The Fabulous,* 320–21.

304 Sketch approved: quoted ibid. 323.

304 Great murals: "Industrial Detroit," *Fortune,* 2/33, 48.

304 a mighty clutter: *NYT Magazine,* 11/20/32.

304 main lobby, strewn: Bloch, *Art in America,* 2/86, 105.

305 PLEASE DO NOT: ibid., 118

305 quit . . . reputedly: ibid., 109

306 the realization: quoted in Herrera, 161.

306   race against drying: "The Frescoer,"
       TNY, 12/26/31, 9.

306   No fixative: RCAC, #125, 3/20/33.

306   Make love: quoted in Herrera, 163.

306   infinitesimal organisms: RFA 2C, B94
       F707, Rivera memorandum, plans for
       mural.

306   lending me: Rivera, *Portrait,* 24. Carrel
       was identified as his adviser by David
       Rockefeller, author interview, 4/02.

307   Have you seen the final: RCAC, W.
       Todd to Reinhard, Hofmeister, and
       Hood, 3/27/33.

307   could we at this time: RCAC, W.
       Todd memo, 4/7/33.

307   Rivera is now working: RCAC, W.
       Todd to A. J. Taylor, 4/10/33.

307   philosophy of Moscow: *NYT,* 4/2/33,
       VI-10.

307   only ultimate form; hostility and at-
       tack: quoted ibid.

307   We all felt so badly; As you know:
       RFA 2C, B94 F706, Nelson to Rivera,
       4/3/33.

308   the debauched rich: Rivera, *My Art,*
       126.

308   life in a socialist: ibid.

308   It is to prove: Bloch, *Art in America,*
       2/86, 114.

309   Nelson R. called: ibid., 115.

309   Gentlemen, . . . we seem: quoted in
       Kilham, 126–27.

310   very polite: *NYWT,* 4/24/33, 1.

310   Rivera Perpetuates: ibid.

310   I am a worker: quoted ibid.

310   those close: ibid.

310   an afterthought: Bloch, *Art in Amer-
       ica,* 2/86, 116.

311   Who's that, Trotsky?; the fun began:
       MOMA, Ben Shahn, on *The Open
       Mind,* WNBC-TV, Eric Goldman, in-
       terviewer; transcript of 1/17/65 broad-
       cast, 17–21.

311   willing to do work: RFA 2H, B133
       F999, Junior to Nelson, 5/12/33.

311   While in Hanover: RFA 2Z, B1 F10,
       Junior to Abby, 5/19/33.

311   viewing the progress; I am sure: RFA

2C, B94 F706, Nelson to Rivera,
       5/4/33.

312   In 1974, Nelson told: CHK-I, Nelson
       Rockefeller.

312   It was not hard: B. Wolfe, *A Life,* 603.

312   In reply; the sector; I am sure:
       quoted in B. Wolfe, *The Fabulous,* DR
       to NAR, 5/6/33, 326–27. The original
       autograph draft of the letter, in Ben
       Shahn's hand, is in Shahn's papers in
       the AAA.

312   it was [Kahlo]: AAA, Hugo Gellert,
       interviewed by Paul Buhle, 4/4/84.

312   would have been glad: William R.
       Valentiner, from his unpublished ms.
       Remembering Artists, quoted by Sterne,
       196.

313   Communists who made no: *NYHT,*
       5/10/33.

313   taken advantage of: RFA 2C, B94
       F706, Robertson to Rivera, 5/9/33.

313   We know that . . . you will receive:
       ibid.

314   You should never try to fool: quoted
       in *NYT,* 5/15/33.

314   in the case of the Rockefellers: quoted
       in Herrera, 171.

314   princely tendency: Reich, 166.

314   cover the expense: RFA 2C, B9 F706,
       Nelson to Alan Blackburn, 12/16/33.

314   touch up: RFA 2C, B9 F706, Todd to
       Nelson, 12/15/33.

314   It will last: RCAC, #125, 3/20/33.

315   for its destruction: "Radical Mural-
       ists," *Time,* 2/26/34, 42.

315   Rivera mural has been removed:
       RCAC, #393, 2/12/34.

315   Rather than mutilate: quoted in B.
       Wolfe, *The Fabulous,* DR to NAR,
       5/6/33, 326–27.

315   venereal disease germs: Rivera, *My
       Art,* 129–30.

315   Riot cars: "Diego Rivera's Mural in
       Rockefeller Center Rejected," *Newsweek,*
       5/20/33, 29–30.

316   Have instructions from General Mo-
       tors: quoted in B. Wolfe, *The Fabulous,*
       330.

316   class solidarity: Balfour, 187.

316   **In order to get here:** quoted in *NYT,* 5/14/33, 1.

316   **wrest control:** *NYT,* 5/16/33, quoted by Herrera, 169.

316   **Bloomfield is answered:** *Workers Age,* 6/15/33, 4.

316   **the money extorted:** Rivera, *Portrait,* 31.

316   *Soy Católico:* quoted in Marnham, 311.

316   **included an address; Hitler and Rockefeller:** *NYT,* 5/18/33.

317   **This is most important:** RFA 2C, B94 F706, Robertson to Abby, 5/15/33.

317   **brought us particularly; fills my heart:** quoted in *Rockefeller Archive Center Newsletter,* Spring 2002, 7.

317   **Your letter . . . has been referred:** quoted in Marnham, 255.

317   **The incident attracted:** Todd, *Living,* 130.

318   **too many teats:** Lawrie, *Boy Wanted,* unpublished ms., quoted in Garvey, 210.

318   **I shall never be happy:** RFA 2C, B78 F581, Junior to Todd, 9/19/33.

318   **a fact which has never:** RFA 2Z, B3 F30, Junior to Senior, 2/17/34.

318   **outraged by the vulgarity:** COHP, Holger Cahill, 281–82.

318   **have been officially:** RCAC, #327, 12/33.

318   **he had encountered:** *NYHT,* 9/15/33, 14.

319   **no human interest:** "Peculiarly British," *NYT Book Review,* 1/24/26.

319   **of full and splendid; flat-chested:** quoted in *Daily Mail,* 11/2/32.

319   **women symbolic:** quoted ibid.

319   **fine, strapping wench:** Belleroche, 116.

319   **Wailing Wall:** RFA 2C, B94 F709, Laurance Rockefeller to Nelson, 4/16/37.

319   **try to catch a train:** RCAC, Todd memo summarizing meeting with Junior ("Mr. David"), 3/20/34.

319   **do the job:** RFA 2C, B78 F582, Todd to Junior, 8/2/33. Todd's letter, the only known evidence regarding these previously unreported negotiations, rings true in the context of his relationship with Junior.

319   **mural painter must:** *NYWT,* 4/25/33, 3.

320   **man on a scaffold:** Allen, "Look at Rockefeller Center," *Harper's,* 10/38, 513–15.

320   **Five characters:** *NYWT,* 4/20/43.

320   TAKE THINGS EASY: RFA 2Z, B3 F30, Senior to Junior, 2/19/33.

General sources for Chapter 18: **Manship:** Rand; Rather. **Faulkner:** Adams *et al.;* author interview, Tim K. Smith, 9/98. **Lawrie:** *Century Association Yearbook, 1964;* Garvey. **Rivera:** B. Wolfe (both); Hamill; Herrera; Marnham. **Rivera in Detroit:** Sterne. **Rivera in New York:** Bloch, in *Art in America.* **Kahlo:** Herrera. **Sert:** Gold and Fizdale. **Brangwyn:** Belleroche.

CHAPTER 19: *I Was Not Interested in Sitting and Listening*

321   **I did not want to go:** quoted in Bleecker, 26.

321   **an omen:** Chernow, 507.

321   **Sistine Madonna:** quoted in Reich, 64.

322   **where Nelson and Laurance:** quoted by George Dudley, ibid., 30.

322   **I have a terrible:** quoted ibid., 28.

322   **Harver Club:** RFA 4A, B3 F25, NAR diary, 5/11/33.

322   **Harryson:** ibid., intermittently throughout.

323   **I would think of making:** quoted in Reich, xii.

323   **I simply want:** quoted in Rockefeller Center, *John D. Rockefeller Jr.,* Nelson to Junior, 7/3/33, 35.

323   **depressed and discouraged:** RFA 2.1.2, B31 F288, Junior to "Babs and boys," 10/6/33.

323 After all the carping; If Mr. Rockefeller: *TNY,* 12/9/33, 17.

324 White himself elsewhere: article in
Saturday Evening Post, quoted in
"Rockefeller Center," *Fortune,* 12/36.
139.

324 I wish that you: quoted in Fosdick,
268.

324 Jacobs: Hellman, *Mrs. DePeyster's,*
249–50.

325 Except, perhaps: ibid., 225 (reprinted
from *The New Yorker*).

325 a libel: ibid., x.

325 showed everybody how: T. Wolfe,
From Bauhaus, 23.

325 his opinion was: www.lecorbusier-
centre.com.

325 pathetic paradox; tumult; hairgrowth;
petrified: quoted in Koolhaas, 261.

325 rational, logically conceived: Le Corbusier, 62.

325 architectural life: ibid., xv.

326 The monkey business: HRC, Geddes
Papers, F95b, Hood to Geddes,
12/14/33.

326 no smokee: HRC, Geddes Papers,
968.1, Hood to Geddes, 12/15/33.

326 Hood and his: Wright and Mumford,
128.

326 good old: ibid., 337–38.

326 apotheosis of megalomania: R. A.
Cram, "Radio City—And After," *American Mercury,* 7/31, 291–96.

326 I am not sure: L. H. Robbins, "Our
'City Within a City' Lifts Its Final
Towers," *NYT Magazine,* 2/13/38, 7.

327 was a good egg: Wright to Paul Frankl,
in Pfeiffer, 86.

327 understood the economic necessity:
H. W. Corbett, "Raymond Mathew-
son Hood," *AF,* 8/34.

327 What if he had had: AL, Hood Papers,
D. M. Douglass to Walter Kilham,
5/3/70.

327 paper architecture: Mumford, *TNY,*
10/12/35, 63.

327 absolutely no influence: AL, Harrison Papers, B6 F01, Harrison response
to Alan Balfour queries, 1/75.

327 Corbu's chief sponsor: Gill, 155–56.

327 We will treat him: RCAC, Todd
memo on "meeting with Mr. David,"
3/20/34.

327 I have just heard: RCAC, Todd to
Harrison, 10/25/34.

328 not a conventional: Newhouse, 97.

328 Mr. Jones: Persico, 118.

328 Mrs. John and I: RFA 2H, B123 F913,
JDR3 to staff member, 11/5/44.

328 was as likely: Gelernter, 216.

329 It would be well: RCAC, Brown to
W. Todd, 7/29/36.

329 personally: RFA 2C, B91 F683, Debevoise to Nelson, 2/9/33.

329 Nelson needs art: quoted in Reich,
151.

329 much as a lesser: ibid., 152.

330 as a way of helping: RFA 4C, B15
F132, file note, n.d.

330 I stressed: RFA 4C, B15 F135,
Kirstein to Nelson, 6/14/35.

330 most satisfactory: RFA 4C, B15 F135,
Nelson to Kirstein, 6/17/35.

330 I have never squandered: quoted in
Reich, 12.

330 office boy: ibid., 379.

330 Mr. Rockefeller should not: RCAC,
R. Palmer to N. A. Kenworthy, 2/1/34.

330 We will get: RFA 2C, B78 F582,
Nelson to Junior, 3/17/34.

330 As a result of our various: RFA 5.1,
B31 F288, Nelson et al. to Junior,
5/1/33.

331 good prime minister: Harr and Johnson, *Century,* 377–78.

331 Dear Pa: RFA 2Z, B5, various.

332 Nelson's temperament: RFA 2.1, B3
F28, Junior to Senior, 2/11/32.

332 I never wanted: quoted as title in
Kramer and Roberts, *I Never.*

332 Had lunch: RFA 5.1.1, B5 F46,
JDR3 diary 1/2/35.

332 at my suggestion: RFA 5.1.1, B5
F46, JDR3 diary 3/25/35.

332 Had lunch with Nel: RFA 5.1.1, B5
F46, JDR3 diary 2/13/36.

332 had a long talk: RFA 5.1.1, B5,
JDR3 diary 12/18/36.

332 **to be assumed by John:** RFA 2H, B133 F999, Junior to Nelson, 3/10/33.

332 **I talked with John:** RFA 2H, B133 F999, Nelson to Junior, 5/25/33.

333 **the position of chief:** RFA 5.1, B5, JDR3 diary, 1/2/35.

333 **I have discussed:** RFA RG5.1, B31 F289, Junior to JDR3, 9/21/35.

333 **chafing at being:** Harr and Johnson, *Century,* 371.

333 **I hoped very much:** RFA RG5.1.1, B5 F46, JDR3 diary, 10/11/34.

333 **to outline to me; very interesting:** RFA RG5.1.1, B5 F46, JDR3 diary, 12/18/36.

333 **Within a month:** Harr and Johnson, *Century,* 375.

335 **his easy acceptance:** Newhouse, 97.

335 **The things:** quoted ibid., 97.

335 **the Group:** Harr and Johnson, *Century,* 388–89.

335 **usefulness:** quoted in Reich, 469.

335 **Do you want:** AL, Harrison Papers, B1 F5, interview 2/9/76.

335 **said to be the largest:** RCAC, #448, 4/16/34.

335 **architectural development of:** ibid.

336 **all-metal; intercepted; useful:** RCAC, #1331, 5/4/36.

336 **could not see any reason:** RFA RG5.1.1, B6 F48, JDR3 diary, 5/27/38.

336 **There has been:** quoted in Ernst, 213–14, Junior to Senior, 12/7/35.

336 **a full-size replica:** RCAC, press release, no number, 6/16/36.

336 **I am proud:** RFA 2L, B36 F303, Nelson to Junior, 10/1/36.

336 **substantially; and the best:** NYA, T. J. Ross to Hellman, 4/27/36.

337 **it would never be possible:** CA, Robertson to Goetze, 1/25/49.

338 **expresse[s] his great:** CA, Goetze to Butler, 1/28/36.

339 **the only man:** CA, Goetze to Butler, 2/20/36.

339 **The questions at issue:** CA, Butler to Cromwell, 1/20/36.

339 **I realize the consummation:** CA, Cromwell to Butler, 2/20/36.

339 **The effulgence:** Butler Papers, Rare Book and Manuscript Division, Columbia University, Cromwell to Butler, 4/3/42.

339 **Mr. Cromwell still:** CA, Goetze to Butler, 4/21/36.

341 **Go over:** AL, Harrison Papers, B6 F02, 2/2/65.

341 **for putting a rock:** author interview, Francis Morrone, 5/17/98.

341 **had gradually become:** CHRIS-2, 94.

342 **Hardly ever:** COHP, Wallace Harrison, 142.

General sources for Chapter 19: **Young Nelson:** Reich. **Le Corbusier:** Hellman; Jacobs; Koolhaas; Le Corbusier. **Nelson and John:** Harr and Johnson, *Century;* J. A. Morris, *Those;* Persico; Reich; author interview, David Rockefeller, 4/02. **Nelson and Harrison:** Newhouse.

CHAPTER 20: *Visitors Give Him Dollars*

343 **You have achieved:** RFA 2C, B88 F664, Junior to Roxy, 12/28/32.

343 **After the show opened:** author interview, Margaret Dunne, 6/18/99.

343 **almost inaudible:** *NYHT,* 12/30/32.

343 **seat 3,700:** ibid.

344 **with a view of seeing:** RFA 2C, B10 F84, Junior to Todd, 9/8/33.

344 **to get people; office rentals; If we can; Our first step:** RFA 2C, B107 F804, Todd to Junior, 11/18/33.

345 **The Fall of:** quoted in "Trouble in Paradise," *Newsweek,* 10/25/71.

345 **very saucy:** quoted in *NYT,* 2/2/33, 21.

345 **impressively and poetically:** quoted in "Helen Keller SEES Rockefeller Center," *RCW,* 10/1/34.

346 **Living in a self-centered:** quoted in Hall, 26.

346 **With cheeks trembling:** *New York Sun,* 1/13/36.

346 COMMAND ME: RFA 2C, B88 F264, Roxy to Nelson, 1/22/34.

346 Death is just: quoted in Hall, 256.
346 vision of a demented: Atkinson, 182.
347 no drawn out: Minnelli, 60–61.
347 pushed me to creative: ibid., 62.
347 dynamic, diminutive: *New York American*, 5/13/34.
347 masochistic loyalty: Gann, 120–22.
347 grab Leonidoff: Francisco, 46; Raymond Paige identified by anonymous source.
348 Number fourteen; Turn me out: quoted in Barbara Anne Heggie and Robert Lewis Taylor, "Idea Flourisher," *TNY*, 2/5/44, 28.
348 Sit down: quoted in NYA, original typescript, by Barbara Anne Heggie, of Erno Rapee profile. The language in the original is more credible than the slightly cleaned-up version that eventually appeared in print.
348 Once out of sight: Heggie and Taylor, "Idea Flourisher," 2/5/44.
348 My basic inclination: Rich, 15.
348 a certain type of act: quoted in "Trouble in Paradise," *Newsweek*, 10/25/71.
349 first class symphony: quoted in *NYHT*, 6/2/63.
349 exquisite: quoted in Rockefeller Center, *John D. Rockefeller Jr.*, 33–34.
349 My, they look: quoted in *NYDN*, 11/1/45.
349 learned a lesson: *NYT*, 10/5/39.
349 As long as a Rockette: quoted in *NYDN*, 11/1/45.
349 part of a regiment: quoted in *NYDN*, 5/7/39.
350 Malted Milk: Robert Roman, "Hide Your Daughters, Here Comes Russ Markert," *Dance Magazine*, 9/69.
350 I've lost; Never mind: ibid.
350 The girls still have: quoted in Francisco, 69.
350 a merciless round: Love, 35–37.
350 In the old days: Marc Platt, quoted in William Como, "How High the Corn at Radio City?," *Dance Magazine*, 8/66, 36–40.

351 crotch-watchers: Love, 60.
351 patron wants: RCMHA, *St. Louis Post-Dispatch*, 11/9/47.
352 singing over crackling: quoted in H. Robinson, *Last*, 253.
352 We do all this: RCMHA, quoted by Janice Herbert in interview, 1989, on tape.
352 I went to: *Film Daily*, 7/20[?]/43; date unclear on clipping.
353 tiny things; you can hold: "Tiny Collection," *TNY*, 7/27/37, 10–12.
353 Mr. Rockefeller gives: *Portland (Maine) Press Herald*, 2/14/37.
353 Say what you want: *TNY*, 3/4/33, 9.
353 hard to cast: HRC, Selznick Papers, B1677, F: Story Dept. Plays, 3/7.
354 air conditioning stacks: *NYT*, 7/19/33, 19.
354 be versed in: *RCW*, 2/27/36.
354 to stand there and talk: Merton, 156.
355 a powerful forsythia: Hellman, "The Man Behind Prometheus," *TNY*, 11/14/36.
355 Uncle Winthrop's: RFA 2C, B78 F582, Nelson to Junior, 5/26/33.
355 rooves: RCAC, Arthur Shurcliff to Brown, 5/25/33.
355 designed Miss Choate's: RFA 2C, B78 F581, Junior to Todd, 4/10/33.
355 Courances: RFA 2C, B78, Bosworth to Junior, 9/14/34.
356 Here the buds of pink: *NYT*, 4/14/35.
356 The scheme . . . will be: *Racine Journal News*, 8/29/31.
356 The gardens are an attraction: RCAC, unsigned memo [probably by Todd], 7/14/36.
356 to eat excess: "Midtown Fauna," *TNY*, 5/4/35, 12.
357 half the males: *Toledo Blade*, 1/21/41.
357 they become nuisances: RCAC, J. Brown memo, 5/10/34.
357 People look down: quoted in L. H. Robbins, "Our 'City Within a City' Lifts Its Final Towers," *NYT Magazine*, 2/13/38, 6.
358 pinwheeling: Krinsky, 154.

358   lines of communication: Fitch and Waite, 13.

358   the catacombs: *NYT,* 2/21/91, Sec. 14, 1.

359   best Catholic choir; wizardry: RFA 2C, B81 F614, Crowell to Woods, copy to Nelson, 12/15/33.

359   flew around the area: *NYT,* 11/28/67.

360   a great decision: Jerzy W. Soltan, quoted in Jordy, 20–21.

360   management . . . still; salvag[e] the Center's: Joe Alex Morris, "The City Where Nobody Lives," *Saturday Evening Post,* 9/17/49, 32.

360   poor, never-not-doomed: "Last Word," *TNY,* 8/21/54, 20.

361   free from the French-pastry: Hugh Blake, "The New Roxy," *TNY,* 2/17/32, 36.

361   extraordinarily beautiful theater: *NYT,* 12/30/32, 14.

361   overpoweringly chic: *New York Sun,* 12/17/32.

361   America's only ice: RCAC, caption, Tenants.

361   has been a bit chilly: RFA 2C, B70, Turnbull to Nelson, 5/24/45.

362   extremely risqué; Hippodrome; gorgeous and impressive: RFA 2G, B89 F669, Van Schmus, "Report to the Theatre Committee," 3/10/34.

362   holding four thousand: Harriman, 89.

363   expected the industry: Krinsky, 142.

363   the flicker: quoted in *NYT,* 10/29/33, VII-24.

364   may enter the studio: *NYT,* 11/4/34, 13.

364   vice president in charge: quoted in *NYT,* 1/18/56.

364   the conductor was as well known: *Life,* 11/27/39.

365   everything that makes: quoted in *RCW,* 10/18/34.

365   the first: MBW papers, Arents Library, Syracuse University, B70, notes.

365   I am not: *RCW,* 11/1/34.

366   Jack Rockefeller's saloon: Westbrook Pegler, syndicated column, 11/22/34.

366   Throughout his life: RFA 2C, B96 F722, *NYDN,* 9/29/34.

366   If you hadn't: *NY Mirror,* 9/3/34.

366   to dress high: Castle, 186.

366   much as I might like: RFA 2C, B91 F683, Junior to Woods, 3/23/33.

366   Not being sufficiently familiar: ibid.

367   If you behave: quoted in *NYP,* 12/29/87.

367   SWANK CROWD: *New York Journal,* 10/4/34.

367   five or six hundred: Castle, 186.

367   a manager, a pianist: *Time,* 10/8/34, 30.

367   I am the slave: *NYP,* 9/26/34.

367   slightly purple: Castle, 188.

368   seems like a terribly: RFA RG5.1.1, B6 F49, JDR3 diary, 5/11/37.

368   made it fashionable: *ANB,* Elsie De Wolfe.

368   not as a room: unattributed quotation, cited in *Restaurant Business,* 6/10/88.

368   greatest and most pretentious: JB/RR, Drawer I, F60.

368   As the quality: CHRIS-2, "Rider."

368   nonflashy strata: "Rockefeller Center," *Fortune,* 12/36, 139.

369   very impressive and dignified: RFA 4L, B275, Edward Seay to John Roy, 10/12/35.

369   Cohen: RCAC, #1026, 10/3/35.

369   go up to the Rainbow: RR/JB, B-Red-34, D. Fairbanks Jr. interviewed by Irena Chalmers, circa 1990.

369   might create: "Rockefeller Center," *Fortune,* 12/36, 139.

369   Dacron not Dunhill: RR/JB, Joseph Baum, office memo, 5/2/84.

369   tango-rhumba; goes with the lease: *Variety,* 1/18/39.

369   Of course our family: *NYDN,* 6/7/39.

370   boy with the patent-leather: Worden, 39.

370   My friends and I: *TNY,* 6/9/73, 5.

370   college boys [who]: RFA 4L, B275, Seay to Roy, 10/12/35.

370 Manhattan Mecca: RCAC, ad in *Yale Man's Guide Book,* n.d.

370 freak dance: *NYT,* 8/14/37.

370 combination of Truckin': *NYDN,* 8/14/35.

370 I loathe the: Saks advertisement, RFA 4L, B275, 1938.

371 You know the group: RFA 2C, B96 F720, Roy to Nelson, 8/4/42.

371 sky-high temple: Middleton, n.p.

371 climax to her career: RFA 4L, B275, by George Pepper, source not indicated on clipping.

372 a nice gesture: George Ross in *NYWT,* date unclear on clipping, circa 9/14/39.

372 very becoming: RFA 4L, B275, *NY Journal-American,* date unclear on clipping, ca. 11/12/39.

General sources for Chapter 20: **Van Schmus:** *NYT* obit, 1/14/42. **Rapee:** Hall. **Leonidoff:** Francisco; Gann; Hall. **Markert and Rockettes:** Francisco; Love. **Schoen:** Balfour. **Bourke-White:** V. Goldberg. **Toscanini:** Chotzinoff; J. Horowitz, *Understanding;* Marek; Sachs.

CHAPTER 21: *The Snake Changing Its Skin*

373 Enclosed please find: RFA 2C, B95 F716, NAR to Van Schmus, 1/27/34.

373 our restaurant: RFA 2C, B96 F720, Nelson to Mrs. W. W. Aldrich, 5/23/34.

373 Dudley & Cole: RCAC, cited in John Roy to James J. Atkinson, 10/27/34.

373 right kind of people: RCAC, Roy to Robertson, 4/10/35 and 4/11/35.

374 art diver; I am very: RFA 2C, B96 F722, Fauntz to Nelson, 6/6/36; see also RFA 4A, B4 F27, B4 F28.

374 As for old "Promiscuous": Fauntz to Nelson, 6/6/36.

374 personally favor: RFA 2C, B96 F720, Meyer Davis to Nelson, 8/30/34.

374 from a financial point: JB/RR, Nelson to Barney Richter, 5/10/35.

374 big shot: RCMHA, *St. Louis Post-Dispatch,* 11/9/47.

375 loaded foodstuffs: *NYHT,* 4/12/35.

375 the sheer oppressive: *NYT,* 3/25/01.

375 Naturally, I have: RFA 2C, B92 F698, Nelson to Robertson, 4/12/35.

375 brutally destroyed: RFA 2C, B92 F699, Charpentier to Nelson, 4/11/35.

375 You might talk plenty: RFA 2C, B92 F699, Charpentier to Junior, 9/26/41.

375 insurmountable difficulties; organizations; whirlwind: RFA 2C, B78 F582, Nelson to Executive Committee, 3/10/36.

376 changing; is now: "Rockefeller Center," *Fortune,* 12/36, 139.

376 You have caught: quoted ibid.

376 something that has not: RFA 2.1, B3 F32, Junior to Senior, 1/17/35.

376 I really do get; please excuse: RFA 2C, B78 F582, Junior to Brown, 5/8/35.

376 assume things are: RFA 2C, B78 F590, Junior to Turnbull, 7/22/35.

377 overlooking the river: quoted in Fosdick, 263, Junior to Robert Moses, 10/23/35.

377 Keep moving; gentle art: RFA 2C, B79 F596, Crowell, draft statement to press, 10/2/38.

377 may have given millions: *Lincoln (Nebraska) Evening Journal,* 11/12/38.

378 platform for kibitzers: RFA 4L, B214 F2160, "Rhododendrons and Public Relations," draft ms. by Ken Clark, circa 1939.

378 three loud cheers: RFA 2C, B79 F596, C. D. Jackson to Robertson, 11/10/38.

378 This was an idea: RFA 2C, B79 F596, Robertson to Jackson, 11/14/38.

378 It's a better: *Chicago Daily News,* 11/12/38.

378 pit their construction: RFA 2C, B79 F596, "Current information," 6/27/57.

378 By 1937 Mr. Rockefeller saw: Rockefeller Center, *John D. Rockefeller Jr.,* 35.

378 jealousies, friction: RFA 2C, B97 F732, Francis T. Christy memorandum, 9/17/34.

378 They have done a stupendous: RFA 2C, B97 F731, Debevoise memorandum, 10/29/34.

379 Only three copies; public and official: RFA 2C, B78 F587, Debevoise to Nelson, 1/2/36.

379 walking plaza: AL, Harrison Papers, B16 F5, interview, 2/9/76.

380 Mother's Museum: Persico, 176.

380 illegitimate offspring: quoted in Shaw, 10.

380 used to be a speakeasy: RFA 5.1.1, JDR3 diary, 8/20/40.

380 Laughing Room: Batterberry, 268.

381 equally adapted: Lynes, 176.

382 Finally, in April: Reich, 128–29.

382 I did not want; very bad: RFA 2C, B78 F582, Todd to Debevoise, 7/28/36.

382 miscellaneous notes; collection of early: NYA, 4/23/36, unsigned memo to Hellman.

383 substantially correct; would like for the article: NYA, T. J. Ross to Hellman, 4/27/36.

383 A journalist: quoted in Hellman, *Mrs. DePeyster's*, ix.

383 some modifications; to see how the latest: NYA, Hellman to T. J. Ross, 10/31/36.

383 more or less agreed: NYA, T. J. Ross memorandum, 11/18/36.

383 would that not be an act: RFA 2C, B78 F587, Debevoise to Nelson, 1/2/36.

384 not have his son's: RFA 5.1.1, B6 F290, JDR3 to Junior, 8/26/36.

384 My dear Mr. Rockefeller: RFA 2C, B7 F583, Todd to Junior, 5/18/38.

384 In spite of all Mr. Todd's: RFA 2C, B7 F583, Debevoise to Junior, 8/10/38.

384 There is no plaque: CHRIS-2.

385 Up the street, blocking: Kingsley, n.p.

385 The contrast of affluence: quoted in Kingsley, 77.

385 the opening shot: quoted in Sanders, 62.

385 suggested an unpleasant: RFA 2C, B81 F610, Caroline Hood report, 7/47.

385 The great masters: Le Corbusier, 42.

385 the building, rushing giddily: *TNY*, 6/10/33, 7–8.

386 [if] you find the work: RFA 2H, B135 F1002, Gumbel to C. J. Charles, 6/9/33.

386 a quick-draw: RFA 2H, B136 F1010, JDR3 to Gumbel, 12/23/41.

387 The chances are: RFA 2H, B135 F1002, Gumbel to Miss Spencer, 1/30/46.

387 He will get up from: J. A. Morris, *Nelson,* 333.

387 an ardor startling: Reich, 168.

387 radio set: RFA 2C, B95 F717, Nelson to Merlin Aylesworth, 12/20/32.

388 City Hall: Collier and Horowitz, 225.

388 You know the animus: RFA 2H, B122 F909, Heydt to Woods, 12/28/33.

388 Chief Tax Dolee: W. H. Allen, *Why,* 79.

388 reference to Rockefeller tax: COHP, W. H. Allen, 282.

389 the customary 90%; without protest : RCAC, Executive Committee Draft Minutes, 10/11/34.

389 with intent to deceive; a provision: RCAC, Lester Abberley to Charles Poletti, 3/30/37.

390 I did piqué turns: RCMHA, Janice Herbert interview, 1989.

390 Neither scorn: quoted in Persico, 166.

390 They have very little: RFA 2Z, B3 F30, Junior to Senior, 5/3/34.

390 I believe that employers: RFA, B100 F757, Junior to Robertson, 3/10/38.

391 the oldest, toughest: "Strikebreaking," *Fortune,* 1/35, 56.

391 tough as a teamster: *CB*43, 631.

392 long and bitter: *Detroit News,* 5/29/38.

392 Labor Utopia: *New York Journal-American,* 8/19/40.

392 Nelson is satisfied: Goulden, *Meany,* 404.

General sources for Chapter 21: **Junior's other activities:** Fosdick. **"21":** Kaytor. **Nelson's takeover:** Reich. **Political influence:** CHRIS-1, CHRIS-2.

CHAPTER 22: *The Kingdom of the World*

393 **In all the building history:** *Washington Star,* undated clipping in RFA 2C, B141.

393 **a maximum of return:** RFA 2C, B80 F598, Nelson to Junior, 2/25/39.

394 **imagination and brilliant:** quoted in Rockefeller, *The Last Rivet,* 45.

394 **go to work on:** Selznick, quoted in Behlmer, 218–19.

395 **Looking out my:** Kazin, *Jew,* 73.

395 **come in at a rate:** quoted in *RCM,* 9/38, 9.

395 **I could sell carloads:** Swanson, 453–68.

396 **delighted with the lunchroom:** RFA 2Z, B3 F30, Junior to Senior, 6/19/34.

396 **Please see me:** J. Horowitz, *Understanding,* 308–9.

396 **Trees should have no:** quoted in Eyssell.

397 **smoke and a box; interfering:** RFA 2C, B70, Barton Turnbull to Nelson, 8/8/04.

397 **Looking out on:** F. L. Allen, *Harper's,* 10/38, 513.

397 **lively sounds:** *NYWT,* 6/28/38.

399 **feel the tingle:** F. L. Allen, "Look at Rockefeller Center," *Harper's,* 10/38, 506–13.

399 **Special Officer Doormen:** *NYHT,* 11/20/55.

399 **greet important people:** RCAC, J. R. Todd to Todd & Brown, 11/1/33.

399 **interfere[d] with the general:** RCAC, Brown to N. A. Kenworthy, 1/30/34.

400 **showing also:** RCMHA, J-145, Clark to Clary and Eyssell, 9/5/41.

400 **but he says there's no use:** *RCW,* 5/2/35, 2.

400 **scientific massage; as new as:** *RCW,* 11/21/35.

400 **seats so capacious:** unattributed quote in Adams et al., 210.

401 **Can I import:** quoted in undated clipping from *RCM,* in HRC, Norman Bel Geddes Papers, JF424, XT-2, I-2.

401 **national clearing house:** *RCW,* 10/18/34, 9.

401 **mounted tenderly:** "National Poetry Center," *TNY,* 12/22/34, 7.

401 **refreshment headquarters:** *RCM,* 4/37, 28.

401 **corps of trained men:** *RCW,* 10/10/35, 17.

401 **Chichen Itza:** Bernays and Kaplan, *Back,* 300.

402 **Aside from the fact:** RFA 2.1, B5 F54, Junior to Farley, 12/11/39.

402 **roasted English:** JB/RR, J-17, caption, 1938.

402 **ascertained that . . . 'lunch':** RCAC, RC Luncheon Club minutes, 7/12/34.

402 **men do not like:** RFA 2C, B96 F722, Debevoise to Nelson, 1/8/34.

403 **As you probably know; Mr. Ellinger:** RFA 4L, B215 F2177, Nelson to Admissions Committee, 10/24/35.

403 **room for a few:** RFA 4L, B215 F2177, John Roy to Nelson, 8/31/38.

403 **light and give service:** Rockefeller, *Last Rivet,* 27.

403 **bring the operation as near:** RFA 2C, B78 F580, Todd to Junior, 11/18/33.

404 **intimately lives and has:** *RCW,* 3/21/35, 4.

404 **female Simon:** union lawyer Louis Ferkin, quoted in *NYT,* 9/23/43.

404 **petticoated:** picket sign, cited in *NYT,* 9/25/43.

405 **see if you can put:** quoted in Rockefeller, *Last Rivet,* 35.

406 **at the door:** quoted ibid., 36–41.

406 **Rivet practice:** RFA 2Z, B12 F121, Junior's diary, 11/1/39.

406 **He's pretty good:** *New York Sun,* 11/2/39.

406 **And so the story:** quoted in Rockefeller, *Last Rivet,* 45.

General sources for Chapter 22: **Last Rivet ceremony:** Rockefeller, *Last Rivet.* **Sarnoff's office:** Lewis. **Whitney's office:** Kahn.

CHAPTER 23: *The Demand Is Almost Unbelievable*

407 The demand for additional: RFA 2C, B91 F685, Junior to his sons, 2/11/46.

407 The White House has; Send it: quoted in *RCM*, 1/42, 12–13.

408 Goeden Morgen: "Dutch Treat," *TNY*, 3/30/40, 15–16.

409 marrying the customers: Farr, 297.

409 a plane ride: ibid., 186–91.

409 the Rickenbacker line: Adamson, 246.

409 I tolded; darkies: Farr, 297–305.

409 Airline history: *NYHT*, 6/13/40.

410 liberally blamed: *NYHT*, 8/2/41.

410 an un-neutral: quoted in RFA 5.1.1, B6 F53, JDR3 diary, 1/27/41.

410 Miss Bernice Thimm: RCAC, caption, Pers. 3, 3/14/41.

410 These winter evenings: quoted in Balfour, 221.

411 Mr. Bailey: TIA, O. P. Swift to Larsen, 2/4/41.

411 They have tough: quoted in Stevenson, 270.

411 exotic Nipponese: *NYHT*, 6/25/42.

412 distressing ignorance: "How to Tell Japs from the Chinese," *Life*, 12/22/41.

412 PLEASE COOPERATE: JB/RR, C-Pink-11, menu, 12/16/42.

412 all the good dyes: quoted in *NYDN*, 11/11/45.

412 We may have to lose: RFA 2C, B100 F762, Borella to Robertson, 8/5/40.

412 *Où est:* JB/RR, H-41, Caroline Hood presentation.

412 Mr. H.S.R. did not: RFA 2C, B88 F664, Van Schmus file memo, 2/29/40.

413 almost like New Year's: *New York*, 11/6/41.

413 operation of these rooms; well received: RFA 2C, B96 F720, Turnbull to Junior, 9/21/42.

413 increasing shortage: RFA 4L, B207 F2081, undated press release.

413 president privately thanking: RFA 4L, B207 F2081, David Siegal to Robertson, 11/12/42.

413 many deep expressions: quoted in *Variety*, 1/6/43.

414 need to be brought: RFA 2C, B70, Turnbull to Nelson, 6/5/42.

414 t-room: Chauncey, 197, 207.

414 skeptical that we can: RFA 2C, B70, Turnbull to Nelson, 6/12/42.

414 the barrel jumper: RFA 2C, B70, Turnbull to Nelson, 11/7/42.

414 the second largest: RFA 2C, B70, Turnbull to Nelson 1/3/41.

415 The Center is now: RFA 5.1.1, B6 F53, JDR3 diary, 12/11/41.

415 Our October statement: JB/RR, x-Blue-8, Robertson to Junior, 11/23/42.

415 How pleased I am: JB/RR, x-Blue-8, 11/27/42.

415 the saturation point: *NYT*, 5/5/44.

415 notified all of our own: RFA 4L, B207 F2081, Turnbull to Nelson, 9/30/43.

415 Already, and quite: RFA 2H, B124 F920, Junior to Heydt, 10/29/45.

416 Gee, Pa; Nelson, . . . whom: quoted in PBS series, *The American Experience:* "The Rockefellers."

417 protective storage: system explained in *RCM*, 8/42, 19.

417 rather live on pate: Elson, *1941–1960*, 178.

417 with tears in his eyes: RFA 4L, B218 F2214, Nelson to Robertson, 5/27/44.

418 some special mark: RFA 4L, B21 F2214, E. A. Maulme to Nelson, 12/21/45.

418 Dear Nelson: RFA 4L, B21 F2214, Geddes to Nelson, 4/9/46; Sherwood to Nelson, 5/6/46.

418 In view of the fact: RFA 4L, B21 F2214, Nelson to Turnbull and F. L. Corcoran, 3/7/46.

418 almost unbelievable: RFA 2C, B91 F685, Junior to his sons, 2/11/46.

418 Because this center: RFA 4L, B219 F2225A, Nelson to Junior, 7/12/48.

419 was probably the greatest: Baker Library, Harvard Business School, Aldrich Papers, B239, W. W. Aldrich interviewed by Arthur M. Johnson, 12/10 and 12/18/65.

419   **I really belong:** *Richmond Times-Dispatch,* 12/7/41, quoted in Fosdick, 429.

General sources for Chapter 23: **Rickenbacker:** Farr; Rickenbacker. **Time Inc.:** Elson (both).

EPILOGUE

421   **take this blow:** quoted in Reich, 473.
421   **the purifying fire:** John D. Rockefeller, Jr., "I Believe," inscription on memorial stone, Rockefeller Center.
421   **We know little; But there they are:** quoted in Fosdick, 429.
421   **It might surprise people:** D. Rockefeller, *Memoirs,* 54.
422   **by far the largest:** Harr and Johnson, *Conscience,* 557–58.
422   **the salvation of:** Harr and Johnson, *Century,* 197–98.
422   **Father did a lot:** quoted in Reich, 390–91.
422   **Often a man gets:** quoted in Fosdick, 266.
422   **No further efforts:** RFA 2Z, B31 F247, file memo, 9/5/58.
423   **Concrete excited:** Persico, 201.
423   **You have always indicated:** quoted in D. Rockefeller, *Memoirs,* 349.
424   **probably the largest-grossing:** quoted in Metz, 75.
425   **It represents the image:** Loth, 115–16.
425   **I was shocked:** RFA 4L, B212 F2132, Goetze to Robertson, 1/17/49.
425   **extremely excessive; if such a complaint:** CA, Robertson to Goetze, 1/25/49
425   **quite improper:** RFA 4L, B219 F2224, Nelson to Robertson, 3/16/49.
425   **You should, I think:** RFA 4L, B219 F2224, Robertson to Nelson, 3/18/49.
426   **We must not forget:** RFA RG2, 2H, Junior to Debevoise, 10/11/57.
426   **I urge you:** RFA R 2H, B57 F422, Junior to Debevoise, 10/23/58.

426   **Harrison's publicity campaign:** letter to editor, *Ohio Architect,* 2/27/53.
427   **Wally Harrison, who built:** *New York Mirror,* 1/26/49.
427   **credit not due:** see *Newsday,* 5/17/02— "He designed Lincoln Center, Rockefeller Center and the United Nations . . ."
427   **incoherent splatter:** quoted in Balfour, 224.
427   **new buildings, with their broad:** RCAC, caption, SpEv IV-C, 8/5/71.
427   **the sinister:** quoted in J. Morris, *Manhattan,* 16.
427   **I saw a car:** quoted in C. Hood, 222.
427   **After a lifetime:** Newhouse, 281.
427   **I'm sure all the critics:** AL, Harrison Papers, from *Boston Globe* obituary, 12/4/81.
427   **compliant servant:** Gill, 155–56.
427   **ruined . . . by the German:** AL, Harrison Papers, B16, F7, WKH essay, 4/27/77.
428   **homos who found:** AL, Harrison Papers, B16, F7, notes for "WKH Book," 4/25/77, 3.
428   **puzzled and:** August Heckscher, in *Century Association Yearbook, 1982,* 237.
429   **to make the dirt:** *NYT,* 3/2/65, 1.
429   **the one place where:** TIA, *Time* reporter memos to writer; carbons of 7/25/61, 8/2/61.
429   **those French and Italian:** CHK-I, Gus Eyssell.
429   **there is no assurance:** RFA 4L, B208 F2091, Eyssell to Dilworth et al., 1/22/69.
429   **Music Hall has been hit:** *Variety,* 10/72, exact date unclear; reproduced in *Marquee,* vol. 4, number 4.
429   **Some of the things:** unnamed dancer quoted in "Tune Out for Radio City?," *Time,* 10/23/72, 82.
430   **By making a fetish:** Frank Rich, "Last Picture Show," *Time,* 3/13/78.
430   **It was like the Catholic:** author interview, Alton Marshall, 5/5/00.

431   It's dead: COHP, Wallace Harrison, 122–23.

431   Williamsburg-level: JB/RR, A-Red-General, Michael Whiteman to Peter Rummell, 5/21/84.

431   mix[ing] the Dacron: RR/JB, Joseph Baum, office memo, 5/2/84.

431   Hope diamond: *NYT,* 9/12/95.

431   singular real estate: response to author query, 4/30.

432   Rockefeller Center amounts to: introduction to Karp, 7.

433   An infinite number: Koolhaas, 289.

433   Rockefeller Center begets: "Rockefeller Center," *Fortune,* 12/36, 139.

BIBLIOGRAPHY

Abramson, Daniel M. *Skyscraper Rivals: The AIG Building and the Architecture of Wall Street.* Princeton: Princeton Architectural Press, 2001.

Adams, Janet; Marjorie Pearson; and Anthony W. Robins. *Rockefeller Center Designation Report.* New York: City of New York Landmarks Preservation Commission, 1985.

Adams, Thomas. *The Building of the City: Regional Plan of New York and Its Environs, Vol. 2.* New York: Regional Plan Association, 1931.

Adamson, Hans. *Eddie Rickenbacker.* New York: Macmillan, 1946.

Allen, Frederick Lewis. *Since Yesterday: The 1930s in America.* New York: Harper & Row, 1972.

Allen, William H. *Rockefeller: Giant, Dwarf, and Symbol.* New York: Institute for Public Service, 1930.

———. *Why Tammanies Revive.* New York: privately published, 1937.

Alpern, Andrew, and Seymour Durst. *New York's Architectural Holdouts.* Mineola, NY: Dover, 1996.

American National Biography. New York: Oxford University Press, 1999.

Angly, Edward, ed. *Oh, Yeah?* New York: Viking, 1931.

Atkinson, Brooks. *Broadway.* New York: Macmillan, 1974.

Balfour, Alan. *Rockefeller Center.* New York: McGraw-Hill, 1978.

Barnouw, Erik. *A Tower in Babel: A History of Broadcasting in the United States, to 1933.* New York: Oxford University Press, 1966.

———. *The Golden Web: A History of Broadcasting in the United States, 1933 to 1953.* New York: Oxford University Press, 1968.

Batterberry, Michael, and Arianne Batterberry. *On the Town in New York: A History of Eating, Drinking and Entertainments from 1776 to the Present.* New York: Scribner, 1973.

Beard, Patricia. *Growing Up Republican: Christie Whitman, the Politics of Character.* New York: HarperCollins, 1996

Beaton, Cecil. *Cecil Beaton's New York.* London: B. T. Batsford, 1938.

Behlmer, Rudy, ed. *Memo from David O. Selznick.* Hollywood, CA: Samuel French, 1989.

Behr, Edward. *Prohibition: Thirteen Years That Changed America.* New York: Arcade, 1996.

Belleroche, William de. *Brangwyn's Pilgrimage.* London: Chapman and Hall, 1948.

Bender, Thomas. *New York Intellect: A History of Intellectual Life in New York City, from 1950 to the Beginnings of Our Own Time.* New York: Knopf, 1987.

Berger, Meyer. *Meyer Berger's New York.* New York: Random House, 1953.

Bernays, Anne, and Justin Kaplan. *Back Then: Two Lives in 1950s New York.* New York: Morrow, 2002.

Bernays, Edward L. *Biography of an Idea: Memoirs of Public Relations Counsel Edward L. Bernays.* New York: Simon & Schuster, 1965.

Bilby, Kenneth. *The General: David Sarnoff and the Rise of the Communications Industry.* New York: Harper & Row, 1986.

Bleecker, Samuel E. *The Politics of Architecture: A Perspective on Nelson A. Rockefeller.* New York: Rutledge Press, 1981.

Bletter, Rosemarie, and Cervin Robinson. *Skyscraper Style: Art Deco New York.* New York: Oxford University Press, 1975.

Breeze, Carla. *New York Deco.* New York: Rizzoli, 1993.

Briggs, John. *Requiem for a Yellow Brick Brewery.* Boston: Little, Brown, 1969.

Brooks, Walter R. *New York: An Intimate Guide.* New York: Knopf, 1931.

Bunyan, Patrick. *All Around the Town: Amazing Manhattan Facts and Curiosities.* New York: Fordham University Press, 1999.

Burchard, Dr. John, and Albert Bush-Brown. *The Architecture of America: A Social & Cultural History.* Boston: Little, Brown, 1961.

Burns, Ric, and James Sanders. *New York: An Illustrated History.* New York: Knopf, 1999.

Butler, Nicholas Murray. *Across the Busy Years, Vol. 1.* New York: Scribner, 1939.

————. *Across the Busy Years, Vol. 2.* New York: Scribner, 1940.

Canato, Mario. *Pragmatic Thinking in the Ideas of the Skyscraper Architects of the 1920s.* Unpublished dissertation, University of Pennsylvania, 1992.

Caro, Robert. *The Power Broker.* New York: Knopf, 1974.

Case, Josephine, and Everett Needham Case. *Owen D. Young and American Enterprise: A Biography.* Boston: David R. Godine, 1982.

Castle, Molly. *Round the World with an Appetite.* London: Hodder & Stoughton, 1936.

Castro, Jan. *The Art & Life of Georgia O'Keeffe.* New York: Crown, 1985.

Century Association Yearbook. New York: Century Association, various years.

Chase, Mary Ellen. *Abby Aldrich Rockefeller.* New York: Macmillan, 1950.

Chauncey, George. *Gay New York: Gender, Urban Culture, and the Making of the Gay World, 1890–1940.* London: HarperCollins Flamingo, 1994.

Chernow, Ron. *Titan: The Life of John D. Rockefeller, Sr.* New York: Random House, 1998.

Christy, Francis. Unpublished memoir, n.d.

Ciment, Michel. *Conversations with Losey.* New York: Routledge, 1985.

Club Members of New York, Vol. IX. New York: Club Members of New York, 1925.

Collier, Peter, and David Horowitz. *The Rockefellers: An American Dynasty.* New York: Holt, Rinehart and Winston, 1976.

Collins, Theresa. *Otto Kahn: Art, Money and Modern Time.* Chapel Hill and London: University of North Carolina Press, 1968.

Condit, Carl W. *American Building: Materials and Techniques from the Beginning of the Colonial Settlements to the Present.* Chicago and London: University of Chicago Press, 1968.

Conrad, Peter. *The Art of the City.* New York and Oxford: Oxford University Press, 1984.

Corbusier, Le (Charles E. Jeanneret-Gris). *When the Cathedrals Were White: A Journey to the Country of Timid People.* New York: Reynal & Hitchcock, 1947.

Cowart, Jack; Juan Hamilton; and Sarah Greenough. *Georgia O'Keeffe: Art and Letters.* Boston: Little, Brown, 1987.

D'Agostino, Carla. *The Christmas Tree at Rockefeller Center.* New York: Lickle Publishing, 1997.

Daley, Robert. *The World Beneath the City.* Philadelphia and New York: Lippincott, 1997.

Dau, Frederick. *Dau's New York Blue Book 1927.* New York: Dau's, 1927.

Dean, Arthur H. *William Nelson Cromwell 1854–1948: An American Pioneer.* New York: Privately published, 1957.

Desmond, James. *Nelson Rockefeller: A Political Biography.* New York: Macmillan, 1964.

DeZemler, Charles. *Once Over Lightly: The Story of Man and His Hair.* New York: Privately published, 1939.

Dolkart, Andrew S. *Morningside Heights: A History of Its Architecture and Development.* New York: Columbia University Press, 1998.

Douglas, Ann. *Terrible Honesty: Mongrel Manhattan in the 1920s.* New York: Farrar, Straus & Giroux, 1995.

Dreher, Carl. *Sarnoff: An American Success.* New York: Quadrangle, 1977.

Eaton, Quaintance. *The Miracle of the Met.* New York: Meredith, 1968.

Eisler, Benita. *O'Keeffe and Stieglitz: An American Romance.* New York: Doubleday, 1991.

Elson, Robert T. *The World of Time Inc.: The Intimate History of a Publishing Enterprise, 1923–1941.* New York: Atheneum, 1968.

———. *The World of Time Inc.: The Intimate History of a Publishing Enterprise, 1941–1960.* New York: Atheneum, 1973.

Ernst, Joseph. *"Dear Father"/"Dear Son": Correspondence of John D. Rockefeller and John D. Rockefeller, Jr.* New York: Fordham University Press in cooperation with Rockefeller Archive Center, 1994.

Eyssell, Gustav S. *Rockefeller Center: Its Current History, 1948–1952.* Unpublished manuscript, RFA 2C.

Farr, Finis. *Rickenbacker's Luck: An American Life.* Boston: Houghton Mifflin, 1979.

Federal Writers' Project. *The WPA Guide to New York City.* New York: Federal Writers' Project, 1939.

Ferriss, Hugh. *The Metropolis of Tomorrow.* New York: Ives Washburn, 1929.

Fifth Avenue Association. *Fifty Years of Fifth.* New York: International Press, 1957.

Fitch, James Marston, and Diana Waite. *Grand Central Terminal and Rockefeller Center: A Historic-critical Estimate of Their Significance.* Albany: NY State Department of Parks & Recreation, 1974.

Fosdick, Raymond. *John D. Rockefeller, Jr.: A Portrait.* New York: Harper and Brothers, 1956.

Francisco, Charles. *The Radio City Music Hall: An Affectionate History of the World's Greatest Theater.* New York: E. P. Dutton, 1979.

Gabler, Neal. *An Empire of their Own.* New York: Crown, 1988.

———. *Winchell: Gossip, Power and the Culture of Celebrity.* New York: Knopf, 1994.

Gann, Ernest K. *A Hostage to Fortune.* New York: Knopf, 1978.

Garvey, Timothy. *Lee O. Lawrie: Classicism and American Culture, 1919–1954.* University of Minnesota, unpublished doctoral dissertation, 1980.

Gatti-Cassaza, Giulio. *Memories of the Opera.* New York: Scribner, 1941.

Geddes, Norman Bel. *Miracle in the Evening.* New York: Doubleday, 1960.

Gelernter, David. *1939: The Lost World of the Fair.* New York: Free Press, 1995.

Giedion, Sigfried. *Space, Time and Architecture: The Growth of a New Tradition.* Cambridge, MA: Harvard University Press, 1941.

Gill, Brendan. *A New York Life: Of Friends and Others.* New York: Poseidon Press, 1990.

Gold, Arthur, and Robert Fizdale. *Misia: The Life of Misia Sert.* New York: Knopf, 1980.

Goldberg, Vicki. *Margaret Bourke-White: A Biography.* New York: Harper & Row, 1986.

Goldberger, Paul. *The City Observed: New York.* New York: Knopf, 1979.

———. *The Skyscraper.* New York: Knopf, 1981.

Goodyear, A. Conger. *The Museum of Modern Art: The First Ten Years.* New York: MOMA, 1943.

Goulden, Joseph C. *Meany.* New York: Atheneum, 1972.

Graham, Martha. *Blood Memory.* New York: Doubleday, 1991.

Grant, James. *The Trouble with Prosperity.* New York: Times Books, 1996.

Gray, Christopher. *Changing New York: The Architectural Scene.* New York: Dover, 1992.

Hall, Ben M. *The Best Remaining Seats.* New York: Bramhall House, 1961.

Hamlin, Talbot. *Architecture Through the Ages.* New York: Putnam, 1940.

———. *Forms and Functions of Twentieth Century Architecture.* New York: Columbia University Press, 1952.

Hanks, David A. *Donald Deskey: Decorative Designs and Interiors.* New York: E. P. Dutton, 1987.

Harr, John Ensor, and Peter J. Johnson. *The Rockefeller Century: Three Generations of America's Greatest Family.* New York: Scribner, 1988.

———. *The Rockefeller Conscience: An American Family in Public and in Private.* New York: Scribner, 1991.

Harriman, Margaret. *Take Them Up Tenderly.* New York: Knopf, 1944.

Hawes, Elizabeth. *New York, New York: How the Apartment House Transformed the Life of the City (1869–1930).* New York: Holt, 1993.

Heckscher, August. *Alive in the City: Memoir of an Ex-Commissioner.* New York: Scribner, 1974.

———. *When La Guardia Was Mayor: New York's Legendary Years.* New York: Norton, 1978.

Heilbrun, Margaret. *Inventing the Skyline: The Architecture of Cass Gilbert.* New York: Columbia University Press, 2000.

Hellman, Geoffrey. *Mrs. de Peyster's Parties, and Other Lively Studies from The New Yorker.* New York: Macmillan, 1963.

Herrera, Hayden. *Frida.* New York: Harper, 1983.

Hiebert, Ray Eldon. *Courtier to the Crowd: The Story of Ivy Lee and the Development of Public Relations.* Ames: Iowa State University Press, 1966.

Hills, Patricia. *Stuart Davis.* New York: Harry N. Abrams, 1996.

Hitchcock, Henry-Russell, and Philip Johnson. *The International Style.* New York: W. W. Norton, 1966.

Hood, Clifton. *722 Miles: The Building of the Subways and How They Transformed New York.* Baltimore and London: Johns Hopkins University Press, 1933.

Horowitz, Joseph. *Understanding Toscanini.* New York: Knopf, 1987.

Horowitz, Louis J. *The Towers of New York: The Memoirs of a Master Builder.* New York: Simon & Schuster, 1937.

Huxtable, Ada Louise. *Kicked a Building Lately?* New York: Quadrangle, 1976.

Ickes, Harold. *The Secret Diary of Harold Ickes, Vol. II, 1936–1939.* New York: Simon & Schuster, 1954.

The International Competition for a New Administration Building for the Chicago Tribune, MCMXXII. Chicago: The Tribune Company, 1923.

Irish, Sharon. *Cass Gilbert, Architect: Modern Traditionalist.* New York: Monacelli, 1998.

Jackson, Kenneth T., ed. *The Encyclopedia of New York City.* New Haven and London: Yale University Press, 1995.

Jacobs, Jane. *The Death and Life of Great American Cities.* New York: Random House, 1961.

James, Marquis. *The Metropolitan Life: A Study in Business Growth.* New York: Viking, 1971.

Johnson, Arthur M. *Winthrop W. Aldrich: Lawyer, Banker, Diplomat.* Boston: Graduate School of Business Administration, Harvard University, 1968.

Jordy, William H. *American Buildings and Their Architects: The Impact of European Modernism in the Mid-Twentieth Century.* Garden City, NY: Anchor Press/Doubleday, 1972.

Kahn, E. J. Jr. *Jock: The Life and Times of John Hay Whitney.* New York: Doubleday, 1981.

Kaiser, Charles. *The Gay Metropolis: 1940–1996.* Boston: Houghton Mifflin, 1997.

Kamin, Blair. *Tribune Tower: American Landmark.* Chicago: Tribune Company, 2000.

Karp, Walter. *The Center: A History and Guide to Rockefeller Center,* introduction by Brendan Gill. New York: American Heritage, 1982.

Kaytor, Marilyn. *"21": The Life and Times of New York's Favorite Club.* New York: Viking, 1975.

Kazin, Alfred. *Starting Out in the Thirties.* Boston: Atlantic Monthly Press, 1965.

———. *New York Jew.* New York, Knopf: 1978.

Kert, Bernice. *Abby Aldrich Rockefeller: The Woman in the Family.* New York: Random House, 1993.

Kessner, Thomas. *Fiorello H. La Guardia and the Making of Modern New York.* New York: McGraw-Hill, 1989.

Kilham, Walter H. Jr., *Raymond Hood, Architect: Form Through Function in the American Skyscraper.* New York: Architectural Book Publishing Company, 1973.

Kingsley, Sidney, with Nene Couch, ed. *Five Prizewinning Plays.* Columbus: Ohio State University Press, 1995.

Kinney, Harrison. *James Thurber: His Life and Times.* New York: Henry Holt, 1995.

Kirstein, Lincoln. *Mosaic.* New York: Farrar, Straus & Giroux, 1994.

Kobler, John. *The Magnificent Otto: The Life of Otto Kahn.* New York: Scribner, 1988.

———. *Ardent Spirits: The Rise and Fall of Prohibition.* New York: DaCapo Press, 1993.

Kolodin, Irving. *The Story of the Metropolitan Opera: 1883–1950.* New York: Knopf, 1953.

———. *The Metropolitan Opera: 1883–1966, A Candid History.* New York: Knopf, 1966.

Koolhaas, Rem. *Delirious New York.* New York: Monacelli, 1994.

Kramer, Hilton. *The Sculpture of Gaston Lachaise.* New York: The Eakins Press, 1967.

Kramer, Michael, and Sam Roberts. *"I Never Wanted to Be Vice-President of Anything."* New York: Basic, 1976.

Kriendler, H. Peter, with H. Paul Jeffers. *21: Every Day Was New Year's Eve, The Memoirs of a New York Saloonkeeper.* Dallas: Taylor, 1999.

Krinsky, Carol Herselle. *Rockefeller Center.* New York and Oxford: Oxford University Press, 1978.

Kroessler, Jeffrey A. *New York Year by Year: A Chronology of the Great Metropolis.* New York and London: New York University Press, 2002.

Kundera, Milan. *The Unbearable Lightness of Being.* New York: HarperPerennial, 1991.

Léger, Fernand. *Functions of Painting.* New York: Viking, 1973.

Lessard, Suzannah. *The Architect of Desire.* New York: Dial, 1996

Lewis, Tom. *Empire of the Air: The Men Who Made Radio.* New York: HarperCollins, 1991.

Lisle, Laurie. *Portrait of an Artist: A Biography of Georgia O'Keeffe.* New York: Seaview Books, 1980.

Lorenz, Lee. *The Art of The New Yorker: 1925–1995.* New York: Knopf, 1995.

Loth, David. *The City within a City.* New York: William Morrow, 1966.

Love, Judith. *Thirty Thousand Kicks: What's It Like to Be a Rockette?* Hicksville, NY: Exposition Press, 1980.

Lynes, Russell. *Good Old Modern.* New York: Atheneum, 1973.

Lyons, Eugene. *David Sarnoff.* New York: Harper & Row, 1966.

McDonagh, Don. *Martha Graham: A Biography.* New York: Praeger, 1973.

Mackay, Donald A. *The Building of Manhattan.* New York: Harper & Row, 1987.

Manchester, William. *A Rockefeller Family Portrait: From John D. to Nelson.* Boston: Little, Brown, 1959.

Marek, George R. *Toscanini.* New York: Atheneum, 1975.

Marnham, Patrick. *Dreaming with His Eyes Open: A Life of Diego Rivera.* New York: Knopf, 1998.

Marrin, Albert. *Nicholas Murray Butler.* Boston: Twayne Publishers, 1976.

Masters, Margaret Dale. *Hartley Burr Alexander: Writer-in-Stone.* Lincoln, NE: Jacob North, 1992.

Matz, Mary Jane. *The Many Lives of Otto Kahn.* New York: Macmillan, 1963.

Mayer, Martin. *The Met: One Hundred Years of Grand Opera.* New York: Simon & Schuster, 1983.

Merton, Thomas. *The Seven Storey Mountain.* New York: Harcourt Brace, 1948.

Metz, Robert. *The Today Show.* Chicago: Playboy Press, 1977.

Middleton, Scudder. *Dining, Wining, and Dancing in New York.* New York: Dodge, 1938.

Miller, Donald L. *Lewis Mumford: A Life.* New York: Weidenfeld & Nicolson, 1989.

Miller, Ross. *Here's the Deal: The Buying and Selling of a Great American City.* New York: Knopf, 1996.

Minnelli, Vincente. *I Remember It Well.* Garden City, NY: Doubleday, 1974.

Mitchell, Joseph. *Up in the Old Hotel.* New York: Vintage, 1993.

Morris, Jan. *Manhattan '45.* New York and Oxford: Oxford University Press, 1987.

Morris, Joe Alex. *Those Rockefeller Brothers: An Informal Biography of Five Extraordinary Young Men.* New York: Harper and Brothers, 1953.

———. *Nelson Rockefeller: A Biography.* New York: Harper and Brothers, 1960.

Morris, Lloyd. *Incredible New York: High Life and Low Life from 1850 to 1950.* Syracuse: Syracuse University Press, 1996.

Museum of Modern Art. *Diego Rivera.* New York: Museum of Modern Art, 1931.

———. *Murals by American Painters.* New York: Museum of Modern Art, 1932.

Nasaw, David. *The Chief: The Life of William Randolph Hearst.* Boston: Houghton Mifflin, 2000.

The National Cyclopaedia of American Biography. New York: James T. White & Co., 1907.

Nelson, Jane. *Carl Milles in the United States.* University of Minnesota, unpublished doctoral dissertation, 1986.

Nevins, Deborah. *Grand Central Terminal: City within the City.* New York: Municipal Art Society, 1982.

Newhouse, Victoria. *Wallace K. Harrison, Architect.* New York: Rizzoli, 1989.

Noguchi, Isamu. *A Sculptor's World.* New York: Harper & Row, 1968.

Nordland, Gerald. *Gaston Lachaise: The Man and His Work.* New York: George Braziller, 1974.

North, Arthur. *Raymond Hood.* New York: Whittlesey House, 1931.

Page, Max. *The Creative Destruction of Manhattan, 1900–1940.* Chicago: University of Chicago Press, 1999.

Persico, Joseph E. *The Imperial Rockefeller.* New York: Simon & Schuster, 1982.

Pfeiffer, Bruce. *Letters to Apprentices: Frank Lloyd Wright.* Fresno: California State University Press, 1986.

Porzelt, Paul. *The Metropolitan Club of New York.* New York: Rizzoli, 1982.

Pritchett, V. S. *New York Proclaimed.* New York: Harcourt, Brace & World, 1965.

Pyle, Tom, and Beth Day. *Pocantico: Fifty Years on the Rockefeller Domain.* New York: Duell, Sloan and Pearce, 1964.

Ramsaye, Terry. *A Million and One Nights: A History of the Motion Picture.* New York: Simon & Schuster, 1954.

Rand, Harry. *Paul Manship.* Washington and London: Smithsonian Institution Press, 1989.

Rather, Susan. *Archaism, Modernism, and the Art of Paul Manship.* Austin: University of Texas Press, 1993.

Reed, Henry. *Beaux-Arts Architecture in New York.* New York: Dover, 1988.

Reich, Cary. *The Life of Nelson A. Rockefeller: Worlds to Conquer 1908–1958.* New York: Doubleday, 1996.

Rewald, John. *The John Hay Whitney Collection.* Washington, DC: National Gallery of Art, 1983.

Reynolds, Donald. *Architecture of New York City: Histories and Views of Important Structures, Sites and Symbols.* New York: Macmillan, 1994.

Rich, Frank, with Lisa Aronson. *The Theatre Art of Boris Aronson.* New York: Knopf, 1987.

Rickenbacker, Eddie. *Rickenbacker: An Autobiography.* Englewood Cliffs, NJ: Prentice-Hall, 1967.

Rivera, Diego. *Portrait of America.* New York: Covici and Friede, 1934.

———. *My Art, My Life.* New York: Dover, 1991.

Robbins, Christine Chapman. *David Hosack: Citizen of New York.* Phaladelphia: American Philosophical Society, 1964.

Robinson, Harlow. *The Last Impresario: The Life, Times and Legacy of Sol Hurok.* New York: Viking, 1994.

Robinson, Roxana. *Georgia O'Keeffe.* New York: Harper & Row, 1989.

Rochfort, Desmond. *The Murals of Diego Rivera.* London: South Bank Board/Journeyman, 1987.

Rockefeller Apartments. New York: New York City Landmarks Preservation Commission, 1982.

Rockefeller Center. *Rockefeller Center.* New York: 1932.

———. *John D. Rockefeller, Jr.: Founder of Rockefeller Center.* New York: Rockefeller Center, 1961

Rockefeller, David. *Memoirs.* New York: Random House, 2002.

Rockefeller, John D. Jr. *The Last Rivet.* New York: Columbia University Press, 1940.

Rogers, Meyric R. *Carl Milles: An Interpretation of His Work.* New Haven: Yale University Press, 1940.

Rosenman, Mervin. *Forgery, Perjury and an Enormous Fortune: 2,303 Claimants to the Ella Wendel Estate.* New York: Beach Hampton Press, 1984.

Sachs, Harvey, *Toscanini.* Philadelphia and New York: Lippincott, 1978.

Saleski, Gdal. *Famous Musicians of a Wandering Race.* New York: Bloch, 1927.

Sanders, James. *Celluloid Skyline.* New York: Knopf, 2001.

Schenkel, Albert F. *The Rich Man and the Kingdom: John D. Rockefeller, Jr. and the Protestant Establishment.* Minneapolis: Fortress Press, 1995.

Selznick, Irene Mayer. *A Private View.* New York: Knopf, 1983.

Shachtman, Tom. *Skyscraper Dreams: The Great Real Estate Dynasties of New York.* Boston: Little, Brown, 1991.

Shaw, Arnold. *The Street That Never Slept.* New York: Coward, McCann and Geoghegan, 1971.

Shultz, Earle, and Walter Simmons. *Offices in the Sky.* Indianapolis: Bobbs-Merrill, 1959.

Silver, Nathan. *Lost New York.* Boston: Houghton Mifflin, 1967.

Simon, Kate. *Fifth Avenue: A Very Social History.* New York: Harcourt Brace Jovanovich, 1978.

Sobel, Robert. *RCA.* Briarcliff Manor, NY: Stein and Day, 1986.

Solomonson, Katherine. *The Chicago Tribune Tower Competition.* Cambridge and New York: Cambridge University Press, 2001.

Stasz, Clarice. *The Rockefeller Women.* New York: St. Martin's Press, 1995.

Stein, Gertrude. *Everybody's Autobiography.* New York: Random House, 1937.

Stern, Robert. *Raymond Hood.* New York: The Institute for Architecture and Urban Studies, 1982.

Stern, Robert; Gregory Gilmartin; and John Massengale. *New York 1900.* New York: Rizzoli, 1983.

Stern, Robert; Gregory Gilmartin; and Thomas Mellins. *New York 1930.* New York: Rizzoli, 1987.

Stern, Robert; Thomas Mellins; and David Fishman. *New York 1960.* New York: Monacelli, 1997.

Sterne, Margaret. *The Passionate Eye: The Life of William Valentiner.* Detroit: Wayne State University Press, 1980.

Stevenson, William. *A Man Called Intrepid: The Secret War.* New York: Harcourt, 1976.

Stone, Edward Durell. *The Evolution of an Architect.* New York: Horizon Press, 1962.

Strouse, Jean. *Morgan: American Financier.* New York: Random House, 1999.

Swanberg, W. A. *Citizen Hearst.* New York: Bantam Books, 1963.

———. *Luce and His Empire.* New York: Scribner, 1972.

Swanson, Gloria. *Swanson on Swanson.* New York: Random House, 1980.

Talmey, Allene. *Doug and Mary and Others.* New York: Macy-Masius, 1927.

Tauranac, John. *The Empire State Building: The Making of a Landmark.* New York: Scribner, 1995.

Taylor, Robert. *Fred Allen: His Life and Wit.* Boston: Little, Brown, 1989.

Taylor, William R. *In Pursuit of Gotham: Culture and Commerce in New York.* New York: Oxford University Press, 1992.

Terkel, Studs. *Hard Times.* New York: Pantheon, 1970.

Thomas, Bob. *Winchell.* Garden City, NY: Doubleday, 1971.

Todd, John R. *Prince William's Parish and Plantations.* Richmond, VA: Garrett & Massie, 1935.

———. *Living a Life.* Privately published, 1947.

Vanderbilt, Cornelius, Jr. *Farewell to Fifth Avenue.* New York: Simon & Schuster, 1935.

Vanderlip, Frank A. *From Farm Boy to Financier.* New York and London: Appleton-Century, 1935.

Walker, Ralph. *Each Day Anew.* Unpublished manuscript, Arents Library, Syracuse University.

Wecter, Dixon. *The Saga of American Society: A Record of Social Aspiration, 1607–1937.* New York: Scribner, 1970.

Weisman, Winston. *The Architectural Significance of Rockefeller Center.* Unpublished dissertation, Ohio State University, 1942.

White, E. B. *The Fox of Peapack.* New York: Harper, 1938.

———. *Here Is New York.* New York: Harper, 1949

White, Norval. *The Architecture Book.* New York: Knopf, 1976.

White, Norval, and Elliot Willensky. *AIA Guide to New York City, Fourth Edition.* New York: Three Rivers Press, 2000.

Willis, Carol. *Form Follows Finance: Skyscrapers and Skylines in New York and Chicago.* Princeton, NJ: Princeton Architectural Press, 1995.

———. *Building the Empire State.* New York: W.W. Norton, 1998.

Wilson, Edmund. *The Thirties.* New York: Farrar, Straus & Giroux, 1980.

Wist, Ronda. *On Fifth Avenue: Then and Now.* New York: Birch Lane Press, 1992.

Wolfe, Bertram D. *The Fabulous Life of Diego Rivera.* Briarcliff Manor, NY: Stein and Day, 1963.

———. *A Life in Two Centuries.* Briarcliff Manor, NY: Stein and Day, 1981.

Wolfe, Tom. *From Bauhaus to Our House.* New York: Bantam, 1991.

Worden, Helen. *Here in New York.* New York: Doubleday, Doran, 1939.

Wright, Frank Lloyd. *An Autobiography.* New York: Horizon Press, 1977.

Wright, Frank Lloyd, and Lewis Mumford. *Frank Lloyd Wright and Lewis Mumford: Thirty Years of Correspondence.* Princeton, NJ: Princeton Architectural Press, 2001.

Zorach, William. *Art Is My Life.* Cleveland and New York: World, 1967.

ACKNOWLEDGMENTS

Even Merle Crowell would be impressed by the number of people to whom I owe thanks. Without their varied gifts of imagination, generosity, tolerance, and toil, this book simply would not exist, and this author would have to find another line of work. Understanding that most readers will skip over a long list of unfamiliar names, I must immediately mention two before the orchestra starts playing and the director cuts to a commercial: Barbara Grossman and Liz Darhansoff.

This book was Barbara's idea. I wasn't looking for a book project, and when Liz called me to suggest that I listen to Barbara's pitch, it would have been very easy to brush off both of them. But I like Barbara, and I like Wendy Wolf (they were colleagues at the time; more about Wendy later). When they suggested lunch, "Why not?" seemed more appropriate than "Thanks but no thanks," so long as they remained aware of a critical caveat: I wasn't interested in starting a new book. We met on a lovely April Friday in the garden of a restaurant in downtown Manhattan, and we blew most of the afternoon catching up, gossiping, bragging, and otherwise avoiding the topic that had occasioned our lunch in the first place. I think it was around the time Barbara asked for the check that I finally said, "All right, go ahead, I'm curious—what's the idea that I'm not going to write a book about?" Barbara said, "History of Rockefeller Center," and I said, "It's a deal."

One might think that this is where Liz steps in. Liz is my agent, and she definitely did make the deal. But she stepped in long, long before that. Liz has been my agent for more than twenty years, and I've known her for more than thirty. She is the perfect agent, her advice invariably sound, her commitment constant, her negotiating skills almost embarrassingly acute. But it's a lot easier, and a lot less important, to be a perfect agent than to be a perfect friend, and Liz is that as well—to me, to my wife, to my children. She earns every cent I pay her to be my agent, but her friendship is a treasure beyond price.

Barbara and Liz launched *Great Fortune;* a vast crew sustained it. If I didn't owe my brother Larry so much, I would have dedicated this book to the research librarians and archivists of America. These are people who devote their careers to preserving the past and making it available to those of us who would try to bring it to life. Their work is entirely selfless, shamefully undervalued, and conducted in total anonymity. The latter condition is redressed only in acknowledgments such as these. Dear reader, if you've ever wondered why writers go on at such length listing all these unfamiliar names, *trust us!* They earn all we can say, and more.

In this category, first mention must go to Darwin Stapleton, director of the Rockefeller Archive Center in Sleepy Hollow, New York; his staff; and his sponsors. It is impossible to imagine an archive better maintained, more efficiently managed, or more welcoming to researchers. During the years that I (and for a long period, my associate Hildy Anderson) worked through thousands of documents pertaining to Rockefeller Center and the Rockefeller family, Dr. Stapleton's entire staff was helpful and generous. I would especially like to note the specific assistance of the wonderful archivists serially assigned to this lengthy project and the tiresome entreaties of its author: Anke Voss-Hubbard, John LeGloahec, Tom Rosenbaum, and Amy Fitch; Michele Hiltzik guided me through the Archive Center's extensive photography holdings. I would also like to thank the members of the Rockefeller family who decided to preserve this extraordinary collection of documents and make it available to researchers without limitation, encumbrance, or preselection.

Jim Reed, of the Rockefeller Center Archive Center (located behind an unmarked door in a certain midtown Manhattan office development), endured my presence and my inquiries off and on for nearly five years. No one knows Rockefeller Center as well as Jim does, loves it as much, or has been as consistently helpful to me. Janet Parks presides over the Department of Prints and Drawings in the Avery Architectural Library at Columbia University, one of the nation's finest collections of letters, documents, plans, and other papers pertaining to twentieth-century architecture. Janet's familiarity with her vast holdings is intimate and informed. She is herself a superb architectural historian.

I also visited or communicated electronically with a large group of dedicated and helpful archivists whom I wish to acknowledge here. The roll call: Judith Throm, of the Archives of American Art; the archivist of the Century Association, Russell Flinchum; my former colleague Bill Hooper, archivist at Time Inc.; at the Chase Manhattan Bank, archivist Shelly Diamond; at the Columbiana collection, Columbia University, Jocelyn Wilk and Hollee Haswell; on Janet Parks's staff at the Avery Library, Lou DiGennaro, Jim Epstein, and Anne-Sophie Roure; at the Columbia Oral History Project, Columbia University, Mary Marshall Clark and Ronald Grele; Lawrence Adams of Toronto's Dance Collection Danse; at the Detroit Historical Museum, Patience Nauta; at the Baker Library, Harvard Business School, Historical Collections Department, Nicole Hayes, Timothy J. Mahoney, and Laura Linard; at the Schlesinger Library, Harvard University, Anne Engelhart, Kathy Herrlich, and Sarah Hutcheon; at the Michelle Smith Performing Arts Library, University of Maryland, Bonnie Jo Dopp, curator of Special Collections; at the Metropolitan Opera Archives, Robert Tuggle and John Pennino; at the Museum of Modern Art, librarian Milan Hughston, and in the Drawings Study Center, curator Kathy Curry; at the New York City Municipal Archives, Kenneth R. Cobb; at the Local History and Genealogy Department of the New York Public Library, Jim Falcone; Christopher Shay and his colleagues Erin Overbey and Stacy McGoldrick, librarians at *The New Yorker* (I must also thank the magazine's editor, David Remnick, for the invitation to take advantage of both the library's staff and its irresistible files); at the Van Pelt Library, University of Pennsylvania, Dan Traister; at the Firestone Library of Princeton University, Don Skemer; at the Radio City Music Hall Archives, Diane Jaust; at the Arents Library, Syracuse University, Carolyn Davis; at the Wadsworth Atheneum, in Hartford, Gene Gaddis; and various staff members at the archives of the Cooper-Hewitt National Design Museum; the Seeley Mudd Library at Princeton University; the Humanities Research Center at the University of Texas in Austin; and the Manuscript Division of the New York Public Library.

The bibliography that begins on page 473 lists most of the books it has been my pleasure to read (or read in) during my attempt to understand twentieth-century New York, American architecture, popular entertainment in the 1920s and 1930s, the Great Depression, Prohibition, the Rockefeller family, and all the other tributaries that lead to Rockefeller Center. But special acknowledgment must be extended to a handful of writers. On the architectural history of Rockefeller Center, the early scholarly work of Winston Weisman, preserved in both his 1942 Ph.D. dissertation and in articles published in the *Journal of the Society of Architectural Historians* in 1951 and 1959, is the Rosetta Stone. His successors Alan Balfour and Carol Herselle Krinsky, authors in the 1970s of separate studies entitled—sensibly enough—*Rockefeller Center,* added to Weisman's work and deepened it as well. Nearly thirty years ago, Professor Krinsky was able to interview several of the principal figures involved in the creation of Rockefeller Center, a privilege the passage of time has since rendered impossible. She generously allowed me to read the transcripts of those interviews, for which she earns my special gratitude.

No one can write about the Rockefeller family without reading and making constant reference to Ron Chernow's great biography of the first John D., *Titan.* Cary Reich wrote about the dominant member of the third Rockefeller generation in *Nelson Rockefeller: Worlds to Conquer 1908–1958*; Reich's tragic death—there is no other adjective—prevented him from writing the second, concluding volume of his excellent biography. There is no similarly ambitious or accomplished biography of the key figure in the interceding generation, namely Junior; I hope I've been able to indicate how much this complicated and misunderstood man deserves one.

Three volumes of New York architectural history by David A. M. Stern and various colleagues—*New York 1900, New York 1930, New York 1960*—are as valuable as they are exhaustive (together, the three books total more than 2,700 pages). Charles B. Fowler never wrote his planned biography of Roxy Rothafel, but through the courtesy of Diane Jaust I was fortunate to be able to make use of his extensive notes. Similarly, Francis Christy's unpublished history-cum-memoir of the first two decades of Rockefeller Center provided material that would otherwise be lost to the modern researcher.

A number of others generously provided information, access, hospitality, and other necessities of the researcher's life: Susan Arons, Charles Baum, Andy Blau, David Boorstin, Barbara Baker Burrows, David Childs, Barbara Cohen and Judith Stonehill (whose late New York Bound bookstore is the departed element of Rockefeller Center that I miss even more than the Rivera mural), Theresa Collins, Clifford J. Corcoran, Alan Fields, Andrew Freeman, Paul Goldberger, Tom Goldstein, Kate Griggs, Hugh Hardy, Ernie Jacks, Peter Johnson, the late Tibor Kalman, Deborah Kirschner; Norman Cohen, Dan Klein, and Peter Kunhardt of Kunhardt Productions; Patrick Marnham, Ann Marshall, Francis Morrone, Nancy Resnick, David Rockwell, Christine Roussel, Jolie Smith, Elisabeth Sussman, Allene White, and Richard Zuckerman. Candor requires me to acknowledge my outright theft of one irresistible metaphor from the late sportswriter Bugs Baer.

I am deeply grateful as well to those people whom either I, or my associate Randy Hartwell, was able to interview. These include Arthur H. Christy (who also provided me with transcripts of his father's taped memoirs), Margaret Dunne, Muriel Kilduff "Duffy" Hake, Dottie Hoarton-Eyl, Violet Holmes, Frederick Kellers, Leon Leonidoff, Jr., Madeleine Leonidoff, Alton Marshall, Emmanuel Mohlo, Leonard Nole, Martin Quigley, Trientje Hood Reed, David Rockefeller, Arthur Rothafel, Vivian Smith Shears, Ruth Reinhard Stewart, Hicks Stone, Steve Stumpf, Thelma Corey Stumpf, and John A. Wenrich.

All of my friends have had to listen to me and otherwise suffer me during my years of obsession with Rockefeller Center. Several also provided specific assistance, particularly Stephen Adler, Nelson Aldrich, Taylor Branch, Sheldon Czapnik, Melissa Easton, Lisa Grunwald, Jonathan Harr, David Klatell, Jane Nelson Magnuson, Sharon McIntosh, Ann Morrell, Joe Nocera, Dick Pollak, Michael Rosenthal, Susan Berns Rothchild, Sam Schulman, Tim Smith, Jean Strouse, Glen Waggoner, and Jill Whedon. Norman Pearlstine allowed me to take two leaves of absence while I was working for him as an editor at large at Time Inc.; without his generosity, which enabled me to begin writing after three years of false starts, I do not think this book would ever have made it to the printer. Henry Steinway, for seven years, supplied a very specific inspiration: if this book could satisfy any one person, I'd like it to be him.

Other friends went further: they actually read the manuscript, large sections of the manuscript, or in some cases the same section of the manuscript over and over. They proved themselves the dearest and most tolerant of friends, and their encouragement was as generous as it was, for me, essential: Suzie Bolotin, Betsy Carter, Greg Curtis, Lee Eisenberg, Jim Gaines (the best editor I have ever known), Kathy Hourigan, John Huey, Michael Janeway, Bob Nylen; John, Donald, and Lily Rothman; Tony Schulte, and Kate Steinway. None, I hope, will be insulted by my awarding the coveted Very Best Reader prize to Bruce McCall, whose enthusiasm for exactly this kind of book is just one of his many endearing peculiarities.

Seven people were, at various times, my Team Rockefeller, and each of them deserves profound credit for his or her role in making this book possible. For the first two years of the project, Hildy Anderson was my indefatigable research assistant; her prodigious labors in the Rockefeller Archive Center and elsewhere were a blessing to me. Hildy was succeeded by Randy Hartwell, who knows more about New York in the 1930s than any Mississippian born in the 1970s has the right to know, and whose own excellent writing was, I fear, put on hold because of his endless and invaluable exertions in my behalf. Vivette Porges found, secured rights to, and helped me select the photographs. Barbara Fox transcribed notes, entered book excerpts in my database, and otherwise helped bring order to a disorderly process. Steve Walkowiak set up my database program (and ought to market a version of it to other writers); Melanie Wertz maintained it whenever it began acting up; and Paul Nocera enabled me to survive countless other digital crises.

Two old friends were midwives to this book. Wendy Wolf, my editor at Viking, has been part of this project from the beginning. She was there at the lunch when the idea was first broached; she was there with appropriate doses of encouragement, remonstration, and threat as my work (and nonwork) dragged through the years; and she was there during the final months of editing and revision that brought it to completion. Amazingly, we're still friends. Chris Jerome and I, after too many years of little contact, are friends again. There is not a sentence in the world that could not be improved by Chris's copyediting, and my own sentences gave her challenges that would have daunted Strunk, White, Fowler, and Bernstein working as a tag team. Any she failed to wrestle into comprehension and clarity can be blamed on my stubbornness. Thank you, Wendy, and thank you, Chris.

Finally, my family. Anyone who knows my remarkable mother, who turned ninety while I was writing this book, knows that Gizella Okrent is as sharp, as funny, and as intellectually alive as she has ever been. Anyone who knows my astonishing wife knows how blessed I am by Becky's support, her companionship, her sense of humor, and her love. Not only could this book not have been written without her, but virtually anything I accomplish in life, professionally and personally, can be directly attributed to the inspiration, the encouragement, and the vast tolerance she provides me daily. Anyone who knows our children, John and Lydia, understands why the delight they give me, and the pride I have in them, are limitless. These four Okrents are *my* great fortune.

ILLUSTRATION CREDITS

INDEX

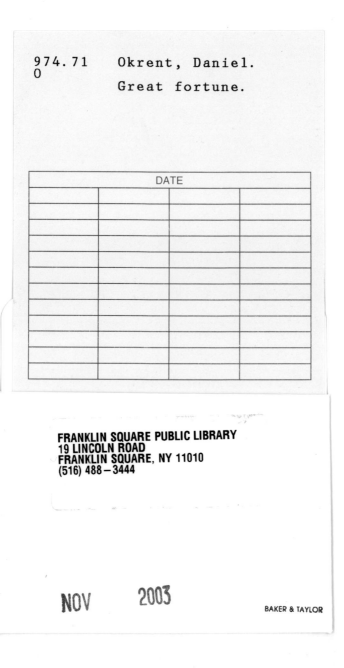

974.71
O

Okrent, Daniel.

Great fortune.

DATE			